The Complete Digital SLR Handbook

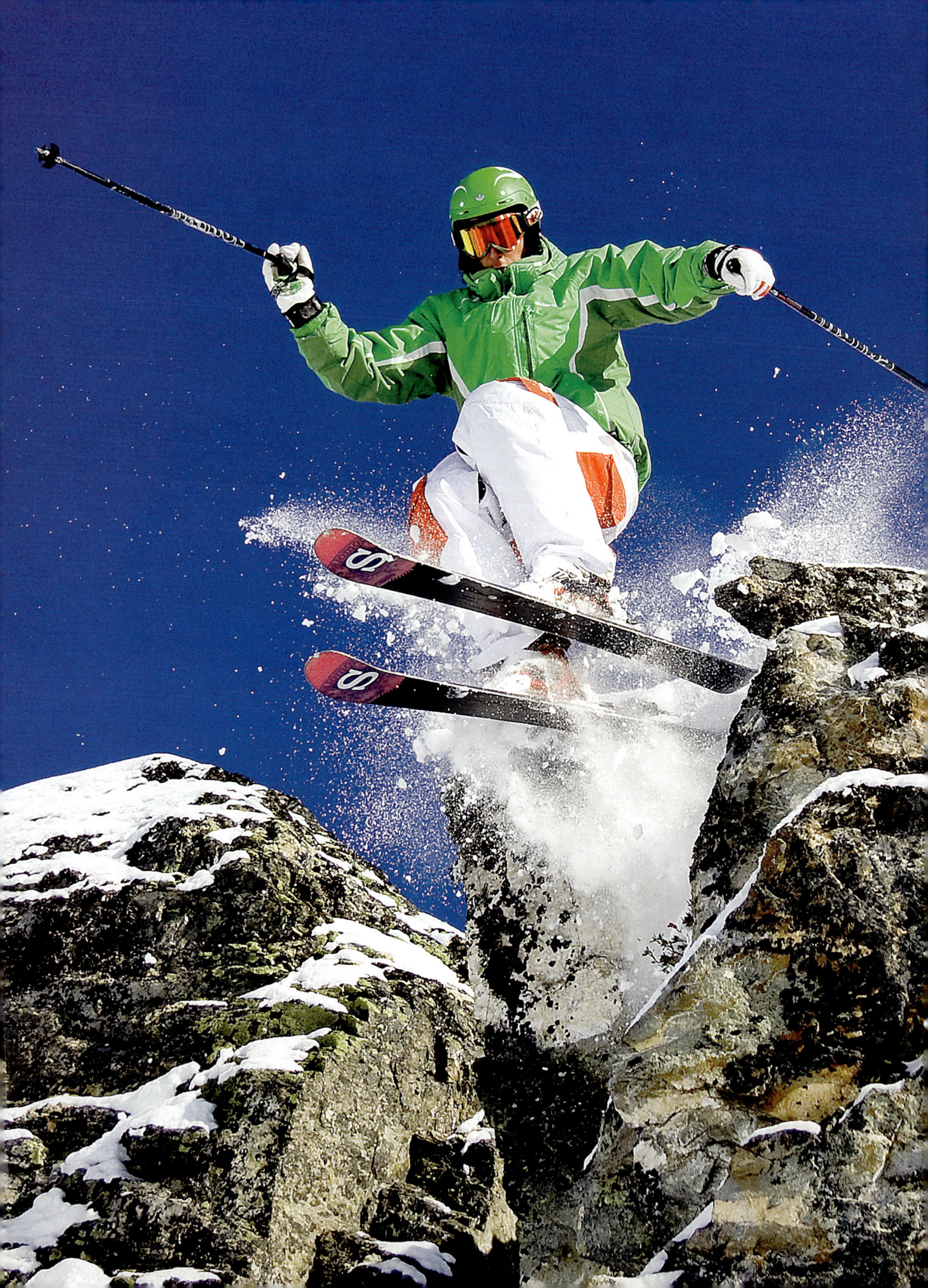

The Complete Digital SLR Handbook

Master Your Camera
to Take Pictures Like a **Pro**

BY EDITORS OF
PhotoPlus
MAGAZINE

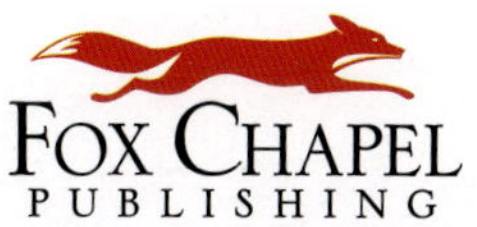

FOX CHAPEL
PUBLISHING

The Complete Digital SLR Handbook is an original work, first published in 2011 in the United Kingdom by Future Publishing Limited in magazine form under the same title. This title printed and distributed in North America under license.

ISBN 978-1-56523-717-9

To learn more about the other great books from Fox Chapel Publishing, or to find a retailer near you, call toll-free 800-457-9112 or visit us at *www.FoxChapelPublishing.com*.

Note to Authors: We are always looking for talented authors to write new books. Please send a brief letter describing your idea to Acquisition Editor, 1970 Broad Street, East Petersburg, PA 17520.

Printed in China

First printing

The Complete Digital SLR Handbook

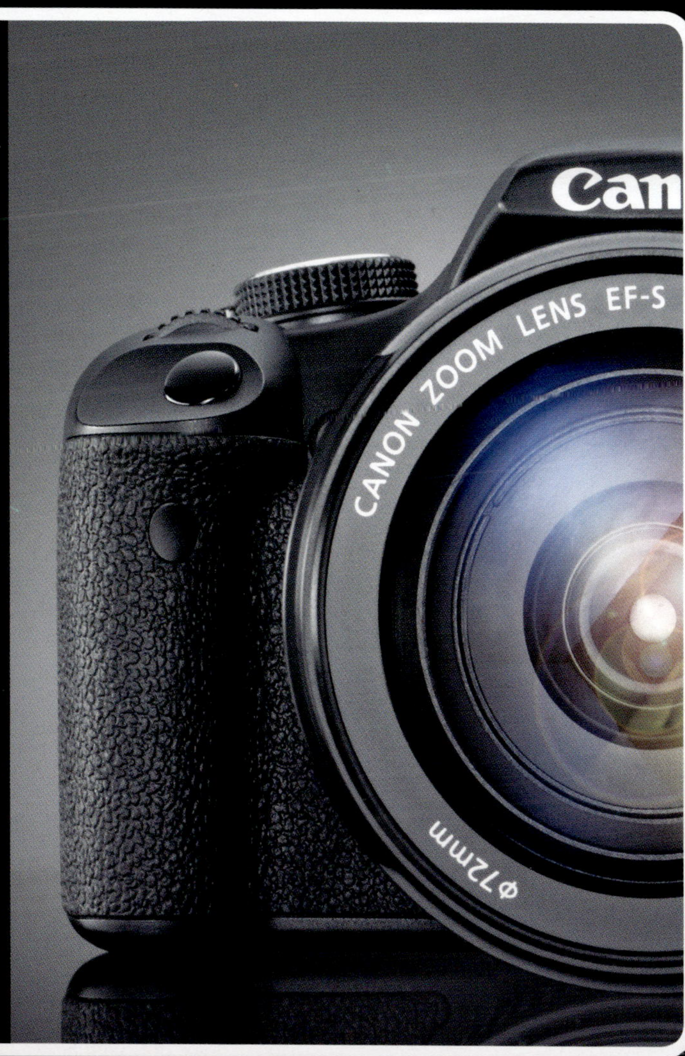

Welcome

We all want to take great photographs and the explosion in affordable digital SLRs has given many of us the chance to own a truly powerful camera for the first time. But with great power comes great complexity. The latest models are packed with features and controls that can appear bewildering to even experienced photographers.

This special handbook will teach you everything you need to know in order to get the best from your digital SLR. We'll demonstrate how to master advanced controls, turning the dial from Auto and on to manual settings where you'll be able to create exactly the look you're after. Of course, great photography isn't just about technical skills – you also need to develop your eye and a special relationship with your subject, whether it's your pet spider or a magnificent mountainous landscape. Our dedicated guides will enable you to tackle popular subjects head on, with real-world advice and tips on getting the best possible shot.

To aid your quest for better photos, we also have in-depth reviews of must-have lenses and accessories, from telephoto zooms to macro flashes. And to put the icing on the cake, our dedicated Photoshop section explains how to enhance your images with the minimum of time and effort, so your photos are always as good as they possibly can be. Enjoy!

Adam Ifans
Editor

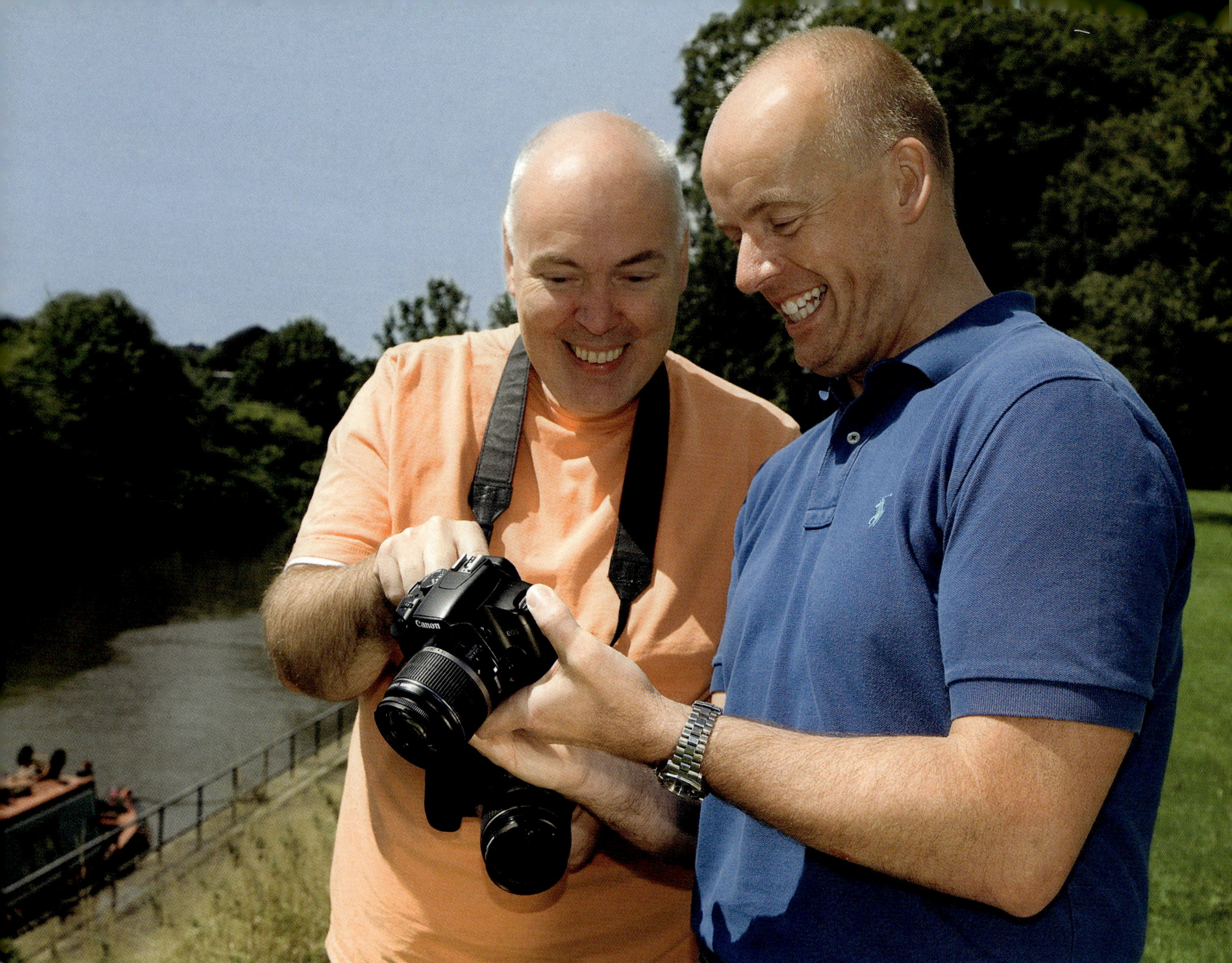

Contents

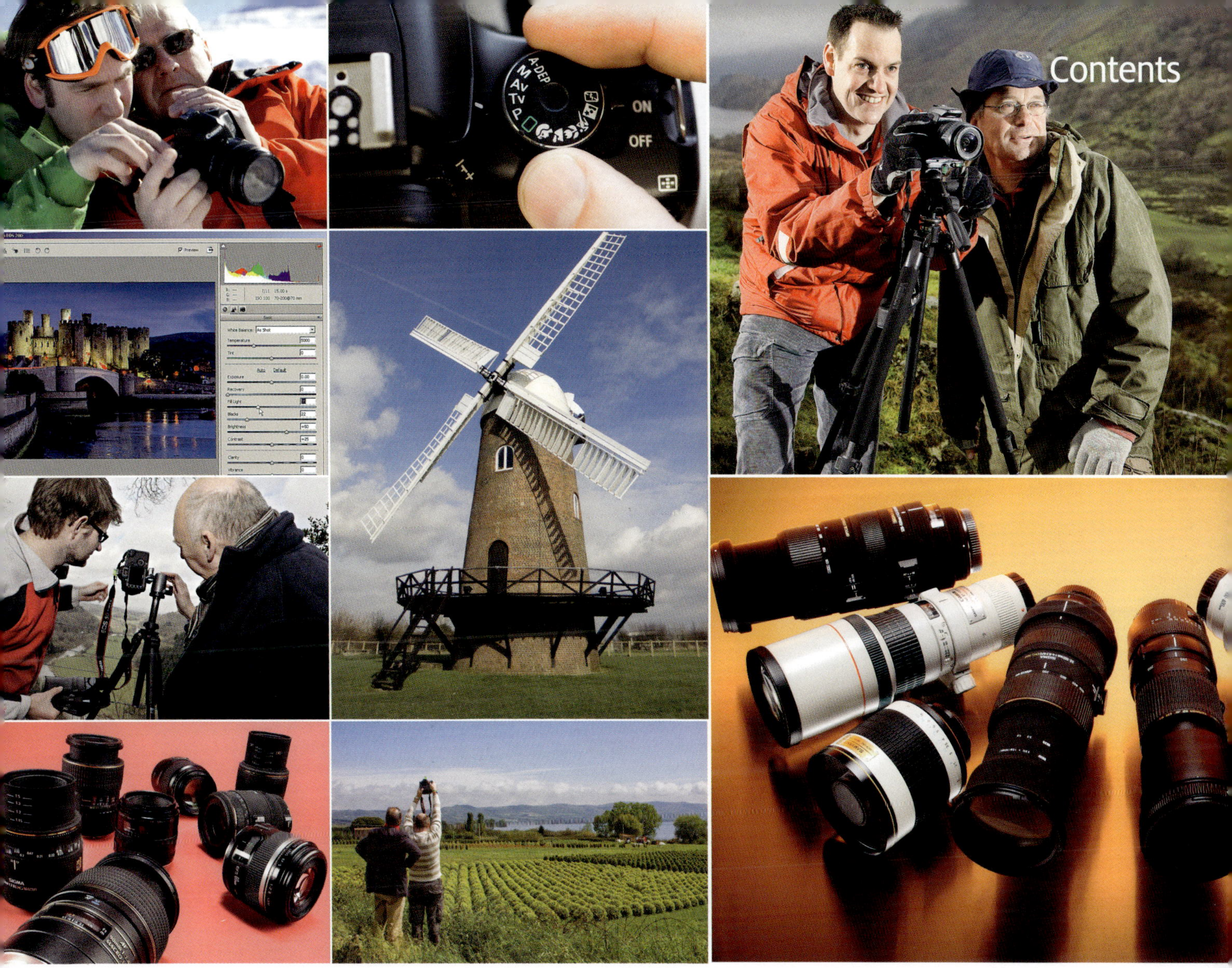

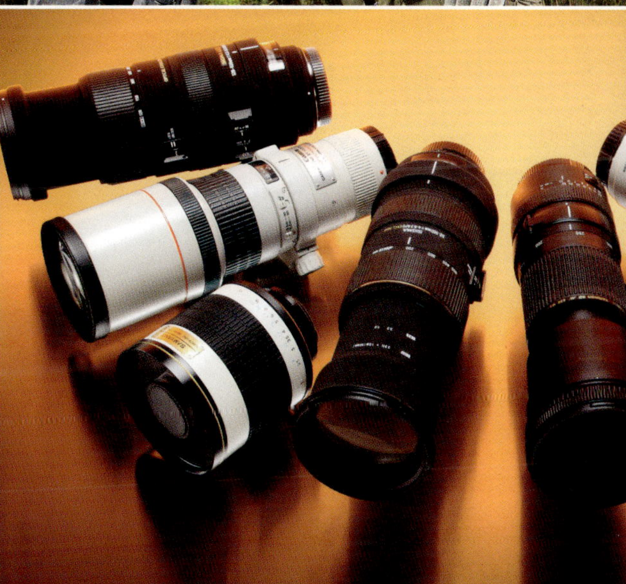

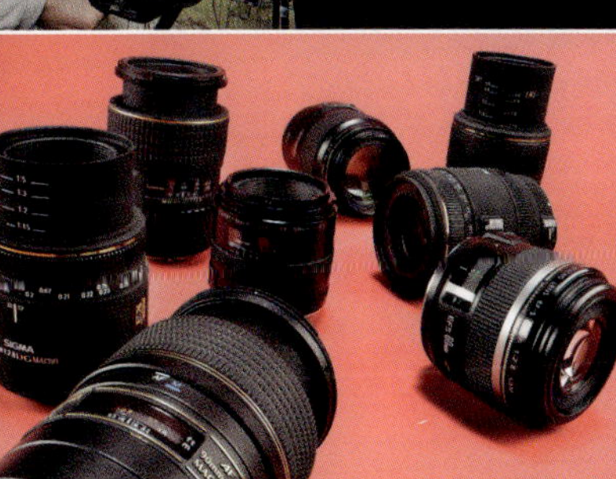

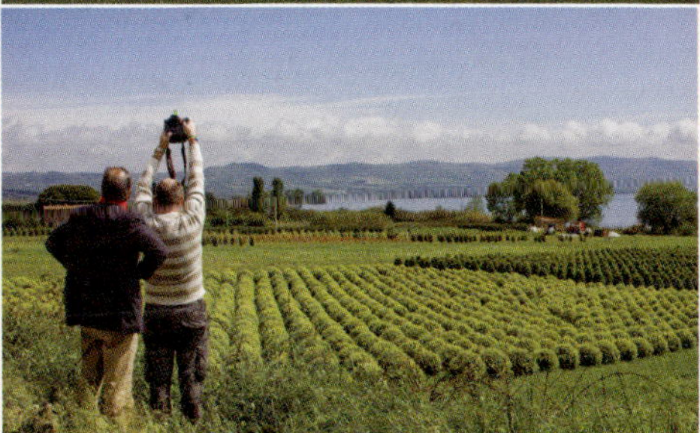

Look out for this badge when reading a tutorial. It shows you that the image we have used in the tutorial is on the free CD – so you can follow our step-by-step advice using the same picture as us!

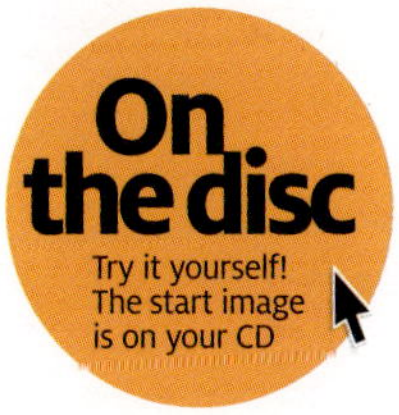

On the disc
Try it yourself! The start image is on your CD

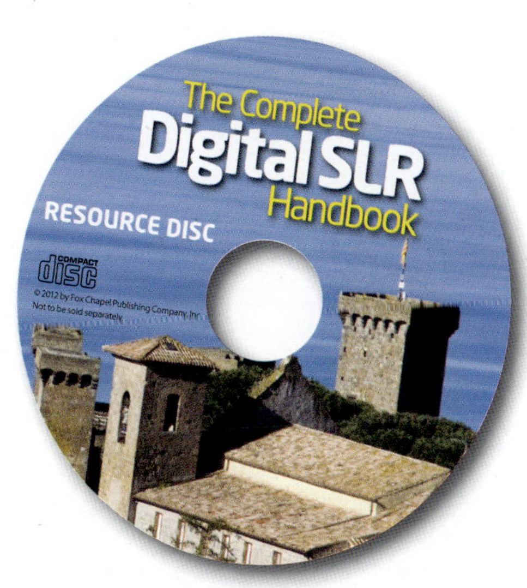

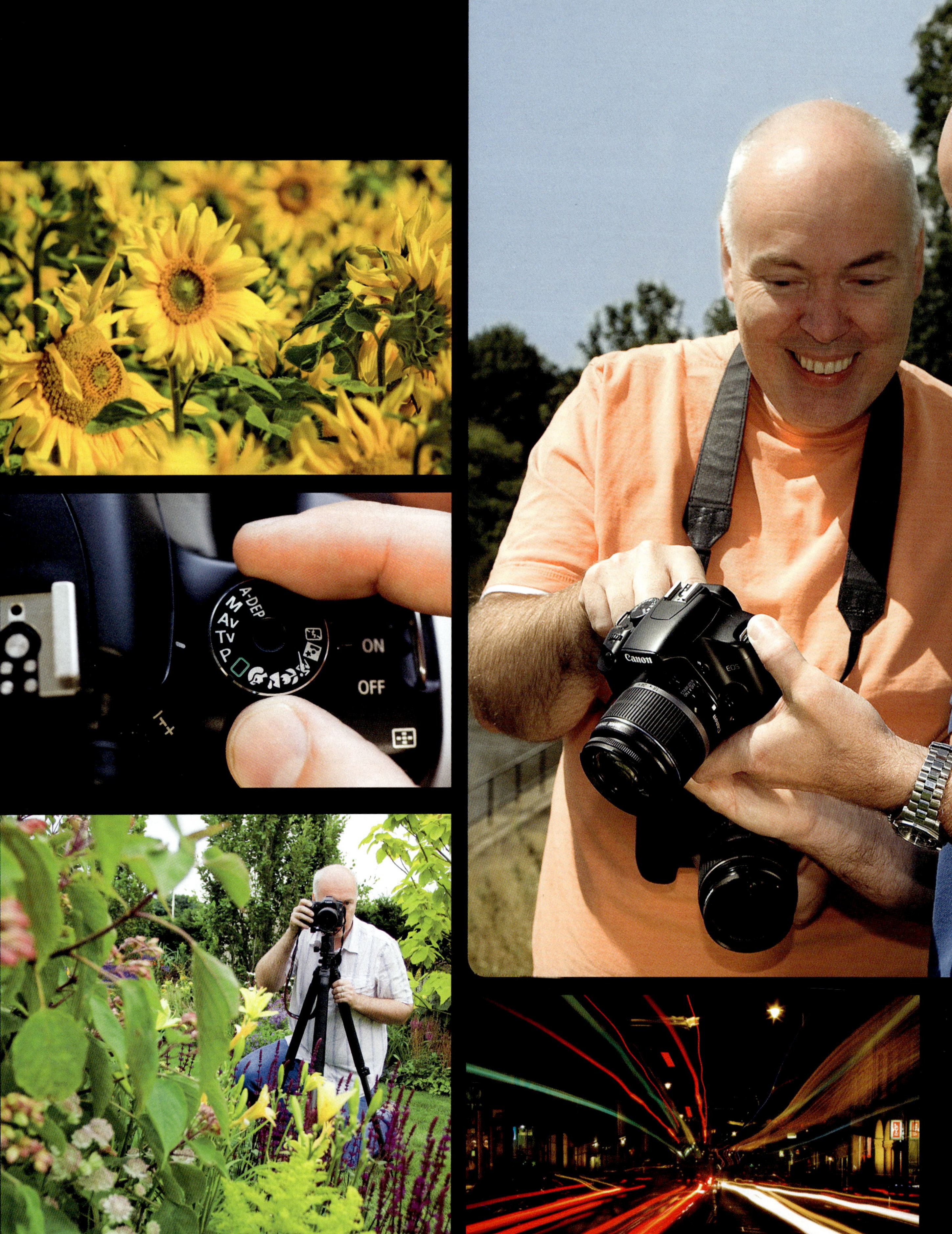
A-DEP
M
Av
Tv
P
ON
OFF
Canon
EOS

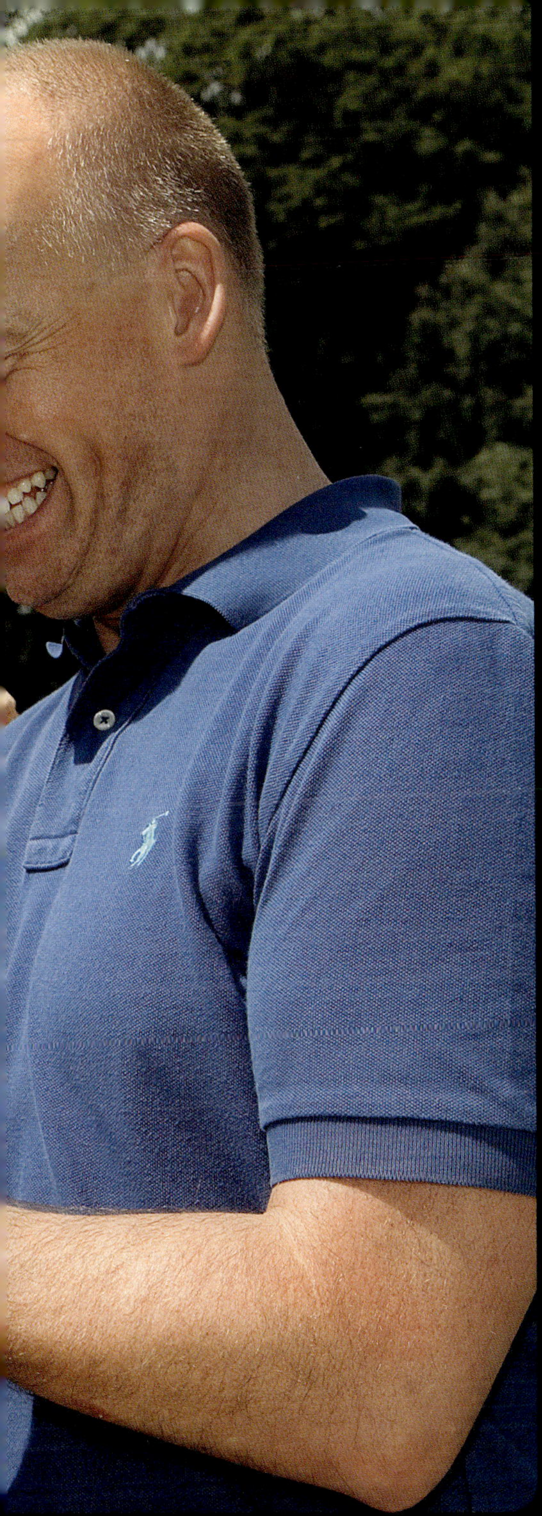

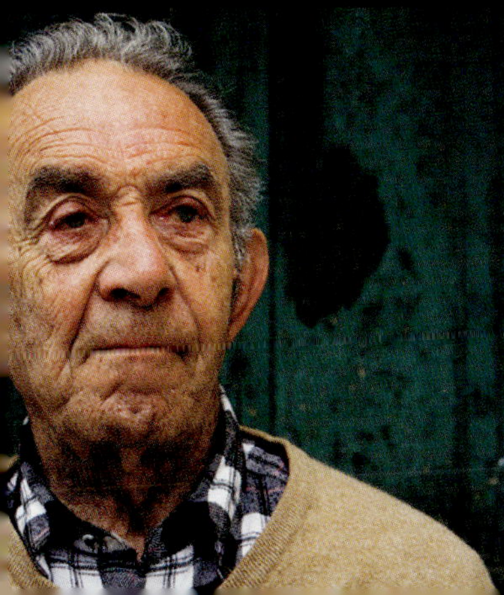

LEARN NEW TECHNIQUES!

Essential SLR skills revealed

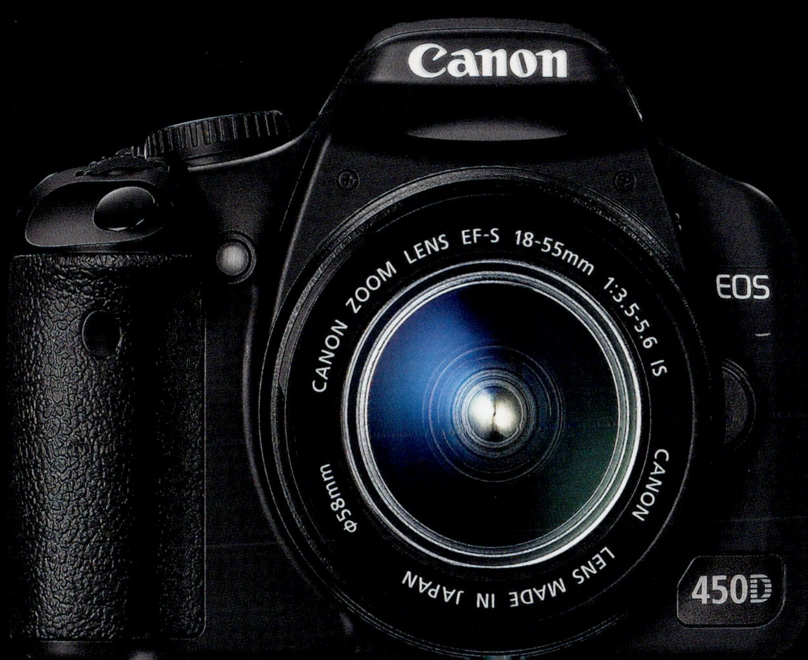

TAKE BETTER SHOTS TODAY!

DIGITAL SLR CRASH COURSE

Words: Chris George (Future)

Whether you're new to digital SLRs, or an experienced user looking for a refresher course, you'll find plenty of great tips in this major feature on getting more from your camera. It's time to get creative!

No matter how long you've had your digital SLR, there's always something to learn. And if you've just bought your first SLR, the learning curve can seem impossibly steep. But it needn't be a painful slog. In this feature we'll help you get the most from your digital SLR by explaining some of the key creative controls, ensuring you get much better shots as a result.

Your digital SLR is a very clever and complicated device that is quite capable of taking all the hard work out of taking great pictures. But although all you need to do is set up the shot in the viewfinder and press the shutter, what makes your SLR different from a mass-market compact camera is the option to take full control of the photographic process. You can decide how dark or light your pictures appear, for example, control the exact degree of focus, ensure that even the fastest-moving objects are frozen in time, or deliberately blurred for fantastic effect. The creative possibilities are endless.

However, to start taking control of your camera in this way you need to master its settings. So where, and how, do you start with such a complex device?

Relax. In this feature we'll reveal how you can go a long way to better pictures by mastering just *three* fundamental controls. Learn how to set the focus, aperture and shutter speed and you'll not only avoid the obvious mistakes, but also start to get the results you want. So fasten your seat belts for our digital SLR crash course!

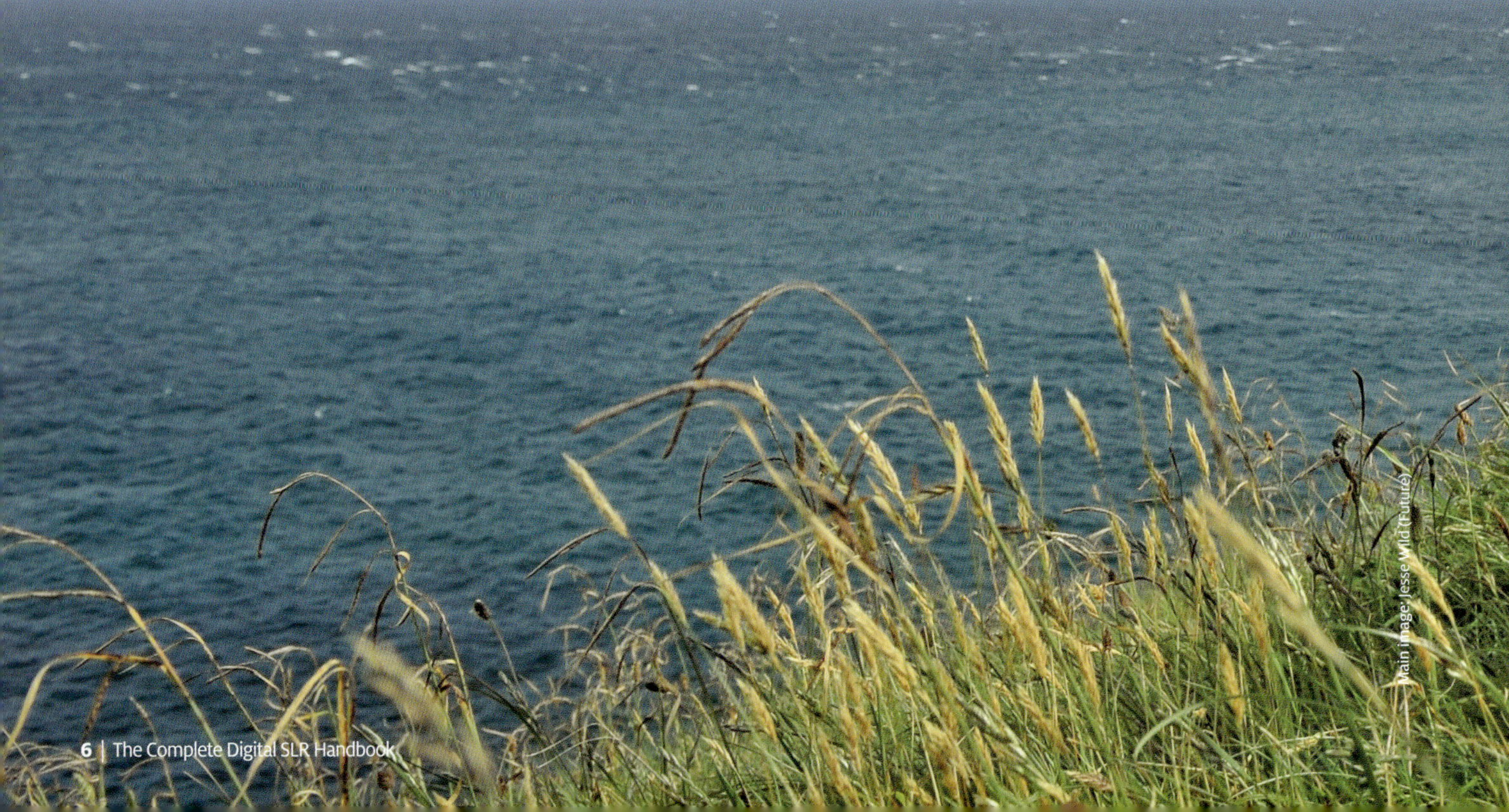

Main image: Jesse Wild (Future)

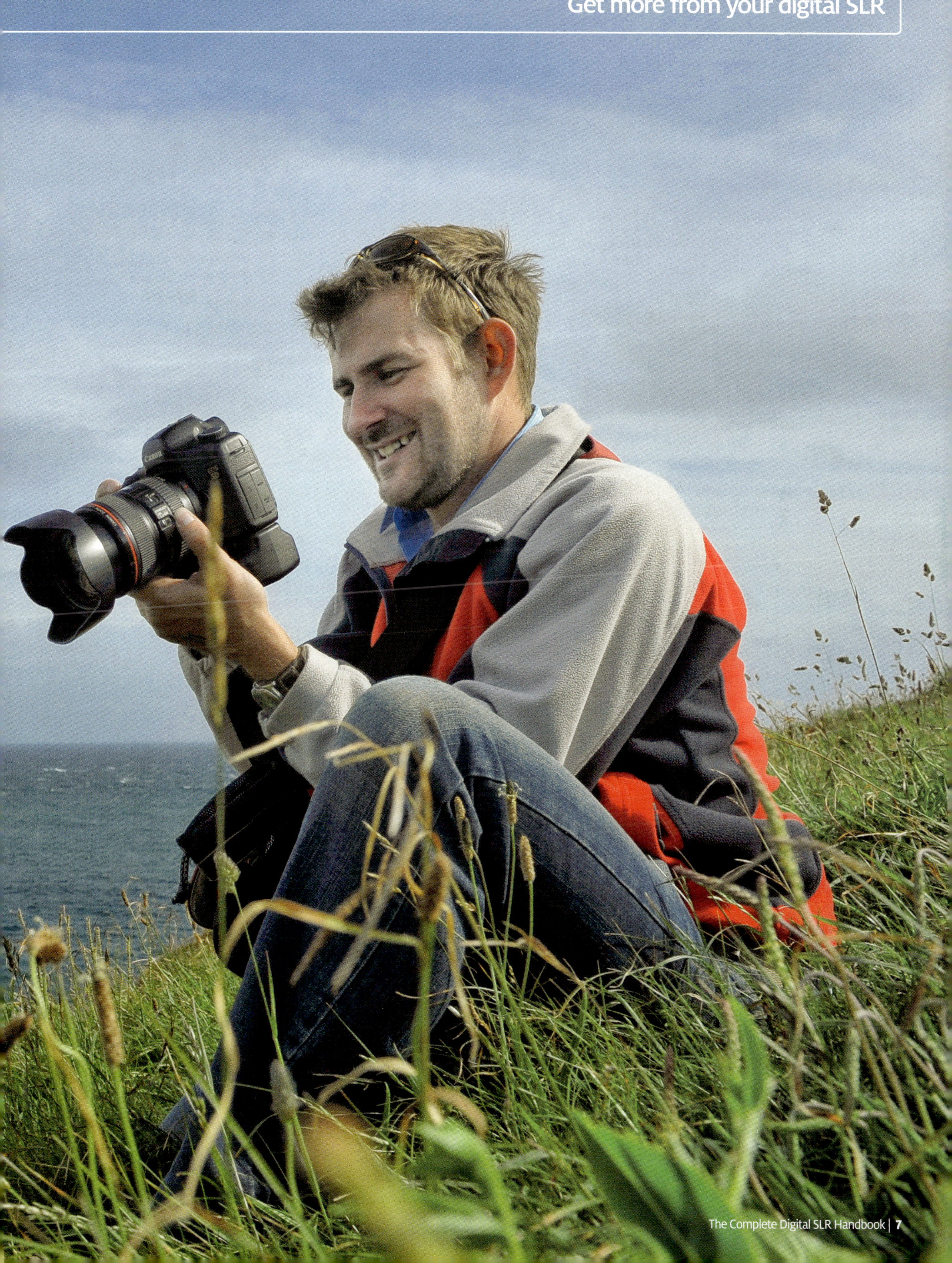

YOUR DIGITAL SLR EXPLAINED

The Canon EOS 500D is a typical digital SLR. Controls identical or similar to the ones described here can be found on Nikon and other makes, too...

FROM THE FRONT

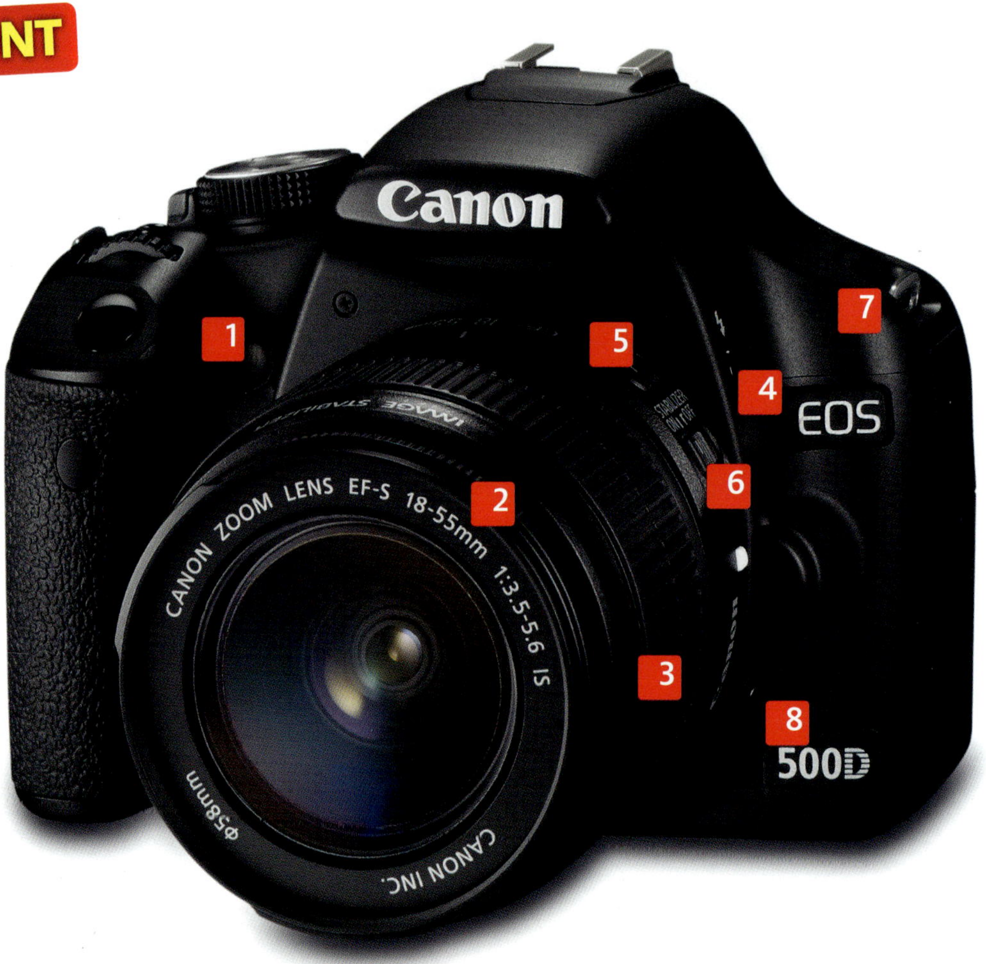

Red-eye reduction

1 To stop the flash bouncing off the subject's retinas and causing glowing red eyes this lamp will emit a burst of light to make the subject's pupils shrink before the flash is triggered. The lamp also acts as a handy self-timer countdown indicator.

Focusing ring

2 In Auto Focus mode this ring rotates until the camera has focussed on the subject. In Manual Focus mode you can rotate the focus ring with your hand to focus on a specific subject.

Zoom ring

3 Rotate this ring clockwise to zoom out for a wide-angle view. Rotate it anti-clockwise (counter-clockwise) to zoom in for a close-up on your subject.

Flash button

4 When shooting using the Creative Zone or manual modes you can tell the built-in flash to pop up by pressing here.

Focus mode switch

5 Leave this set on AF (Auto Focus) if you want the camera to control the focussing. Flip the switch to MF (Manual Focus) when you want to control the focus yourself. In MF mode you can still use the AF points in the viewfinder to tell you when the subject is in sharp focus.

Image Stabilizer switch

6 The lens's IS (Image Stabilizer) is designed to stop blur caused by camera shake (which is especially noticeable when you're zoomed in on a distant subject. Nikon IS lenses have a similar VR (Vibration Reduction) switch.

Built-in microphone

7 Cameras such as the Canon 500D and the Nikon D90 can also record video. Sound to go with it is recorded through a microphone like this (though it will also record camera handling noises like the zoom ring being rotated!).

Depth of Field preview button

8 By pressing here, you can get the camera to stop down to the lens's current aperture setting. You can then preview how much of the shot will be in focus by looking through the viewfinder or by checking the Live View display.

ROUND THE BACK

Aperture/ Exposure Compensation button

1 On Manual mode hold this button down and turn the Main dial to open or close the aperture. In some other modes (like Aperture Value) you can set the camera to open up or close down a stop using this button and the Main dial.

AF point selection

2 Press this button then rotate the Main dial to select which Auto Focus point the camera will use. It also enables you to zoom in on a shot when you play it back on the camera's LCD.

AE Lock button

3 This button enables you to lock the camera's exposure once you've taken a reading of the scene's lighting. You can also use it to zoom out of a shot when viewing it on the LCD in playback mode. It also lets you focus the camera when using Live View.

Live View

4 Press here to display what the camera will capture on the LCD screen. Most new D-SLRs have a live LCD function, which saves you from having to look through the viewfinder.

Cross keys

5 These cross key buttons allow you to navigate through the camera's menus and sub-menus. You can then press the Set button to choose a specific menu setting. Nikon calls these buttons the Multi-selector. Each button also acts as a shortcut to popular functions like WB (White Balance) or AF (Auto Focus).

Self-timer

6 This cross key button lets you change the camera from Single shooting to Continuous shooting mode (or change the self-timer settings).

Playback button

7 The Playback button enables you to review the shots that you've captured on the camera's memory card.

Erase button

8 The universal trashcan symbol lets you delete the file you're currently viewing on the camera's LCD screen.

Menu button

9 Click here to access a vast array of menus and sub menus so that you can alter the way it behaves to suit your requirements. This button lets you access and change the Quality settings for example.

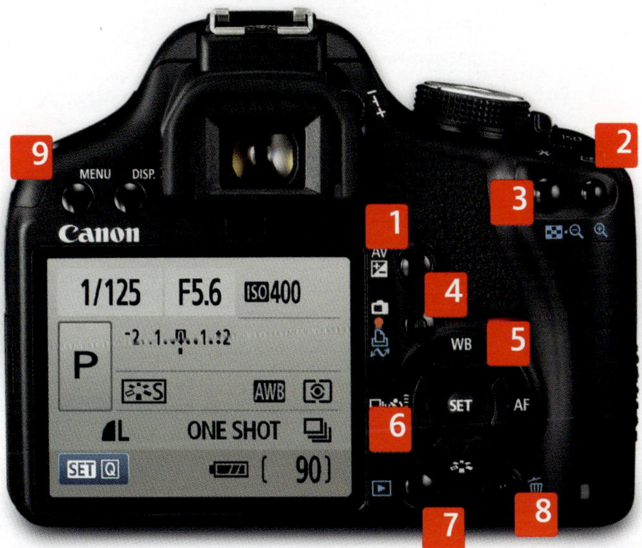

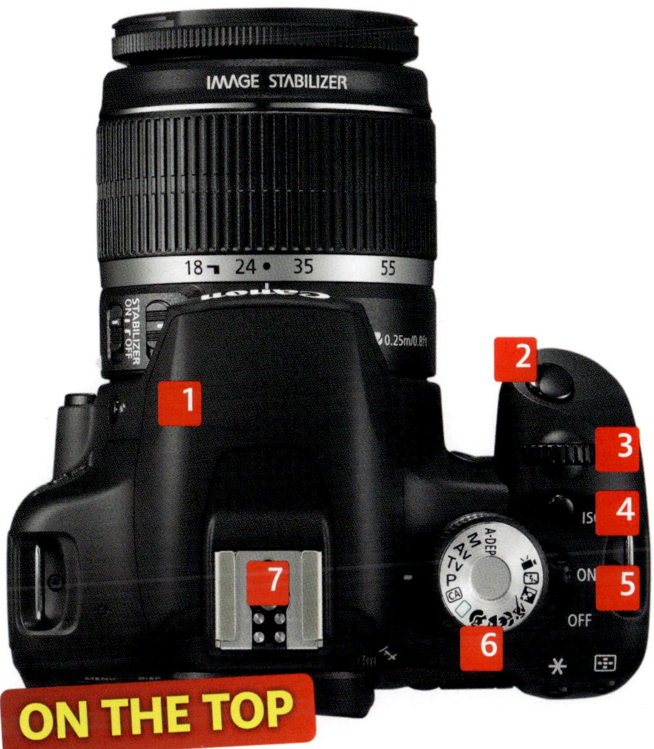

ON THE TOP

Built-in flash

1 When there's not enough available light to capture a decent exposure, your digital SLR's built-in flash can pop-up to shine some light on the situation. In some modes, you may need to pop it up manually. If there's not enough light for the camera's Auto Focus to function the flash unit can also produce a burst of light to help, called an AF-assist beam.

Shutter button

2 Press this button all the way down to capture a shot. Press it half way down to focus and take an exposure reading of the scene's lighting. Also press here to wake the camera up after it has gone into sleep mode.

Main Dial

3 Rotating this dial enables you to manually set the camera's aperture or shutter speed. It's called the Command dial on a Nikon.

ISO button

4 Click here to choose an ISO speed for the camera to use. You can then use the Main Dial to select a faster ISO speed to make the camera more sensitive to low light. You can also set the ISO speed manually by going through the menu system on most digital SLRs and many compacts.

On/off switch

5 Turn the camera off when not in use (though it will automatically fall asleep to save power after 30 seconds).

Mode Dial

6 Rotate this dial to choose a shooting mode. The camera will then set the appropriate aperture and shutter speed setting (as well as processing colour in different ways depending on the mode). There are Basic shooting modes for every type of subject (like Portrait or Landscape).

Flash hot shoe mount

7 All D-SLRs enable you to mount a more powerful flashgun on top of the camera so that you can illuminate distant subjects (and perform more creative and effective flash-related shots).

Exposure: the basics

We take the obfuscation out of f-stops and the shake out of shutter speeds

Photography is all about writing with light, and even in today's digital era, this is still how cameras create pictures. Your SLR's sensor needs a fixed measure of light to create a recordable signal. The camera controls the exposure – the amount of light that reaches the sensor – so you can still take great pictures on the darkest nights or in the brightest conditions.

Two key things control exposure. First is the shutter speed – the length of time that the sensor records for before the shutter curtains are closed. This has a huge range, from a fraction of a millisecond to whole minutes.

Second is the aperture – the size of the iris-like hole in the lens. The larger the aperture, the shorter the shutter speed needed. The range of aperture sizes is limited, and depends on the lens.

Lighter or darker?

Your SLR measures the brightness of a scene and uses this information to set (or help you select) the best aperture and shutter speed. Although the meter works well in most situations, it doesn't always get it right, and pictures can appear too dark or too light. Check them carefully on the LCD. If you need to make the shot lighter use Exposure Compensation to set a positive value and shoot again; to go darker set a negative number instead. White, bright scenes will often look grey and need more exposure. Dark, black subjects will need less.

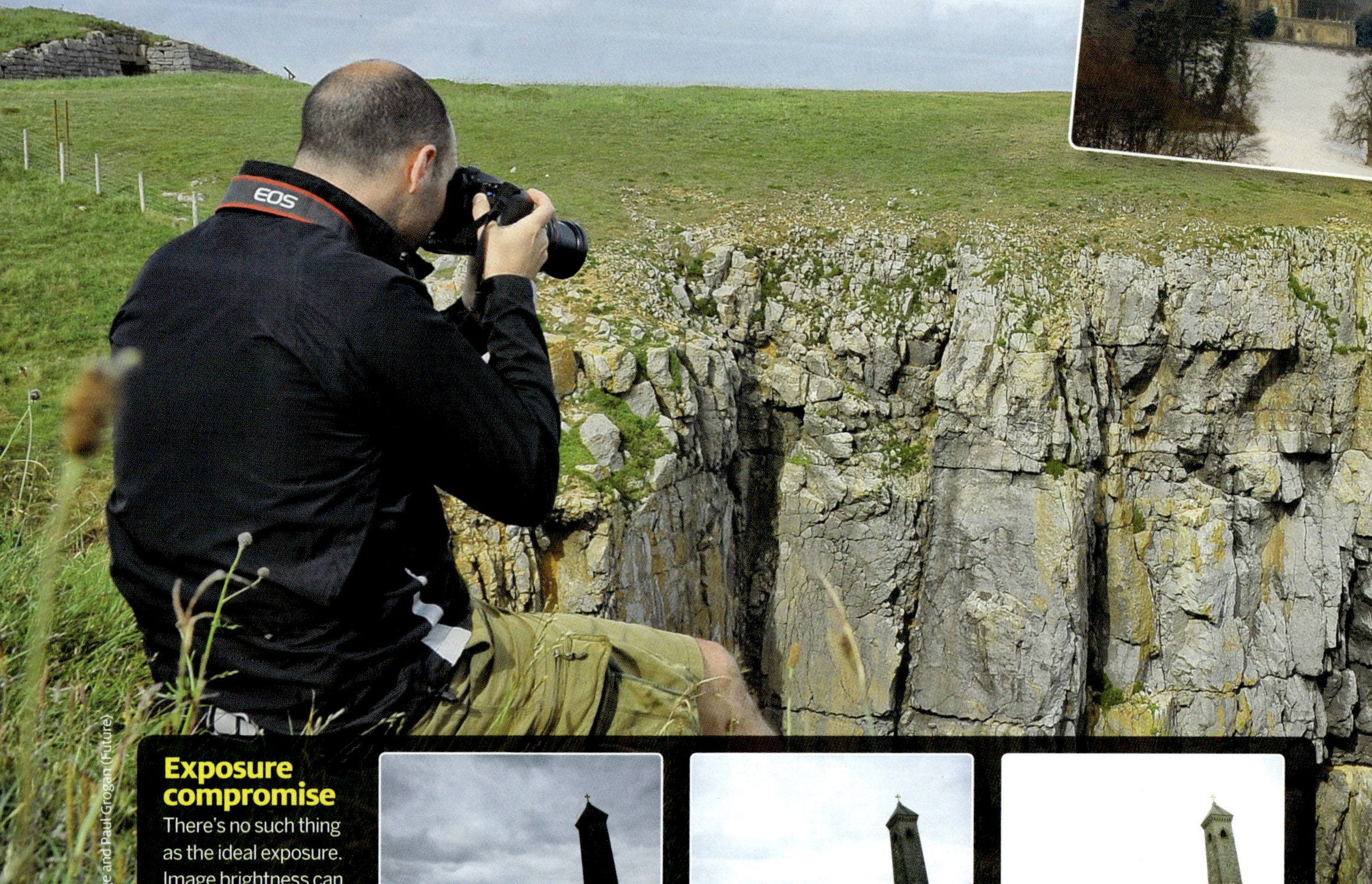

All photos: Jade Lord, Chris George and Paul Grogan (Future)

Exposure compromise

There's no such thing as the ideal exposure. Image brightness can be a matter of taste. With high-contrast shots, one exposure can struggle to capture brightness correctly in every area at the same time.

1 Taken at 1/125 sec at f/8
This image looks too dark overall, but the exposure is perfect for the cloudy sky dominating the frame.

2 Taken at 1/125 sec at f/4
This compromise exposure gives some detail in the tower and some in the sky, but it's not ideal.

3 Taken at 1/60 sec at f/4
The brightest exposure gives the best shot of the tower, but the sky has gone completely white.

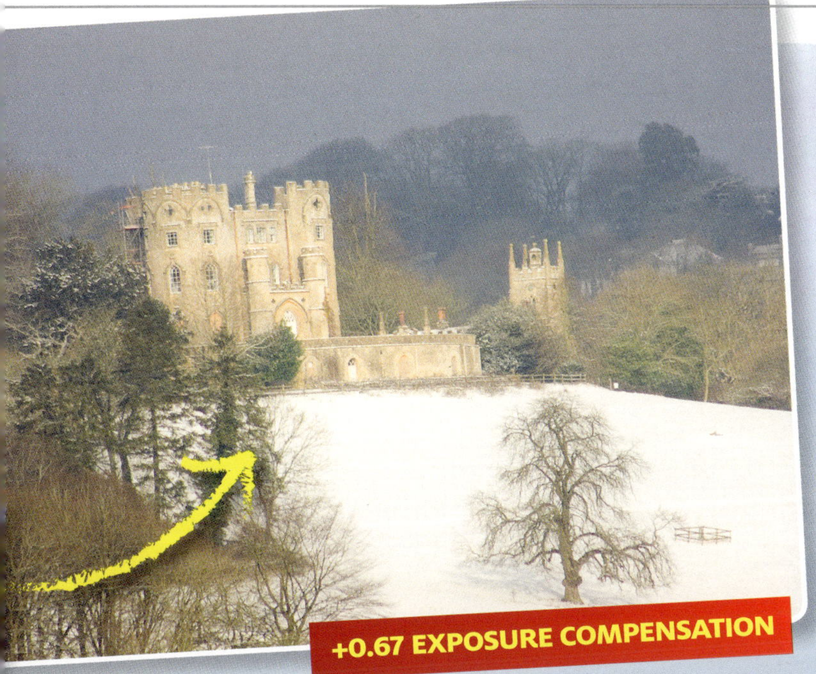

+0.67 EXPOSURE COMPENSATION

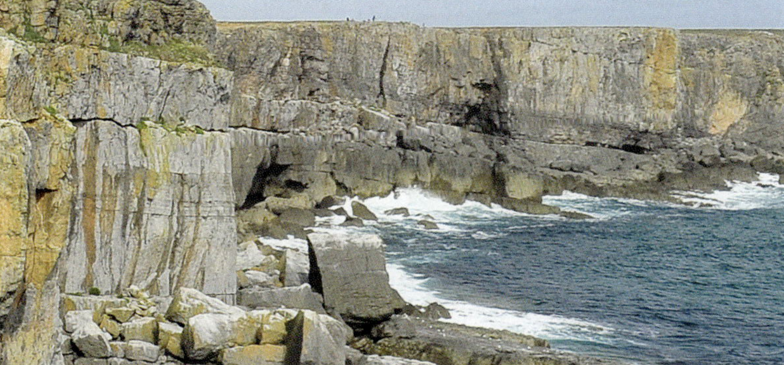

Pick the best aperture

Aperture sizes are measured in f-stops using a curious non-linear scale. It is worth learning the main 'full stop' sequence. The setting you use alters the depth of field (how much of the image is sharp, see p34). The aperture also affects image quality.

FULL STOPS	HALF STOPS	THIRD STOPS
f/2.8		
		f/3.2
	f/3.5	
		f/3.5
f/4		
		f/4.5
	f/4.5	
		f/5
f/5.6		
		f/6.3
	f/6.7	
		f/7.1
f/8		
		f/9
	f/9.5	
		f/10
f/11		
		f/13
	f/13	
		f/14
f/16		
		f/18
	f/19	
		f/20
f/22		

One stop

Half a stop

Third of a stop

Two stops = double the f-number

Wide apertures

Wider apertures = less depth of field

Mid apertures = best image quality

Smaller apertures = more depth of field

Small apertures

Camera shake and shutter speeds

The first thing to ensure when picking a shutter speed (and aperture) is that it is fast enough to avoid camera shake. To avoid blurry, unsharp shots caused by unsteady hands, check the shutter speed is 1/60 sec or faster whenever possible. However, with longer telephoto lenses and zooms you need faster shutter speeds still. With a 200mm zoom, set the shutter speed to 1/250 sec or faster. ▶

If you can, sit or lie down to get a steadier shot

WITH SHAKE 1/15 SEC

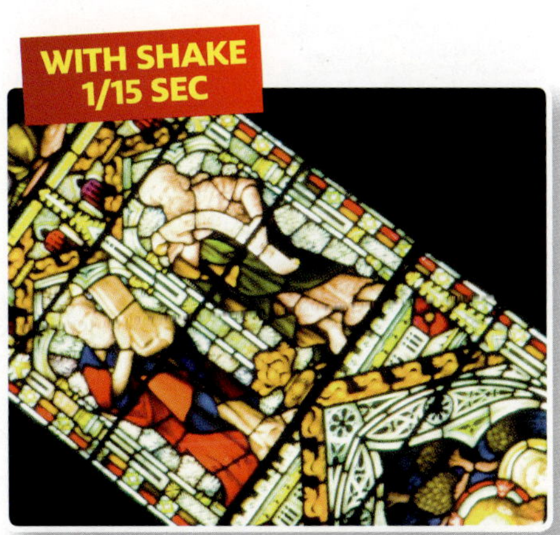

NO SHAKE 1/125 SEC

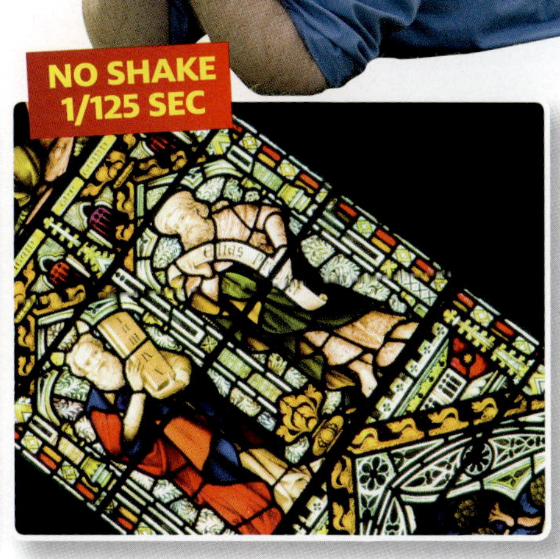

Jargon buster

f-number
Measure of the size of the aperture – an iris-like opening on the lens. The number is derived by dividing the focal length of the lens by the diameter of the aperture. Typical settings for a lens range from f/4 to f/22. As well as the traditional 'full stop' settings, your SLR offers intermediate 'half stop' or 'third stop' settings.

Resolution
Measure of lens quality and the amount of fine detail it can make out. Lenses give their best quality when NOT used at their smallest or widest aperture settings.

Depth of field

How much of a shot is sharp depends partly on the aperture used

The aperture setting that you or your SLR decide to use does not just change the overall exposure or shutter speed for the shot. It also has an important creative effect on how the scene is recorded.

The narrower the aperture (the larger the f-number), the more of the image that appears in sharp focus. It's all to do with depth of field, an optical phenomenon that means that, although a lens can only focus precisely on one plane at a time, there is a zone in front and behind that plane that will appear pin sharp.

How deep this zone of depth of field is does not just depend on the aperture size. It is also affected by the focal length or zoom setting you use – and on how close you are to the subject.

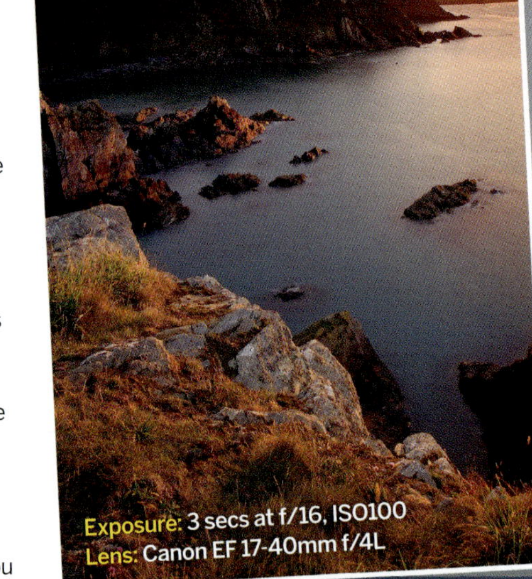

Maximise depth of field with small apertures for classic landscapes

Exposure: 3 secs at f/16, ISO100
Lens: Canon EF 17-40mm f/4L

Focusing points

The less depth of field that you have in a scene, the more crucial it is that the lens is focused accurately. The longer the telephoto setting you use, the wider the aperture selected and the closer you get to the subject, the more any focusing inaccuracies will show up.

In these situations, don't let the camera pick the AF (autofocus) point for you. Switch to Manual AF Point Selection and use the point in the viewfinder that sits on top of the area you want to focus on.

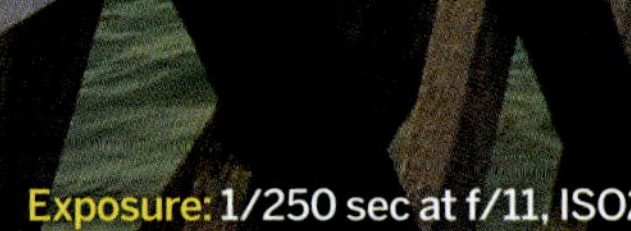

Shot at f/4 at close distance, depth of field is limited. Focusing at different points creates two very different pictures

Exposure: 1/250 sec at f/11, ISO200
Lens: Sigma 10-20mm f/4-5.6 EX

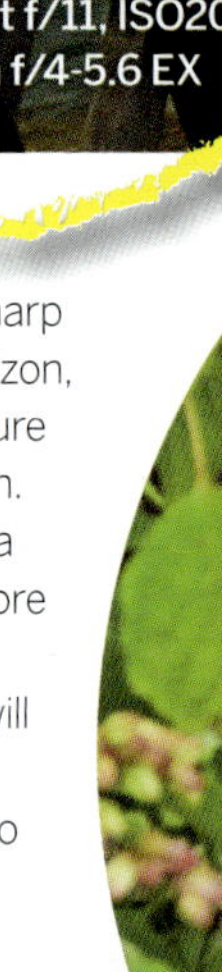

Wide view

If you want everything sharp from your feet to the horizon, using the smallest aperture will not usually be enough. You will also need to use a wide lens setting. The more wide-angle the lens, the more depth of field you will get. Try focusing a third of the way up the frame to maximise depth of field.

All photos: Chris George and Paul Grogan (Future) and Lee Beel

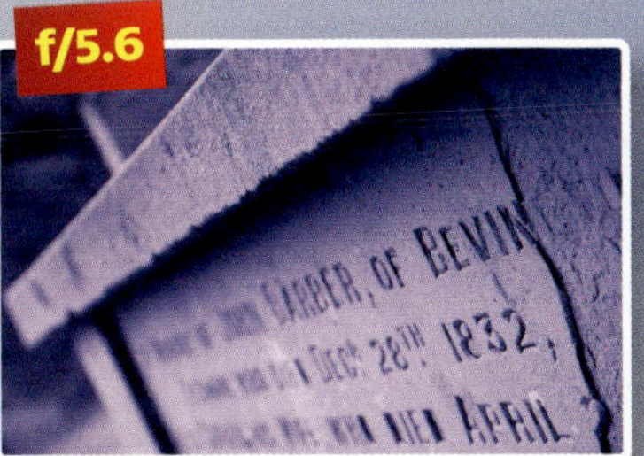
f/5.6

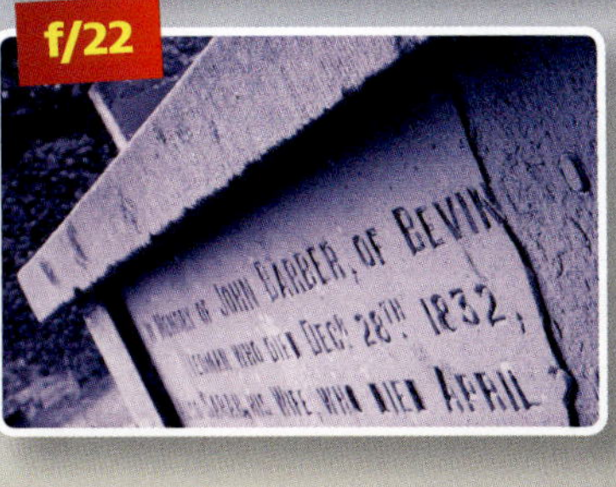
f/22

Tripods add depth

In an ideal world, you would have the full range of apertures to choose from every time you took a picture – allowing you complete control over the amount of depth of field in the scene. In reality, the range of apertures on offer is often limited because you need a shutter speed that is fast enough to avoid camera shake.

You can avoid such compromises, however, if you use a tripod for your shots, because you can then use the smallest apertures in any light. This works best if the subject is stationary – a good alternative if you don't have a tripod, or with moving targets, is to boost the ISO.

The simplest way to alter the aperture is to switch to Av mode on the Mode dial, then use the thumbwheel to dial in the aperture that you want. You can see the setting change in the viewfinder as you do this.

Getting blur to work for you

Any part of the shot that falls outside the depth of field zone is, by definition, unsharp. These blurred areas in an image are an important way of taking the emphasis away from some parts of a scene, so the main subject becomes more prominent. However, just because an area is unsharp does not mean that is is no longer recognisable or distracting. You may need to use a wider aperture to make the depth of field shallower and make these areas appear more blurred. When setting the depth of field, controlling the degree of blur in out of focus areas is often as important as controlling subject sharpness.

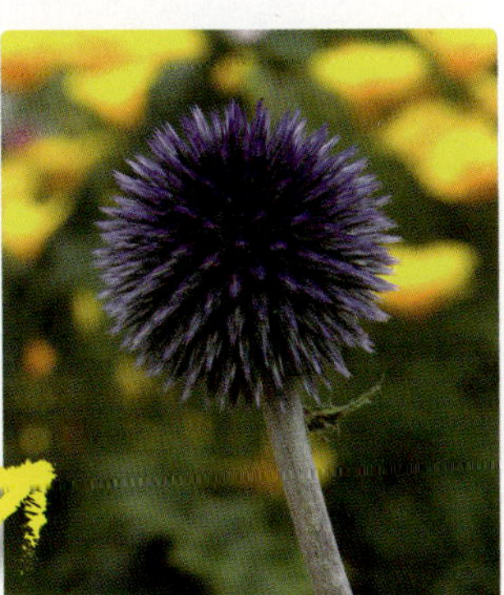

1 200mm at f/32
All the flower is sharp; the background is out of focus but is distracting.

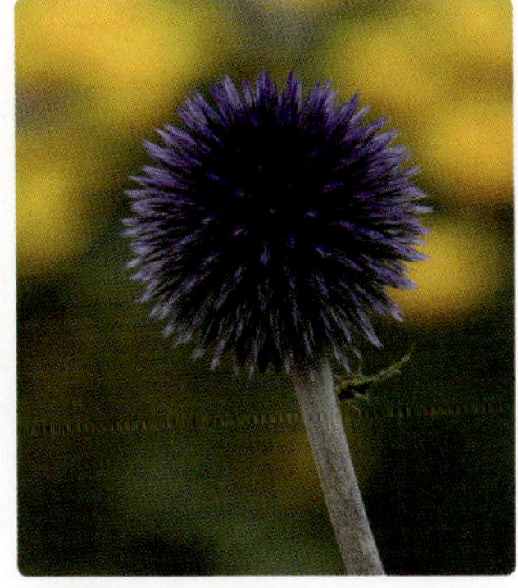

2 200mm at f/11
Most of the flower is sharp; the background is more out of focus but yellow shapes are still visible.

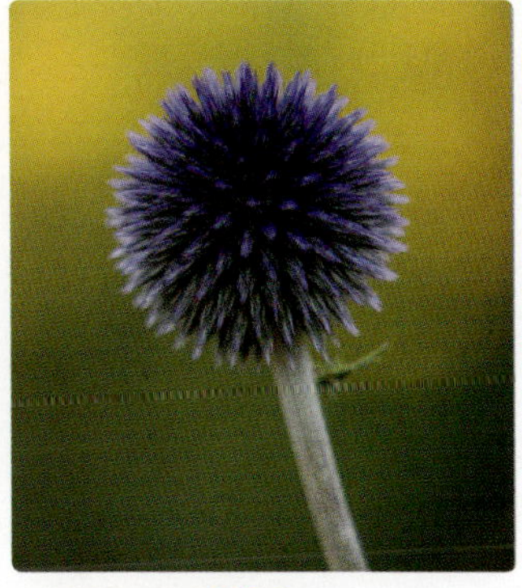

3 200mm at f/2.8
Only some of the flower is sharp, but the background is beautifully blurred and undistracting. ▶

Jargon busters

Focal length
Measurement in millimetres of the optical length of a lens. In practice, it is used to describe the angle of view and the magnification provided by a lens or zoom setting. The shorter the focal length, the wider the angle of view. The longer the focal length, the bigger the image magnification at a given distance.

Depth of field
A measure of how much of a picture is in focus, from the nearest point in the scene to the camera that looks sharp to the furthest point that looks sharp.

Shutter speed and movement

How best to capture the action with your shutter speed setting

Like aperture, shutter speed selection is not just useful for controlling exposure (or just for avoiding camera shake, see p32). Speed also has its creative uses.

The shutter speed you set is crucial when you are shooting a subject that moves. Often, you want to pick a speed that allows you to freeze the movement in the frame – whether it be a jet plane, galloping horses or a tree swaying in the breeze. Picking the right speed to do this will depend not only on the subject speed, but also on its direction of movement in the frame, and how big it appears in the shot.

However, the beauty of an SLR is that you can decide that you don't want the moving parts to be sharp – opting to go slow and get artistic blur instead.

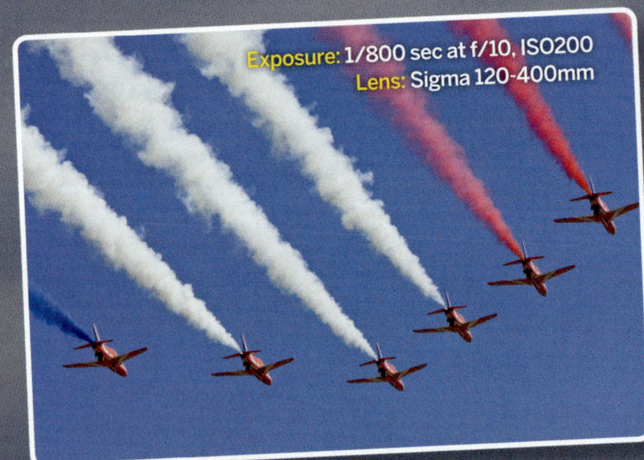

Exposure: 1/800 sec at f/10, ISO200
Lens: Sigma 120-400mm

Half sharp, half blurred

Using slow shutter speeds to blur movement often works best when at least some part of the frame is sharp. One method (as in the shot below) is to use a tripod, so the static surroundings stay pin sharp, then use a long shutter speed so that anything moving in the frame is blurred. Another similar idea is to pop up the flash when using a slow shutter speed, creating a ghost image around a flash-frozen foreground subject.

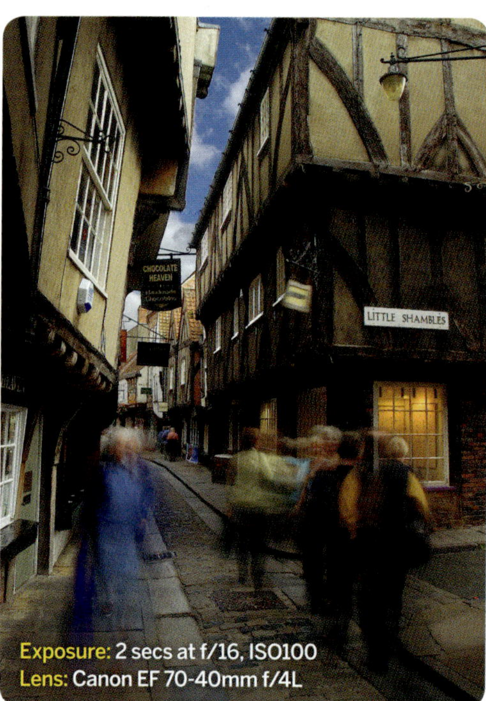

Exposure: 2 secs at f/16, ISO100
Lens: Canon EF 70-40mm f/4L

All photos: Chris George (Future) and Lee Beel

Focus modes

Your digital SLR probably has three autofocus modes. One Shot AF mode is ideal for static subjects. It will not take a photo until it thinks the lens is focused, and will let you lock focus by half pressing down the shutter button. AI Servo AF is designed for moving targets. The focus re-adjusts as you half-press the shutter, and continues to do so until the picture is taken. AI Focus AF switches between One Shot and AI Servo AF for you, so is great for all-round use.

The speed for speed

The shutter speed you need to freeze a moving object in the frame depends on how fast it is moving in the viewfinder. This depends on the actual speed of the subject, but also on how big it appears in the frame, and in which direction it is travelling. To freeze a train 50m away with a wide-angle lens, a shutter speed of 1/500 sec should give a sharp shot, but crop in close with a 200mm telephoto setting and a speed of 1/2500 sec or faster would be needed.

The setting you need also depends on whether the subject is heading towards you or crossing the frame. If moving straight across the viewfinder you will need a shutter speed that is four times faster than if the subject is heading straight towards you.

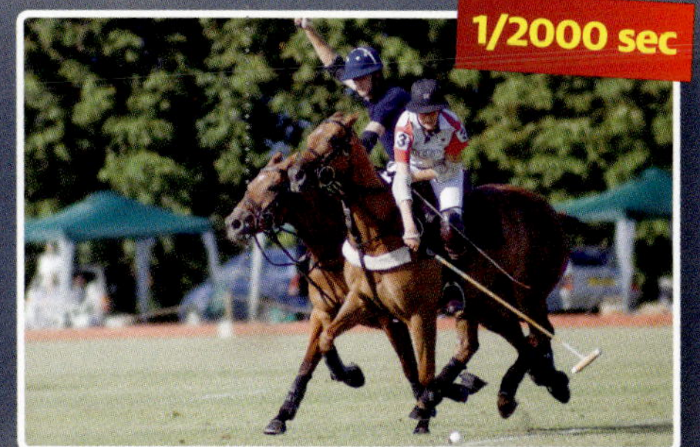

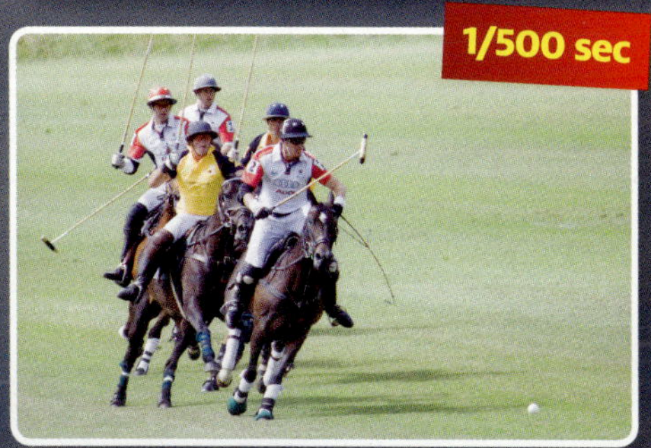

Jargon busters

Tv mode
Time Value (Tv), or Shutter Priority, is an exposure mode that allows you to set the shutter speed you want for a particular subject using the thumbwheel. The camera then tries to set an aperture that ensures a suitable overall exposure.

P mode
In Program (P) mode the camera will set the aperture and shutter speed for you to give what the meter thinks is a suitable overall exposure. However, you can still use the thumbwheel to override the settings and choose a particular shutter speed or aperture if you wish.

ONE SHOT AF

Choose One Shot AF for static subjects and AI Servo AF if your subject is moving

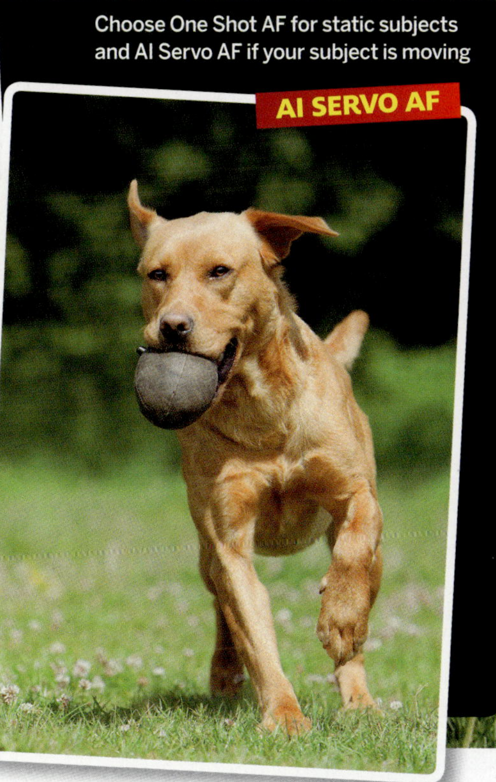

Shutter speeds explained

Common shutter speed values are measured in fractions of a second; an exposure of 1/125 sec is twice as long as one of 1/250 sec. Be warned: confusingly, the camera may display these as 125 and 250 on the LCD and in the viewfinder.

FULL STOPS	HALF STOPS	THIRD STOPS
1/4000		
		1/3200
	1/3000	
		1/2500
1/2000		
		1/1600
	1/1500	
		1/1250
1/1000		
		1/800
	1/750	
		1/640
1/500		
		1/400
	1/350	
		1/320
1/250		
		1/200
	1/180	
		1/160
1/125		
		1/100
	1/90	
		1/80
1/60		
		1/50
	1/45	
		1/40
1/30		
		1/25
	1/20	
		1/20
1/15		
		1/13
	1/10	
1/8		1/10

One stop

Half a stop

Third of a stop

One stop = shutter open twice as long

Fast shutter speeds

Fast speeds = sharp images of moving subjects

Slow speeds = blurred images of moving subjects

Slow shutter speeds

BETTER PHOTOS GUARANTEED!

Learn to see like a photographer

Words and photos: Chris George & Peter Travers (Future)

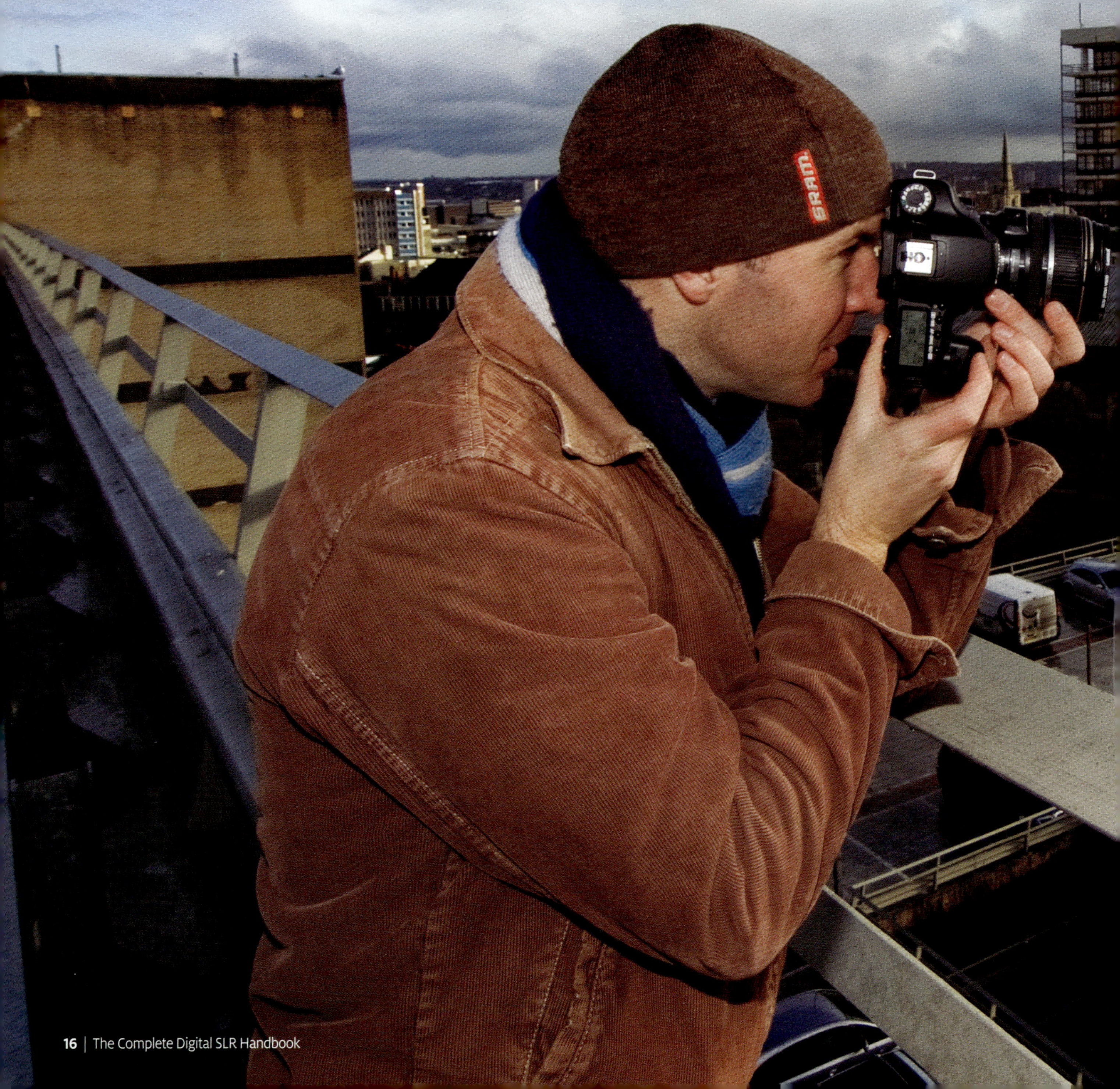

You don't have to go far to find great shots, if you know where – and how – to look. Here's how to take outstanding images in your back yard...

If you want to take great photographs you need to learn to see the world around you with fresh eyes. There's no need to travel to exotic locations or drive deep into the countryside to take fantastic shots. The pictures are already all around you – you just need to learn to see them. Developing an eye for composition is something everyone can learn, and something that everyone gets better at with practice. And there is no better place to start than in your own home town.

Taking pictures on your own doorstep is a tough test for any photographer. Everything is so familiar that you become blind to the potential shots that surround you. So here we'll share great tips and ideas to help you rediscover the magic of your own manor.

Learning to 'shoot local' is also a great way to save money during the recession. There's no need to get in a car or board a plane – just open the door and start shooting!

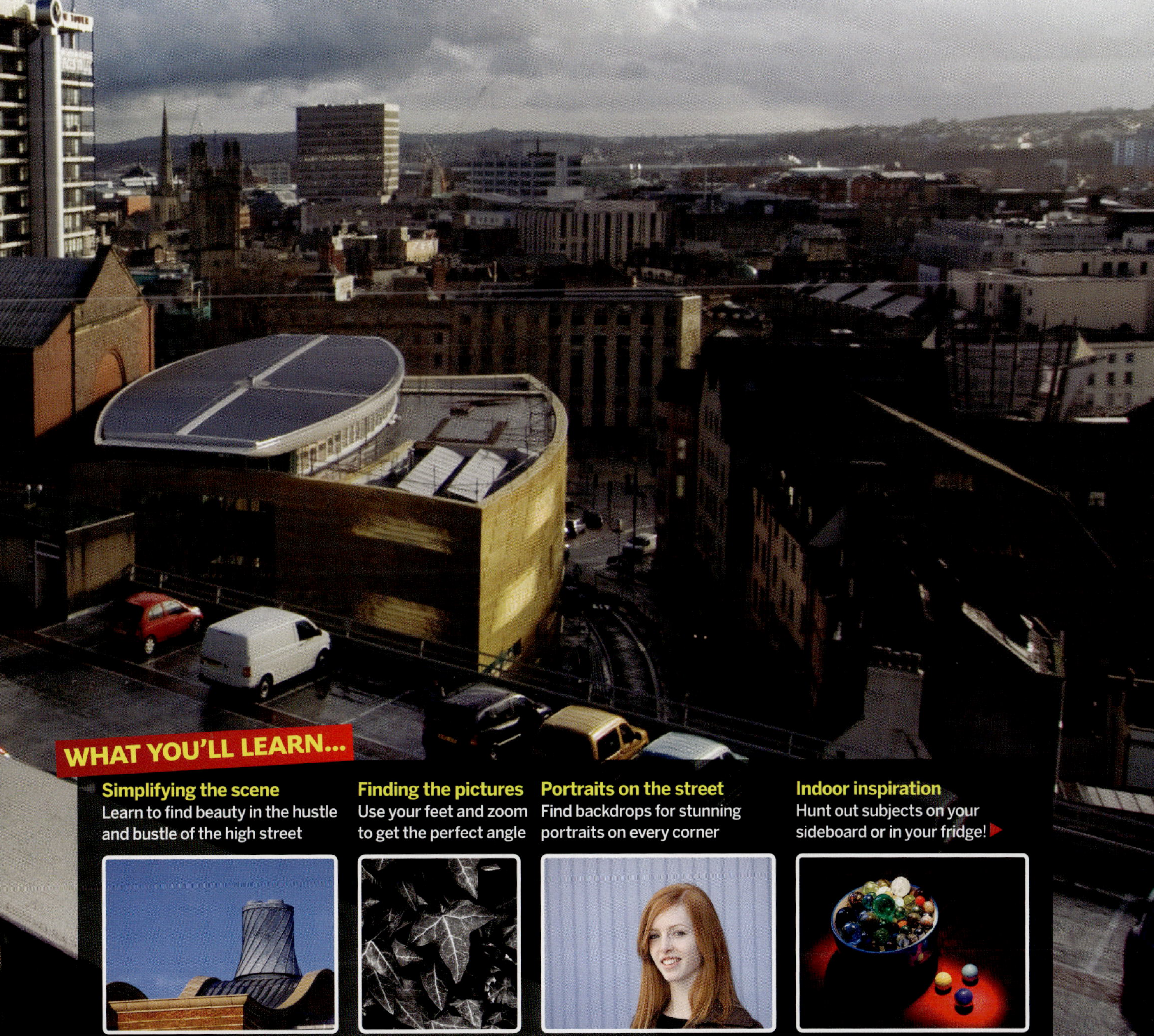

WHAT YOU'LL LEARN...

Simplifying the scene
Learn to find beauty in the hustle and bustle of the high street

Finding the pictures
Use your feet and zoom to get the perfect angle

Portraits on the street
Find backdrops for stunning portraits on every corner

Indoor inspiration
Hunt out subjects on your sideboard or in your fridge!

Simplifying the scene

The secret of effective composition is to remember that it's not only what you frame within your viewfinder that's important. Just as critical is what you leave out. We live in a busy, exciting yet messy world, so don't make the mistake of thinking that you must attempt to capture everything you see within a scene. In fact, often you need to do just the opposite – only capturing a suggestion of the scene in front of you if you want to get quality shots.

Painters can just ignore and leave out the things they don't want on the canvas, but the photographer needs to be more inventive if he or she is to get a clean, uncluttered composition. Try zooming in, or physically moving in, for a tighter shot. This will simplify the scene and your shots will soon begin to transform from casual snaps into eye-catching photos.

Check out professional travel photos of a busy Moroccan market, for example, and you'll often see that the best shots are not of the entire colourful scene. The shots with the most impact are those that focus on a single market stall with a small selection of vibrantly coloured goods. You can use these same techniques in your home town. Read on to find out how...

Picking out photos

The key to getting good results when shooting in cities is to crop out the messy world to find clean compositions. Photos work best when you extract the abstract possibilities rather than trying to photograph the surroundings 'warts and all'. This photo of a chimney with its shapes and curves shows what's possible when you look for it – we shot this from the top of a car park on the other side of the road! We just had to zoom in and wait for the sun to create shadows and for the clouds to clear from the frame. This created a more pleasing background.

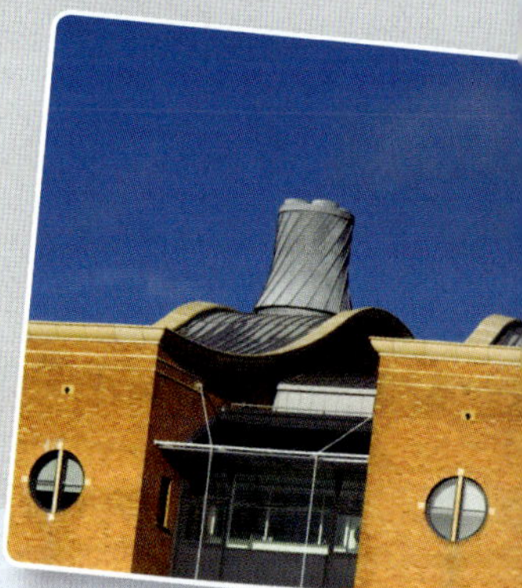

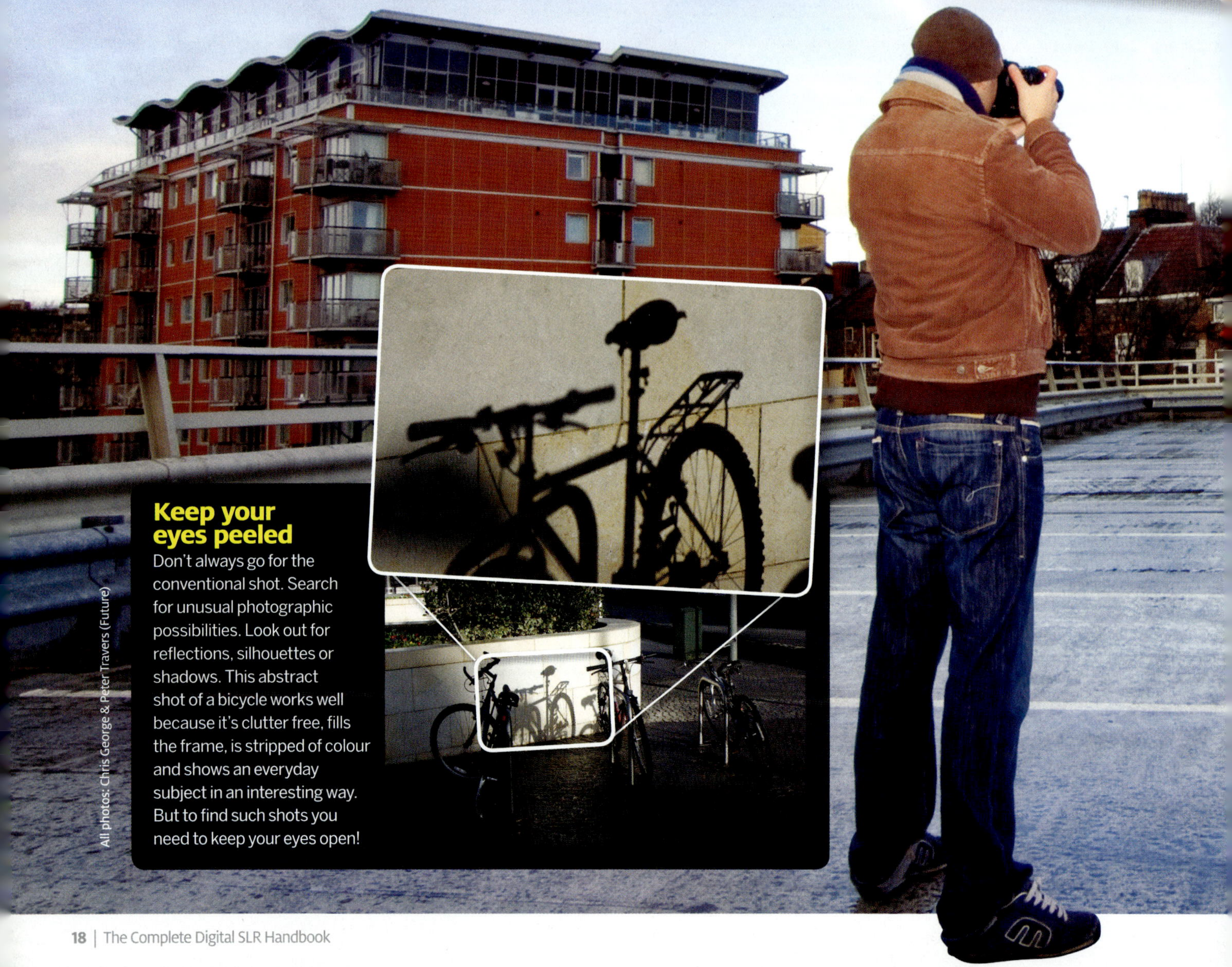

Keep your eyes peeled

Don't always go for the conventional shot. Search for unusual photographic possibilities. Look out for reflections, silhouettes or shadows. This abstract shot of a bicycle works well because it's clutter free, fills the frame, is stripped of colour and shows an everyday subject in an interesting way. But to find such shots you need to keep your eyes open!

All photos: Chris George & Peter Travers (Future)

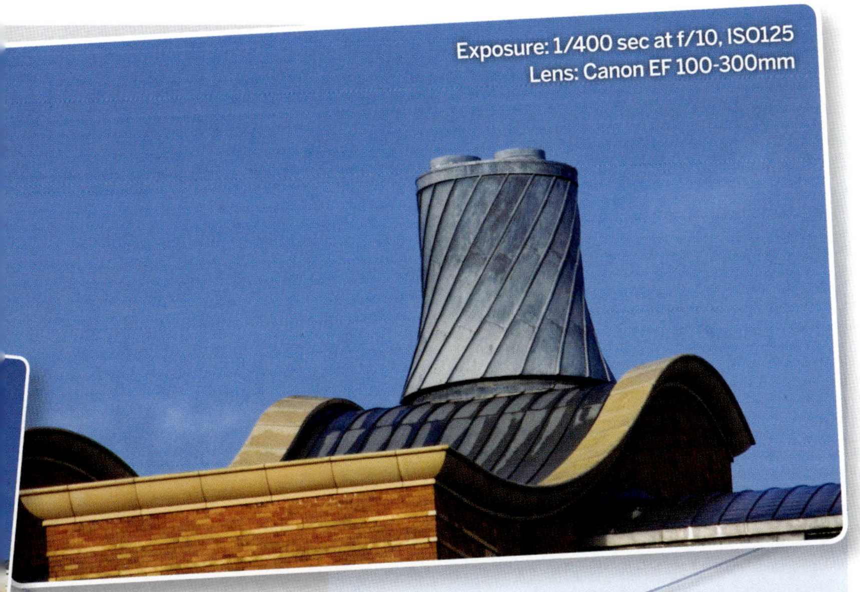

Exposure: 1/400 sec at f/10, ISO125
Lens: Canon EF 100-300mm

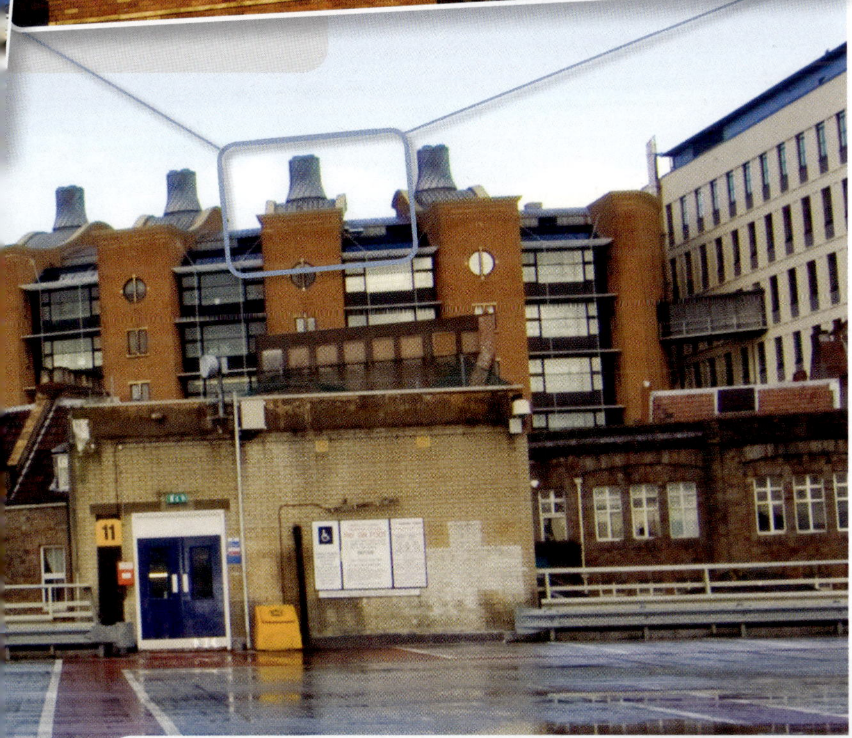

Photoshop potential?

Keep an eye out for photos with potential – shots that, although initially might not look all that, could be turned into little gems with some cunning Photoshop trickery.

This leafless silver birch tree stood amongst green foliage, but in colour it looked a bit lifeless, with little light or shadows. A quick black-and-white conversion and some boosted contrast later, and it's transformed into a fine-art beauty that features lovely white tones standing proudly against a newly created black background.

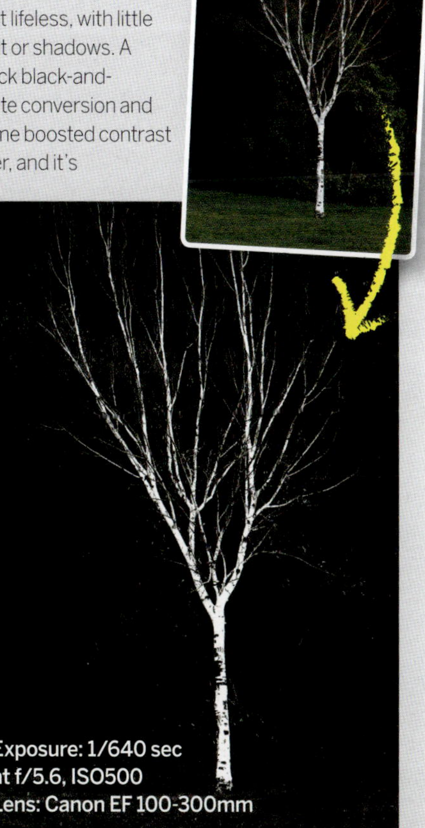

Exposure: 1/640 sec at f/5.6, ISO500
Lens: Canon EF 100-300mm

Clean up city streets

If you live in Paris or Prague, elegant nightscapes are easy to find. However, most UK high streets are chaotic – cluttered with people, cars and ugly shops. You can solve the problem by shooting a long exposure and filling your scenes with light trails. This time of year is ideal for photos like this because it's dark when rush-hour is in full flow. Look out for double-decker buses and lorries, as their upper lights will fill the top half of your photos with a second line of light trails. Use a tripod and shoot on Self-timer to avoid camera shake. Shoot in Manual, using your narrowest aperture (usually f/22) with a shutter speed of 15-25 seconds.

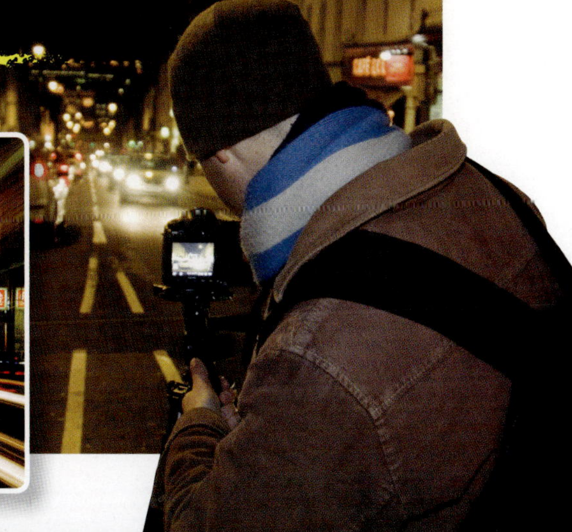

We used a shutter speed of 13 sec at f/29 for this abstract rush-hour shot

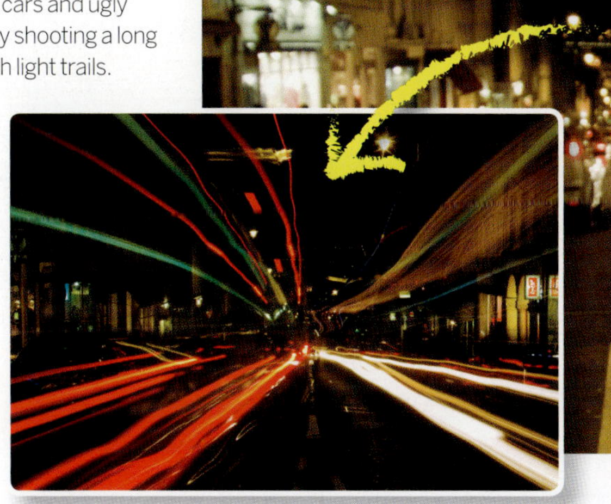

Finding the pictures

It's easy to overlook great photo opportunities in your home town simply because you see the same sights all the time, but there are some useful tricks you can use to help you see the picture potential in scenes you've walked by hundreds of times before.

It may sound obvious, but because buildings aren't moveable you need to move to get the best angle. Circumnavigate your chosen subjects from all sides and try to find different heights to discover improved views that will add more impact to your shots.

Look through your camera's viewfinder each time you find a new angle to see which composition works best. Also look at scenes through different lenses and different focal lengths, from 18mm on a wide-angle lens to 200mm on a telephoto lens. Changing the focal length is not just a simple cropping tool, it will also change the composition of your picture. As you zoom in and out, or move about, you can frame your subject with different foregrounds and backgrounds. A long zoom setting, for instance, is great for framing your subject against the one bit of blue in an otherwise grey sky.

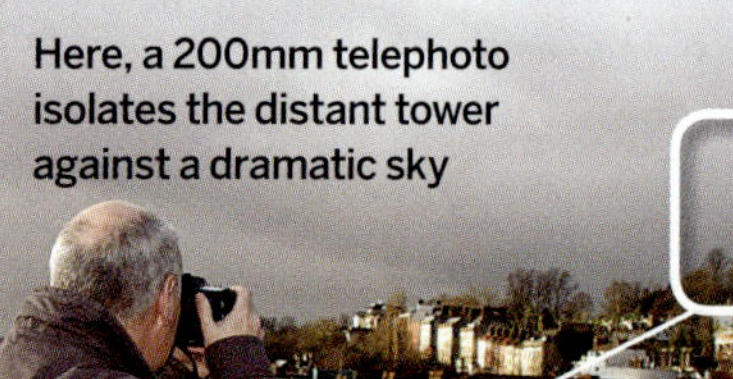

Here, a 200mm telephoto isolates the distant tower against a dramatic sky

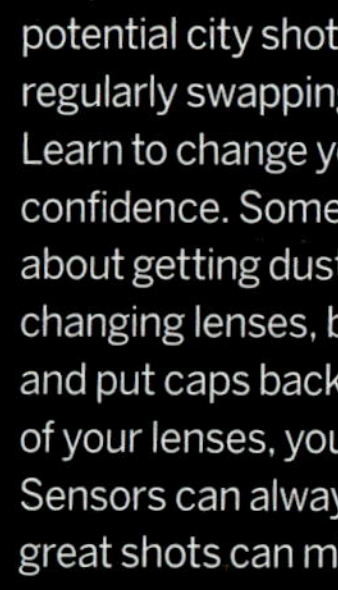

Zoom in!

Not all photo opportunities will be right in front of you. They could be miles away, so carry a telephoto zoom lens (with a focal length of 200-300mm) and look all around the horizon to identify potentially interesting images. If you shoot sights in your home town, you have no excuse not to find the best angle – and to wait for the best light to shoot it in. This shot of a city centre tower was shot from the same car park as the image on the previous page. You only need a suggestion of surrounding buildings for people to get an idea of where your photo was taken.

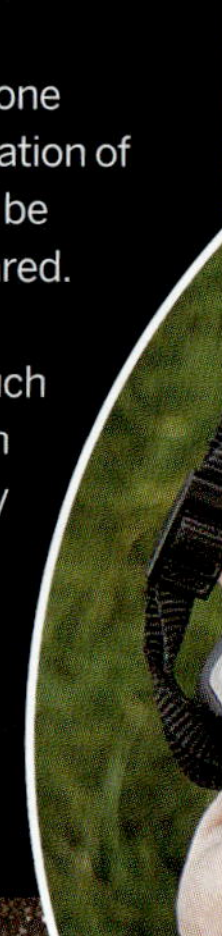

Keep swapping lenses

You'll need at least one wide-angle and one telephoto zoom lens to capture the variation of potential city shots, which means you'll be regularly swapping lenses. Don't be scared. Learn to change your lenses with confidence. Some people worry too much about getting dust on their sensor when changing lenses, but if you swap quickly and put caps back on the camera-end of your lenses, you minimise the risk. Sensors can always be cleaned, but great shots can missed if you don't use the best lens for the job.

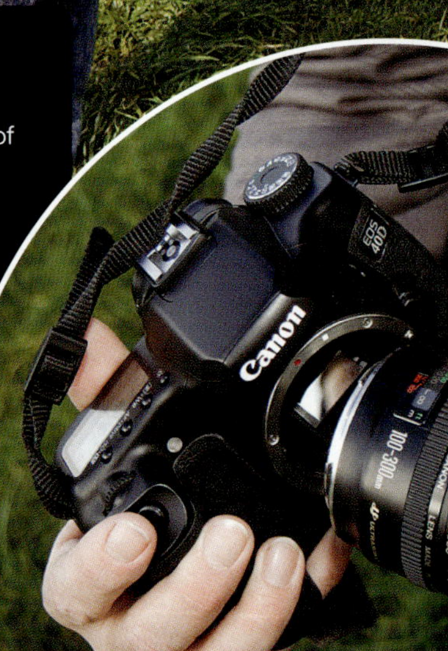

All photos: Chris George & Peter Travers (Future)

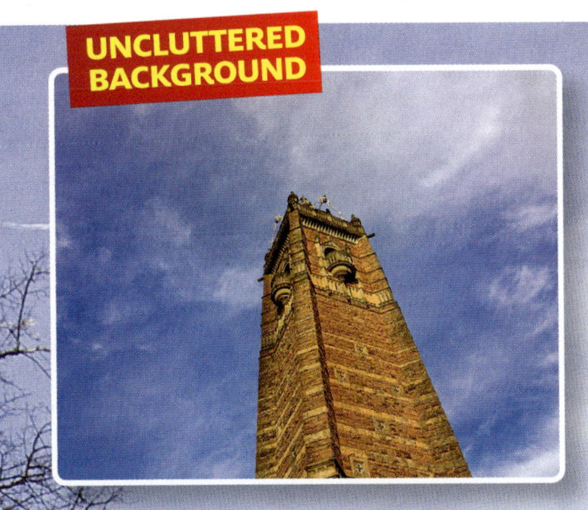

FOREGROUND INTEREST

Walk around your subject

Don't just stand in one spot and zoom in until you've got your subject in the frame before taking your shot. Walk around your subject. This not only creates a different angle, but also, most importantly, changes the foreground and background for an improved composition. By removing any foreground you'll make your subjects more prominent, but by adding more foreground interest your subject is no longer star of the show and will become just another part of your scene. Both techniques work well, but try both, because one will generally work better than the other for a specific photograph.

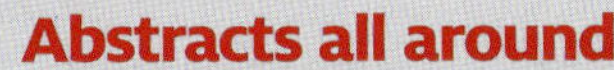

Abstracts all around

Abstract images exist everywhere – you just need to look for them. Even brickwork or bark can look great when tightly composed to show off their contrasting textures and tones. Keep a look out for man-made patterns. Details of buildings work particularly well, so try using your telephoto zoom lens and compose tight shots to create conceptual images from boring office blocks. Lighting can make all the difference to these shots, so make the effort to go back later if the sun is not co-operating. ▶

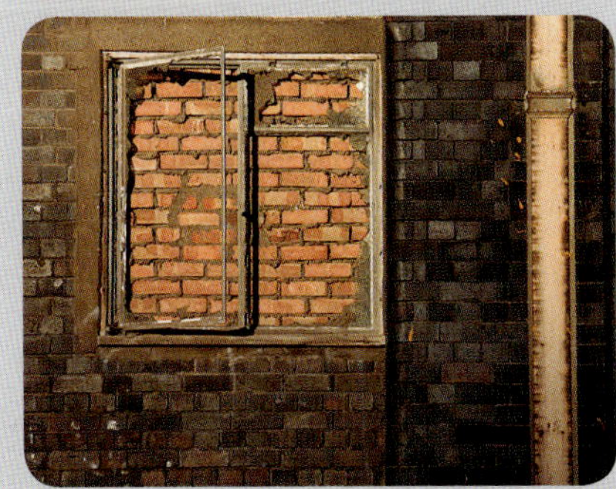

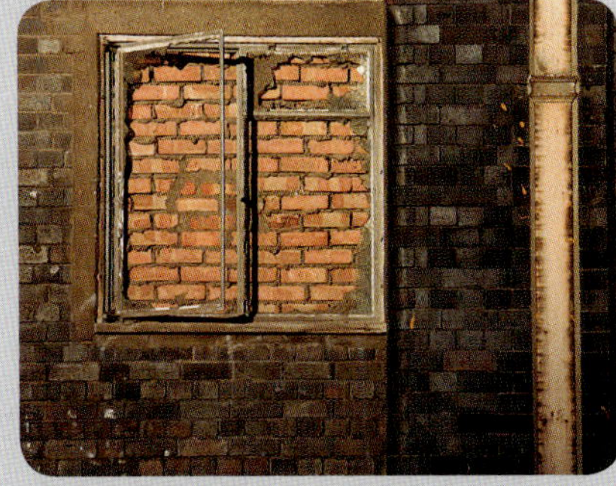

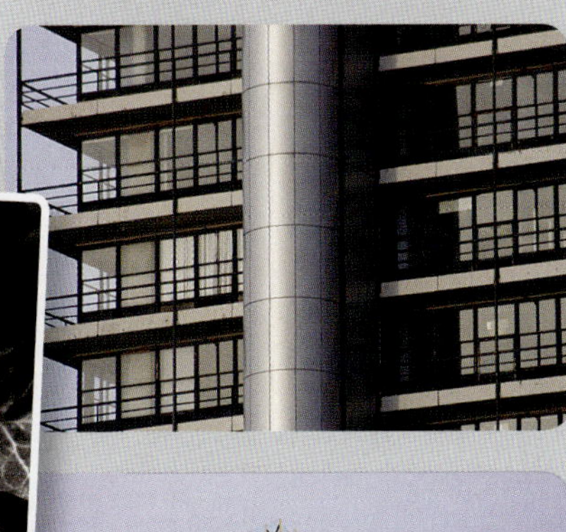

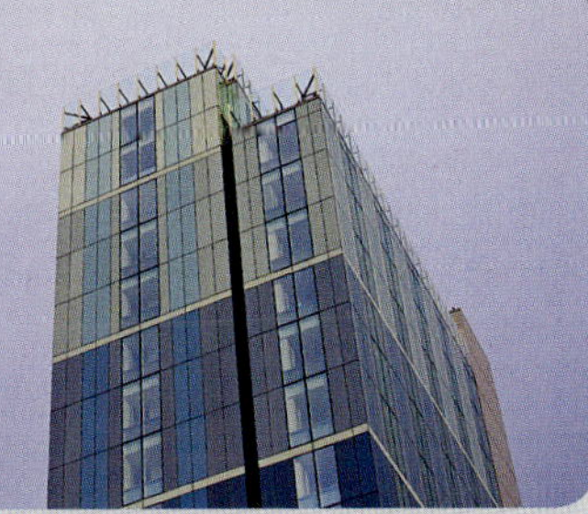

Patterns in nature

Opportunities to shoot plants exist in every town, and it's not just brightly coloured flowers that make cracking pictures. Think of your photos as a way of capturing patterns and look closely at trees and plants for interesting options. Even ivy makes great images, especially when converted to black and white. This emphasises its vein-filled leaves and natural shape. You don't need a macro lens either – just zoom right in with your telephoto.

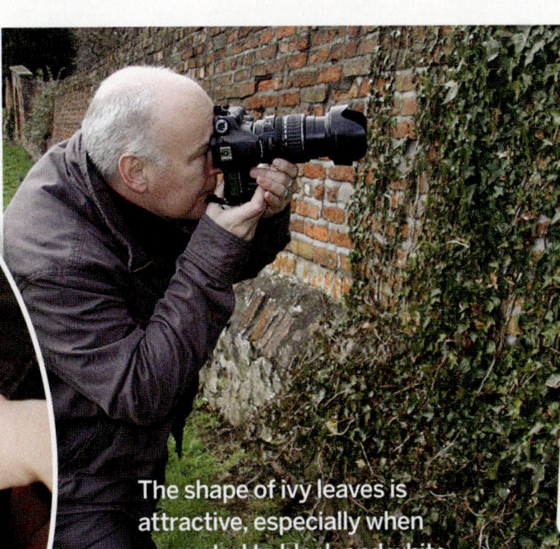

The shape of ivy leaves is attractive, especially when converted to black and white

Portraits on the street

Wherever you live, you rarely have to look far to find photogenic faces. Whether it is the person's natural beauty that inspires you, or their character and clothes, your local streets are a great place to shoot striking portraits.

There's no need to set up or hire a studio to get great pictures of people. Just step outside and you'll be surrounded by local architecture that provides backdrops in every pattern and colour that you can imagine.

Bizarrely, it's the parts of modern buildings hidden from view that often provide the richest pickings. The loading bays of shops, or small industrial units, often have large doors and panelled walls that offer a range of clean backdrops perfect for the job.

Keep things simple and use natural light. You will get the best results if you shoot on a bright day, and then capture your portraits in the shade. You can then use a reflector to balance the light. There's no need to buy a reflector – a sheet of white cardboard will do the job. Alternatively, pop up your built-in flash to help soften shadows and add catchlights to the eyes.

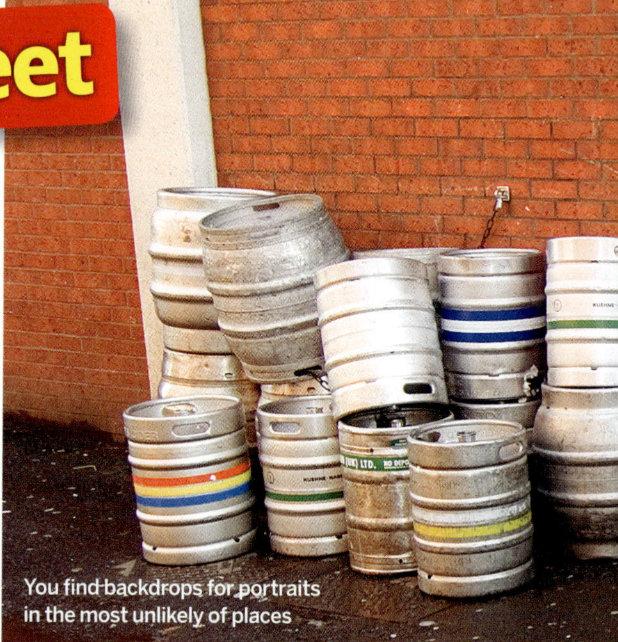

You find backdrops for portraits in the most unlikely of places

MAKE THE MOST OF ANY BACKGROUND...

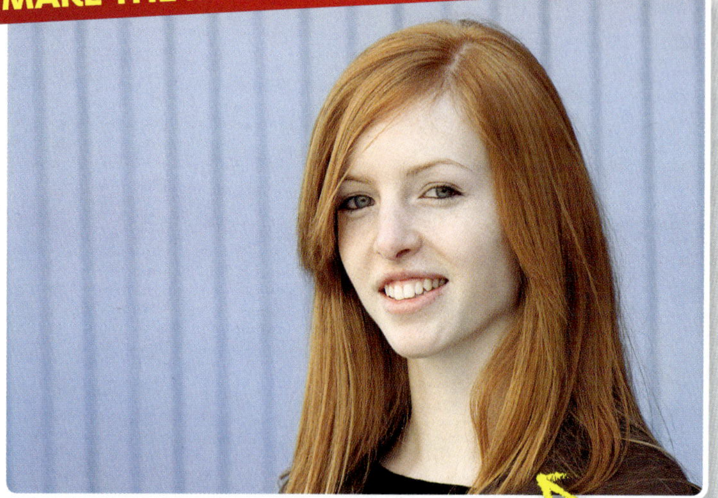

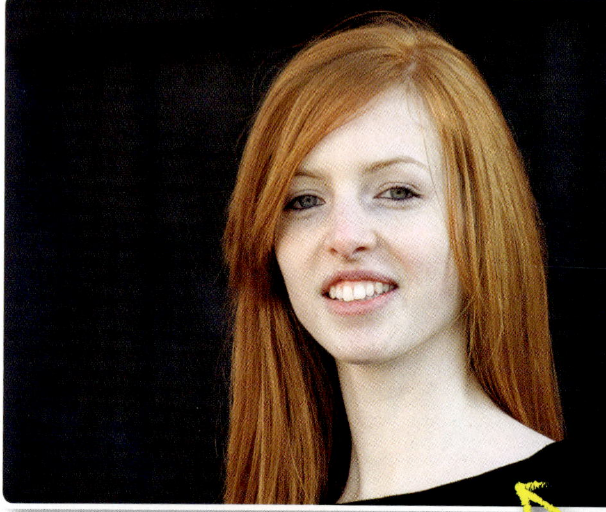

#1 BACK GATE

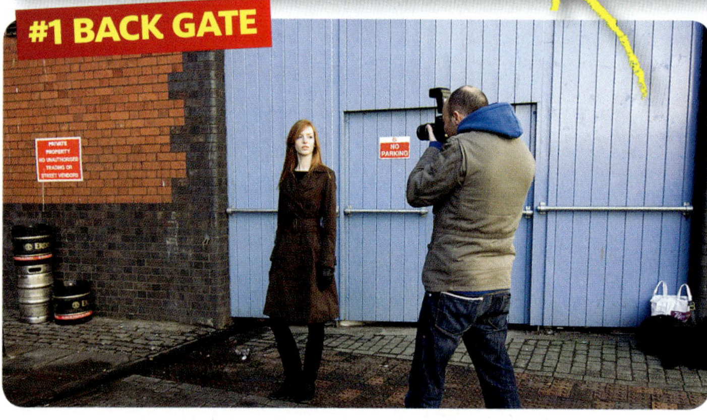

All photos: Chris George & Peter Travers (Future)

#2 RUBBISH BINS

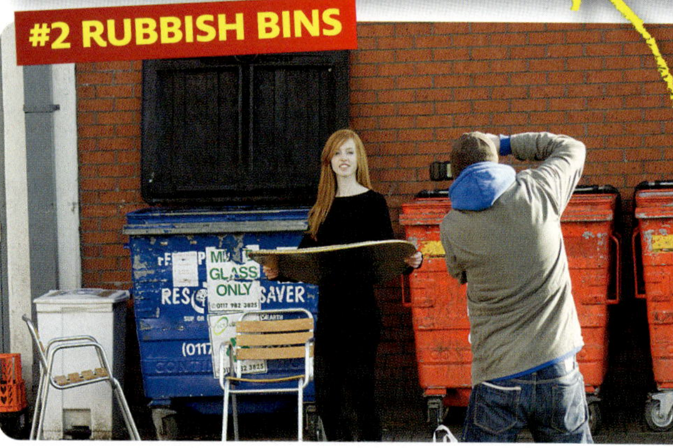

How much backdrop do you need?

You need a large expanse of backdrop for full-length portraits, and the sides of industrial units are great for giving you the wash of colour you need. But with head-and-shoulder shots you can make do with much smaller areas of colour or texture. If you find an area you want to use as a background and there is not much of it, shoot from further back with a longer telephoto zoom setting so that even a small door or bin lid will fill the frame.

Softly softly with the aperture

Makes sure your subject is positioned a few feet in front of the backdrop, and use the widest aperture your lens allows (typically between f/2.8 to f/5.6) in Av mode. These two tricks will ensure that the background is slightly unsharp, so the subject stands out. However, it's essential to ensure you have the lens focused accurately on the person's eyes.

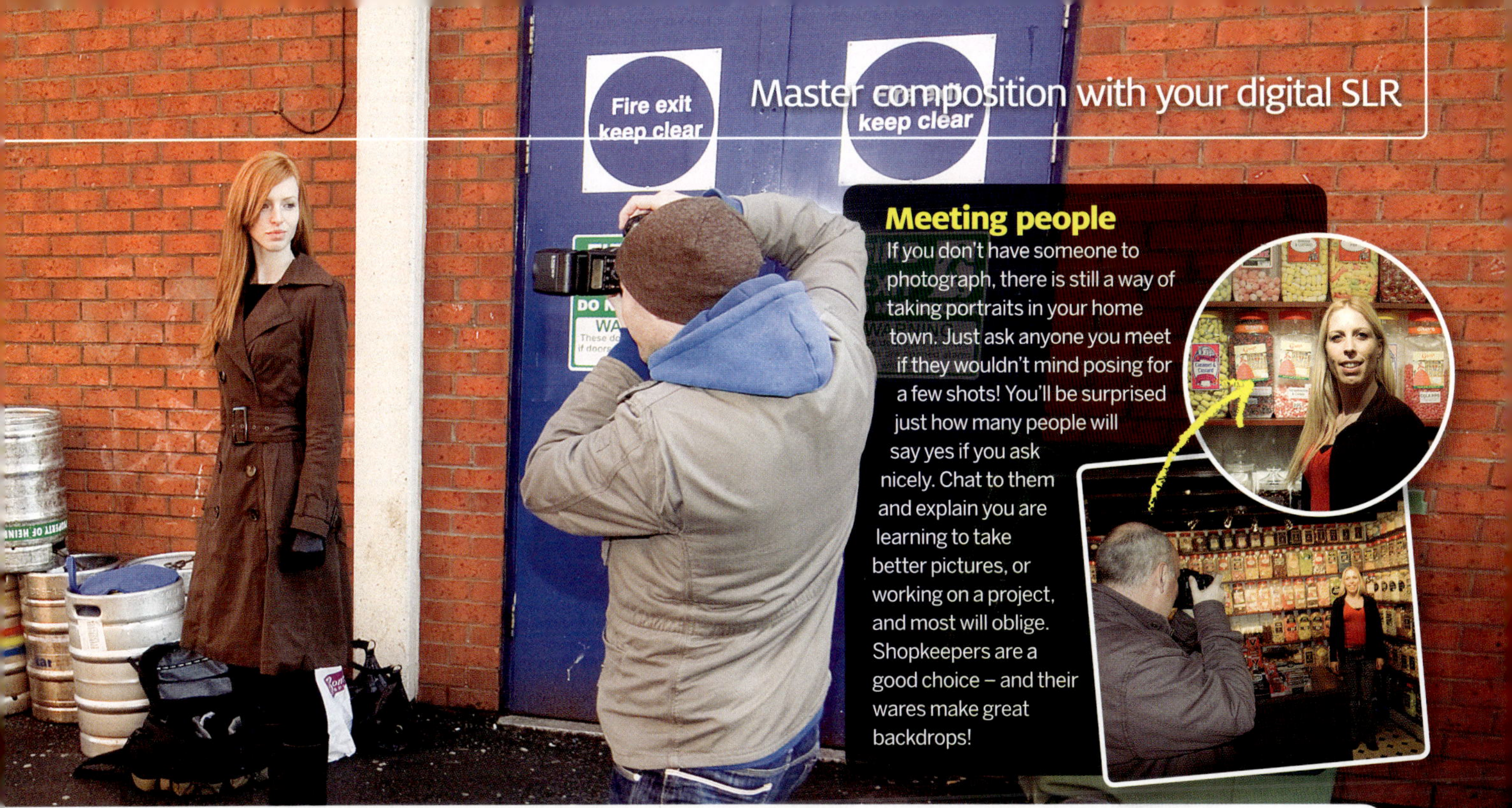

Meeting people

If you don't have someone to photograph, there is still a way of taking portraits in your home town. Just ask anyone you meet if they wouldn't mind posing for a few shots! You'll be surprised just how many people will say yes if you ask nicely. Chat to them and explain you are learning to take better pictures, or working on a project, and most will oblige. Shopkeepers are a good choice – and their wares make great backdrops!

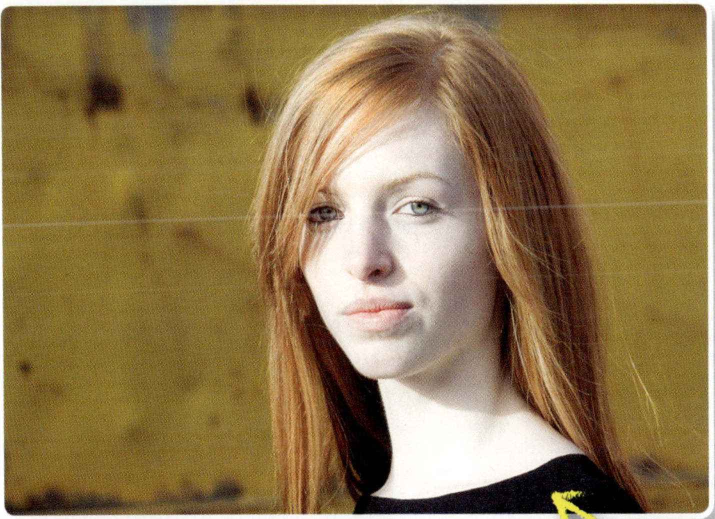

#3 SKIP

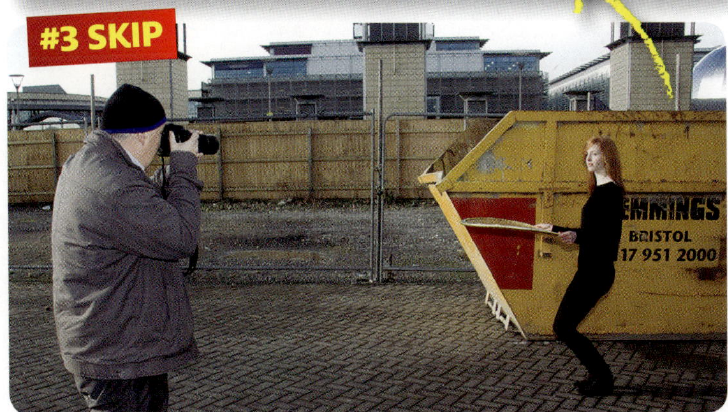

Off with their head...

When framing close-up portraits, it is easy to end up with your subject's head sitting squarely in the centre of the frame. It's better to give your subject room to breathe – and to include more of the beautiful backdrop you have found! A simple posing trick is to get your model to stand with their shoulders at a 45° angle to the camera and wall, then to turn their head or eyes to face the camera. Leave more space on the side of the frame their body is facing, and less behind them.

Candid camera

As you walk the streets with your camera you will see all sorts of interesting characters that would make a great subject for a candid portrait. Most photographers find these easier to shoot from a distance, shooting, say, from the other side of the street. This approach is usually easier in a busy market, than on a quiet back street. Once you have found your subject, wait for the best pose – or try to find a way of framing them so that the surroundings add something to your portrait.

You are within your rights to photograph people in public places (in the UK, at least). But use your common sense to avoid upsetting people. It's best to avoid taking candids of children, unless you have their parents' permission. ▶

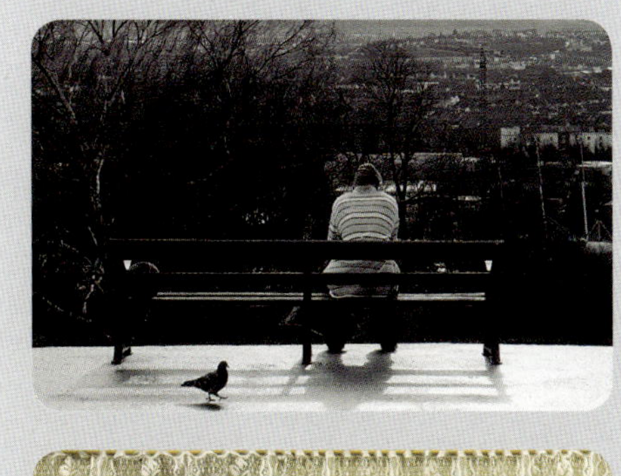

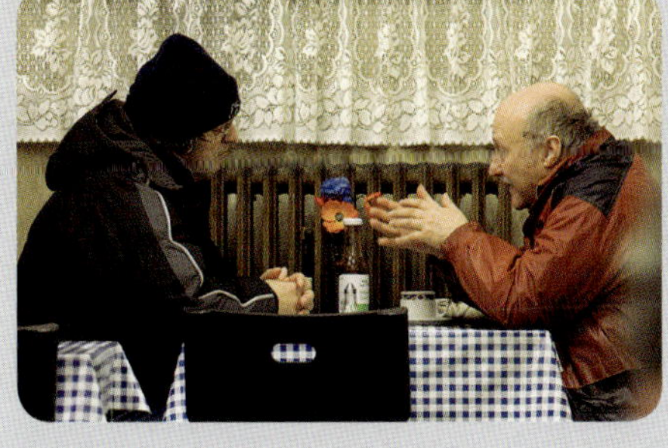

Indoor inspiration

Even using all these tips and ideas, there will be times when you really struggle to capture decent pictures around your home town. If it is pouring with rain, for example, there may be little point in trying to take great photos. But there's no excuse to give up.

You can find plenty of great objects around your home that can be turned into impressive still-life subjects. Your sideboard and shelves are probably stacked with suitable knick-knacks and mementoes for you to shoot. However, we think your fridge should be your first port of call. Plenty of professional photographers make good money photographing food – and the raw ingredients in your kitchen are perfect.

Artists learn to paint with bowls of fruit and bottles of wine, and you too can get great pictures from these subjects. Try shooting food that has interesting three-dimensional form – such as red and green peppers. You'll find great texture on cabbages and broccoli. Just make sure you use the best specimens...

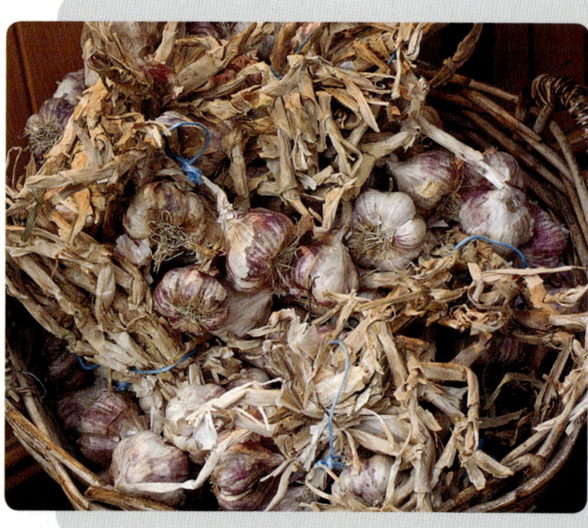

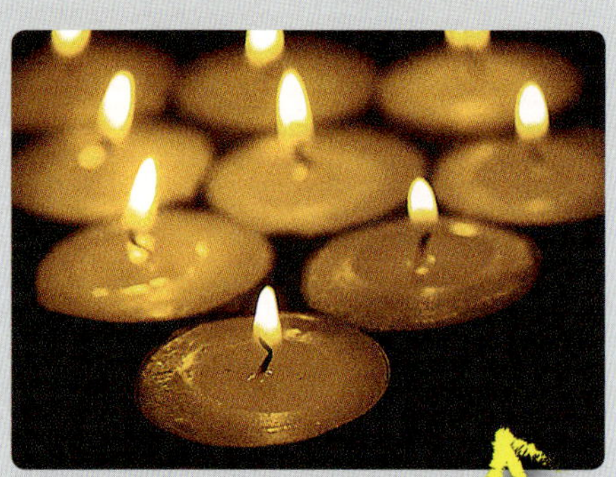

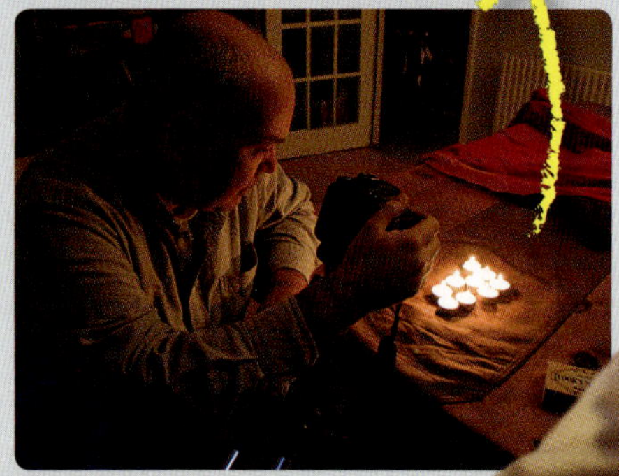

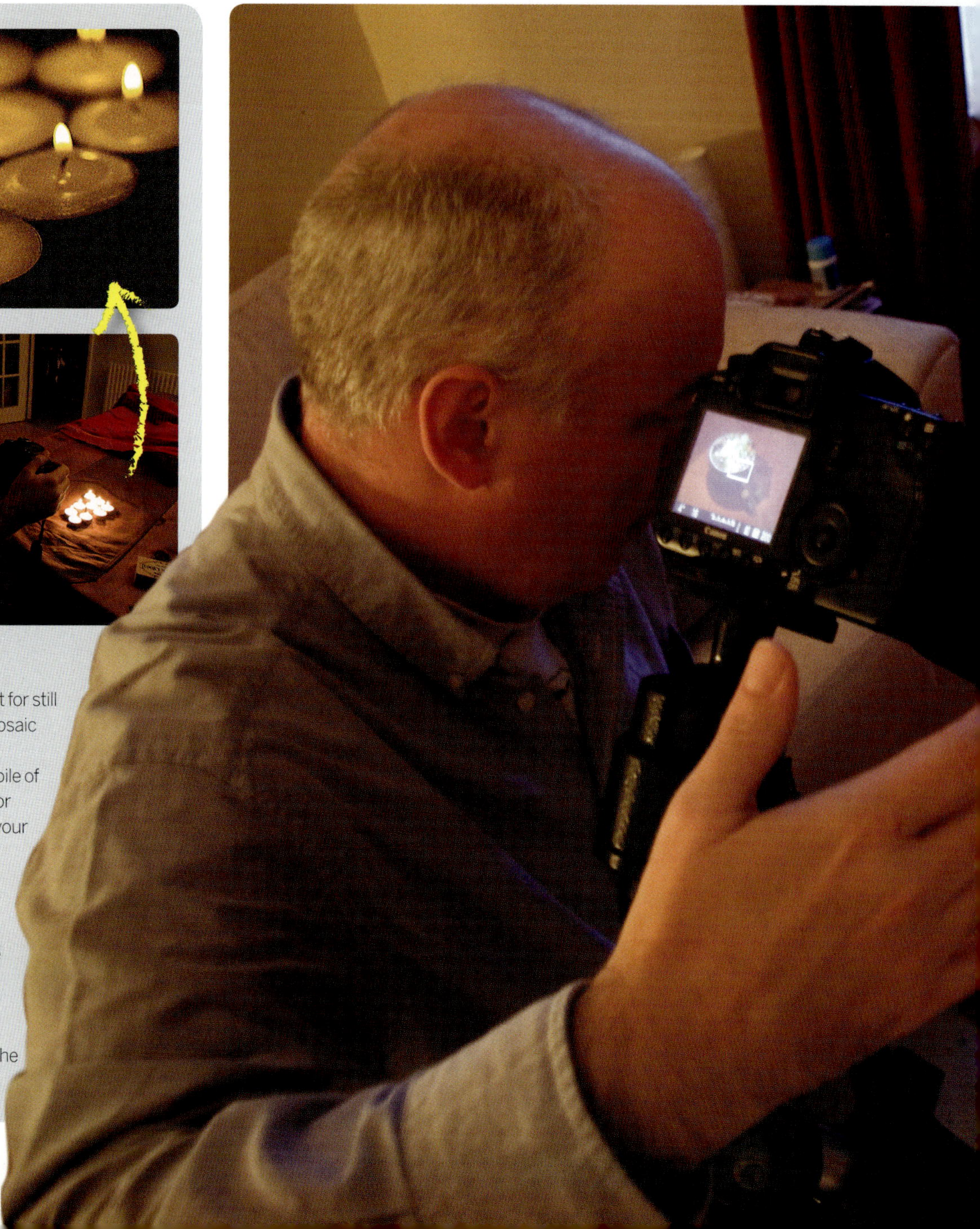

Shooting by candlelight

Groups of objects are great for still lifes, and even the most prosaic of subjects often work well photographed this way. A pile of screws from your toolbox or coloured paperclips from your desk look good captured up close. Here, a bag of tealights provided us with inspiration. The flickering flames make a nice picture – we simply tweaked the colour balance in Photoshop and added a grainy filter to accentuate the low-light look.

All photos: Chris George & Peter Travers (Future)

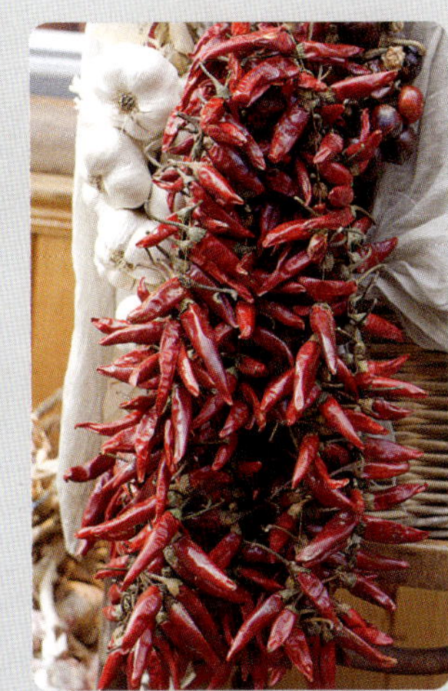

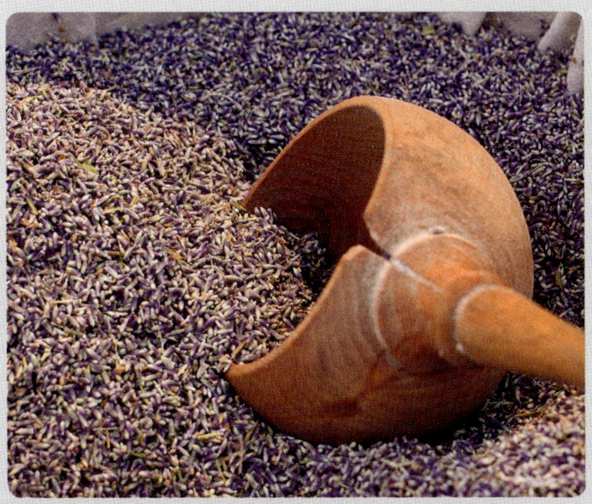

Still life on the street

Nothing in your fridge? Cupboards clutter-free? If you can't raid other people's houses for inspiration, you should just go down to the shops. There's no need to buy anything, you can just photograph the things you find in situ. Markets and shops are full of enticing displays ready for you to work with. Windows are dressed and merchandise is arranged to attract the eye – all you need to do is find the angle and the crop to pick out the most interesting bits from what you see. You probably won't be able to use a tripod, so increase the ISO as necessary to ensure the shots are shake free. ■

Think about lighting

When shooting still lifes you can get great results simply using natural light. As the subjects are small, find a window that is bright – but avoid direct sunlight. You can create your 'set' here – with the subject, backdrop and any props you need. For the shot on the right, a chopping board created a great frame for the asparagus, while the fabric of a footstool creates the backdrop. If it is dark, try using a small torch to light your subject (see below). Mount your camera on a tripod and select a small aperture so that the shutter speed is several seconds long. As the trigger is fired, paint your scene with the torch light – ensuring that you keep the torch itself just out of shot. Move the light, spotlighting the areas you want to accentuate.

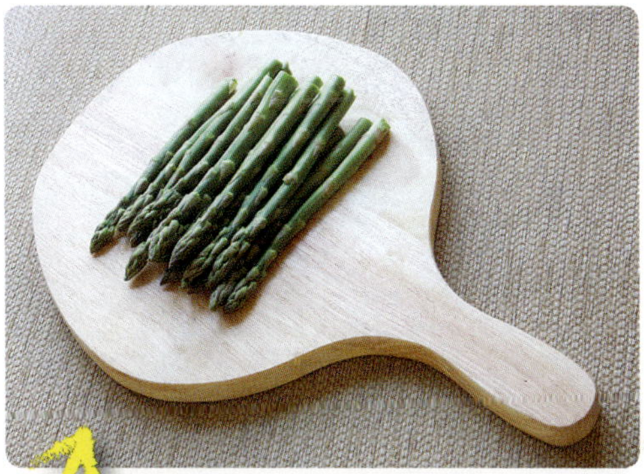

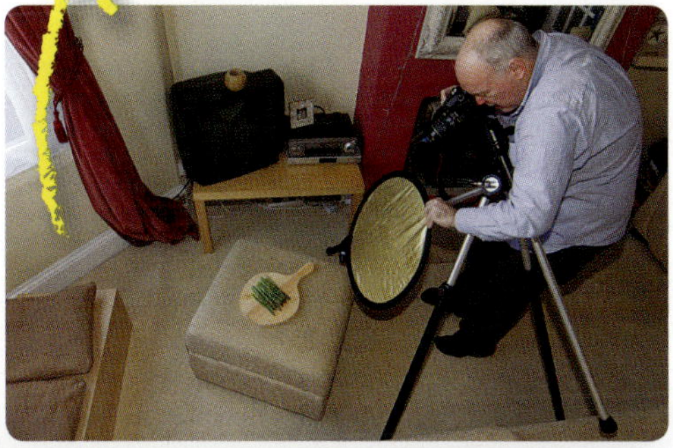

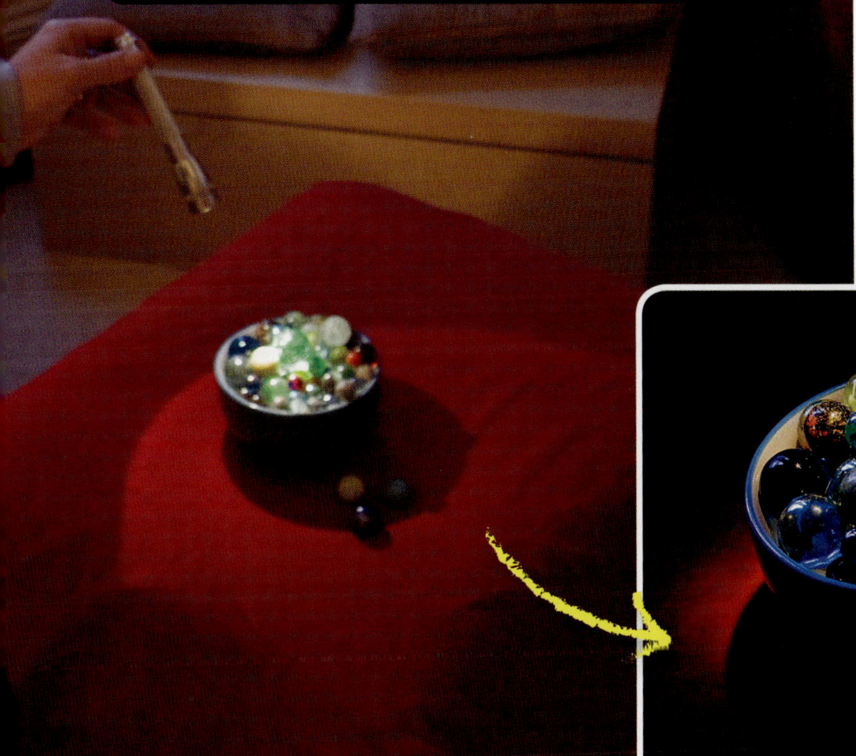

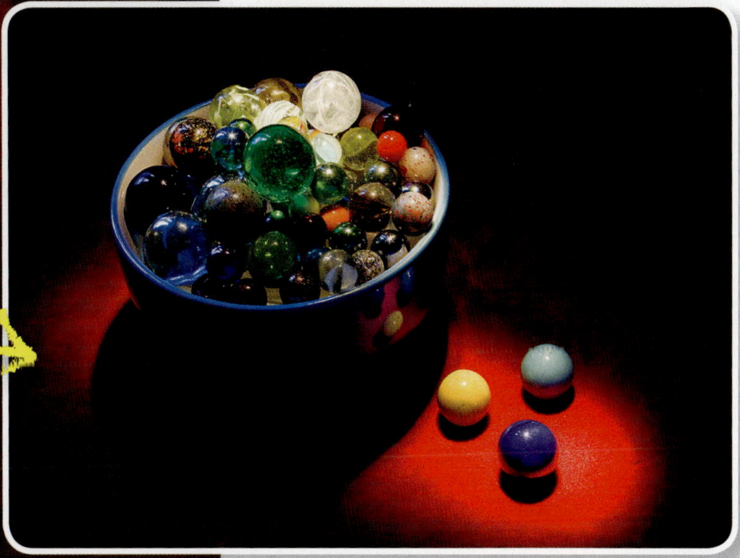

These marbles were shot with a four-second exposure at f/16, using a torch to create a spot-lit effect

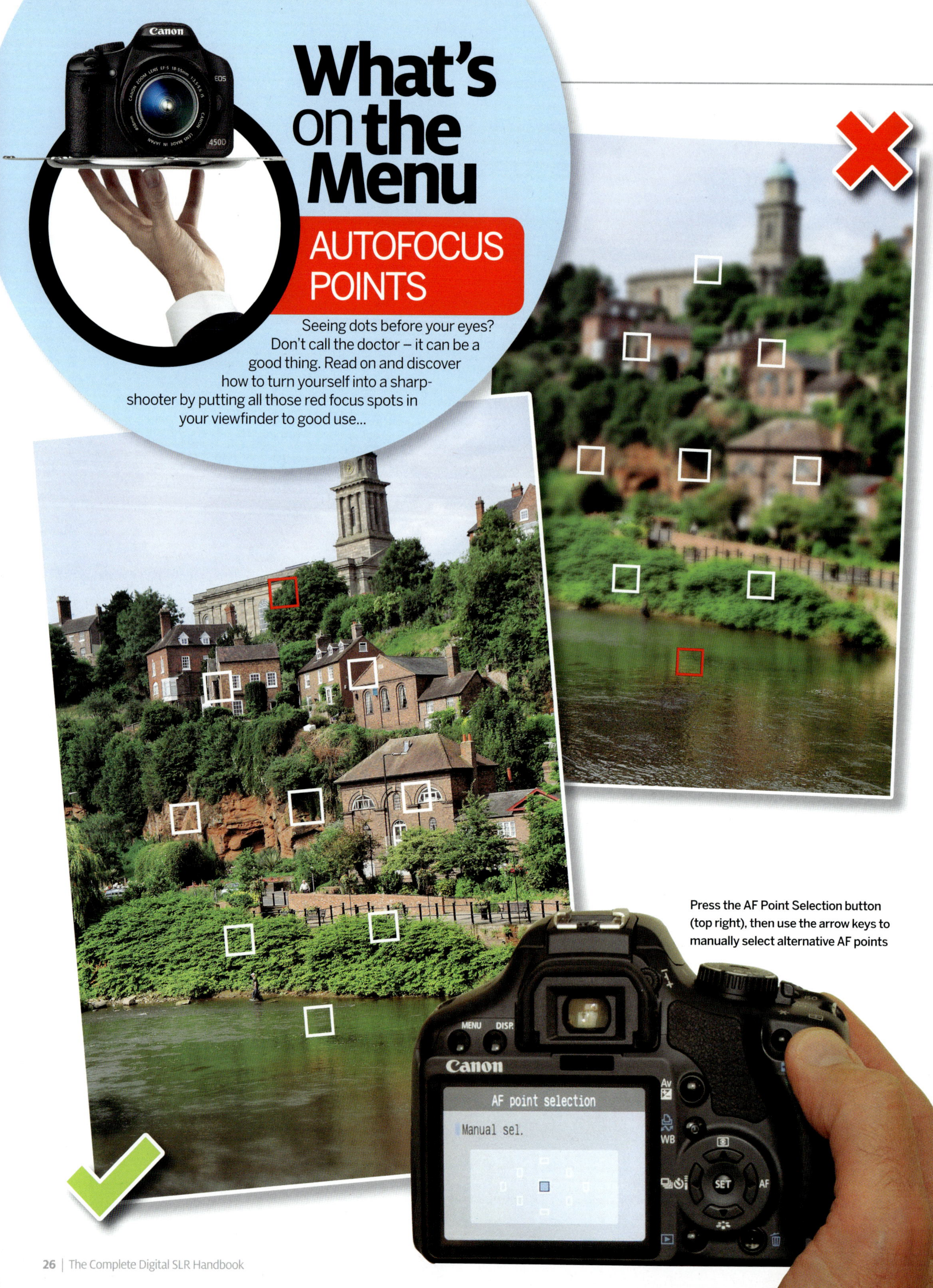

What's on the Menu

AUTOFOCUS POINTS

Seeing dots before your eyes? Don't call the doctor – it can be a good thing. Read on and discover how to turn yourself into a sharp-shooter by putting all those red focus spots in your viewfinder to good use...

Press the AF Point Selection button (top right), then use the arrow keys to manually select alternative AF points

Focusing has never been so simple. Use any of the Basic Zone shooting modes – Full Auto, Portrait or Landscape – and your camera does all the work for you. It's almost too easy. A light press on the shutter button is all you need and, 99 times out of a 100, the camera will focus in a split-second and you're ready to fire. So why is it that many shots simply aren't sharp in the places that matter, such as the eyes in a portrait or the rolling hills of a landscape? The answer lies in the way that the autofocus system actually works.

Left to its own devices, a D-SLR like the 450D or 50D uses all of its nine autofocus sensors, which are spread out in a wide array around the image frame, as shown in the walkthrough below. There's one AF point at the centre, one both above and below it, another two to the left and right, and a final pair positioned towards the extreme left and right sides of the frame. More advanced cameras, including the 5D Mark II, feature an additional six 'AF Assist' points, although these, unlike the first nine, can't be selected manually.

Near and far

To achieve autofocus in Basic Zone shooting modes, as well as under default conditions in most Creative Zone modes, your camera uses information from all nine AF points. It works out the distance of each part of the scene from the camera, chooses the closest object that coincides with an AF point and locks the autofocus at that setting. This is fine if you want to focus on the nearest object in a scene, but often that's not the case. If you're shooting a sweeping landscape, for example, you don't want to focus on the grass in the foreground.

In these cases it's better to select a Manual AF point. And in close-up or telephoto photography, especially with a large, wide aperture that reduces the depth of field, pinpoint accuracy becomes even more critical.

MAKE THE MOST OF AF POINTS

It pays to be picky when deciding which focus point to use

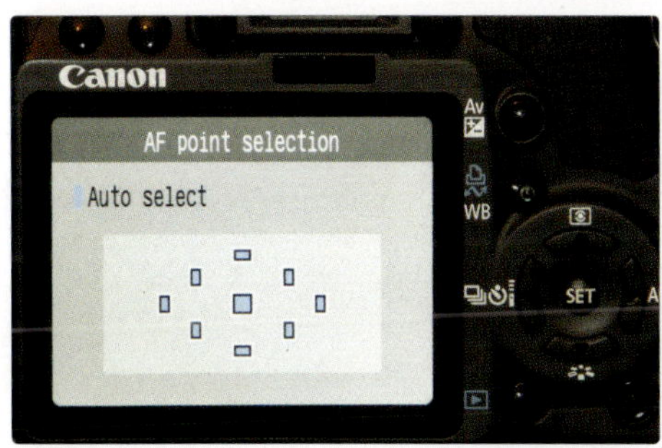

Auto select

1 By default, your SLR uses every AF point in each shooting mode but, in most Creative Zone modes, you can choose AF points manually. Press the AF Point Selection button at the top-right of the rear of the camera and the display will confirm that multi-point Auto Select AF is in use.

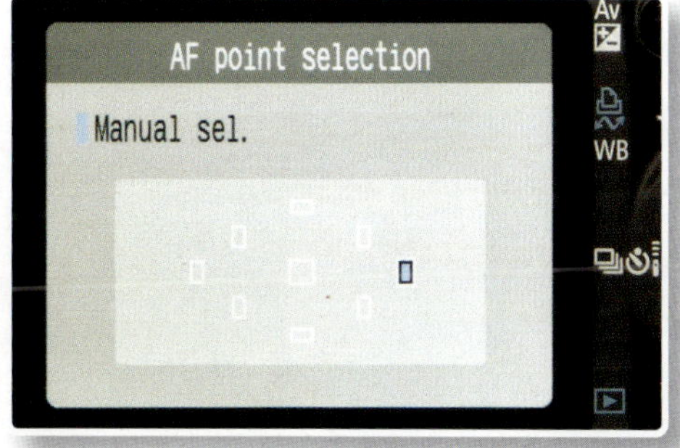

Change the AF point

3 You're not limited to using the central AF point in Manual Select mode. After switching to single-point AF, you can use the arrow keys (or the Multi-controller on cameras such as the 50D) to switch to any of the other eight AF points. To return to the central AF point, press the Set button again.

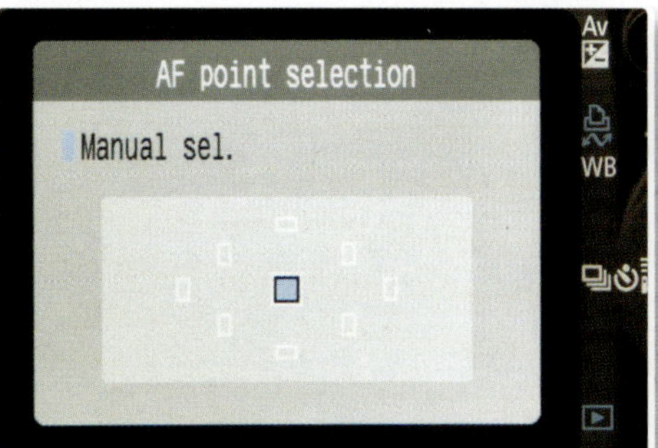

Manual select

2 To switch from AF Auto Select to Manual Select mode, press the AF Point Selection button as in the previous step, but then press the Set button. The camera will now switch from multi-point selection to using only the central AF point for autofocus. Press the Set button again to revert to multi-point Auto Select.

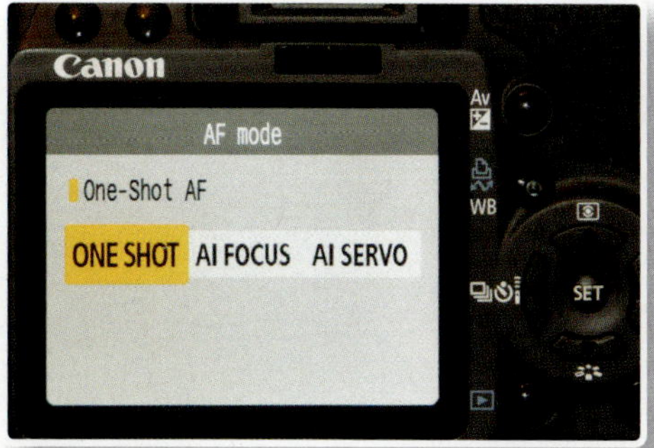

AF modes

4 Manual AF point selection works in any of the various AF modes, so you can couple use of selective AF points with One Shot AF for stationary subjects, AI Focus AF for erratic subjects, or AI Servo AF for tracking moving subjects. Select the most appropriate AF mode by pressing the AF arrow key. ▶

Phrase Book

AF point
The 450D uses nine AF points, with a central cross-type AF point that can focus on vertical and horizontal lines simultaneously. The other eight can only resolve either horizontal or vertical lines. The 50D uses the more advanced cross-type AF points for all nine sensors.

Central AF point
The central AF point is twice as sensitive as those positioned around the edge of the frame. This can deliver greater precision in tricky conditions or when using a lens with a maximum aperture of at least f/2.8, such as the EF 50mm f/1.8 or the EF-S 60mm f/2.8 Macro.

Rule of thirds
This is a composition technique where the image is divided into thirds, a bit like an elongated noughts and crosses grid, and points of interest are placed as close as possible to intersecting imaginary lines. Wide-area AF points are positioned with this in mind.

Super Tip!

"You can use AF points as a guide even when focusing manually. Switch the lens to MF (Manual Focus), lightly press and hold the shutter button, and the AF points will flash red when that area of the shot comes into focus as you adjust the focus ring."

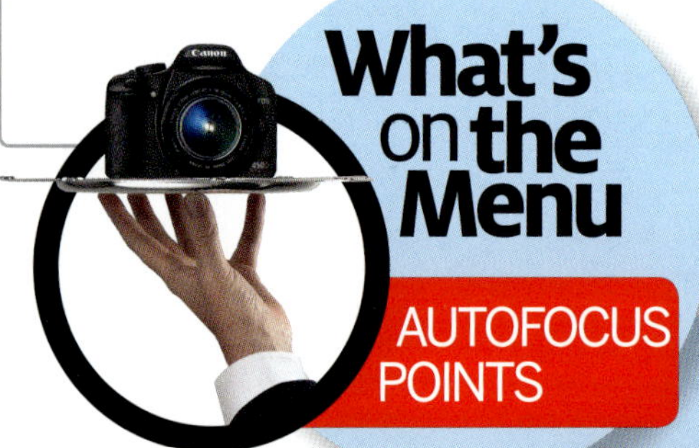

TAKE CONTROL OF FOCUS

Master AF points to transform a variety of shots

Super Tip!

"A particularly creative yet automatic use of AF points is available via the A-DEP (Auto Depth of Field) shooting mode. This special mode in the Creative Zone uses all of the nine available AF points to gauge the relative distances of various objects and areas within the overall scene. It then automatically combines the optimum focus setting with the required aperture, giving a sufficiently large depth of field that will keep as much of the scene in focus as possible. The A-DEP mode is particularly good for group portrait shots as well as for landscape photography. The AF points will flash red in the viewfinder for all corresponding parts of the frame that will be rendered sharply."

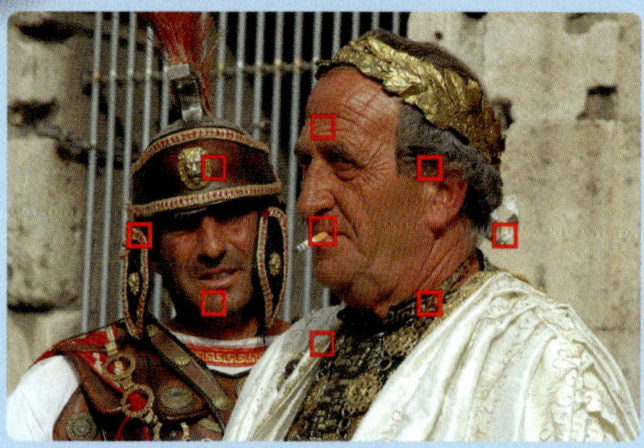

Auto Select

1 When you generally want to focus on the closest object in a scene and you need to react quickly to what's going on around you, Auto Select is a good option. It saves potentially missing a shot because you're too busy adjusting AF point selection, and is also good for tracking action (for more on this see the opposite page).

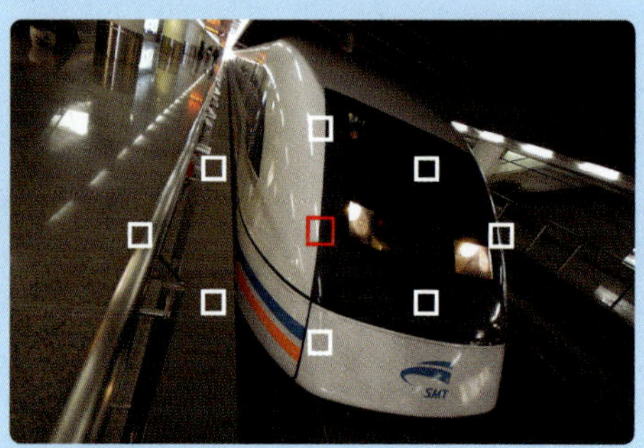

Central AF point

2 The central AF point is the most sensitive and accurate of all, so it's great for use in very dull or extremely bright lighting conditions, when other AF points can struggle to achieve autofocus. It's also perfect for when the main object of interest is at the centre of the frame.

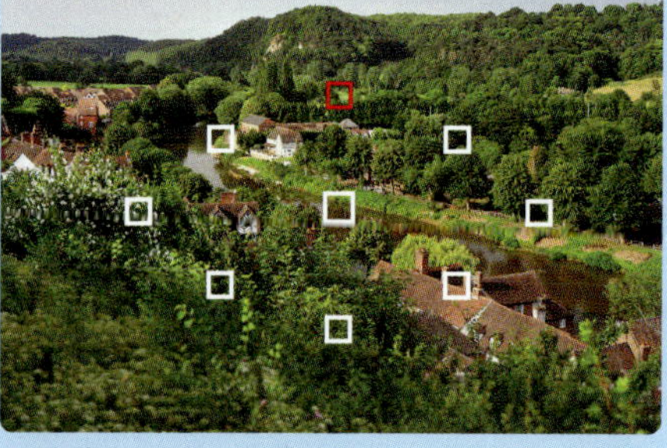

Upper AF point

3 When you're taking a landscape shot and your emphasis is on distant scenery rather than the foreground, select the upper AF point. This stops the camera focusing on spurious foreground objects or areas that happen to coincide with a lower AF point.

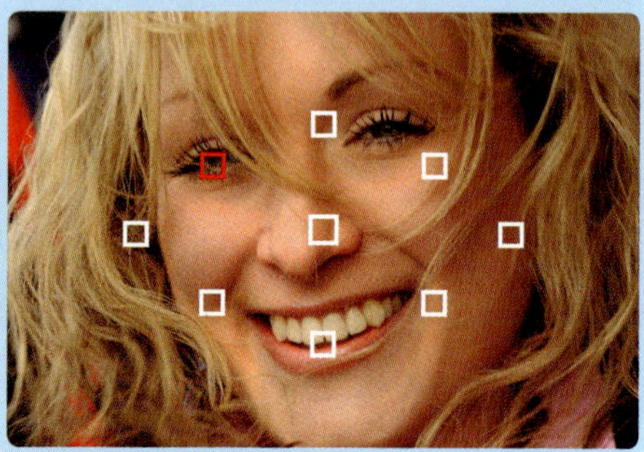

Diagonal AF point

4 Portraits usually work best when the subject is slightly off-centre in the frame. Shooting in landscape or portrait orientation, choose the appropriate diagonal AF point and focus on one of the subject's eyes. If the face is at an angle to you, focus on the eye that's closest.

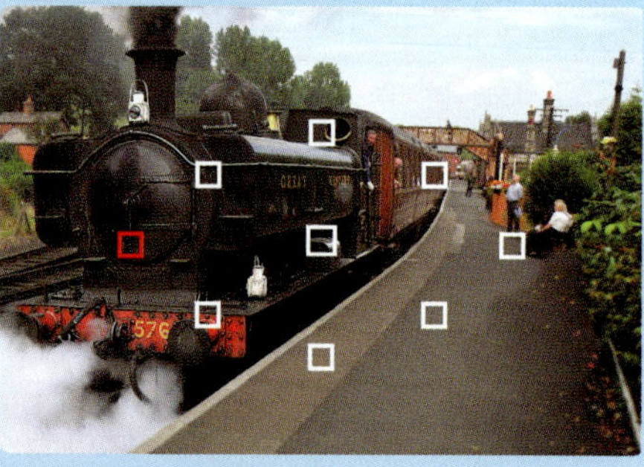

Edge AF point

5 The AF points positioned at the far left- and right-hand sides of the image frame are very handy when you want to throw foreground areas into soft focus, concentrating on a more distant subject that's positioned on one side of the frame.

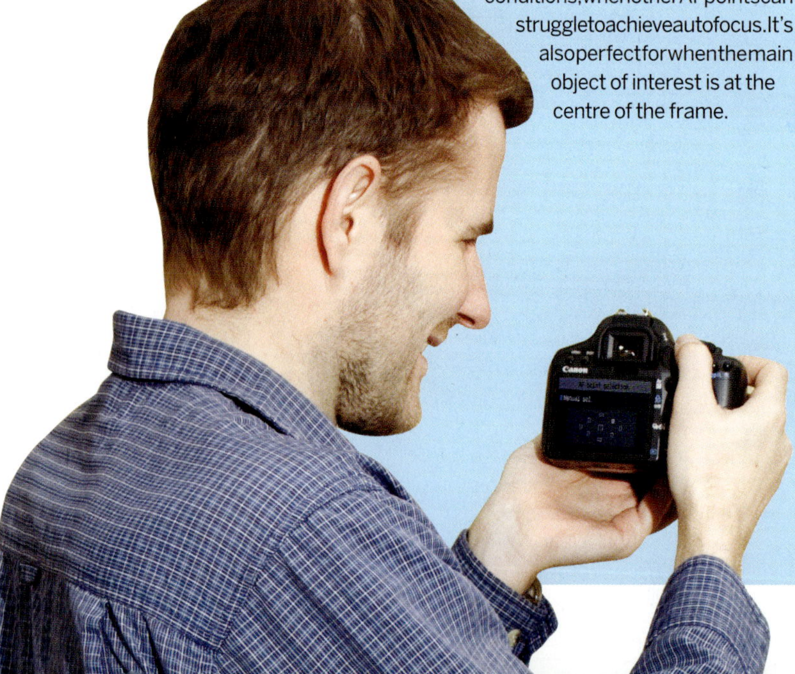

How to pick your spot

With so many AF points to choose from, which should you use?

While for most of us, nine selectable AF points are more than enough, top-end professional cameras, such as the EOS-1Ds Mark III, have an incredible 26 to choose from. You can even choose multiple AF points in small groups. Whichever camera you've got, knowing which AF point to select can, understandably, be a challenge.

Often it seems easiest is to stick with the central AF point, position it over the object you want to focus on, then lightly press the shutter button to achieve AF (or press the AF-On button on cameras like the 50D). You can lock the AF setting by holding the shutter button, recompose the shot, then fully press the shutter to take the shot. This often works, but it's easy to come unstuck.

The main problem with only using the central AF point is that a light reading is also taken, and the exposure value locked, at the same time. If, for example, you focus on an object that's in shadow, then recompose to include brighter areas, your image will be over-exposed.

Get the point

One answer is to press the AE Lock (star) button after recomposing the image, thereby taking a new light reading, while still holding the shutter button to keep autofocus locked. But it's usually easier to pick the AF point that's closest to the point you want to focus on, so any subsequent camera movement will be minimal.

Selecting the most appropriate AF point not only ensures more accurate light metering, but focusing as well, because there's less camera movement after AF has been locked. Plus, AF point placement is based on the rule of thirds (see Phrase Book), aiding composition.

Super Tip!

"Pay attention to the red and green lights in your viewfinder display. The large green dot that illuminates at the bottom-right signifies that autofocus has been achieved and set. To find out which parts of the frame have been focused on, keep an eye on the blinking red dots that correspond to the AF points positioned in the frame."

GRAB A PIECE OF THE ACTION

AF point trickery can help you to track moving targets

Unlike One Shot AF mode, which locks the focus setting as soon as autofocus is achieved, AI Servo AF mode automatically tracks moving targets, from kids and pets at play to racing cars or roaming wildlife, adjusting the focus as necessary up to and including the moment when the shot is taken.

It's tempting to manually select a single AF point that corresponds to the position of the moving target within the frame, but this often demands an incredibly steady pair of hands and an almost superhuman panning technique.

Switch to the Auto Select AF Point (multi-point) setting when using AI Servo AF and the camera will initially focus and track moving subjects using only the central AF point. If the target strays from the centre of the frame, alternative AF points will be automatically used as necessary, so the camera can continue to track its movement.

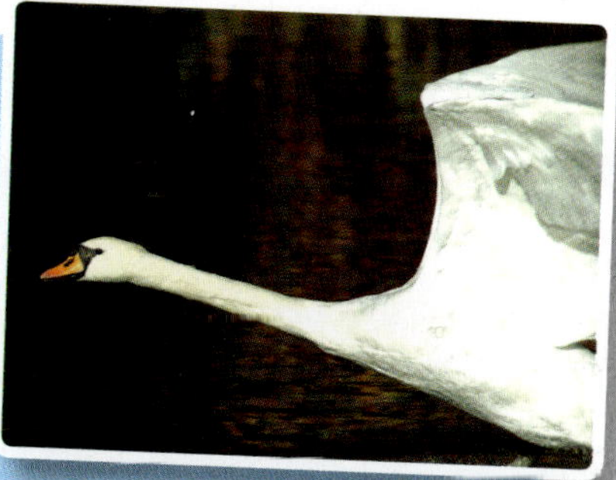

Use the Auto Select AF mode with AI Servo autofocus to effectively track moving subjects

MASTER HYPERFOCAL DISTANCE

Wouldn't it be nice if you didn't have to bother with focus at all?

Particularly popular before the introduction of autofocus cameras, the use of 'hyperfocal distance' is still a really neat trick for times when your camera struggles to autofocus in difficult lighting conditions – such as misty mornings. It's basically the distance that you can focus to at any given aperture, where the resulting depth of field will retain sharpness in the scene from as far away as infinity to the closest possible point. The depth of field increases greatly when combining smaller apertures with wider-angle zoom settings, so use of hyperfocal distance is particularly useful for landscape photography, especially when you're using a lens that has a built-in distance scale. The table on the right shows the hyperfocal distance for a range of apertures, complete with the nearest and furthest points that will be retained in focus, when using an 18mm zoom setting on a camera such as the 400D or 40D. ■

Hyperfocal distances in metres for a 400D with an 18mm zoom setting

(see www.dofmaster.com for other lenses)

Aperture	Hyperfocal distance	Nearest/furthest distance kept sharp in image
f/2.8	6.05m	3.03m to infinity
f/3.5	5.09m	2.55m to infinity
f/4	4.28m	2.14m to infinity
f/5.6	3.03m	1.52m to infinity
f/8	2.15m	1.08m to infinity
f/11	1.53m	0.76m to infinity
f/16	1.08m	0.54m to infinity
f/22	0.77m	0.39m to infinity
f/32	0.55m	0.28m to infinity

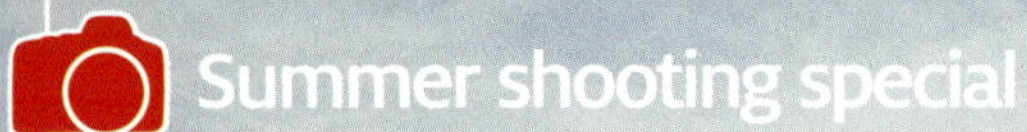

LEARN ESSENTIAL DIGITAL SLR SKILLS

STOP WASTING

Follow the easy tips in our guide to getting perfect shots from your camera and guarantee great results every time you press the trigger

Your digital SLR is capable of taking award-winning shots of anything you point it at, but it can't do this all on its own, and every photographer makes mistakes. Inevitably, a proportion of your images will end up being a bit blurred, a touch out of focus, poorly lit or badly framed. But the real indicator of success is just how many of those wasted shots you get on each memory card that you fill up.

With photography, if your settings are wrong, practice doesn't make perfect. We are all forever learning how to get the most out of our SLRs and striving to get the best possible picture out of every scene

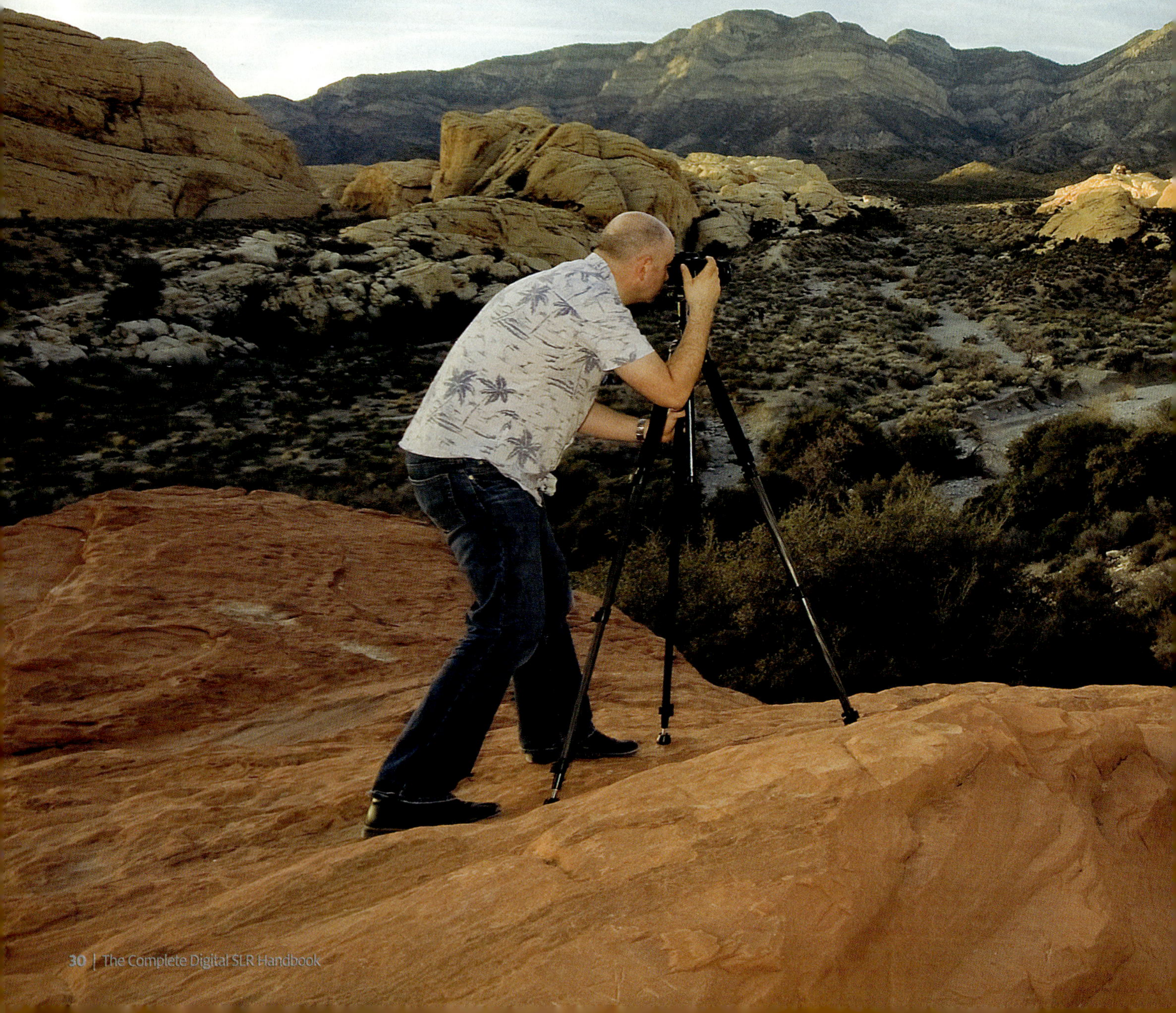

SHOTS

MAKE EVERY SHOT A WINNER!

Words: Chris George & Peter Travers (Future)

we see. However, there are plenty of simple ways in which to improve your hit rate – and cut down on those shots that are only fit for the Delete button.

Over the following pages we'll show you how to set up your camera every time you go out, so that you will never miss a shot because you're using the wrong setting. We'll then show you how to make your shots sharper and cut accidental blur from your pictures. The next step is to learn to look at the light, and master exposure to make the most of every photo opportunity.

Take all these tips on board, and we guarantee an instant improvement, so grab your camera and get ready to take better shots today!

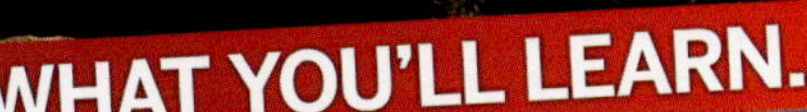

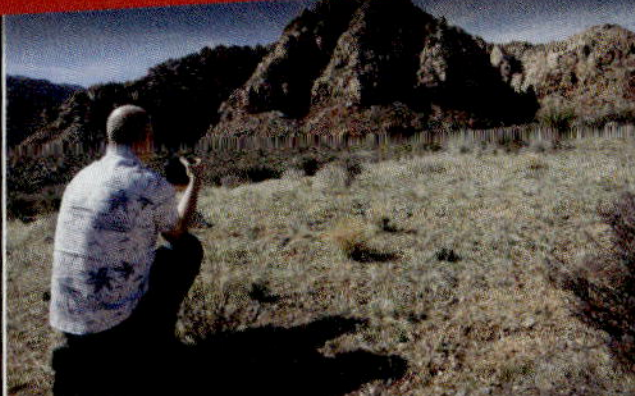
Essential set-up tips

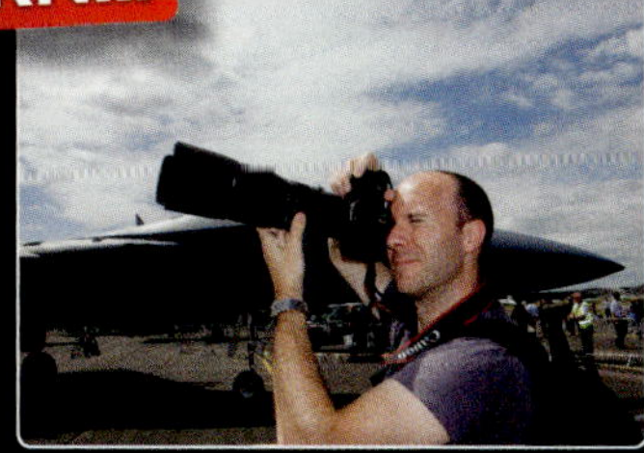
How to ensure sharpness

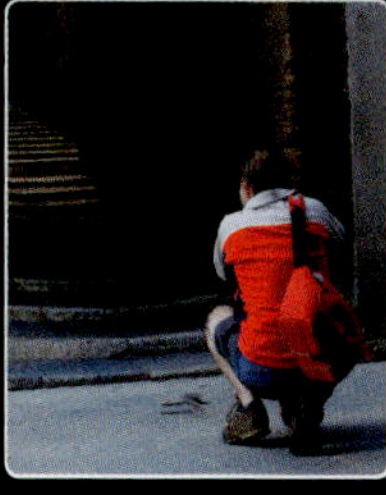
Exposure rules

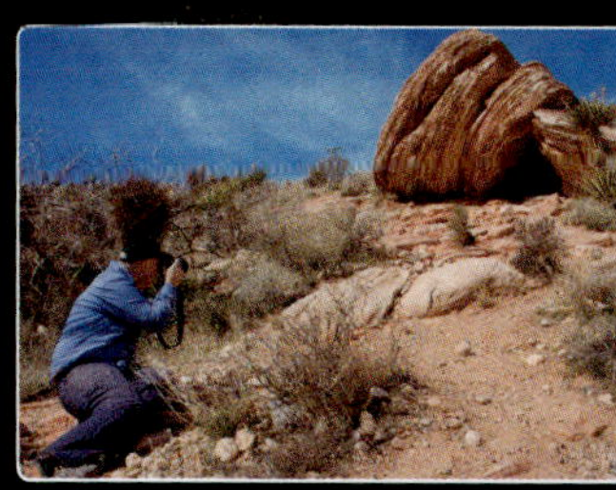
Fail-safe composition tricks

Get set up

Check your camera settings carefully every time you pick up your SLR

CARD CARE

The more spare memory the merrier

Before you set off, press the playback button on your SLR and check you have enough space on your memory card. If there are pictures, have they been saved and backed-up on your PC? If so, use the Delete All or Format command. It's much easier to clean the card in one fell swoop, rather than scrabbling around deleting the older shots one at a time when you find you've run out of memory later in the day. Get into the habit of downloading your shots as soon as you return from a shoot.

Always carry two or more spare memory cards. The price of Compact Flash and SDHC cards has fallen dramatically in the last couple of years, so ensure you have more capacity than you'll ever need wherever you shoot.

BATTERY CHECKS

Power-up and get ready to fire

It's all too easy to miss shots, or end up with awful results, simply because your camera isn't set up properly. The last thing you want is to turn up at a wedding, only to realise halfway through the day that your SLR is set to Fluorescent White Balance and ISO12,800, and that all the shots you've taken of the bride look green and grainy.

The first step to avoiding wasted shots and missed opportunities is to check over your camera carefully before you go out. Before you even leave the house you need to do two fundamental things. Start by checking the battery. Your SLR won't take any pictures if there is no power. Charge it up if necessary, and be warned that the battery indicator is just a guide, and can mislead you into thinking you have plenty of juice when it's actually about to run dry. For this reason, you should always carry one or more spare batteries, and charge them as soon as you return from a shoot.

Secondly, make sure there is a memory card in the camera! It may sound obvious, but it's easy to leave it sitting in your card reader as you head out into the sun.

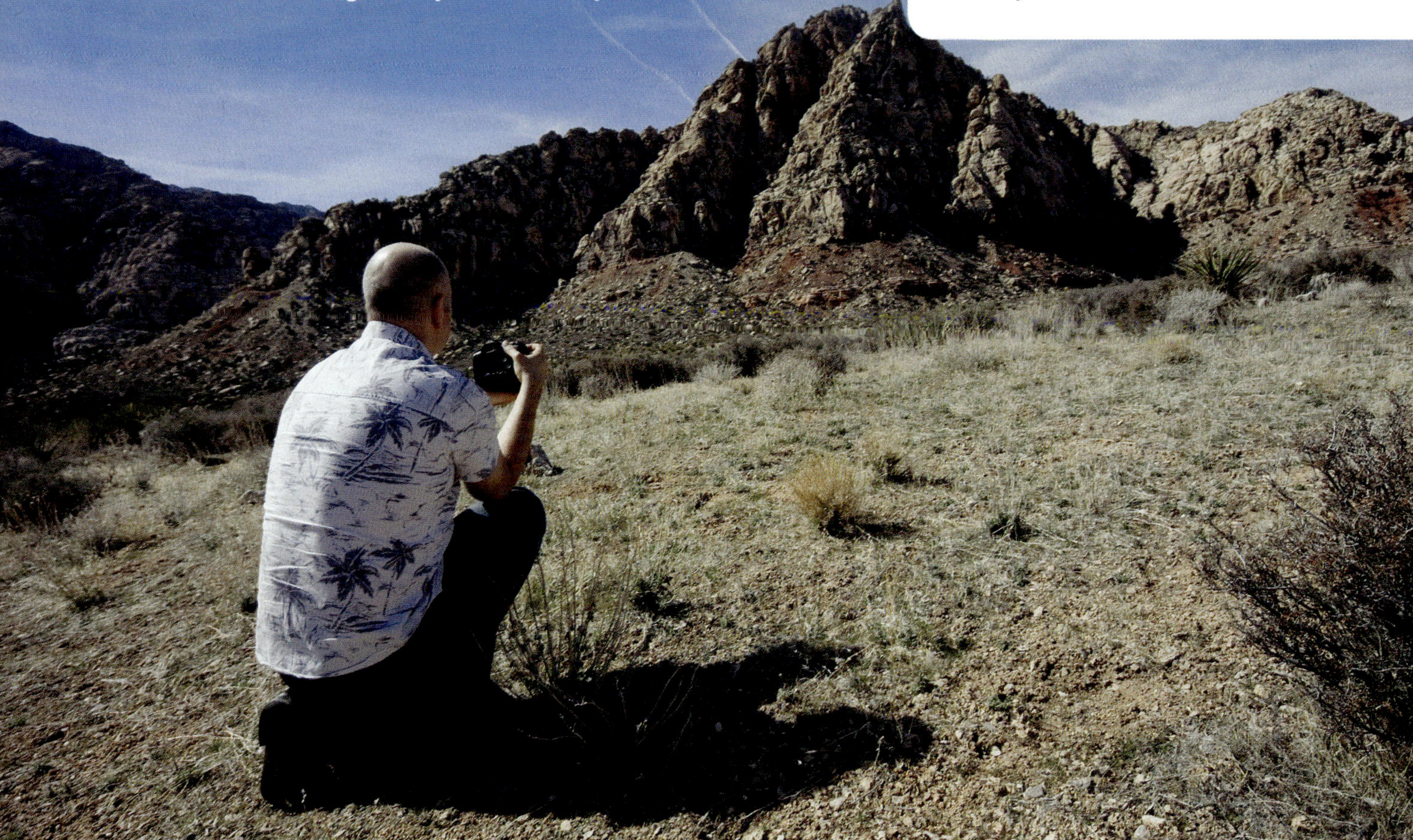

SYSTEMS CHECK

Check over and reset all your camera's key settings

Sometimes you know what you are going to photograph when you head out with your camera, but often you must be ready for anything. In the course of the day, you may change modes and functions to suit the subject in hand, but if you want to avoid missing shots, it pays to choose settings that will be capable of dealing with the vast majority of shooting situations.

Return to the following 'default' modes before you start and you'll be ready for anything...

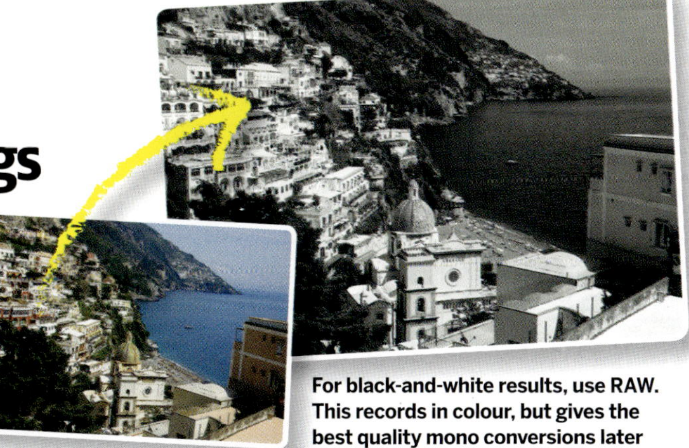

For black-and-white results, use RAW. This records in colour, but gives the best quality mono conversions later

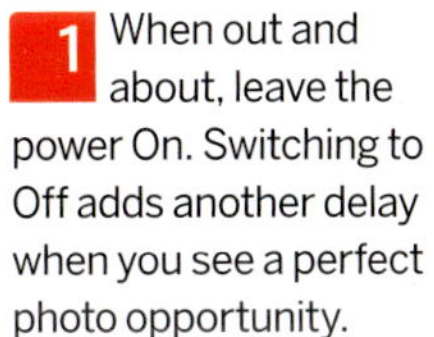

1 When out and about, leave the power On. Switching to Off adds another delay when you see a perfect photo opportunity.

2 Your camera gives lots of Quality options, but to get the best from your SLR use the RAW setting.

3 See if your card has enough space (see left). The 'remaining frames' counter only gives an estimate, and will change depending on the Quality setting used.

4 Check the power (see left).

5 The Evaluative metering mode is a good starting setting.

6 Reset Exposure Compensation to 0.

7 Don't set this too high, unless you know you're going to be shooting in low light without flash or a tripod. Start off between ISO100 and ISO200.

8 Your SLR gives lots of colour balance options, but your default ready-for-action setting should be Auto AWB.

9 The best all-round exposure mode for creative photography is Av (Aperture Priority). This allows you to adjust the aperture or shutter speed to suit the subject, simply by turning the thumbwheel left of right.

10 If using your camera's Av mode, make sure your starting aperture isn't too wide or too narrow. A mid aperture between f/5.6 and f/8 is the best bet.

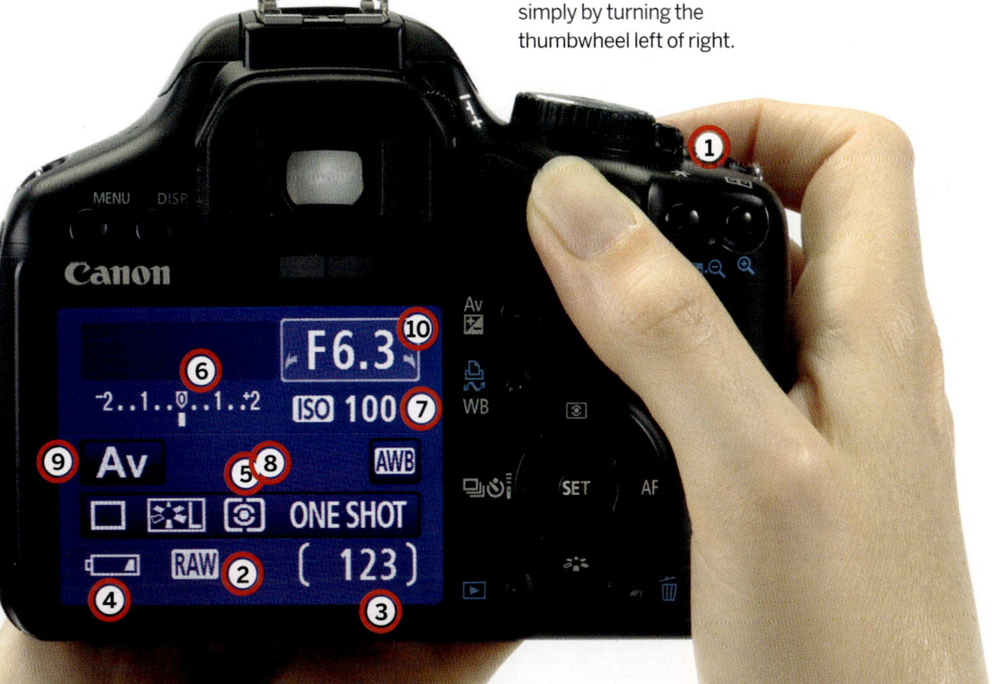

WHITE BALANCE

Get perfect colour with RAW and AWB

The White Balance options on your SLR allow you to change the colour balance of your shots for more accurate results in the full gamut of lighting conditions you may find yourself shooting in. They can also be used simply for artistic effect. However, if you set your camera to AWB (Auto White Balance), and record in RAW, your results will be close enough in colour – and you can then change the balance on your computer if necessary. ▶

RAW VERSION 1

RAW VERSION 2

RAW VERSION 3

Images by Chris George & Peter Travers (Future)

Sharpness

Essential techniques for sharp shooters

DEPTH OF SHARPNESS

Select the correct aperture

You don't always need to ensure the entire scene you're shooting is sharp from front to back for an image to be successful. In fact, the opposite can often be true. By using a wide aperture of f/5.6 (rather than a narrow aperture of f/22) when taking a photo of this statue, for example, we created a shallow depth of field. This ensured the main subject appeared sharp but the background blurred. This helps to maintain focus in the right place – on your subject.

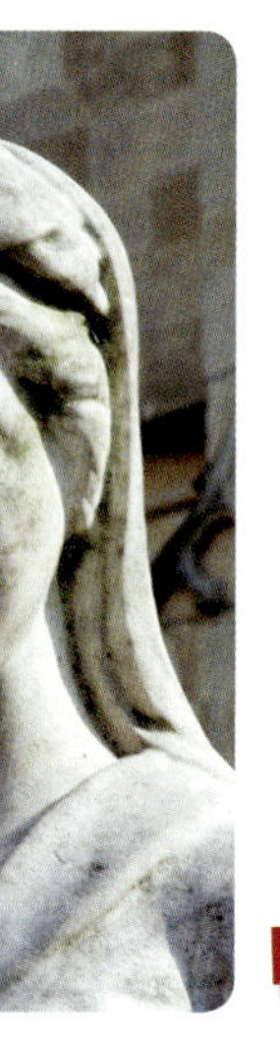

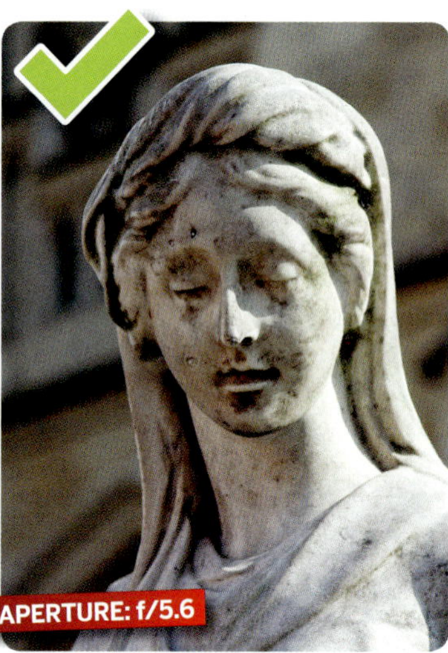

Images by Chris George & Sophie Spicer (Future)

STAY SHARP

Choosing the point of focus

If you leave your camera on its factory settings it will be set up to use Auto AF Point Selection. This is fine when photographing stationary subjects, but when you're shooting moving targets your SLR will focus on whatever's nearest to you.

In the first shot of the Red Arrows, below, the camera has tried to focus on the closer smoke trails rather than the distant planes. Switch to Manual AF Point Selection (see right) so you control what you focus on and you'll guarantee sharper shots.

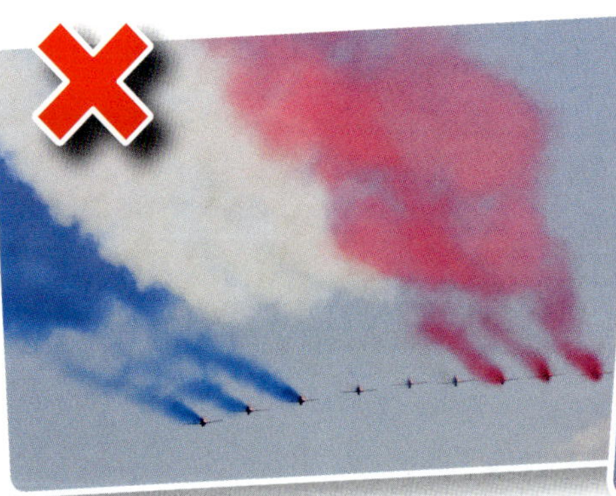

BE AFRAID OF BLUR

Take control of the shutter speed

In most cases a blurred image is a bad image, but it's easy to ensure your images remain sharp. The longer the zoom setting you use, the faster your shutter speed must be to avoid camera shake.

When using a telephoto zoom lens at a focal length of, say, 300mm, the rule of thumb is that the shutter speed should be faster than 1/300 sec. But play safe, if you can. When shooting the sunflowers in our example (right), we used a shutter speed of 1/1600 sec to avoid blur.

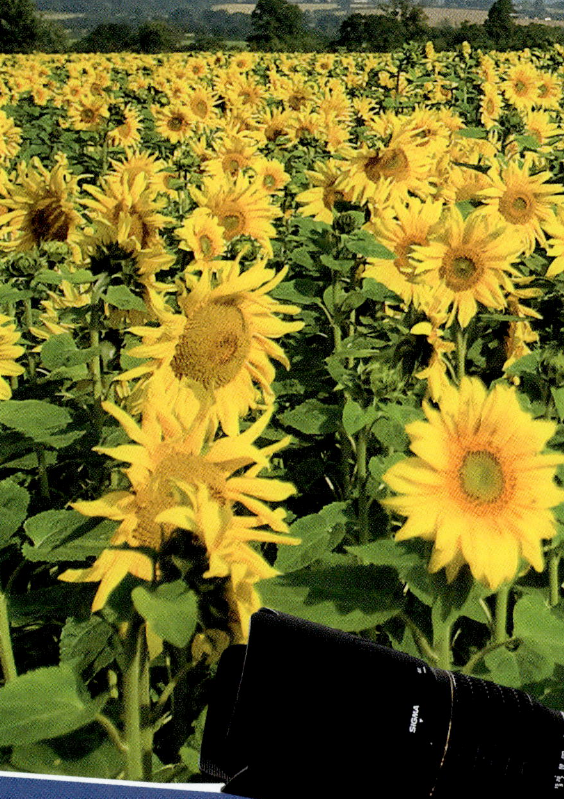

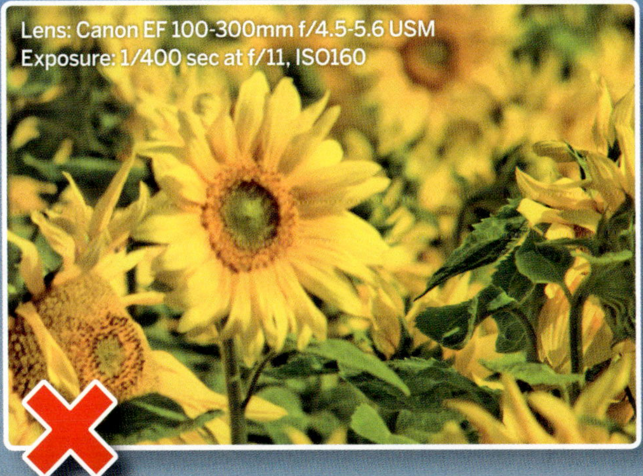
Lens: Canon EF 100-300mm f/4.5-5.6 USM
Exposure: 1/400 sec at f/11, ISO160

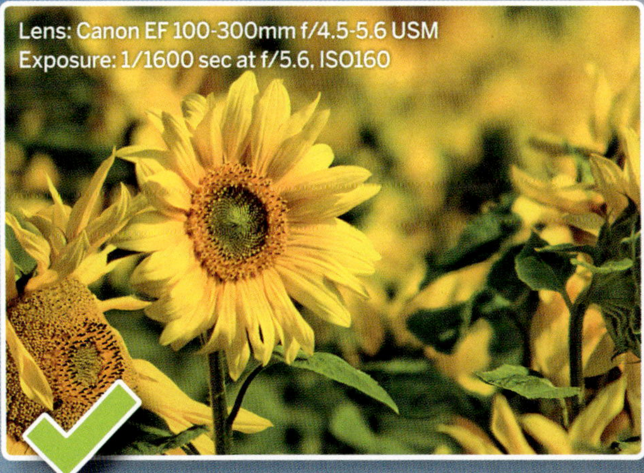
Lens: Canon EF 100-300mm f/4.5-5.6 USM
Exposure: 1/1600 sec at f/5.6, ISO160

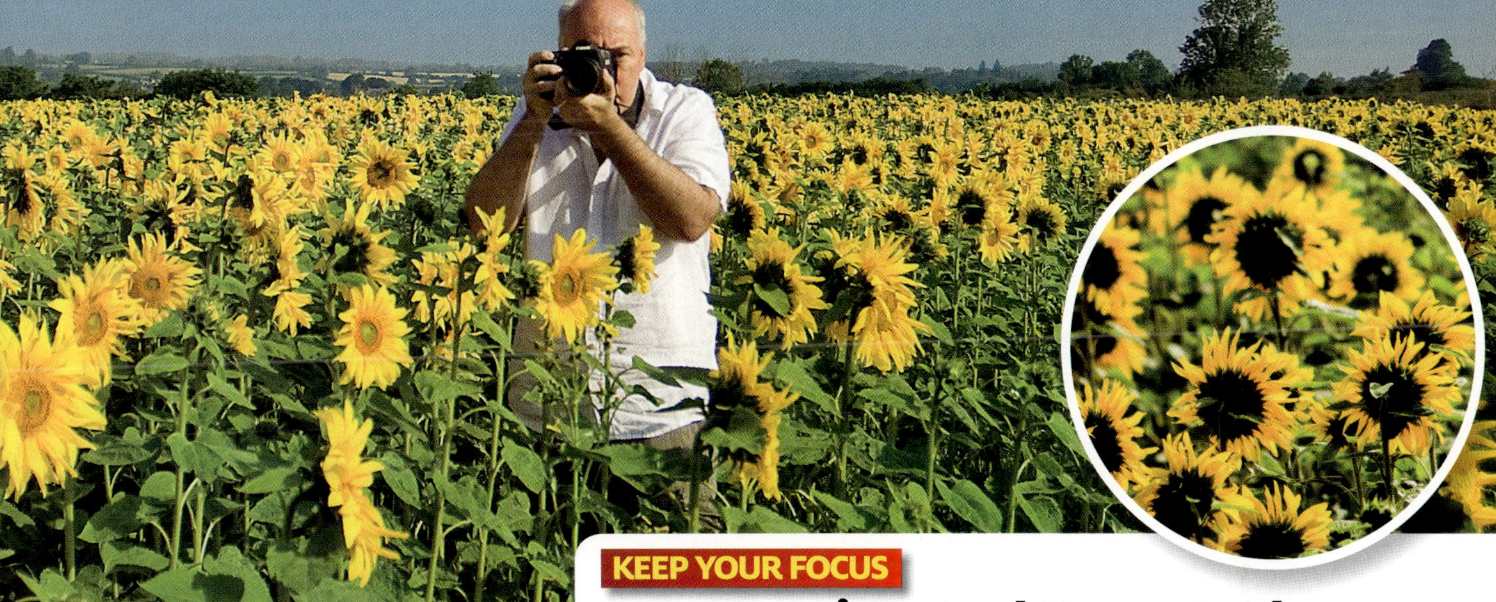

KEEP YOUR FOCUS

Set AF points and Focus Lock

Learn how to take control of your camera's Autofocus (AF) Point Selection and how to lock your focus to reduce the amount of shots you waste...

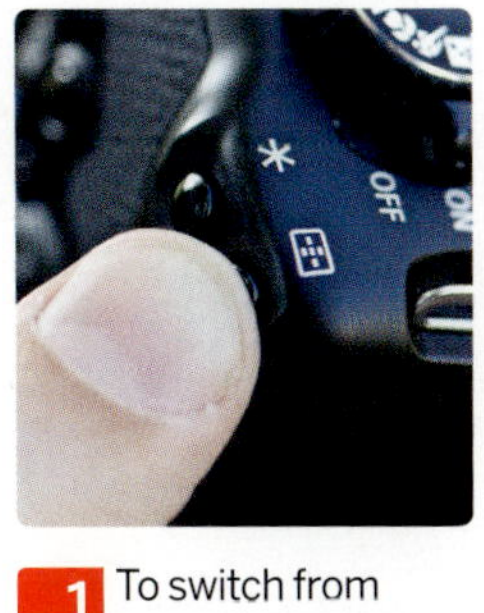

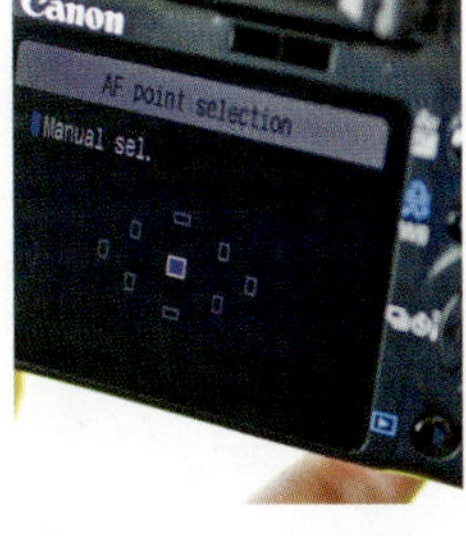

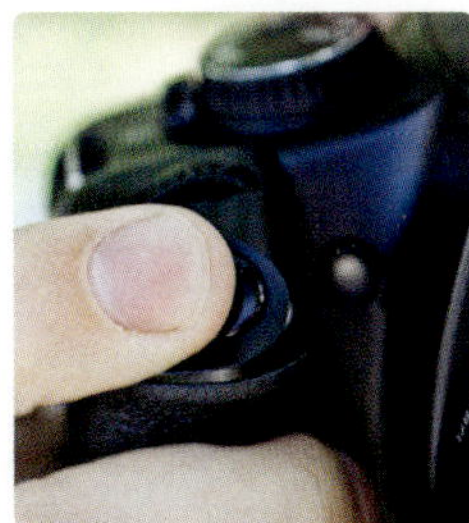

1 To switch from basic Auto AF Point Selection, which uses all nine AF points, to Manual AF Point Selection, first press the AF Point Selection button on the back of your camera (top right).

2 Now look through the viewfinder or at the rear LCD screen (or top LCD if your camera has one) and use the top dial behind the shutter release button to select which AF point you want to use. Begin by selecting the central AF point.

3 Now you can use Focus Lock by half-pressing the shutter release button to focus on your main subject. Try recomposing to position subjects away from the centre of the frame for more eye-catching results. ▶

Exposure

Easy-to-learn skills for sure-fire success

LOW-LIGHT SHOTS

Increase ISO when shooting after dark

So, you're out late one evening with your camera and you spot a photo opportunity, but you don't have a tripod. This doesn't mean you have to accept your shots will be shaky or give up. Instead, use your D-SLR's ISO range to its fullest and enjoy the freedom of shooting hand-held in low light. It's inspiring to see the details and tones your camera can capture when – to the naked eye – it's dark as night. Also consider that when shooting at ISO1600 or above, the grain can actually enhance the mood.

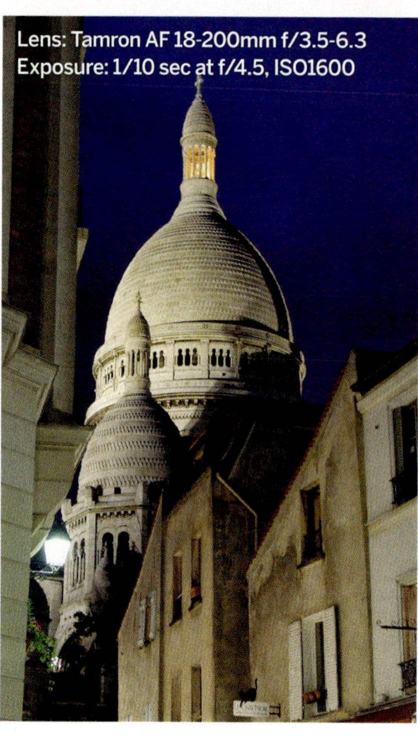
Lens: Tamron AF 18-200mm f/3.5-6.3
Exposure: 1/10 sec at f/4.5, ISO1600

EXPOSURE COMPENSATION

Control exposure to make images lighter or darker

Your SLR's clever, but it still makes mistakes and sometimes over- or under-exposes photos – especially if there's a mixture of lighting or tones in a scene. When shooting in Av or Tv use Exposure Compensation to increase or decrease your image's exposure.

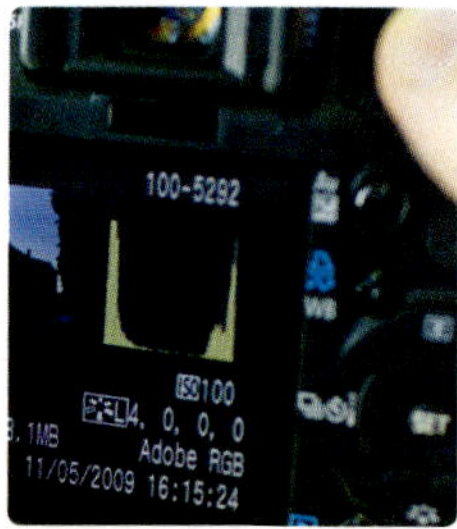

1 Use the histogram when reviewing shots on your D-SLR's LCD to see if your photos are over-exposed (data is clumped to the right) or under-exposed (data is pushed to the left).

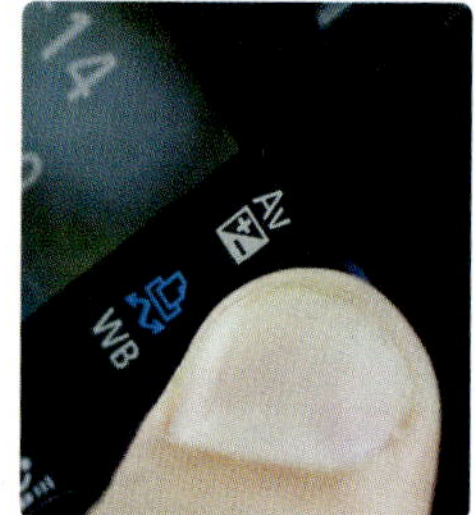

2 To adjust the exposure, hold down the Av+/- button on the back of your SLR and use the top dial to increase or decrease the compensation on the exposure level indicator.

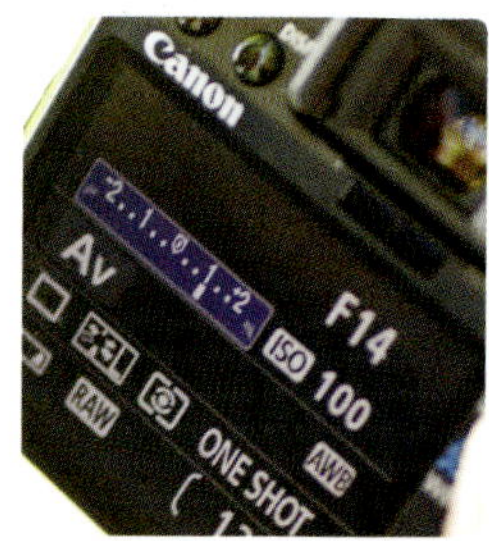

3 You can increase/ decrease exposures from 1/3 of a stop to two full stops. To darken over-exposed shots, decrease the exposure (eg -1 stop). To lighten under-exposed shots try entering +1 stop.

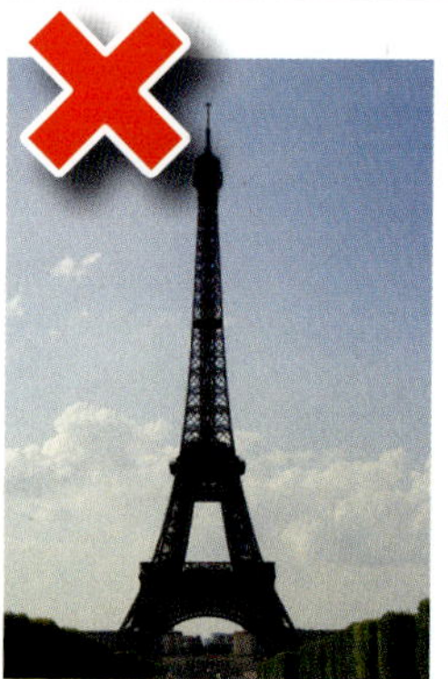

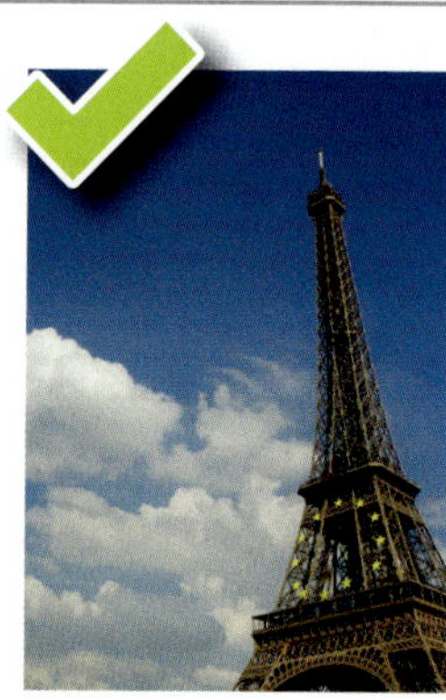

SUN WORSHIPPING

Effective positioning

Knowing where the sun is in relation to your scene or subjects can make the difference between a wonderful shot and a wasted opportunity. You'll generally find it's more beneficial to shoot with the sun at your back so the light highlights whatever you're photographing. This also has the added bonus of producing more vibrantly coloured skies and more vivid overall tones.

Shoot directly into the sun and you'll get correctly exposed subjects and over-exposed skies or under-exposed subjects and still overly bright skies.

WASTE NOT, WANT NOT

Wait for good light

Don't just point and shoot regardless of the lighting conditions. Watch the clouds to see if a gap is likely to appear for the sun's rays to break through and brighten up the scene. The difference will be dramatic. The winning shot will look dazzling and full of life, as the light and shadows reveal more detail, colour and contrast. The losing shot will look flat and lifeless, and will more than likely end up in the trash can.

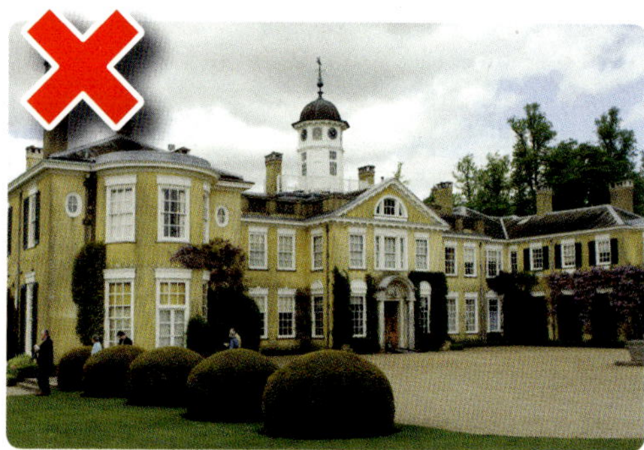

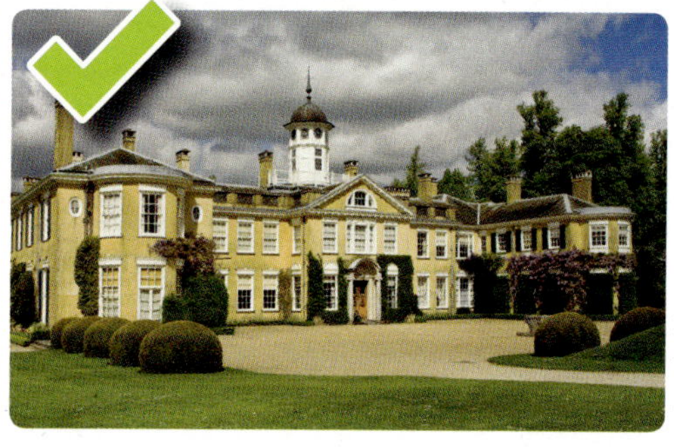

Images by Chris George, Paul Grogan & Sophie Spicer (Future)

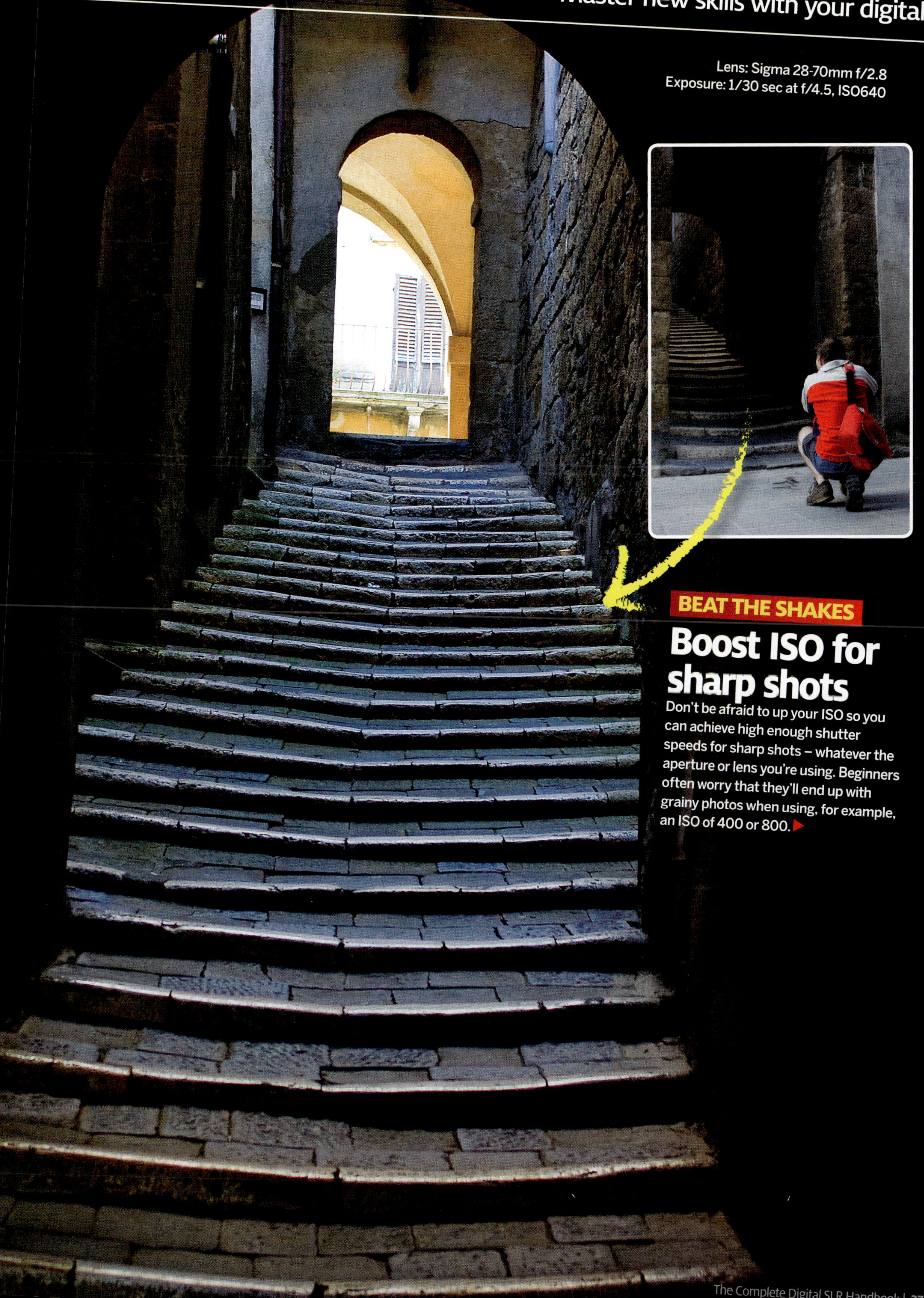

Lens: Sigma 28-70mm f/2.8
Exposure: 1/30 sec at f/4.5, ISO640

BEAT THE SHAKES

Boost ISO for sharp shots

Don't be afraid to up your ISO so you can achieve high enough shutter speeds for sharp shots – whatever the aperture or lens you're using. Beginners often worry that they'll end up with grainy photos when using, for example, an ISO of 400 or 800. ▶

Composition

Successful strategies for finding and framing shots

WATCH YOUR BACK

Background checks

Try not to get to too carried away with the main event and forget about everything around it. You may capture the subject perfectly, but if the background is cluttered it will be a distraction in your final still image.

Get into the habit of looking carefully at the background in every shot and try another camera angle to find something plainer if possible. Alternatively, use a wide aperture to knock it out of focus.

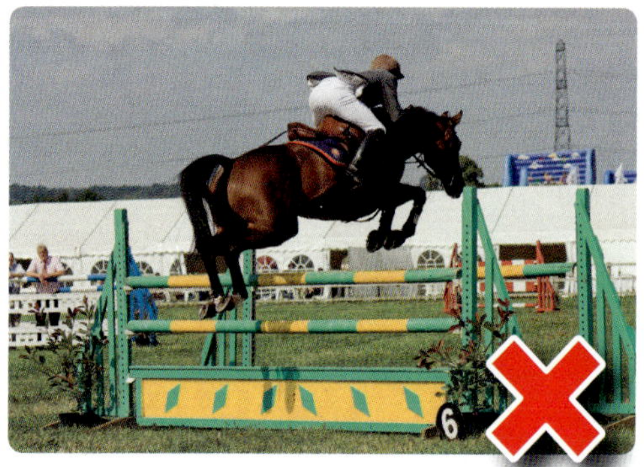

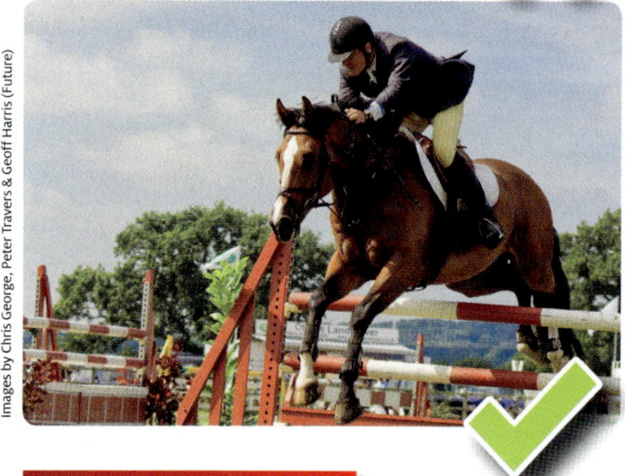

Images by Chris George, Peter Travers & Geoff Harris (Future)

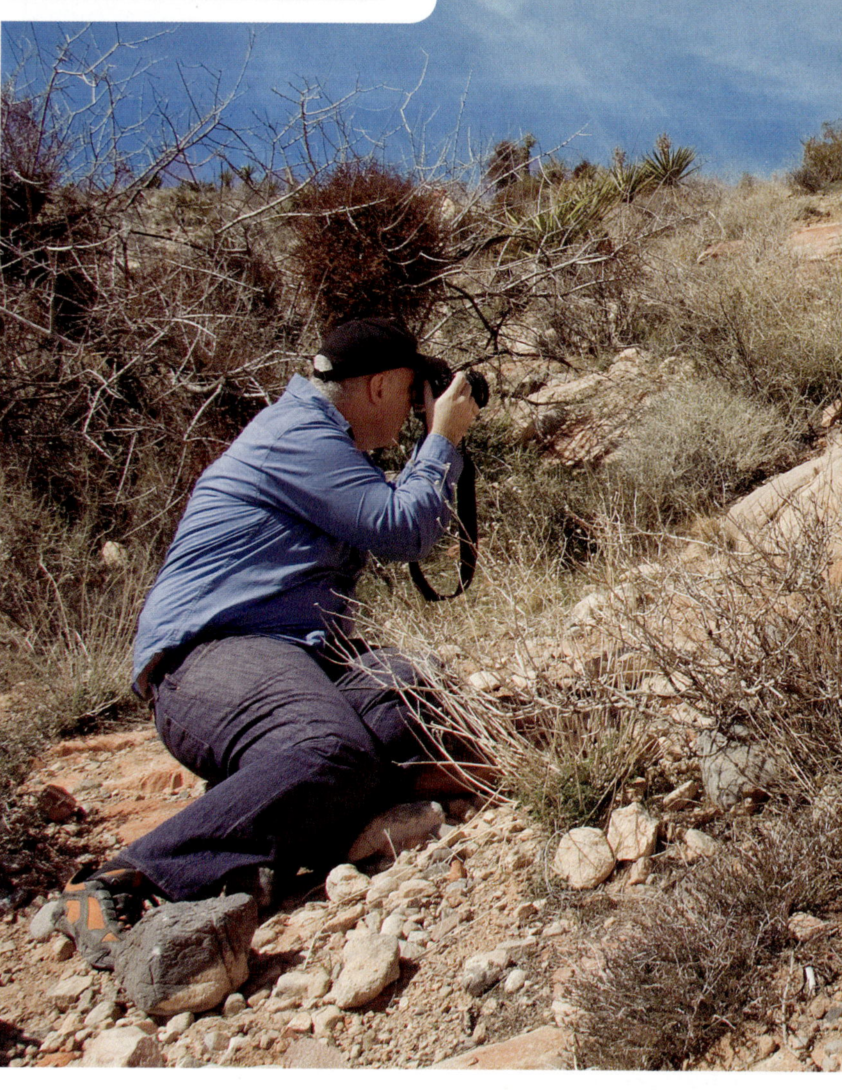

FILL THE FRAME

Don't waste the space

The first rule of composition is to make good use of the frame. As the legendary war photographer Robert Capa said, "If your pictures aren't any good it's because you're not close enough."

Do your best to fill the frame with the subject. Crop in close so that you get as much detail as possible, and only include the surroundings if they actually add something. There's a natural tendency for photographers to try and fit too much into each picture, but photos usually work best if you simplify the scene as much as possible.

Concentrate on the subject by making good use of your zoom – narrowing the angle of view to cut out unwanted foregrounds and backgrounds. Even better, let your feet do the work, getting closer into the scene rather than relying on your lens's telephoto setting.

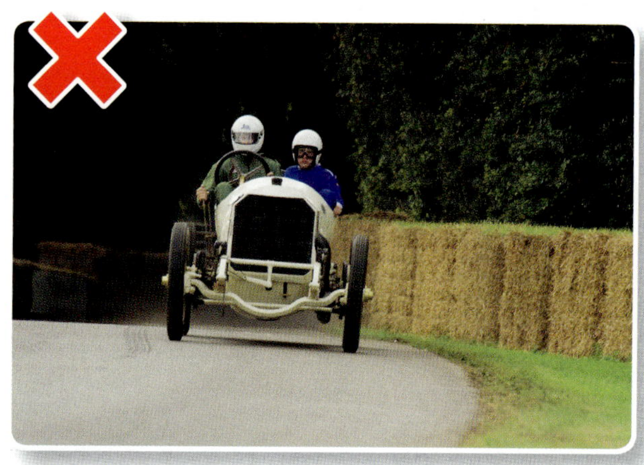

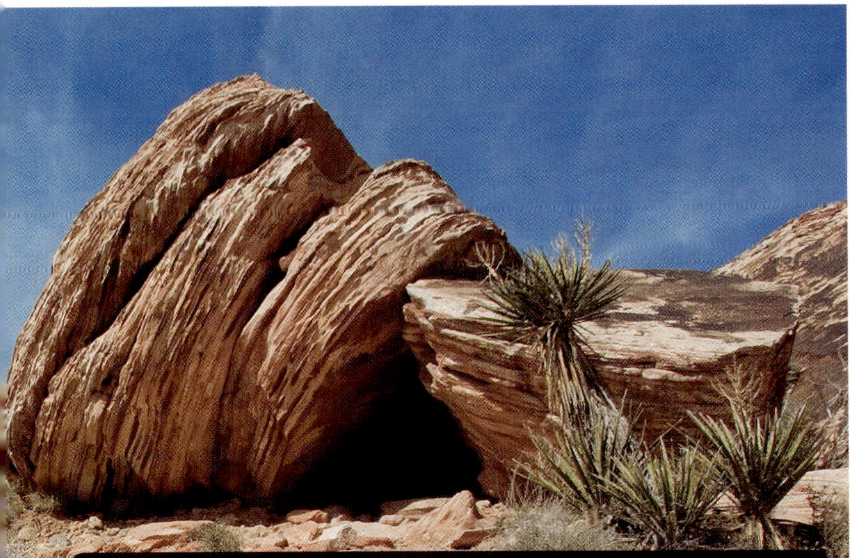

MOVE THE CAMERA

Keep changing the angle and height

Try to change your shooting position. Don't simply find a good spot and then take all your pictures with your camera at head height.

You will be able to get much more from the scene if you constantly look at ways in which to move around the subject to find a more interesting angle. At the same time, explore ways to get the camera higher or lower, for a worm's eye or bird's eye view of what is going on. Struggle for your art and get down on the ground if necessary, and look for things you can safely climb up onto in search of an elevated shooting platform.

EYE LEVEL

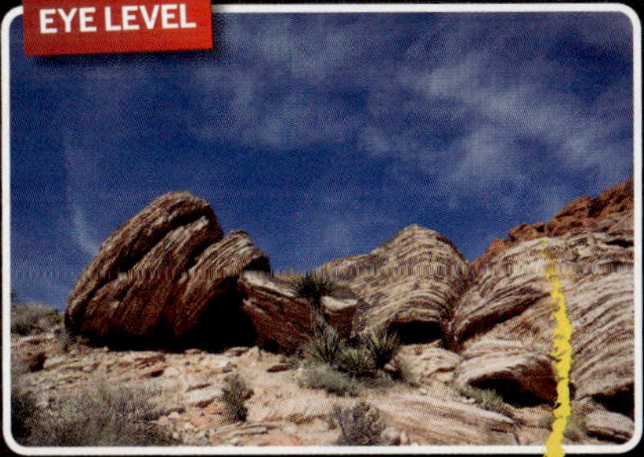

GROUND LEVEL

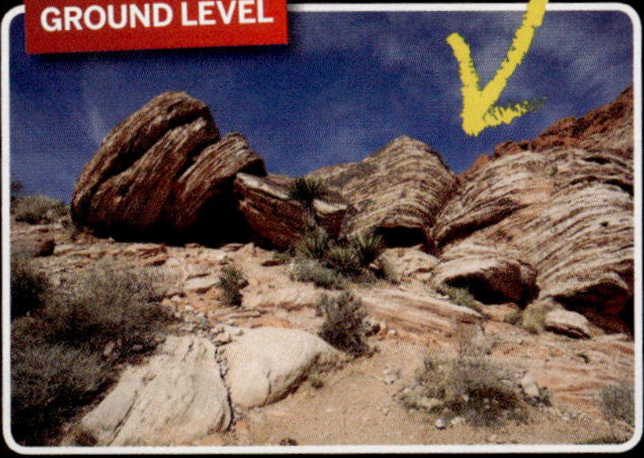

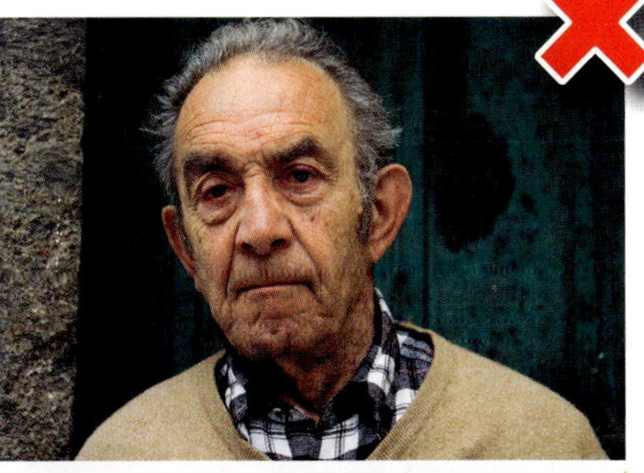

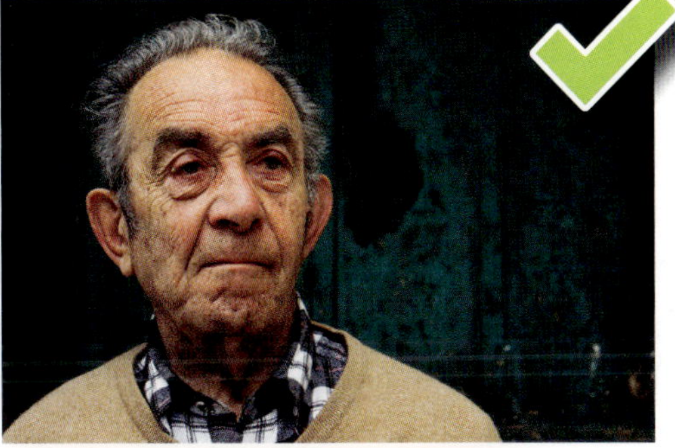

OFF-CENTRE FRAMING

Be eccentric and get perfect balance

The viewfinder markings and focusing system of your SLR encourage you to place your subject in the centre of the frame. Although this can work well sometimes, your compositions will look more dynamic if the main subject – or the main focal point in the picture – is positioned away from the centre of the frame.

Some photographers swear by the 'rule of thirds', where key points in the picture are placed one-third of the way in from two of the frame edges. Key lines, such as a horizon, are similarly placed one third of the way in from one of the edges. However, there is no need to be slavish – your pictures will often look more dramatic if you shift the focus of the composition away from the centre. The more off-centre the positioning of the subject, the more dramatic the final composition will look.

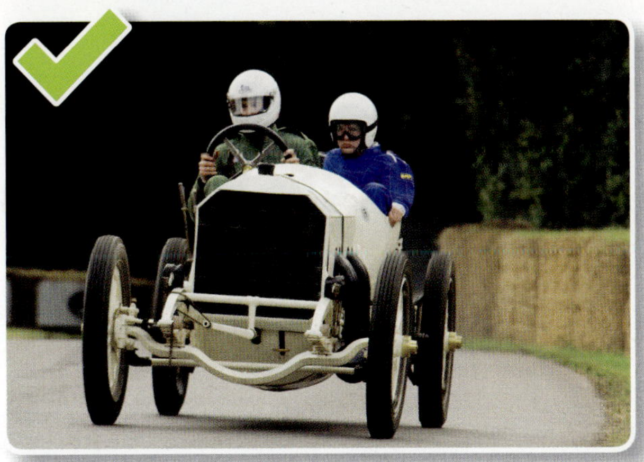

WASTE MANAGEMENT

Learn to be trigger happy

Although it's the golden goal of all photographers to take as many great pictures as possible, don't get too hooked up with the idea that every shot should be pixel perfect. The more pictures you take, the wider the variety of shots you can head home with – and you are more likely to come away with a winner.

One of the main advantages of digital photography is that it doesn't cost anything to take extra shots – and no-one needs to see the ones that don't make the grade! ■

TAKE EVEN BETTER SHOTS!

Fast fixes for digital SLRs

Follow our easy-to-use flow charts for hands-on advice to cure your exposure and focusing headaches and to soothe your composition and colour complaints...

Whether you're an experienced enthusiast or you've just bought your first digital SLR, everybody has problems with their pictures now and then. It's nothing to be embarrassed about. In fact, if you're less than perfectly happy with your shots, it only goes to prove that you're eager to improve your D-SLR shooting skills. And, as the saying goes, you can always learn from your mistakes!

However, working out how to solve your dilemmas on your own can prove to be a real headache. Which menu option or control do you need to use to make your pictures look better? Well, you can rest easy, because our team of D-SLR doctors are here to cure all of your camera complaints.

Whether your highlights are looking blown out and over-exposed, or your photos are suffering from camera shake, we've got the solutions to your problems. If you're finding it impossible to capture photos with a sense of impact, or your images' colours look out of whack, we'll help you resolve your issues.

Read on to learn the quick and easy way to restore your shots back to health.

HAVE YOU HAD THESE PROBLEMS?

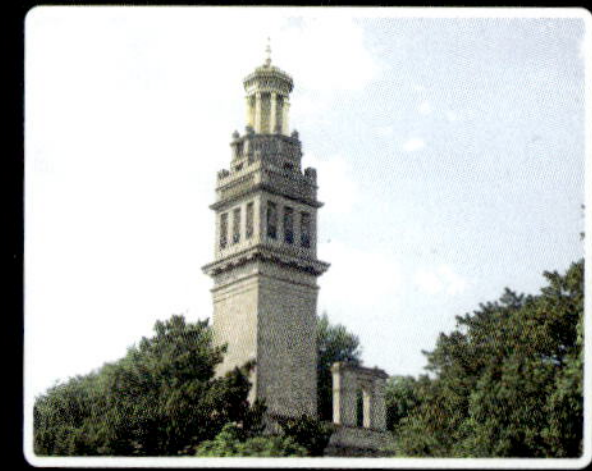

Why are the brighter parts of my shots blown out?
We help you improve exposure

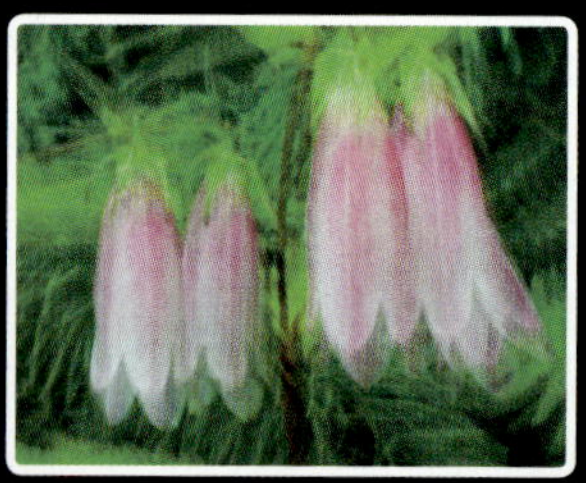

Why are all my photos blurry and out of focus?
How to ban blur for good

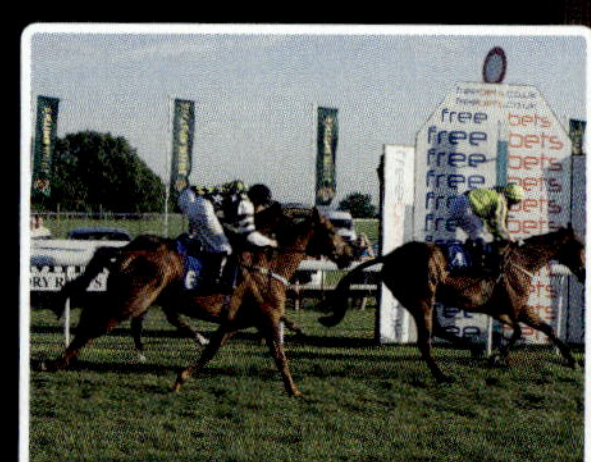

Why do my images look so cluttered?
Quick fixes for composition

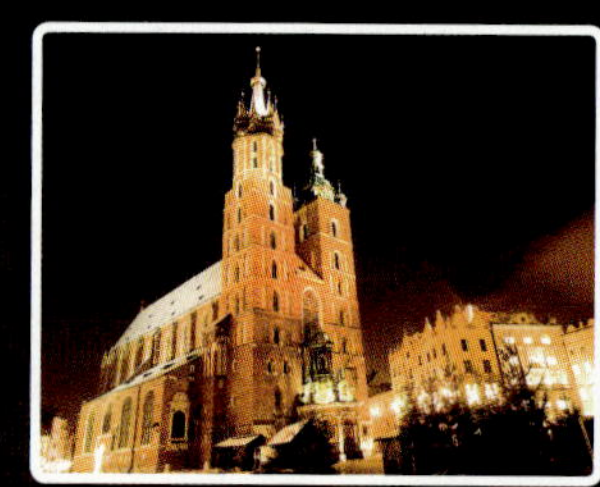

Why have my colours come out wrong?
White Balance woes sorted

Main image: Paul Grogan (Future)

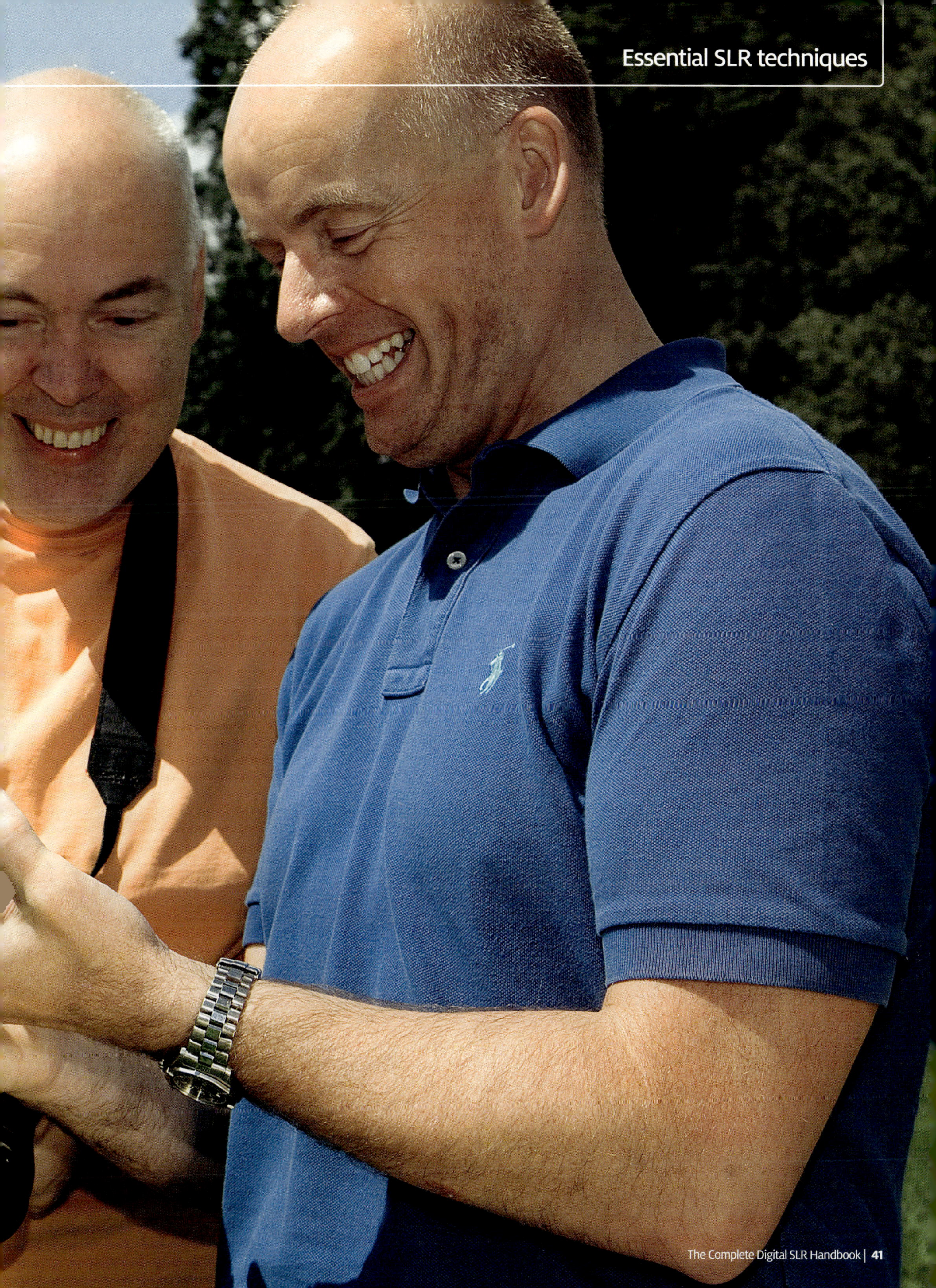

EXPOSURE

Q Why are all my shots blown out?

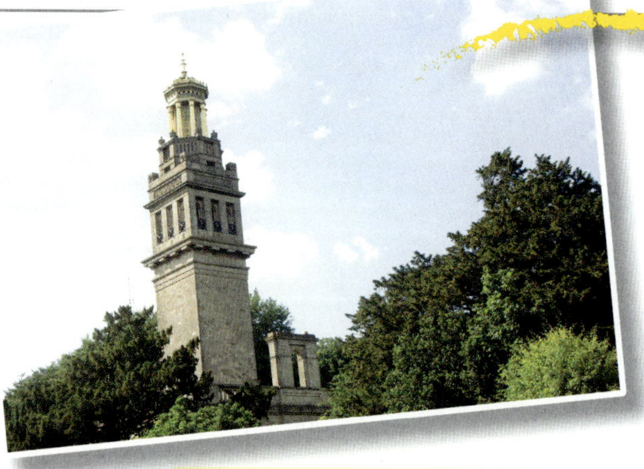

Were you shooting in bright daylight?

Photographing landscapes under midday sun can prove problematic. For the best colours and problem-free exposures, try to shoot your scenes with your back to the sun. If that's not an option, here are two other possible solutions...

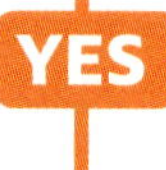

YES

Did you use an ND Grad filter?

In landscapes, a standard exposure will either result in overly bright skies lacking detail, colour and impact, or striking skies and excessively dark foregrounds.

NO

Using ND Grad filters

By using a Neutral Density (ND) Gradient filter when photographing landscapes, you make the brightness of the scene more even. You'll be able to capture the foreground detail as well as the beautiful colour and texture of clouds in the sky.

Did you try using Exposure Compensation?

Left to its own devices, your digital D-SLR can sometimes produce pictures that look lighter or darker than you would like them to. Switch to Av (Aperture Priority) mode and use Exposure Compensation to tweak the overall brightness.

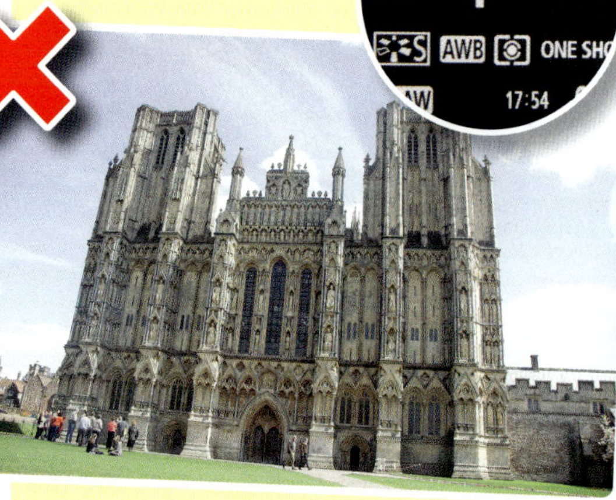

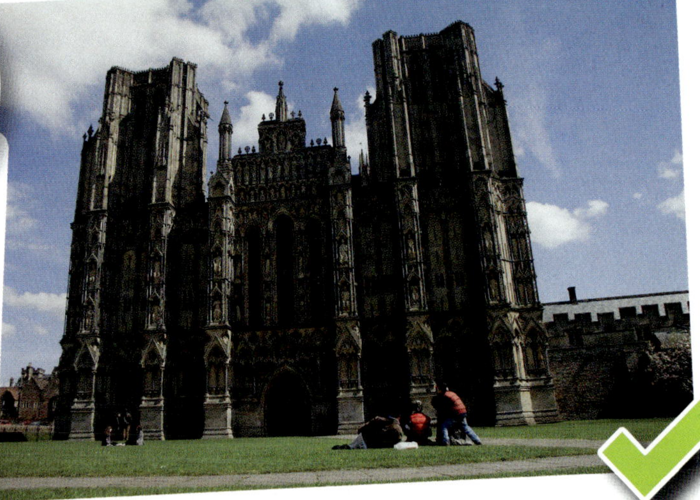

Try using histograms

When reviewing your shots on your camera's LCD, get into the habit of checking histograms as well to see if your shots are too bright or dark. You can also check histograms in Levels in Photoshop.

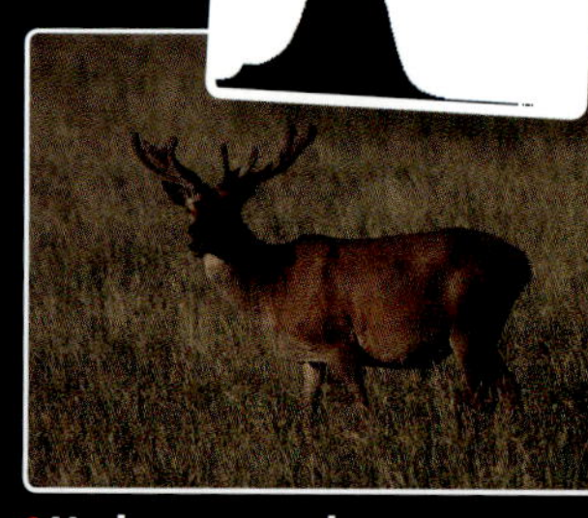

1 Under-exposed
This shot of a stag is too dark. The majority of the tones are stacked on the left of the histogram.

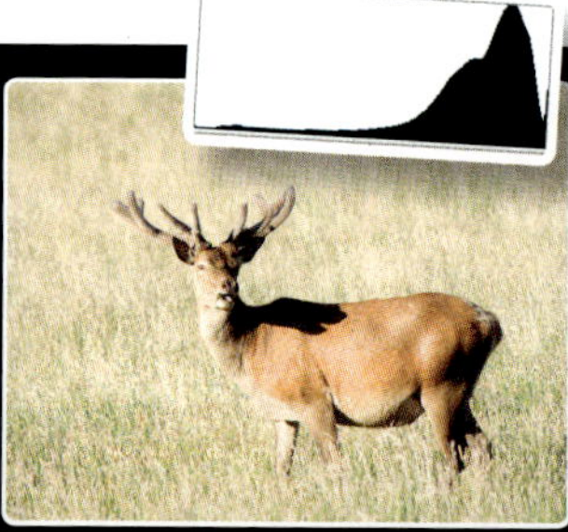

2 Over-exposed
This shot is too bright. The majority of the tones are now bunched up on the right of the histogram.

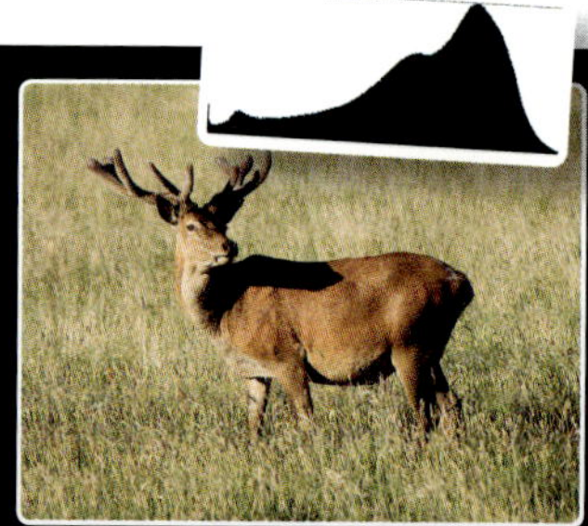

3 Correctly exposed
This shot is bang on. There's an even spread of shadows, midtones and highlights on the histogram.

All images: Peter Travers, Chris George (Future)

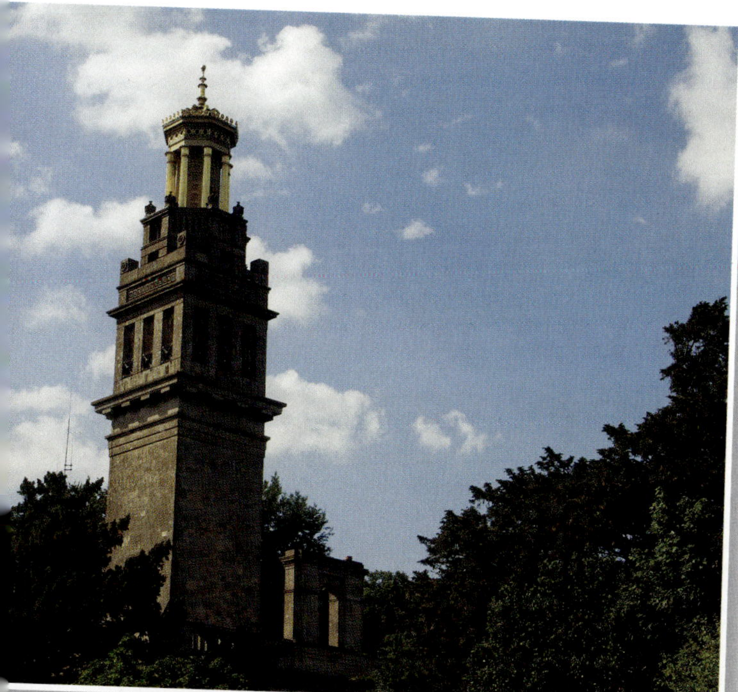

DULL PHOTOS

Q Why do my landscape shots look so flat?

Did you wait for the best light?

Dull, overcast days generally mean dull landscape shots because the lack of light creates too little contrast. However, being patient often pays off – even a brief break in the clouds can completely transform the scene.

NO

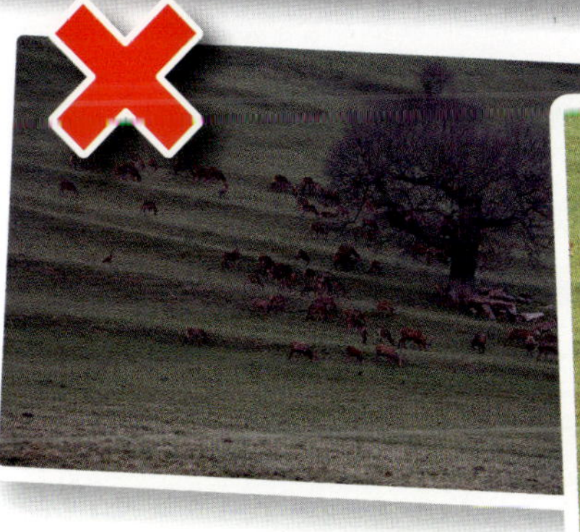

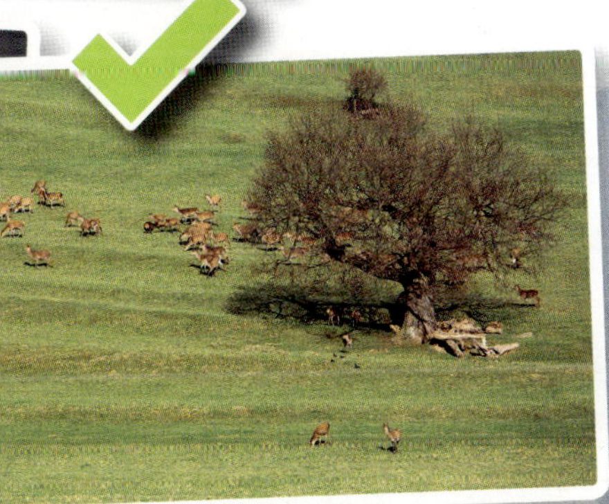

Shooting in the sunshine

The sun will instantly brighten up your shots. Colours appear more vibrant and the sunlight will also add shadows, and therefore more contrast, to your scenes. Better still, go back at around sunrise or sunset for the 'magic hour' – the sun is lower at these times, so the light will be softer, shadows will be longer and the sky is likely to be full of breathtaking colour.

PORTRAITS

Q Why do my skies look white and washed out?

Can you change position?

If you position your subjects with bright sunlight behind them you'll not only end up with distracting, dazzling backgrounds, but also a portrait with too much contrast and very little light actually falling on your subject.

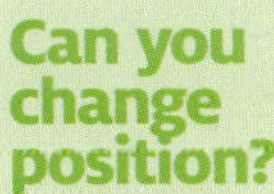

NO

Can you shoot in the shade?

Take portraits in the shade to produce an even light. Ask your subject to move out of the sun to remove any shadows from their face, and to reduce harsh highlights in the background.

NO

No shade? Use fill flash

If there's no shade and you want to shoot with the sunlight behind your subject, then use some 'fill flash' to fill in the shadows and capture a cracking, colourful portrait. Use your on-camera flash, shoot in Av (Aperture Priority) mode and dial in -1 stop of Exposure Compensation to capture more colour and detail in the bright sky and background.

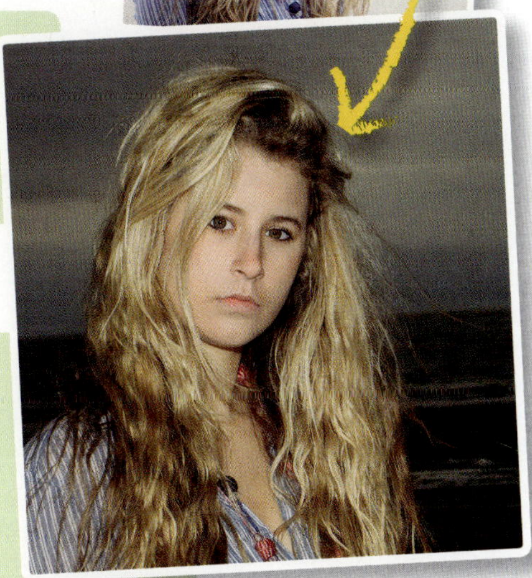

SHARPNESS

Q Why are my photos blurry & out of focus?

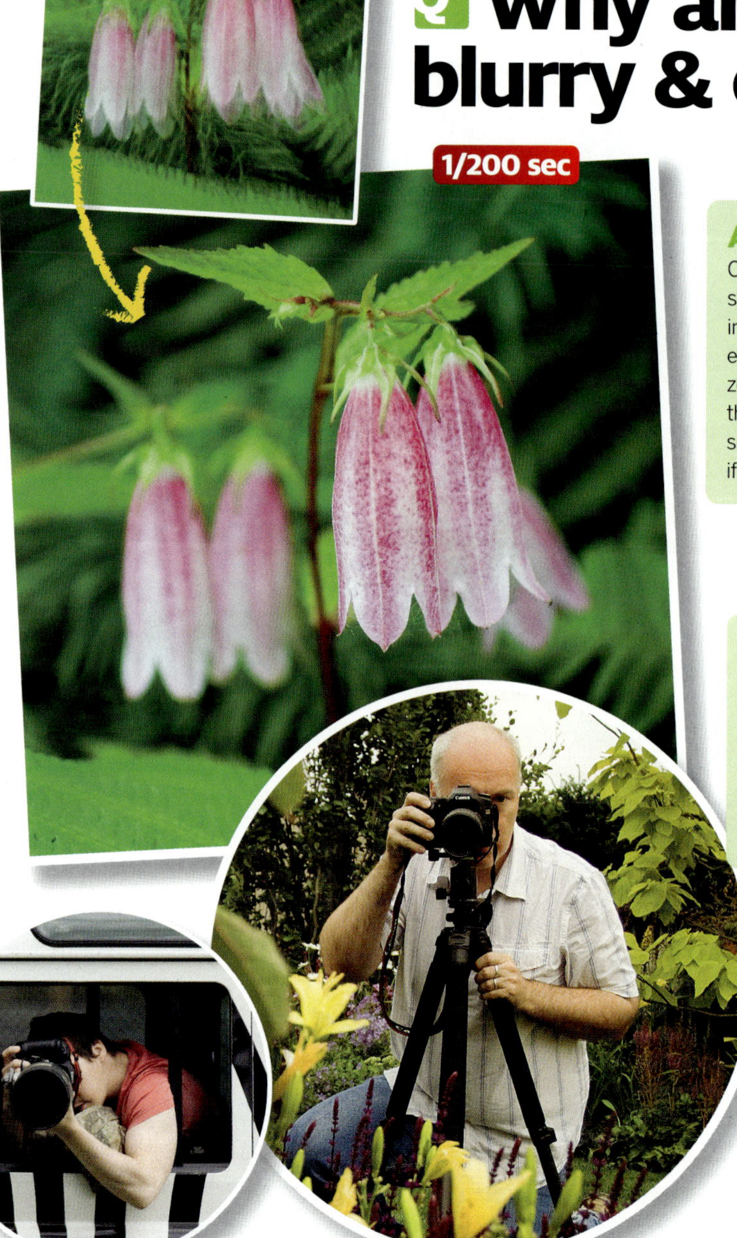

Are you shooting handheld?

Camera shake could be your problem. Make sure you're using a fast enough shutter speed in relationship to your focal length – for example, if you're using a 200mm telephoto zoom, your shutter speed needs to be faster than 1/200 sec to obtain sharp shots when shooting handheld. Increase your ISO setting if necessary to achieve a faster shutter speed.

YES

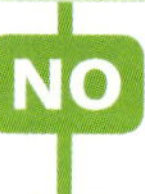

Are you using a tripod?

A tripod, monopod or beanbag can eliminate or reduce camera shake by keeping your D-SLR totally still. This means that, however slow your shutter speeds, you can capture pin-sharp shots. It also means you can use narrow apertures in any light to give greater depth of field and keep everything in focus.

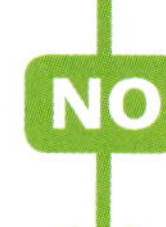

Brace yourself

If you don't have a tripod and are shooting in low light, and have no choice but to use a shutter speed too slow to shoot handheld, then brace yourself against something to keep your camera steady when pressing the shutter button. A tree, fence post or even your car door are better than nothing.

All images: Peter Travers, Chris George (Future)

AF point selection

Your digital SLR enables you to choose specific autofocus (AF) points which can help you to achieve perfect focus of whatever you're shooting. Here's how to set your camera up and get sharp shots...

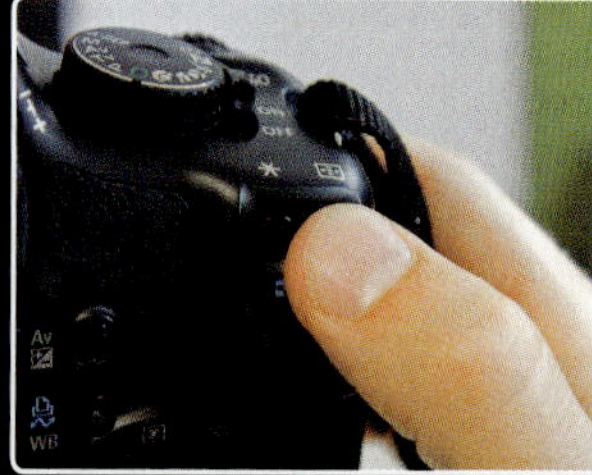

1 AF point selection button Press the button in the top-right corner on the back of your D-SLR to access the AF point selection.

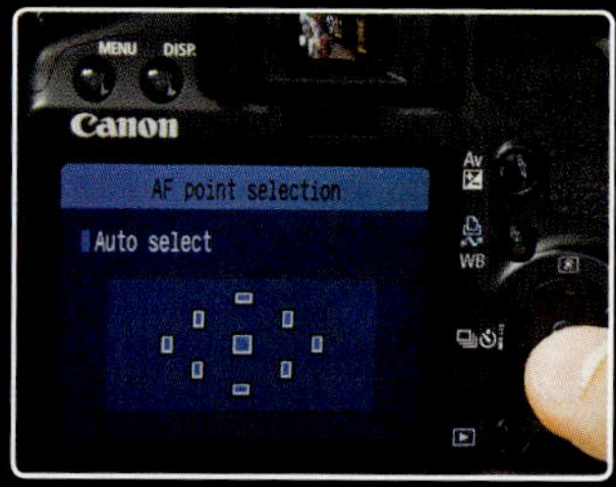

2 Auto AF point selection If all the AF points light up then this means Automatic AF point selection is switched on...

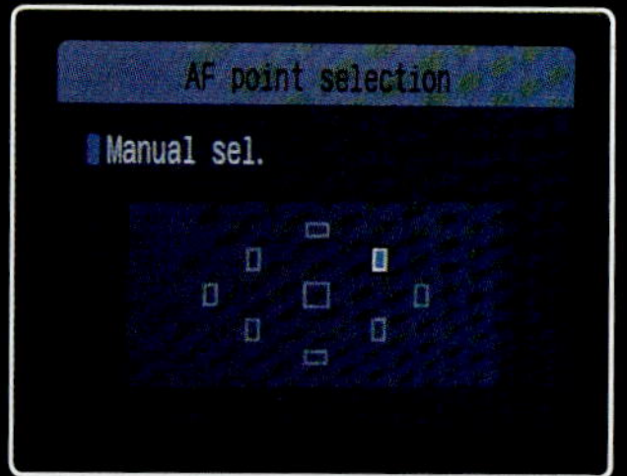

3 Manually select AF points ...but we'd suggest manually selecting a specific AF point. Use the arrow keys and then the Set key.

Are you using an IS lens?

Many modern lenses now come equipped with Image Stabilization (IS), which can reduce a certain amount of camera shake, enabling you to take sharper shots.

YES

Switch on IS

We'd recommend using IS most of the time. With the Canon EF-S 18-55mm IS kit lens at its 55mm focal length, you can obtain sharp results even at relatively slow shutter speeds (such as 1/10 to 1/40 sec).

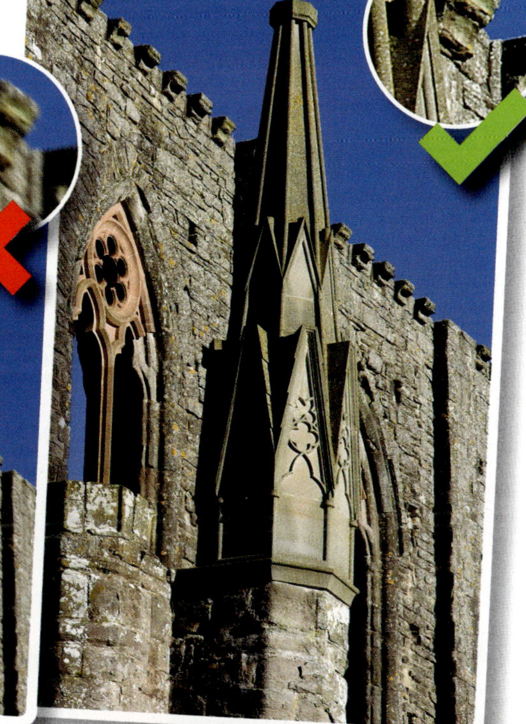

AUTOFOCUS MODES

Q How do I focus on moving targets?

Are you using AI Servo?

If your subjects are moving then you should switch to the AI Servo AF (autofocus) mode and leave it to your digital SLR to adjust the focus as your subject (and its focusing distance) moves around in your frame.

YES

Have you set an AF point?

Don't rely on automatic AF (autofocus) point selection to achieve focus on your moving target. Pick a single AF point for more accurate results (see left).

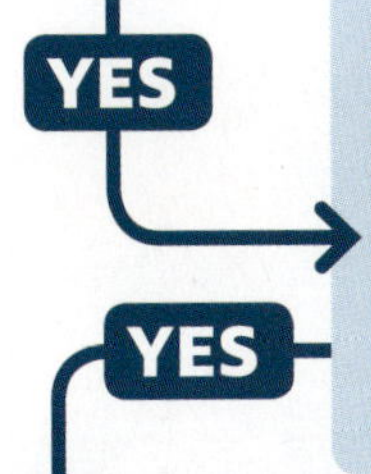

Drive mode on?

Use the high-speed Continuous Drive mode to increase your chances of getting the shot. An EOS 450D offers 3.5 frames per second, while a 40D rattles off a machine gun-like 6.5fps.

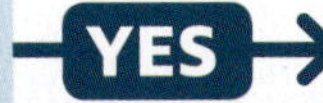

Manually pre-focus

If you know where you subject will appear, try switching to manual focus and pre-focus on that spot – whether it's a branch a bird might land on or, as above, the high jump bar. Then just press the shutter button at the right moment!

COMPOSITION

Q Why do my photos look so cluttered?

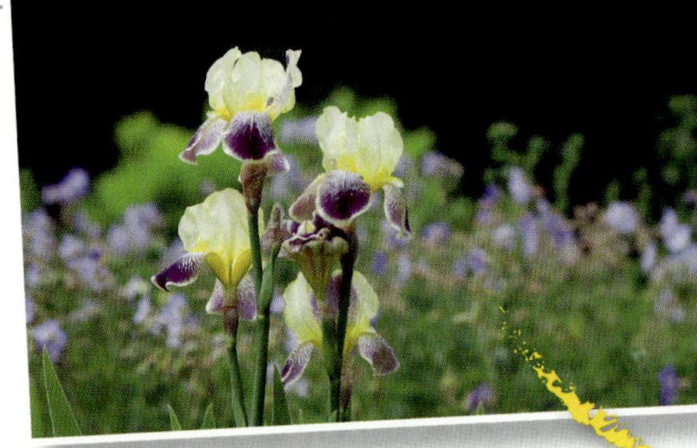

Are your backgrounds distracting?

It's easy to forget the importance of your backgrounds, so let us remind you – they can make all the difference! Here are three solutions to tidy up your cluttered photos...

YES

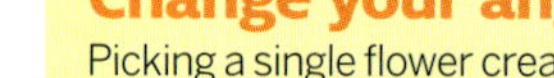

Change your angle of view

Picking a single flower creates a much cleaner composition than trying to photograph a bunch. Move around your subject, trying both low and high camera angles until you find a clean background that makes your subject stand out.

Use a wider aperture

Shooting with an aperture that's too narrow means that more of the background behind your subject will be in focus – and therefore more distracting. Choose a wider aperture (around f/2.5 to f/4) to create a shallower depth of field. This will knock the background out of focus and isolate your subject in the frame, making it 'pop'. See below for how to use your SLR's Aperture Priority (Av) shooting mode.

Use a slower shutter speed

When backgrounds behind sporting subjects are leading the eye away from your main focal point, select a slower shutter speed and pan (see right). Done well, this will blur only the background.

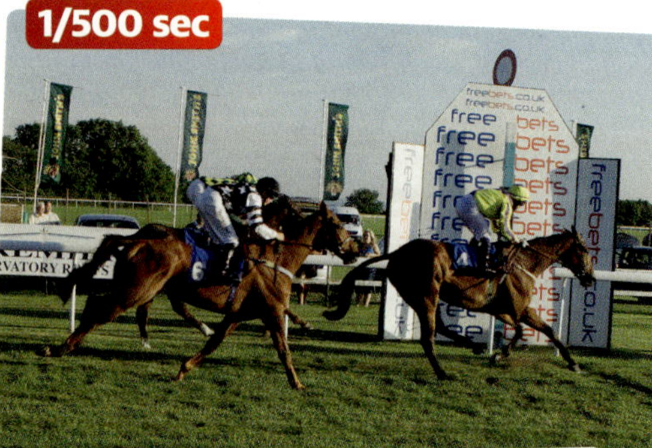

1/500 sec

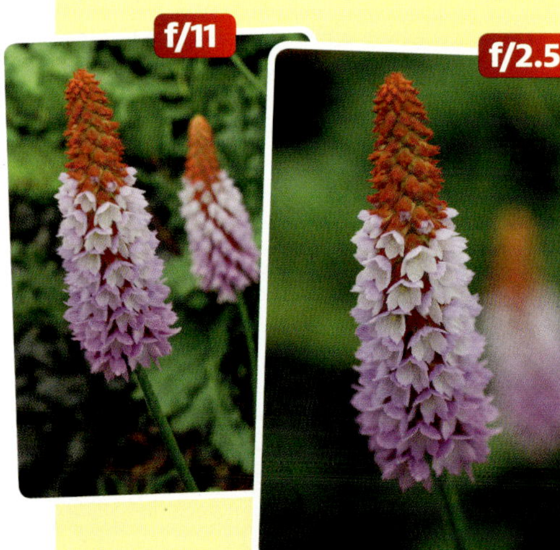

f/11

f/2.5

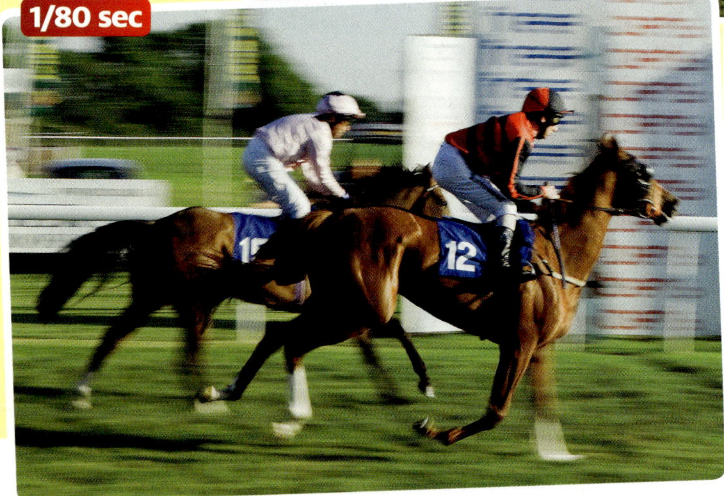

1/80 sec

How to use the Av and Tv modes

Learn to take control of your digital SLR and set your aperture and shutter speed using the Av and Tv modes to avoid capturing any clutter in your backgrounds. Here's how it's done...

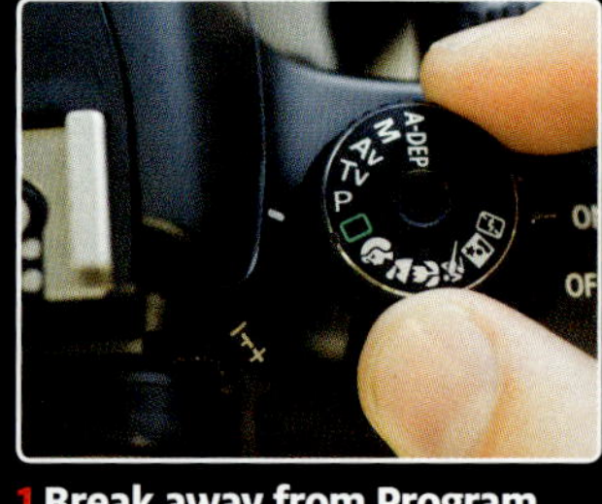

1 Break away from Program
It's a good starting point, but the camera will set both aperture and shutter speed as it sees fit.

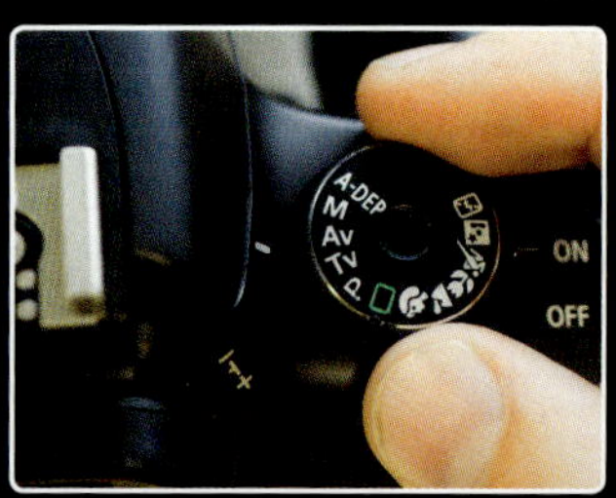

2 Control your apertures
Use the Av (Aperture Priority) mode so you control the aperture – your camera will set the shutter speed.

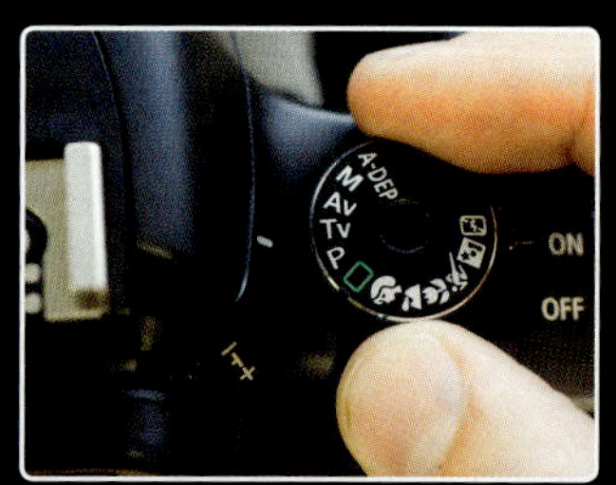

3 Control your shutter speeds
Use the Tv (Shutter Priority) mode so you control the shutter speed – your camera will set the aperture.

All images: Peter Travers, Chris George (Future)

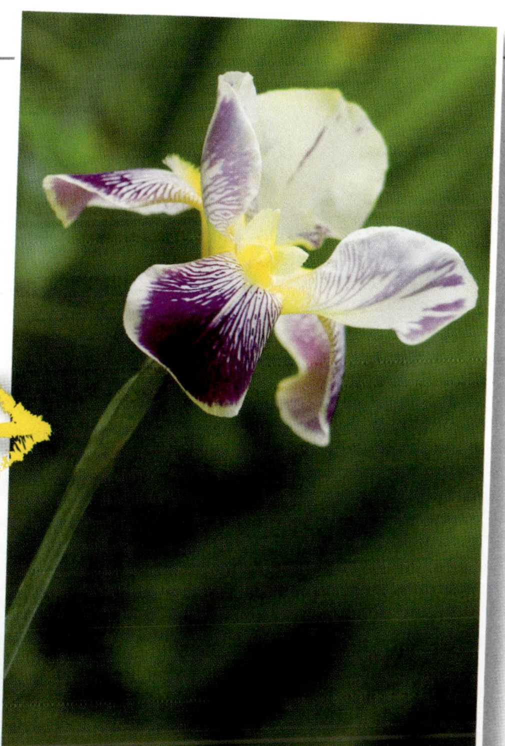

ADD EMPHASIS

Q Why do my images lack any impact?

Have you filled the frame?
A common mistake is to try to capture the entire scene as you see it, rather than focusing only on the best part.

NO →

Zoom in!
You'll get better results with more impact if you zoom in and fill the frame with the area of real interest.

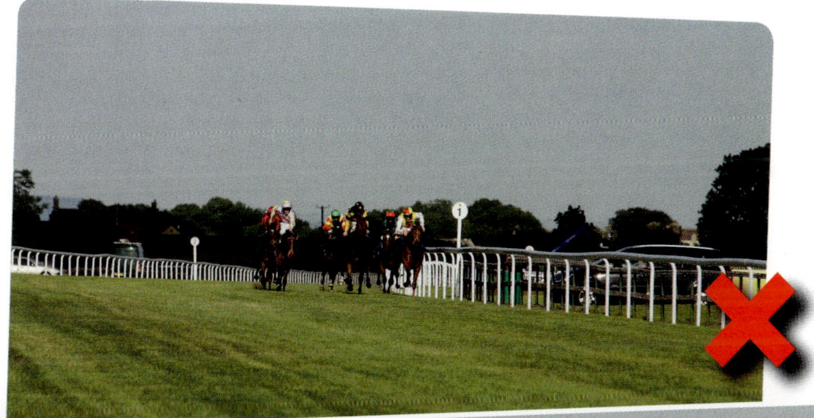

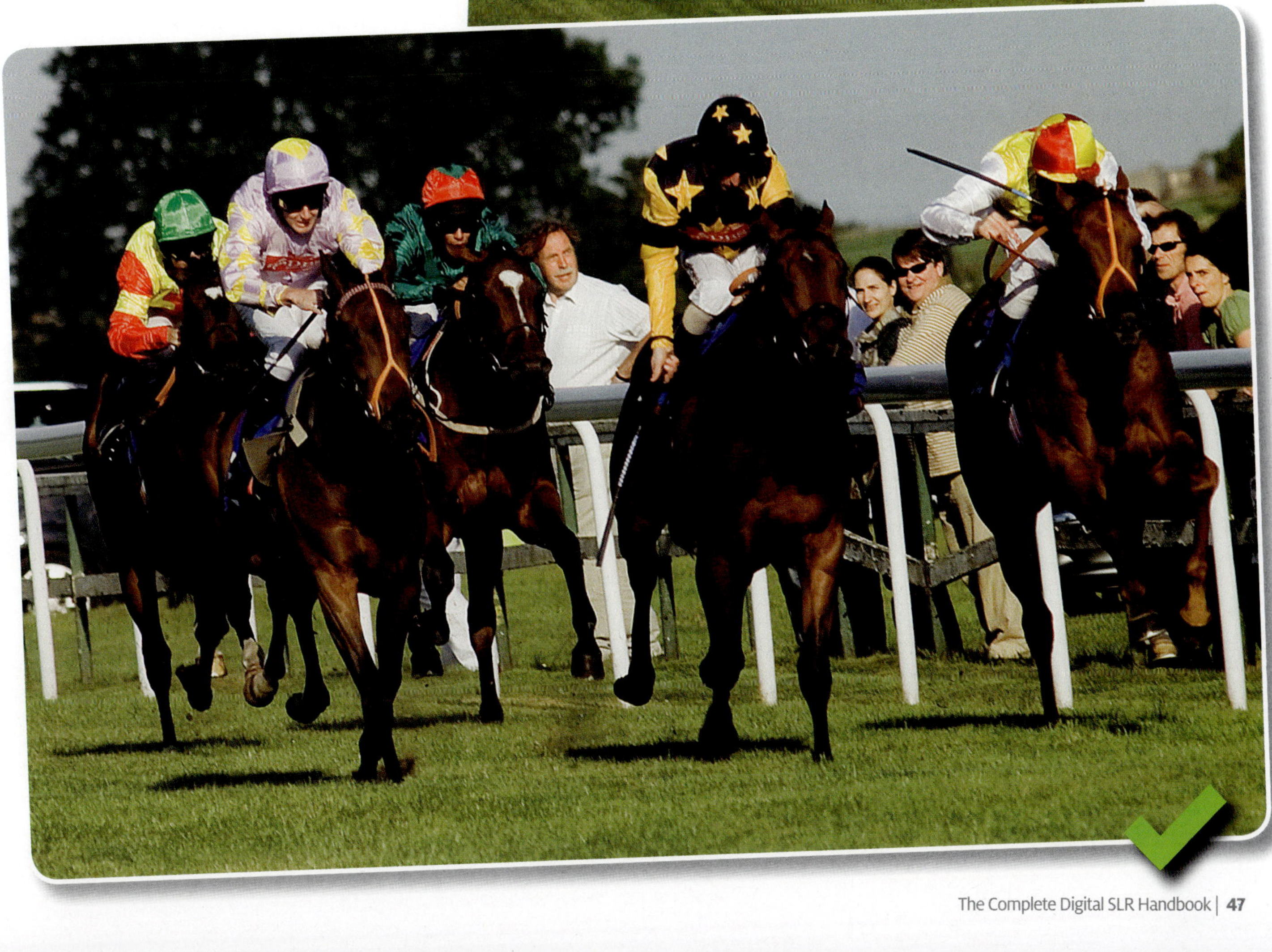

PANNING MADE EASY

Q Why do my action shots look boring?

Have you captured the movement?

If you want to freeze any action shots then shoot with a fast shutter speed (1/500 sec or 1/1000 sec), but remember that these shots often lack any sense of speed or movement. Sometimes, the subject looks so frozen it seems stationary.

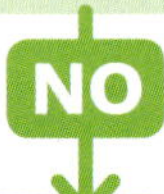

Panning techniques

Switch to a slow shutter setting to capture a sense of speed. Try 1/100 or 1/80 sec (go slower as you gain confidence) and track your subjects smoothly through the frame, shooting as they travel past. The blurred background will add a feeling of movement.

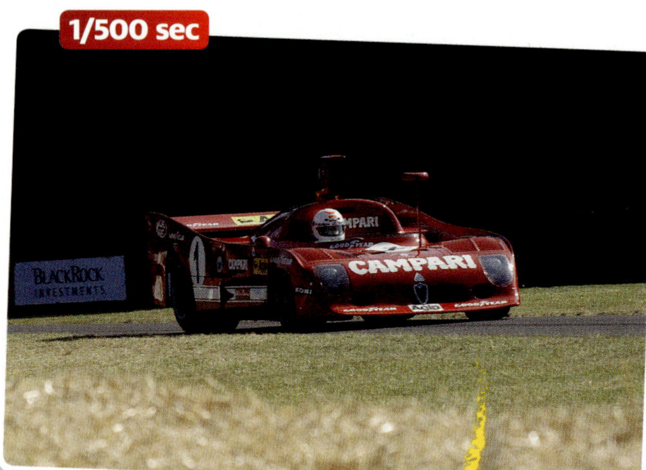

1/500 sec

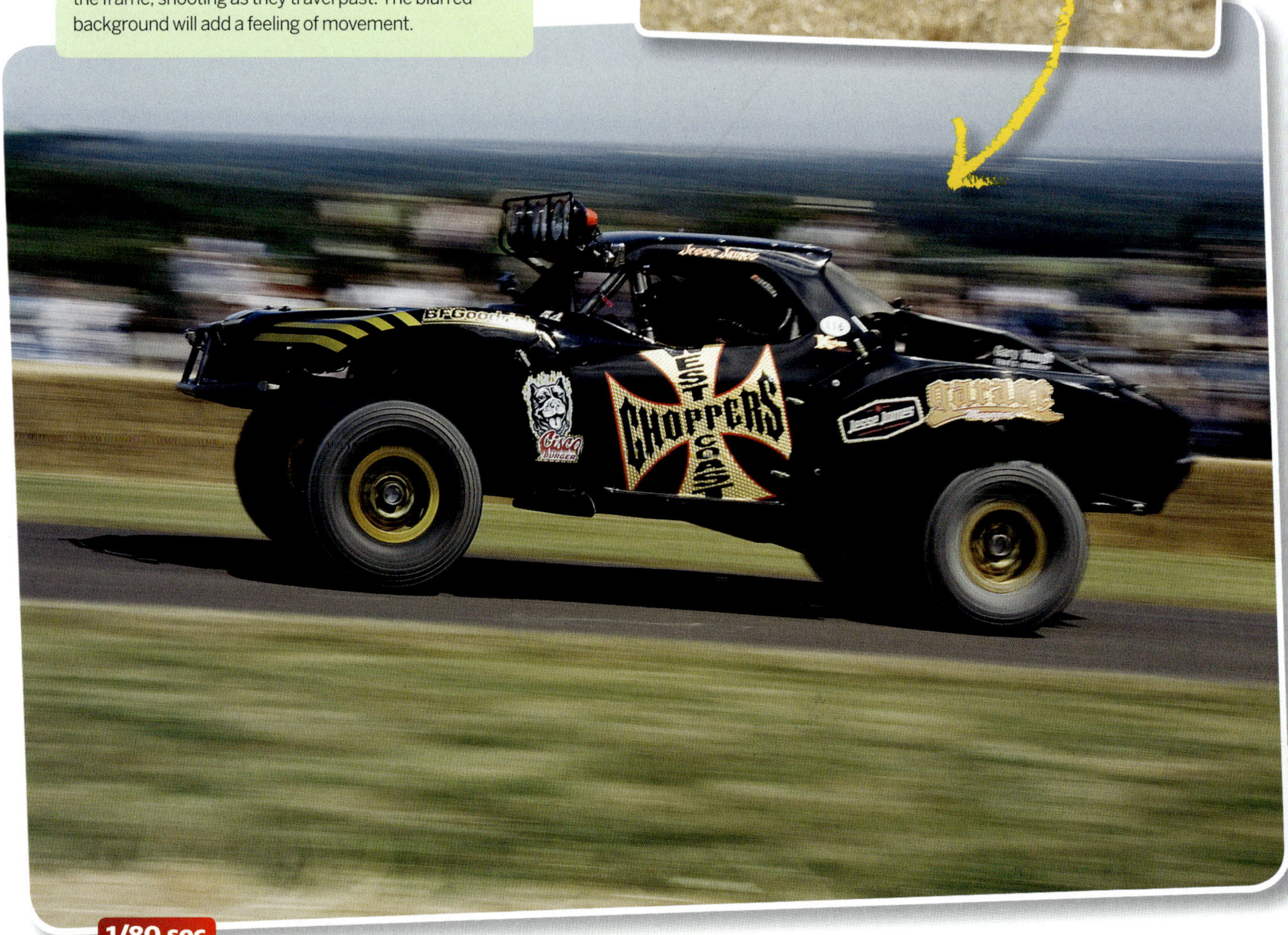

1/80 sec

WHITE BALANCE

Q Why do my colours look all wrong?

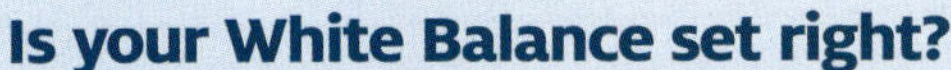

Is your White Balance set right?

Your digital camera is a clever piece of kit, but it can't take perfect shots every time by itself. If you notice that the colours in your photos look inaccurate – a little too warm (orange) or too cold (blue) – then it's likely that you need to take a look at your camera's White Balance settings.

NO

Are you shooting indoors?

If you've ever taken portraits indoors, you'll know what a difference each lighting source can make to your results. Set your White Balance according to the lights – Fluorescent or Tungsten – to ensure whites and skin tones don't appear overly warm. (See below to learn how to set your White Balance.)

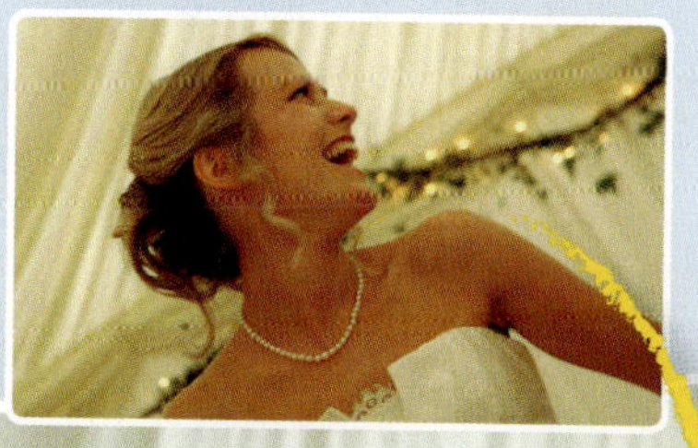

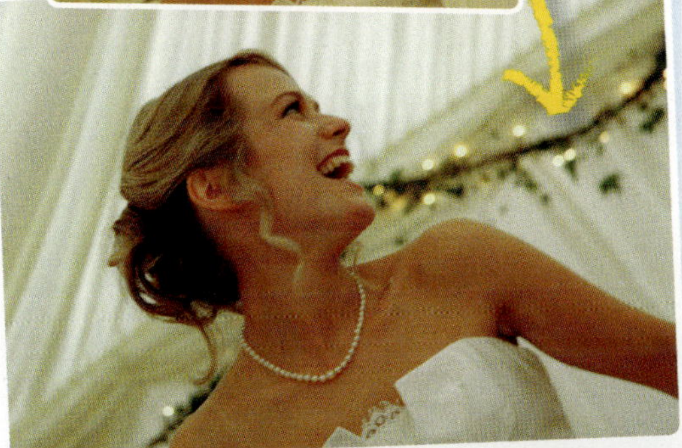

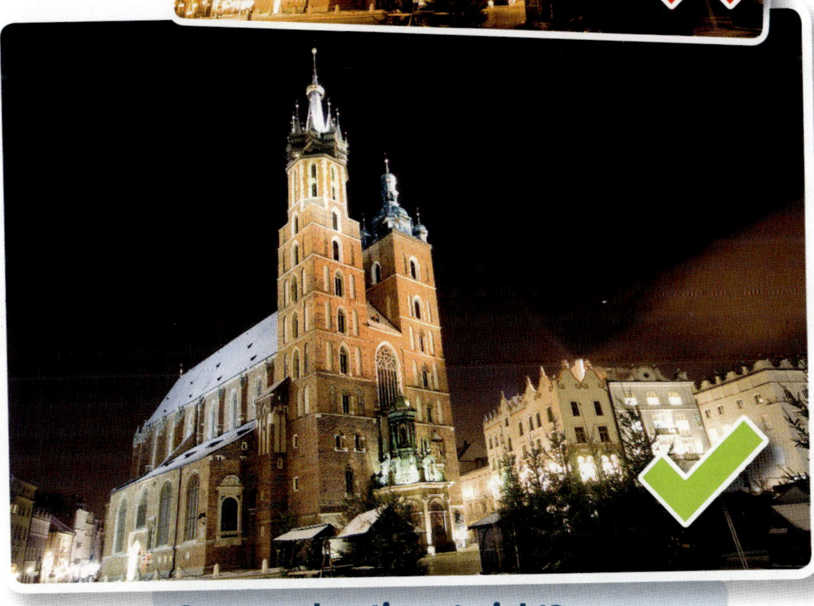

Are you shooting at night?

If you're shooting city scenes at night, it's very easy for the ambient light and street lights to be out of range of the usual Auto White Balance setting. Customise your White Balance using the Custom WB menu option, you'll need a Grey Card (see below) or a sheet of white paper to make sure your colours look correct and your cities look cool.

Setting your White Balance

How you set your digital SLR's White Balance (WB) will determined how the whites in your shots appear. Set your WB correctly and your shots will be whiter than white.

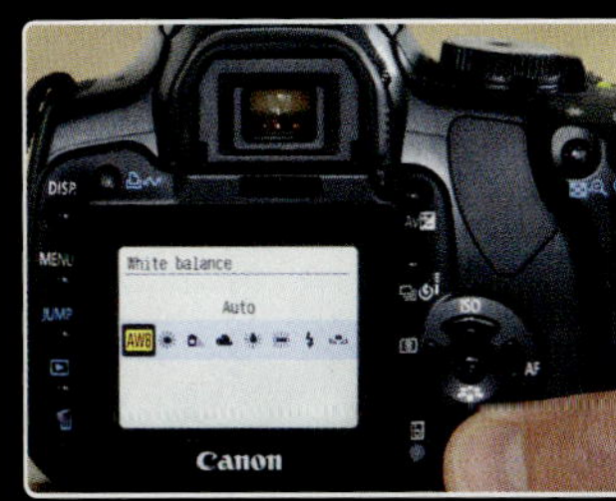

1 Auto White Balance
The Auto WB setting will accurately capture the correct colour temperature for most situations.

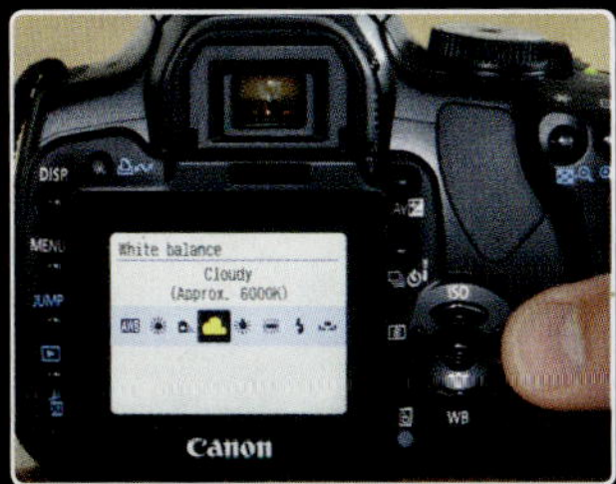

2 White Balance presets
If you want to set the WB so it's consistent for your lighting source, then use the built-in WB settings.

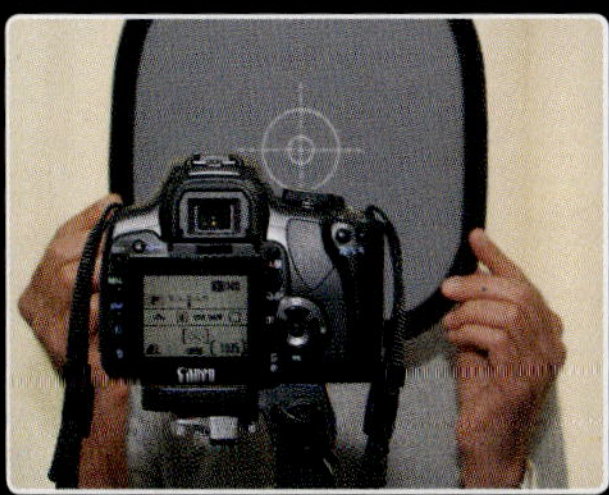

3 Custom White Balance
For truly accurate results you can create a Custom WB setting. You'll need a Grey Card to do this.

All images: Peter Travers, Chris George (Future)

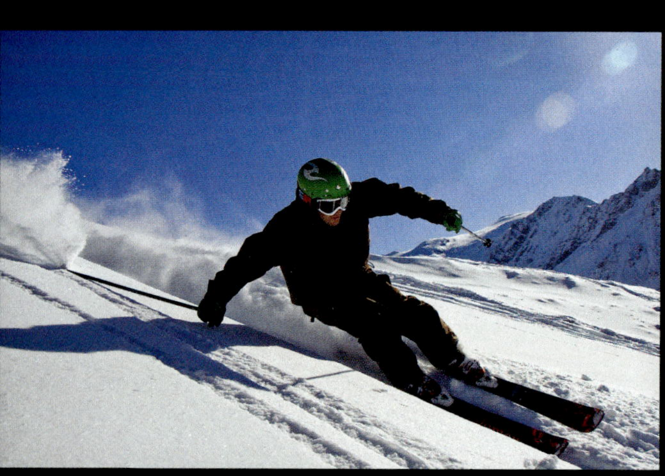

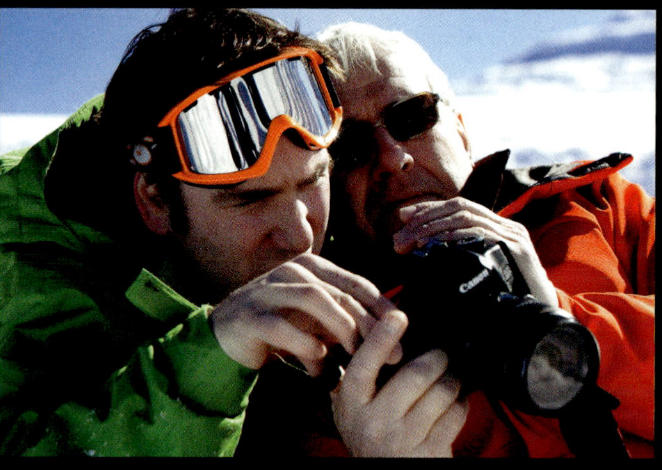

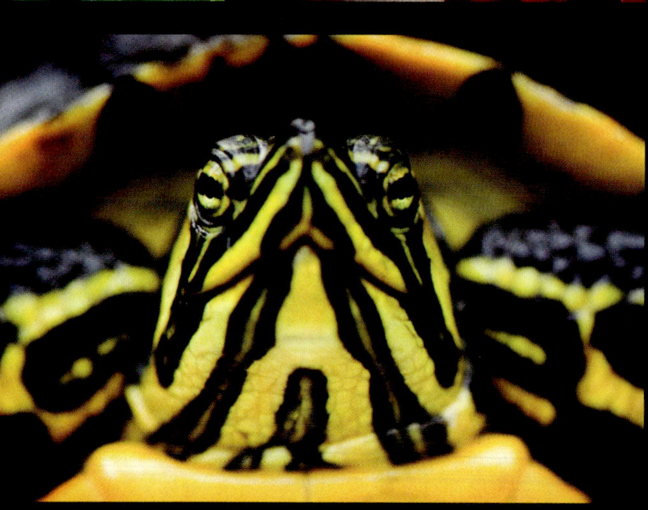

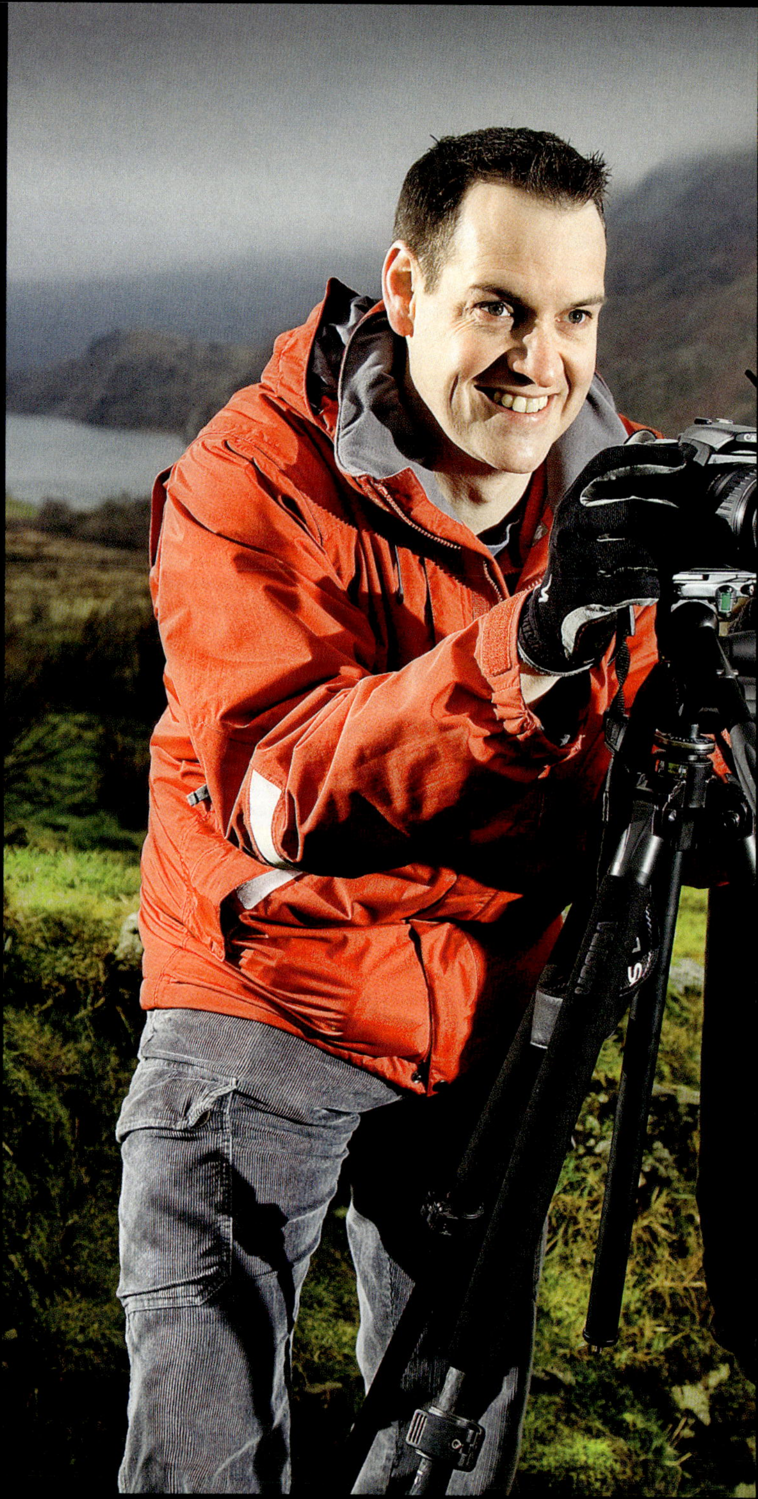

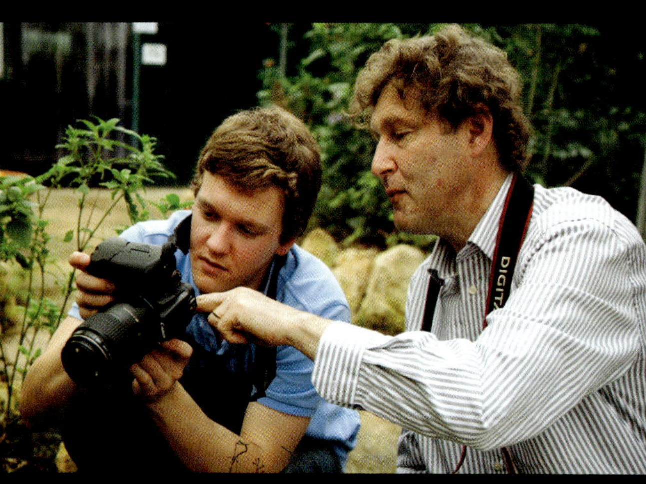

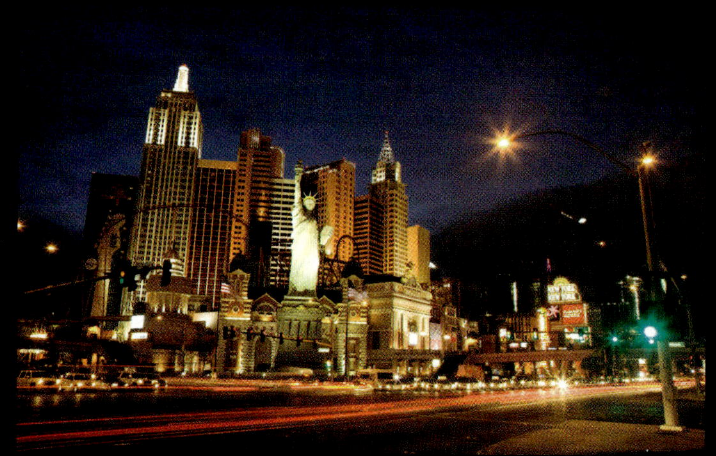

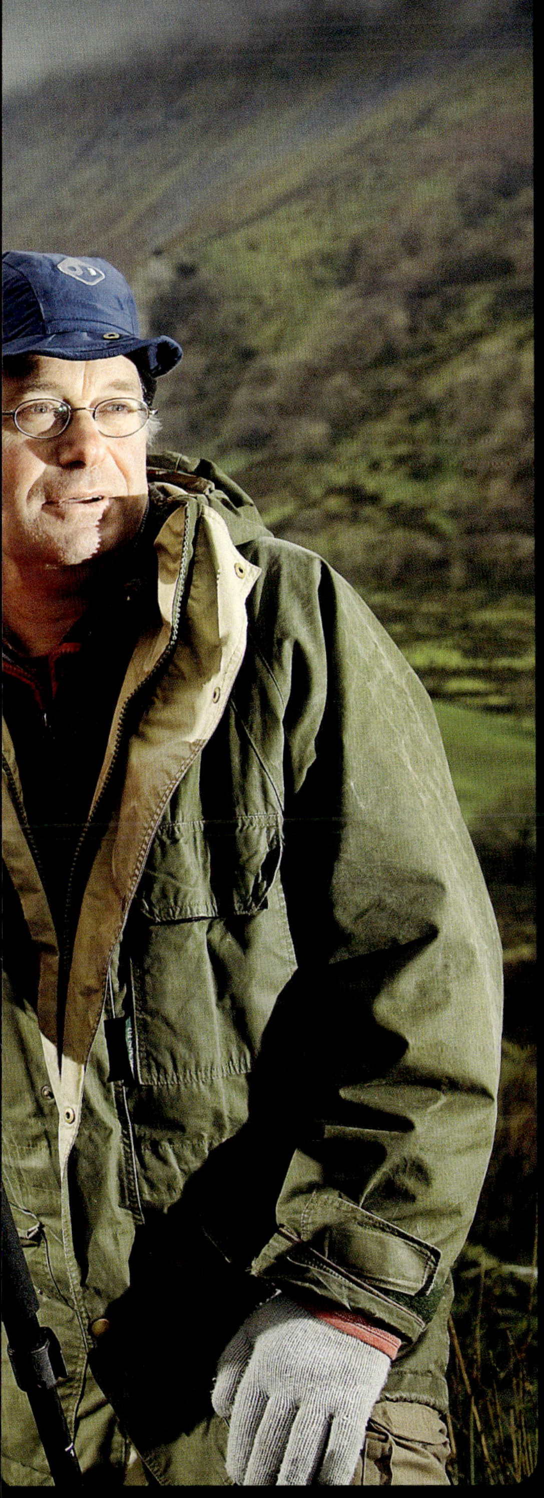

TAKE BETTER PHOTOS!

Real-life photography

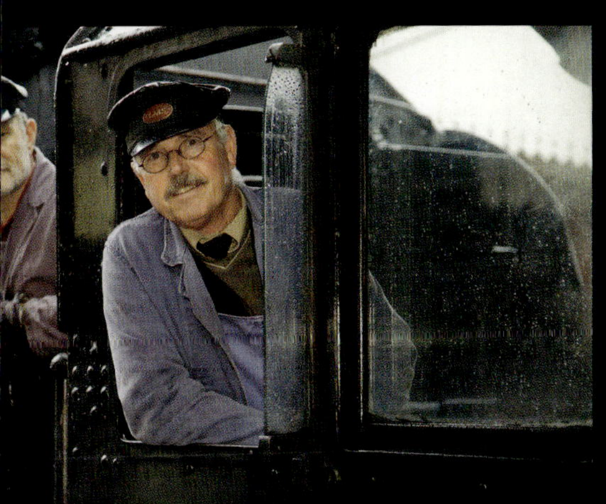

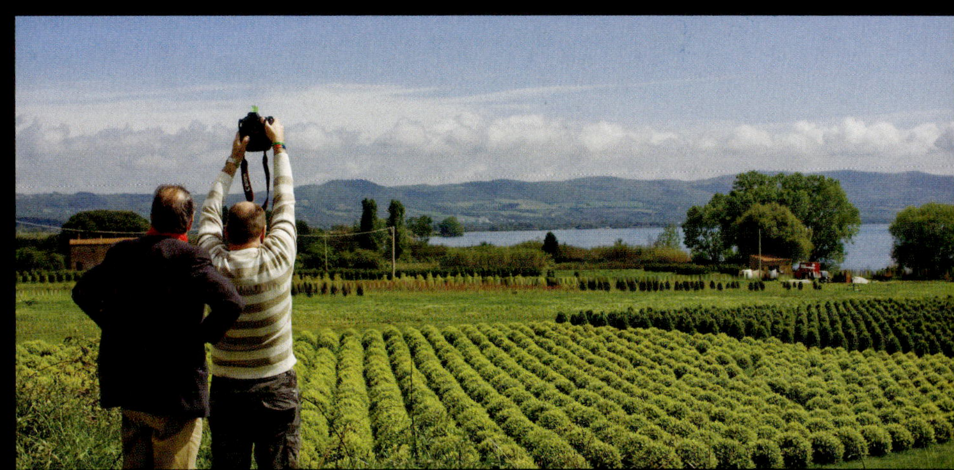

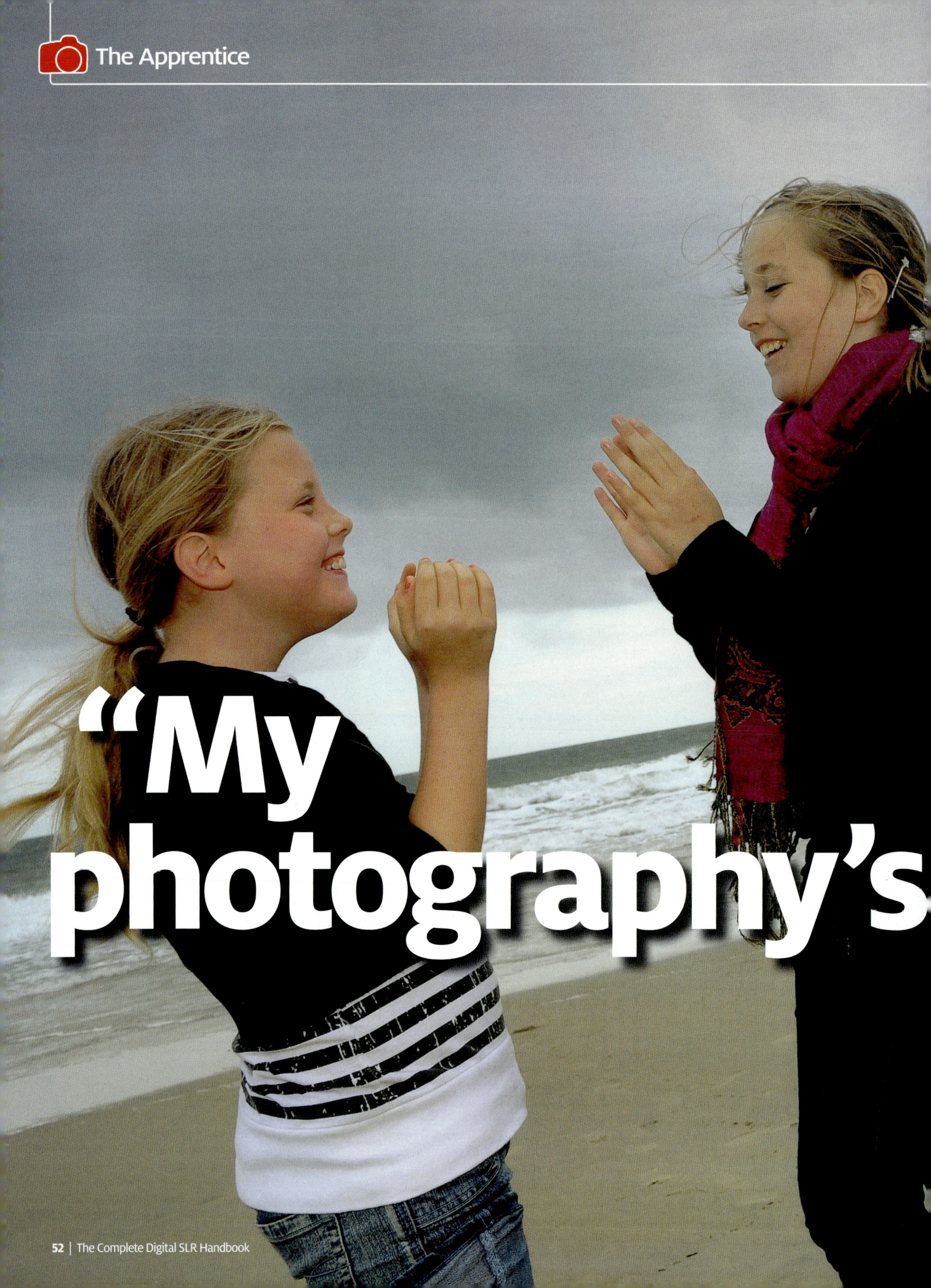

"My photography's

THE APPRENTICE...

Name: **Sarah Milne**
Camera: **Canon EOS 50D**

Sarah, 38, is a single mum and amateur photographer from Croydon. After buying her first Canon D-SLR (an EOS 450D) 18 months ago, she enrolled on an Open College of the Arts photography course and has never looked back. Sarah's work has progressed quickly (check out her project at www.giftsoflife.co.uk), but she wants advice on how to photograph her daughters.

THE PRO...

Name: **Paul Smart**
Camera: **Canon EOS-1D Mark III**

Paul, 30, was born in Leicester and studied photography in Australia before settling in Devon. He works from his studio in Exeter and has been a successful family portrait specialist for five years. Check out his website at www.maxamphotography.com.

a family affair!"

Words: Peter Travers • Location shots: Rob Scott (Future)

Learn how to take fantastic family portraits as our Apprentice heads to Bournemouth to get top tuition from Canon portrait photographer Paul Smart

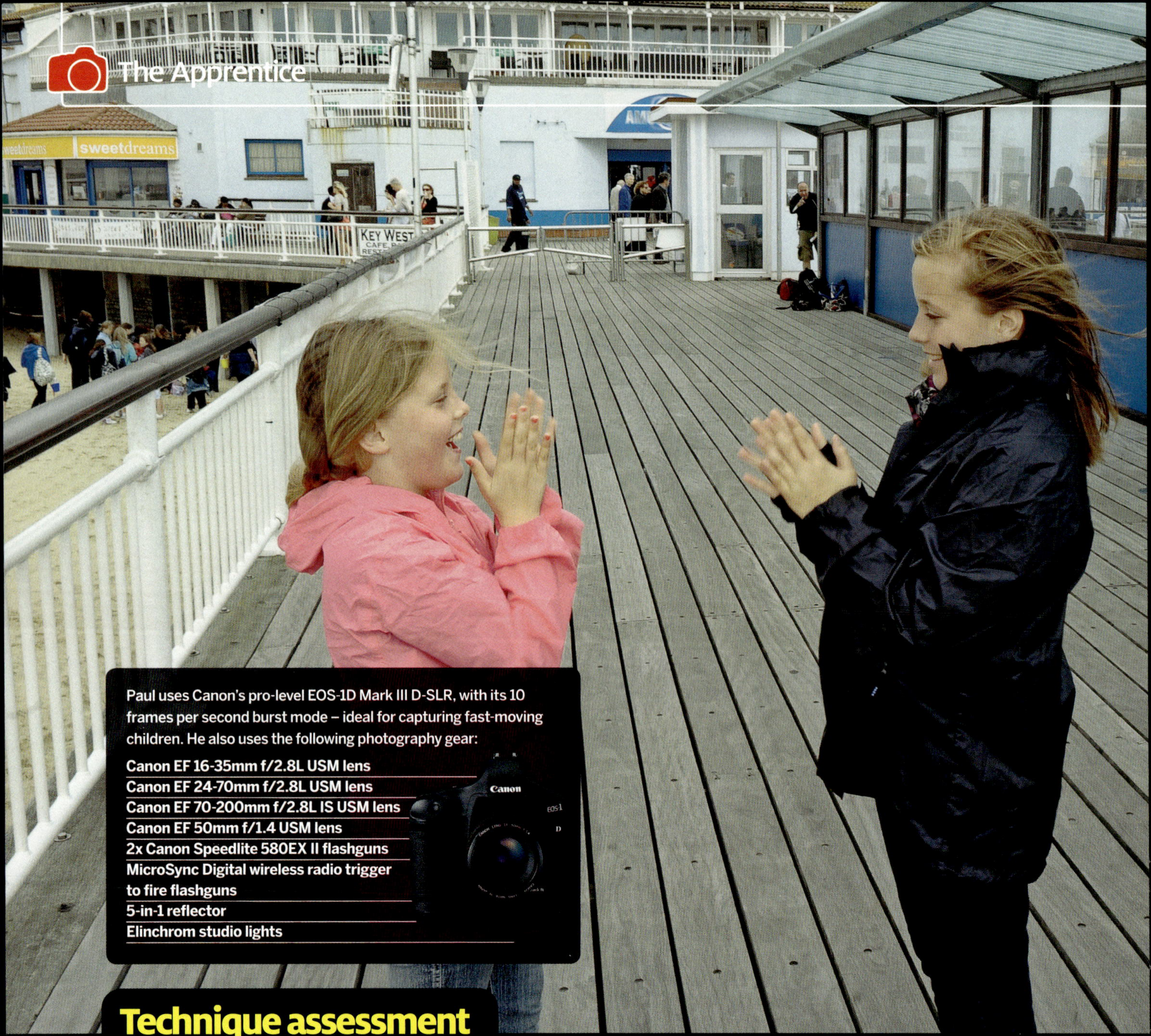

Paul uses Canon's pro-level EOS-1D Mark III D-SLR, with its 10 frames per second burst mode – ideal for capturing fast-moving children. He also uses the following photography gear:

- Canon EF 16-35mm f/2.8L USM lens
- Canon EF 24-70mm f/2.8L USM lens
- Canon EF 70-200mm f/2.8L IS USM lens
- Canon EF 50mm f/1.4 USM lens
- 2x Canon Speedlite 580EX II flashguns
- MicroSync Digital wireless radio trigger to fire flashguns
- 5-in-1 reflector
- Elinchrom studio lights

Technique assessment

Is Sarah ready to shoot portraits?

After Sarah had warmed up and taken a few portraits of her two daughters, Paul noticed a few ways she could improve her technique...

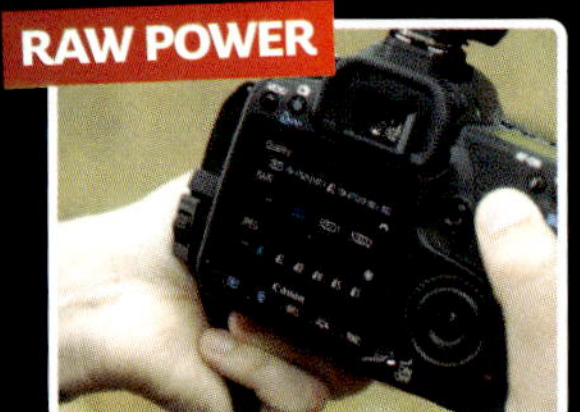

RAW POWER

Switch to RAW image quality

"Sarah had her Canon EOS set up to capture just JPEGs," says Paul. "JPEGs are fine if you manage to get the shot perfect every time, but it's better to shoot in RAW as it's the highest image quality setting and gives you many more options to accurately enhance your shots in Adobe Camera Raw if they need a boost."

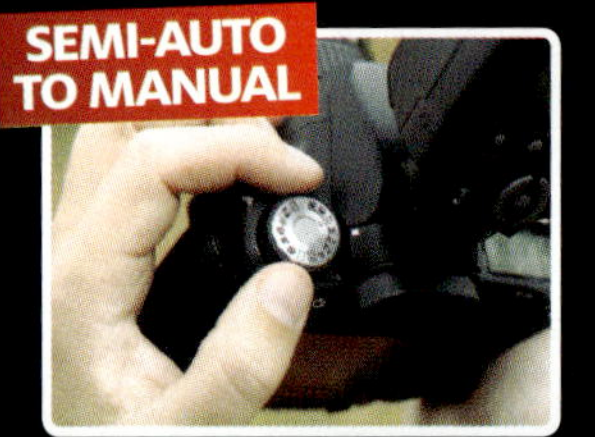

SEMI-AUTO TO MANUAL

Switch shooting modes

"Sarah was relying on Av (Aperture Priority) mode, but when shooting outdoor portraits in bright daylight, as we were, it's common for cameras to underexpose shots," explains Paul. "I gave Sarah the confidence to shoot in Manual mode, to set her aperture and shutter speed, and to get the portraits she wanted."

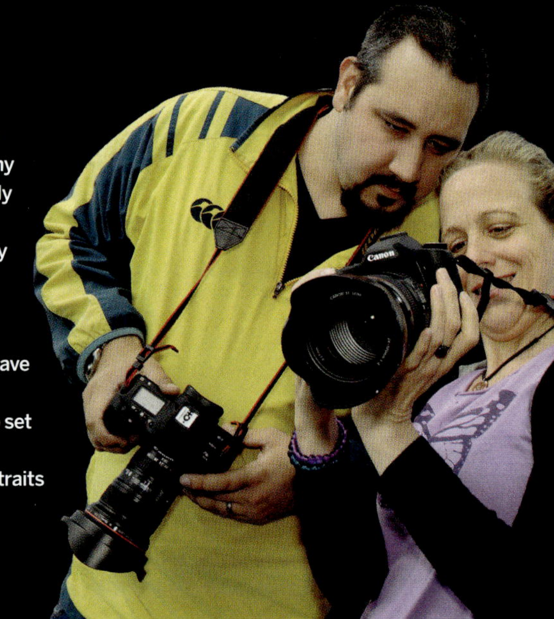

KILLER KIT OF THE PROS #1

'Fast' lenses

"Most of my lenses are from Canon's L-series," says Paul. "They're expensive, but you get the best quality glass, build and accuracy, giving the best portraits. They're 'fast' lenses, so they have a constant aperture of either f/2.8 or f/4, meaning fast shutter speeds for sharp portraits, even in low light."

EXPERT INSIGHT

Stay focused on your subjects

When it came to focusing, Sarah was a little ahead of herself – attempting to manually focus with mixed results. Paul encouraged her to use her lens's autofocus (AF) mode to get consistently sharper shots. "I use AF when photographing children because they rarely keep still, so it's practically impossible to manually focus and ensure sharp shots," Paul explains.

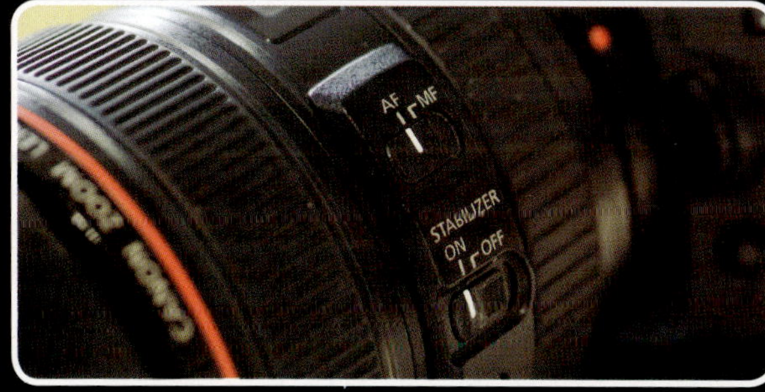

PAUL'S TIP

Start shooting with a mid-range zoom

Paul likes to begin shooting portraits using his Canon EF 24-70mm f/2.8L USM lens. "The 24-70mm on my EOS-1D Mark III enables me to take wide shots of a family of four or five, then zoom in to take individual portraits," says Paul. "Depending on the sort of shot I'm trying to take, I'll then switch to a 16-35mm wide-angle or 70-200mm telephoto zoom as necessary."

HOT SHOT #1

▲ Exposure: 1/60 sec at f/9, ISO100
Lens: Canon EF 24-105mm f/4L IS USM

◀ Sarah's comment

"This was a pleasing start for me. Paul talked about clean compositions and leading lines, which I've tried to put into effect in this shot of Hope and Ellie playing on the pier. I used an aperture of f/9 to keep the length of pier in focus and, shooting in Manual, I dialled-in one stop of overexposure (using the Exposure Level indicator) to correctly expose the girls and make the sea and sky less prominent in the background." ▶

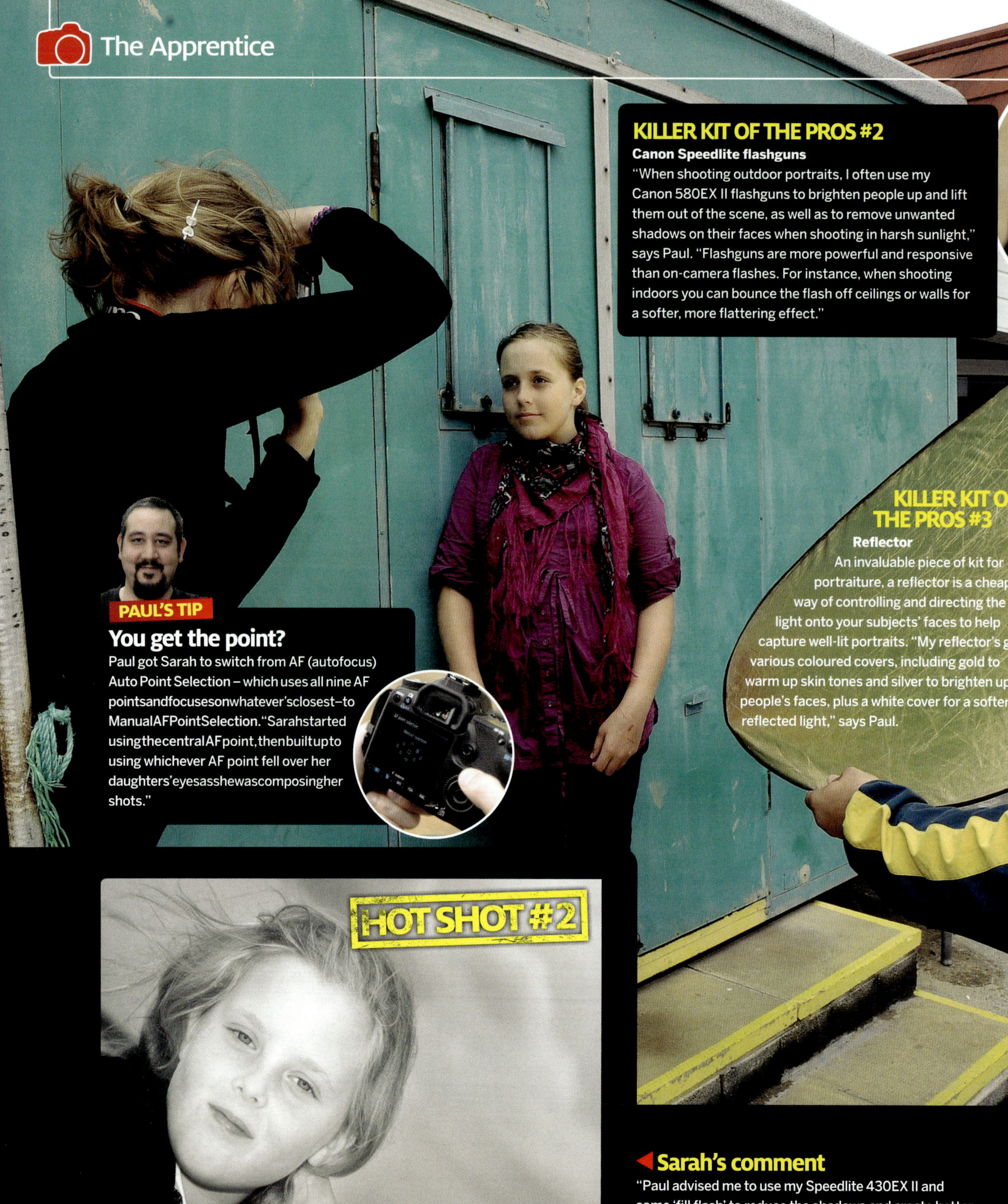

KILLER KIT OF THE PROS #2

Canon Speedlite flashguns

"When shooting outdoor portraits, I often use my Canon 580EX II flashguns to brighten people up and lift them out of the scene, as well as to remove unwanted shadows on their faces when shooting in harsh sunlight," says Paul. "Flashguns are more powerful and responsive than on-camera flashes. For instance, when shooting indoors you can bounce the flash off ceilings or walls for a softer, more flattering effect."

KILLER KIT OF THE PROS #3

Reflector

An invaluable piece of kit for portraiture, a reflector is a cheap way of controlling and directing the light onto your subjects' faces to help capture well-lit portraits. "My reflector's got various coloured covers, including gold to warm up skin tones and silver to brighten up people's faces, plus a white cover for a softer reflected light," says Paul.

PAUL'S TIP

You get the point?

Paul got Sarah to switch from AF (autofocus) Auto Point Selection – which uses all nine AF points and focuses on whatever's closest – to Manual AF Point Selection. "Sarah started using the central AF point, then built up to using whichever AF point fell over her daughters' eyes as she was composing her shots."

HOT SHOT #2

▲ **Exposure:** 1/200 sec at f/7.1, ISO100
Lens: Canon EF 24-105mm f/4L IS USM

◀ Sarah's comment

"Paul advised me to use my Speedlite 430EX II and some 'fill flash' to reduce the shadows and create better skin tones, while still retaining some detail in the bright sky. I used Manual mode and set the aperture to f/7.1 to blur the background, with a shutter speed of 1/200 sec to sync with the flash. I sat down on the beach to get down to her eye level and tilted the horizon to make the final portrait more dynamic, while still including the helter-skelter on the pier in the background as a point of interest. I later converted the shot to black and white."

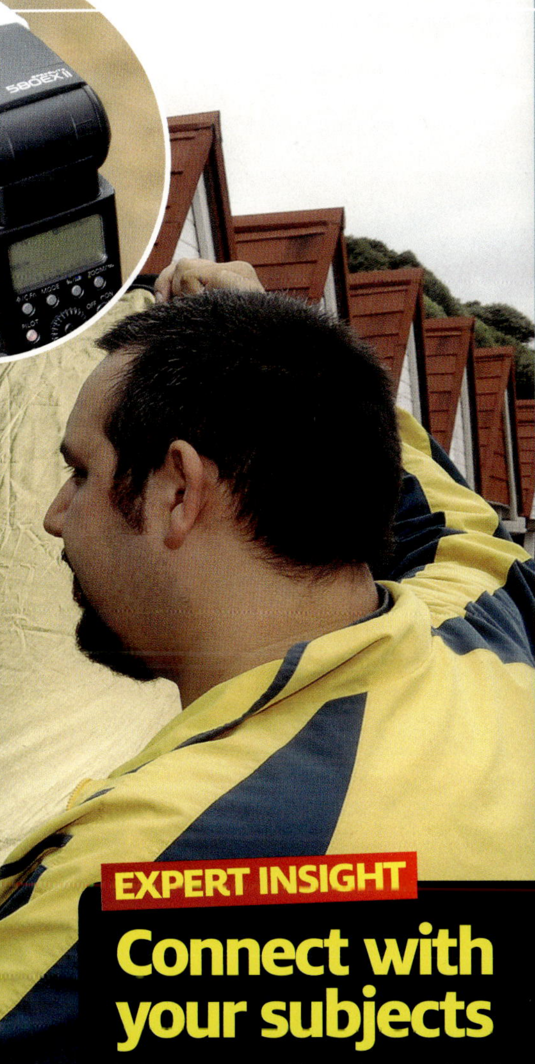

EXPERT INSIGHT

Connect with your subjects

Building a rapport with people you're about to photograph is crucial. If you don't engage with them, your shots will look lifeless. "Normally I'll have an informal chat and a laugh with the kids and parents first, which helps people to relax before the photography begins," says Paul. "Sarah didn't have this problem as she was photographing her own daughters. However, this means a different approach is needed to get the shots, because quite often your children won't listen to you. I made sure Sarah gave the girls clear instructions – while maintaining an all-important sense of fun!"

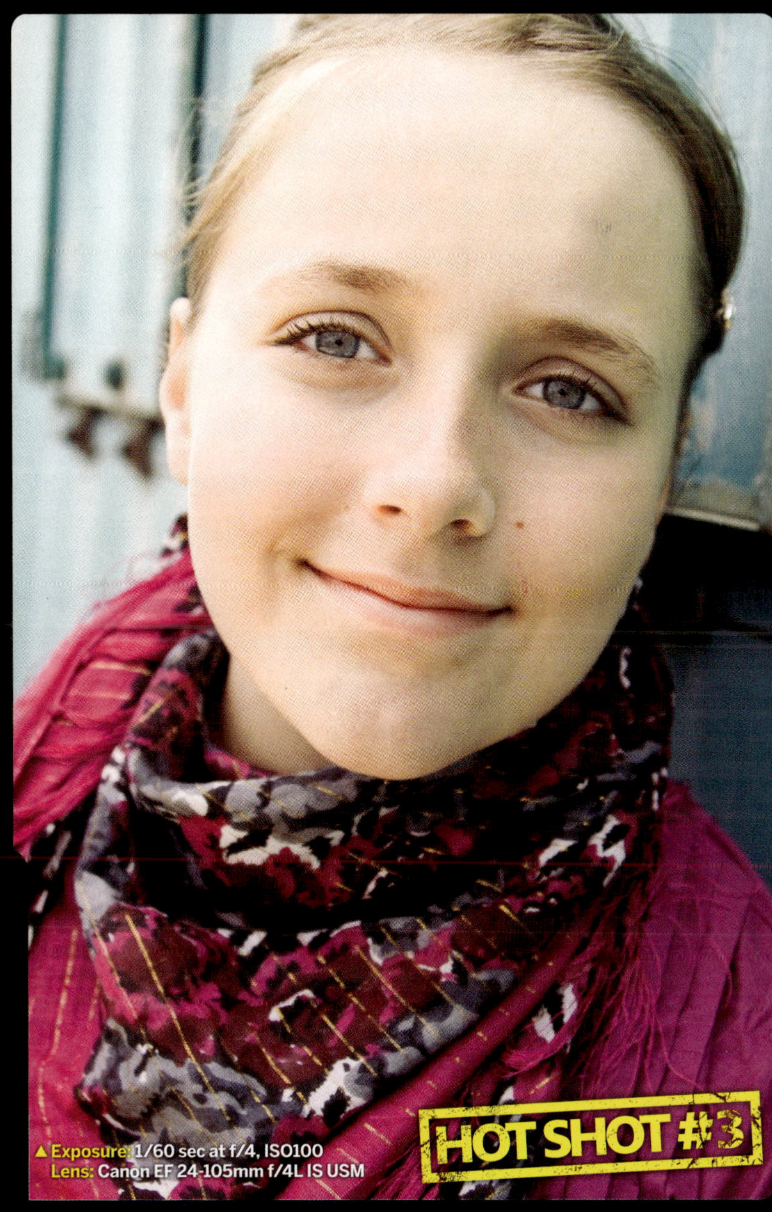

▲ **Exposure:** 1/60 sec at f/4, ISO100
Lens: Canon EF 24-105mm f/4L IS USM

▲ Sarah's comment

"We decided to get individual portraits of the girls, and this is my eldest daughter, Hope, posing against the colourful background of a beachfront building that had a lovely green, weathered exterior. As it was overcast, the natural light was soft and created no unsightly shadows. I chose a wide aperture and focused on Hope's eyes, using a tight composition to fill the frame."

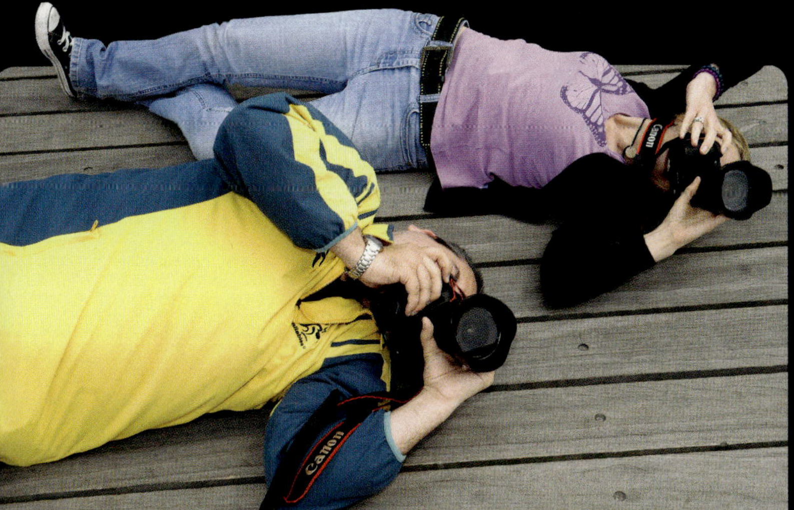

SARAH'S TIP

◀ Change your angle of view

"Paul was very active when taking portraits and encouraged me to move around my subjects to capture more interesting angles of view," says Sarah. "I ended up standing on benches to shoot downwards, lying on my back on the pier to shoot upwards, and crawling around on the beach to get down to my daughters' eye level, all of which helped me capture more inventive shots." ▶

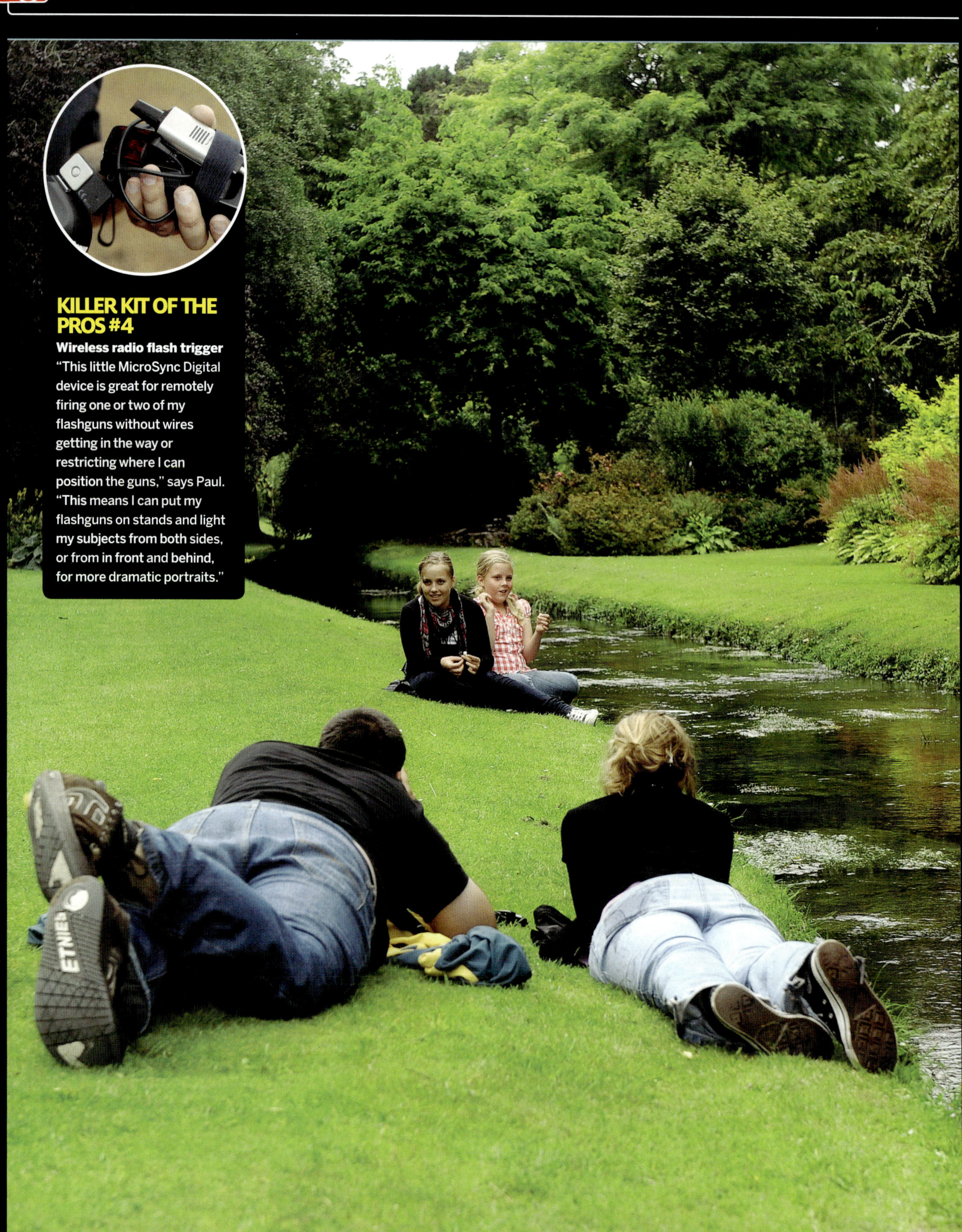

KILLER KIT OF THE PROS #4

Wireless radio flash trigger

"This little MicroSync Digital device is great for remotely firing one or two of my flashguns without wires getting in the way or restricting where I can position the guns," says Paul. "This means I can put my flashguns on stands and light my subjects from both sides, or from in front and behind, for more dramatic portraits."

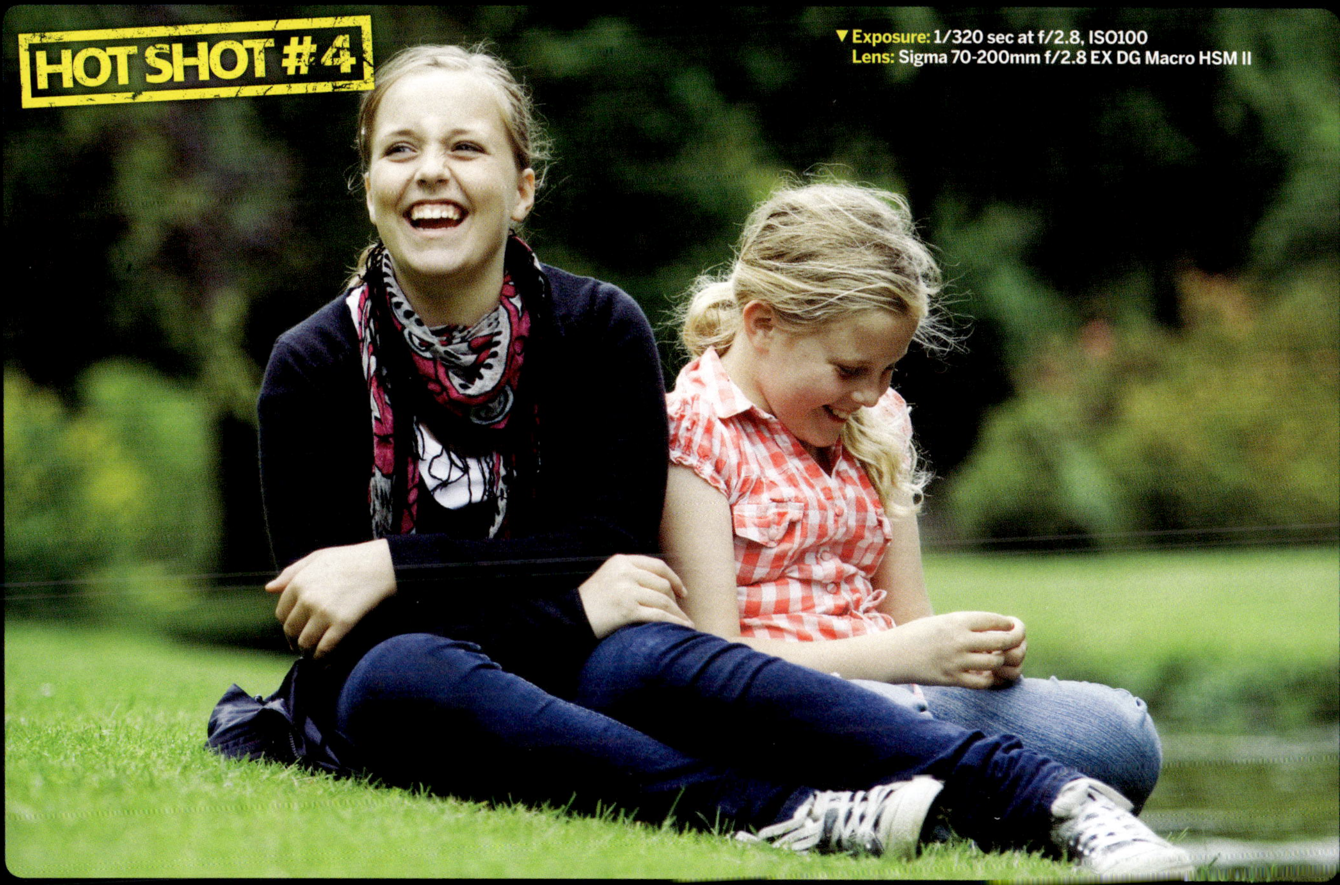

HOT SHOT #4

▼ **Exposure:** 1/320 sec at f/2.8, ISO100
Lens: Sigma 70-200mm f/2.8 EX DG Macro HSM II

▲ **Sarah's comment**

"We walked to the nearby park for these portraits. We found a clearing where the dark greenery was far enough behind the girls so that, by using a wide aperture of f/2.8 and a long telephoto lens, we could knock it out of focus. I got down on my front to reduce the amount of foreground appearing in my frame and fired away on Continuous Shooting mode (6.3 frames per second) as the girls played around. I love the way Hope's cracking up as Ellie giggles while struggling to make a daisy chain."

EXPERT INSIGHT

Capture some action

Once comfortable in front of the camera, one of the great bonuses of photographing children is that they love to show off and pose. The trick is to be ready to capture the action on camera. "Sarah was set with a wide aperture of f/2.8 and a resulting fast shutter speed of 1/500 sec, which meant a perfect exposure that froze any movement the girls made, such as Ellie splashing around in the stream (below)."

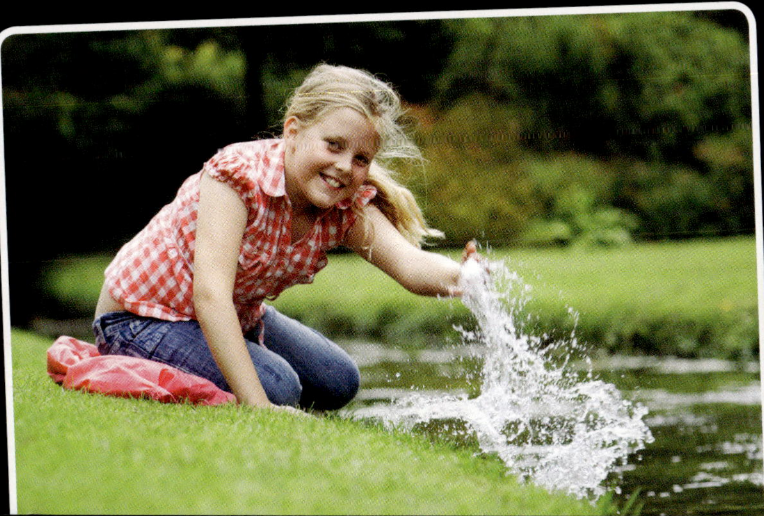

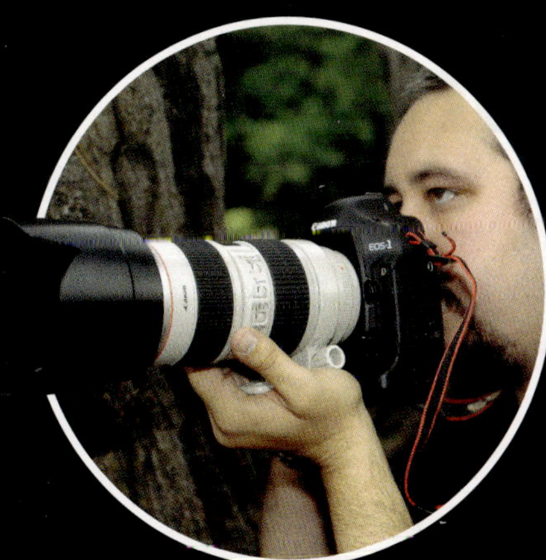

KILLER KIT OF THE PROS #5

Telephoto zoom

"I never go anywhere without my Canon EF 70-200mm f/2.8L IS lens," says Paul. "It's a brilliant portrait lens because at f/2.8, and over a 100mm focal length, I can blur any backgrounds to make people 'pop' out of the shot. Its 200mm focal length also enables me to stand back and give subjects space, meaning better facial expressions and portraits!"

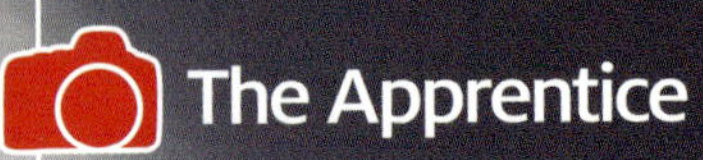

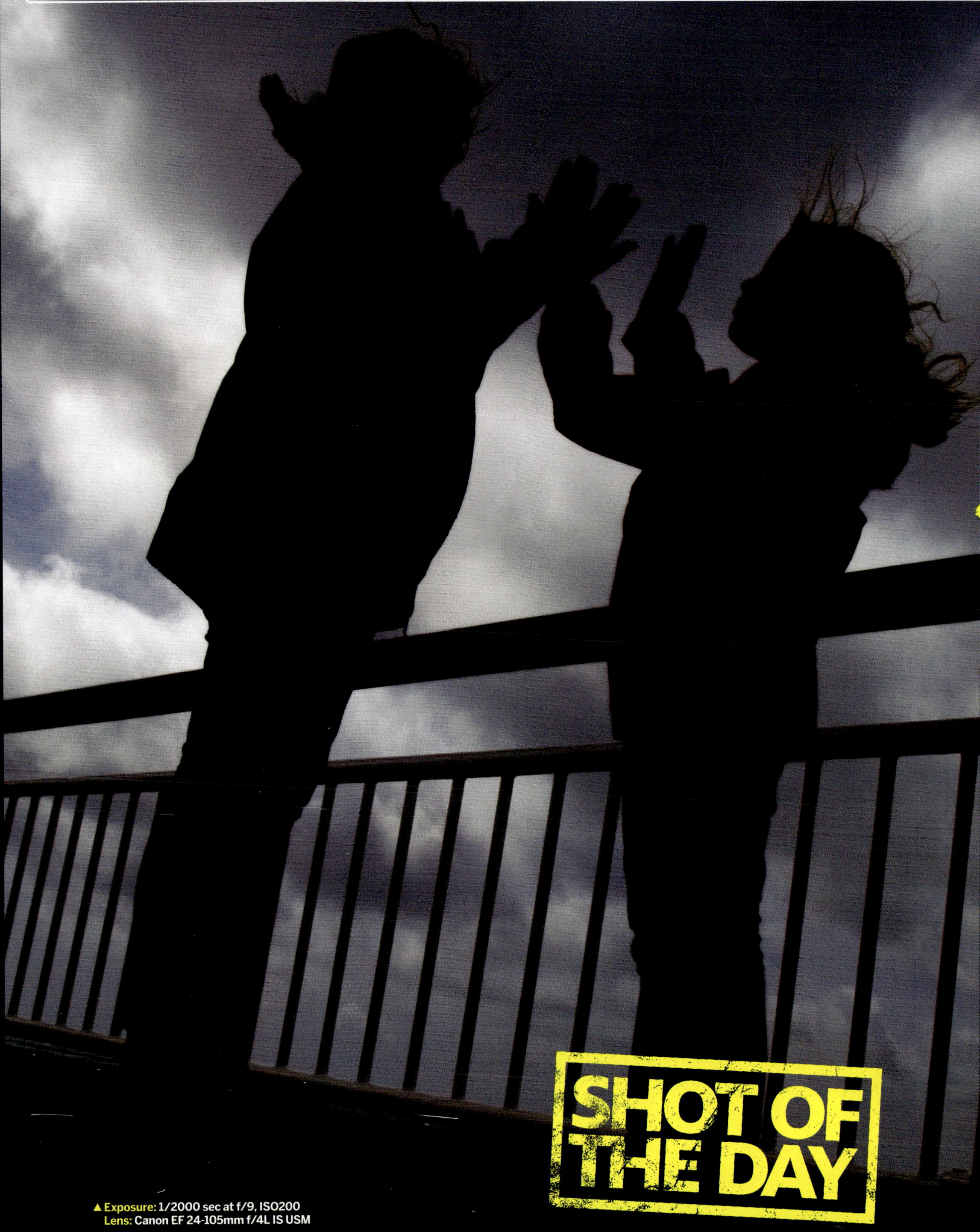

▲ **Exposure:** 1/2000 sec at f/9, ISO200
Lens: Canon EF 24-105mm f/4L IS USM

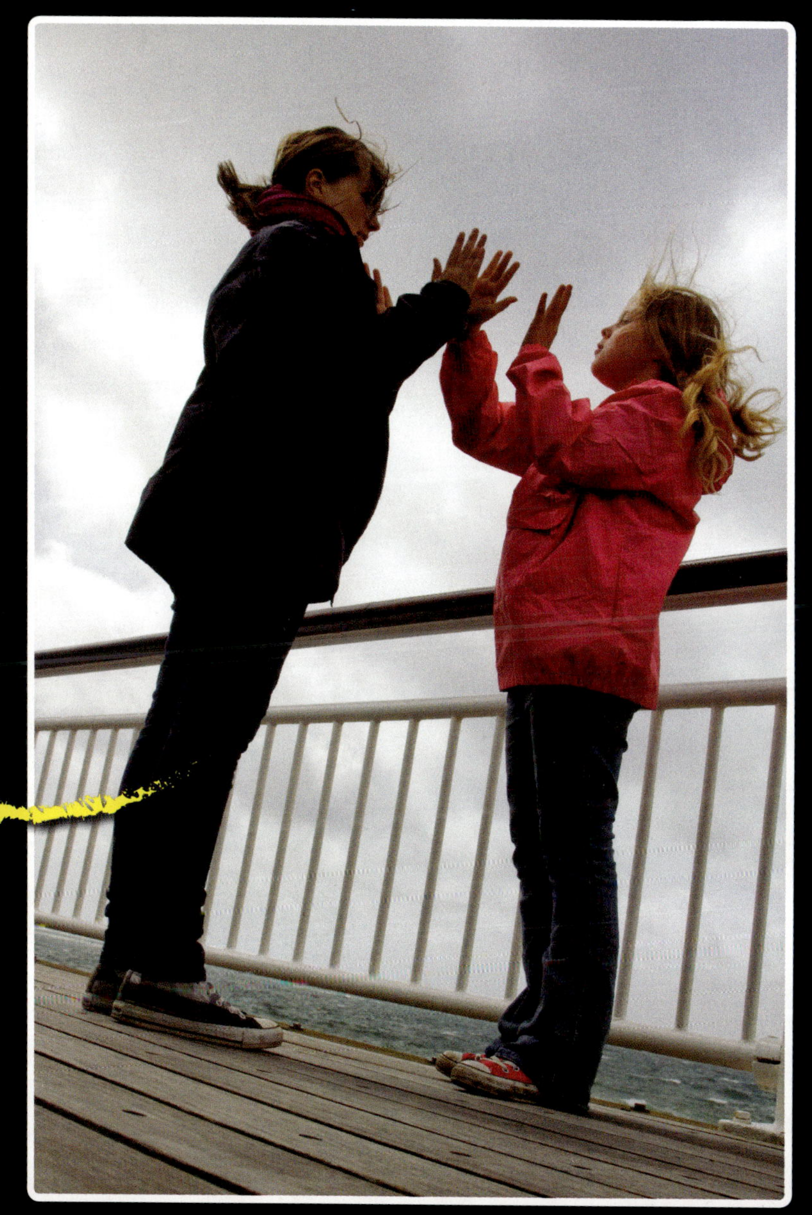

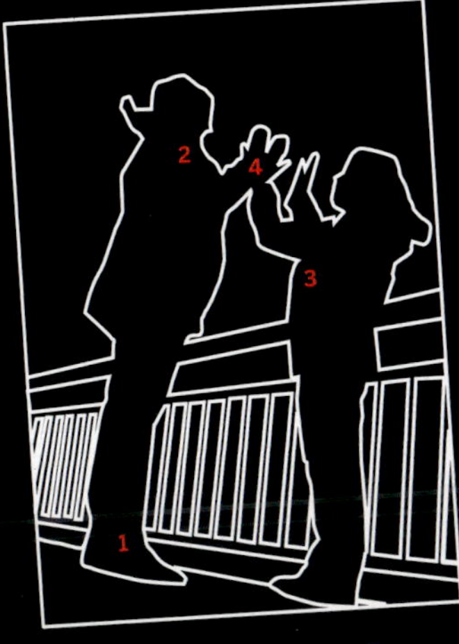

Paul's verdict

"Sarah really impressed me with her natural ability and eye for a shot. The composition is great [1]: Sarah got down low, shooting up towards the girls, so there's more clear sky than distracting foreground. By shooting with a vertical composition she's managed to fill the frame with the girls [2]. By underexposing by two stops Sarah has created a striking silhouette [3] – where you can still see the girls' outline against the moody sky – and has also managed to freeze the motion wonderfully as the girls play [4]."

Sarah's comments

"This is my most creative portrait of the girls. Although I do like the more traditionally exposed shot (see above), where you can clearly see the pier, the girls and their colourful jackets and shoes, I definitely prefer this beautiful silhouette as it has much more impact. I increased the contrast in Photoshop using Curves to make the blacks and whites punchier. Paul gave me confidence to try new things on the day and I'm really chuffed I was able to take such a winning family portrait."

WELL DONE SARAH!

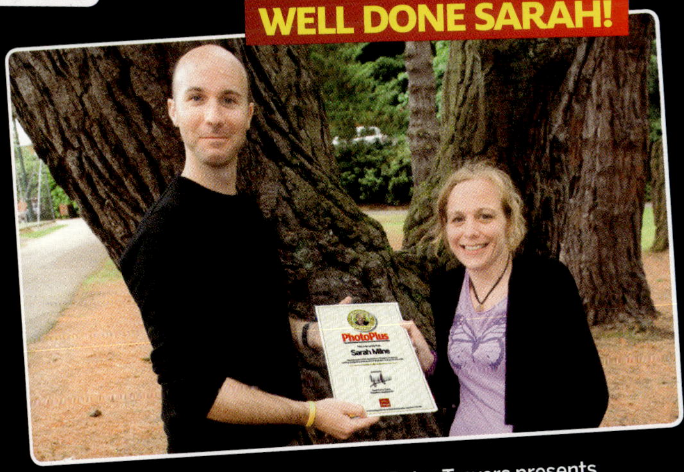

Practice makes perfect! Deputy editor Peter Travers presents Apprentice Sarah with her certificate

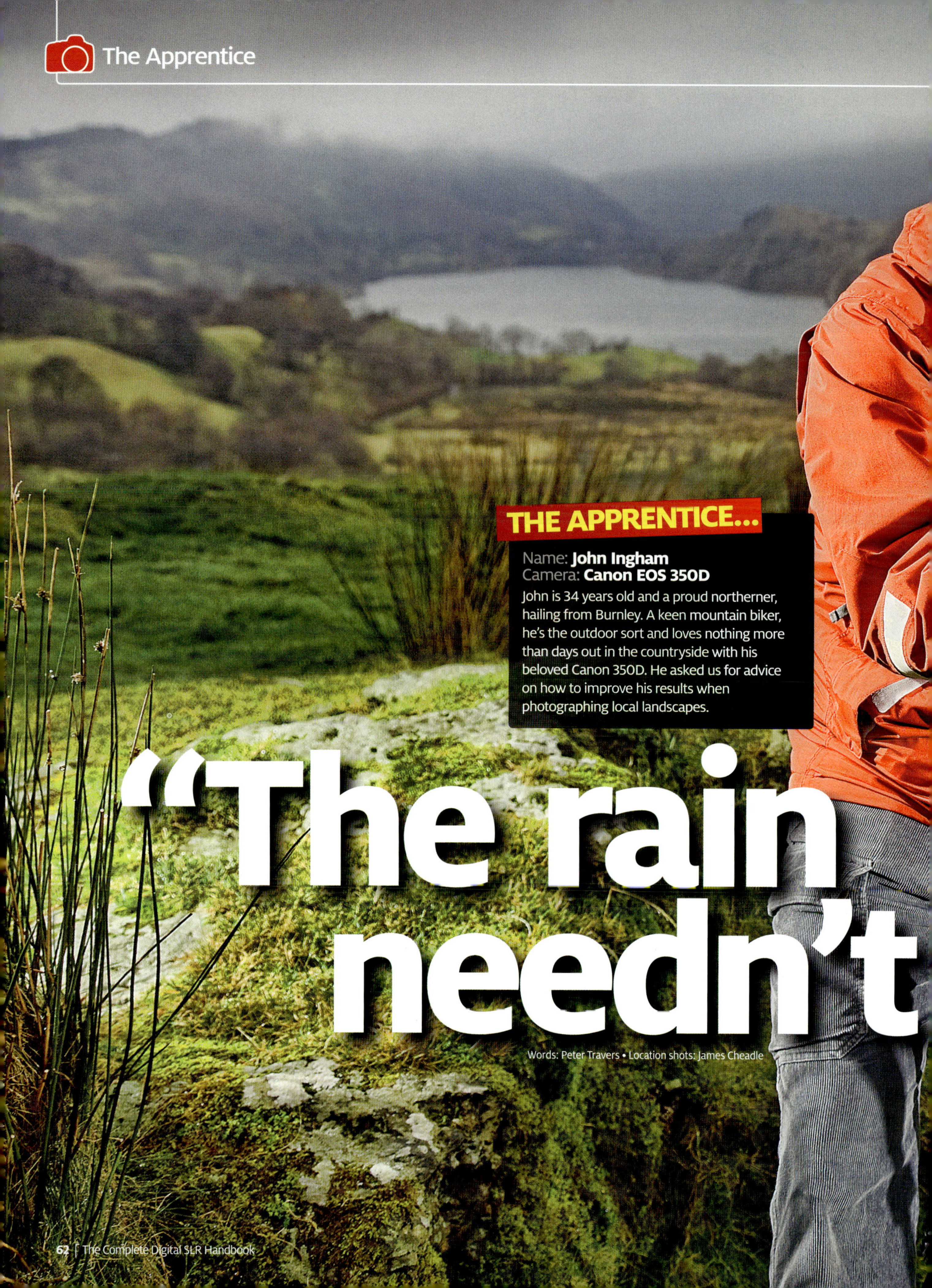

THE APPRENTICE...

Name: **John Ingham**
Camera: **Canon EOS 350D**

John is 34 years old and a proud northerner, hailing from Burnley. A keen mountain biker, he's the outdoor sort and loves nothing more than days out in the countryside with his beloved Canon 350D. He asked us for advice on how to improve his results when photographing local landscapes.

"The rain needn't

Words: Peter Travers • Location shots: James Cheadle

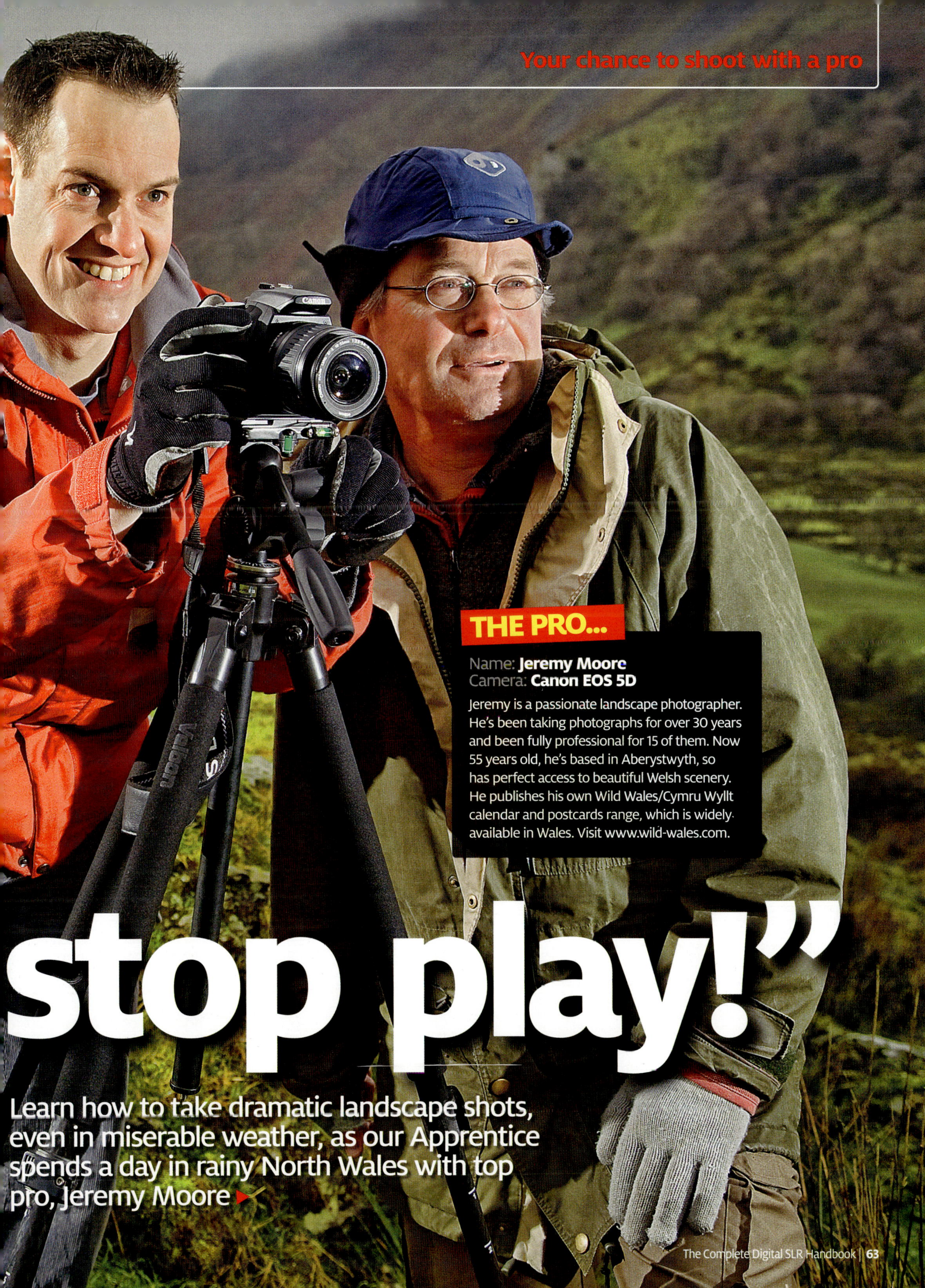

THE PRO...

Name: **Jeremy Moore**
Camera: **Canon EOS 5D**

Jeremy is a passionate landscape photographer. He's been taking photographs for over 30 years and been fully professional for 15 of them. Now 55 years old, he's based in Aberystwyth, so has perfect access to beautiful Welsh scenery. He publishes his own Wild Wales/Cymru Wyllt calendar and postcards range, which is widely available in Wales. Visit www.wild-wales.com.

stop play!"

Learn how to take dramatic landscape shots, even in miserable weather, as our Apprentice spends a day in rainy North Wales with top pro, Jeremy Moore

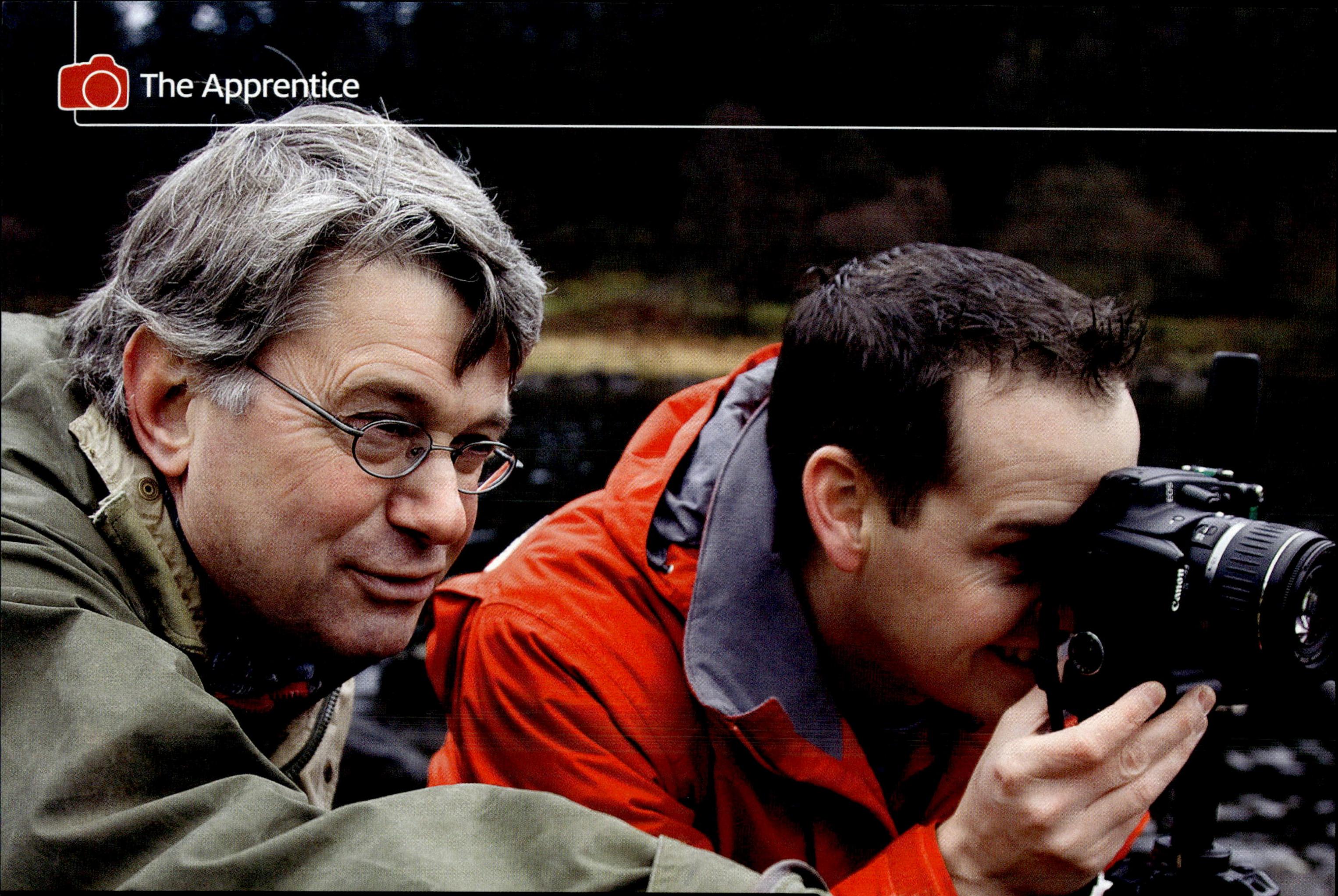

Technique assessment

Ready to shoot?

Following a few lakeside test shots in Snowdonia, Canon pro Jeremy made a few suggestions that helped John to improve his technique...

WARM UP YOUR SHOTS

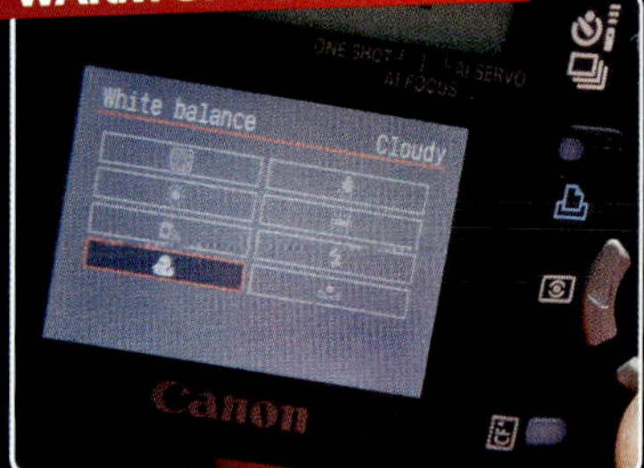

Control White Balance

"John was relying on his camera's Auto White Balance (AWB) setting," says Jeremy. "While this is fine in most situations, your SLR doesn't get it 100% right. To ensure your colours are accurate, set your White Balance setting according to the weather – cloudy for our shoot! Adjust your White Balance to a specific setting and all the photos you take will have a consistent colour 'temperature', so you'll spend less time in Photoshop warming up or cooling down images."

GET FAST SHUTTER SPEEDS

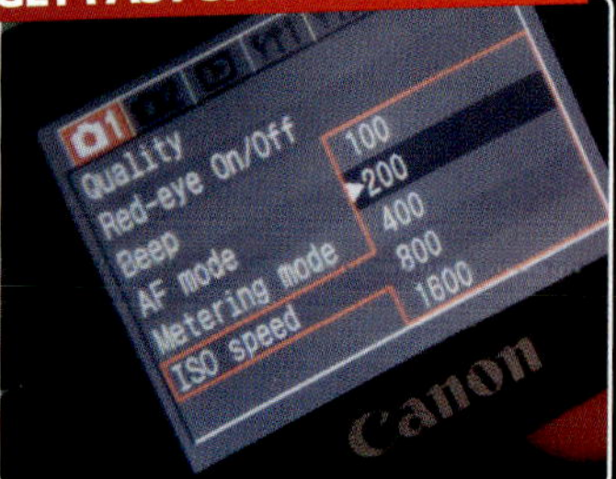

Increase your ISO

"It may seem strange to increase your ISO when using a tripod for landscape photographs, but on really windy days like today your camera will still move, even on a tripod," says Jeremy. "As a result, your shots will look a little soft when using slower shutter speeds. To ensure you get super sharp shots, I recommend increasing the ISO from 100 to 200. This will enable you to use faster shutter speeds, which will produce sharp shots without any noticeable 'noise'."

As well as his favoured, full-frame (no 1.6x crop factor) Canon EOS 5D, Jeremy uses the following kit to capture his stunning landscape photos...

- Canon 17-40mm f/4L USM lens
- Canon 70-200mm f/4L USM lens
- Canon EF 24-105mm f/4L USM lens
- Gitzo GT2531EX Carbon 6X tripod
- MagicBall tripod head
- Hoya polarising filter
- Singh Ray 'Galen Rowell' ND grad filters

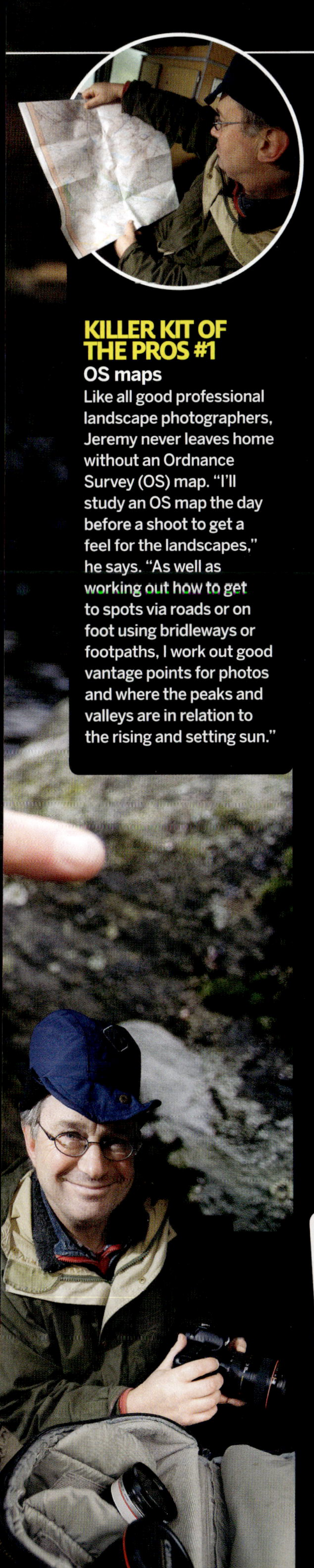

KILLER KIT OF THE PROS #1

OS maps

Like all good professional landscape photographers, Jeremy never leaves home without an Ordnance Survey (OS) map. "I'll study an OS map the day before a shoot to get a feel for the landscapes," he says. "As well as working out how to get to spots via roads or on foot using bridleways or footpaths, I work out good vantage points for photos and where the peaks and valleys are in relation to the rising and setting sun."

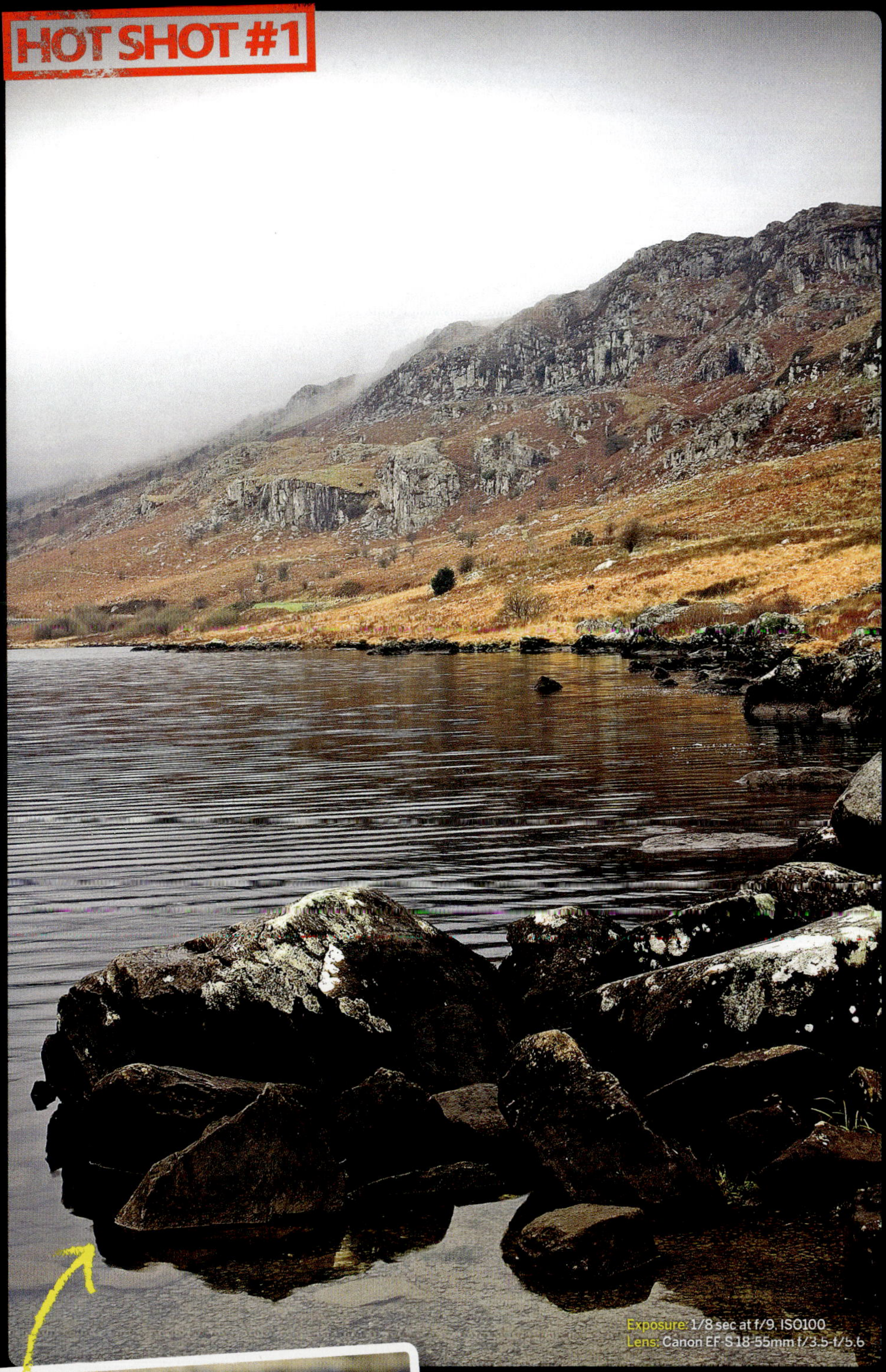

HOT SHOT #1

Exposure: 1/8 sec at f/9, ISO100
Lens: Canon EF-S 18-55mm f/3.5-f/5.6

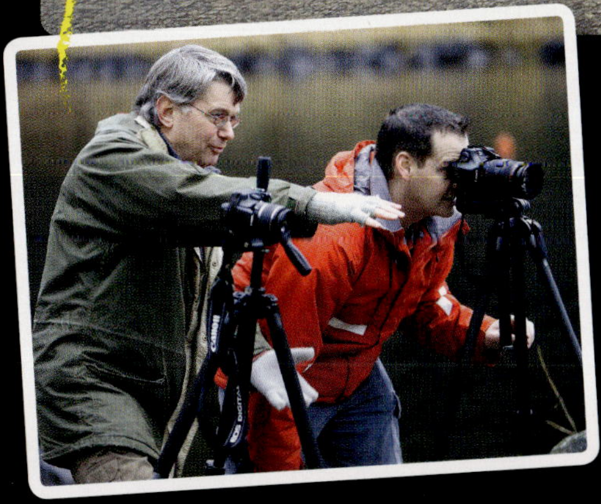

▲ John's comment

"Not bad for my first attempt! Because the wind hadn't picked up the lake was flat, providing a glassy, subtle texture. Following Jeremy's advice, I positioned the rocks in the foreground to add some interest. He also encouraged me to try a vertical composition, which I prefer to the horizontal shots I'd taken before. The cloud and light levels were low, which made my original image look a little flat, so I used Photoshop to boost the saturation and contrast to add some impact." ▶

KILLER KIT OF THE PROS #2

MagicBall tripod head

A tripod's only as good as its head, particularly when photographing landscapes, because you'll regularly set up on uneven ground and need to adjust your head to get your SLR level. "I love this MagicBall head," says Jeremy. "It's very quick and manoeuvrable, making it very simple to position, so I never miss a shot when the weather conditions are constantly changing."

JOHN'S TIP

Three is the magic number

"Jeremy explained how to think about my compositions by splitting the scene into sections of thirds. By doing this I was able to get a good balance across the image by including equal amounts of lake, landscape and sky, which was more pleasing to the eye than half landscape, half sky."

JEREMY'S TIP

Shoot in Manual for maximum control

"Many beginners and amateurs rely on the fully-auto P mode or semi-auto Av (Aperture Priority) shooting modes," says Jeremy. "However, to control my exposures I shoot in Manual. This way I'm able to set the aperture *and* shutter speed to get the results I want, rather than letting my camera dictate what it thinks should be bright and dark. This is especially important if you want to shoot silhouetted landscapes at sunrise or sunset to capture coloured skies."

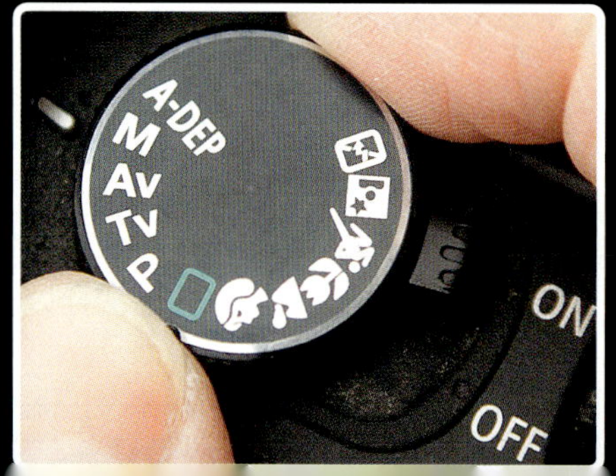

KILLER KIT OF THE PROS #3

Spirit level

"You can ensure horizons are straight using the spirit level built into your tripod head," says Jeremy. "However, don't rely on spirit levels on the tops of tripod legs – found on cheaper tripods – because even if the legs are level, your tripod head and camera might not be, so you'll still end up with wonky skylines."

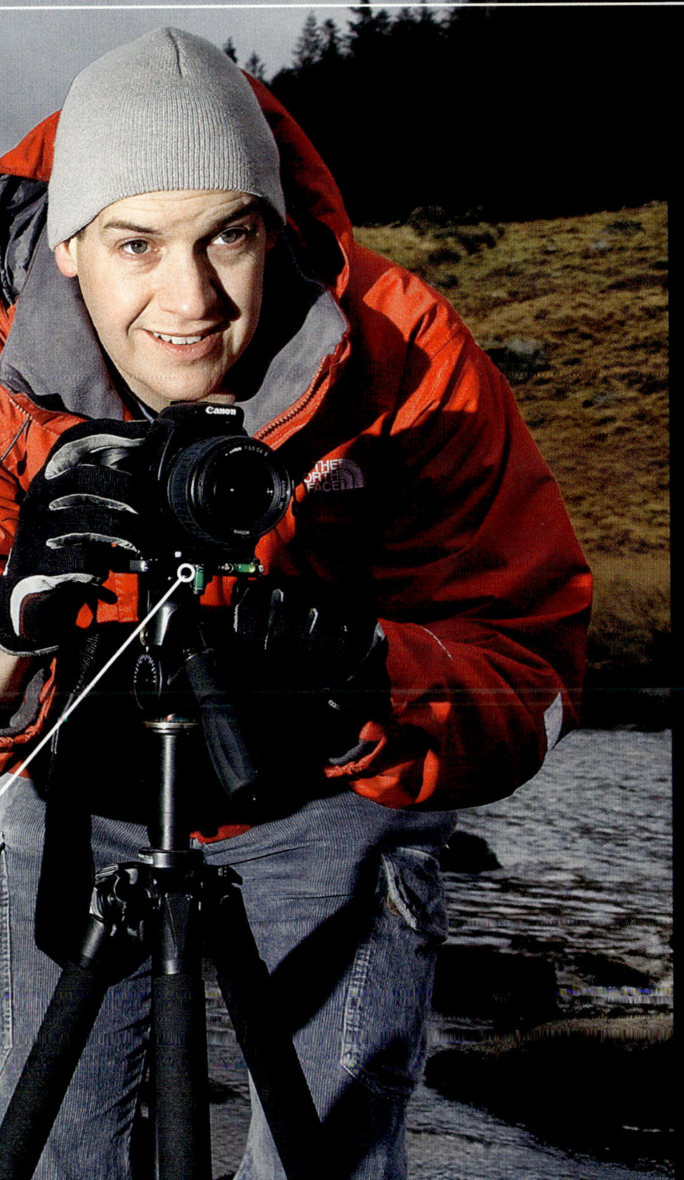

Wonders of the wild Welsh countryside

Jeremy shares three of his favourite Welsh landscapes

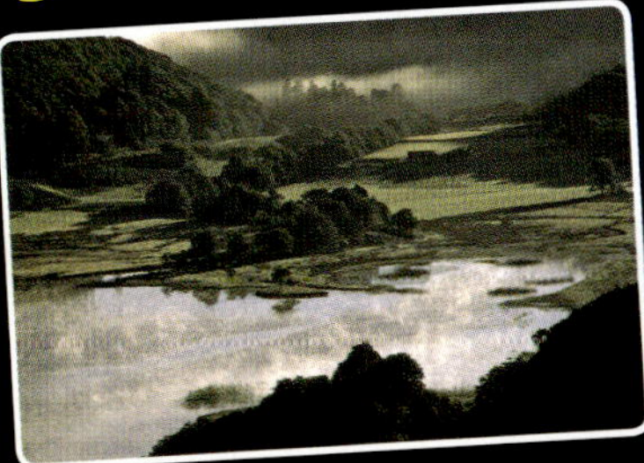

▶ Llyn Dinas, near Beddgelert, Snowdonia

"This is the culmination of a magical morning near Mount Snowdon. After a couple of hours the valley fog lifted, leaving these wisps, which rose from the surface."

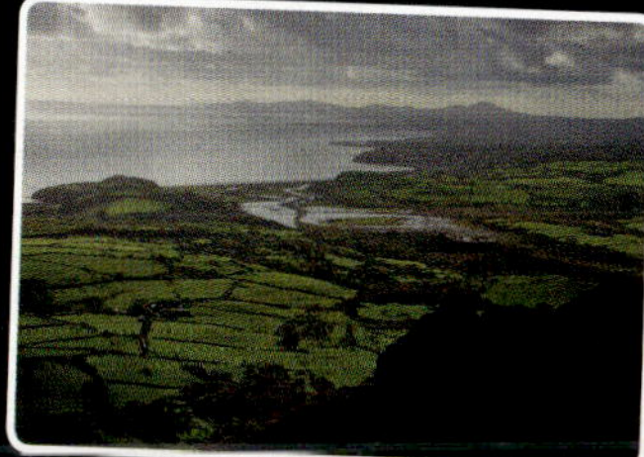

◀ Porthmadog, North West Wales

"Moel-y-Gest is a mountain in miniature near Porthmadog, Wales. It has a great 360-degree view from the summit, including this vista, which stretches down to the Llyn Peninsula."

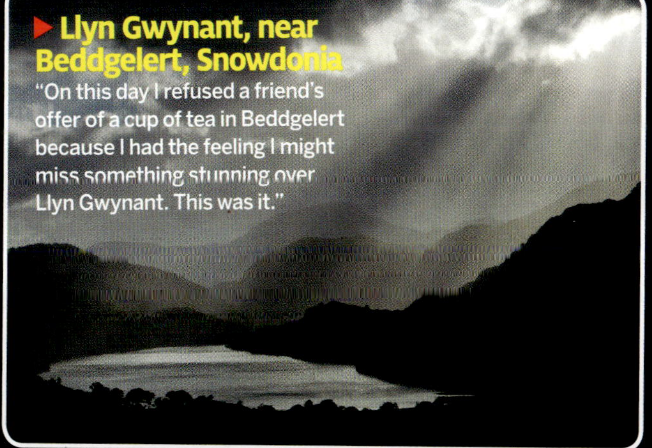

▶ Llyn Gwynant, near Beddgelert, Snowdonia

"On this day I refused a friend's offer of a cup of tea in Beddgelert because I had the feeling I might miss something stunning over Llyn Gwynant. This was it."

HOT SHOT #2

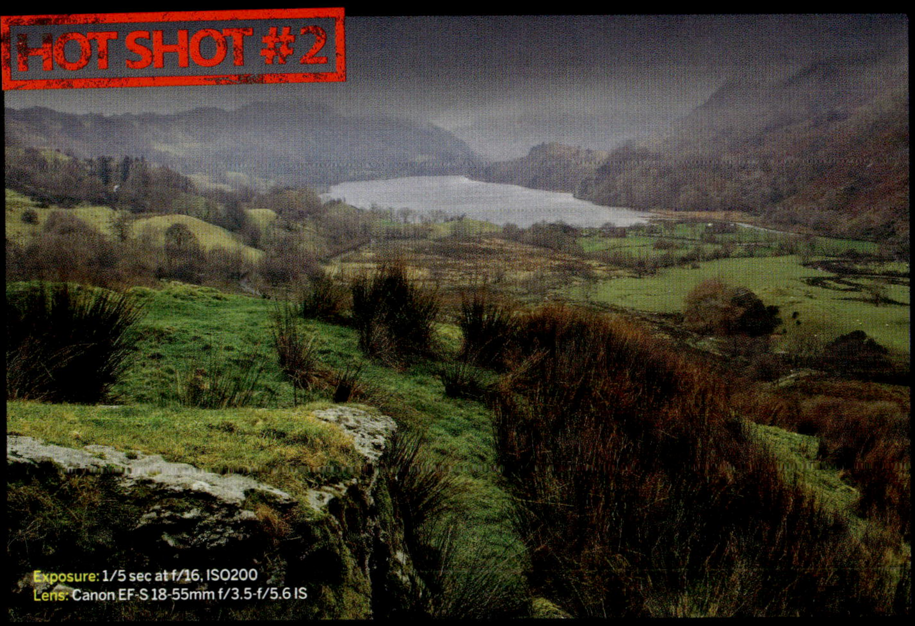

Exposure: 1/5 sec at f/16, ISO200
Lens: Canon EF-S 18-55mm f/3.5-f/5.6 IS

◀ John's comment

"The wind had picked up at this point so, following Jeremy's advice, I increased the ISO to 200 for a slightly faster shutter speed that helped to minimise blur," says John. "Using my tripod, I aimed my 350D downwards to reduce the amount of bland sky that would be in shot. This meant I could use the mossy rocks and tall grass to lead the eye down into the valley towards the lake and mountains I had positioned in the top third. Again, I used Photoshop to boost the contrast and saturation and enhance the greens of the moss and grass." ▶

KILLER KIT OF THE PROS #5

Camper van

Capturing landscapes requires dedication, and you'll regularly need to arrive at your location at first light and stay there until the sun goes down. To avoid spending hundreds of pounds in hotels, Jeremy bought a camper van. "It gives me the freedom to roam all across the country and to be in position to get top shots," he says. "Plus, there's the added bonus of only ever being a few feet from a hot cuppa and a warm bed for afternoon naps!"

KILLER KIT OF THE PROS #4

Filters for dull days

Neutral Density (ND) graduated filters are great for enhancing dull, bright skies because they enable you to darken them while retaining detail in the foreground. Jeremy's very experienced using his filters and is confident enough to simply hold them in front of the lens and turn as necessary to line up the ND grad with the horizon. However, if you're new to filters, use a filter adaptor attached to the front of your lens for greater accuracy.

EXPERT INSIGHT

Focus manually in low light

"Early in the day I got John to use his AF (autofocus) points," says Jeremy. "However, as he gained confidence I convinced him to try his lens's MF (manual focus) option. This is particularly effective in low-light situations when your SLR can struggle to find something bright enough to focus on."

EXPERT INSIGHT

Use Depth of Field Preview

For successful landscape shots you need to make sure you're set up to capture the maximum depth of field (DoF) – how much of your image is acceptably in focus from front to back. "To check how much of your scene will be in focus use the DoF Preview button on the front, bottom-left of your Canon," says Jeremy. "As you're looking through the viewfinder, press the DoF Preview button to 'stop down' to your current aperture setting. You'll notice at narrower apertures (f/16, for example) most of the scene goes dark. Don't worry, your shots won't come out like that. Learn to look past the darkness and you'll be able to see which elements in your background will appear sharp. To see the difference, choose a wide aperture (f/5.6, for example) and press the button again. Your viewfinder won't go as dark and the background will now appear out of focus."

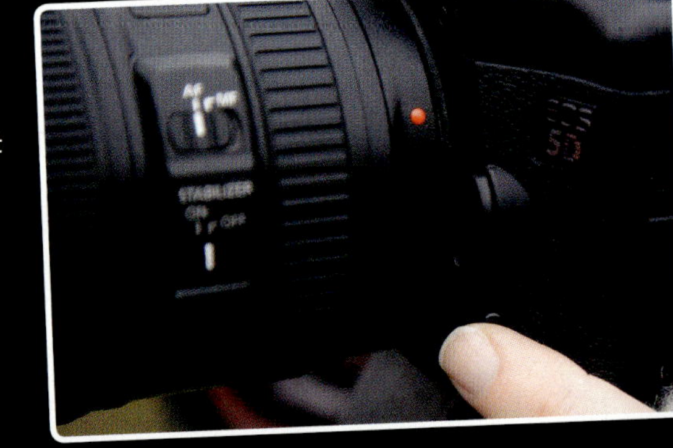

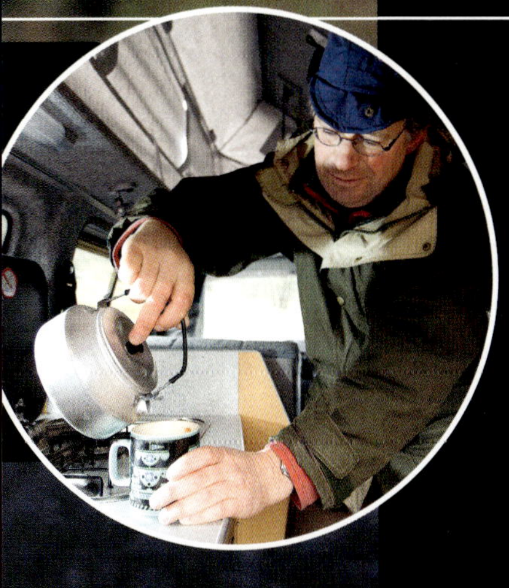

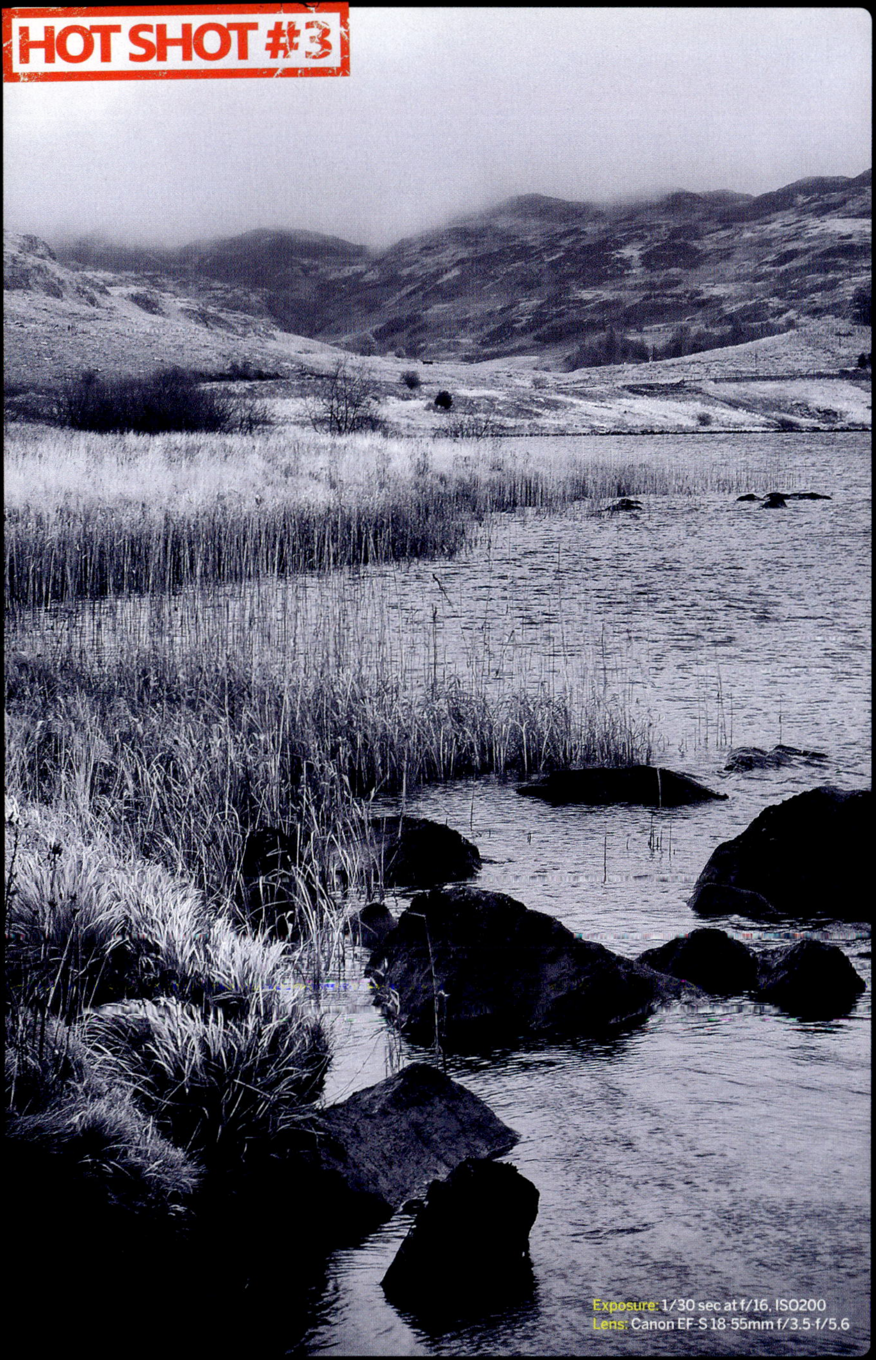

HOT SHOT #3

Exposure: 1/30 sec at f/16, ISO200
Lens: Canon EF-S 18-55mm f/3.5-f/5.6

John's comment

"Jeremy told me that when the sun's out and it's not too windy, you can get some stunning reflections of the mountains in this lake, but it was too overcast and cloudy when we were there! Instead, I composed this shot vertically and used the rocks and long grass as foreground interest, with the grass in the central section leading you into the scene and towards the backdrop of mountains, which disappeared into the cloudy heavens. I cropped the image in Photoshop to lose some distracting rocks at the bottom, used the Clone tool to tidy up the edges, and then converted it to mono."

EXPERT INSIGHT

Remove colour to add impact

Deputy editor, Peter Travers, showed John how to use Photoshop to convert his shot to black and white, which is a great way of 'saving' those bland colour landscapes taken on dull days, which might otherwise be wasted.

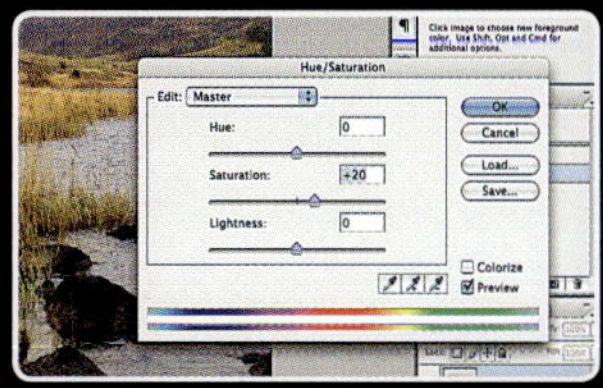

Start with colour image

1 Shoot in colour, then convert. Boost contrast using the Brightness/Contrast window and Saturation with the Hue/Saturation tool. Set both to around +25.

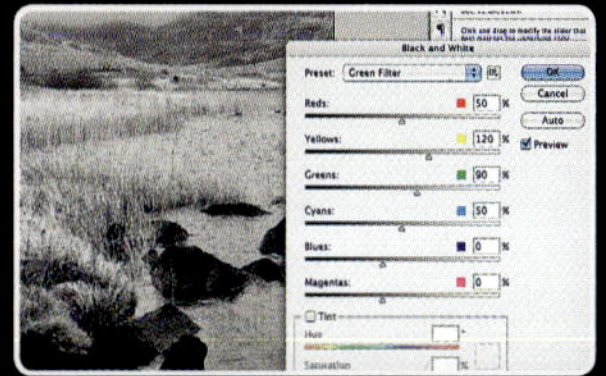

Convert to black and white

2 Use Photoshop's built-in black and white conversion tool. We found the Green Filter preset worked best to bring out the vivid greens in this landscape.

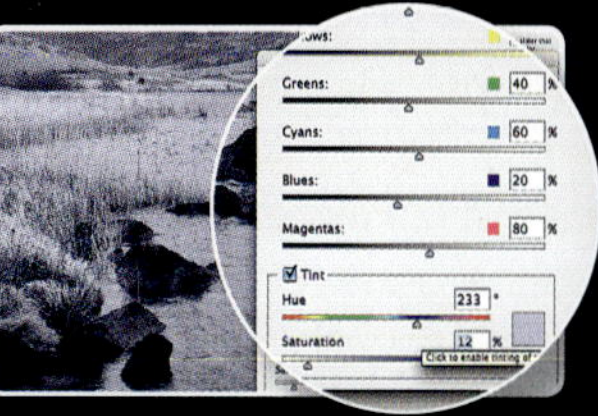

Add a tint for a pro finish

3 Still in the Black and White window, click on Tint and set Hue to 233 and Saturation to 13% for a classy cool-blue tint. Boost the contrast one last time.

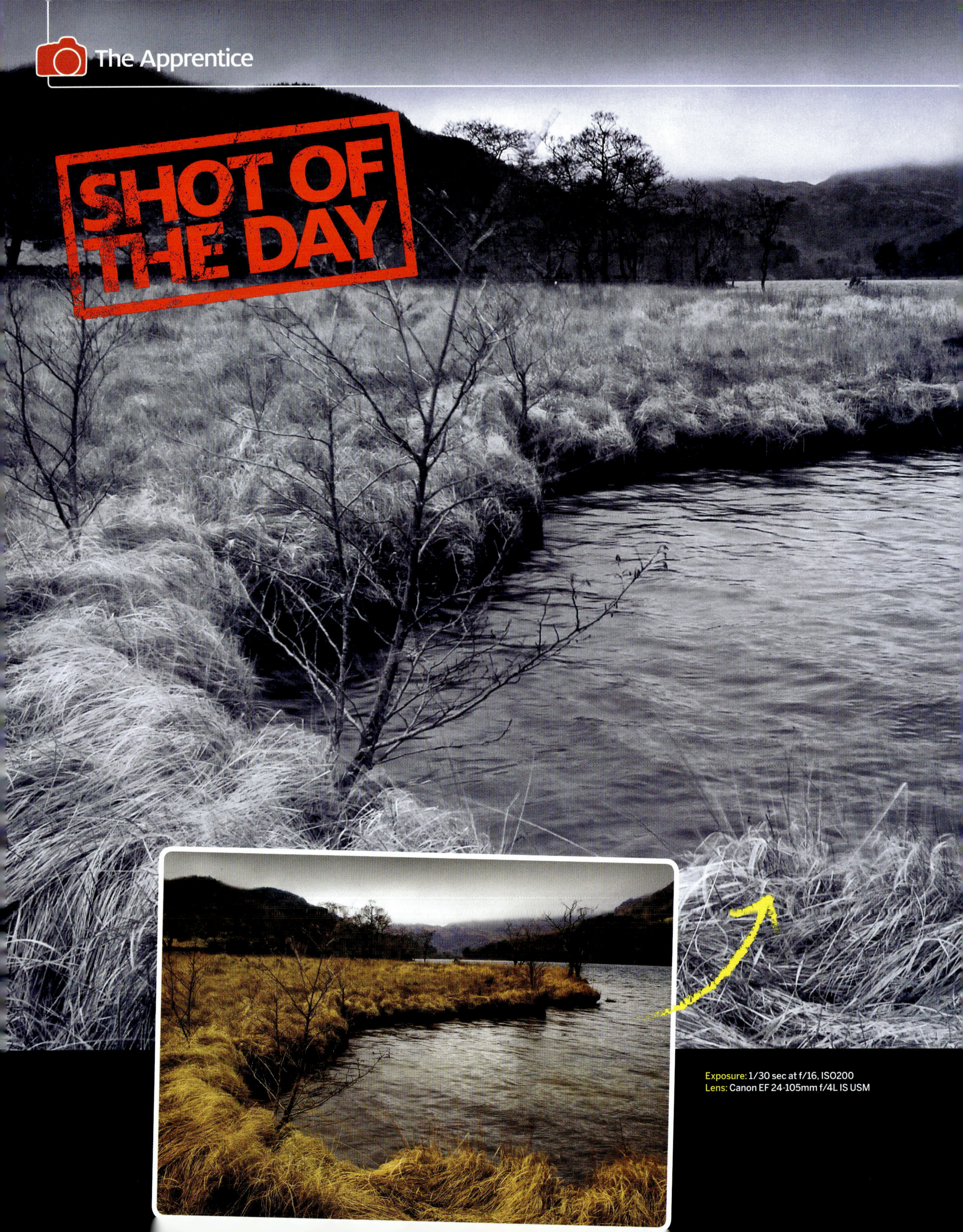

Exposure: 1/30 sec at f/16, ISO200
Lens: Canon EF 24-105mm f/4L IS USM

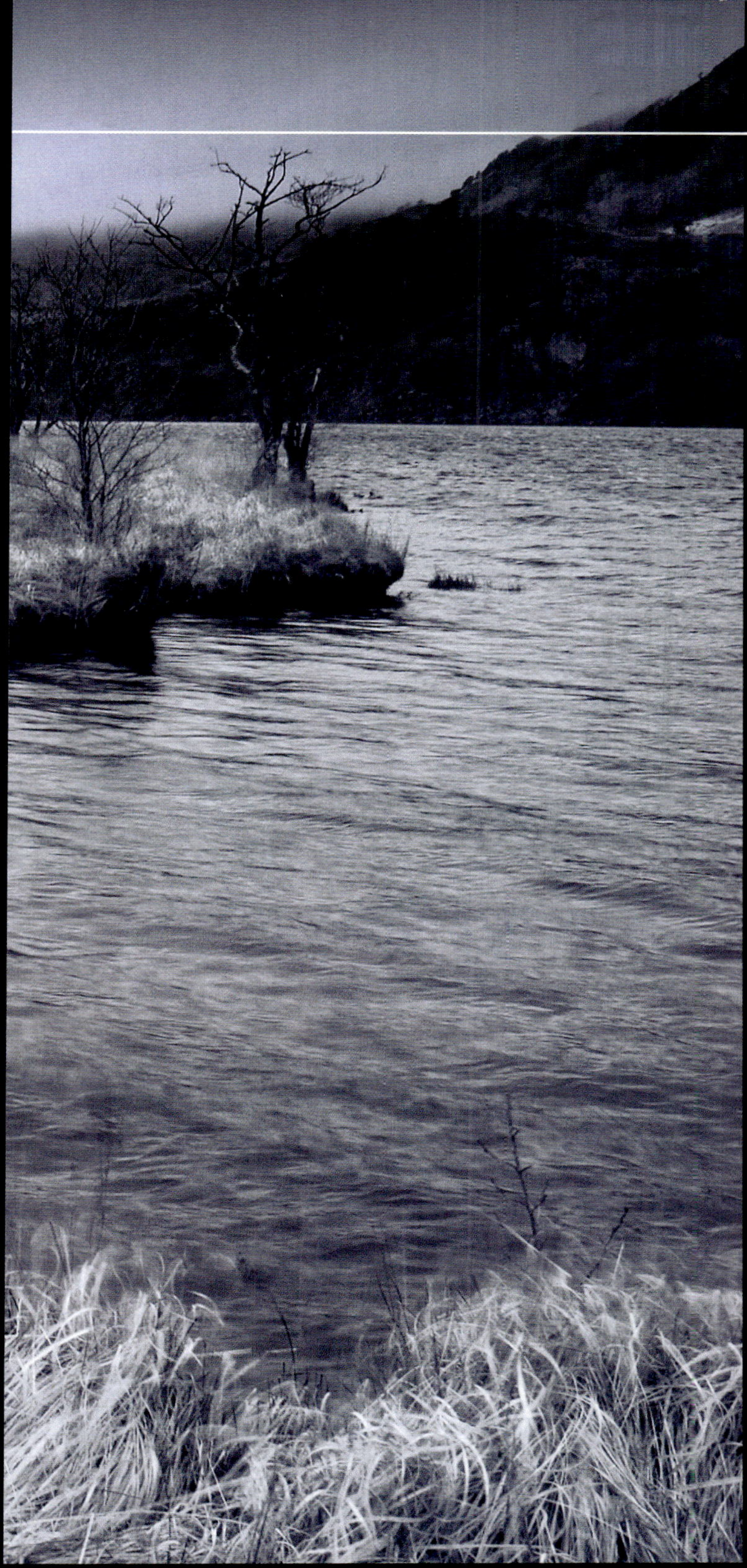

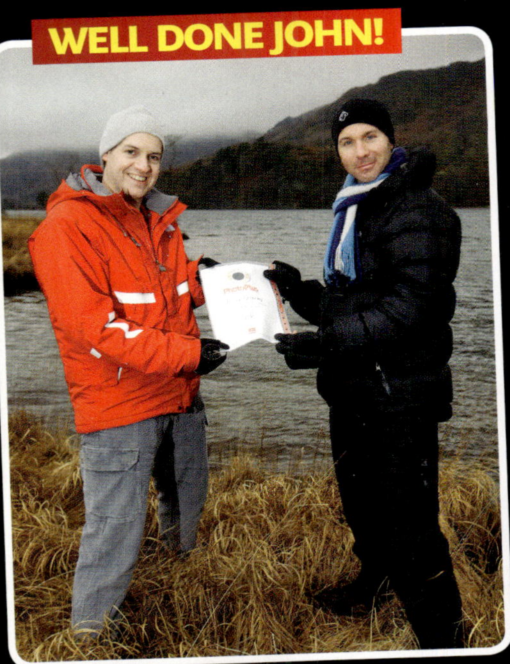

Well done that man! John picks up his certificate from deputy editor, Peter Travers

Jeremy's verdict

"I think John's captured a brilliantly moody landscape here on what was a challenging day with very little light to play around with. He's been very clever with his composition [1] by bringing your eye in from the left and up into the image, utilising the sweeping lakeside grass. I particularly like the stark trees that are dotted around like nature's guards – they make interesting focal points [2]. John also managed to squeeze some beautiful Welsh mountains into the scene while maintaining only a suggestion of the sky [3], which was so grey and boring!"

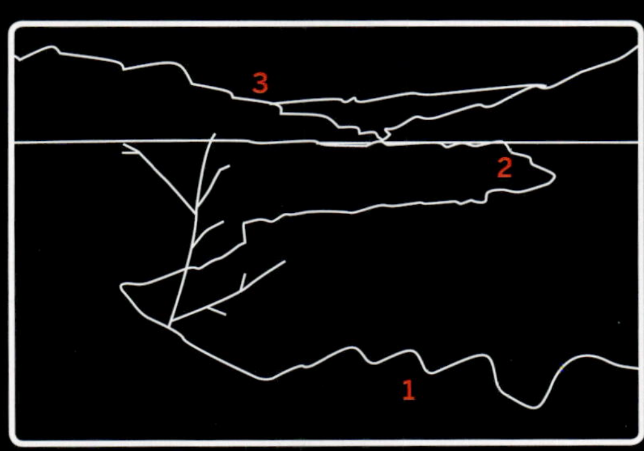

John's comment

"I tried to put all the techniques Jeremy had taught me into this shot. I angled my SLR down to make the most of the grasses and trees, and tried to create a curve from the bottom right through the image. I used Photoshop to increase the saturation, which enhanced the colour of the grass, before I converted it to mono and boosted the contrast." ■

"Now for my

THE PRO...

Name: **David Maitland**
Camera: **Canon EOS-1Ds Mark II**

Although Dr David Maitland only turned full-time in 2006, he's already a prolific nature photographer and has won countless awards for his original and colourful images of reptiles and insects, including several Wildlife Photographer of the Year awards. Originally from St Andrews and a qualified biologist, 52-year-old David now lives in Wiltshire. See his picturesque portfolio at www.davidmaitland.com.

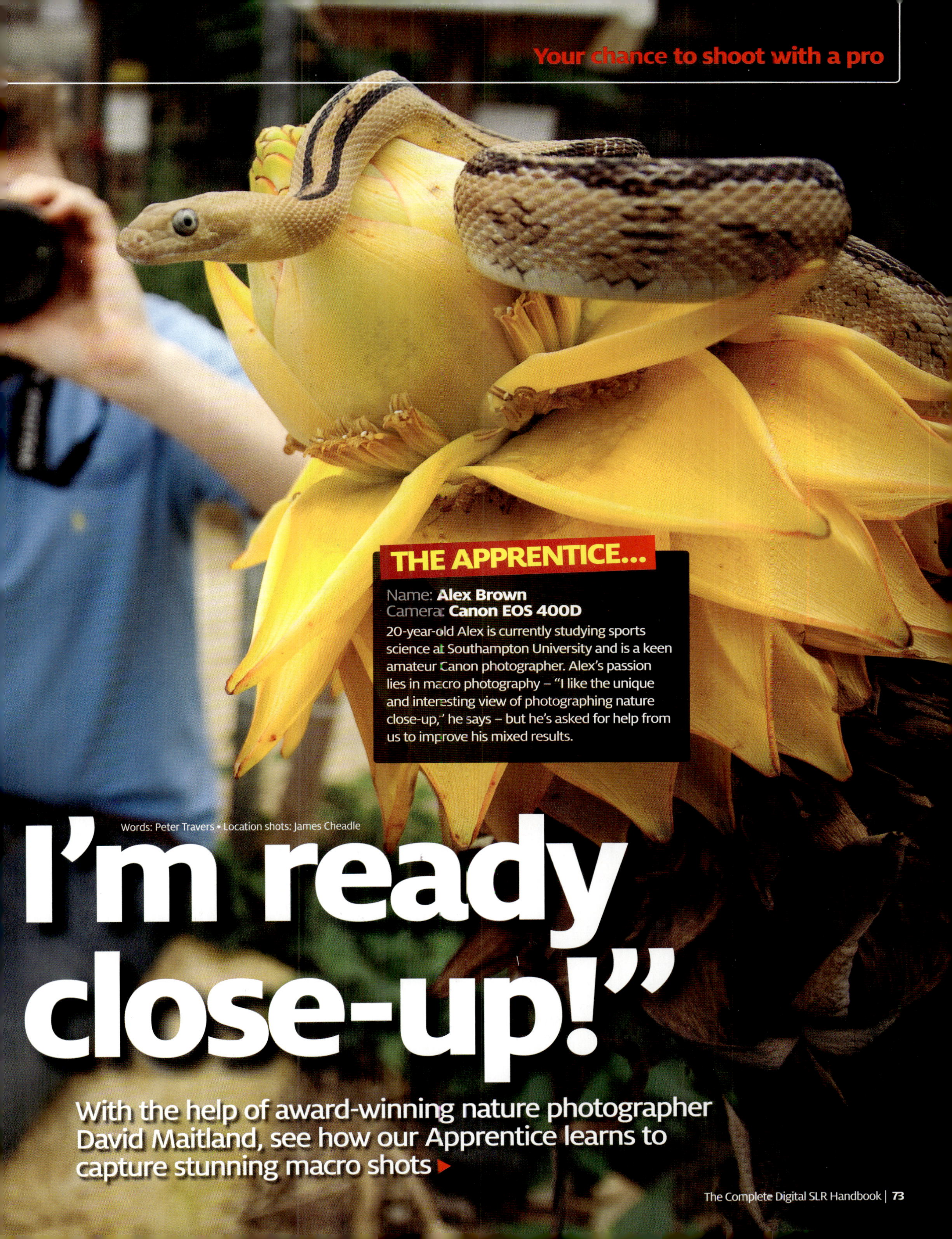

THE APPRENTICE...

Name: **Alex Brown**
Camera: **Canon EOS 400D**

20-year-old Alex is currently studying sports science at Southampton University and is a keen amateur Canon photographer. Alex's passion lies in macro photography – "I like the unique and interesting view of photographing nature close-up,' he says – but he's asked for help from us to improve his mixed results.

Words: Peter Travers • Location shots: James Cheadle

I'm ready close-up!"

With the help of award-winning nature photographer David Maitland, see how our Apprentice learns to capture stunning macro shots ▶

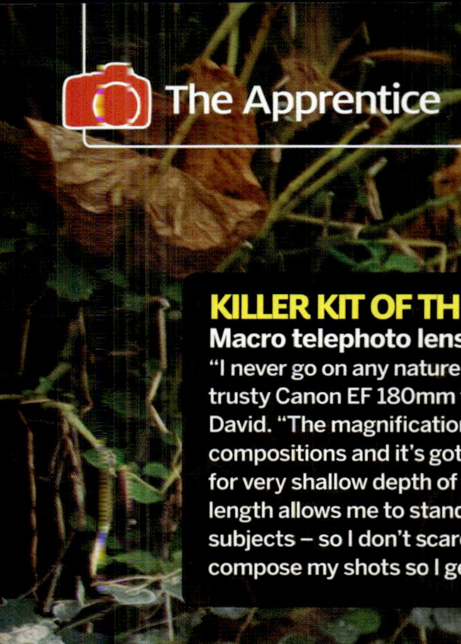

KILLER KIT OF THE PROS #1

Macro telephoto lens

"I never go on any nature shoots without my trusty Canon EF 180mm f/3.5L Macro lens," says David. "The magnification is amazing for close compositions and it's got a wide aperture of f/3.5 for very shallow depth of field. Its 180mm focal length allows me to stand further away from my subjects – so I don't scare them off – but still compose my shots so I get incredible close-up detail."

ALEX'S TIP

Set your alarm

"Get there early. Even though Studley Grange butterfly house doesn't open to the general public until 10am, we agreed with the manager to arrive at 9am," says Alex. "This means you can photograph the butterflies when they're not warmed up enough to fly – so they sit still, making it easier to get great photos. There are also fewer people to get in front of or behind the insects."

Technique assessment

Is Alex ready to take close-ups?

After Alex had taken several practice shots using his own camera settings, David suggested a few ways to help improve his images...

ALWAYS CHOOSE RAW

Quality 3888x2592

L L
M M
S S
RAW+L RAW

Maximise quality

"I always shoot in the RAW format," says David. "JPEGs can lack detail and tone compared to RAW files, which provide the highest image quality and therefore greater scope if I need to boost the colours when processing my shots in Photoshop."

TURN DOWN THE NOISE

ISO speed

100 800
200 1600
400

Minimise artefacts

"With macro photography, the slightest noise becomes much more noticeable. I keep ISO at 50 or 100 (with a maximum of 200) and use a monopod or brace myself against trees to keep the camera still when shooting at slow shutter speeds."

David relies on top Canon gear when photographing nature in far-flung locations. He uses full-frame Canon EOS-1Ds Mark II and 5D Mark II bodies along with the following lenses and kit:

- Canon MP-E 65mm f/2.8 1-5x Macro
- Canon EF 100mm f/2.8 Macro USM
- Canon EF 180mm f/3.5L Macro USM
- Canon EF 70-200mm f/2.8L IS USM
- Canon EF 16-35mm f/2.8L USM
- Manfrotto carbon monopod and RC234 head
- Three Canon Speedlite 580EX II flashguns
- Canon Speedlite Transmitter ST-E2

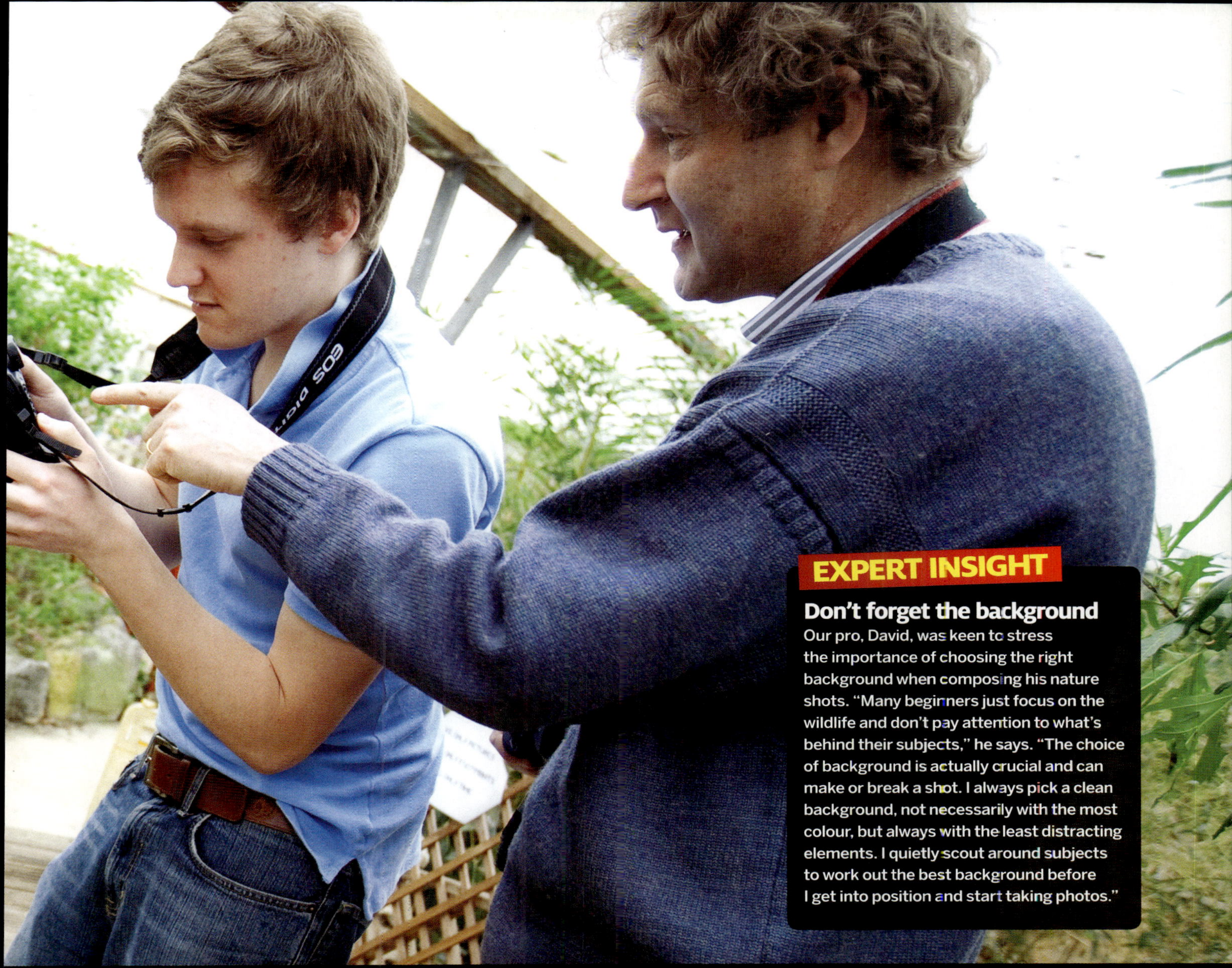

EXPERT INSIGHT

Don't forget the background

Our pro, David, was keen to stress the importance of choosing the right background when composing his nature shots. "Many beginners just focus on the wildlife and don't pay attention to what's behind their subjects," he says. "The choice of background is actually crucial and can make or break a shot. I always pick a clean background, not necessarily with the most colour, but always with the least distracting elements. I quietly scout around subjects to work out the best background before I get into position and start taking photos."

HOT SHOT #1

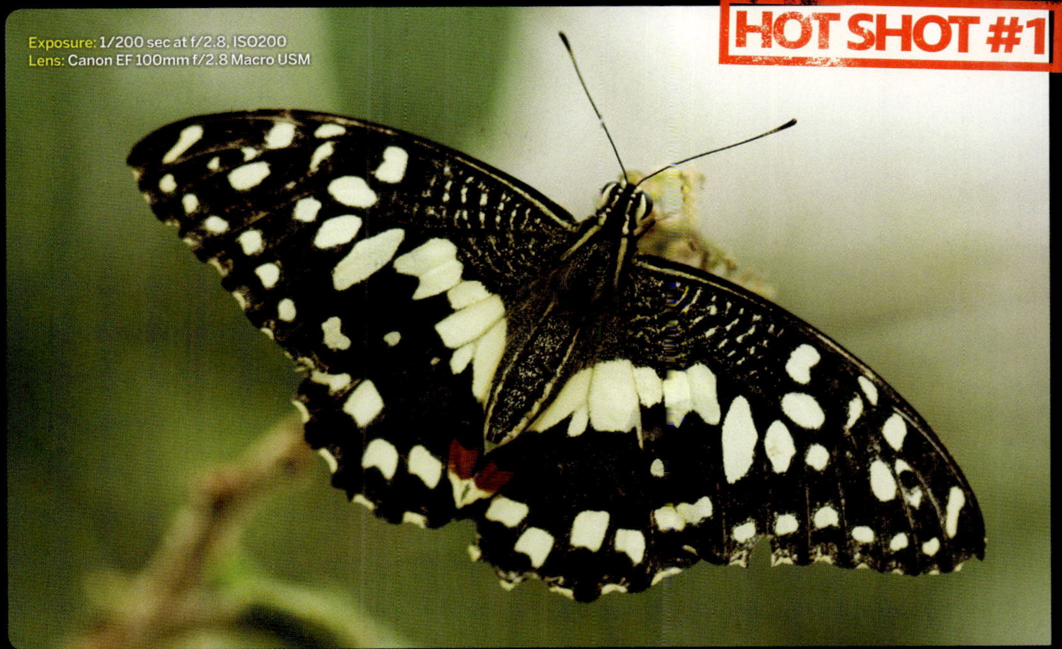

Exposure: 1/200 sec at f/2.8, ISO200
Lens: Canon EF 100mm f/2.8 Macro USM

Alex's comment

"To begin with, David got me to take the 'easy' classic butterfly shot (of a Papilio demoleus). I was looking straight on at the butterfly and focused on its hairy body – which is also on the same plain as its wings – so the entire butterfly was acceptably sharp. Using my EF 100mm Macro lens at its widest aperture of f/2.8 I was able to blur all of the background greenery and the branch trailing off into the corner. By tilting the butterfly slightly in-camera the image is given a more creative feel."

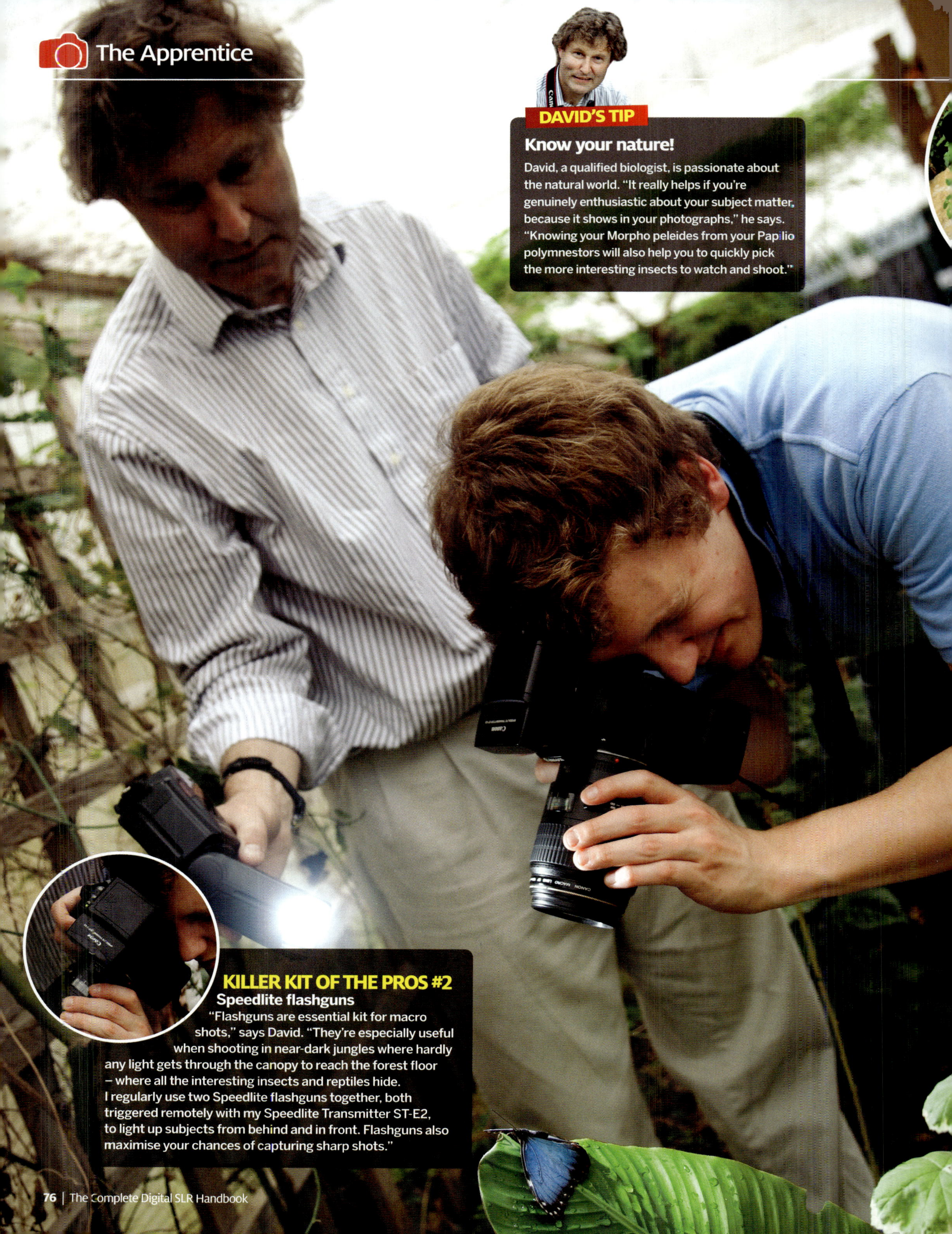

DAVID'S TIP

Know your nature!

David, a qualified biologist, is passionate about the natural world. "It really helps if you're genuinely enthusiastic about your subject matter, because it shows in your photographs," he says. "Knowing your Morpho peleides from your Papilio polymnestors will also help you to quickly pick the more interesting insects to watch and shoot."

KILLER KIT OF THE PROS #2

Speedlite flashguns

"Flashguns are essential kit for macro shots," says David. "They're especially useful when shooting in near-dark jungles where hardly any light gets through the canopy to reach the forest floor – where all the interesting insects and reptiles hide. I regularly use two Speedlite flashguns together, both triggered remotely with my Speedlite Transmitter ST-E2, to light up subjects from behind and in front. Flashguns also maximise your chances of capturing sharp shots."

KILLER KIT OF THE PROS #3

Manfrotto monopod

"I use a monopod for four reasons," says David. "First, it enables me to get sharp shots using slower shutter speeds. Second, I can keep the ISO at 100 to maintain the best quality images and third, it takes the weight of my heavy EOS-1Ds camera and telephoto zoom lens. Finally, it doubles as a walking stick when I'm trekking up steep trails!"

EXPERT INSIGHT

Stay focused

Learning how to focus when using a macro lens can be tricky, but David passed on some expert advice. "I got Alex to switch to Manual AF point selection and choose the AF point closest to his subject's head or eyes. This also encouraged Alex to apply the 'rule of thirds' to position a subject in the top third of his shots."

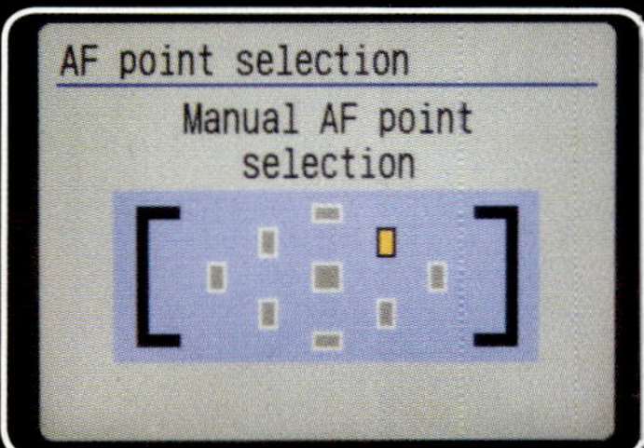

David's macro magic

Canon pro David shares a few of his favourite natural world subjects and their destinations

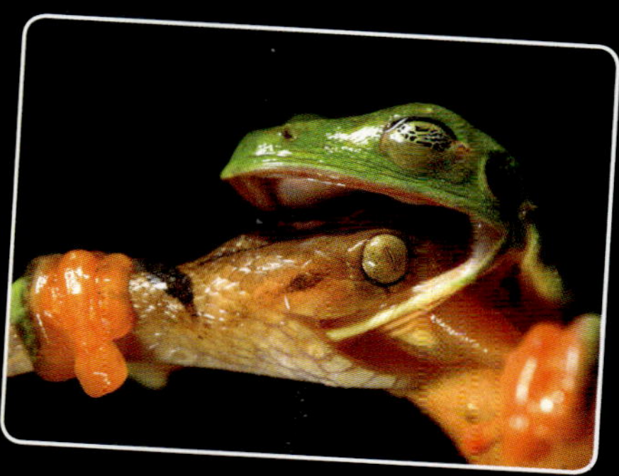

▶ Morelet's Tree Frog and Cat-eyed Snake

"Photographed in Belize, this is a critically endangered Morelet's Tree Frog (Agalychnis moreletii) battling for its life with a Cat-eyed Snake – they're locked in a stalemate. I stayed taking different angles of shots for over three hours."

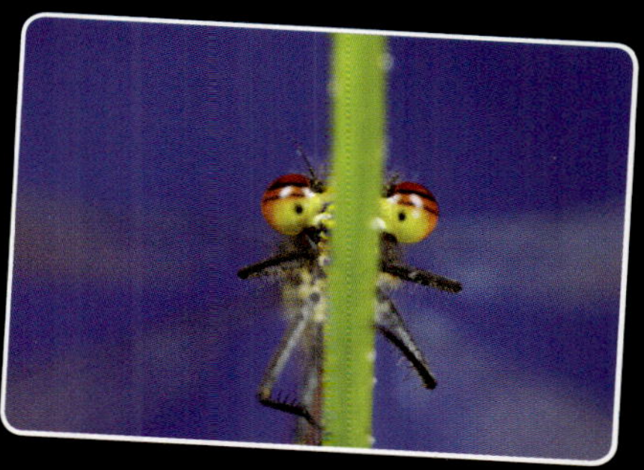

◀ Large Red Damselfly

"This is a Large Red Damselfly (Pyrrhosoma nymphula), which I shot in a local meadow in Wiltshire. I wanted to get a nice Damselfly face showing the two false pupils in its eyes. I waited for one to perch and made sure only the front surfaces of its eyes were in focus."

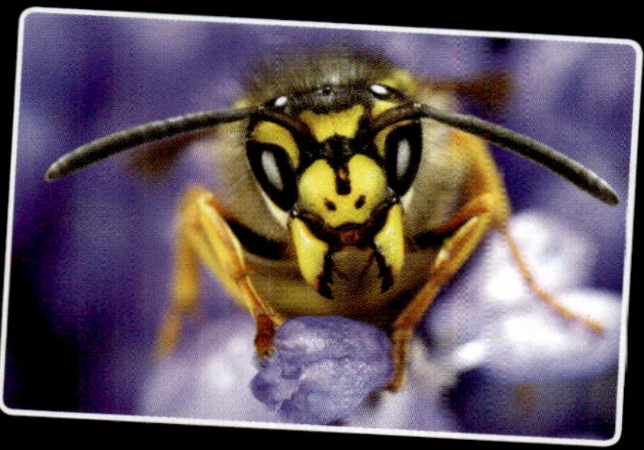

▶ Queen Wasp

"This Common Queen Wasp (Vespula vulgaris) was shot in my back garden! It's reacting to my movement by threatening me with its gaping jaws. This is what really sets this shot apart, together with the colours and the catch-lights nicely positioned in the wasp's eyes. I used an EF 65mm Macro lens at f/11 and flashes behind and in front of the wasp."

HOT SHOT #2

Exposure: 1/250 sec at f/3.5, ISO200
Lens: Canon EF 180mm f/3.5L Macro USM

▶ Alex's comment

"David got me to shoot in Av (Aperture Priority) mode so I could chose a wide aperture to control the shallow depth of field. This Morpho peleides butterfly was warming up its wings, so we were fortunate enough to photograph the brilliant blue colouring. I was gaining confidence, so I got down low and focused on its head, positioning it in the top third of the frame and making sure the green leaf made up most of the background. As I was shooting at an angle and using f/3.5, part of the wings and the leaf are nicely out of focus." ▶

EXPERT INSIGHT

The devil is in the detail

Macro can open up a whole new range of photographic opportunities. Try focusing on the patterns of butterfly wings for startling results. All shots shown here were taken with flashguns remotely triggered at an exposure of 1/200 sec at f/11, ISO100.

"Fill the frame and use markings and veins as leading lines to draw the eyes into the shot," says David. "As it's a flat surface, use a medium aperture of f/11 to capture all the detail. Using a remote flashgun to light the source from the side will reveal more colour, texture and shadow."

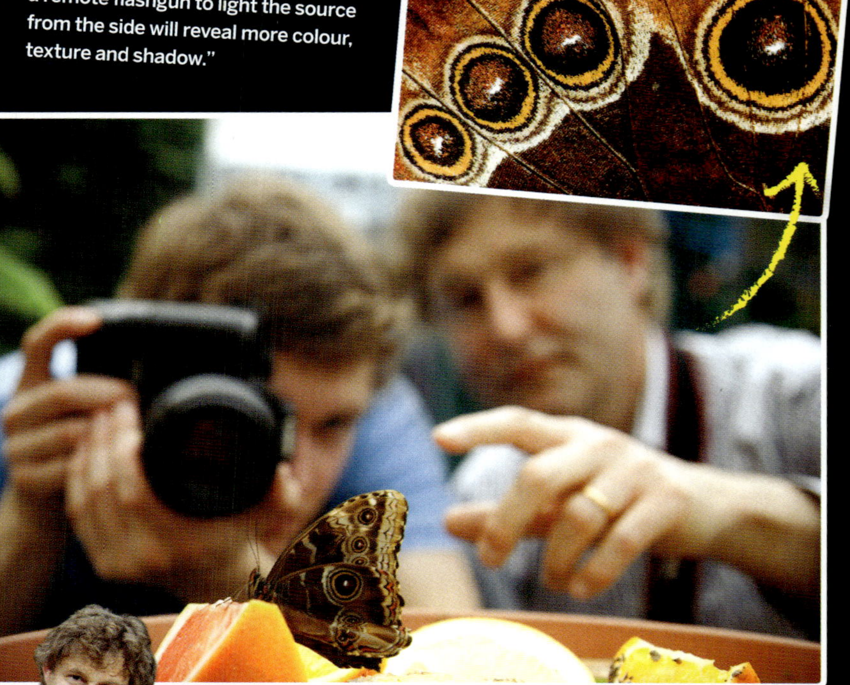

DAVID'S TIP

Patience is a virtue

As well as explaining to Alex that you need to be physically fit and aware of the dangers when attempting deep forest treks in search of wildlife, David emphasised the need for patience: "You may need to sit for hours in the same spot, waiting. I actually love the calm of a forest and I'm quite content to sit on a damp, muddy floor with the bugs, waiting for an elusive insect to come out to play."

KILLER KIT OF THE PROS #4

Novoflex neoprene

"Wonderfully cheap and simple, I use these neoprene wraps to protect my camera bodies and lenses," says David. "I can then slot all my gear safely into my compact backpack, which is much lighter and less bulky than a rigid camera backpack full of protective padding. When I'm going on week-long treks in the jungles of Borneo, for instance, lightweight kit is key. I always travel as light as I can, which is why I sometimes favour my lighter EOS 5D Mark II instead of the rather hefty EOS-1Ds."

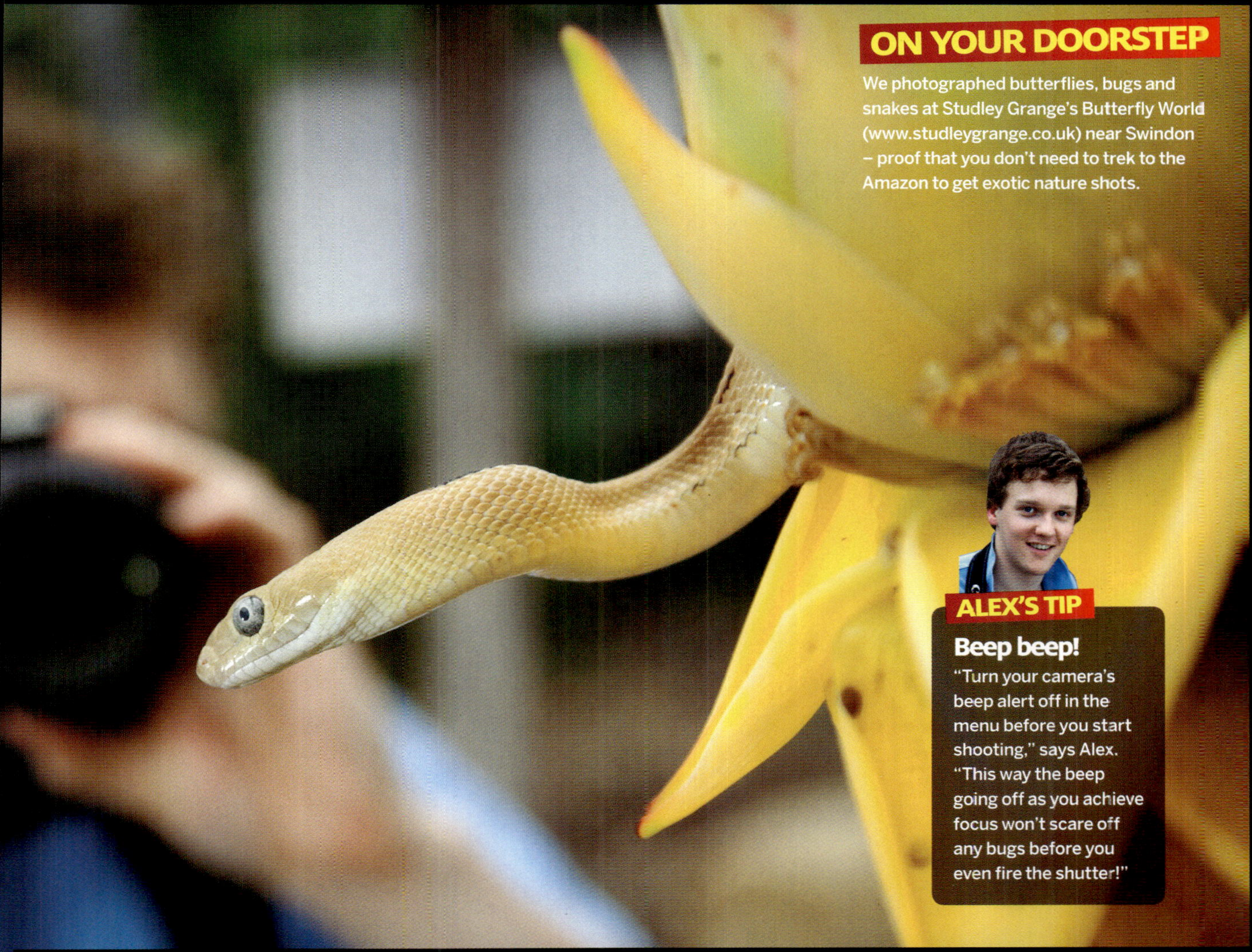

ON YOUR DOORSTEP

We photographed butterflies, bugs and snakes at Studley Grange's Butterfly World (www.studleygrange.co.uk) near Swindon – proof that you don't need to trek to the Amazon to get exotic nature shots.

ALEX'S TIP

Beep beep!

"Turn your camera's beep alert off in the menu before you start shooting," says Alex. "This way the beep going off as you achieve focus won't scare off any bugs before you even fire the shutter!"

HOT SHOT #3

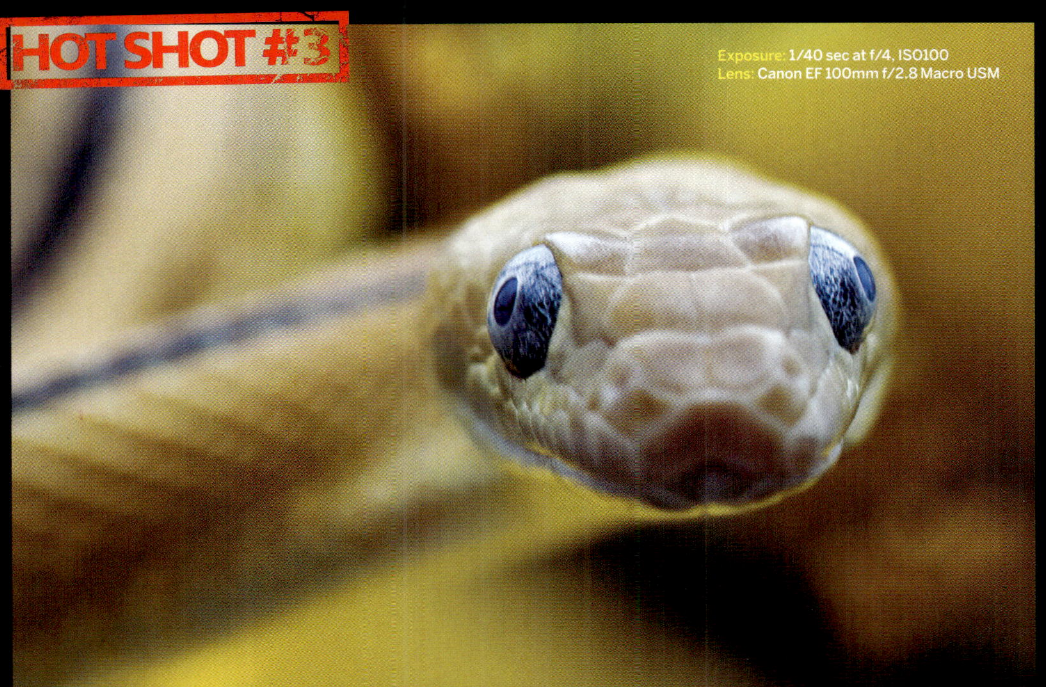

Exposure: 1/40 sec at f/4, ISO100
Lens: Canon EF 100mm f/2.8 Macro USM

Alex's comment

"I loved photographing this charismatic Trans-Pecos Rat Snake. The keeper draped him over a tall Banana Palm plant, enabling us to get down to his eye-level. I focused on his inquisitive eyes – I learned that the eyes are the most important part of nature photos – and used an aperture of f/4 to push his body out of focus. He was constantly slithering around, so I used Continuous Drive mode to take multiple shots, increasing my chances of sharp photos. I cropped the image in Photoshop afterwards to lose some background."

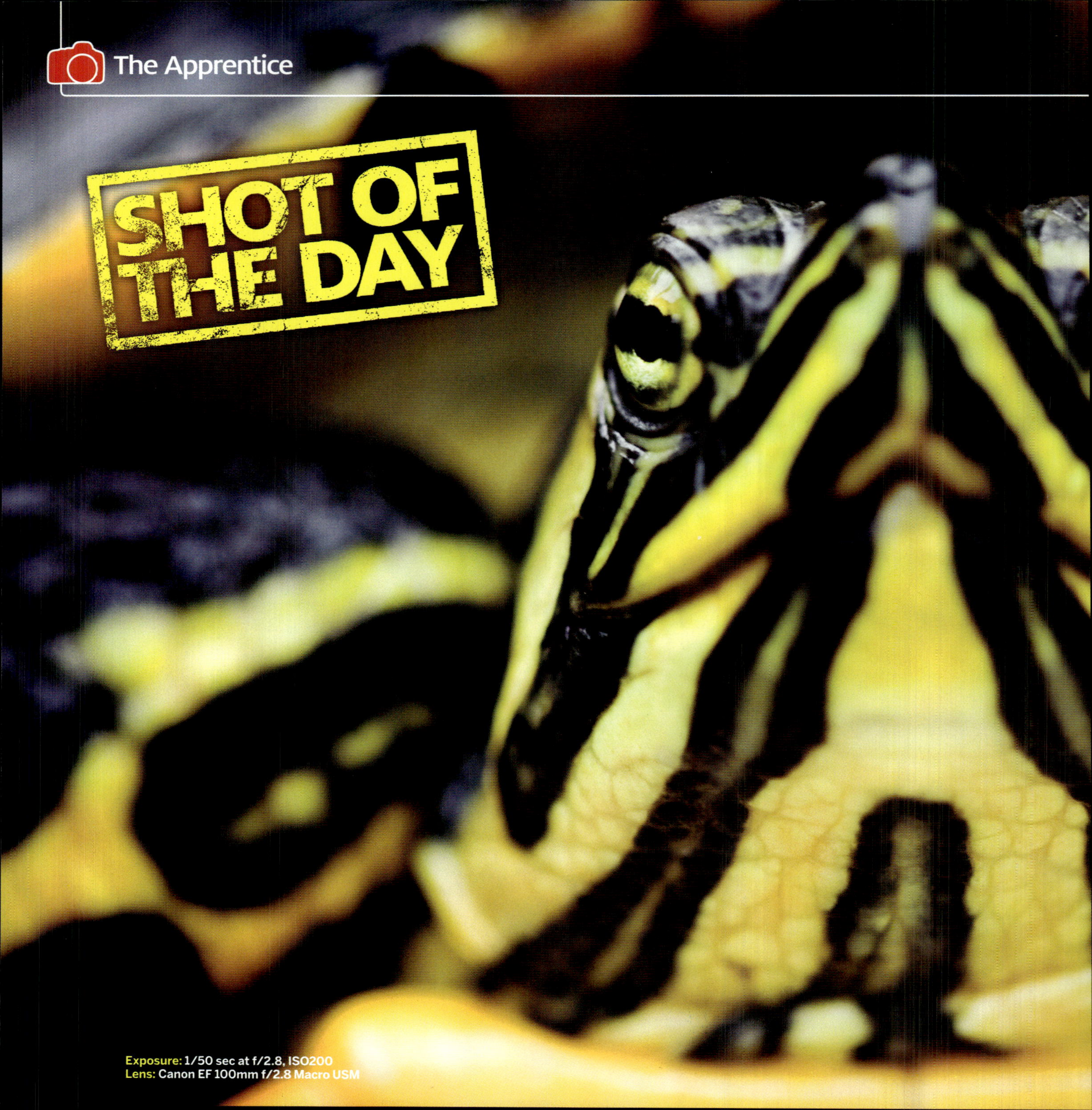

SHOT OF THE DAY

Exposure: 1/50 sec at f/2.8, ISO200
Lens: Canon EF 100mm f/2.8 Macro USM

David's verdict

"Alex's tight composition means the shot is a dazzling mixture of the black and yellow colouring of the Yellow Bellied Terrapin [1]. His focusing is bang on and he's done well to focus on those beady little eyes [2]. By using a wide aperture of f/2.8, Alex has ensured the eyes are pin-sharp, with the legs and shell blurred behind [3]. There's a lovely symmetry to this shot, with the terrapin's nose central in the frame [4]."

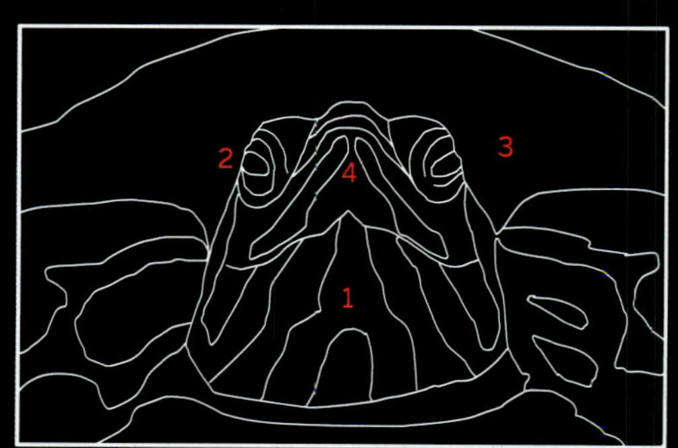

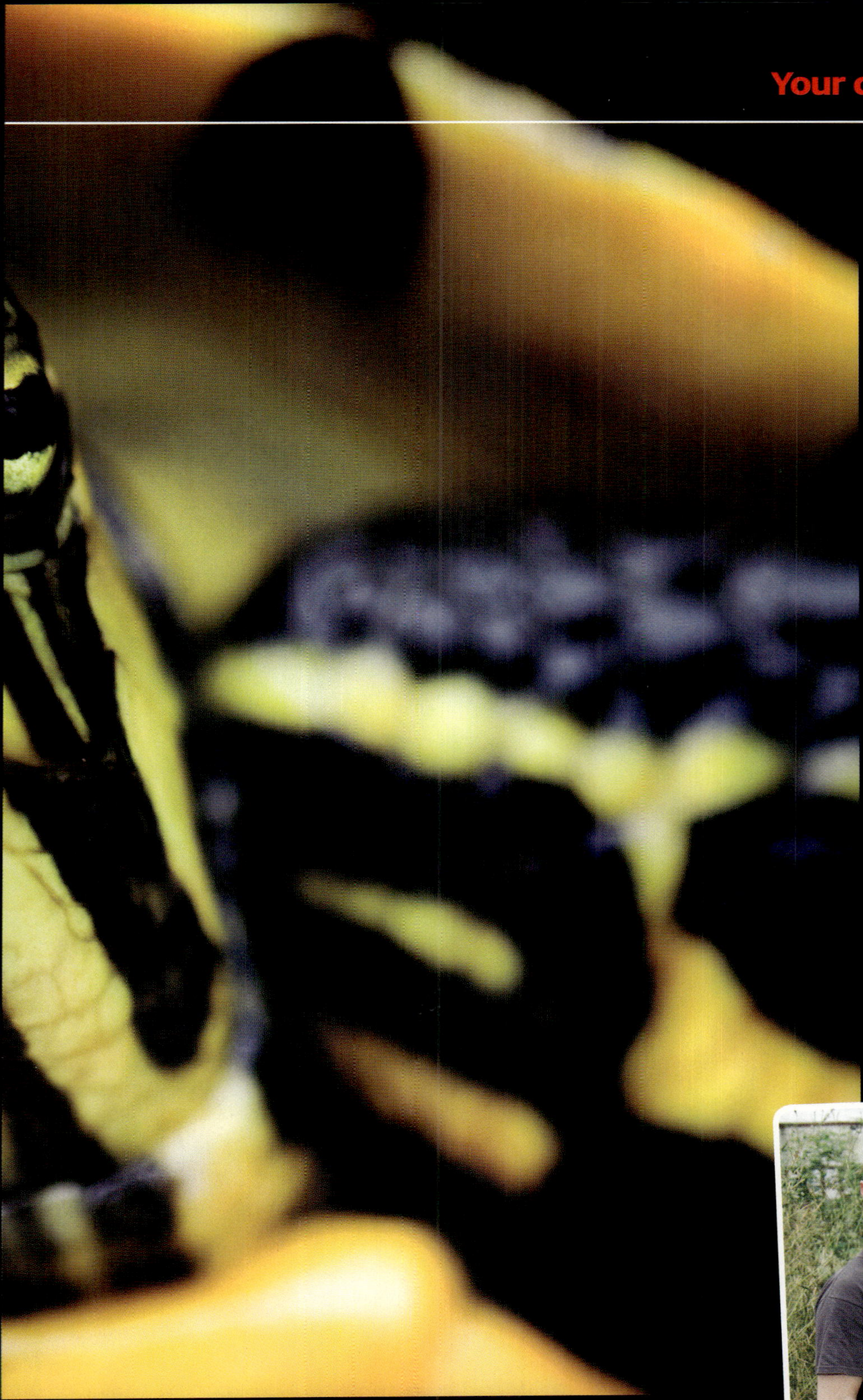

Alex's comment

"Using my Canon EF 100mm Macro lens at f/2.8, I sat on the floor to get down to the Yellow Bellied Terrapin's eye level as he perched on a rock near the pond. I'd tried lots of compositions and with many other shots my focusing was slightly off, so the nose was in focus but not the eyes. I feel I've captured the reptile's character. It's almost as if he's looking down his nose at us!"

WELL DONE ALEX!

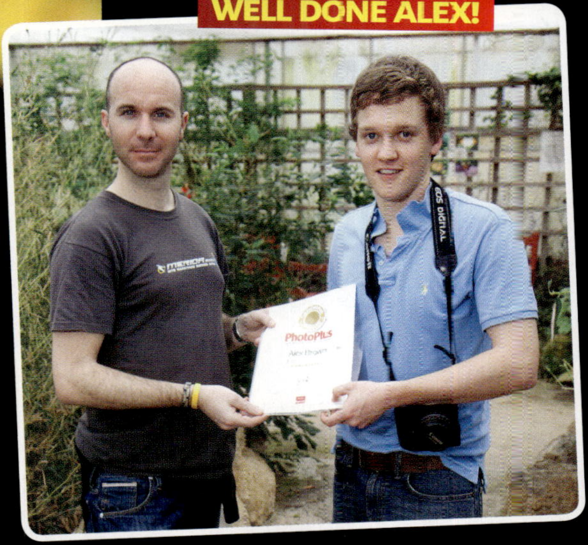

Macro bugs me no more! Alex gets his certificate from deputy editor, Peter Travers

"Shooting needn't be a gamble!"

Going on a summer city break? Learn how to capture the excitement of big cities as a top US photographer helps a reader win big in Las Vegas

THE PRO...

Name: **John Morris**
Camera: **Canon EOS 5D**

John, 38, is a well-established professional photographer with a thriving studio in the Las Vegas area. He specialises in architectural photography for major clients in the city and undertakes a range of other commercial projects. See his website at www.johnmorrisphotography.com.

Words: Geoff Harris (Future) • Location shots: Chris George (Future)

Vegas

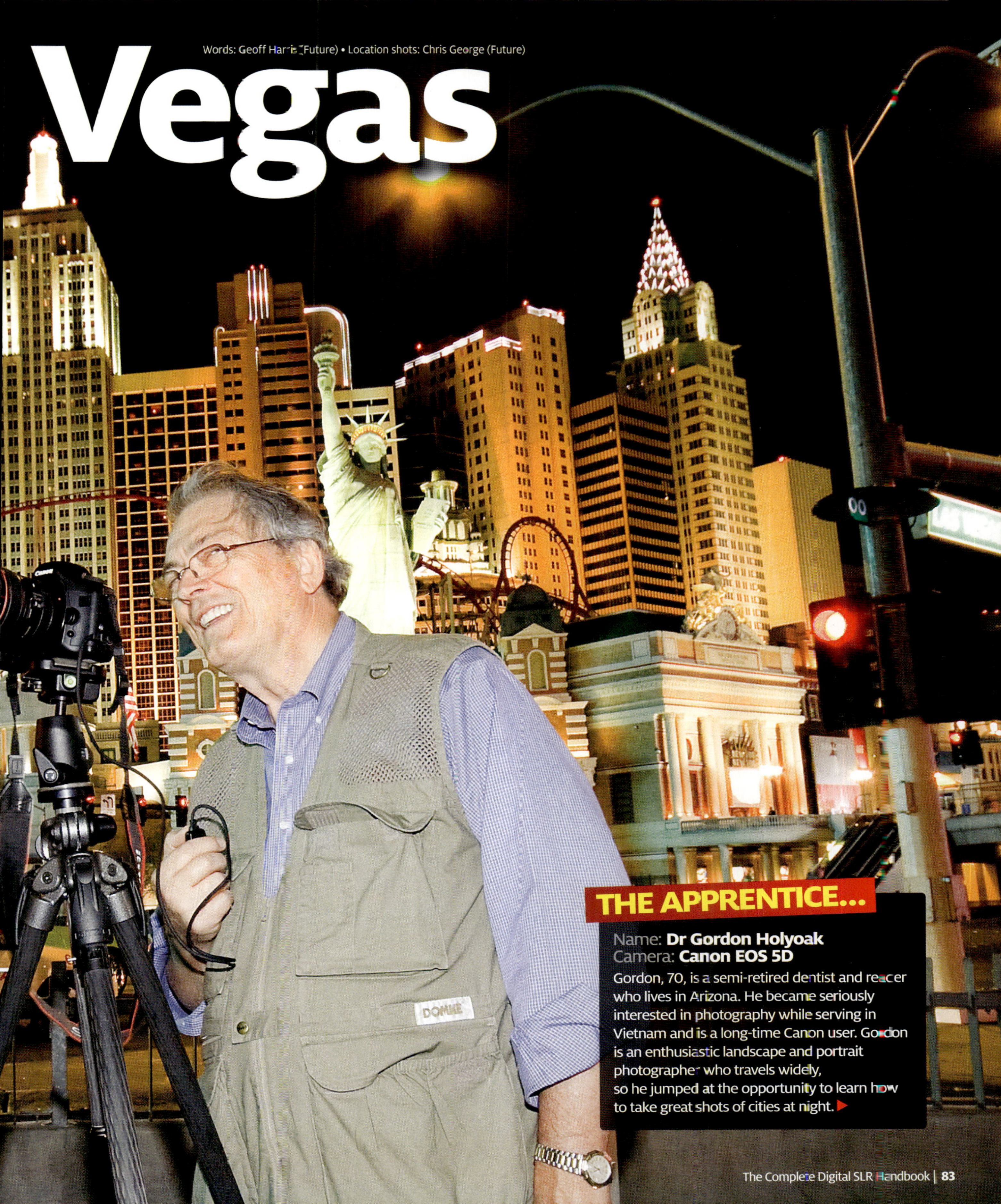

THE APPRENTICE...

Name: **Dr Gordon Holyoak**
Camera: **Canon EOS 5D**

Gordon, 70, is a semi-retired dentist and racer who lives in Arizona. He became seriously interested in photography while serving in Vietnam and is a long-time Canon user. Gordon is an enthusiastic landscape and portrait photographer who travels widely, so he jumped at the opportunity to learn how to take great shots of cities at night. ▶

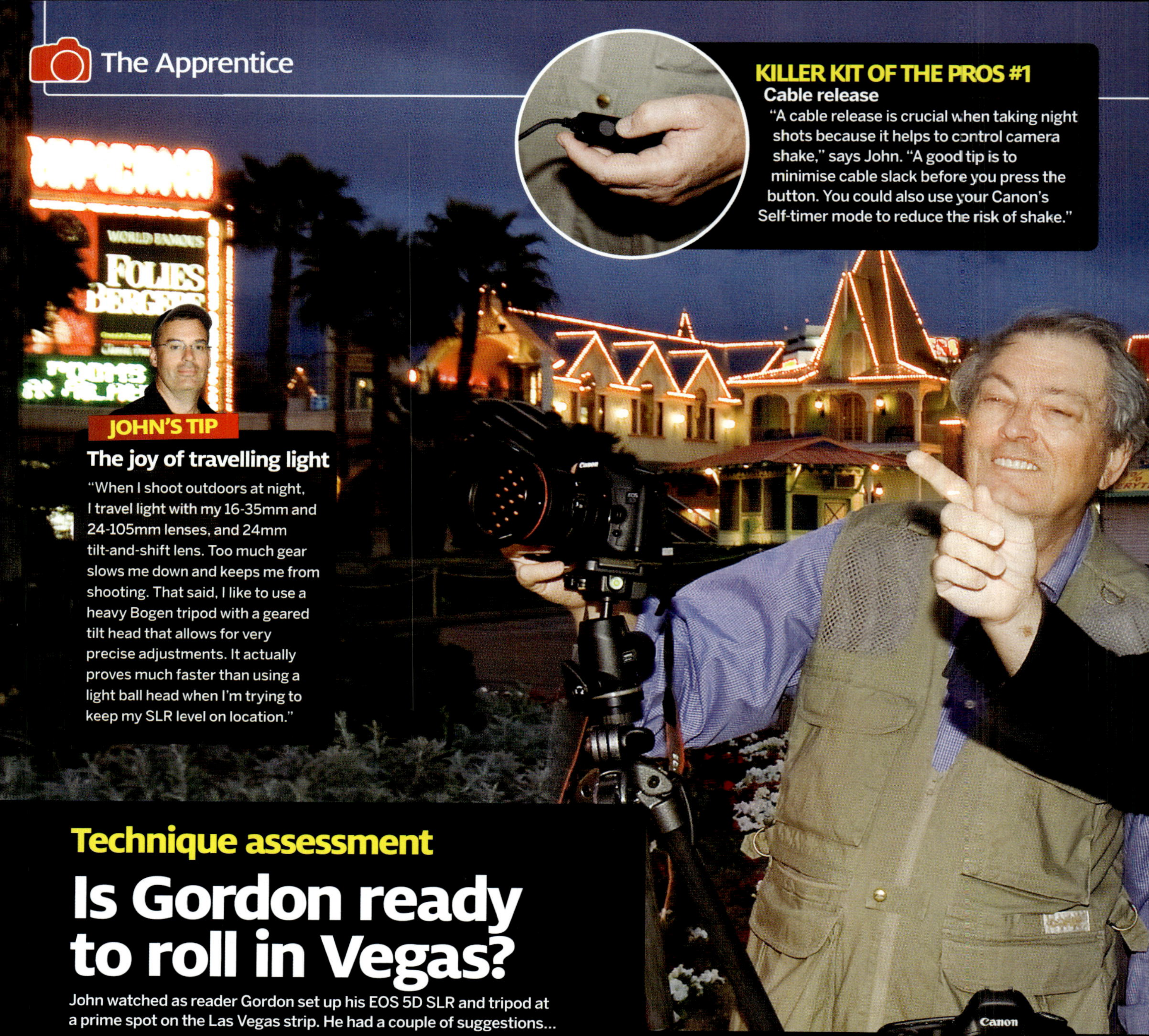

KILLER KIT OF THE PROS #1

Cable release

"A cable release is crucial when taking night shots because it helps to control camera shake," says John. "A good tip is to minimise cable slack before you press the button. You could also use your Canon's Self-timer mode to reduce the risk of shake."

JOHN'S TIP

The joy of travelling light

"When I shoot outdoors at night, I travel light with my 16-35mm and 24-105mm lenses, and 24mm tilt-and-shift lens. Too much gear slows me down and keeps me from shooting. That said, I like to use a heavy Bogen tripod with a geared tilt head that allows for very precise adjustments. It actually proves much faster than using a light ball head when I'm trying to keep my SLR level on location."

Technique assessment

Is Gordon ready to roll in Vegas?

John watched as reader Gordon set up his EOS 5D SLR and tripod at a prime spot on the Las Vegas strip. He had a couple of suggestions...

TAKE MORE CONTROL

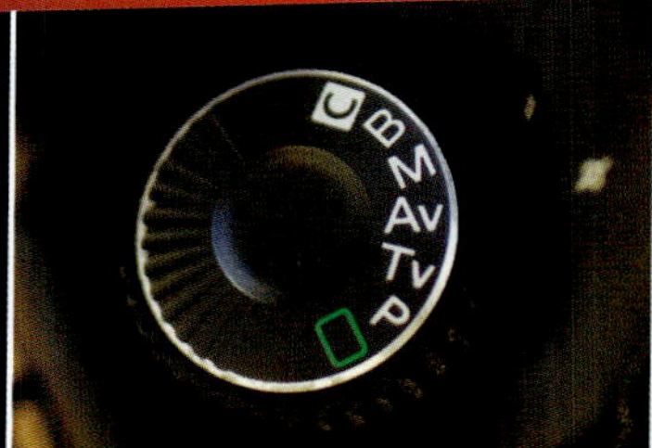

Shoot in Manual mode

"Gordon was shooting in Av mode," says John. "I use Manual because we're shooting a stationary subject (the city) in consistent lighting. In Av, your SLR can over- or under-expose the scene. Also, you can fine-tune the shutter speed in Manual."

WATCH THOSE CENTRE LEGS

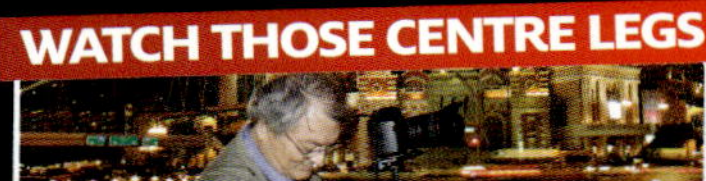

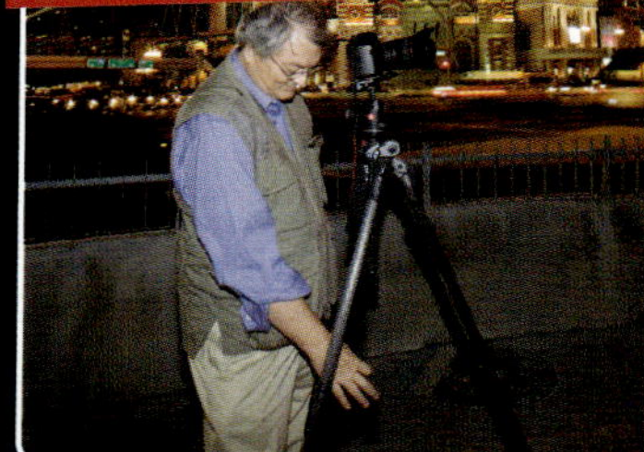

Pro tripod techniques

"Gordon was extending his tripod's centre column. This reduces stability, although it's OK to fully extend the legs in order to form a strong, wide base. It was quite windy, so we attached a bag to the bottom of the centre column for ballast."

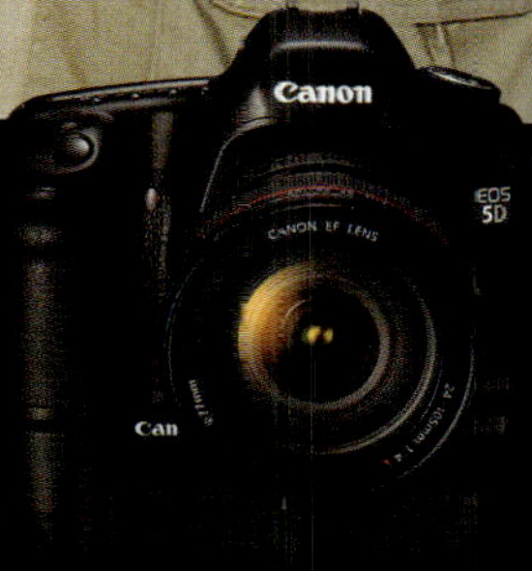

Canon pro John Morris gets asked to photograph everything from swanky hotels to informal weddings. Depending on the job in hand, he uses an EOS 5D, 40D or 30D, along with the following gear:

- Canon EF 70-200mm f/2.8L IS USM
- Canon EF 24-105mm f/4L IS USM
- Canon EF 16-35mm f/2.8L II USM
- Canon EF TS-E 24mm f/3.5L
- Canon EF 50mm f/1.4 USM
- Canon Speedlite 580EX flashguns and PocketWizards
- Bogen 3221 Gear tripod with 3275 3-axis gear head
- Bogen 190mf3 Carbonfibre tripod with medium ball head (486RC2)

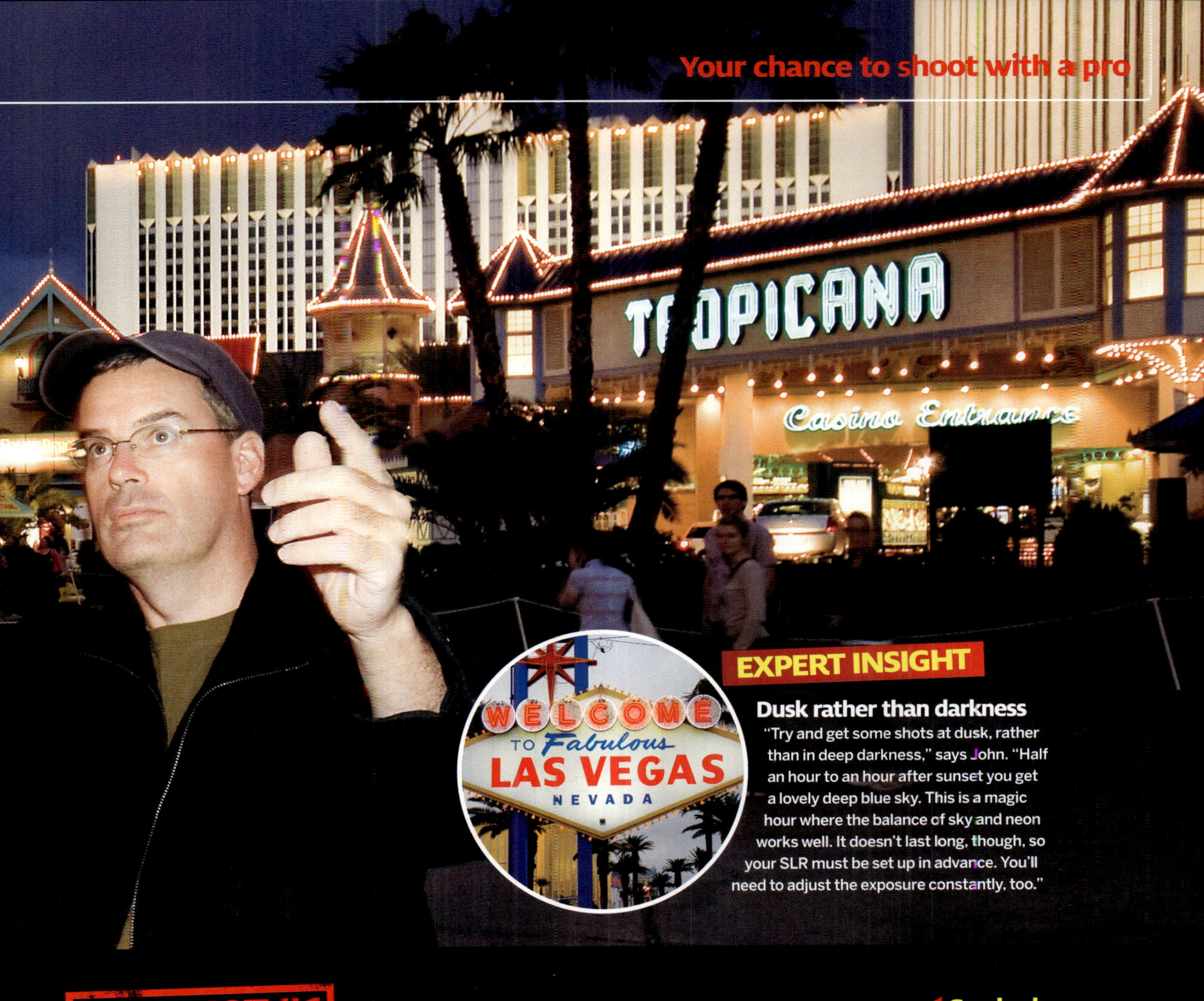

EXPERT INSIGHT

Dusk rather than darkness

"Try and get some shots at dusk, rather than in deep darkness," says John. "Half an hour to an hour after sunset you get a lovely deep blue sky. This is a magic hour where the balance of sky and neon works well. It doesn't last long, though, so your SLR must be set up in advance. You'll need to adjust the exposure constantly, too."

HOT SHOT #1

Exposure: 6 secs at f/11, ISO400
Lens: Canon EF 24-105mm f/4L

◀ Gordon's comment

"I'm pleased with this shot as a first attempt. We spent a lot of time setting up the tripod and camera and practising with the cable release – it kept sticking for some reason. John got me to think carefully about composition and how to to include street elements that couldn't be worked around. I shot this in Manual mode, at a small f/11 aperture. I used a long exposure of six seconds to create light trails from the traffic passing under the bridge. I think it works well." ▶

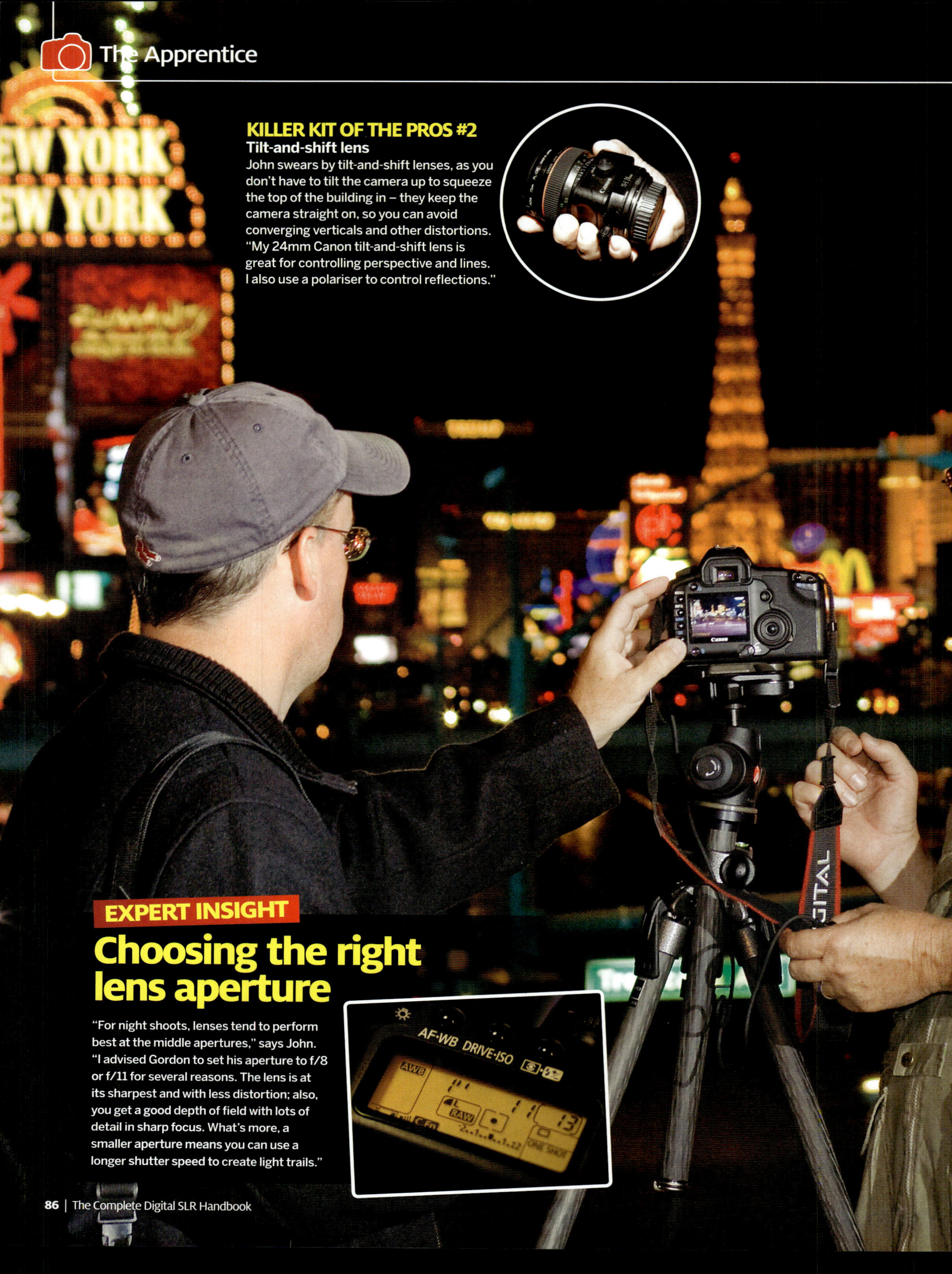

KILLER KIT OF THE PROS #2

Tilt-and-shift lens

John swears by tilt-and-shift lenses, as you don't have to tilt the camera up to squeeze the top of the building in – they keep the camera straight on, so you can avoid converging verticals and other distortions. "My 24mm Canon tilt-and-shift lens is great for controlling perspective and lines. I also use a polariser to control reflections."

EXPERT INSIGHT

Choosing the right lens aperture

"For night shoots, lenses tend to perform best at the middle apertures," says John. "I advised Gordon to set his aperture to f/8 or f/11 for several reasons. The lens is at its sharpest and with less distortion; also, you get a good depth of field with lots of detail in sharp focus. What's more, a smaller aperture means you can use a longer shutter speed to create light trails."

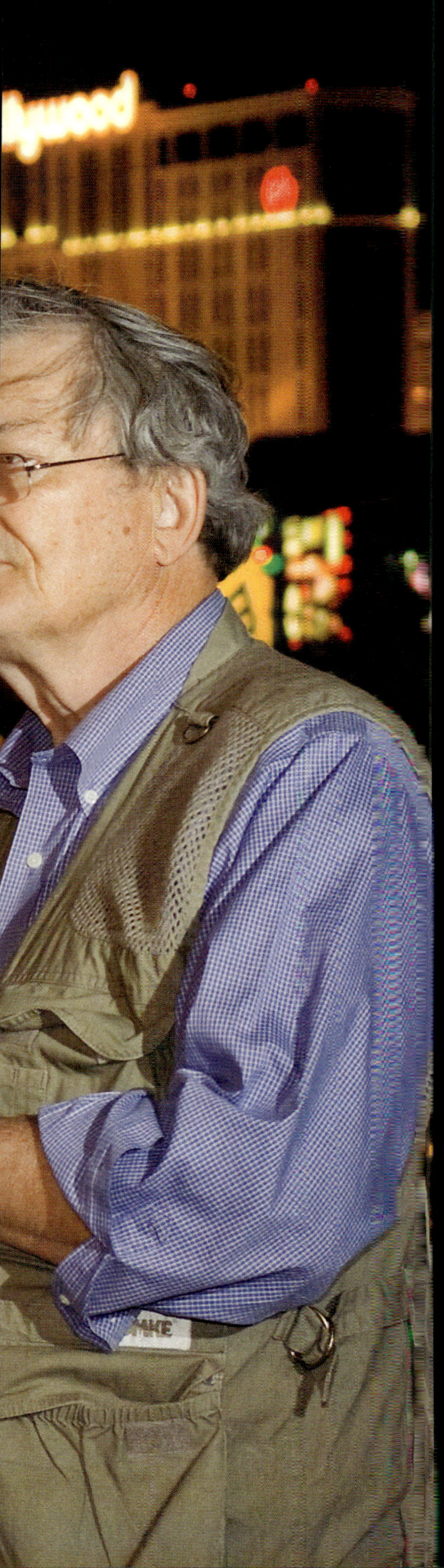

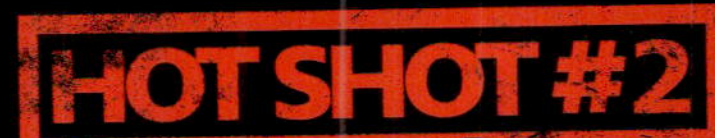

Exposure: 5 secs at f/11, ISO400
Lens: Canon EF 24-105mm f/4L

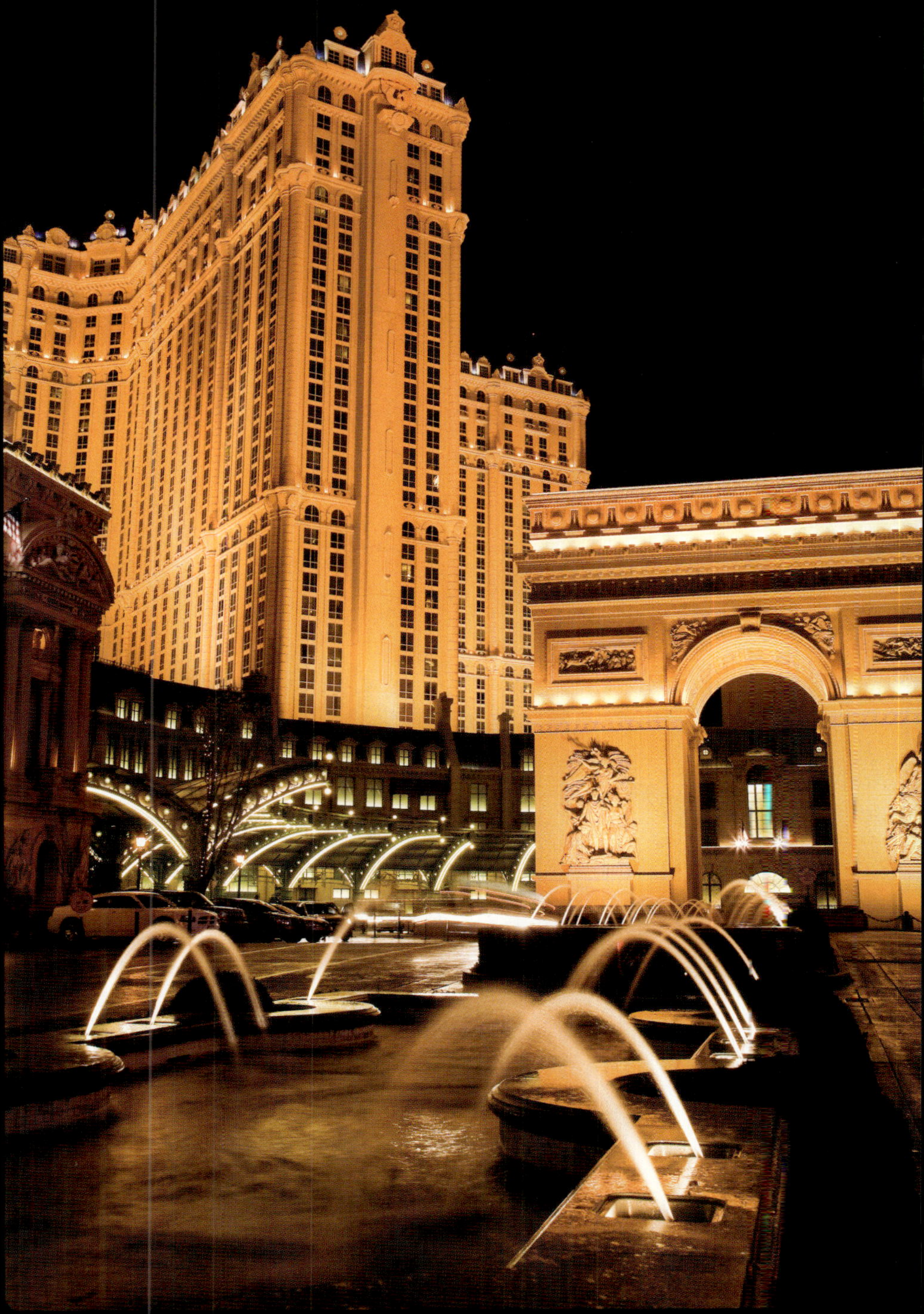

▶ Gordon's comment

"After we had taken some shots of the Las Vegas strip around New York, New York, we moved on to the Paris hotel. It's got some replicas of landmarks from the real Paris, such as the Eiffel Tower and the Arc D'Triomphe. In this shot, we used a slow shutter speed to slow down the fountains and create a pleasing milky effect in the water – at the same time ensuring the shot was well lit." ▶

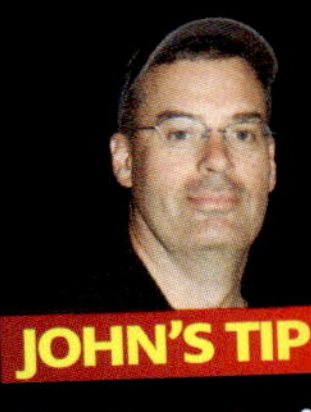

JOHN'S TIP

Spot metering magic

"We used Spot metering to keep the details in the distinct Paris architecture. Had we let the camera decide, it might have tried to expose for the black sky, blowing out the brighter details. In earlier shots, we used the light meter to get a general idea of the settings we needed, and then switched to Manual mode to fine-tune the exposure. Same here, but with Spot metering!"

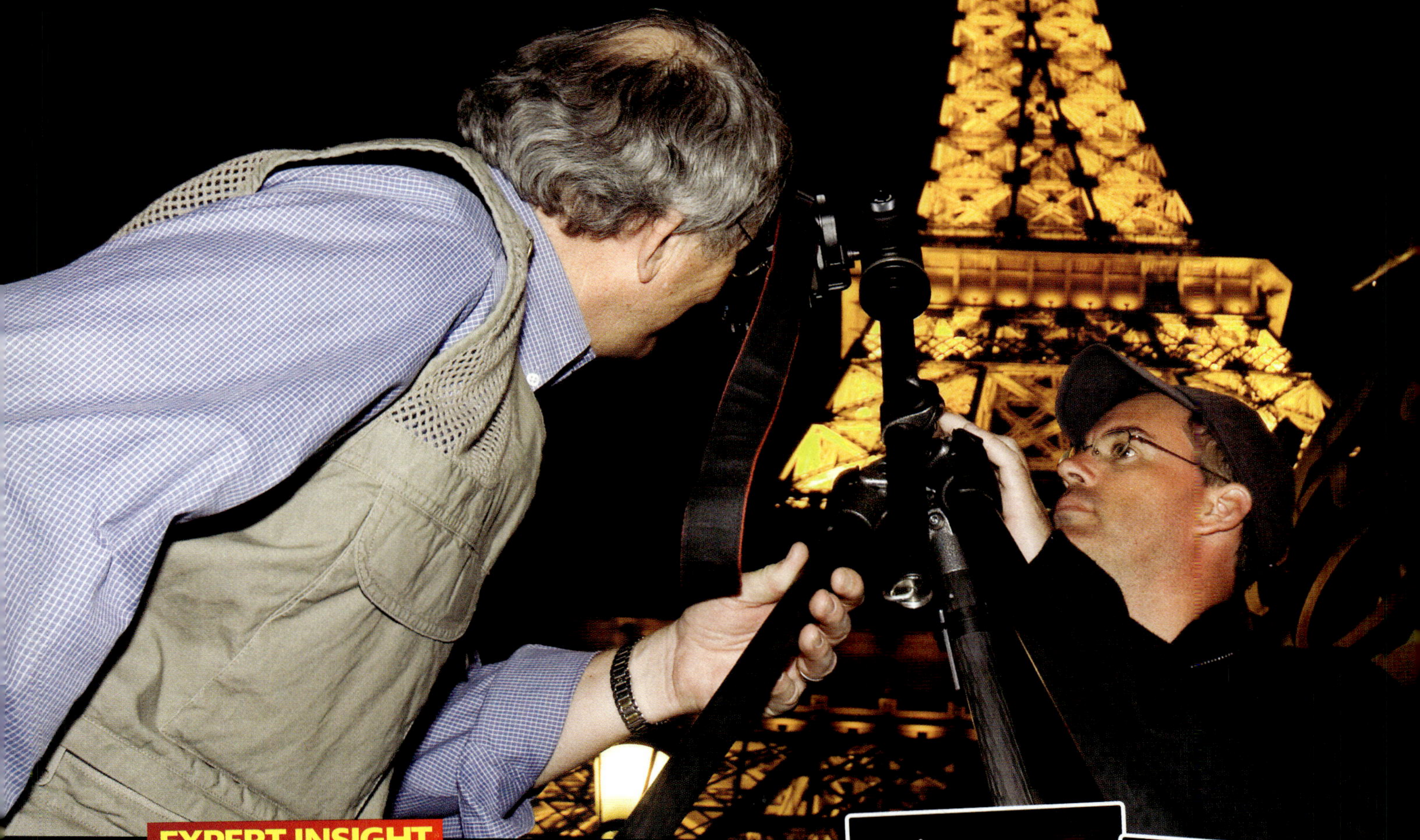

EXPERT INSIGHT

The beauty of bracketing

"A good tip when shooting cities at night is to bracket your exposures," says John. "With bracketing, you take a series of photographs at different exposures (under-exposed, over-exposed, and so on). You can then merge these later in Photoshop, so it's like an insurance policy. Also, if you're taking a night scene that includes bright neon, you have to make compromises between the highlights and shadows, since the camera can only capture a limited range. By bracketing, you can combine elements of the different exposures later to display the full range of dark and light details. High Dynamic Range (HDR) effects can also be applied to create an image closer to what the eye sees."

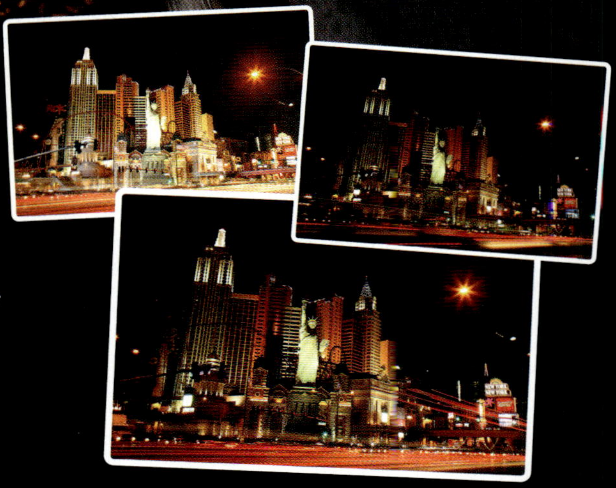

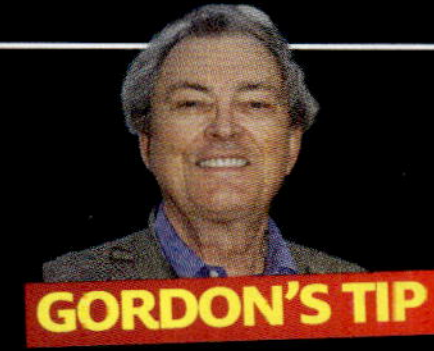

GORDON'S TIP

Know the LCD's limits

"If you're using the rear LCD to check your shots, reduce the brightness in the menu, because Canon tends to set its screens too bright. For accurate exposure checking always use the tone chart or histogram. You should only use the LCD for composition. And remember that you can't tell whether an image is in focus from the LCD either!"

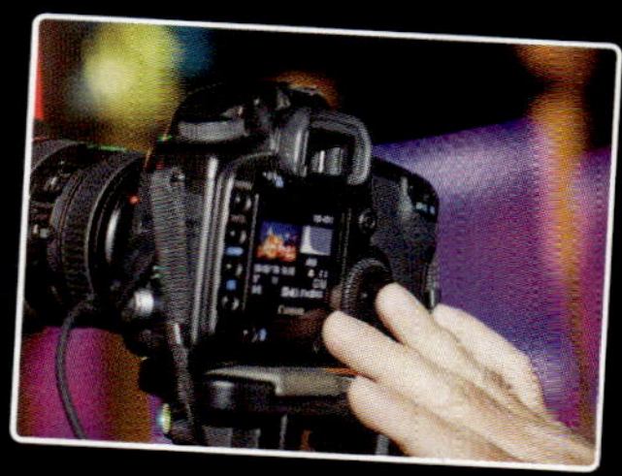

HOT SHOT #3

Exposure: 2 secs at f/11, ISO400
Lens: Canon EF 24-105mm f/4L

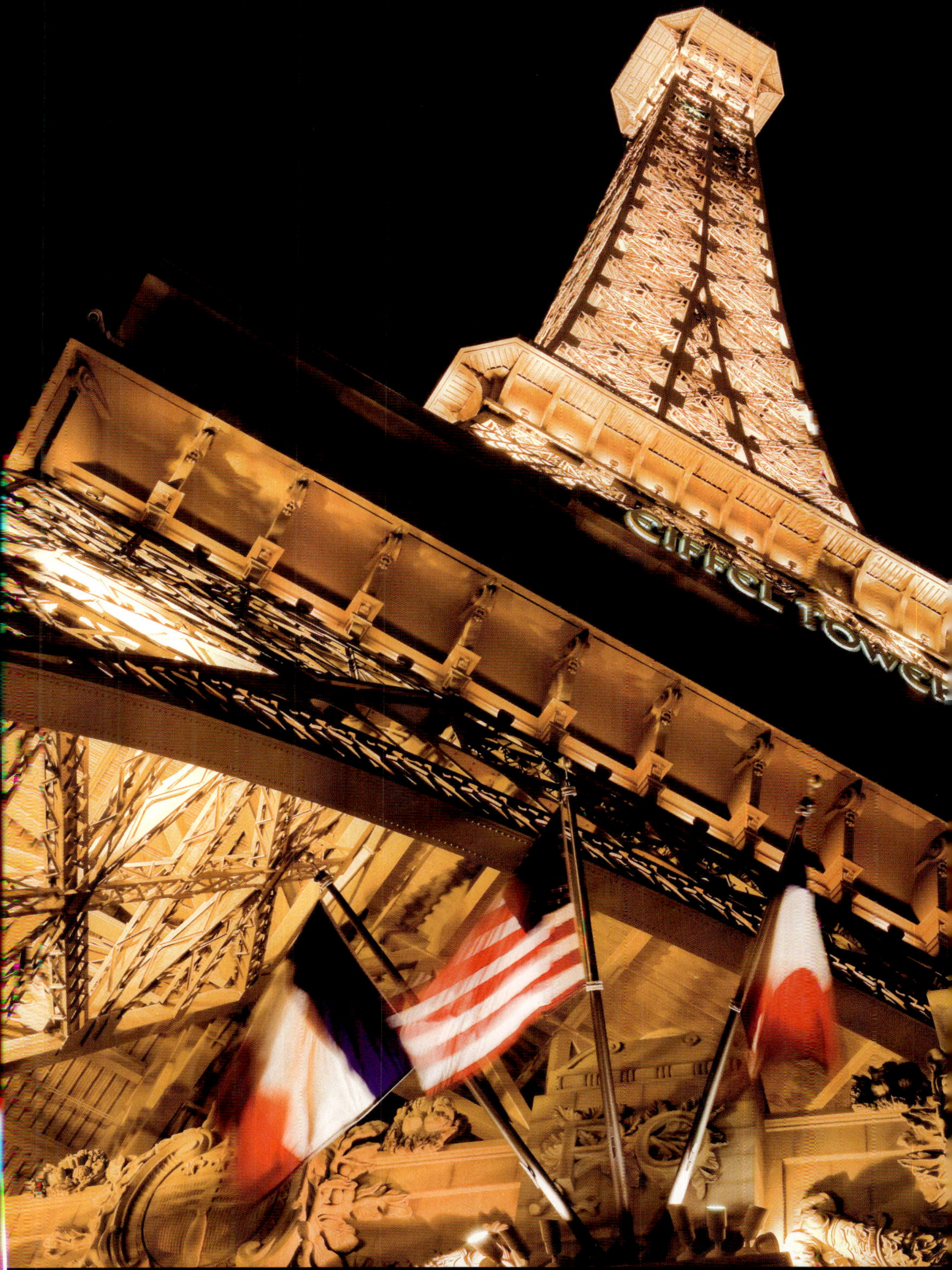

Gordon's comment

"I'm really happy with this shot of the Eiffel Tower near the Paris hotel. Getting it involved writhing around on the sidewalk with a shortened tripod, much to the amusement of all the Las Vegas revellers walking by. It took me a while to get used to using a retracted tripod in this way, but it was essential considering we were shooting at a slow shutter speed of two seconds. This speed also kept enough detail on the flags – as you can see it was quite breezy!"

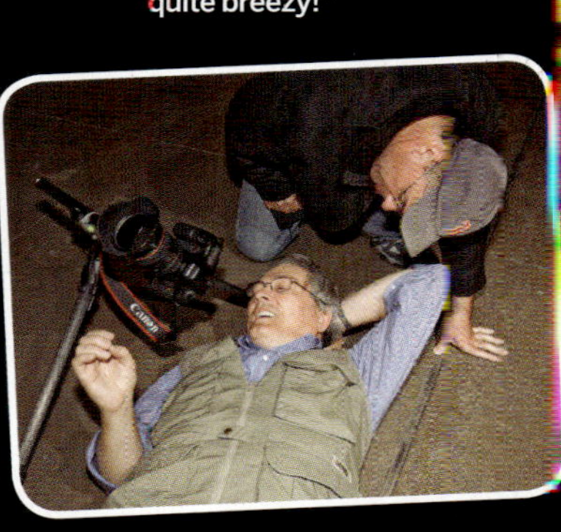

SHOT OF THE DAY

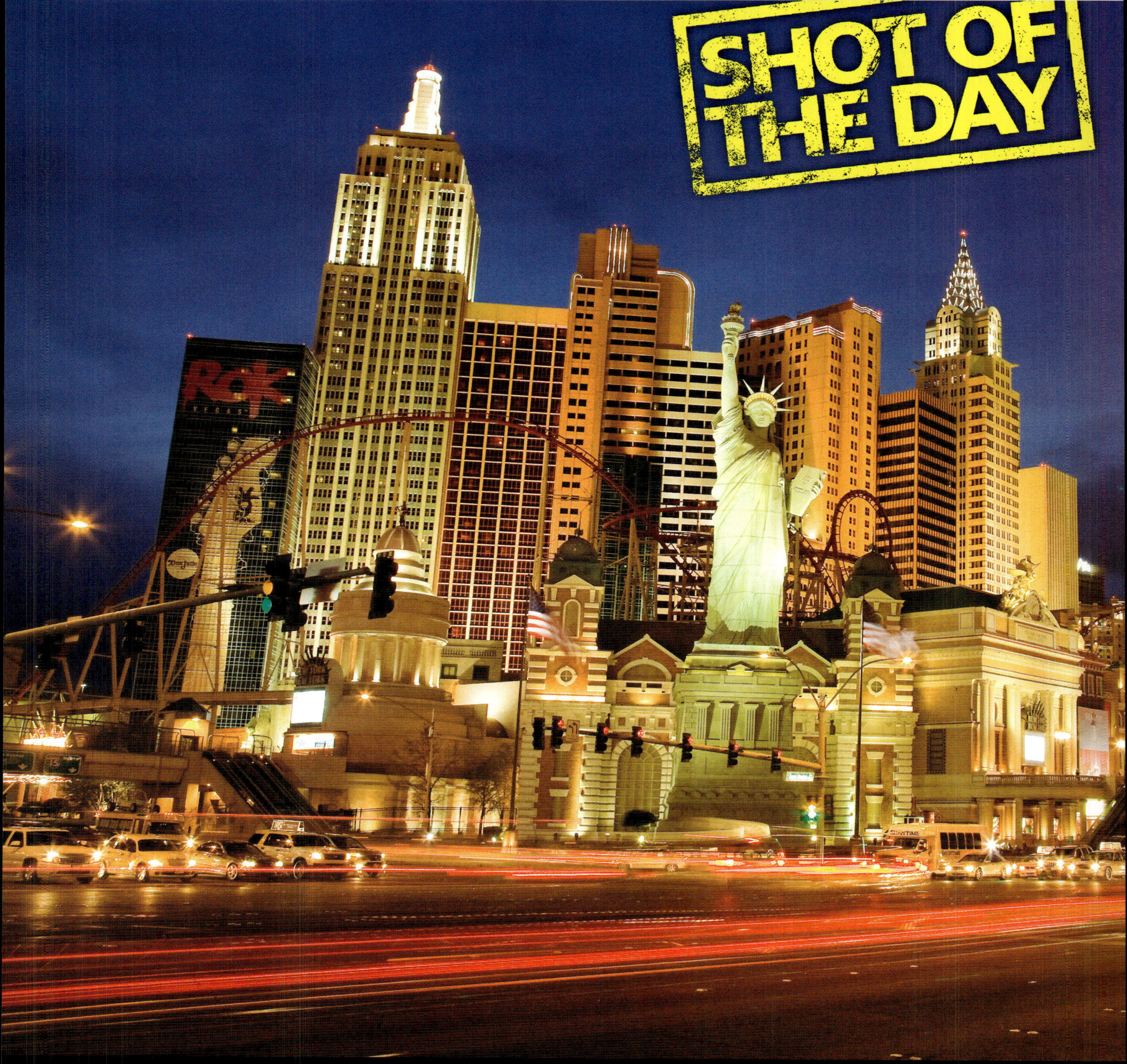

John's verdict

"Good lines and great composition help this shot, but it's the colour that makes it [1]. The deep blues contrast well with the warm orange glow of the tungsten lights, as well as the red taillights and yellow headlights of the cars [2]. The small aperture of f/11 creates attractive star-shaped highlights [3]. Gordon did well to keep it all sharp."

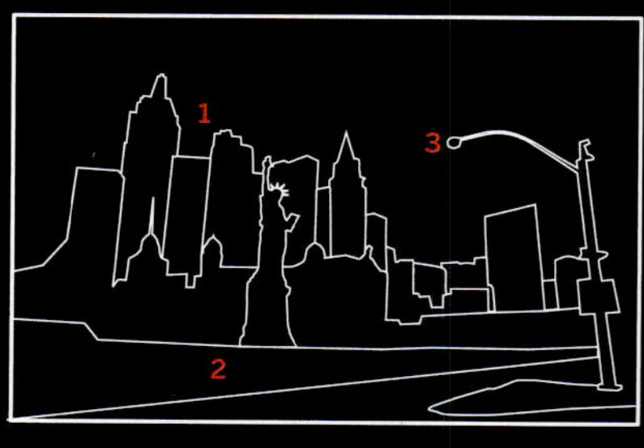

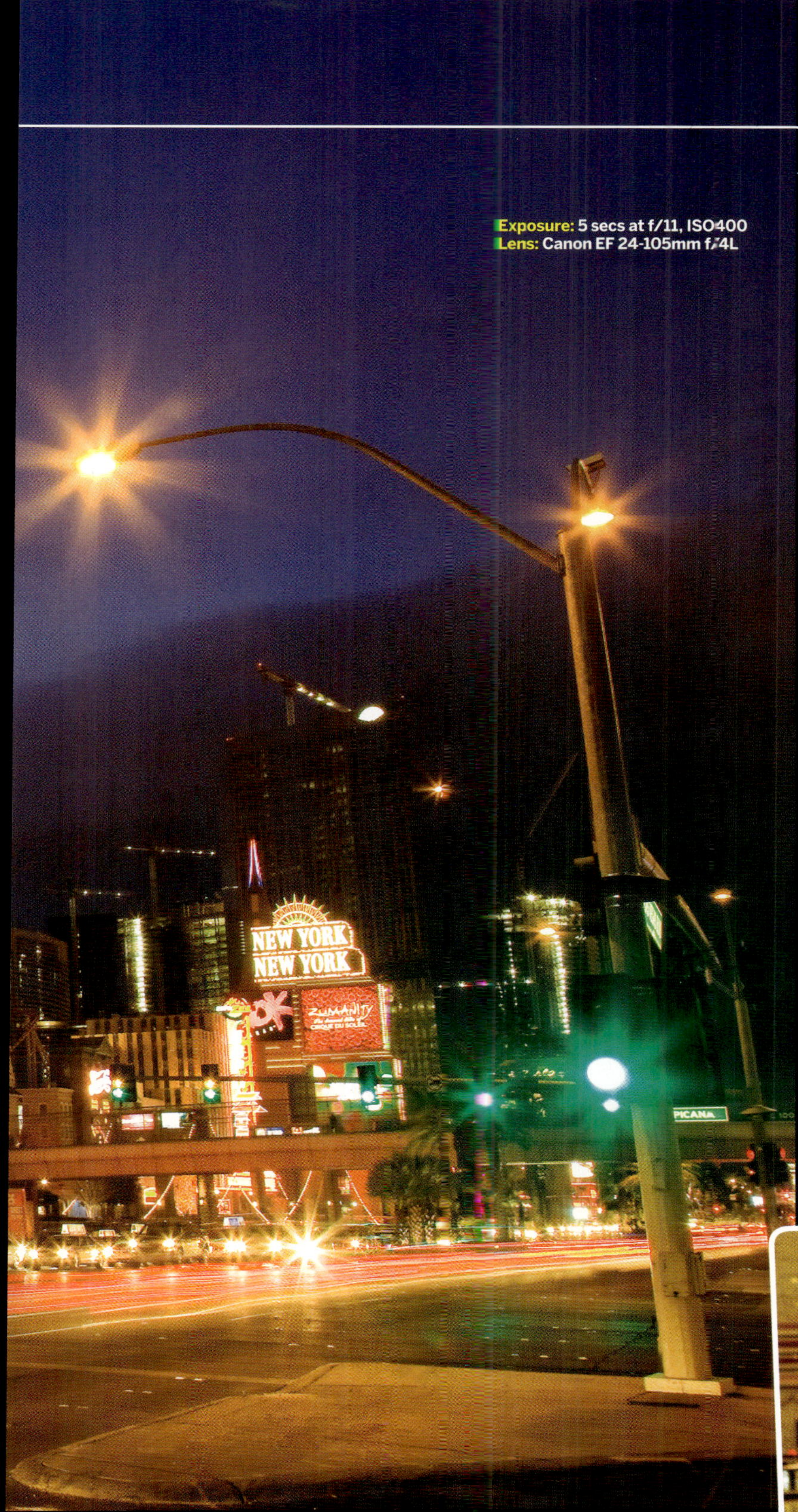

Exposure: 5 secs at f/11, ISO400
Lens: Canon EF 24-105mm f/4L

Gordon's comment

"I'm particularly pleased with this photo because it was an early one. There was a lot of information to absorb, but John was a great teacher. This shot works so well because of the timing – the rich blue light really makes it work. And as John said, thinking carefully about composition and what to include or remove from the frame really pays dividends."

WELL DONE GORDON!

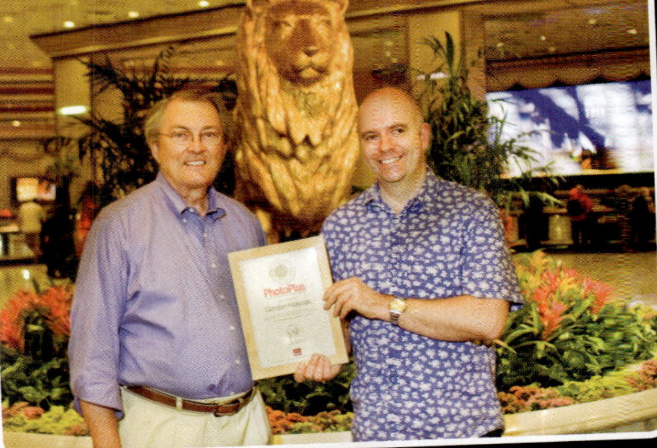

He's the 'mane' man! Intrepid reader Gordon receives his certificate

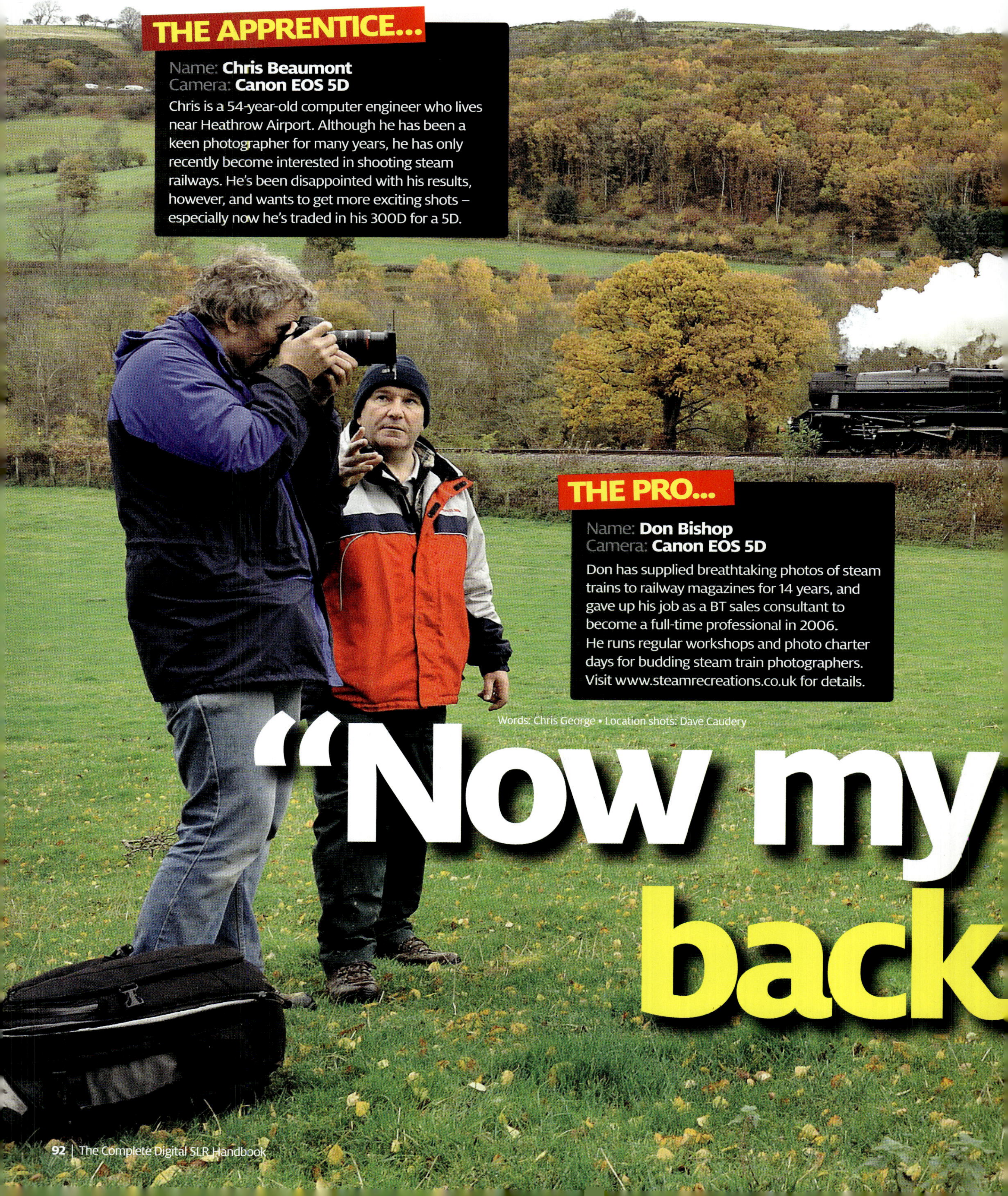

THE APPRENTICE...

Name: **Chris Beaumont**
Camera: **Canon EOS 5D**

Chris is a 54-year-old computer engineer who lives near Heathrow Airport. Although he has been a keen photographer for many years, he has only recently become interested in shooting steam railways. He's been disappointed with his results, however, and wants to get more exciting shots – especially now he's traded in his 300D for a 5D.

THE PRO...

Name: **Don Bishop**
Camera: **Canon EOS 5D**

Don has supplied breathtaking photos of steam trains to railway magazines for 14 years, and gave up his job as a BT sales consultant to become a full-time professional in 2006. He runs regular workshops and photo charter days for budding steam train photographers. Visit www.steamrecreations.co.uk for details.

Words: Chris George • Location shots: Dave Caudery

"Now my back

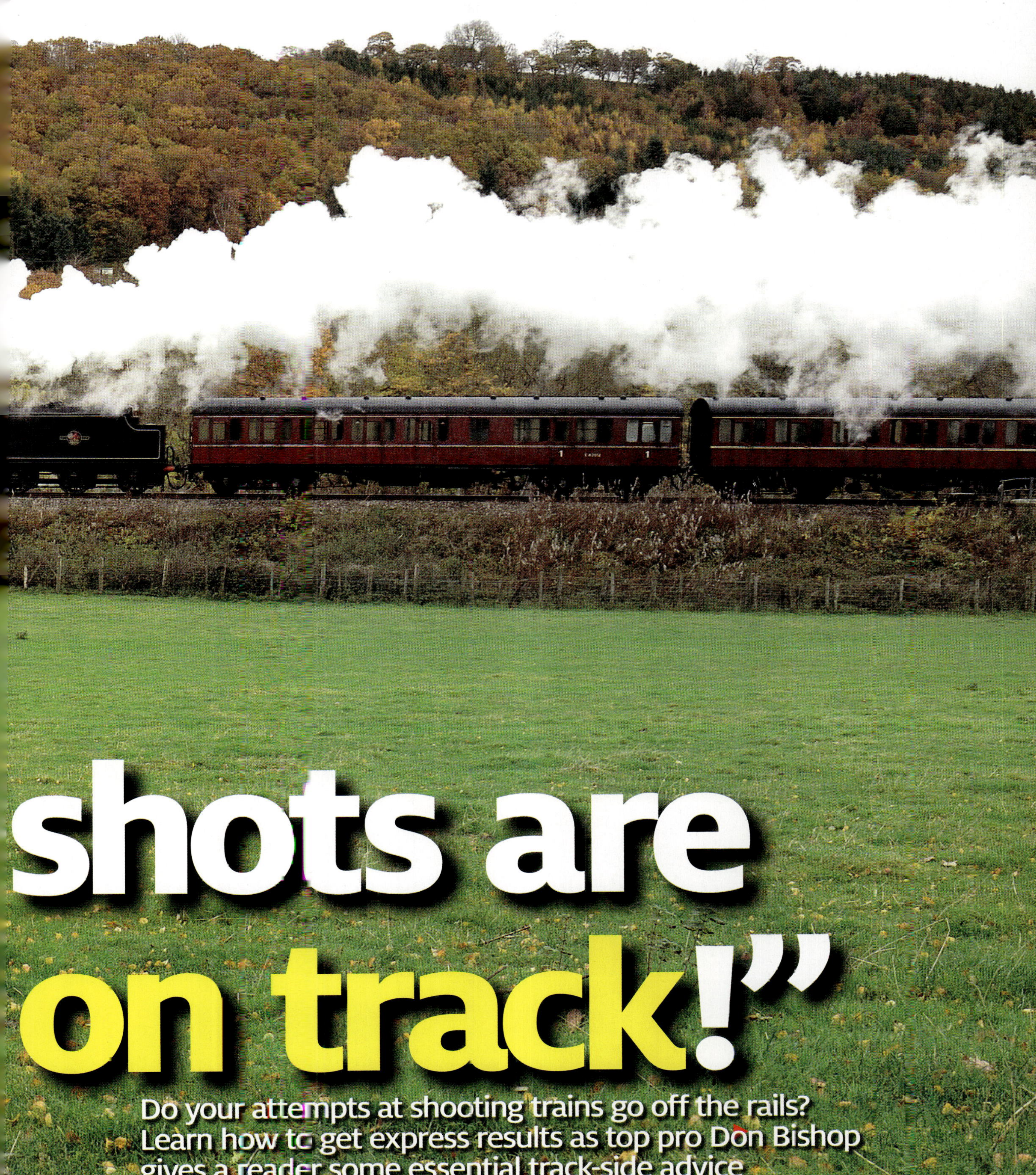

shots are on track!"

Do your attempts at shooting trains go off the rails? Learn how to get express results as top pro Don Bishop gives a reader some essential track-side advice

LADIES

DON'S TIP

Safety first

"Railways are dangerous places, and when photographing trains you must stay safe. Railways have their own safety guidelines, so make sure you know what they are and follow them. Do not trespass. Lineside permits are available at many of the heritage lines around the UK, but access to Network Rail mainlines is not permitted. If you're shooting from the trackside you will be expected to wear an orange high-vis jacket at all times."

Technique assessment

Is Chris ready to go full steam ahead?

After taking a few dozen shots, Don showed Chris the best way to set up his Canon to increase his chances of capturing the action

SHOOTING IN AV?

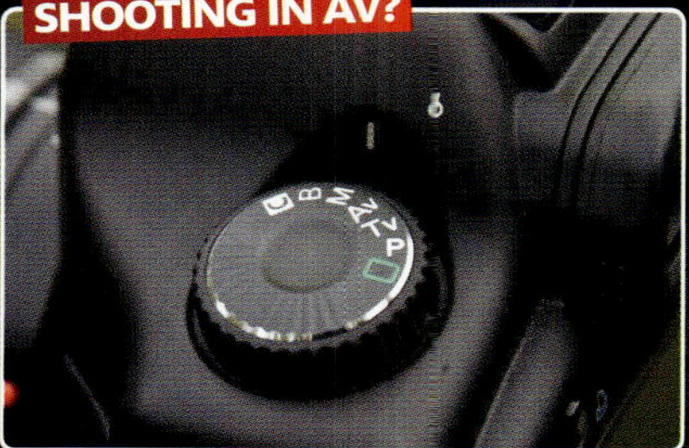

Switch to Manual

"I advised Chris to switch to Manual mode," says Don. "He'd been using Av, but by relying on the built-in meter he had problems with overexposure, with the exhaust of the trains 'blowing out'. With so much white and black in steam train shots, it is best to set the exposure yourself before the train moves into view."

STRUGGLING WITH FOCUS?

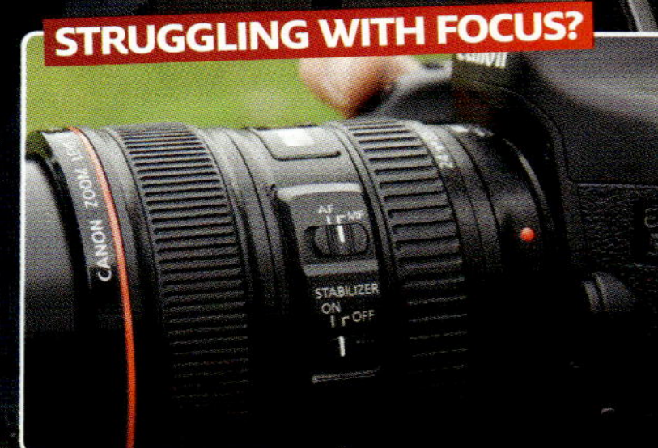

Focus a third of the way in

"If you charter a train, you're in control and it follows a set path, so you can also get focus right before it moves into your frame," says Don. "Visualise where the train will be, and focus on a point about a third of the way along its length using one of the autofocus points. Switch to manual focus to lock on this position."

KILLER KIT OF THE PROS #1

Hotshoe spirit level

"When shooting on inclined tracks and rolling hills it is hard to get the shot level using your eye alone. This spirit level attaches to my camera's hotshoe. You only need to line up the bubble for the horizontal plane – it doesn't matter how the camera tilts forwards or backwards."

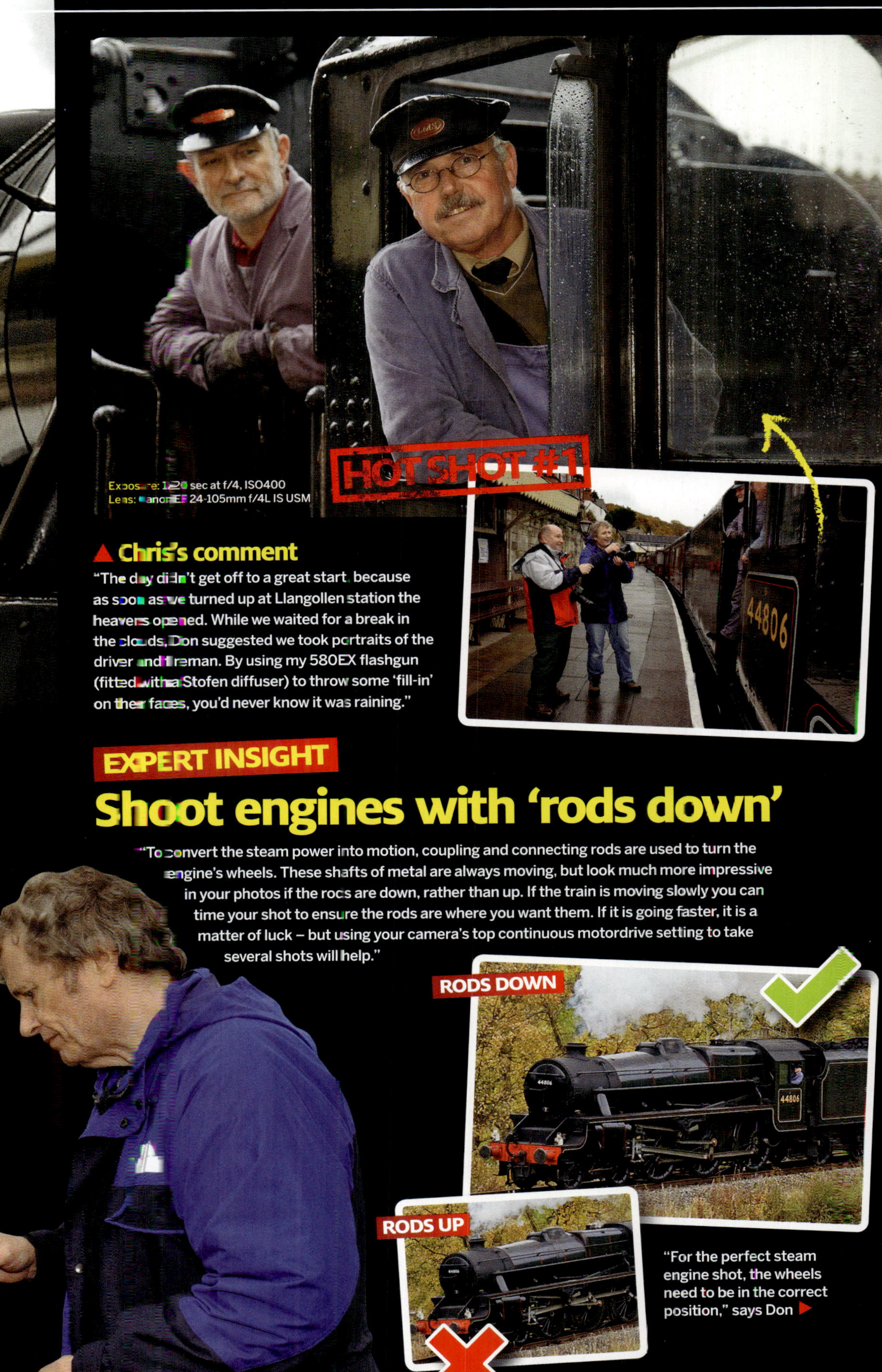

Exposure: 1/20 sec at f/4, ISO400
Lens: Canon EF 24-105mm f/4L IS USM

▲ Chris's comment

"The day didn't get off to a great start, because as soon as we turned up at Llangollen station the heavens opened. While we waited for a break in the clouds, Don suggested we took portraits of the driver and fireman. By using my 580EX flashgun (fitted with a Stofen diffuser) to throw some 'fill-in' on their faces, you'd never know it was raining."

EXPERT INSIGHT

Shoot engines with 'rods down'

"To convert the steam power into motion, coupling and connecting rods are used to turn the engine's wheels. These shafts of metal are always moving, but look much more impressive in your photos if the rods are down, rather than up. If the train is moving slowly you can time your shot to ensure the rods are where you want them. If it is going faster, it is a matter of luck – but using your camera's top continuous motordrive setting to take several shots will help."

"For the perfect steam engine shot, the wheels need to be in the correct position," says Don ▶

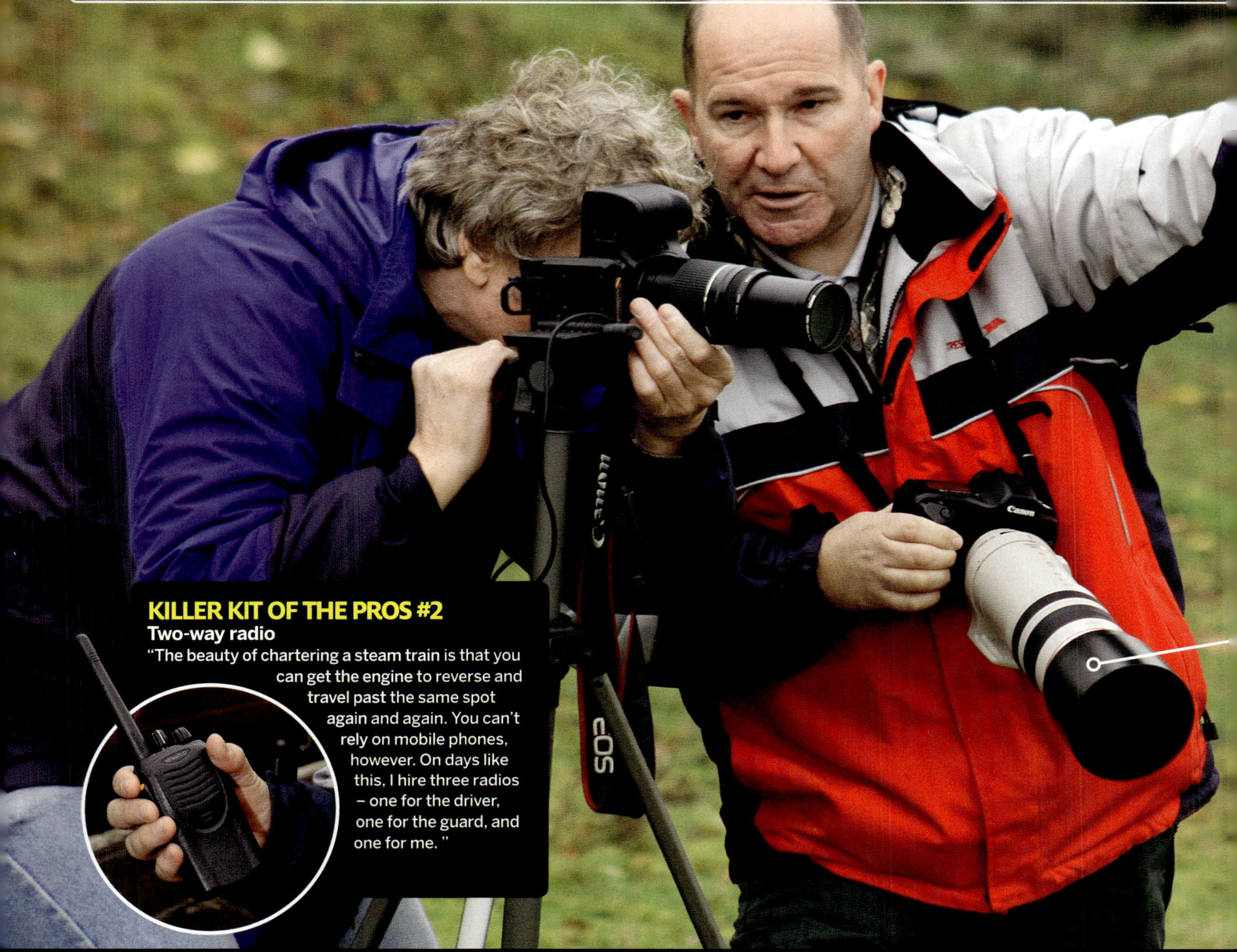

KILLER KIT OF THE PROS #2

Two-way radio

"The beauty of chartering a steam train is that you can get the engine to reverse and travel past the same spot again and again. You can't rely on mobile phones, however. On days like this, I hire three radios – one for the driver, one for the guard, and one for me."

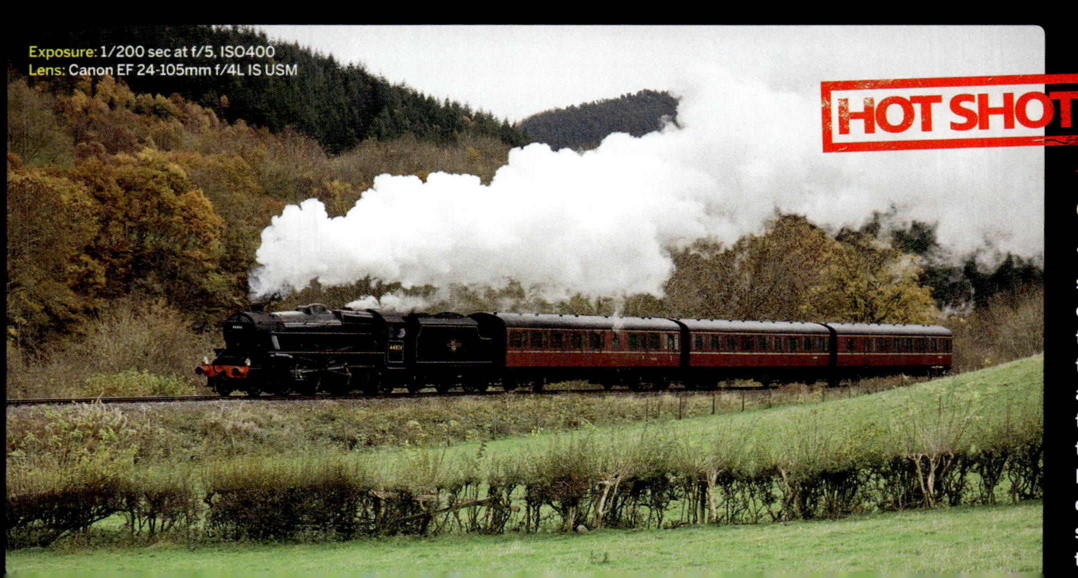

Exposure: 1/200 sec at f/5, ISO400
Lens: Canon EF 24-105mm f/4L IS USM

HOT SHOT #2

Chris's comment

"Fortunately the rain stopped after an hour or so and we were able to head out with the train as planned to try and capture some of the classic 'steam in the landscape' shots I had hoped to take. I deliberately framed the shot to cut out some of the washed-out grey sky."

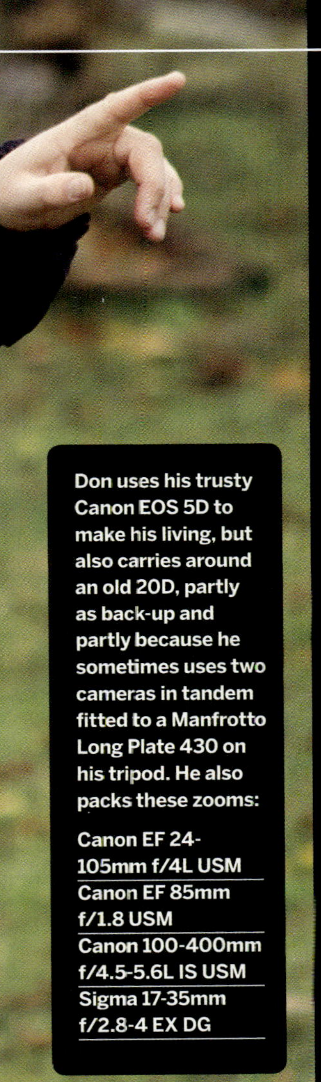

Don uses his trusty Canon EOS 5D to make his living, but also carries around an old 20D, partly as back-up and partly because he sometimes uses two cameras in tandem fitted to a Manfrotto Long Plate 430 on his tripod. He also packs these zooms:

- Canon EF 24-105mm f/4L USM
- Canon EF 85mm f/1.8 USM
- Canon 100-400mm f/4.5-5.6L IS USM
- Sigma 17-35mm f/2.8-4 EX DG

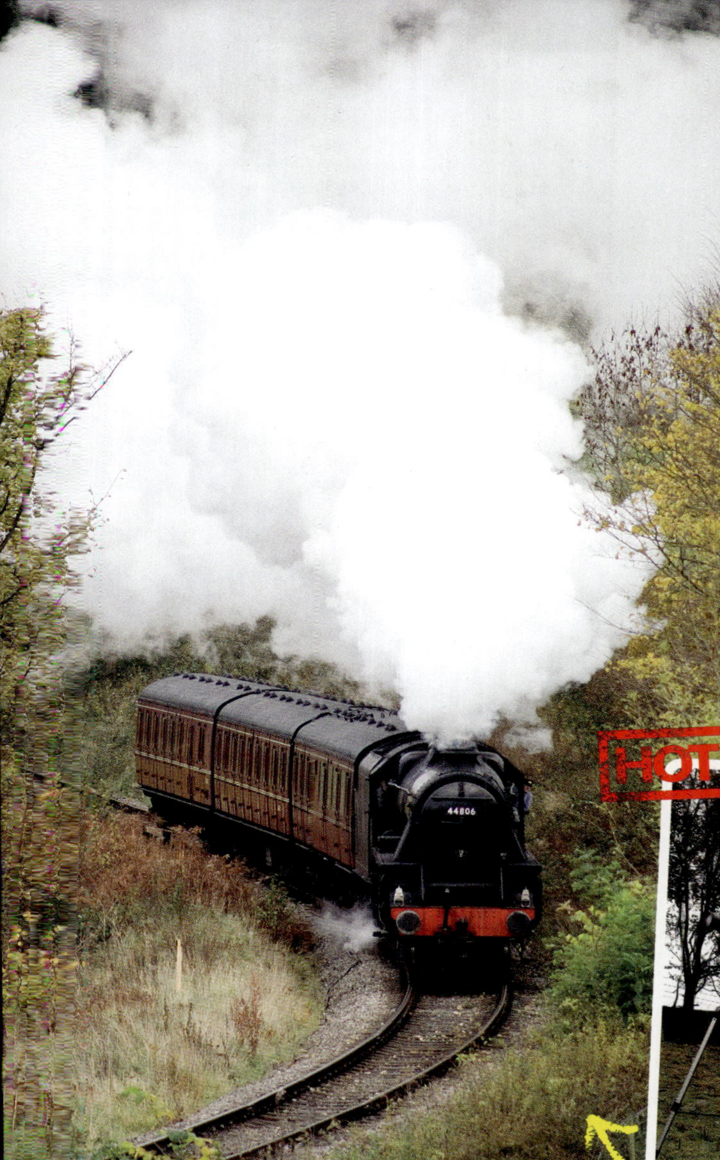

Exposure: 1/320 sec at f/5.6, ISO500
Lens: Canon EF 75-300mm f/4-5.6 III

Chris's comment

"Nearly all of the photographs I took on the day were horizontal format, but I think this vertical shot works very well. The train is working hard as it climbs the hill, but luckily the exhaust is clear of the back carriage. The curve of the track does a brilliant job of leading the viewer's eye into the middle of the shot"

HOT SHOT #3

CHRIS'S TIP

Charter your own train!

"At steam railways you often have to wait ages for the next train to go past, and you can usually only photograph them going one way. When the train is travelling back down the track the engine's chimney or 'smoke box' will be at the back of the engine, and not at the front as it should be. Photo charters are great, because the train can be set up to pass you in the correct direction several times in a matter of minutes. Every pass allows you to perfect your technique and timing, and the position of the smoke is different every time."

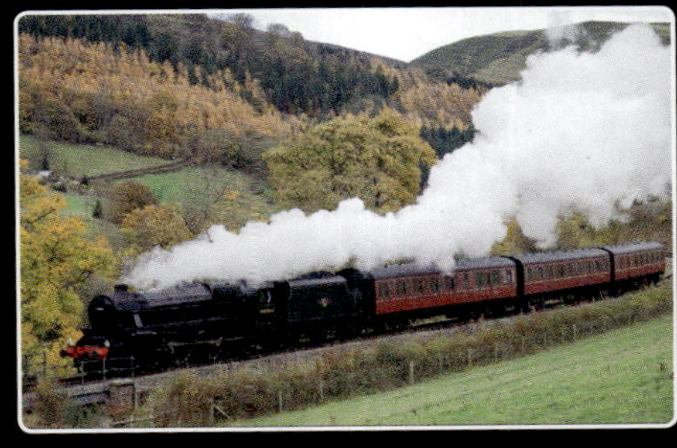

First attempt
In this first shot, the composition works well, but the steam obscures part of the engine.

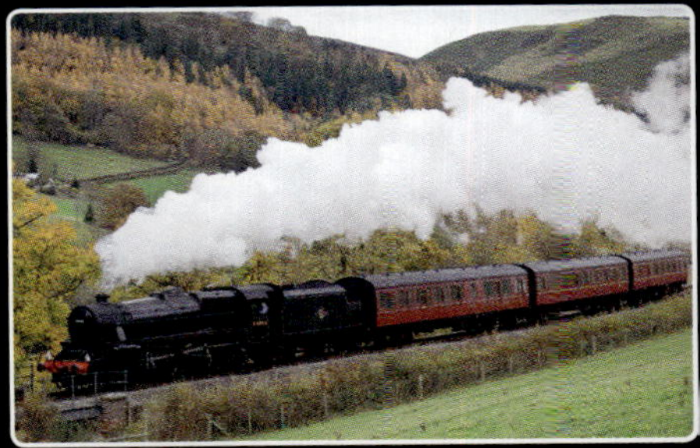

Second attempt
By chartering the train we were able to try again. This time the steam looks perfect!

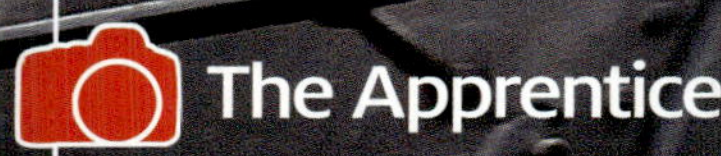

KILLER KIT OF THE PROS #3

Folding pocket secateurs

"To get the best views of the track, you often have to shoot over hedges. Sometimes it is necessary to do a bit of light pruning to ensure your lens has a clear line of sight. This mini multi-purpose tool costs under $10, and stows away safely in my backpack."

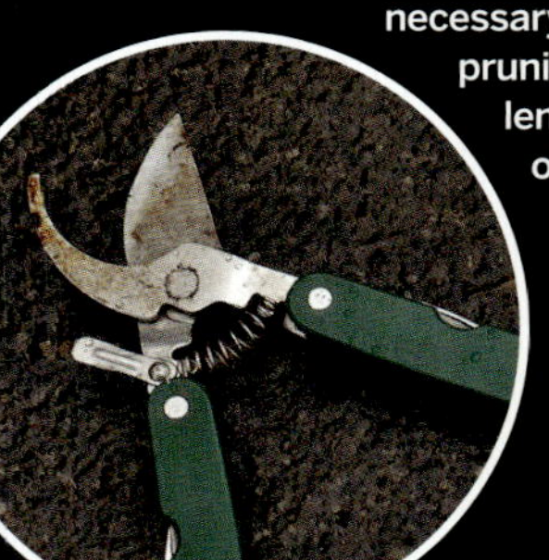

KILLER KIT OF THE PROS #4

Stepladder

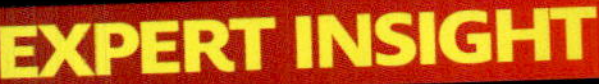

"A stepladder allows you to get a good vantage point, so you can see over hedges and other photographers. Also, on photo charters the train stops where you want it to along the track, so you won't necessarily have a platform from which to board the train. These steps help me clamber on board to be ferried from one location to the next."

EXPERT INSIGHT

Maximise the steam

"The best time to shoot steam railways is between late September and late April. It needs to be cold enough for the engine to produce the right amount of white exhaust. Without this steam, your shots can look a bit lifeless, so you also need to pick a vantage point where the engine is working hard – look for sections of track with a gradient."

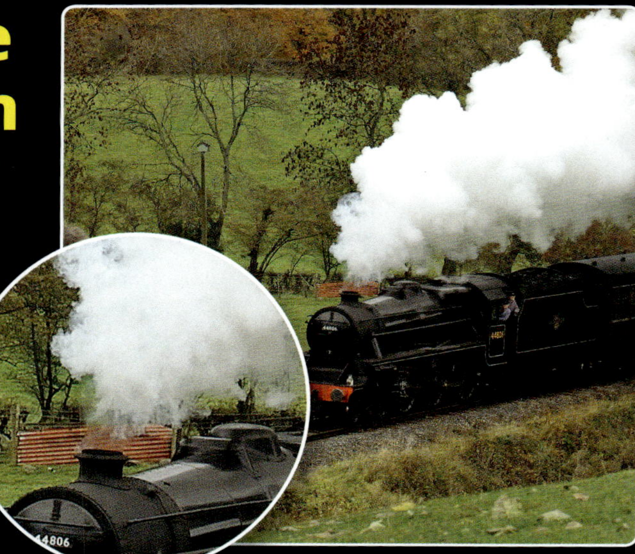

Chris's comment

"This was one of the last shots of the day – and it had started to rain again. However, the angle of the train meant that the wet carriage roofs reflected what daylight there was. The shot's full of atmosphere, and just goes to prove that you shouldn't pack up your kit when the going gets wet!"

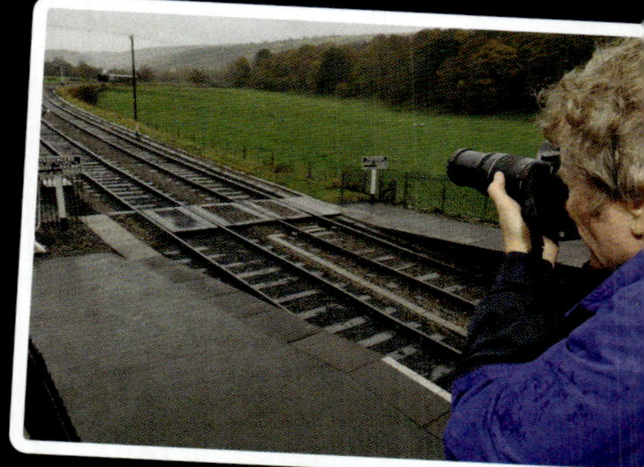

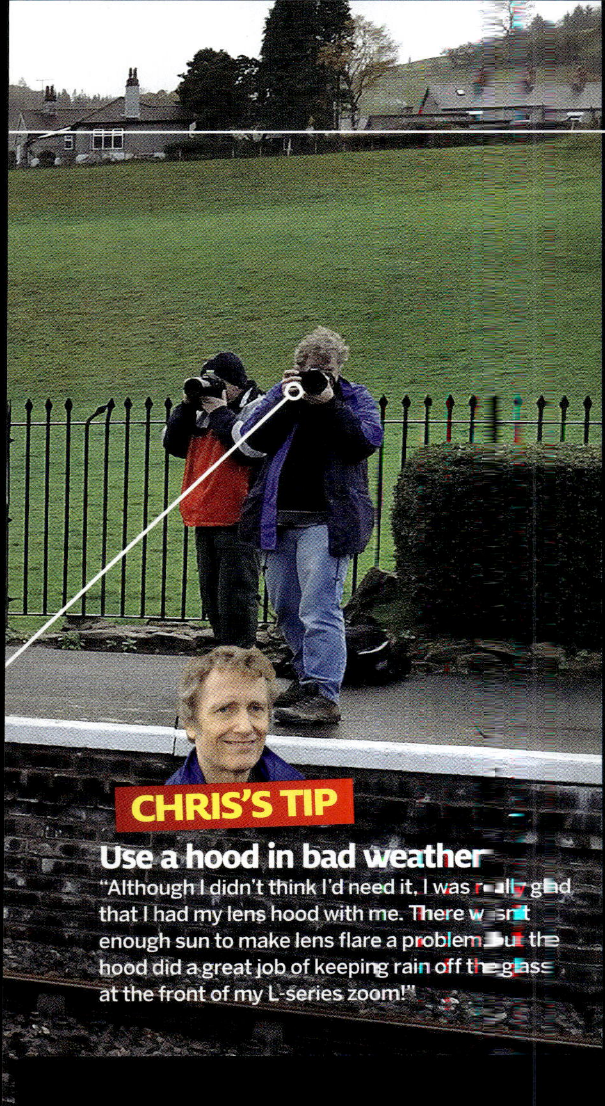

CHRIS'S TIP

Use a hood in bad weather

"Although I didn't think I'd need it, I was really glad that I had my lens hood with me. There wasn't enough sun to make lens flare a problem, but the hood did a great job of keeping rain off the glass at the front of my L-series zoom!"

Don's favourite locations

We went to Llangollen Railway in Wales for our shoot, but Don travels the country in search of great steam train photos. These shots were taken in some of his favourite locations...

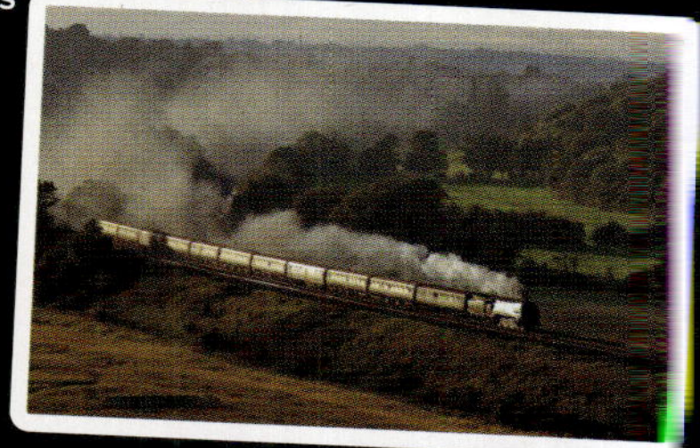

▶ GWR mainline

"This 'Battle of Britain' Pacific No. 34067 'Tangmere' caught the glint of the beautiful evening light as it passed Newton St Loe, near Bath, with a Bristol to London Victoria special in September

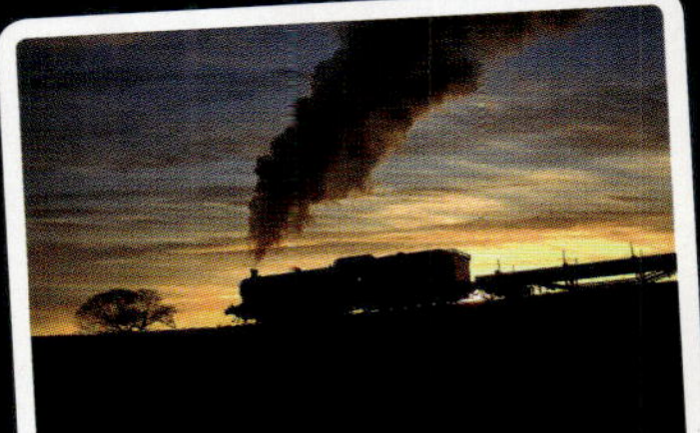

◀ North Yorkshire Moors Railway

"I deliberately threw this Q6 0-8-0 No. 63395 into a dark silhouette against the colourful evening sky. I later enhanced the sky in Photoshop to give the shot a boost."

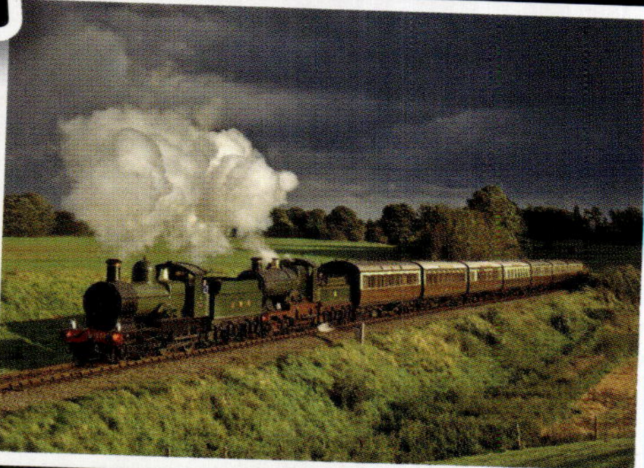

▶ Severn Valley Railway

"No. 9017 Earl of Berkeley and No. 3440 City of Truro pass Eardington summit on the Severn Valley Railway during one of my photo charters. The train looks stunning against the dark, dramatic sky." ▶

HOT SHOT #4

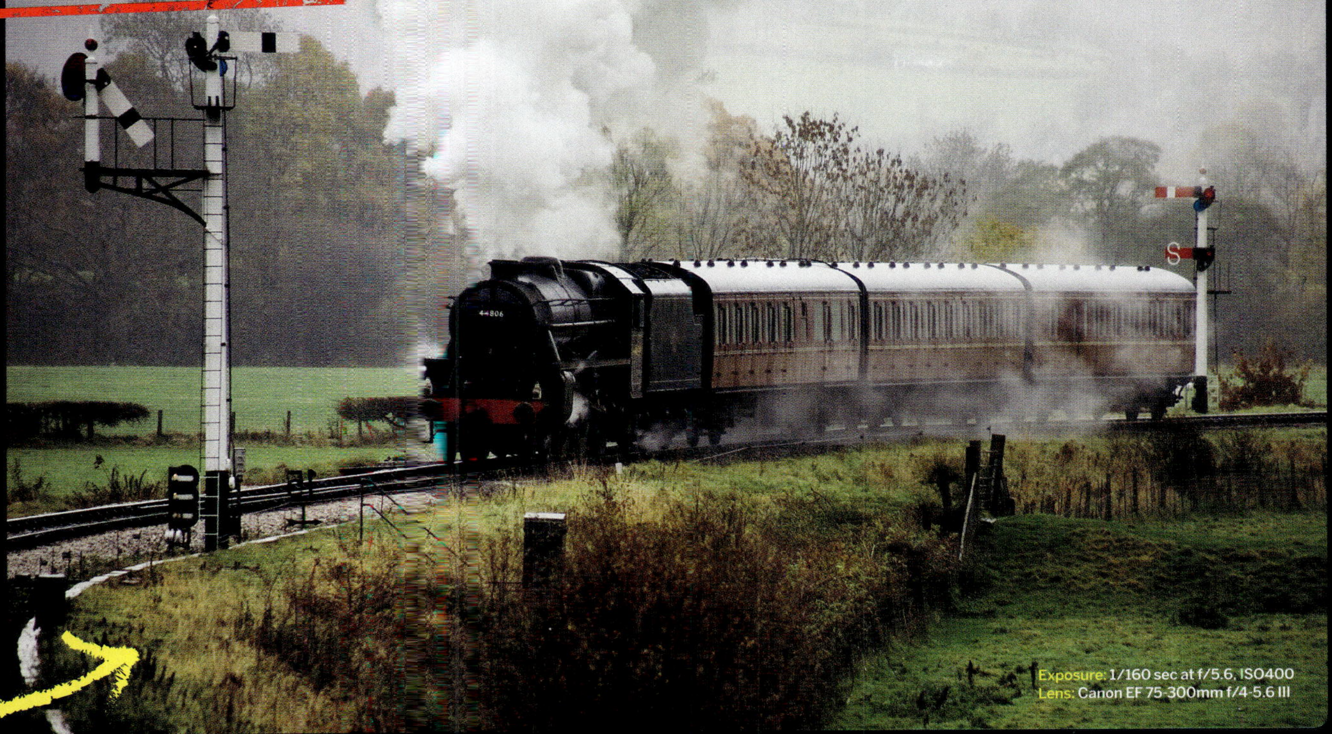

Exposure: 1/160 sec at f/5.6, ISO400
Lens: Canon EF 75-300mm f/4-5.6 III

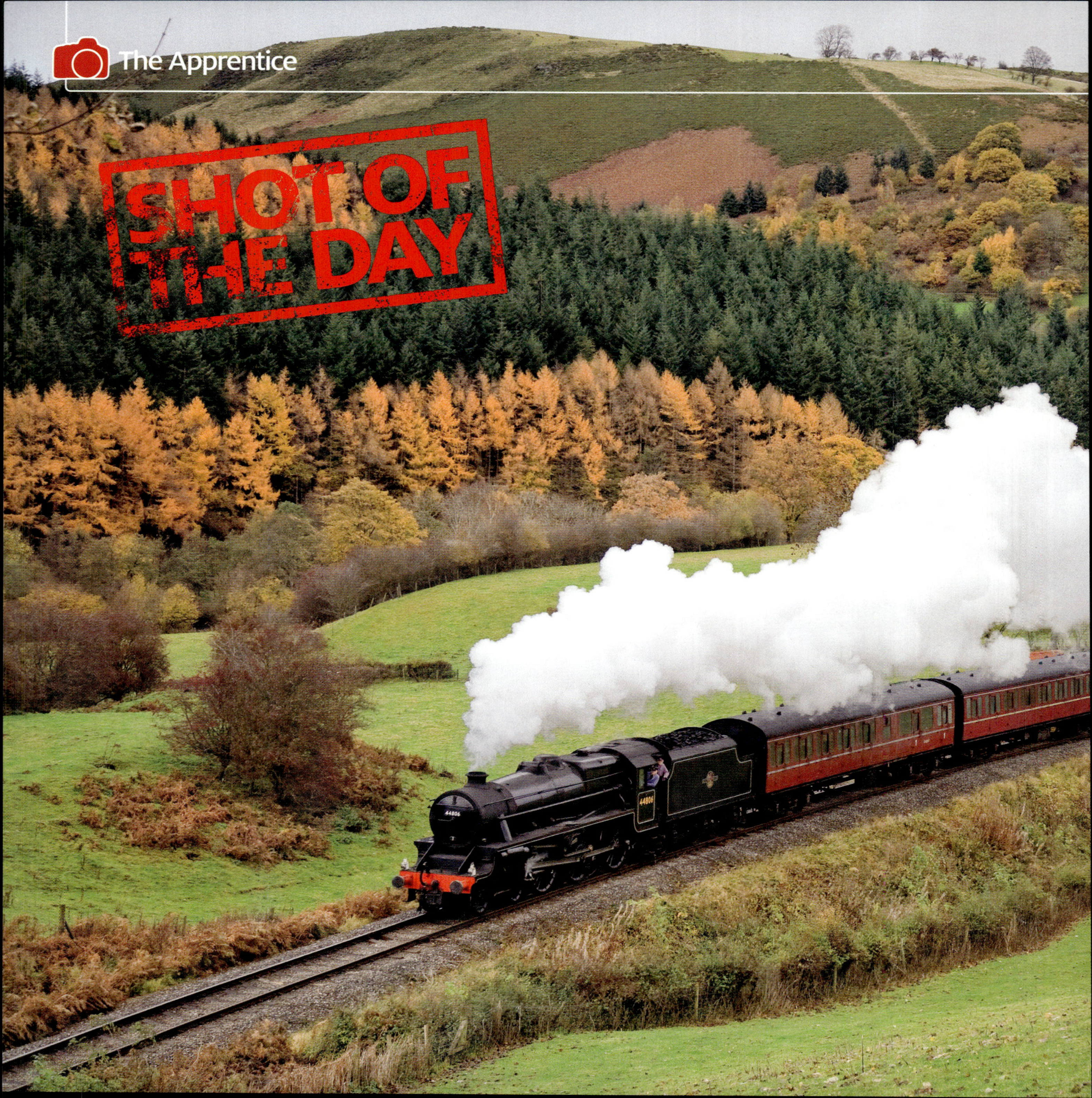

SHOT OF THE DAY

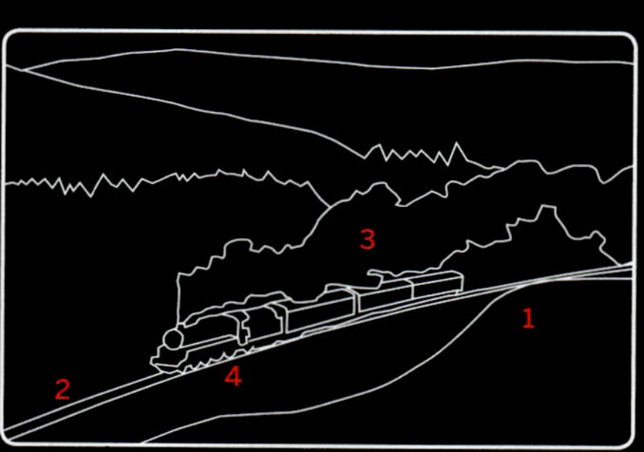

Don's verdict

"I love this picture. It is exactly the sort of shot I had hoped Chris would capture during our day at Llangollen Railway. Steam trains always look their best when they're powering across a landscape, rather than stuck in a station, and despite the weather Chris has done a brilliant job. He has used the dips in the landscape [1] to lead the viewer's eye towards the train, while the track creates a strong, dynamic, diagonal line across the frame [2]. The train's exhaust is well positioned, so that you can see all the carriages within the frame [3], and you can just see the driver and fireman, who are in a perfect position peering off the footplate [4]. A great shot, Chris!"

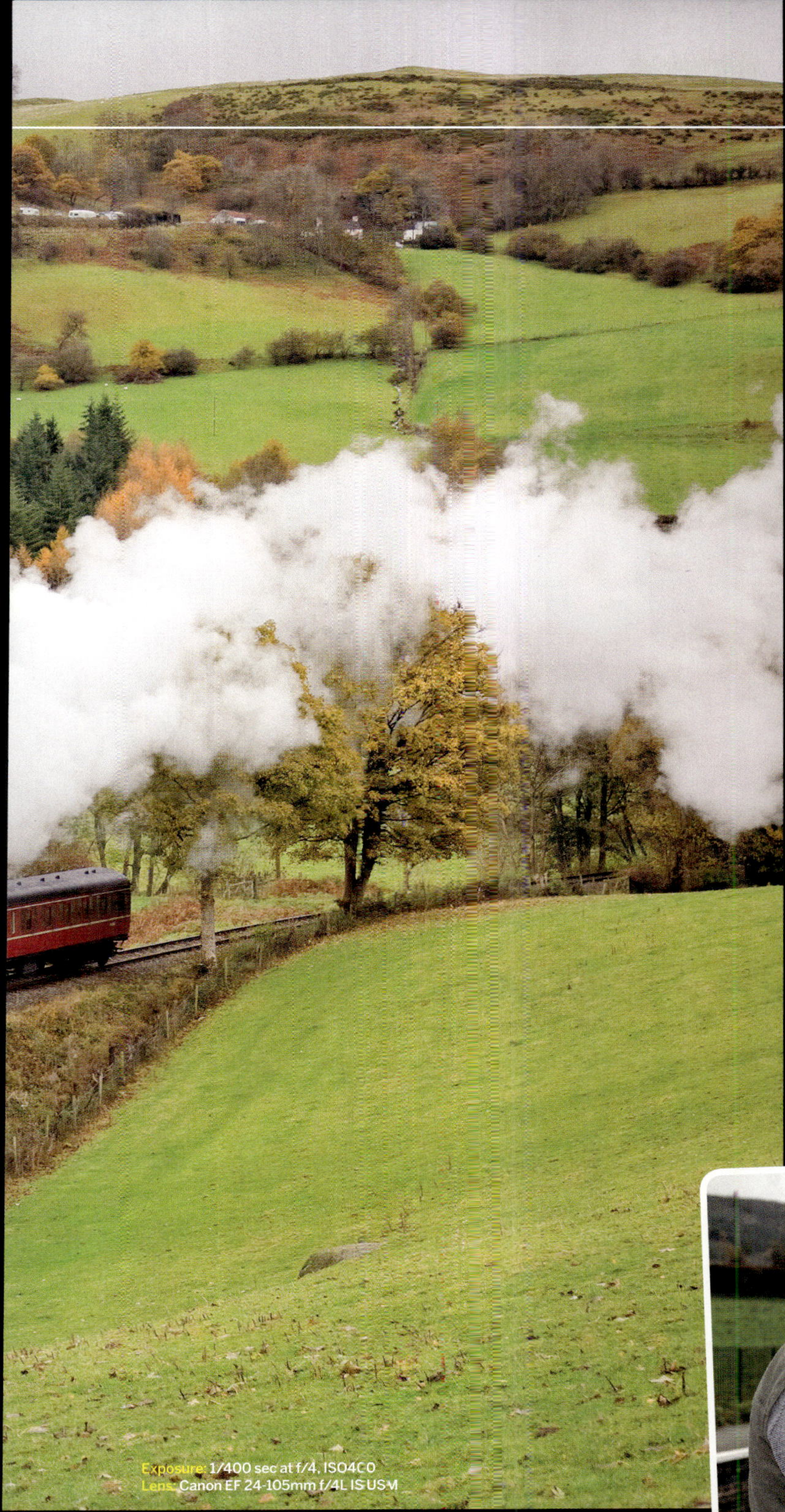

Exposure: 1/400 sec at f/4, ISO400
Lens: Canon EF 24-105mm f/4L IS USM

Chris's comment

"I shot this train from the same position four times. I set up the focus and exposure manually before the train moved into frame. I then fired off a burst of shots to ensure I froze the train in the perfect position. My first shot was slightly overexposed, and on my second attempt the exhaust had dipped down, obscuring some of the train. This shot was taken on the last run." ■

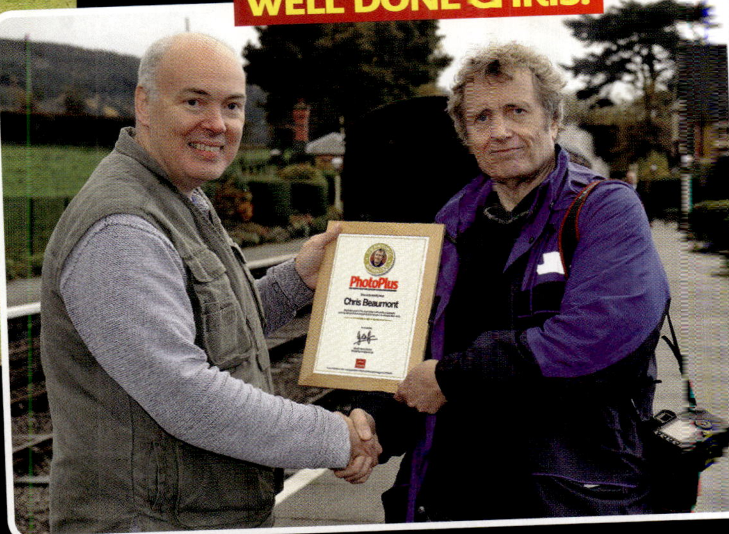

Ticket to ride! Our chuffed Apprentice receives his certificate from associate editor Chris George

"My bird pho really taken

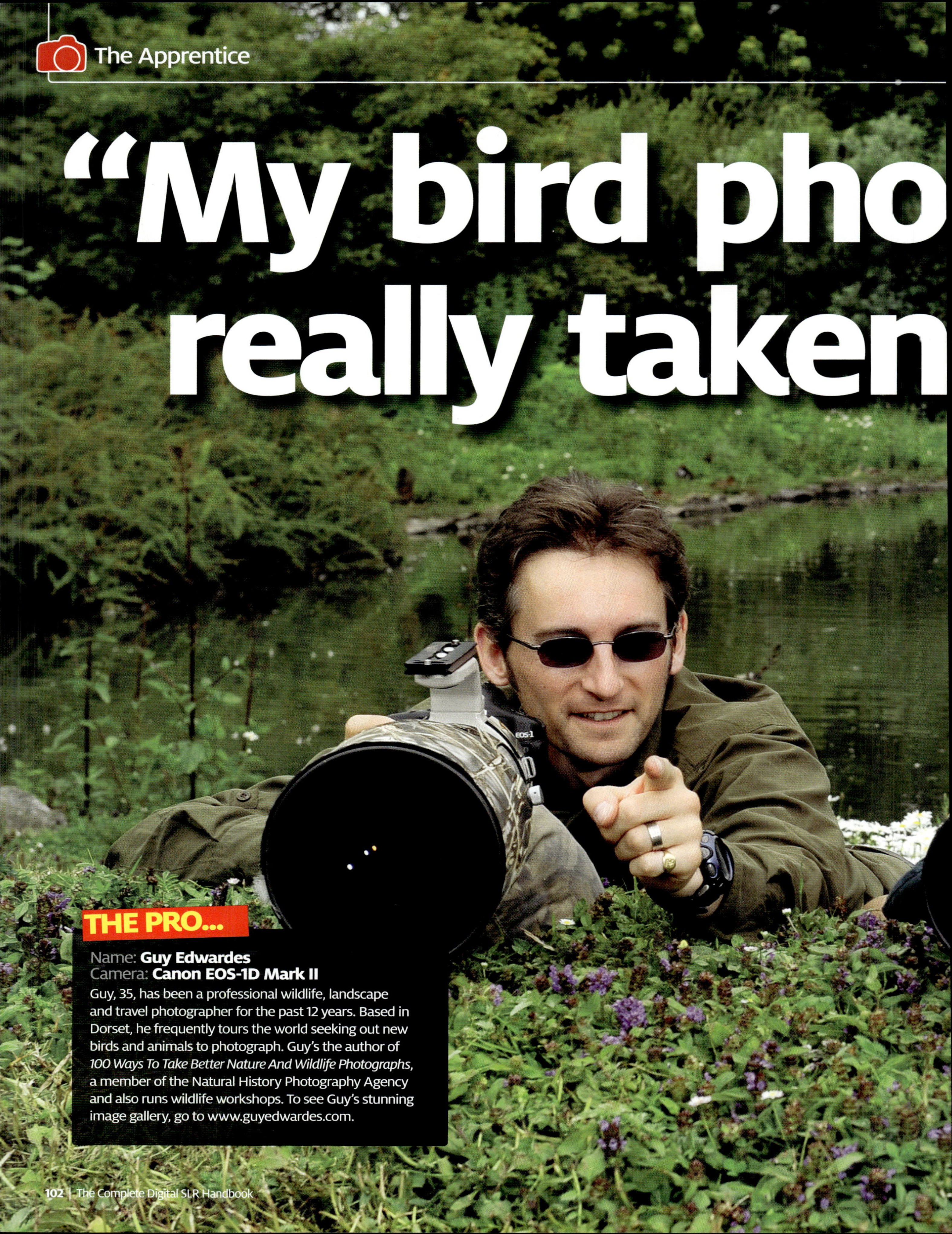

THE PRO...

Name: **Guy Edwardes**
Camera: **Canon EOS-1D Mark II**

Guy, 35, has been a professional wildlife, landscape and travel photographer for the past 12 years. Based in Dorset, he frequently tours the world seeking out new birds and animals to photograph. Guy's the author of *100 Ways To Take Better Nature And Wildlife Photographs*, a member of the Natural History Photography Agency and also runs wildlife workshops. To see Guy's stunning image gallery, go to www.guyedwardes.com.

Words: Peter Travers • Location shots: Jesse Wild (Future)

tography's off!"

Learn how to take beautiful bird photos! Here, our Apprentice visits Slimbridge Wetland Centre to get top pro tuition from wildlife guru Guy Edwardes ▶

THE APPRENTICE...

Name: **Anthony Marston**
Camera: **Canon EOS-1D Mark III**

Anthony is a 52-year-old sales director from Leicester. He's been a keen amateur photographer for over 30 years and often photographed his sons riding BMX bikes and playing rugby. Two years ago he developed an additional interest in wildlife photography. Anthony recently treated himself to a Canon EOS-1D Mk III D-SLR, so is looking for some pro advice to help him take better wildlife shots.

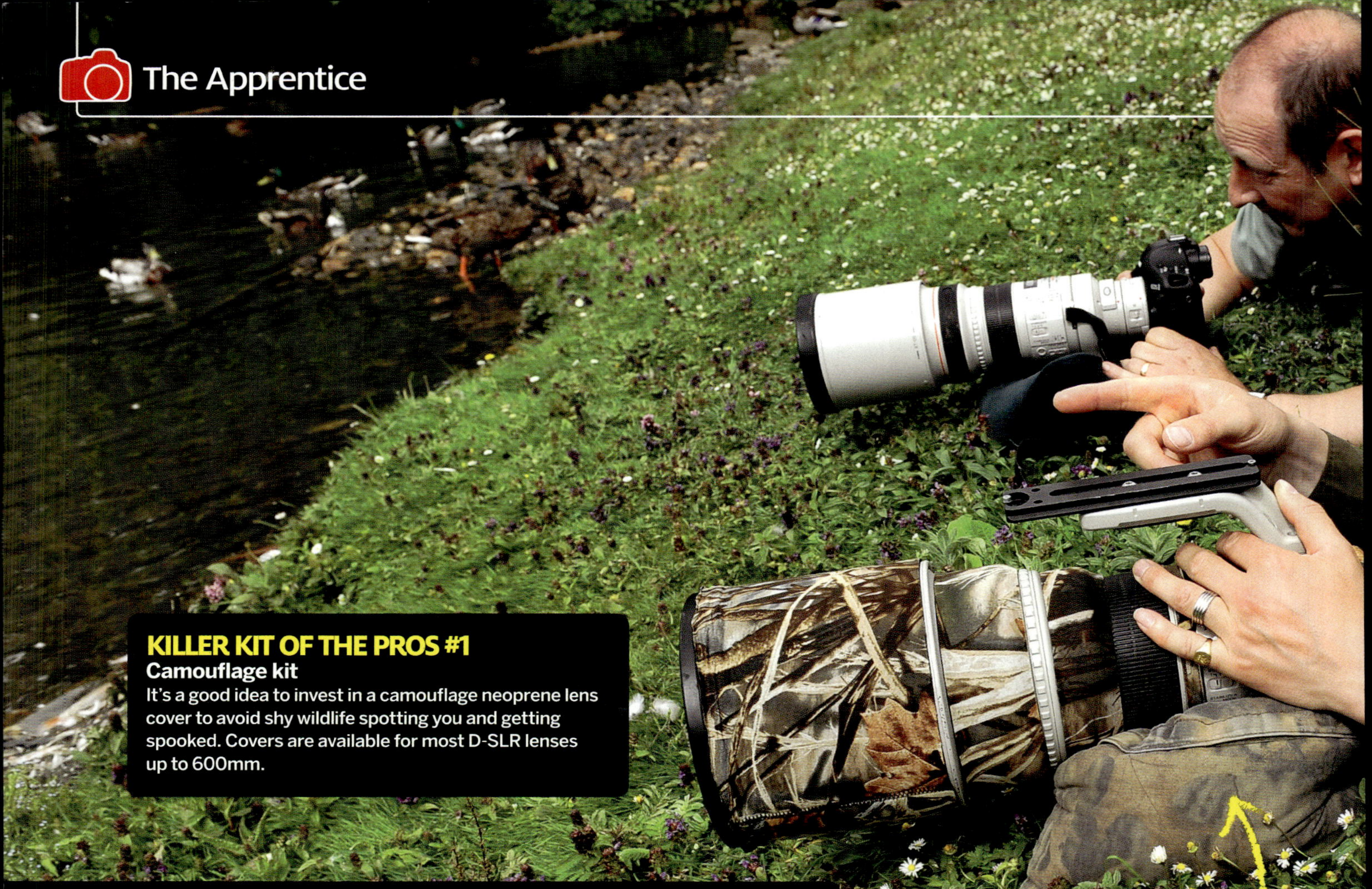

KILLER KIT OF THE PROS #1
Camouflage kit
It's a good idea to invest in a camouflage neoprene lens cover to avoid shy wildlife spotting you and getting spooked. Covers are available for most D-SLR lenses up to 600mm.

KILLER KIT OF THE PROS #2
Bean bag
Guy carries two bean bags on every wildlife shoot. They're perfect for resting telephoto lenses on fence posts, reducing camera shake. Guy's top tip? "Fill the bags with grain so you've always got food to attract the birds."

Technique assessment

Is Anthony ready to capture the wildlife?

After Anthony warmed up with some simple bird shots, using his favoured camera methods, Guy suggested a few ways to improve his D-SLR techniques

WIDER APERTURES

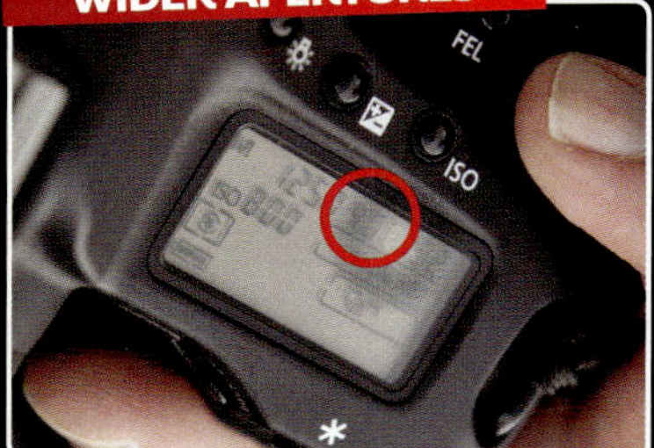

Blow out backgrounds

"Anthony was shooting in Manual mode, but wasn't always using his widest aperture, so some of the backgrounds behind the birds were distracting," says Guy. "Using his 'fast' telephoto lens (a Canon EF 300mm f/2.8L IS) I got him to shoot at f/2.8 or f/4 to blow out the backgrounds and make his subjects more prominent."

FAST SHUTTER SPEEDS

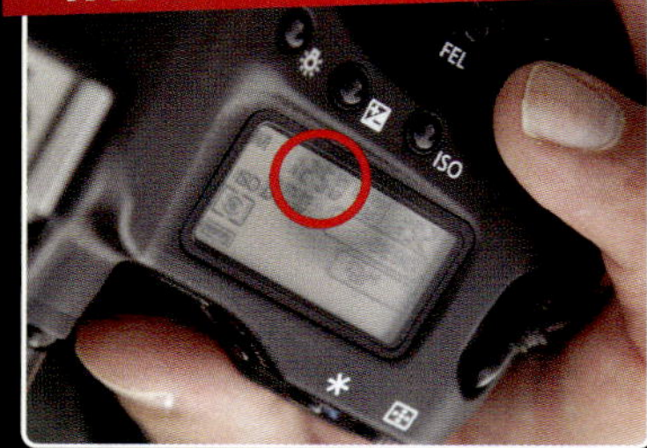

Capture sharp shots

"By using a 'fast' lens you can achieve rapid shutter speeds for sharp shots," says Guy. "I got Anthony to increase the ISO to 400 or 800 as necessary, so that his shutter speeds were around 1/1000 sec. This will be more than fast enough to eliminate camera shake and is also quick enough to freeze the birds' movement."

Guy relies on his ever-faithful pro-level Canon EOS-1D Mark II for his nature photography. It only has a 1.3x crop factor (not 1.6x like the 500D and 50D) and will fire off eight frames per second in motordrive burst mode – ideal for capturing quick-moving birds on the hop. He also carries the following gear:

- Canon EF 400mm f/2.8L IS USM
- Canon EF 400mm f/5.6L USM
- Canon EF 500mm f/4L IS USM
- Canon EF 600mm f/4L IS USM
- Canon EF 16-35mm f/2.8L USM
- Canon EF 70-200mm f/4L IS USM
- Canon EF 24-105mm f/4L IS USM
- Two Canon Speedlite 550EX flashguns, flash bracket, flash extender and off-camera shoe cord
- Two bean bags
- Canon EF 1.4x and 2x Extenders

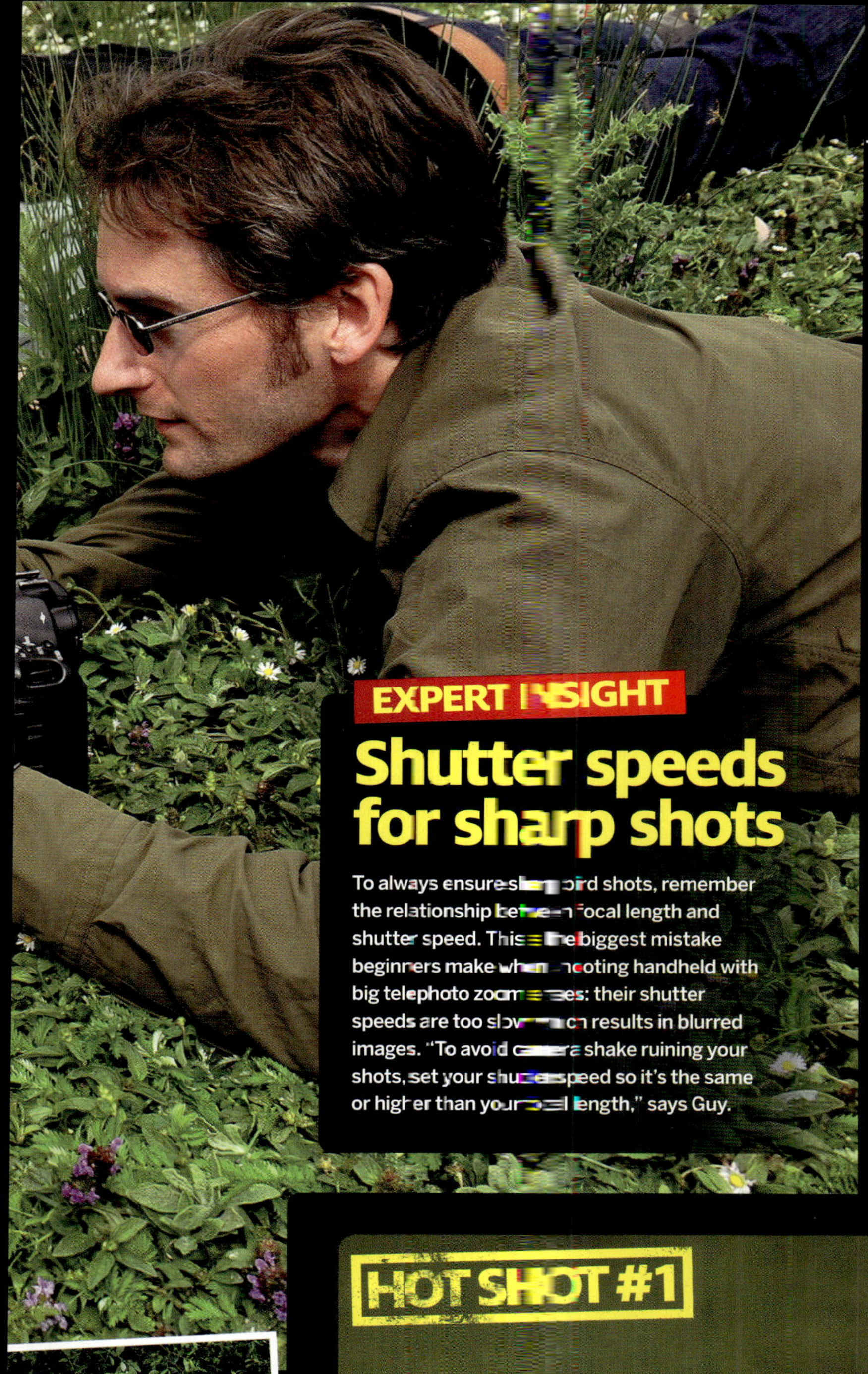

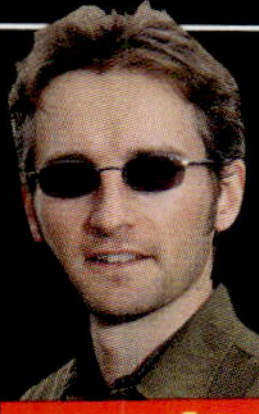

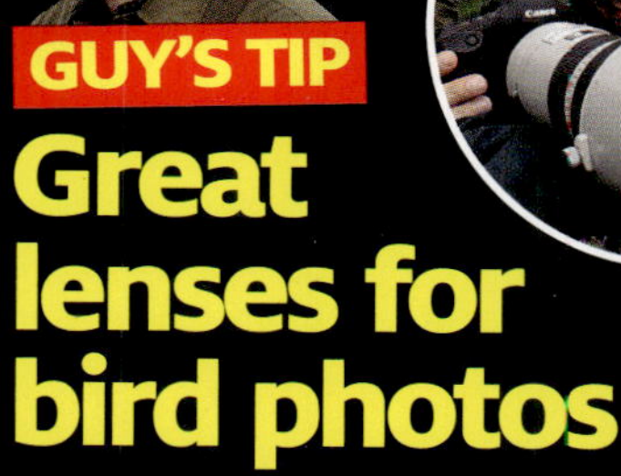

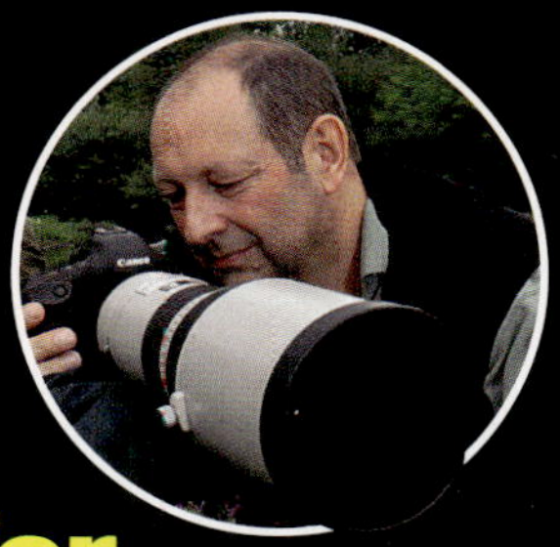

GUY'S TIP

Great lenses for bird photos

For bird photography, Guy recommends investing in the best and biggest telephoto prime (fixed focal length) lenses you can afford. "You'll get the best results with prime lenses as they have the highest quality glass and you'll be able to get close-ups even when birds are relatively far away," he says. "Also, when you're using wide apertures they blur backgrounds more, so your subjects will really stand out."

Anthony's comment

"Not a bad start for me! For this shot of a male American Wigeon, Guy suggested that I get down to the water's edge and the duck's eye level, which meant we were lying on concrete! I used my 300mm lens for a good close-up composition of the duck and its reflection, and used a wide aperture of f/4 so I could blur the background. With the ISO at 400, the resulting shutter speed was 1/1600 sec – easily fast enough to avoid any camera shake and freeze the duck's movement on the water."

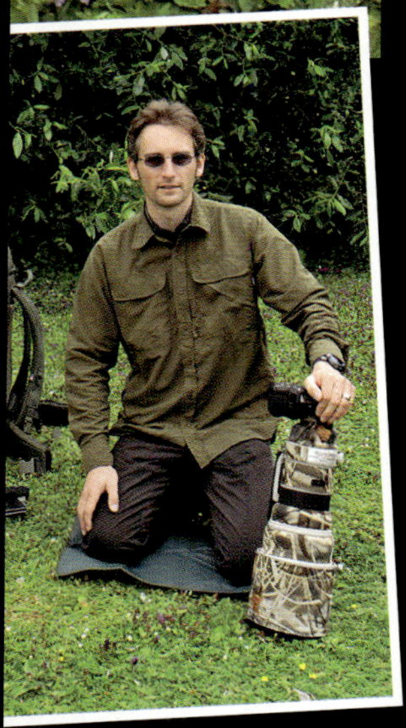

EXPERT INSIGHT

Shutter speeds for sharp shots

To always ensure sharp bird shots, remember the relationship between focal length and shutter speed. This is the biggest mistake beginners make when shooting handheld with big telephoto zoom lenses: their shutter speeds are too slow, which results in blurred images. "To avoid camera shake ruining your shots, set your shutter speed so it's the same or higher than your focal length," says Guy.

HOT SHOT #1

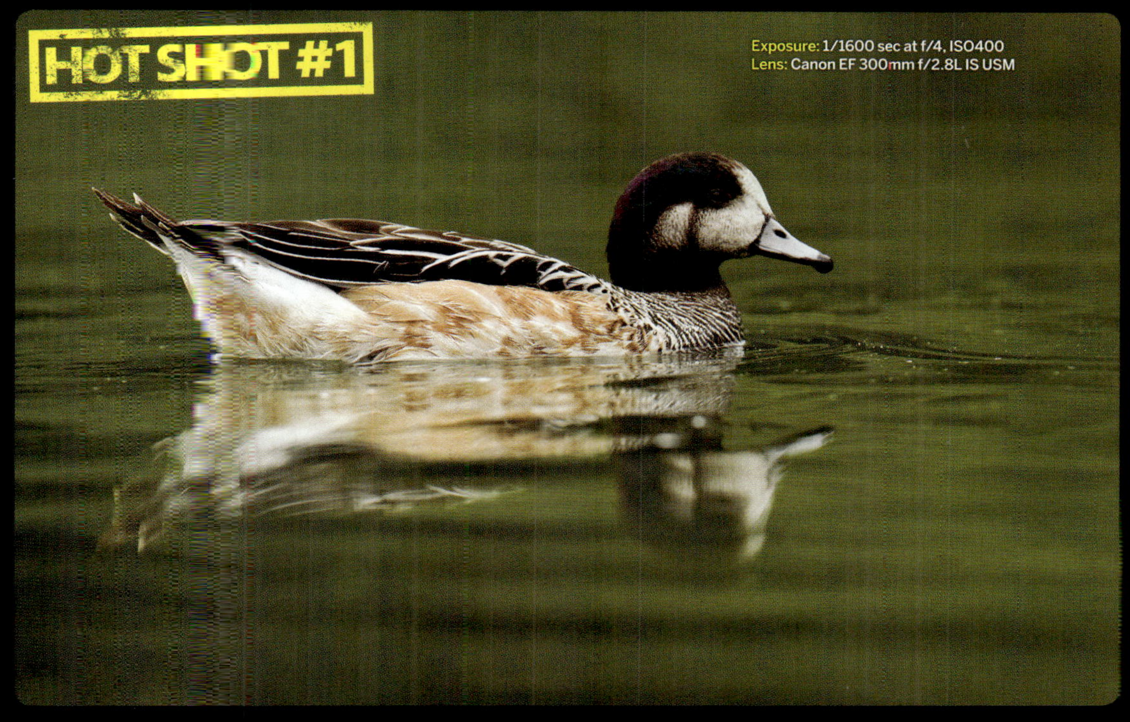

Exposure: 1/1600 sec at f/4, ISO400
Lens: Canon EF 300mm f/2.8L IS USM

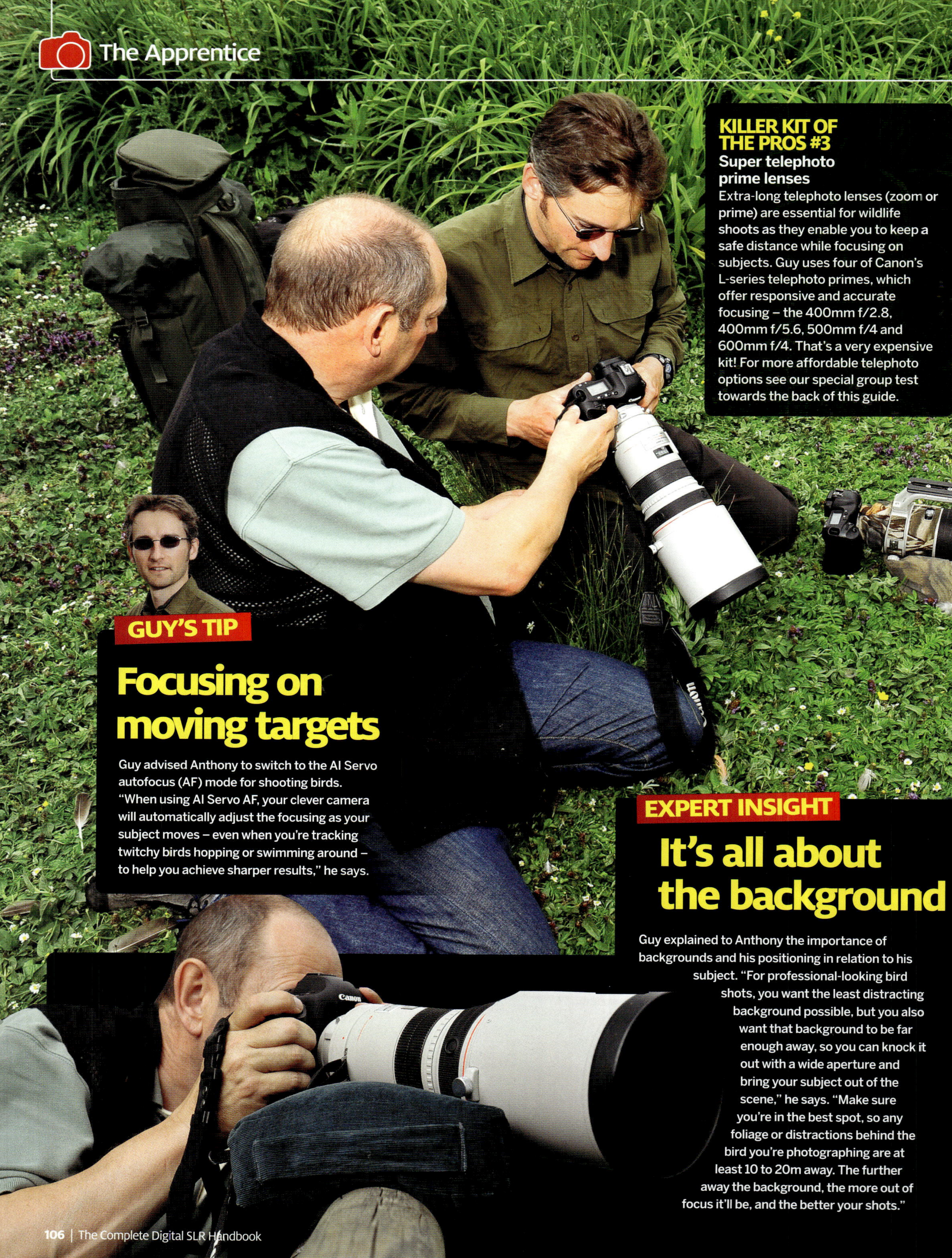

KILLER KIT OF THE PROS #3
Super telephoto prime lenses

Extra-long telephoto lenses (zoom or prime) are essential for wildlife shoots as they enable you to keep a safe distance while focusing on subjects. Guy uses four of Canon's L-series telephoto primes, which offer responsive and accurate focusing – the 400mm f/2.8, 400mm f/5.6, 500mm f/4 and 600mm f/4. That's a very expensive kit! For more affordable telephoto options see our special group test towards the back of this guide.

GUY'S TIP

Focusing on moving targets

Guy advised Anthony to switch to the AI Servo autofocus (AF) mode for shooting birds. "When using AI Servo AF, your clever camera will automatically adjust the focusing as your subject moves – even when you're tracking twitchy birds hopping or swimming around – to help you achieve sharper results," he says.

EXPERT INSIGHT

It's all about the background

Guy explained to Anthony the importance of backgrounds and his positioning in relation to his subject. "For professional-looking bird shots, you want the least distracting background possible, but you also want that background to be far enough away, so you can knock it out with a wide aperture and bring your subject out of the scene," he says. "Make sure you're in the best spot, so any foliage or distractions behind the bird you're photographing are at least 10 to 20m away. The further away the background, the more out of focus it'll be, and the better your shots."

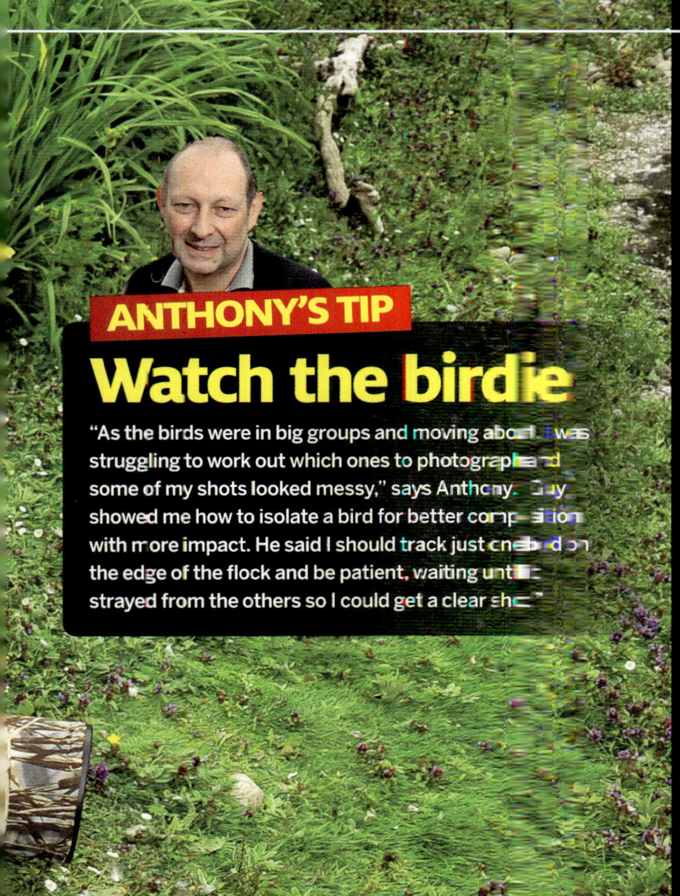

ANTHONY'S TIP

Watch the birdie

"As the birds were in big groups and moving about, I was struggling to work out which ones to photograph and some of my shots looked messy," says Anthony. "Guy showed me how to isolate a bird for better composition with more impact. He said I should track just one bird on the edge of the flock and be patient, waiting until it strayed from the others so I could get a clear shot."

KILLER KIT OF THE PROS #4

Low-level tripod

Some wildlife photographers rely on monopods but, as Guy explains, "you can't get down low enough with a monopod, so I prefer my tripod." Guy favours Gitzo G5540LS tripod legs and a G1380 Fluid Head. It's sturdy enough for hefty telephoto lenses and also collapses so you can use it at a low level. Not all tripods enable you to remove the central column and collapse the whole thing down, so try before you buy to avoid disappointment.

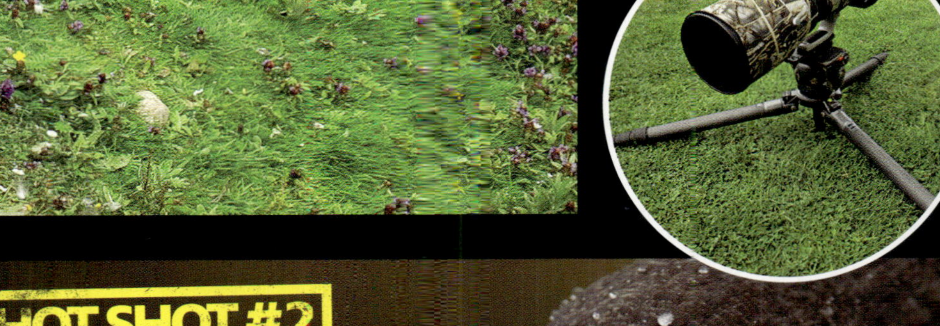

Anthony's comment

"We were lucky to get such close-up shots of this beautiful black swan. He wasn't shy at all about pecking grain from our hands, so Guy fed him while I knelt down to his eye level. Composing the shot, I used my 300mm lens with a 1.4x Extender (to achieve a combined focal length of 420mm) to focus on just his head, beady red eyes and bright red beak. The drop of water from his beak – which has been frozen in time thanks to my 1/1600 sec shutter speed – really adds to the overall shot."

HOT SHOT #2

Exposure: 1/1600 sec at f/4, ISO500
Lens: Canon EF 300mm f/2.8L IS USM + Canon EF 1.4x Extender

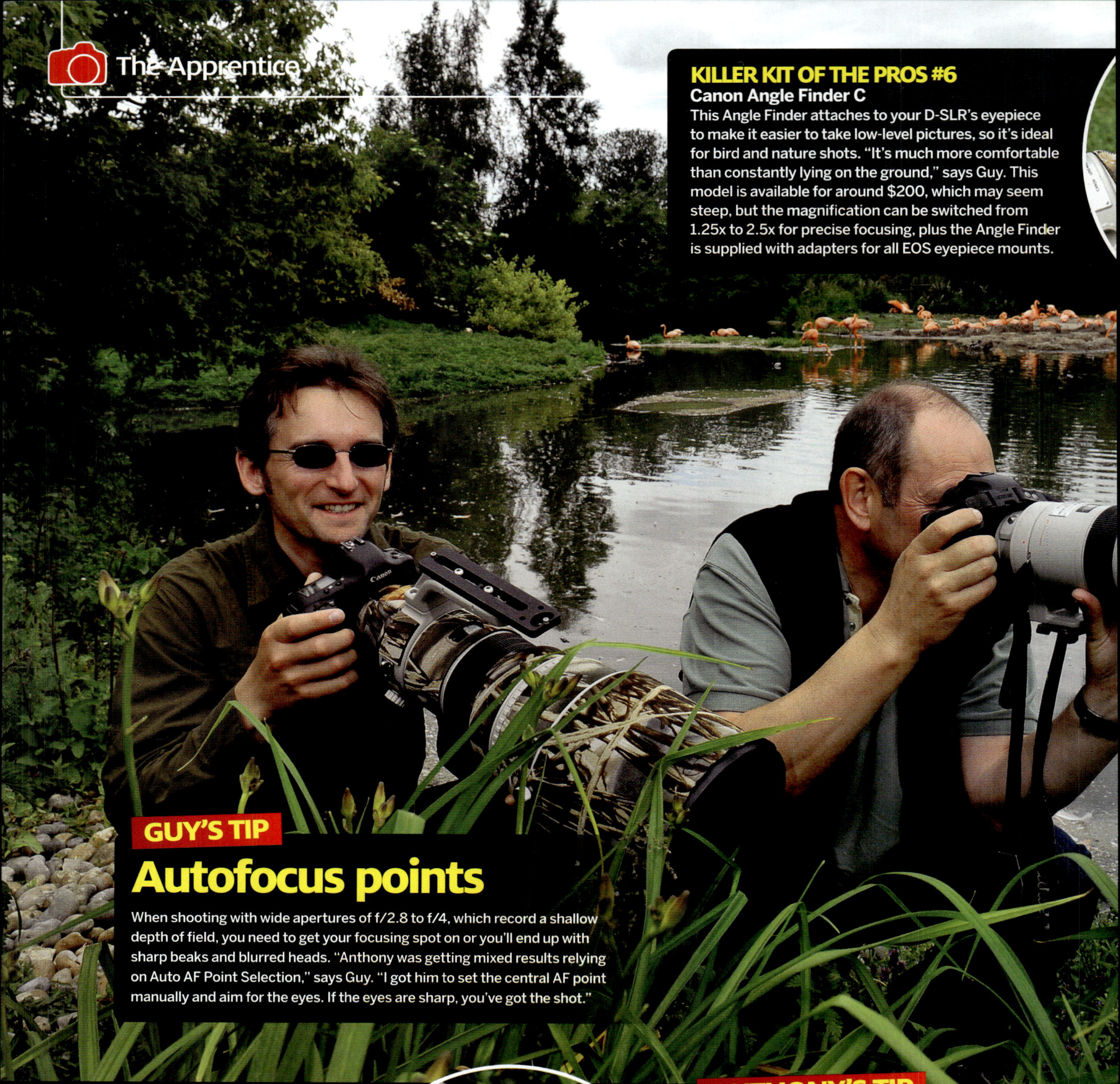

KILLER KIT OF THE PROS #6

Canon Angle Finder C

This Angle Finder attaches to your D-SLR's eyepiece to make it easier to take low-level pictures, so it's ideal for bird and nature shots. "It's much more comfortable than constantly lying on the ground," says Guy. This model is available for around $200, which may seem steep, but the magnification can be switched from 1.25x to 2.5x for precise focusing, plus the Angle Finder is supplied with adapters for all EOS eyepiece mounts.

GUY'S TIP

Autofocus points

When shooting with wide apertures of f/2.8 to f/4, which record a shallow depth of field, you need to get your focusing spot on or you'll end up with sharp beaks and blurred heads. "Anthony was getting mixed results relying on Auto AF Point Selection," says Guy. "I got him to set the central AF point manually and aim for the eyes. If the eyes are sharp, you've got the shot."

KILLER KIT OF THE PROS #5

Lens extenders

Guy encouraged Anthony to use his Canon EF 300mm f/2.8L lens with an EF 1.4x Extender. This increased the lens's focal length to 420mm so he could get closer to the birds. "This also reduces your widest available aperture to f/4," says Guy, "so Anthony needed to up the ISO a little more."

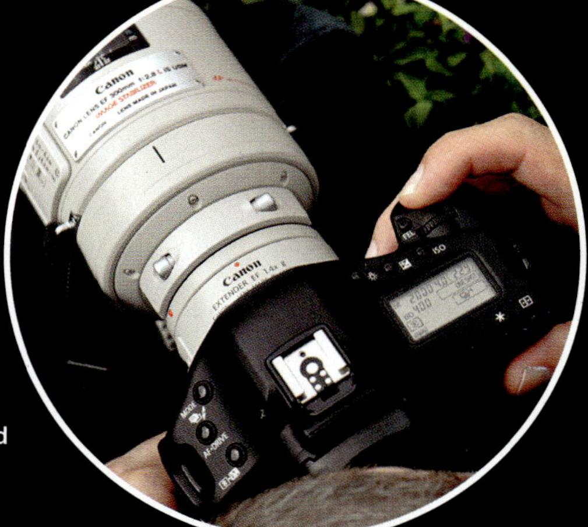

ANTHONY'S TIP

Shoot at high speeds

Guy's Canon EOS-1D Mark II will fire off eight frames per second in Continuous Shooting Drive mode, while Anthony's newer EOS-1D Mark III manages ten. The higher the speed, the better the chance of getting the shot. "Birds are constantly on the move, so to increase my odds of capturing them I used my 1D's super-fast Continuous Shooting mode. It's also great fun firing off a machine gun-like burst of shots!" says Anthony.

HOT SHOT #3

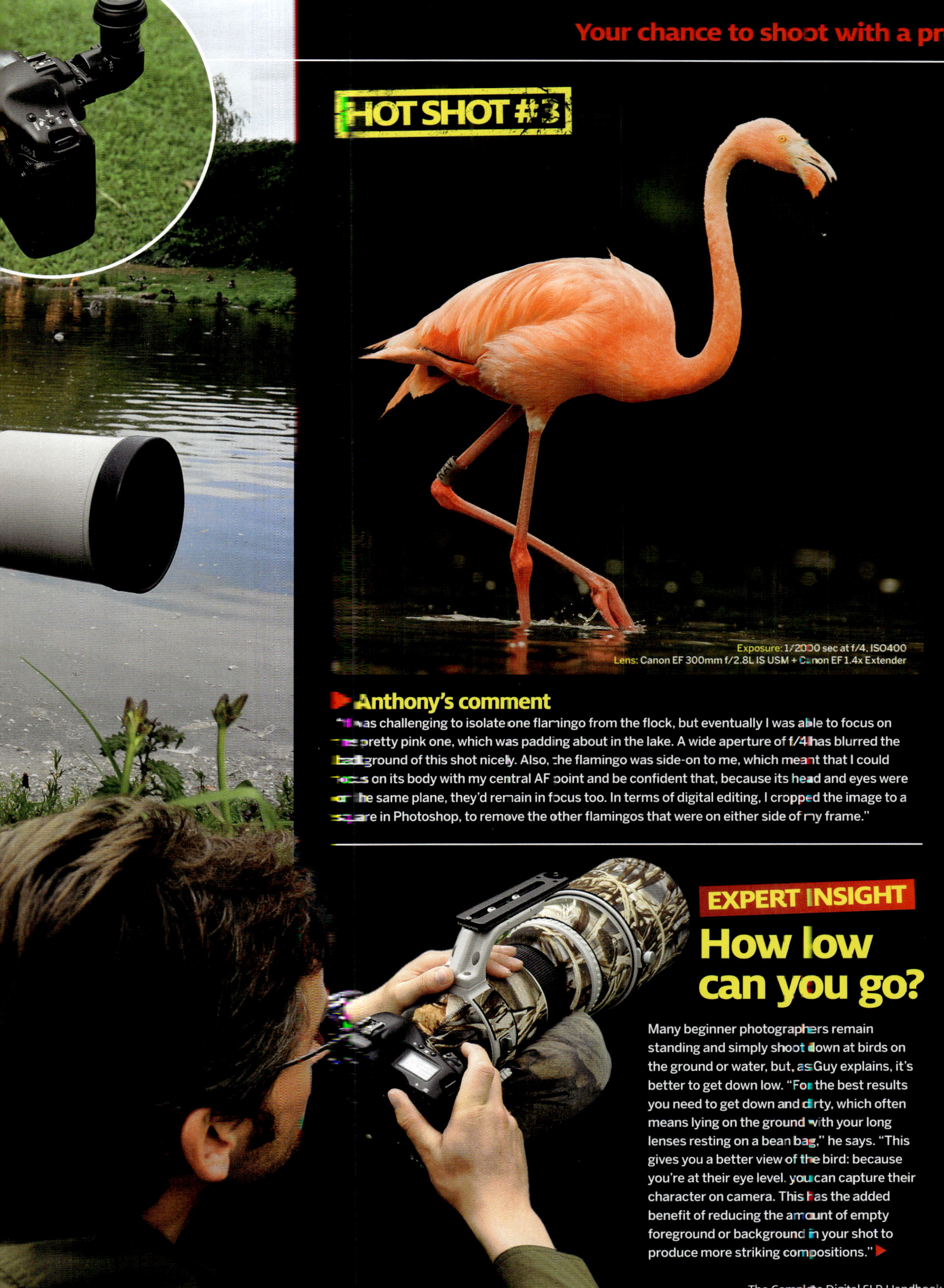

Exposure: 1/2000 sec at f/4, ISO400
Lens: Canon EF 300mm f/2.8L IS USM + Canon EF 1.4x Extender

Anthony's comment

"It was challenging to isolate one flamingo from the flock, but eventually I was able to focus on this pretty pink one, which was padding about in the lake. A wide aperture of f/4 has blurred the background of this shot nicely. Also, the flamingo was side-on to me, which meant that I could focus on its body with my central AF point and be confident that, because its head and eyes were on the same plane, they'd remain in focus too. In terms of digital editing, I cropped the image to a square in Photoshop, to remove the other flamingos that were on either side of my frame."

EXPERT INSIGHT

How low can you go?

Many beginner photographers remain standing and simply shoot down at birds on the ground or water, but, as Guy explains, it's better to get down low. "For the best results you need to get down and dirty, which often means lying on the ground with your long lenses resting on a bean bag," he says. "This gives you a better view of the bird: because you're at their eye level, you can capture their character on camera. This has the added benefit of reducing the amount of empty foreground or background in your shot to produce more striking compositions."

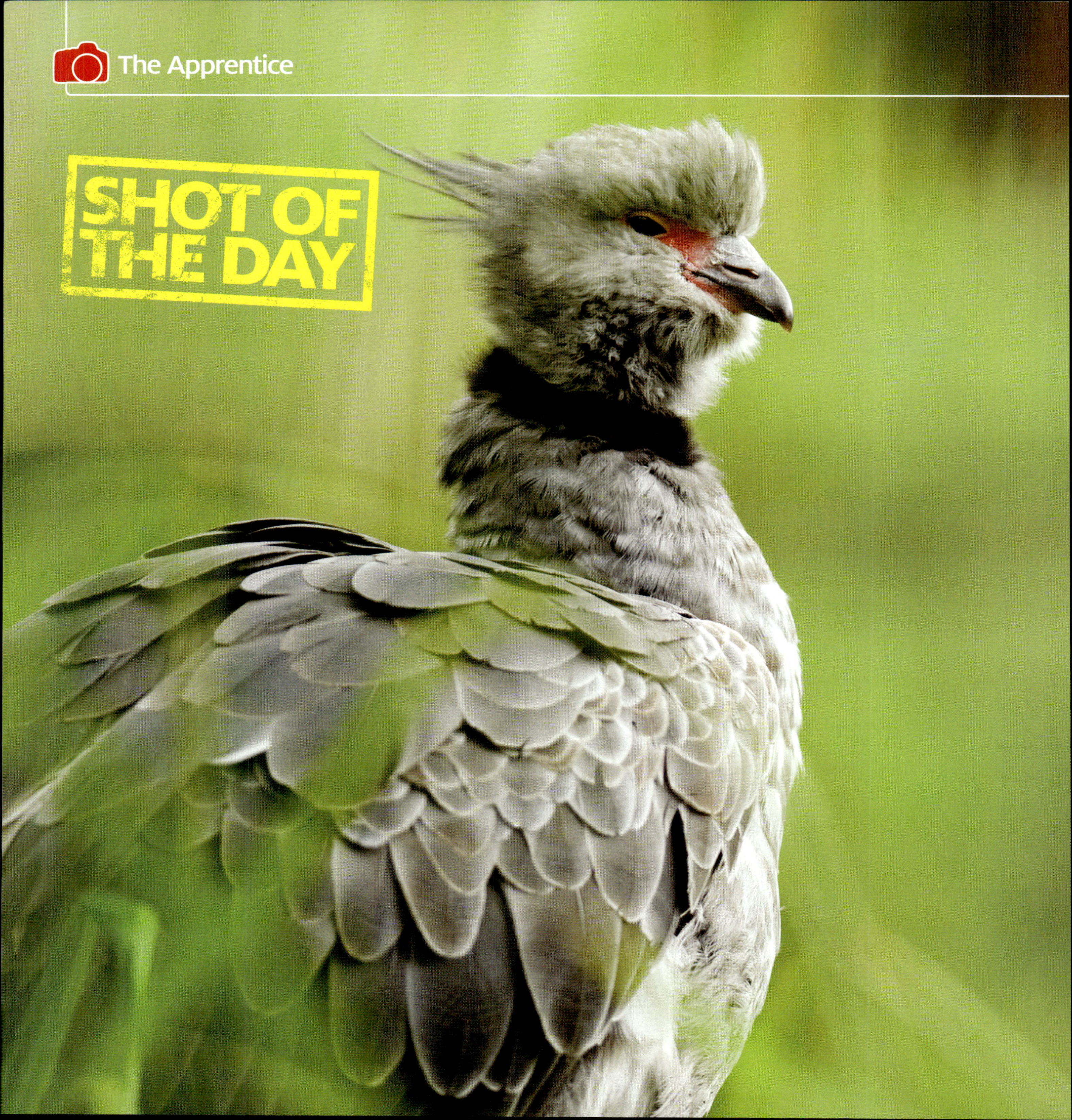

SHOT OF THE DAY

Guy's Verdict

"This is a wonderful photo. Anthony's captured the character of this Southern Screamer while using several techniques he learned throughout the day. By using a wide aperture he's blown out any foliage in the foreground [1] and vegetation in the background [2], which really makes the bird 'pop' out of the picture. The composition is lovely: by applying the rule of thirds and positioning the bird to the left [3], he's created a photo with breathing space and a peaceful feeling. His focusing is bang on, too, which isn't easy when done through a hedge! By using an AF point in the top-left of the frame, Anthony's focused on the bird's head and eyes perfectly [4]. Good skills!"

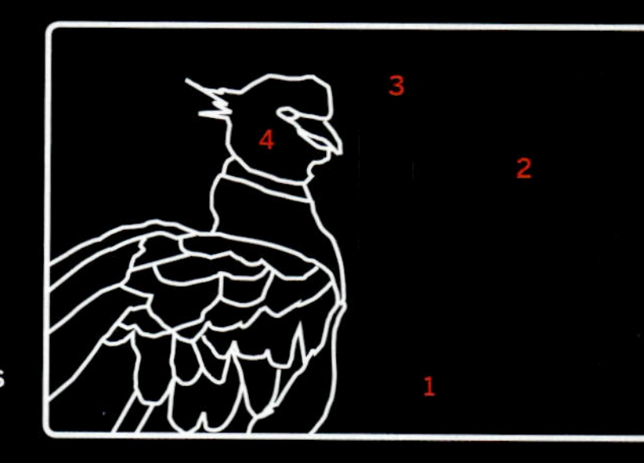

Exposure 1/1000 sec at f/2.8, ISO500
Lens Canon EF 300mm f/2.8L IS USM

Anthony's comment

"We spotted a pair of Southern Screamers through a gap in a hedge. This provided a unique, atmospheric composition and also meant we could photograph them from a distance without disturbing them. I used my 300mm lens at a wide aperture to knock out the foliage, focused on the bird's head and fired away. I like this charming shot of the lone bird just turning its head to give us a cursory glance." ■

WELL DONE ANTHONY!

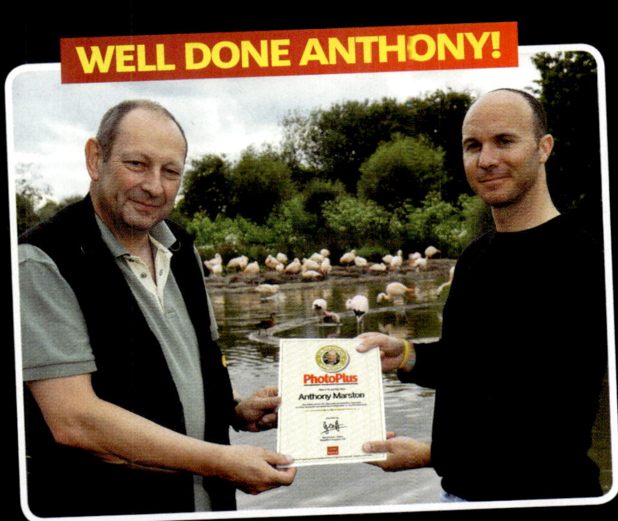

He's earned his wings! Anthony picks up his Apprentice certificate from deputy editor, Peter Travers

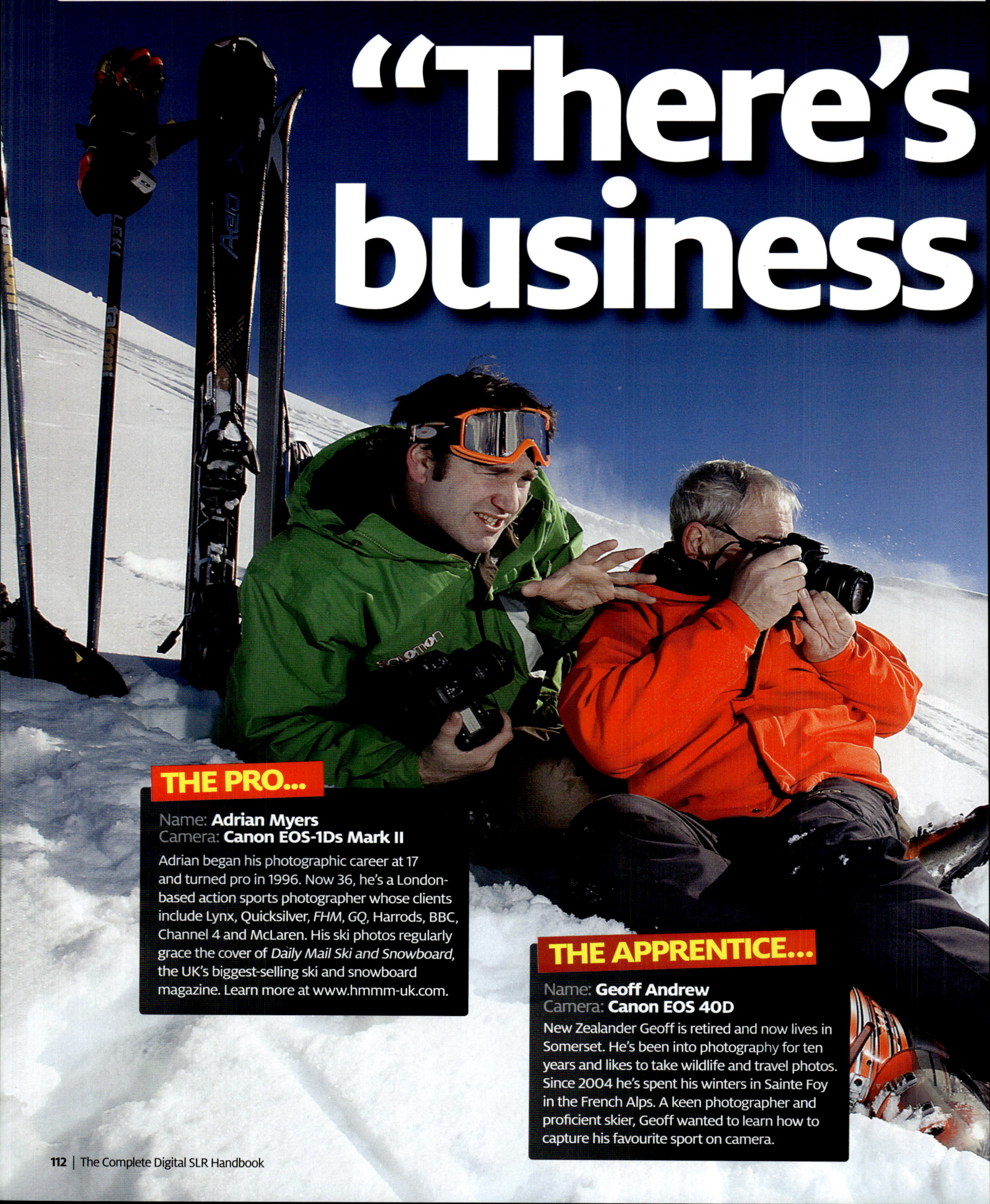

"There's business

THE PRO...

Name: **Adrian Myers**
Camera: **Canon EOS-1Ds Mark II**

Adrian began his photographic career at 17 and turned pro in 1996. Now 36, he's a London-based action sports photographer whose clients include Lynx, Quicksilver, *FHM*, *GQ*, Harrods, BBC, Channel 4 and McLaren. His ski photos regularly grace the cover of *Daily Mail Ski and Snowboard*, the UK's biggest-selling ski and snowboard magazine. Learn more at www.hmmm-uk.com.

THE APPRENTICE...

Name: **Geoff Andrew**
Camera: **Canon EOS 40D**

New Zealander Geoff is retired and now lives in Somerset. He's been into photography for ten years and likes to take wildlife and travel photos. Since 2004 he's spent his winters in Sainte Foy in the French Alps. A keen photographer and proficient skier, Geoff wanted to learn how to capture his favourite sport on camera.

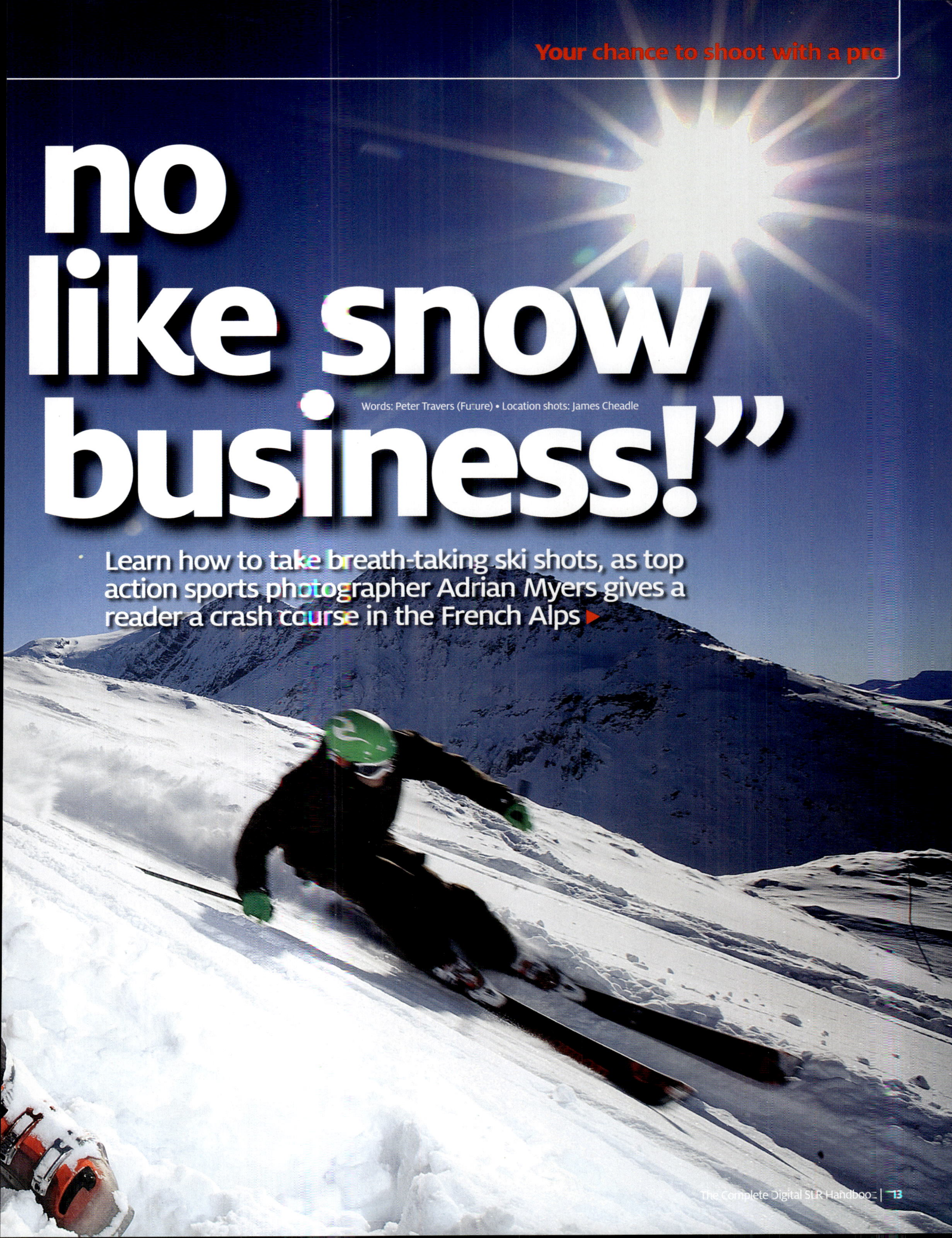

no like snow business!”

Words: Peter Travers (Future) • Location shots: James Cheadle

Learn how to take breath-taking ski shots, as top action sports photographer Adrian Myers gives a reader a crash course in the French Alps ▸

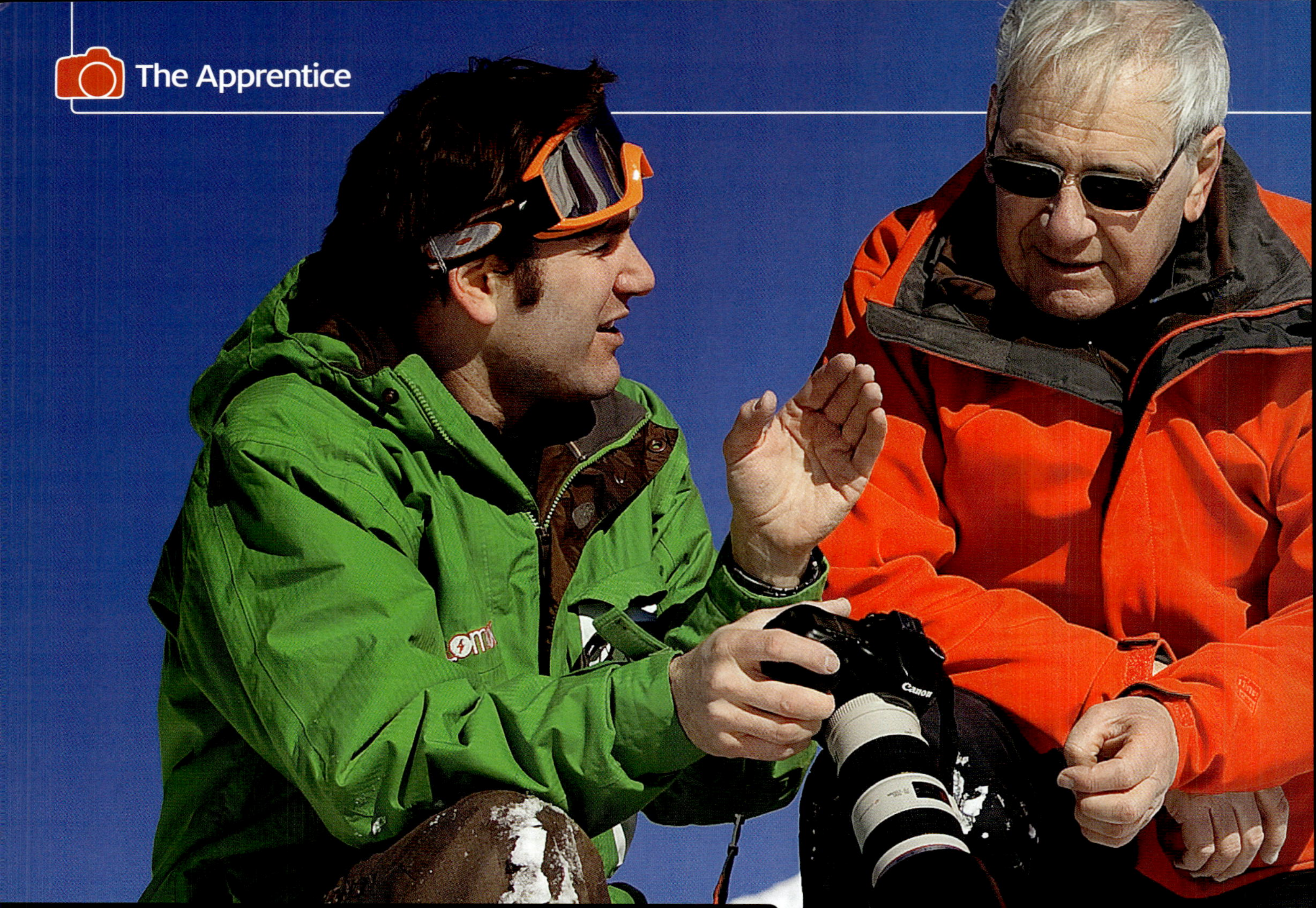

Technique assessment

Is Geoff ready to freeze the action?

After Geoff had literally warmed up and taken a few ski shots, Adrian noticed a few ways he could improve his chances of better shots...

INCREASE YOUR CHANCES

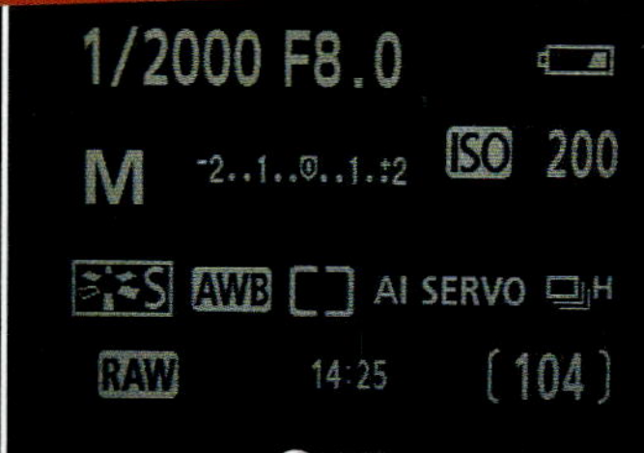

Switch Drive modes

"I got Geoff to switch his Drive mode to High-speed Continuous," says Adrian. "This way his SLR would take 6.5 frames per second and he could take multiple shots every time the skier whizzed past. He could then choose the best image later on."

GET FOCUSED

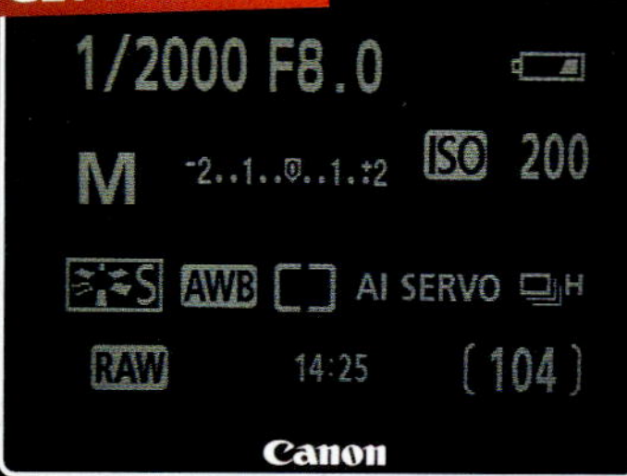

Switch to AI Servo AF

"I changed Geoff's AF mode to AI Servo, which is great for following moving targets when the focusing distance changes," says Adrian. "I showed Geoff how to half-press the shutter button to focus continuously and his results improved instantly."

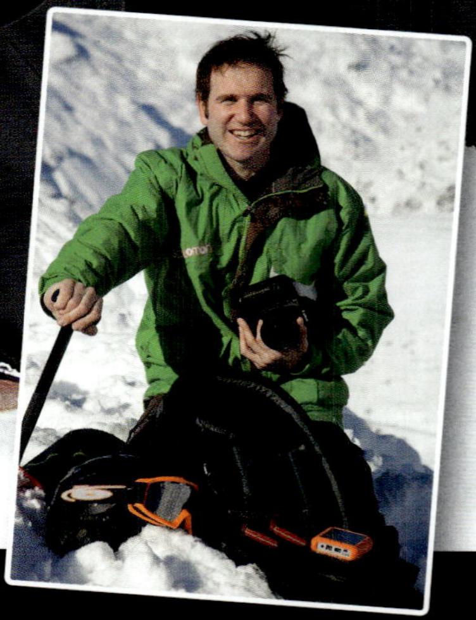

Adrian relies on his pro-level full-frame Canon EOS-1Ds Mark II to capture his stunning action sports images. He also carries an EOS 5D as a back-up, as well as the following kit:

- Canon EF 20mm f/2.8 USM
- Canon EF 70-200mm f/2.8L IS USM
- Canon EF 24-105mm f/4L IS USM
- 4x4Gb, 4x2Gb and 6x1Gb Lexar CompactFlash cards
- Two 500Gb LaCie Rugged portable hard disks

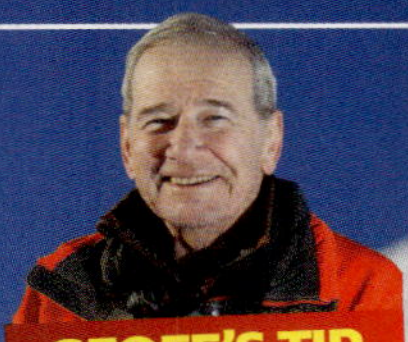

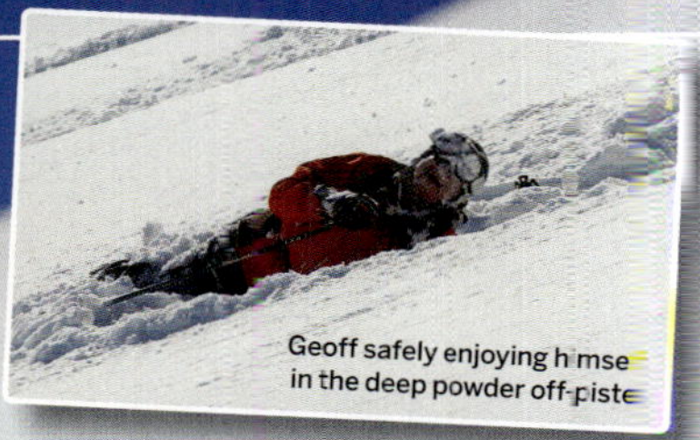

GEOFF'S TIP

Safety first!

Geoff safely enjoying himself in the deep powder off-piste

As an experienced skier, apprentice Geoff offers some sound advice: "Don't head out in bad weather, always tell someone where you're going and what time you'll be back, don't go out alone if possible and take a mobile phone with the mountain rescue number stored. You should also wear a transceiver (see below).

"It's best to wear plenty of layers, a hat, gloves and warm, windproof and waterproof clothing. It's better to wear too many layers (then take one off) than to go cold on the slopes. Be smart and you can have fun safely!"

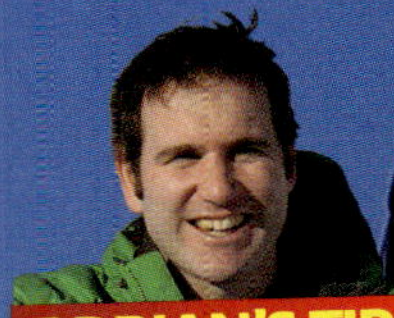

ADRIAN'S TIP

Be a walking wardrobe!

"On important shoots, I'll wear one of the model's outfits up to the location and then we'll swap clothes half-way through the shoot so I can get another set of images with them in different coloured gear. It's surprising how different photos can look with a quick change of clothing!"

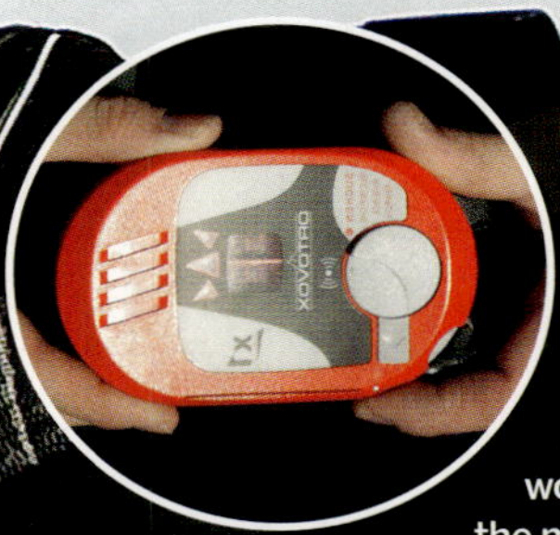

KILLER KIT OF THE PROS #1

Avalanche transceiver

"I always carry my transceiver," says Adrian. "It's just not worth taking a chance on the mountains. On our shoot our ski model Chris, Geoff and myself all wore one. I'm an experienced skier, but when shooting off-piste I could still get caught in an avalanche. Transceivers greatly increase your chance of survival as they send a signal that helps rescuers accurately pinpoint buried avalanche victims."

HOT SHOT #1

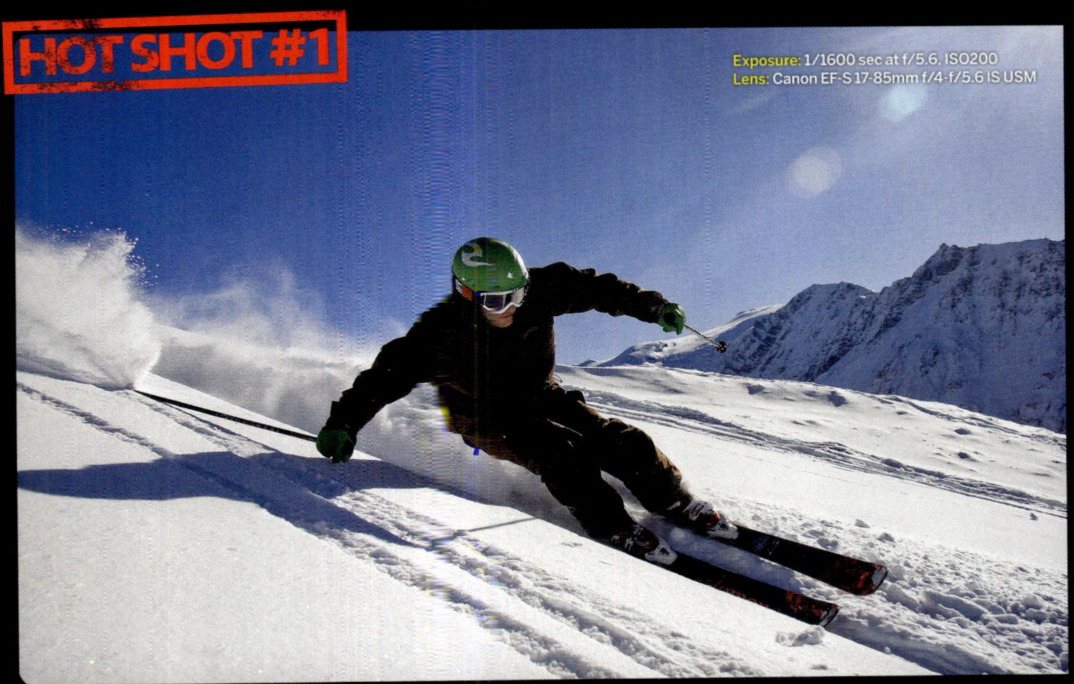

Exposure: 1/1600 sec at f/5.6, ISO200
Lens: Canon EF-S 17-85mm f/4-f/5.6 IS USM

Geoff's comment

"Taken at the start of the shoot, I'm pretty pleased with this shot. It shows both speed and movement and I'm happy with the exposure and focus. The sun was on our right-hand side and I tried to shoot using my wide-angle lens to fit the skier and the trailing ski pole into the frame as he came past and kicked up snow. Adrian pointed out that having the whole sun in the top right was distracting so, following his advice, I cropped the shot in Photoshop to reduce the sun's impact."

EXPERT INSIGHT

Use a wide-angle lens!

"When we started taking ski shots, I advised Geoff that it would be easier to get his eye in by shooting with his wide-angle lens (EF-S 17-85mm IS) at a wider focal length of around 17mm or 20mm to make sure he captured all, rather than half, of the skier in the shot," says Adrian. "He can then simply crop the image slightly in Photoshop afterwards if there's a little too much space around the subject."

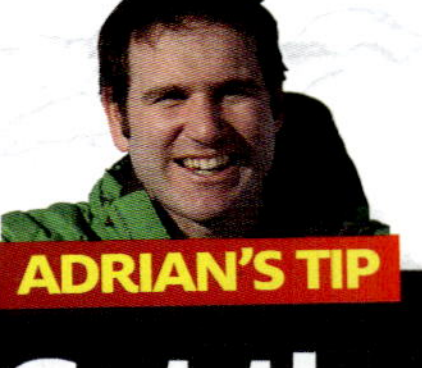

ADRIAN'S TIP

Get the whitest whites

Left to its own devices, your digital D-SLR will try to turn expanses of white snow to grey because it thinks the scene is over-exposed. There's an easy way to get around this. "Shooting in Manual mode, I simply take a meter reading of the snow – I do this by pointing my camera down at the snow near where I'm shooting, autofocusing on the snow and taking a shot," says Adrian. "I do this at, say, f/16, then open up the aperture by two full stops to f/8 to expose correctly for pure white snow."

While we're on the subject of snow, don't venture far off the marked ski runs unless you know the area and are sure there's no avalanche risk. "We were only ever 50-100ft from the smoothed-out and safe ski runs. You won't need to trek far from the beaten track to find good spots with fresh, untouched snow," says Adrian. "Look near the tops of the lifts, where the sun will be, and along the sides of the slopes."

KILLER KIT OF THE PROS #2

Walkie talkies

"Walkie talkies are essential if you need to communicate with the ski model you're photographing. You'll find they're often out of sight or earshot when getting a run-up to your chosen photo spot, so you can use the walkie talkies to let your subject know you're ready to take the shot."

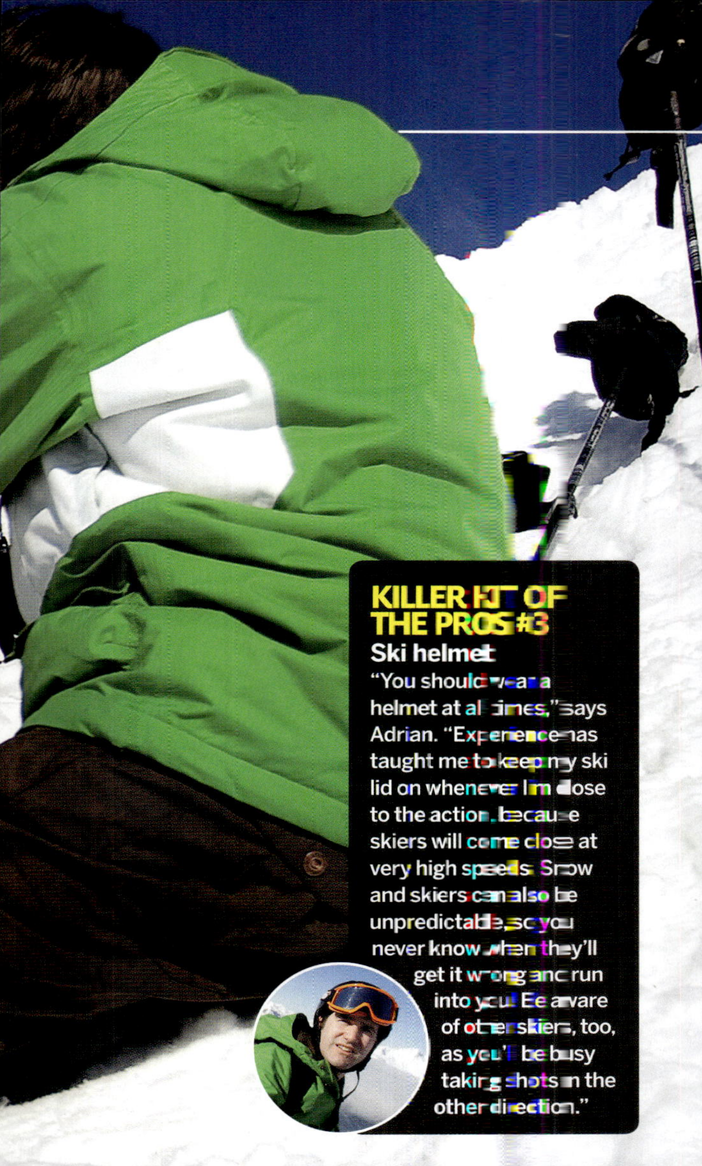

Pole positions

Canon pro Adrian travels the world to take photos of winter sports. Here he shares three of his favourite destinations

▶ Salbach, Austria

"I took this image for a *Daily Mail Ski and Snowboard* cover with my Canon 70-200mm f/2.8L, using a focal length of 90mm to avoid being landed on! This shot is full of action because the skier's coming straight at you, with plenty of space for cover headlines and text."

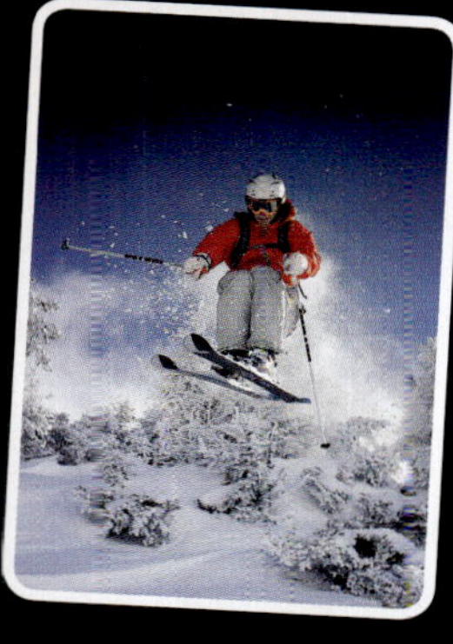

◀ Sainte Foy, France

"Here I got in close as the skier jumped to capture the snow falling off the rock. It can be useful to let the sun backlight the snow to add a sense of drama. The skier sits neatly on the left – perfect for a magazine spread."

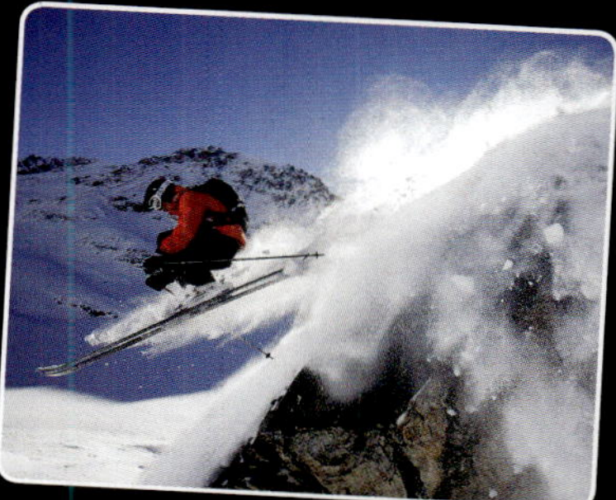

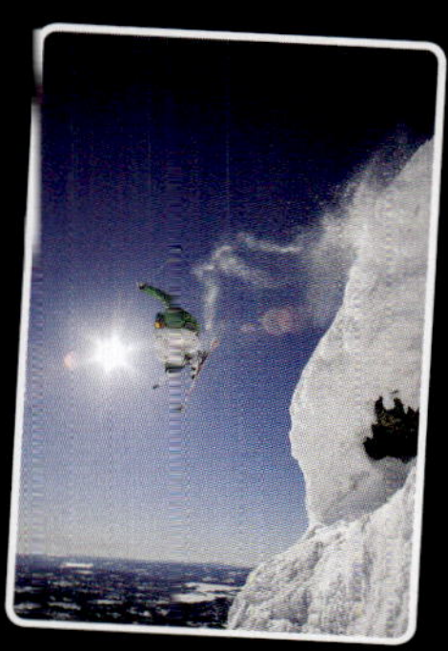

▶ Are, Sweden

"This image was taken with my Canon 20mm f/2.8 wide-angle lens (f/7.1 at 1/1000 sec). I like the way the skier jumps out into the valley. By using a 20mm lens, the size of the cliff was also exaggerated."

KILLER KIT OF THE PROS #3

Ski helmet

"You should wear a helmet at all times," says Adrian. "Experience has taught me to keep my ski lid on whenever I'm close to the action, because skiers will come close at very high speeds. Snow and skiers can also be unpredictable, so you never know when they'll get it wrong and run into you! Be aware of other skiers, too, as you'll be busy taking shots in the other direction."

HOT SHOT #2

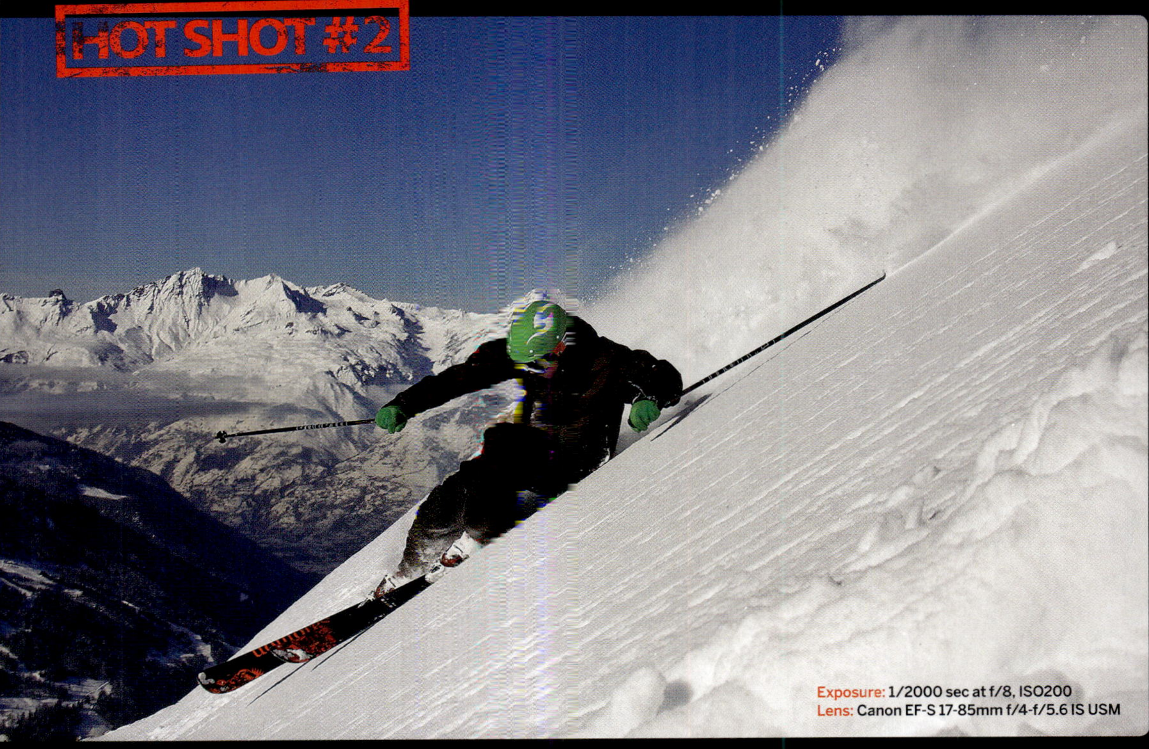

Exposure: 1/2000 sec at f/8, ISO200
Lens: Canon EF-S 17-85mm f/4-f/5.6 IS USM

◀ Geoff's comment

"Staying on the same slope (as Hot Shot #1), this time we faced in the other direction. laid against the slope and got Chris (the ski model) to carve in a big arc around us. I tracked him as he went and like this particular shot – with the mountains and trees below and behind, which add to the alpine atmosphere. My timing and confidence were increasing, so I zoomed in a little using a focal length of 30mm. As the slope was steeper and the snow deeper, Chris was able to get into a more exciting pose, which helps make the shot." ▶

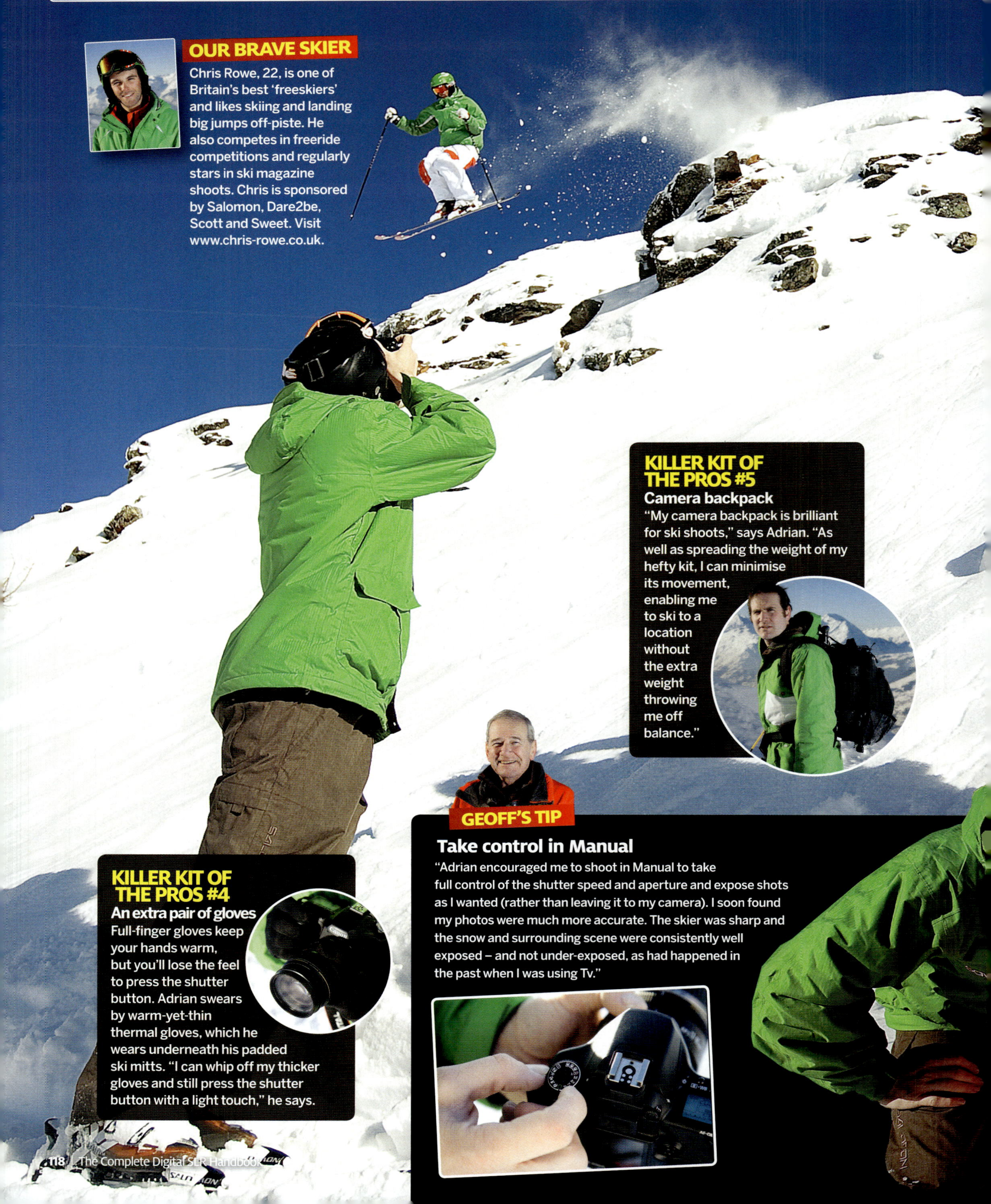

OUR BRAVE SKIER

Chris Rowe, 22, is one of Britain's best 'freeskiers' and likes skiing and landing big jumps off-piste. He also competes in freeride competitions and regularly stars in ski magazine shoots. Chris is sponsored by Salomon, Dare2be, Scott and Sweet. Visit www.chris-rowe.co.uk.

KILLER KIT OF THE PROS #5

Camera backpack

"My camera backpack is brilliant for ski shoots," says Adrian. "As well as spreading the weight of my hefty kit, I can minimise its movement, enabling me to ski to a location without the extra weight throwing me off balance."

KILLER KIT OF THE PROS #4

An extra pair of gloves

Full-finger gloves keep your hands warm, but you'll lose the feel to press the shutter button. Adrian swears by warm-yet-thin thermal gloves, which he wears underneath his padded ski mitts. "I can whip off my thicker gloves and still press the shutter button with a light touch," he says.

GEOFF'S TIP

Take control in Manual

"Adrian encouraged me to shoot in Manual to take full control of the shutter speed and aperture and expose shots as I wanted (rather than leaving it to my camera). I soon found my photos were much more accurate. The skier was sharp and the snow and surrounding scene were consistently well exposed – and not under-exposed, as had happened in the past when I was using Tv."

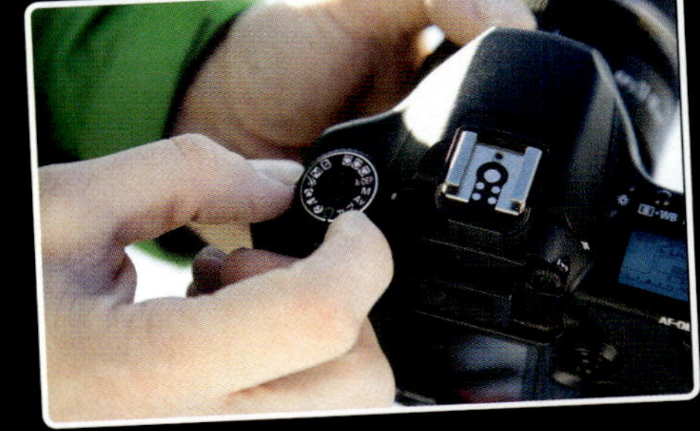

THANK YOU!

Thanks to Sainte Foy Tourist Office (www.saintefoy.net) and Optimum Ski (www.optimumski.com) for their accommodation at Chalet Tarentaise.

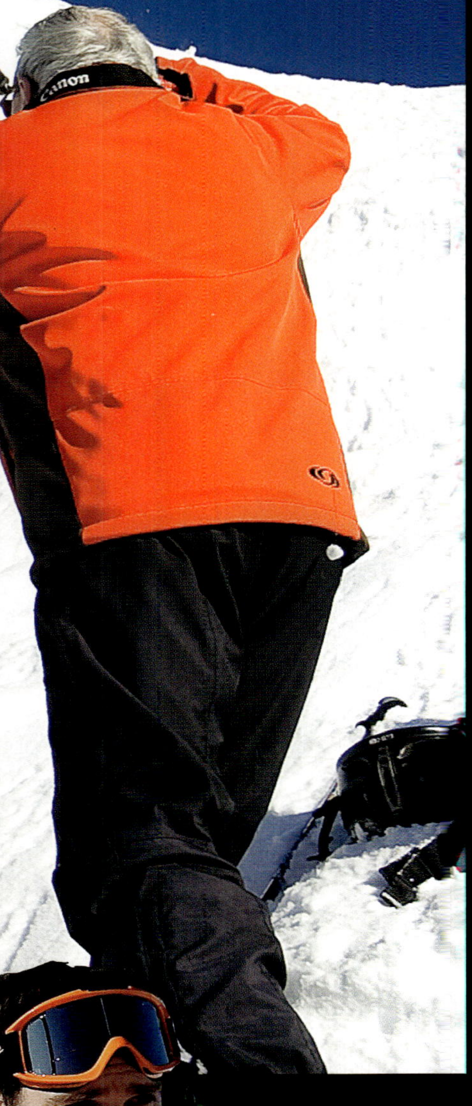

HOT SHOT #3

Exposure: 1/2000 sec at f/6.3, ISO200
Lens: Canon EF-S 17-85mm f/4-f/5.6 IS USM

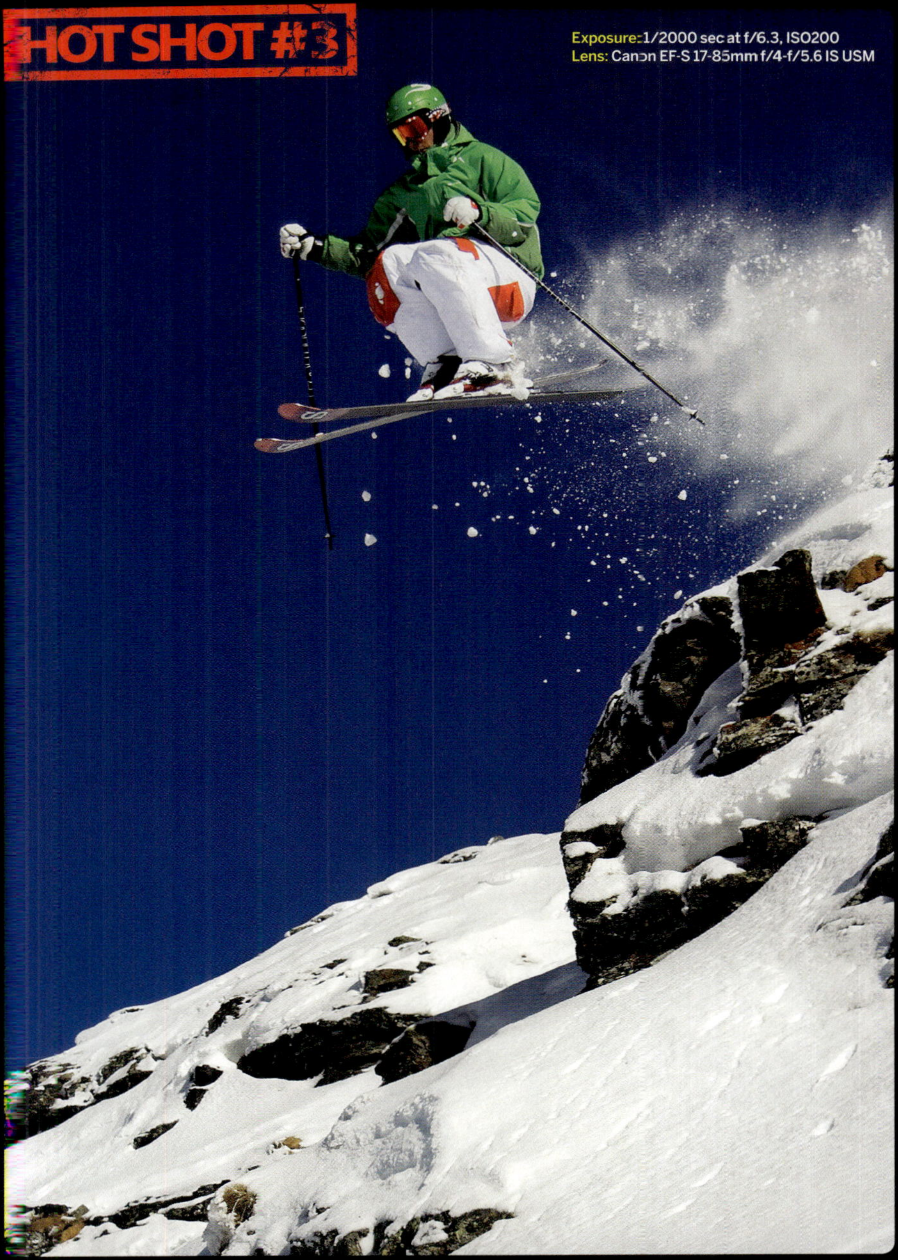

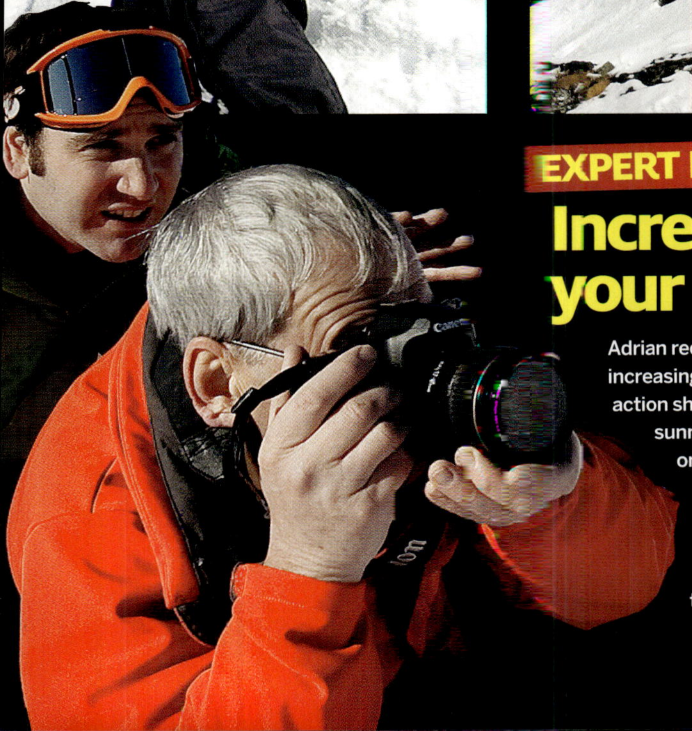

EXPERT INSIGHT

Increase your ISO

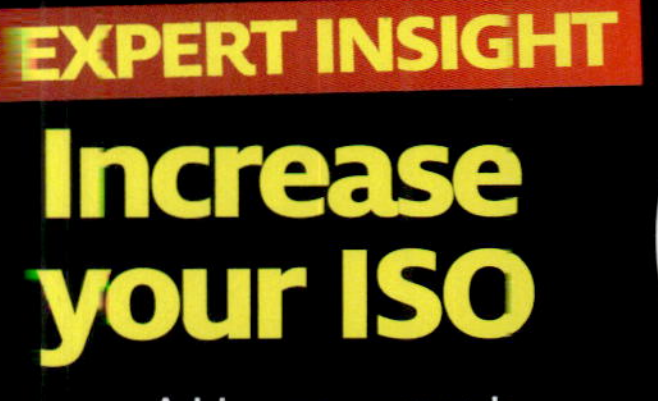

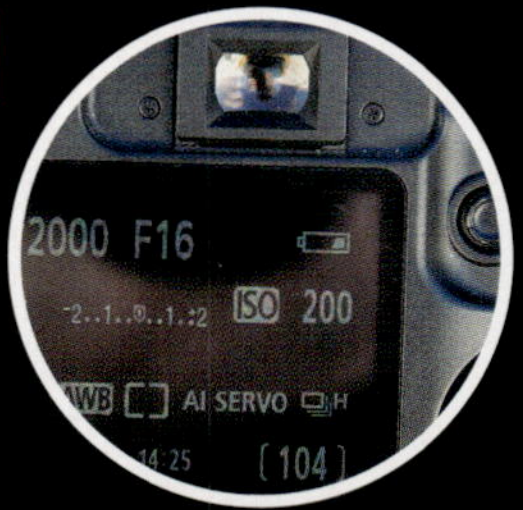

Adrian recommends increasing your ISO for ski action shots – we were shooting on a sunny day and the snow reflected even more light onto our subject. "By upping your ISO from 100 to 200 you'll get faster shutter speeds," says Adrian, "so at f/6.3-f/8 you can shoot at around 1/1600 sec and freeze the action. This will give you sharper shots. At ISO200 there will be no noticeable image noise."

Geoff's comment ▲

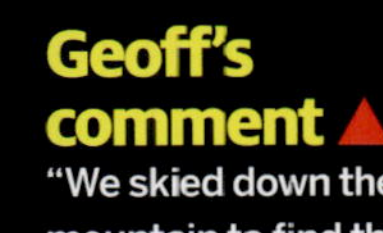

"We skied down the mountain to find this rock, which Chris was more than happy to jump off! Adrian suggested that we shoot from below using a vertical composition to emphasise the height of the drop. I shot with an aperture of f/6.3 and a rapid 1/2000 sec shutter speed so I could clearly capture Chris leaping into the snowy abyss!" ▶

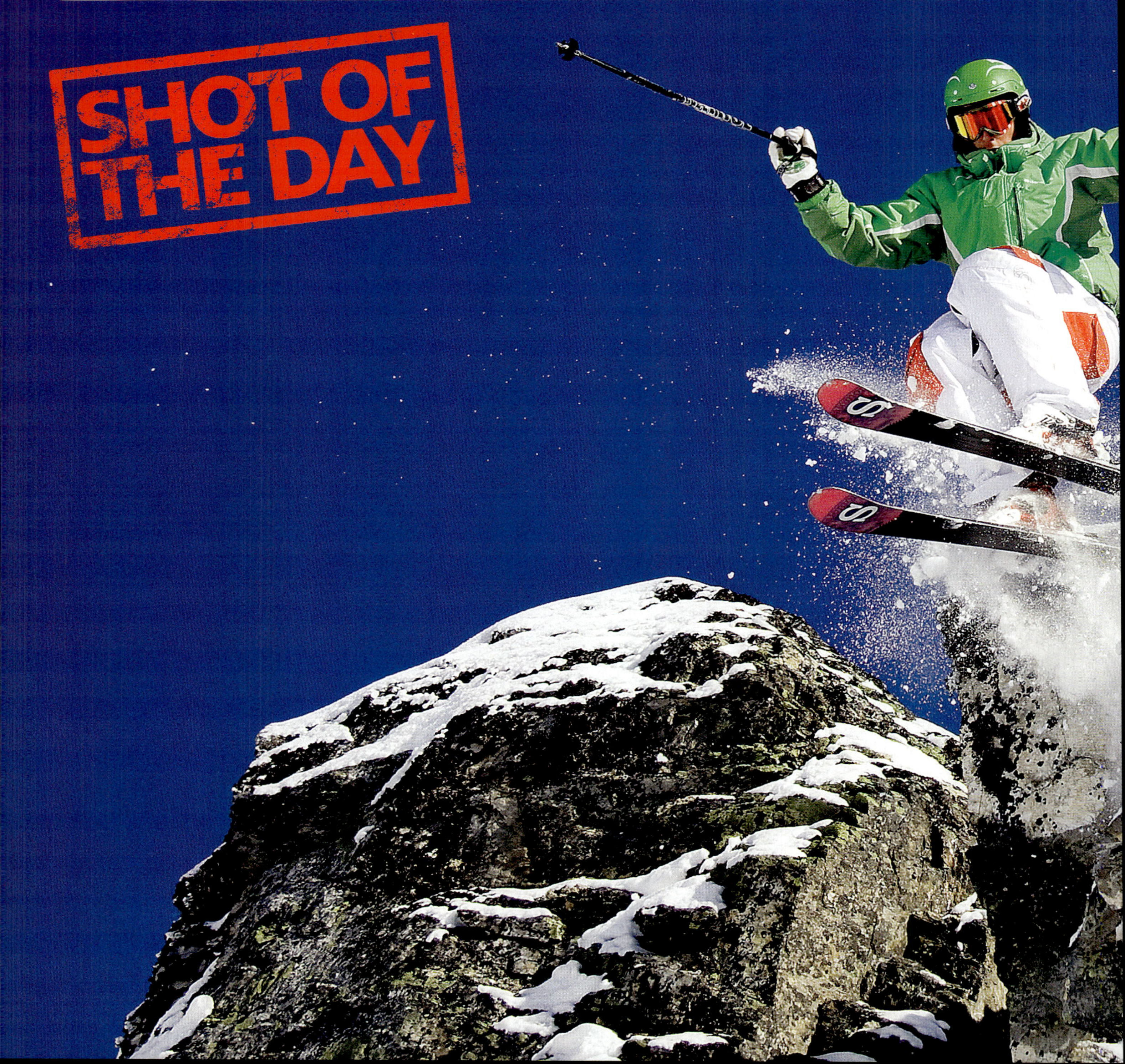

SHOT OF THE DAY

Adrian's verdict

"Geoff was the perfect student – he listened carefully and then acted on my suggestions. He's done really well to capture a shot this stunning after just one day of shooting. After a few initial pointers, I got him to use AF to pre-focus on the lip of the rocks and then switch to MF to ensure that he got sharp shots of Chris. The exposure is great, the snow's white and there's plenty of detail in the rocks [1]. At ISO200 Geoff got a shutter speed of 1/1250 sec, which helped him to 'pause' the action [2]. Finally, the composition is great – he's caught Chris with blue sky behind him [3]. Any later and Chris would probably have been lost against the rocky backdrop [4]."

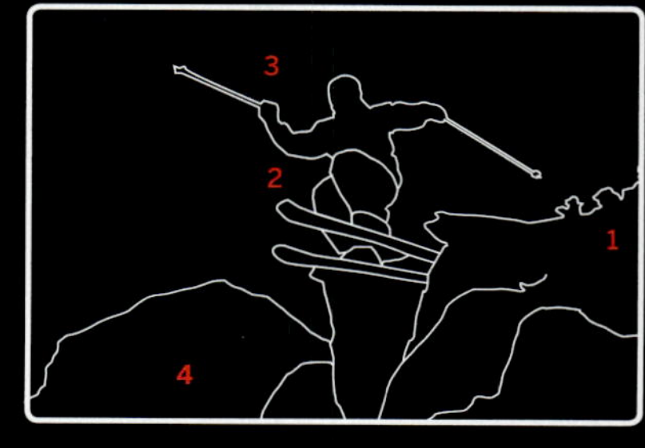

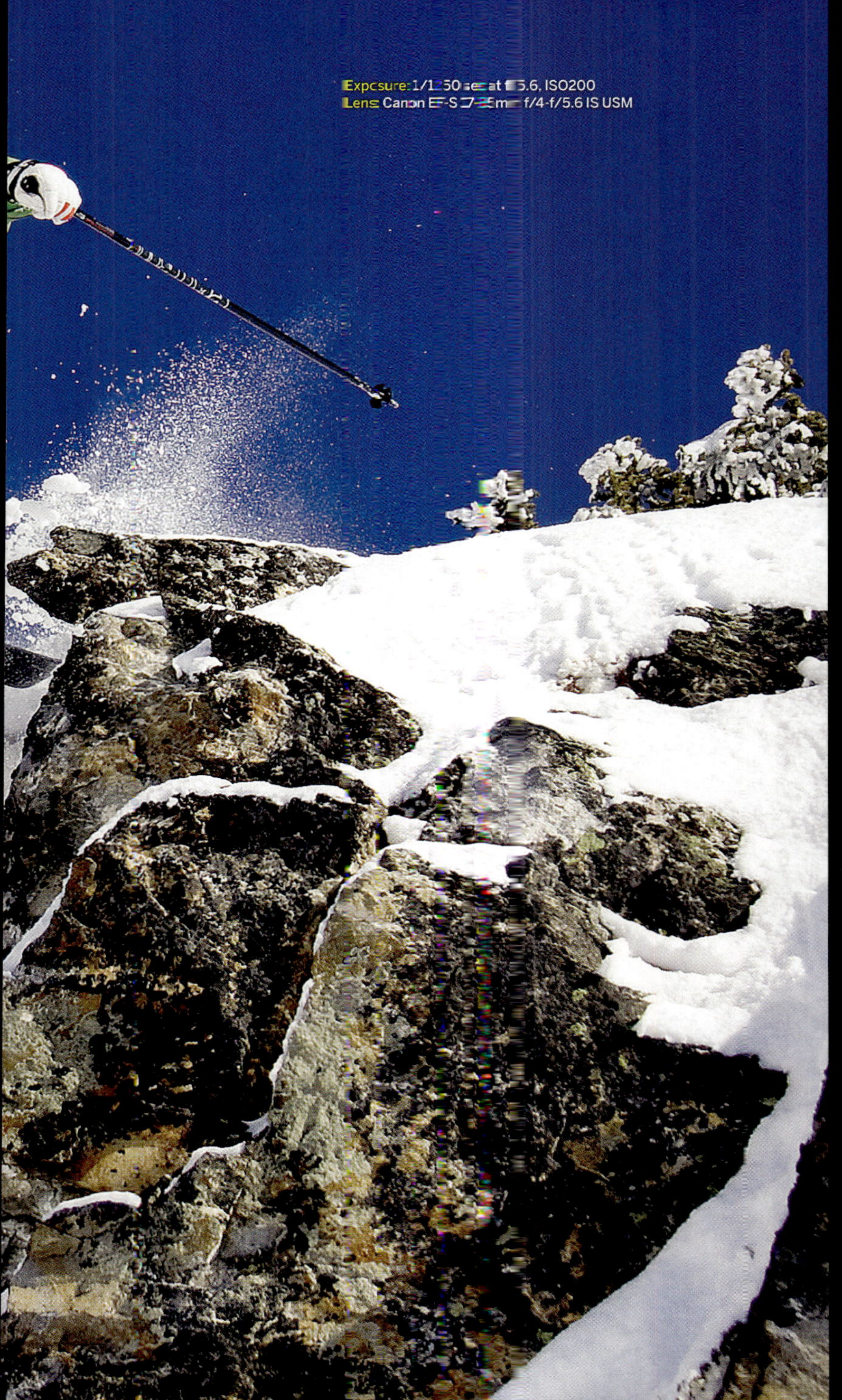

Exposure: 1/1250 sec at f/5.6, ISO200
Lens: Canon EF-S 17-85mm f/4-f/5.6 IS USM

Geoff's comment

"I'm really proud of this shot. I tried to put all the techniques Adrian had taught me together, and think I managed it! Chris was hitting the lip at a fair speed, so Adrian got me to focus manually. I took multiple shots on Continuous Drive mode and decided on this one because it captures the excitement and sense of danger as Chris takes another leap of faith." ■

WELL DONE GEOFF!

How cool! Geoff picks up his Apprentice certificate from deputy editor, Peter Travers

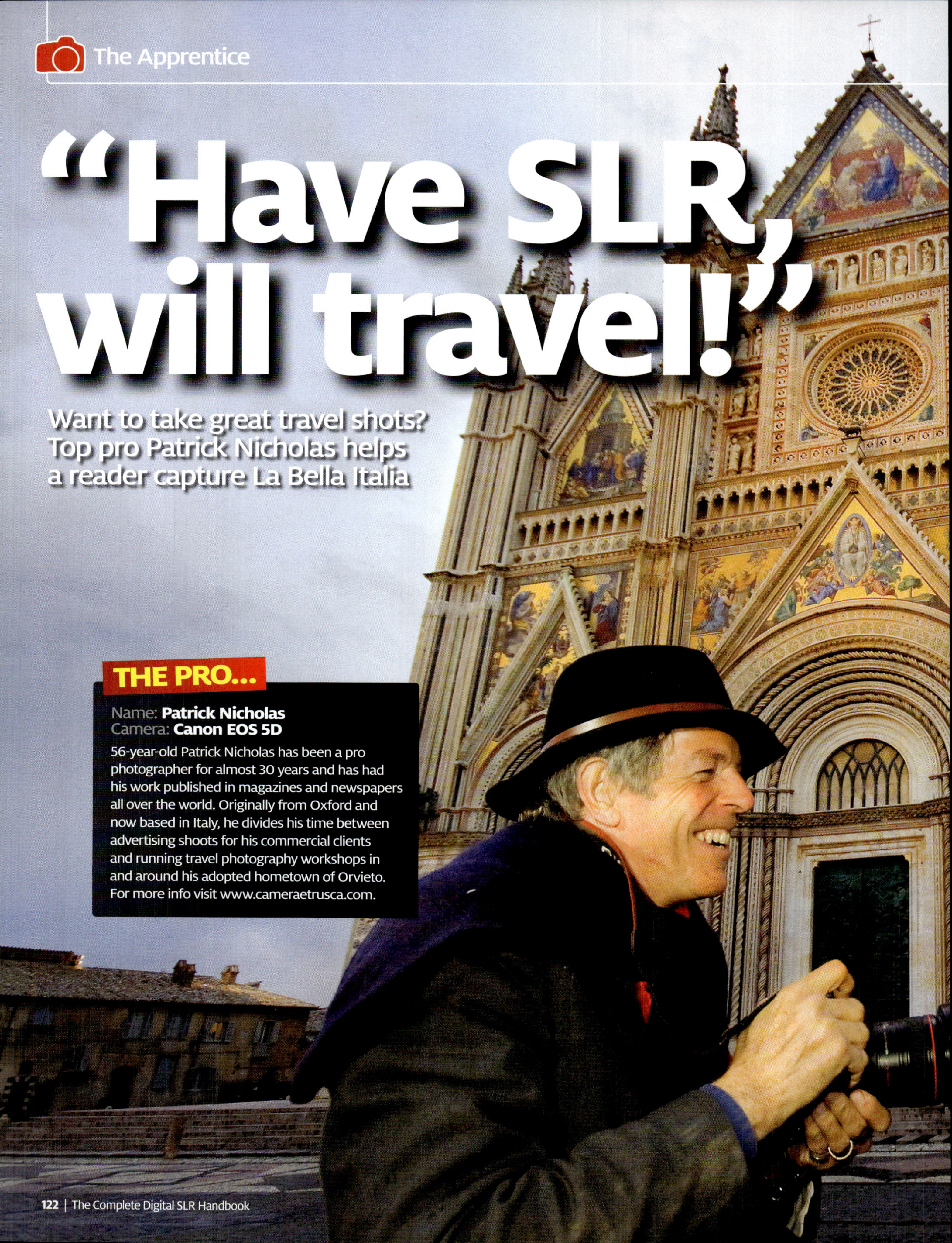

"Have SLR, will travel!"

Want to take great travel shots? Top pro Patrick Nicholas helps a reader capture La Bella Italia

THE PRO...

Name: **Patrick Nicholas**
Camera: **Canon EOS 5D**

56-year-old Patrick Nicholas has been a pro photographer for almost 30 years and has had his work published in magazines and newspapers all over the world. Originally from Oxford and now based in Italy, he divides his time between advertising shoots for his commercial clients and running travel photography workshops in and around his adopted hometown of Orvieto. For more info visit www.cameraetrusca.com.

Words: Paul Grogan (Future) • Location shots: Chris George (Future)

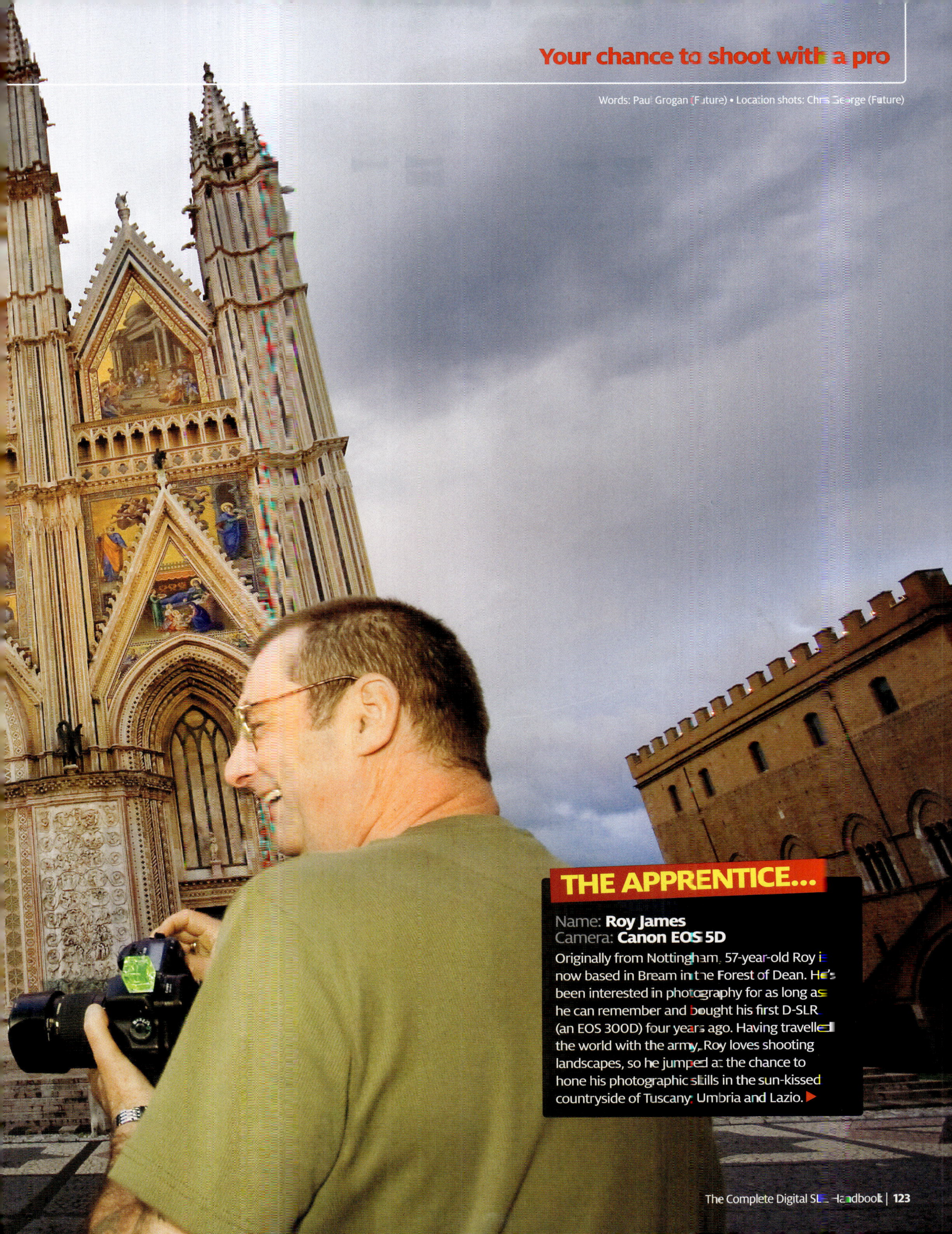

THE APPRENTICE...

Name: **Roy James**
Camera: **Canon EOS 5D**

Originally from Nottingham, 57-year-old Roy is now based in Bream in the Forest of Dean. He's been interested in photography for as long as he can remember and bought his first D-SLR (an EOS 300D) four years ago. Having travelled the world with the army, Roy loves shooting landscapes, so he jumped at the chance to hone his photographic skills in the sun-kissed countryside of Tuscany, Umbria and Lazio.

KILLER KIT OF THE PROS #1

Panoramic tripod head

"A panoramic tripod head is essential for shooting panoramics because it keeps the camera level for every frame, making them much easier to stitch together later in Photoshop," says Patrick. "If you can afford to, buy one that's geared, because this will enable you to fine-tune the left and right adjustments with more precision than a head that swivels freely will allow."

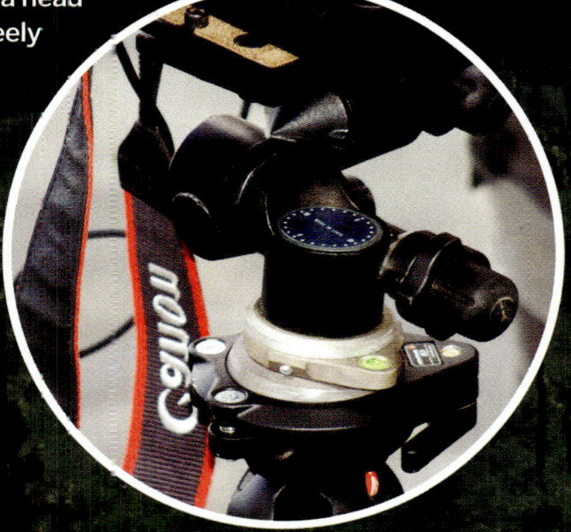

Technique assessment

Is Roy ready to shoot landscapes?

Patrick took a look at the settings Roy was using and recommended a few changes to help him capture the Italian countryside at its best...

OPTIMISE APERTURE

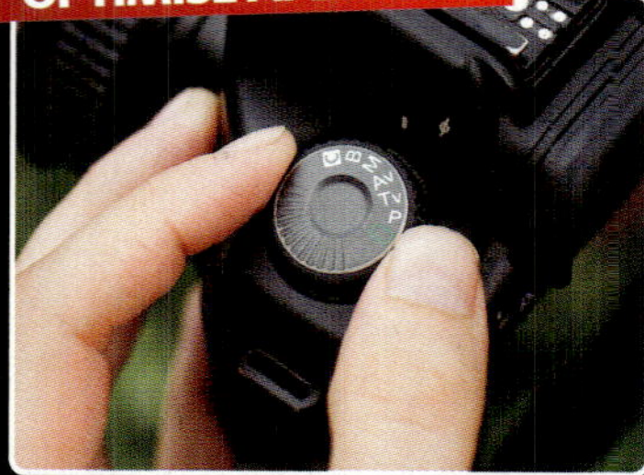

Find your sweet spot

"Roy was shooting in Full Auto mode, but to take complete control you've got to use Manual," says Patrick. "For landscapes, I usually try to set an aperture of between f/8 and f/11, which is generally considered the 'sweet spot' in terms of sharpness."

TURN OFF AUTOFOCUS

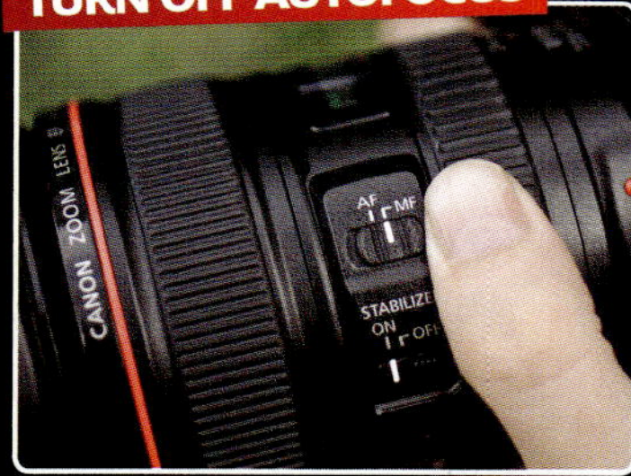

Lock the focal length

"Roy also relied on autofocus," says Patrick, "but when I'm shooting landscapes using a tripod, I prefer to focus in AF mode, then switch to manual so the focus stays locked. This is important if you want to stitch a series of images together."

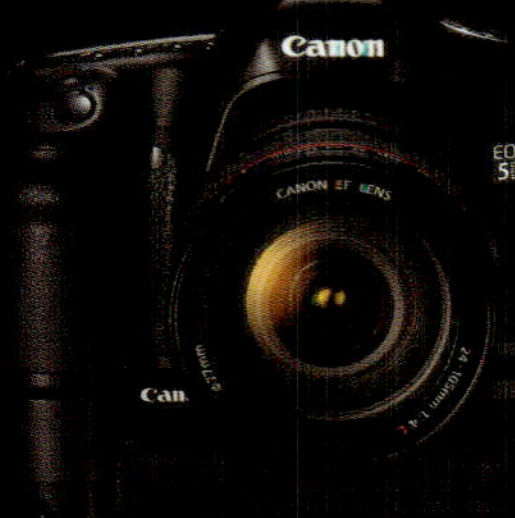

Although Patrick still uses a range of film cameras for his commercial work, he never goes anywhere without his trusty EOS 5D. He travels light on landscape shoots, limiting his kit to the following items:

- Canon EF 24-105mm f/4L IS USM
- Canon EF 100mm f/2.8 Macro USM
- Canon EF 70-300mm f/4-5.6 USM
- Sigma 17-35mm f/2.8-4 EX DG
- Canon 550EX flash and diffuser
- Manfrotto carbon fibre tripod
- Manfrotto 3502 levelling head
- Manfrotto 405 panoramic head
- A selection of Cokin filters

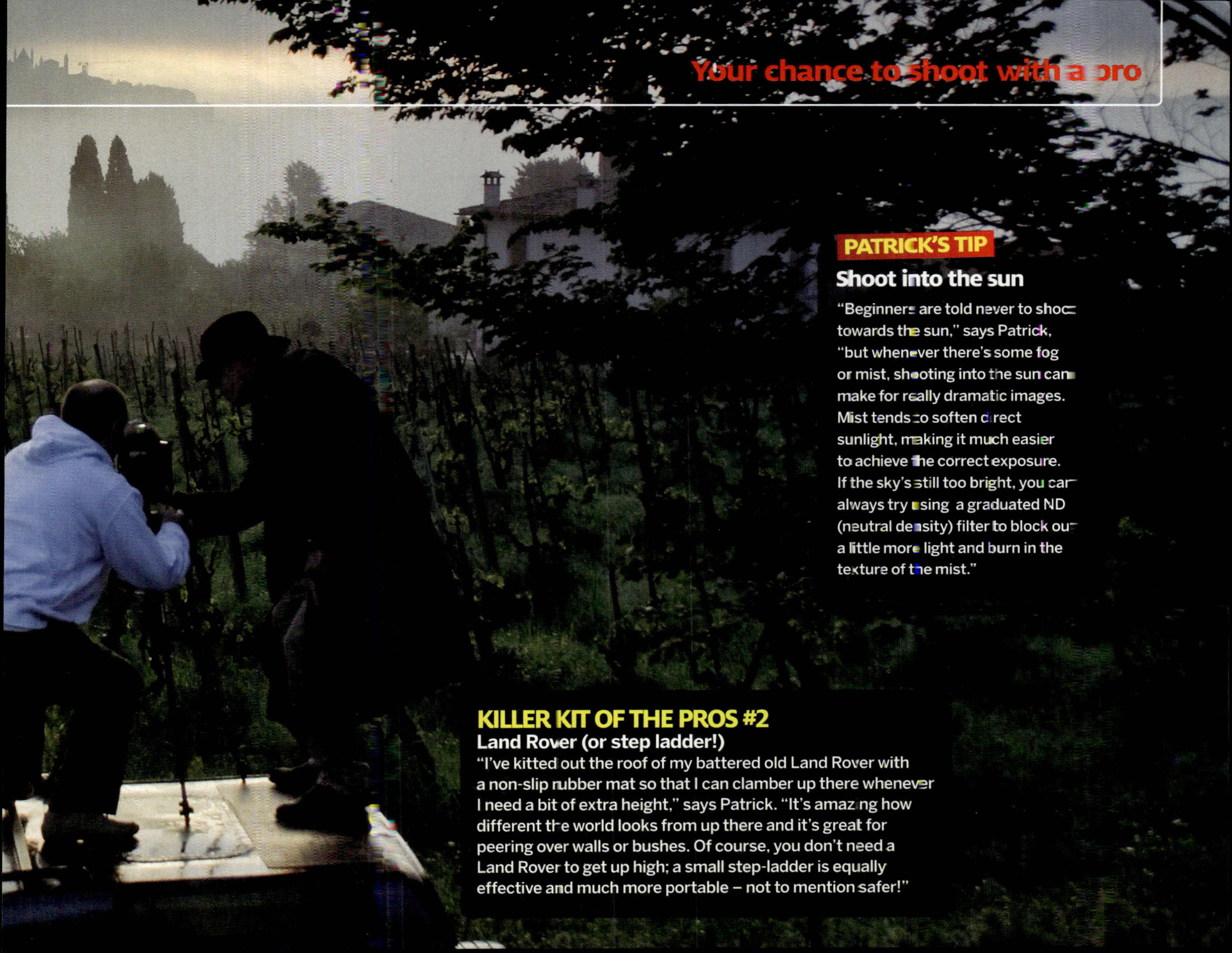

PATRICK'S TIP

Shoot into the sun

"Beginners are told never to shoot towards the sun," says Patrick, "but whenever there's some fog or mist, shooting into the sun can make for really dramatic images. Mist tends to soften direct sunlight, making it much easier to achieve the correct exposure. If the sky's still too bright, you can always try using a graduated ND (neutral density) filter to block out a little more light and burn in the texture of the mist."

KILLER KIT OF THE PROS #2

Land Rover (or step ladder!)

"I've kitted out the roof of my battered old Land Rover with a non-slip rubber mat so that I can clamber up there whenever I need a bit of extra height," says Patrick. "It's amazing how different the world looks from up there and it's great for peering over walls or bushes. Of course, you don't need a Land Rover to get up high; a small step-ladder is equally effective and much more portable – not to mention safer!"

HOT SHOT #1

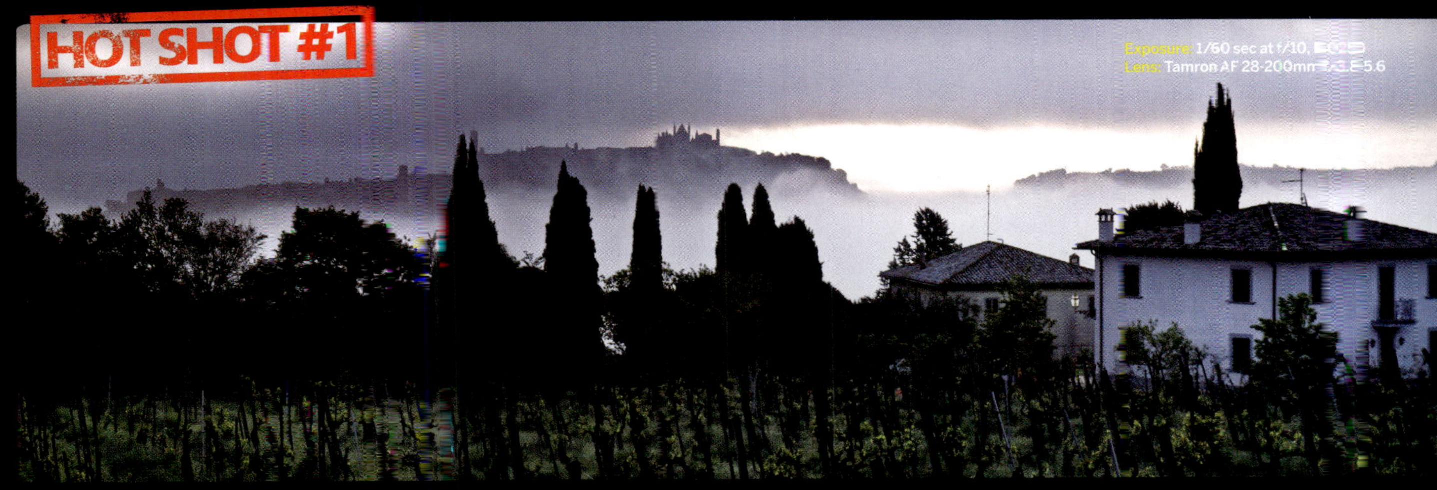

Exposure: 1/60 sec at f/10, [illegible]
Lens: Tamron AF 28-200mm [illegible]-5.6

Roy's comment

"After clambering onto the top of Patrick's Land Rover, we spent quite a long time setting the tripod up and carefully composing the shot. Patrick encouraged me to think in terms of stitching two or three shots together to create a panorama, and suggested using the trees on the left and building on the right to frame the final image. He also showed me how he uses the geared head attached to his tripod to turn the camera exactly the same distance each time. For a first effort, I'm pretty pleased with how this image turned out."

EXPERT INSIGHT

Fine-tune your histogram

"If you want take your photography to the next level, check your histogram," says Patrick. "Ideally you're looking for a bell-shaped curve stretching from the darkest tones on the left to the brightest on the right. If your tones are all bunched up in the middle, increase your exposure slightly to ensure that the histogram reaches all the way to the right, because this is where your camera's sensor is at its most sensitive. Just make sure that it isn't bunched up at the right, because any pixels that are shunted all the way off the end of the graph will print out as pure white."

PATRICK'S TIP

Think abstract

"When shooting landscapes in mist or cloud, it's often a good idea to focus on the more abstract elements of the scene," says Patrick. "If Roy had included a bank of trees in the foreground of Hot Shot #3, for example, it would have added an element of realism that would have ruined the ethereal feel of this otherwise graphic image."

KILLER KIT OF THE PROS #3

Visible Dust sensor cleaner

"When you're shooting travel images, you find yourself changing lenses constantly, which makes keeping your sensor clean all but impossible," says Patrick. "You can't beat getting your sensor professionally cleaned, but when I'm on location I use this sensor cleaning kit from Visible Dust. It's compact and easy to use, it gets rid of all but the most stubborn spots, and it saves hours of cloning out dust in Photoshop."

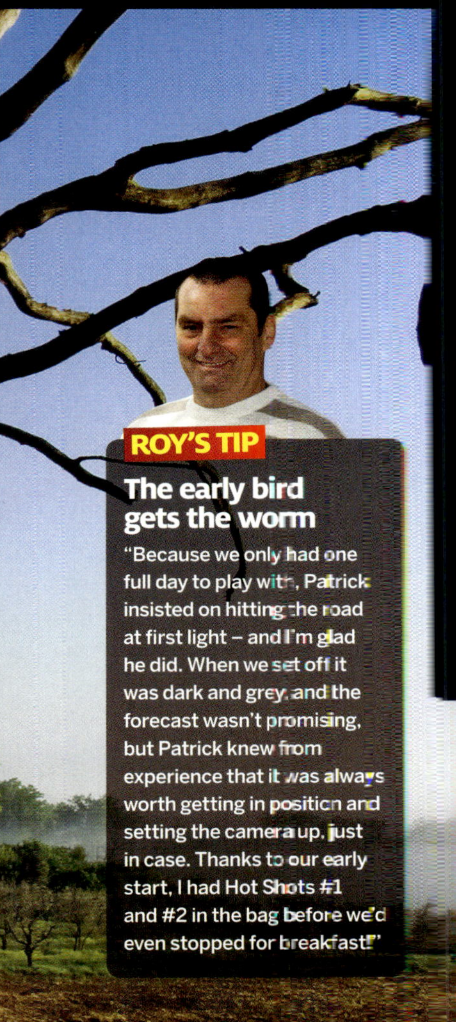

ROY'S TIP

The early bird gets the worm

"Because we only had one full day to play with, Patrick insisted on hitting the road at first light – and I'm glad he did. When we set off it was dark and grey, and the forecast wasn't promising, but Patrick knew from experience that it was always worth getting in position and setting the camera up, just in case. Thanks to our early start, I had Hot Shots #1 and #2 in the bag before we'd even stopped for breakfast!"

Roy's comment

"Here, Patrick encouraged me to zoom in on the tower, to 'pull' the island closer to the foreground. The clouds were changing quite quickly, but for a few seconds two clouds framed the distant island, so I opted for a symmetrical composition with the clouds at the top and the olive trees at the bottom. Finally, I set an aperture of f/16 to ensure maximum depth of field. I really like the bands of colour in this shot, and the way the warm terracotta tiles of the village contrast with the deep blue of the lake."

HOT SHOT #2

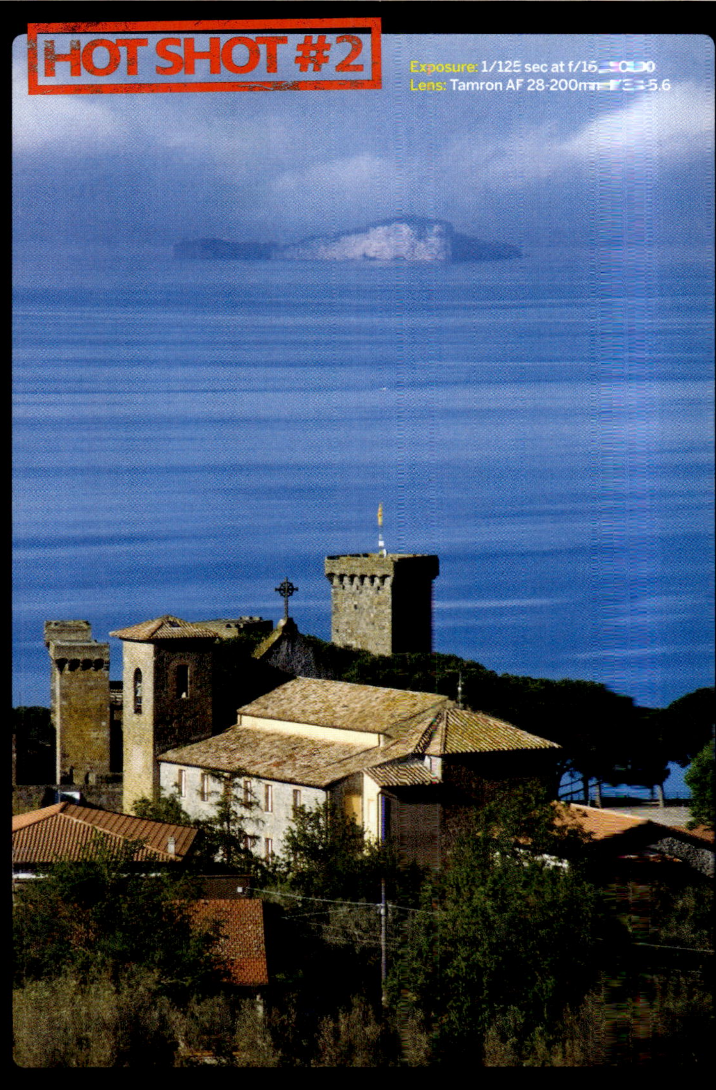

Exposure: 1/125 sec at f/16, ISO100
Lens: Tamron AF 28-200mm f/3.8-5.6

HOT SHOT #3

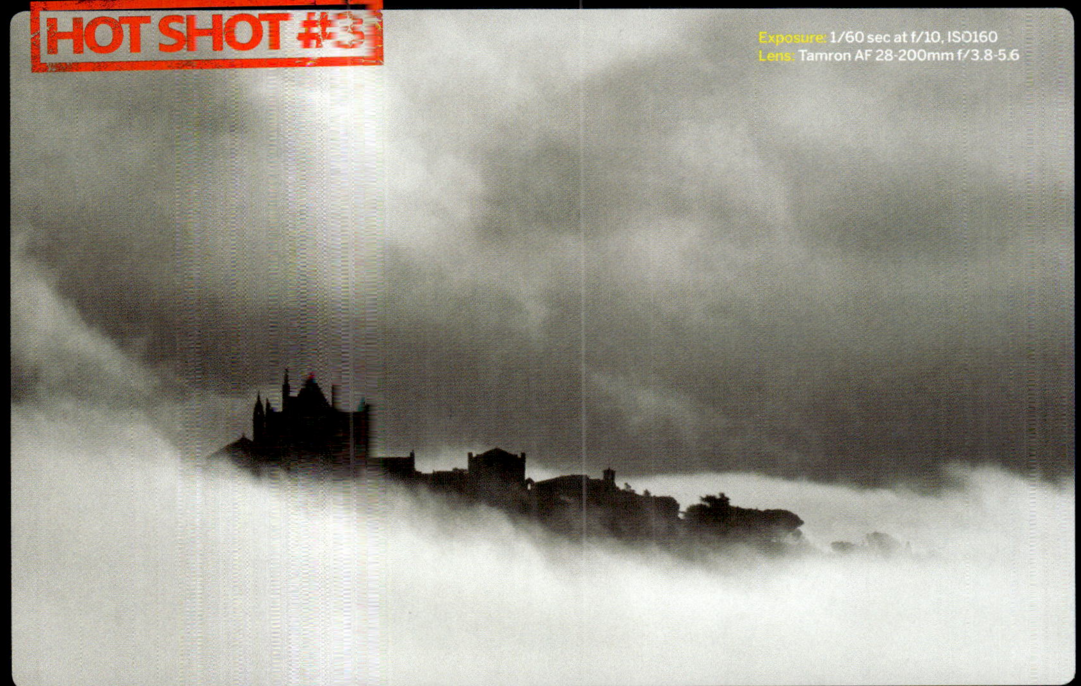

Exposure: 1/60 sec at f/10, ISO160
Lens: Tamron AF 28-200mm f/3.8-5.6

Roy's comment

"For this shot, Patrick urged me to use a long lens to crop in on the cathedral, and to compose it with the silhouette slightly off-centre. He also encouraged me to include more of the moody sky above the cathedral than below, as the sky above was more dramatic. I converted the shot to black and white in Photoshop and burned in some detail in the clouds to make them even more moody and get the result I was looking for."

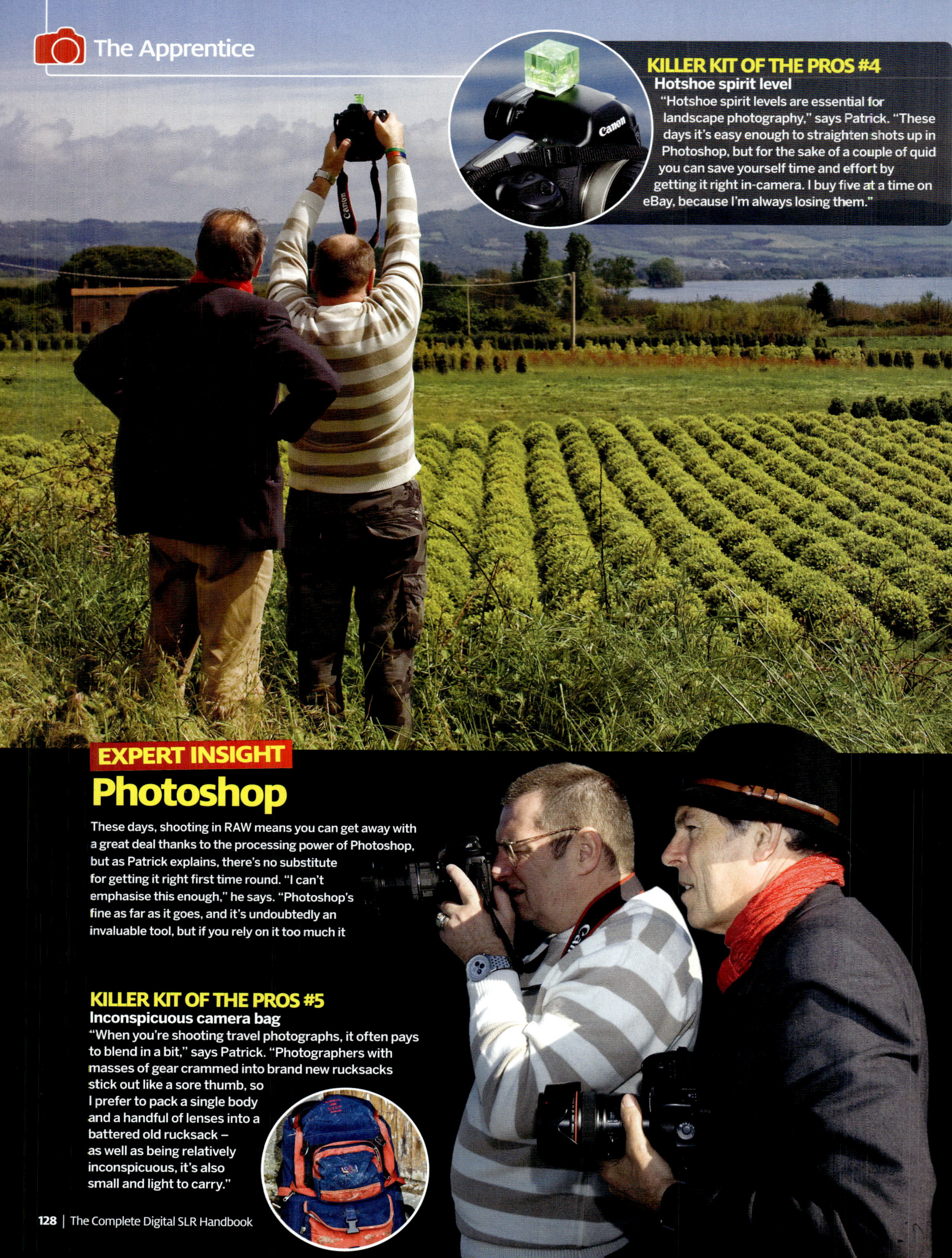

KILLER KIT OF THE PROS #4
Hotshoe spirit level

"Hotshoe spirit levels are essential for landscape photography," says Patrick. "These days it's easy enough to straighten shots up in Photoshop, but for the sake of a couple of quid you can save yourself time and effort by getting it right in-camera. I buy five at a time on eBay, because I'm always losing them."

EXPERT INSIGHT
Photoshop

These days, shooting in RAW means you can get away with a great deal thanks to the processing power of Photoshop, but as Patrick explains, there's no substitute for getting it right first time round. "I can't emphasise this enough," he says. "Photoshop's fine as far as it goes, and it's undoubtedly an invaluable tool, but if you rely on it too much it

KILLER KIT OF THE PROS #5
Inconspicuous camera bag

"When you're shooting travel photographs, it often pays to blend in a bit," says Patrick. "Photographers with masses of gear crammed into brand new rucksacks stick out like a sore thumb, so I prefer to pack a single body and a handful of lenses into a battered old rucksack – as well as being relatively inconspicuous, it's also small and light to carry."

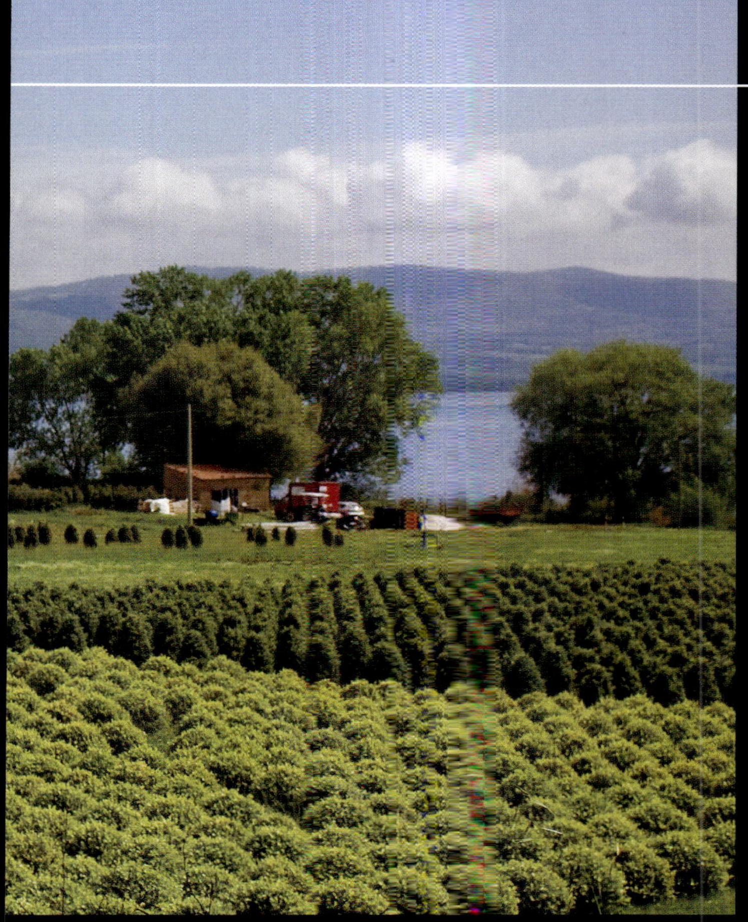

Roy's comment

"Patrick's instructions were to try to get the shrubs into a diamond shape by standing on a rock and holding my camera above my head! To maximise depth of field, he recommended an aperture of f/16 and showed me how to focus a third of the way into the scene to ensure a sharp shot from front to back. He then urged me to disable the autofocus so the lens wouldn't refocus while I was taking the shot. Considering I was more or less shooting blind, it's not bad!"

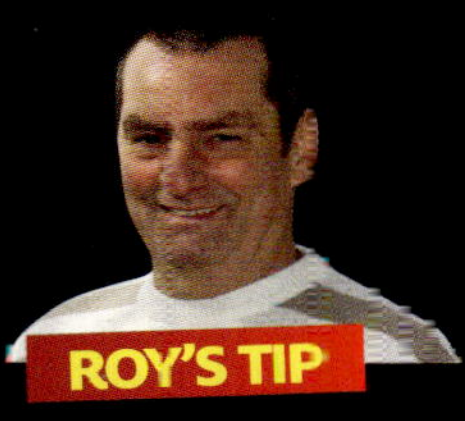

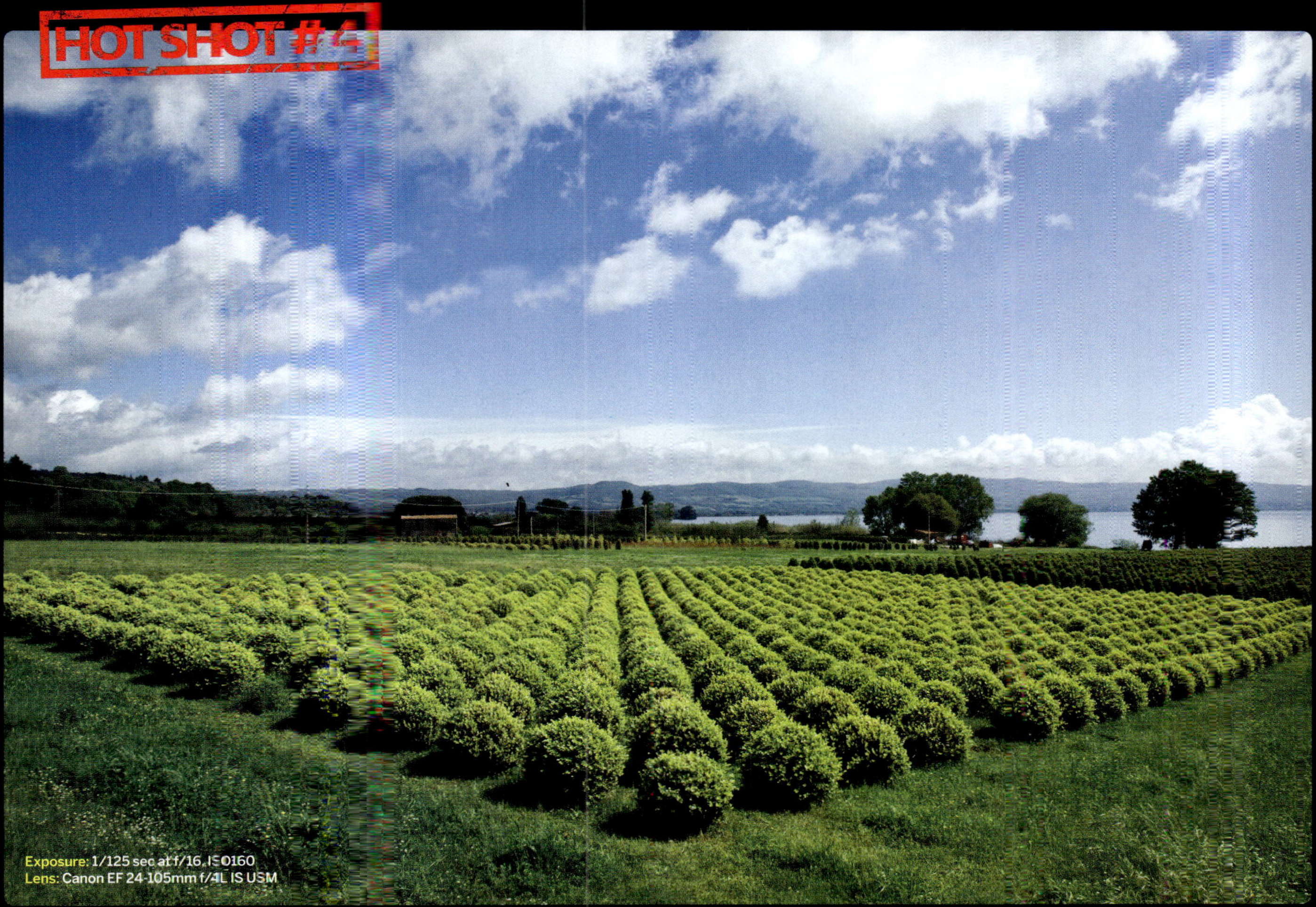

Remember Sunny 16

"Patrick explained the 'Sunny 16' rule to me early on, and it was amazing how often I found myself using it. It's basically a rule of thumb that says if you're shooting on a bright, sunny day at an ISO of 100 and a shutter speed of 1/125 sec, your aperture setting should be around f/16. Once you know that, you can toggle your shutter speed and aperture settings back and forth depending on how much – or how little – depth of field you want. Mind you, Patrick did point out that here in the UK, where the sun isn't quite as bright, it should be the Sunny 13 rule, but somehow that doesn't have quite the same ring to it."

HOT SHOT #4

Exposure: 1/125 sec at f/16, ISO160
Lens: Canon EF 24-105mm f/4L IS USM

SHOT OF THE DAY

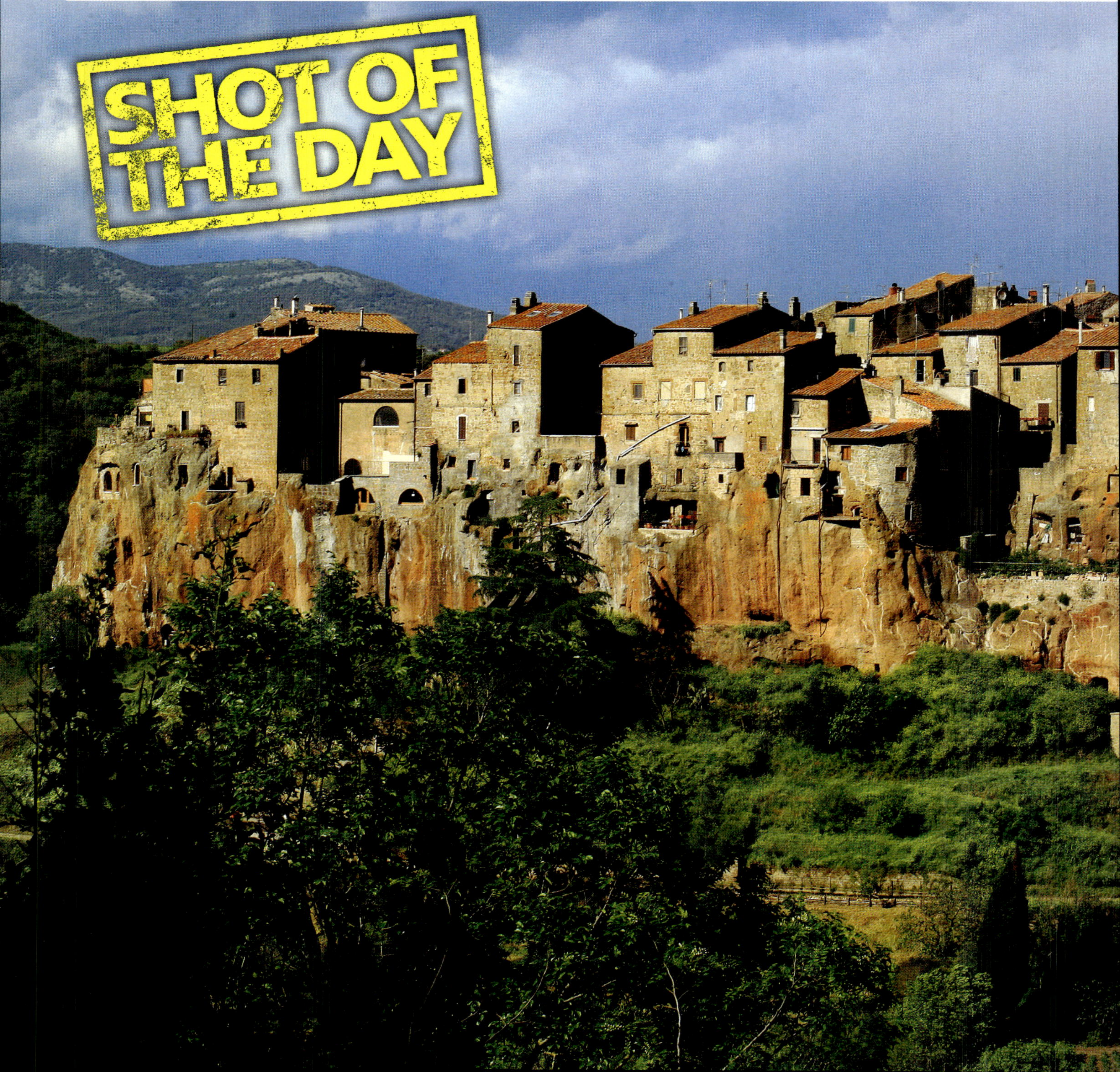

Patrick's verdict

"Roy has avoided the temptation to zoom in to the exclusion of all else and included the mountains and green valley to give a sense of context [1]. His lens has brought the distant volcano into the shot and the colours are striking [2]. Clever framing has focused attention on the buildings erupting from the rock [3]. What a dramatic shot!"

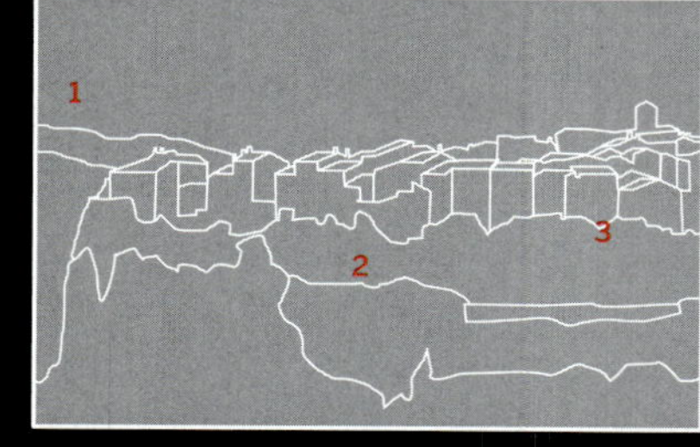

Exposure 1/80 sec at f/22, ISO160
Lens Tamron 70-300mm f/4-5.6 Di LD

Roy's comment

"I'm really pleased with this shot. Using several of the techniques Patrick showed me, I cropped in close enough to emphasise the height of the cliffs, but not at the expense of context. I also included enough of the stormy blue sky to give it a dramatic feel and to emphasise the warmer tones of the buildings and tiles. I just love the way the buildings seem to grow out of the rock."

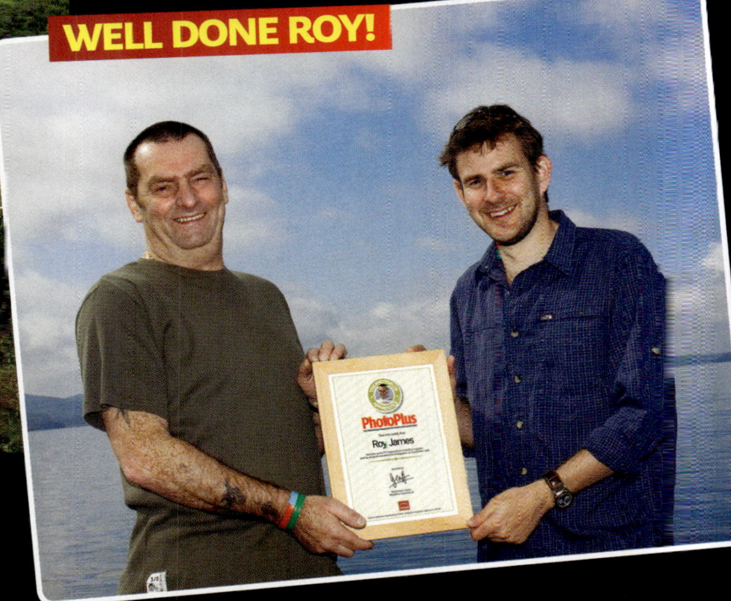

Bad shots are a thing of the pasta! Roy receives his certificate from technique editor, Paul Grogan

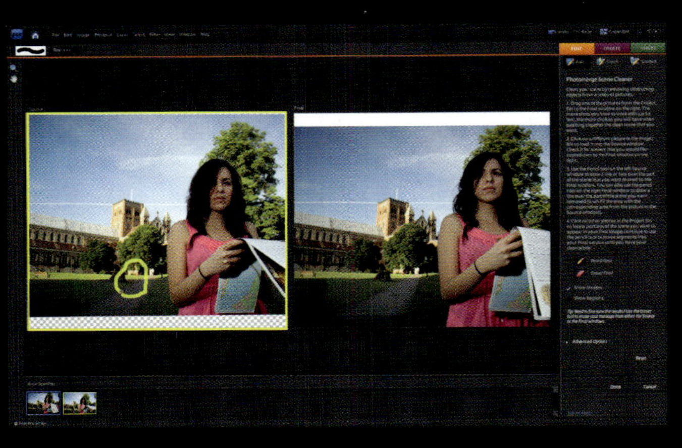

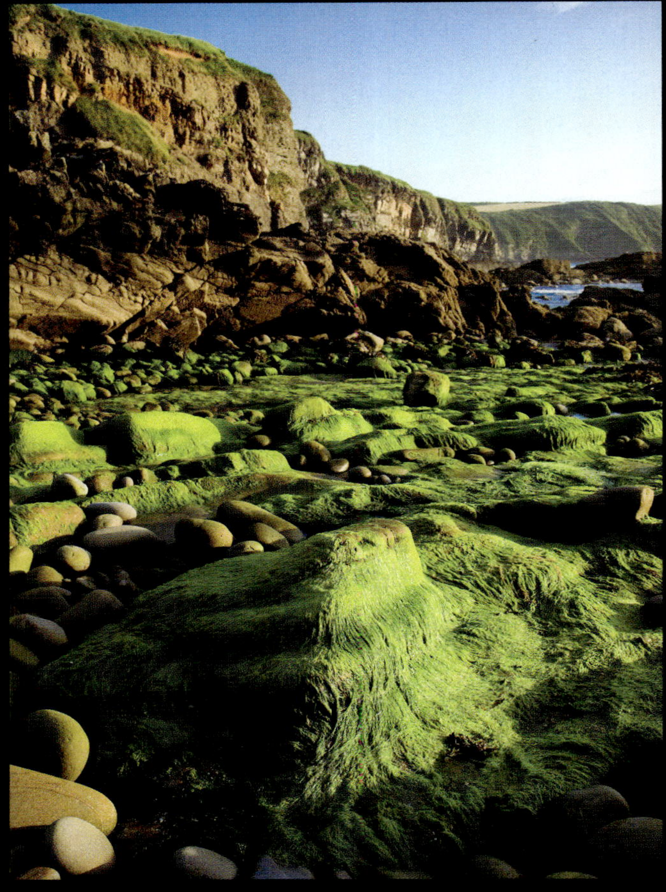

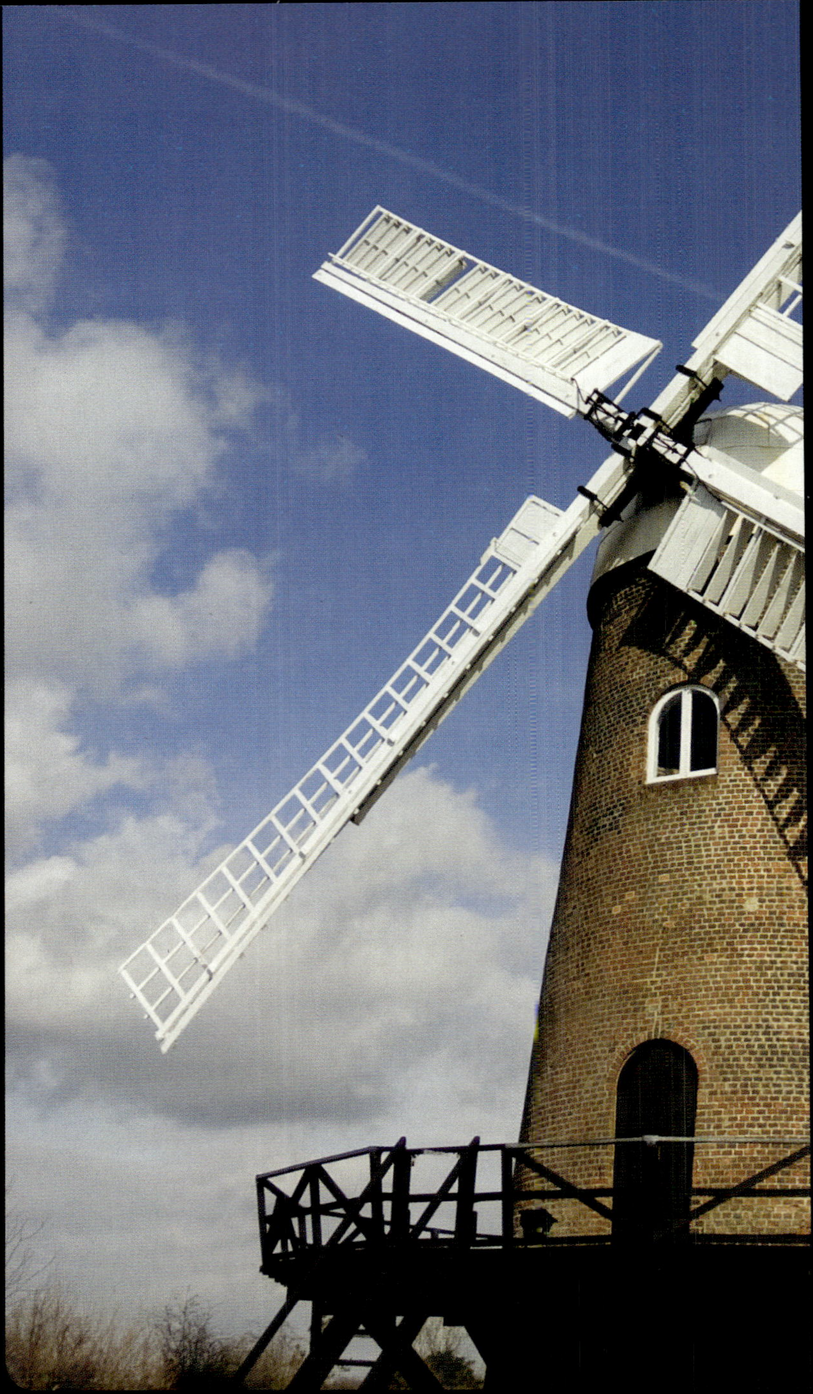

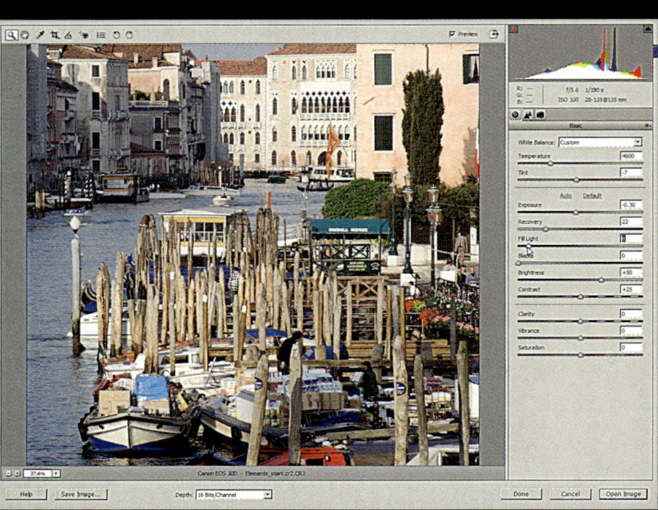

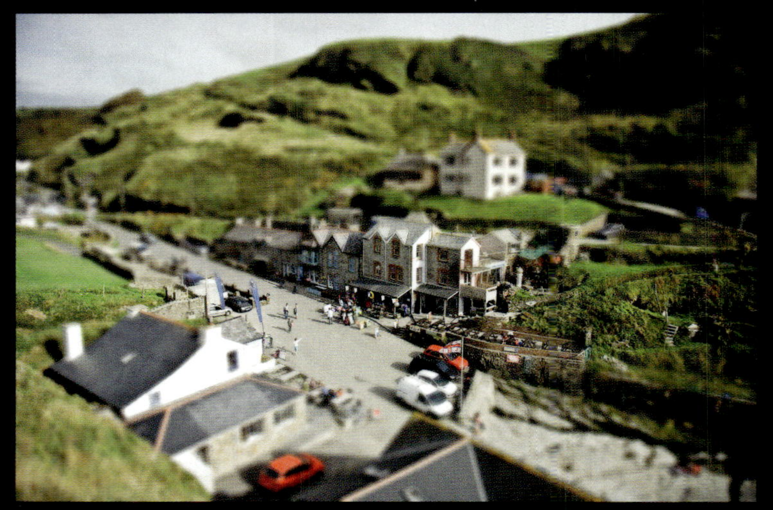

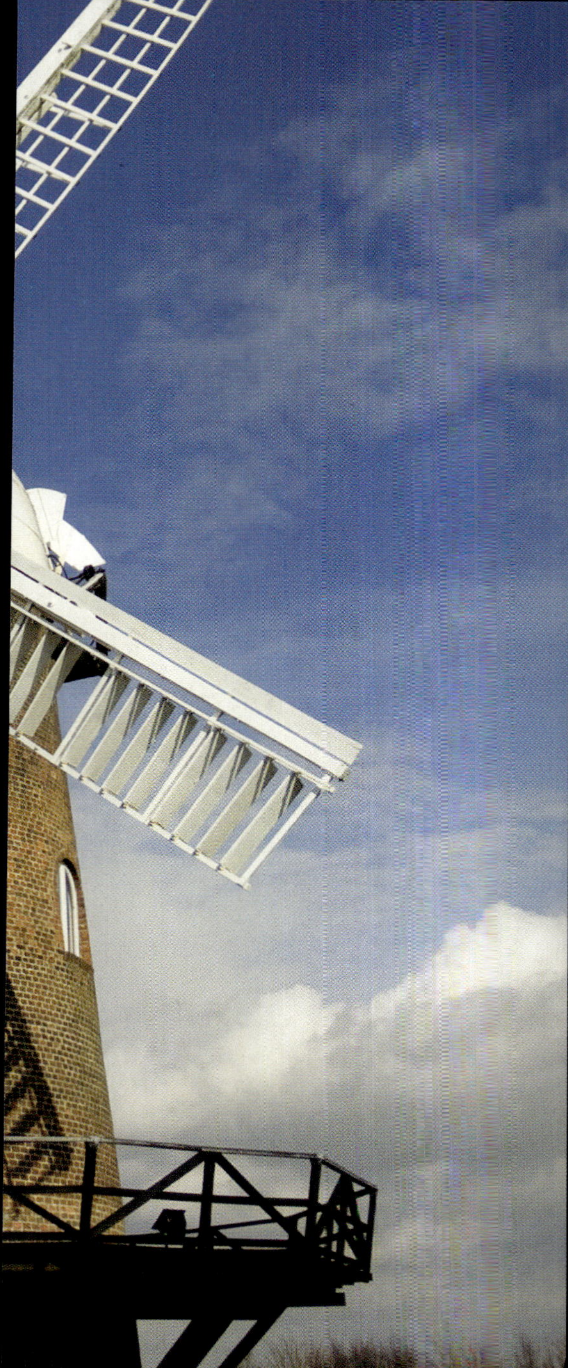

IMPROVE YOUR PHOTOS!

Creative Photoshop

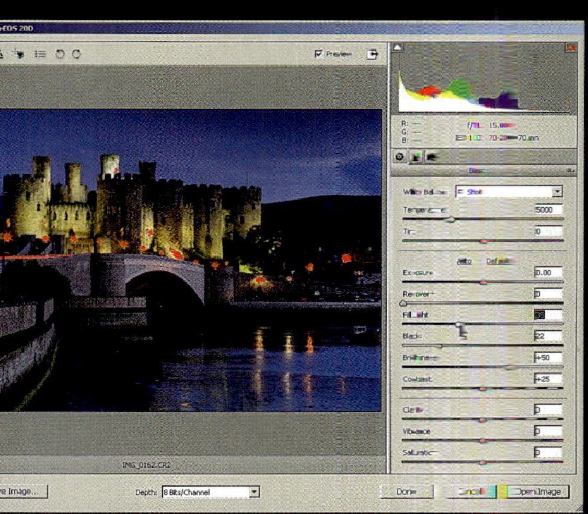

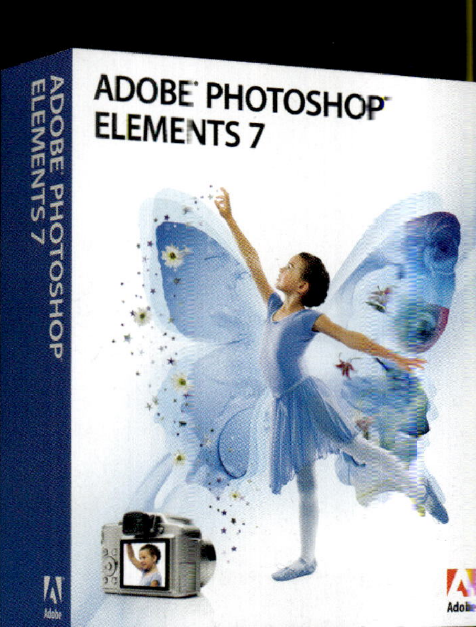

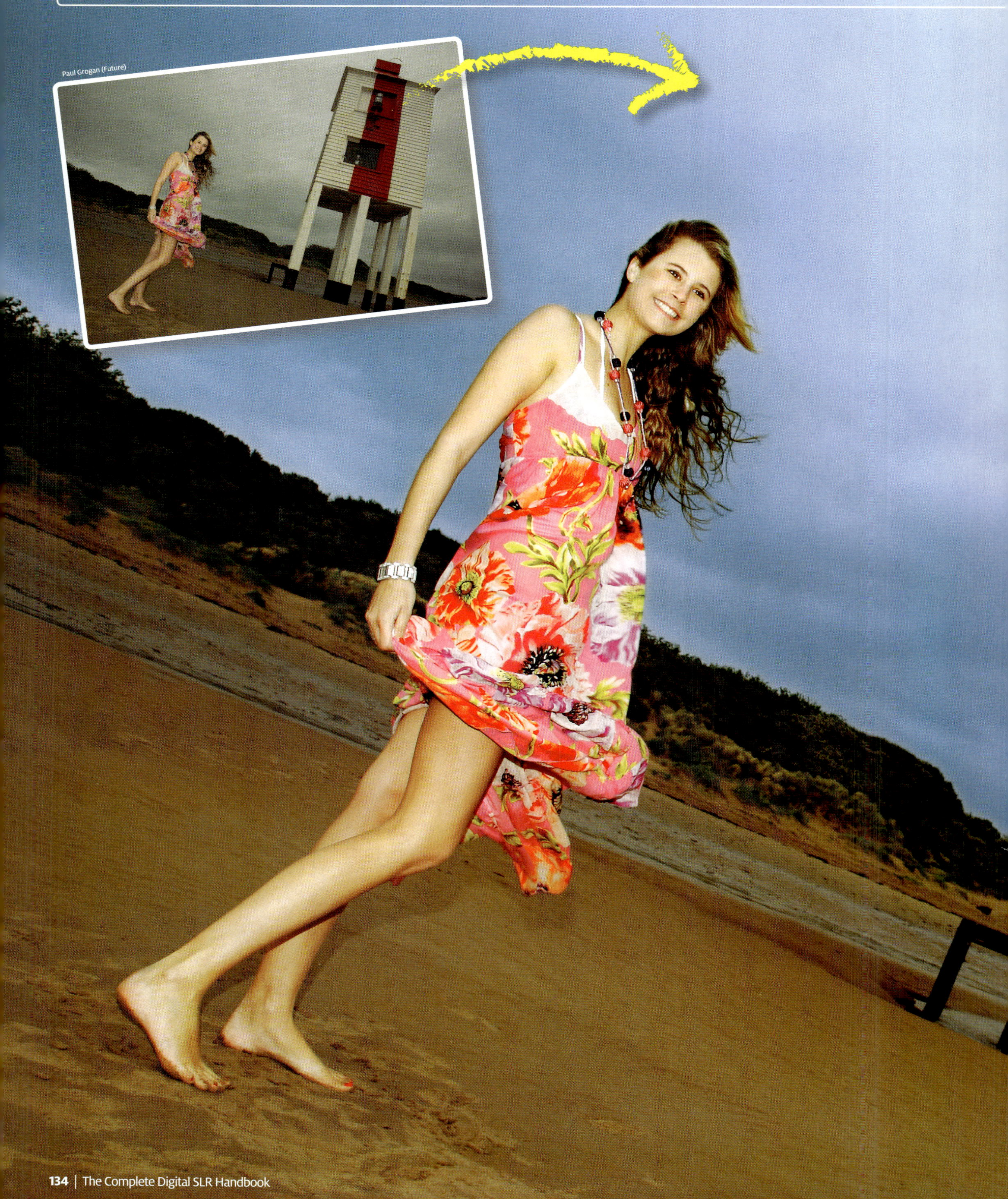

Paul Grogan (Future)

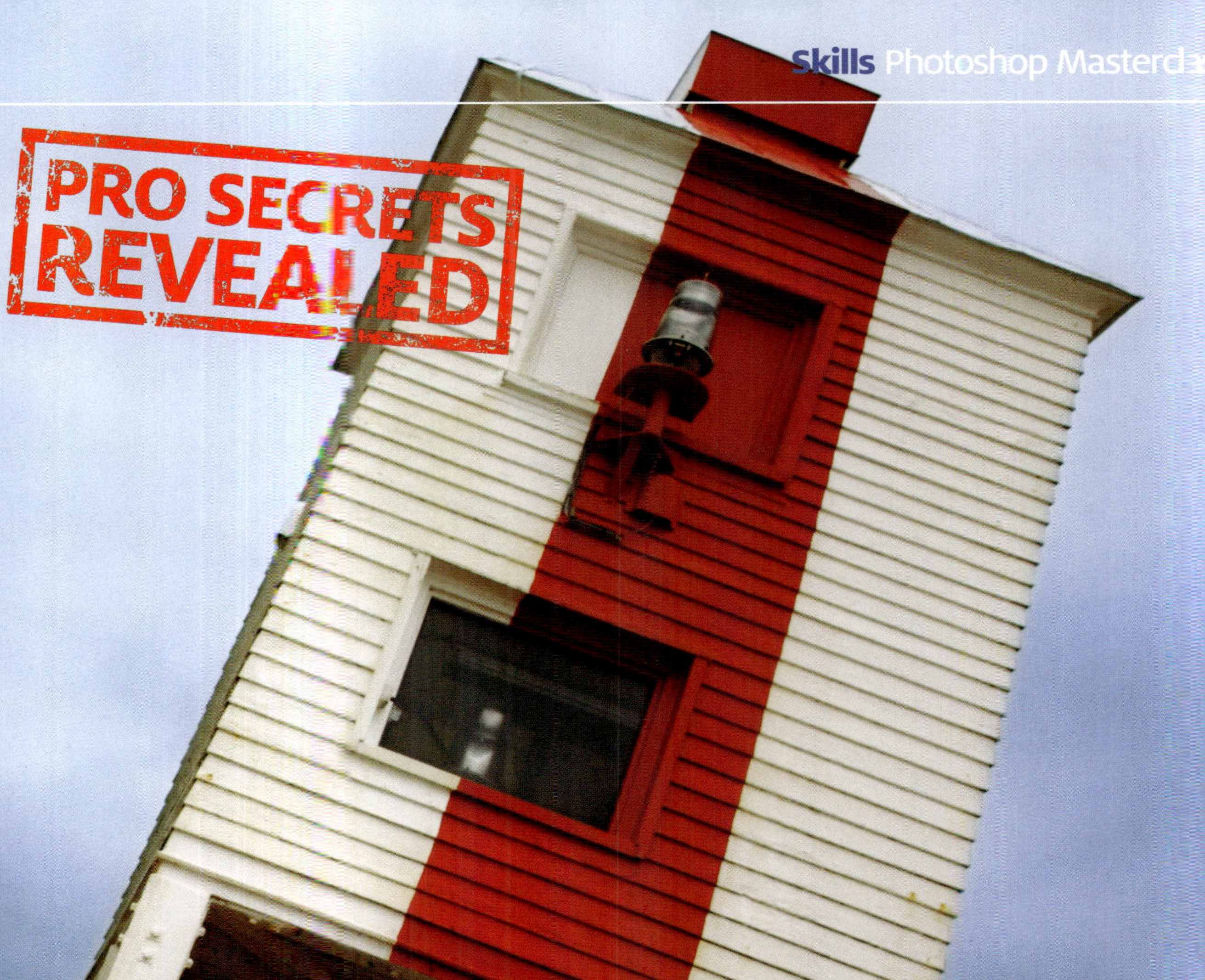

Discover the perfect method for...

Capturing flash-lit fashion portraits

Checklist

What you'll need
Digital Photo Professional
Photoshop CS3 or above

How long it'll take
Half a day

The skills you'll learn
- How to master fill-in flash
- How to boost colour and contrast in DPP
- How to make dull, cloudy skies look more moody
- How to selectively sharpen your subject

Fill-in flash can make portraits shot on location really leap off the page, even when the weather isn't co-operating...

Fashion and portrait photographers regularly use fill-in flash to create colourful, punchy location shots that bring out the best in both the model and the clothes they're wearing. Deliberately under-exposing the background and adding a quick burst of flash to bring out colour and detail in the foreground can really make your subject leap off the page, and the great thing about this kind of flash photography is that the weather doesn't have to be perfect for you to get good results – in fact, dark, overcast skies can provide added drama as you can see in the shot on this page.

The beach is a great place to get to grips with fill-in flash, because there's plenty of room to move around and try out different techniques. For this Photoshop Masterclass, we headed down to blustery Burnham-on-Sea for a fashion shoot.

Here, we'll show you how to make the most of any location shoot, whether you're photographing models on a beach or your kids in a park. We'll look at which settings and equipment to use, how to boost colour and contrast to make your subject stand out, and how to improve dull, grey skies. Turn the page to get started...

STEP BY STEP 1

Flash of inspiration

Top tips guaranteed to help you shoot fill-flash portraits like a pro

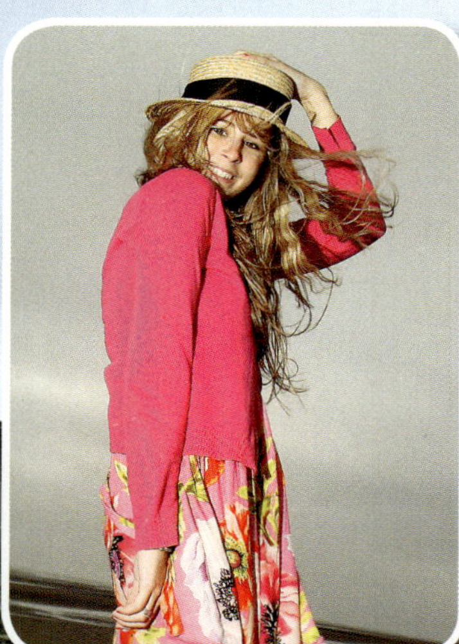

Accessorise!

1 You can add colour and interest to any location portrait by including accessories such as hats and sunglasses, or colourful clothing such as brightly coloured scarves or kaftans. This is particularly true for fashion shoots, but is equally appropriate for beach portraits of friends and family, where props such as surf-boards or brightly coloured beach balls can add a sense of summer fun.

Use off-camera flash

2 If you're serious about portraits, an off-camera flash cord is essential. This enables you to control not just where the flash is coming from, but also exactly where it's pointing, giving you much more creative control. This kind of flash work takes a bit of practice, but the beauty of digital photography is that the only thing limiting how many shots you take is the number of memory cards you're carrying.

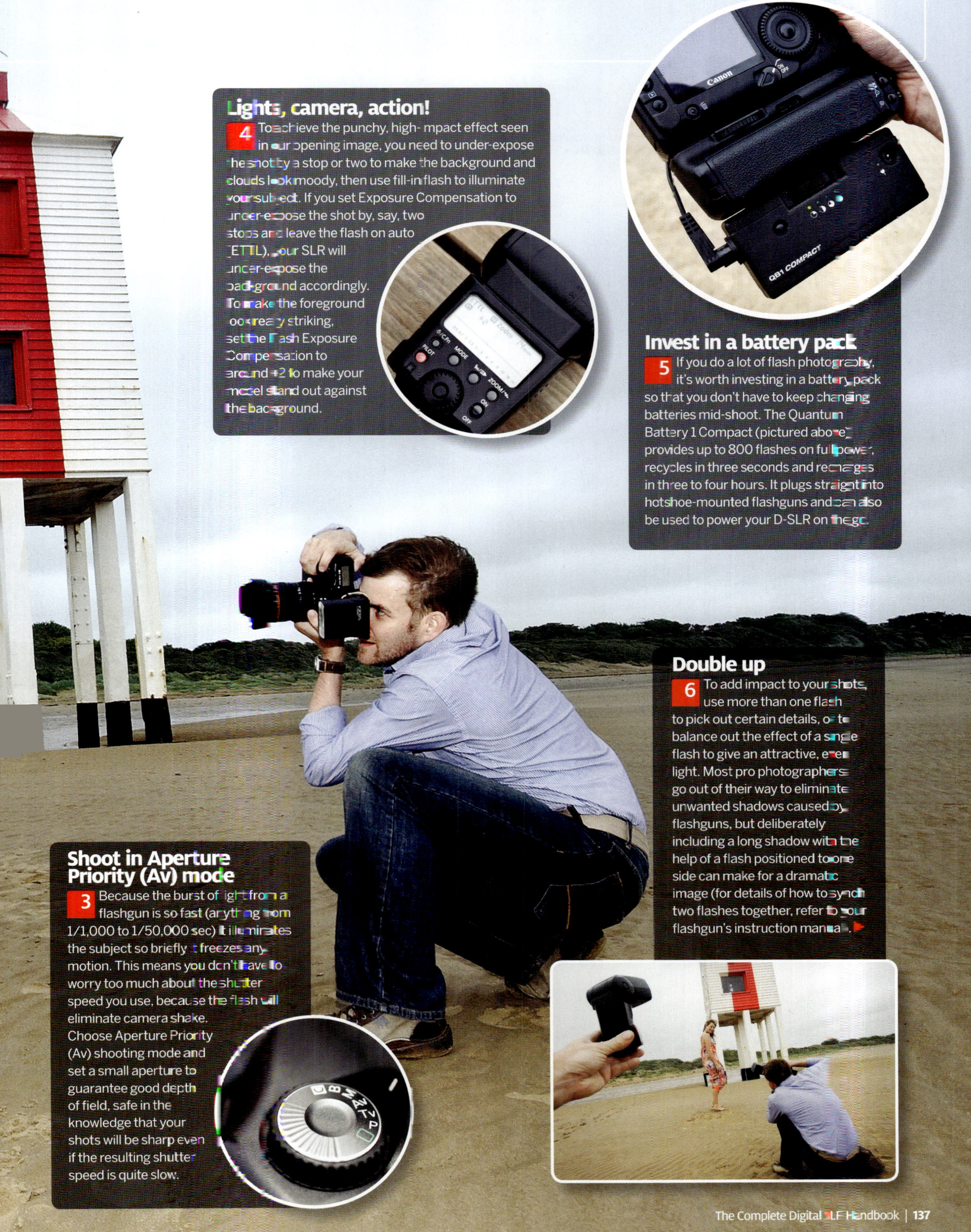

Shoot in Aperture Priority (Av) mode

3 Because the burst of light from a flashgun is so fast (anything from 1/1,000 to 1/50,000 sec) it illuminates the subject so briefly it freezes any motion. This means you don't have to worry too much about the shutter speed you use, because the flash will eliminate camera shake. Choose Aperture Priority (Av) shooting mode and set a small aperture to guarantee good depth of field, safe in the knowledge that your shots will be sharp even if the resulting shutter speed is quite slow.

Lights, camera, action!

4 To achieve the punchy, high-impact effect seen in our opening image, you need to under-expose the shot by a stop or two to make the background and clouds look moody, then use fill-in flash to illuminate your subject. If you set Exposure Compensation to under-expose the shot by, say, two stops and leave the flash on auto (ETTL), your SLR will under-expose the background accordingly. To make the foreground look really striking, set the Flash Exposure Compensation to around +2 to make your model stand out against the background.

Invest in a battery pack

5 If you do a lot of flash photography, it's worth investing in a battery pack so that you don't have to keep changing batteries mid-shoot. The Quantum Battery 1 Compact (pictured above) provides up to 800 flashes on full power, recycles in three seconds and recharges in three to four hours. It plugs straight into hotshoe-mounted flashguns and can also be used to power your D-SLR on the go.

Double up

6 To add impact to your shots, use more than one flash to pick out certain details, or to balance out the effect of a single flash to give an attractive, even light. Most pro photographers go out of their way to eliminate unwanted shadows caused by flashguns, but deliberately including a long shadow with the help of a flash positioned to one side can make for a dramatic image (for details of how to synch two flashes together, refer to your flashgun's instruction manual). ▶

STEP BY STEP 2 Transform your shot post-shoot

Super Tip!

"Digital Photo Professional features a clever tool that enables you to compare the original version of your image with the final edited version at the click of a mouse. This is useful for gauging how far to go with a particular edit, such as tweaking colour or contrast. To compare the two versions, simply go to View>Before/After Comparison and then View>ChangeUp/Down/Left/Right to choose whether to display them side-by-side or one above the other."

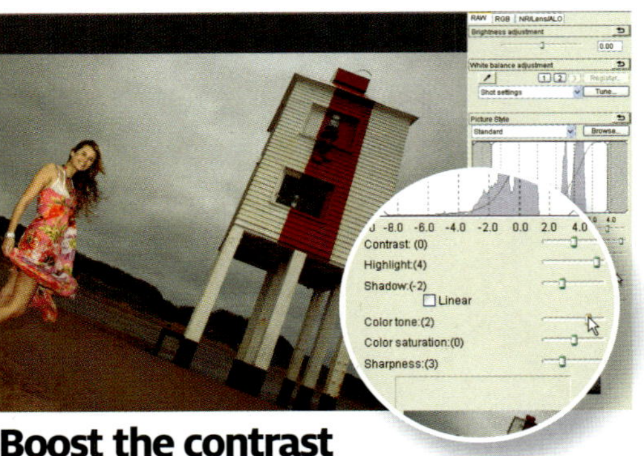

Boost the contrast

1 Launch Digital Photo Professional (DPP) and use the window on the left to navigate to the file named masterclass_start.cr2 on the Video Disc. Select the image and click on the Edit Image Window icon. In the new window that opens up, move the Highlight slider to 4 and the Shadow slider to -2 to bring out detail in the clouds. Now drag the Colour Tone slider to 2 to warm up the model's skin tones.

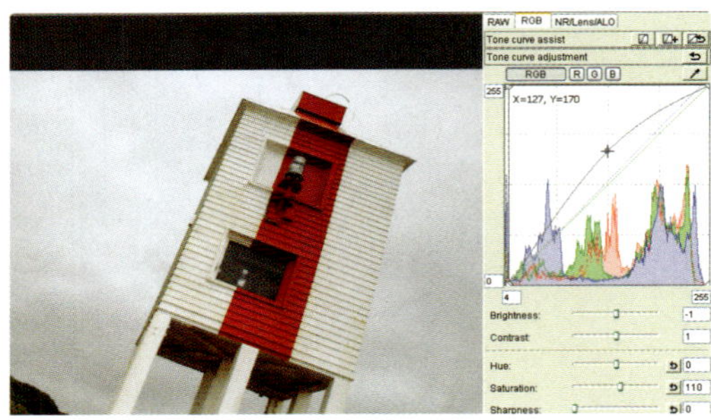

Get richer reds

2 Select the RGB tab at the top of the Tool palette and drag the middle point of the Curves line up so Y=170 and X=127. Drag the Contrast slider to 2 and the Saturation slider to 110 to give the reds in the tower and the model's dress a boost. For a more moody sky, click on the B (Blue) tab in the Curves palette and drag the vertical line at the far right of the histogram to 245.

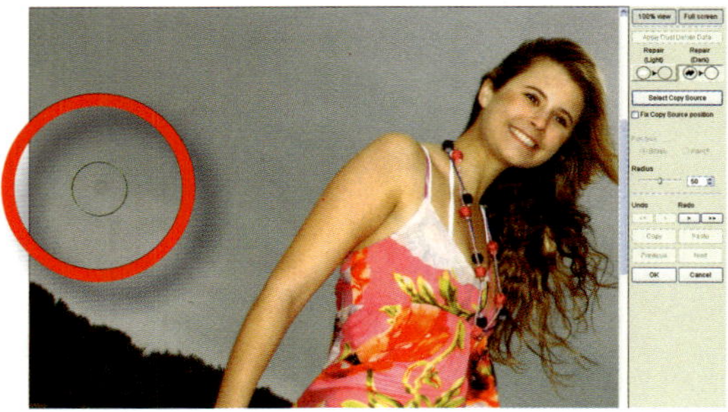

Stamp out spots

3 Go to Tools>StartStampTool and double-click on the sky above the model's shoulder. Click on the Repair (Dark) button, select a brush Radius of 30 and click on any sensor spots in the sky to remove them. Hit OK when finished and go to Tools>Transfer ToPhotoshop to open the image as a 16-bit TIFF.

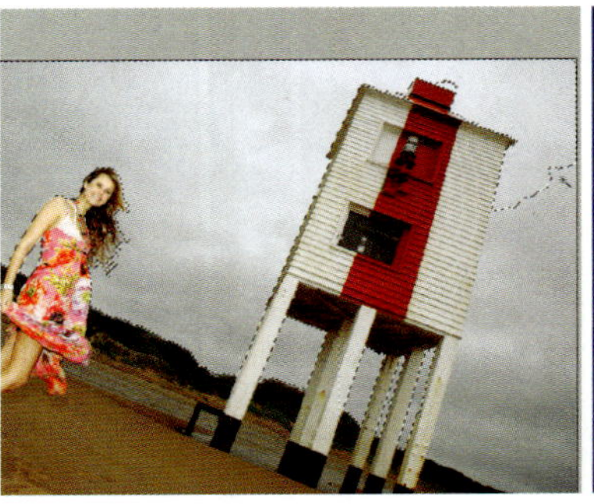

Select the sky

4 With the image now open in Photoshop, go to Layer>DuplicateLayer, click OK and select the Magic Wand tool. Set Tolerance to 10, tick Contiguous and start selecting the sky, holding Shift to add to your selection and Alt to subtract from it. Take care around the tower, but don't worry about the model's hair yet.

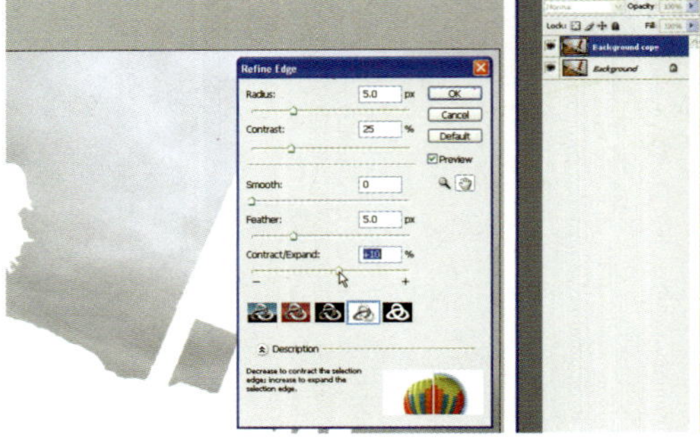

Very refined

5 Click on Refine Edge (introduced with CS3) at the top of the screen, and in the window that appears, drag the Radius slider to 5 pixels, the Contrast slider to 25%, the Feather slider to around 5 pixels and the Contract/Expand slider to +10%. Click OK.

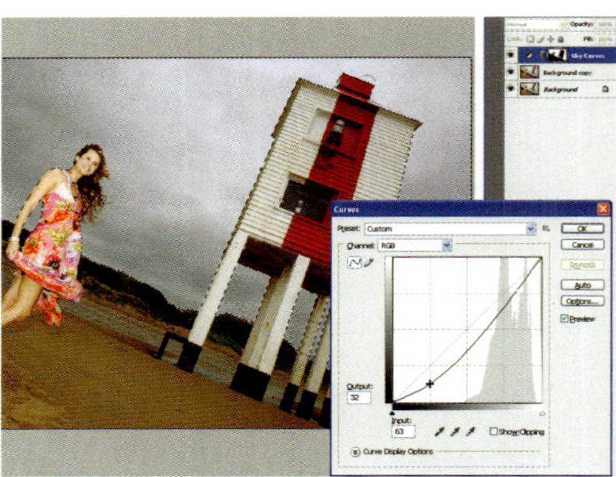

Get moody

6 Once you've made your selection, go to Layer> NewAdjustmentLayer and select Curves from the drop-down menu. Click OK, and in the Curves window that opens up click on the diagonal line about a quarter of the way up and drag it downwards until the figure in the Output box on the left is around 32.

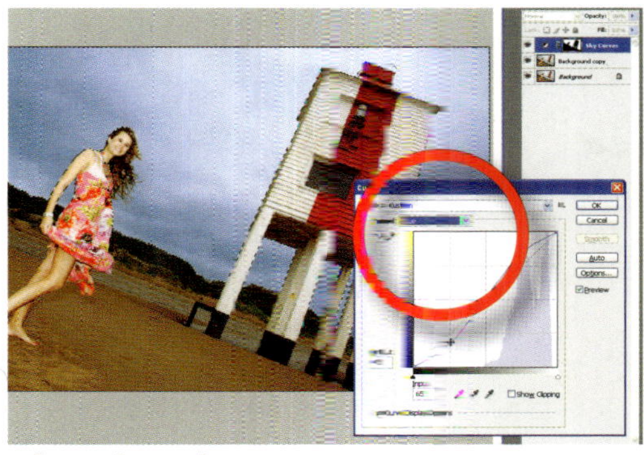

Blue thunder

7 To make the sky even more moody, select Blue from the Channel menu and drag the bottom half of the curve line down and the top half up to create a shallow s-shaped curve. Repeat with the Red channel, clicking a quarter of the way up the line and dragging it down until the Output value is around 40. Click OK.

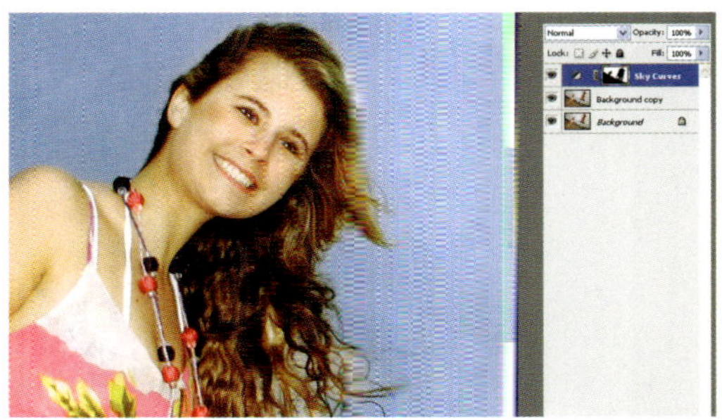

Trim the fringe

8 If you zoom in to 100%, you'll see some coloured fringing around the model and along the edge of the horizon. To remove it, select the Curves layer, set the foreground colour to white and grab the Brush tool. Set Mode to Normal, Size to 50 and Opacity and Flow to 50%, then paint over the areas of grey sky around the model's hair and right arm and along the horizon.

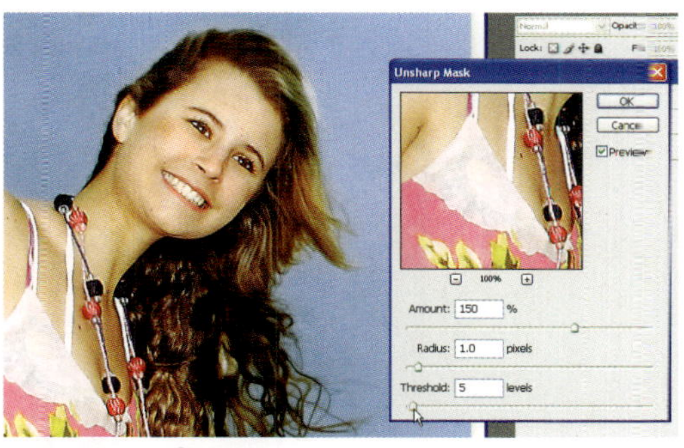

Sharpen it up

9 Merge the visible layers into a new layer by pressing Shift+Ctrl+Alt+E (Shift+Apple+Alt+E on a Mac), then go to Filter>Sharpen>UnsharpMask. Set Amount to 150, Radius to 1 and Threshold to 0. Click OK, then add a Layer Mask by clicking on the icon in the Layers palette. Set the foreground colour to black and press Alt+Delete to mask out the sharp layer.

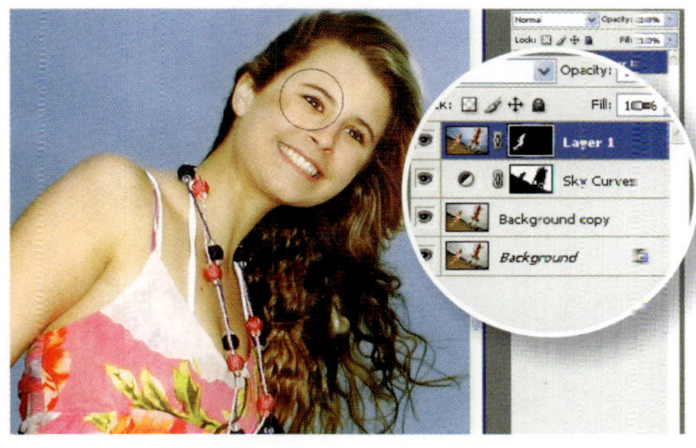

The big reveal

10 To sharpen the model but not the background, change the foreground colour to white, then select a soft-edged brush with a Radius of 100 and set Opacity to 100% and Flow to 80%. Carefully paint over the model's face and dress to reveal the sharpened layer below, then save your final image as a PSD file.

Essential tips

How to get the most out of your location shoots

When you're shooting portraits on location, it's worth mixing things up a little – clothes, backdrop, poses – to make sure you get as much out of your shoot as possible. Here are a few more photos from our evening at Burnham on Sea that illustrate a variety of different approaches to shooting in the same place.

Use the location

Try using elements in the landscape such as these wooden posts (right) to improve composition and add interest to your shots.

Have some fun...

Fashion photography can be quite a serious business, so try lightening up the mood a little by playing around with poses.

...then get all moody

Try to make sure that the expression of your model reflects the mood of the scene as a whole, as demonstrated in this slightly gritty shot (far right).

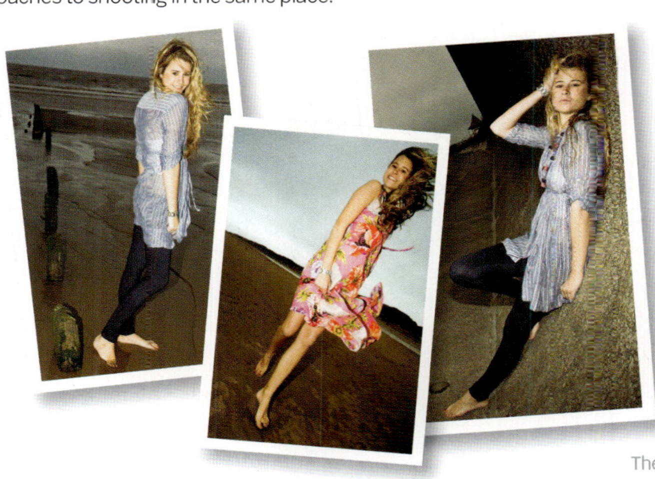

Super Tip!

"If you're shooting wide-angle portraits in which the subject doesn't fill the frame, little blemishes on the skin aren't that obvious. However, if you're shooting a close-up with fill-flash, which tends to highlight every single pimple and wrinkle, it's worth zooming in on the subject's face and cloning out any minor blemishes using the Clone tool or Healing Brush. The Healing Brush is especially effective on skin, because it tends to smooth it out and give it a soft, flattering finish."

Phrase Book?

Bit depth

Bit depth refers to the maximum number of colours or tones an image contains. A JPEG image uses eight bits for each of the red, green and blue colour channels, which provide 256 tones and more than 16 million possible colours. A 16-bit image, meanwhile (see step 3) uses 16 bits for each channel, which provide 65,535 different tones and 281 trillion possible colours. The result is a more detailed image and a smoother gradation between colours. This extra information is useful because even if you lose some during processing, you will still end up with a high quality final image.

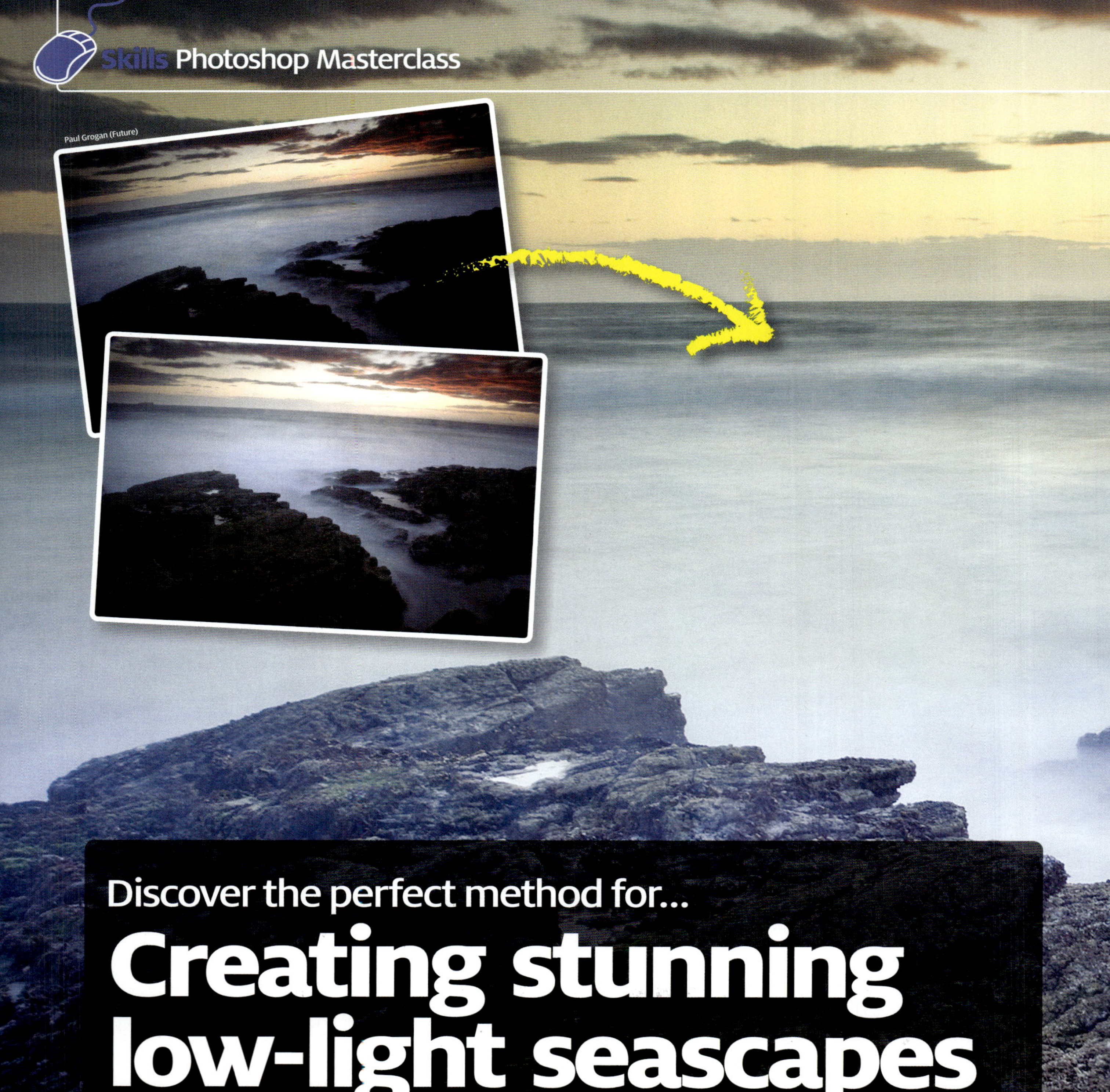
Paul Grogan (Future)

Discover the perfect method for...

Creating stunning low-light seascapes

Checklist

What you'll need
Photoshop CS or above

How long it'll take
Half a day

The skills you'll learn
- How to master long exposures in low light
- How to merge two shots
- How to use layers and masks to enhance selected areas
- How to fix lens distortion

Shooting coastal scenes using slow shutter speeds can result in really dramatic images. Here's how it's done...

Sunset seascapes are the stock-in-trade of many professional landscape photographers. By combining the rich reds of a setting sun with the moody blues of glistening boulders, they can create images as striking as they are serene.

Another favourite trick of seascape specialists is to use slow shutter speeds to blur out movement in the water, resulting in smooth, quicksilver seas.

Here in the UK, we're spoilt for choice when it comes to stunning coastlines, so for this Masterclass we headed to Pembrokeshire for a sunset shoot of our own. Over the next few pages, we'll show you how to make the most of any coastal shoot, and how to give your seascapes that milky, ethereal look. We'll take a look at the settings and equipment to use, and also show you how to fine-tune your exposures using layers and Layer Masks. Finally, we'll explain how to correct the barrelling that's so common in coastal landscapes shot with wide-angle lenses. So let's get started...

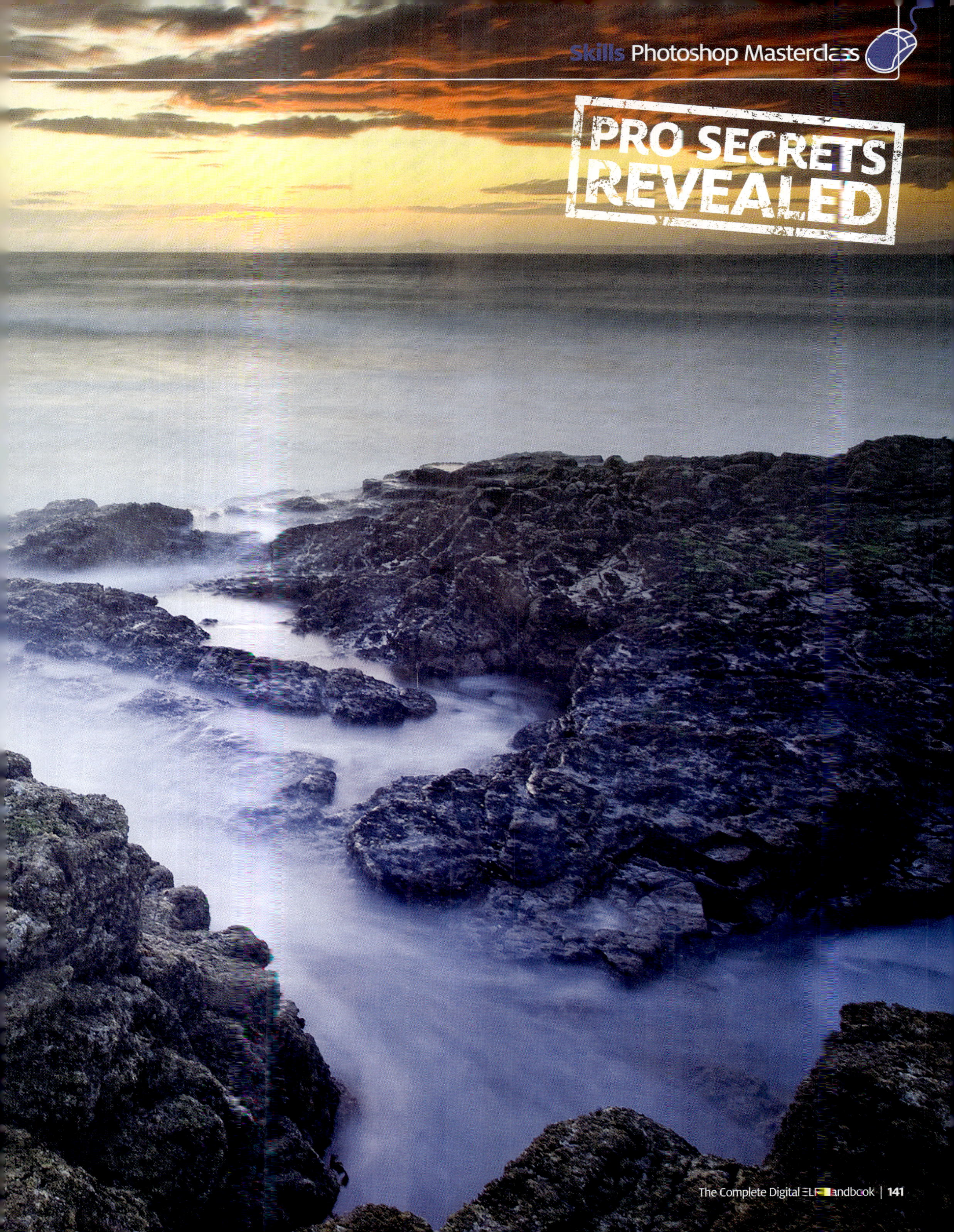
PRO SECRETS REVEALED

STEP BY STEP 1

Capturing the scene

Six top tips for shooting classic seascapes at slow shutter speeds

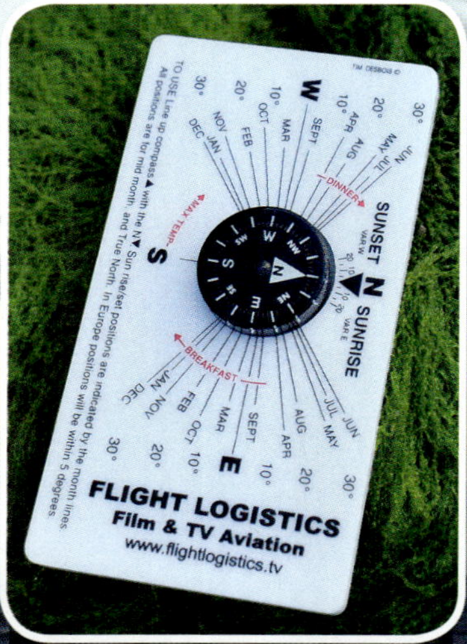

Time your shoot

1 When photographing coastal scenes at dawn or dusk it's essential that you know where and when the sun will rise and set, so you can ensure you're in the right place at the right time. For sunrise and sunset times, check out the excellent www.sunrisesunsetmap.com, and to work out where the sun will come up and go down anywhere in the UK, check out this clever little sun compass (above), available from www.flightlogistics.tv.

Wait for the tide

2 Knowing the times of low and high tide can make all the difference when it comes to shooting seascapes, as this will determine the sort of shot you'll end up with. The key is to time your shoot so that the tide you want coincides with sunrise or sunset. You can always get tide times online before you go, but if you do a lot of coastal photography, it's worth investing in a tide table for your part of the country (visit www.quicktide.co.uk for more info).

Use Av mode

3 If you want both the foreground and background of your scene to be in focus it's important to use as small an aperture as possible. To ensure good depth of field, switch to Av mode and then choose an aperture of f/16 or f/22. This will also allow you to shoot at a very slow shutter speed, which is essential for blurring any crashing waves and giving the sea a silky-smooth finish.

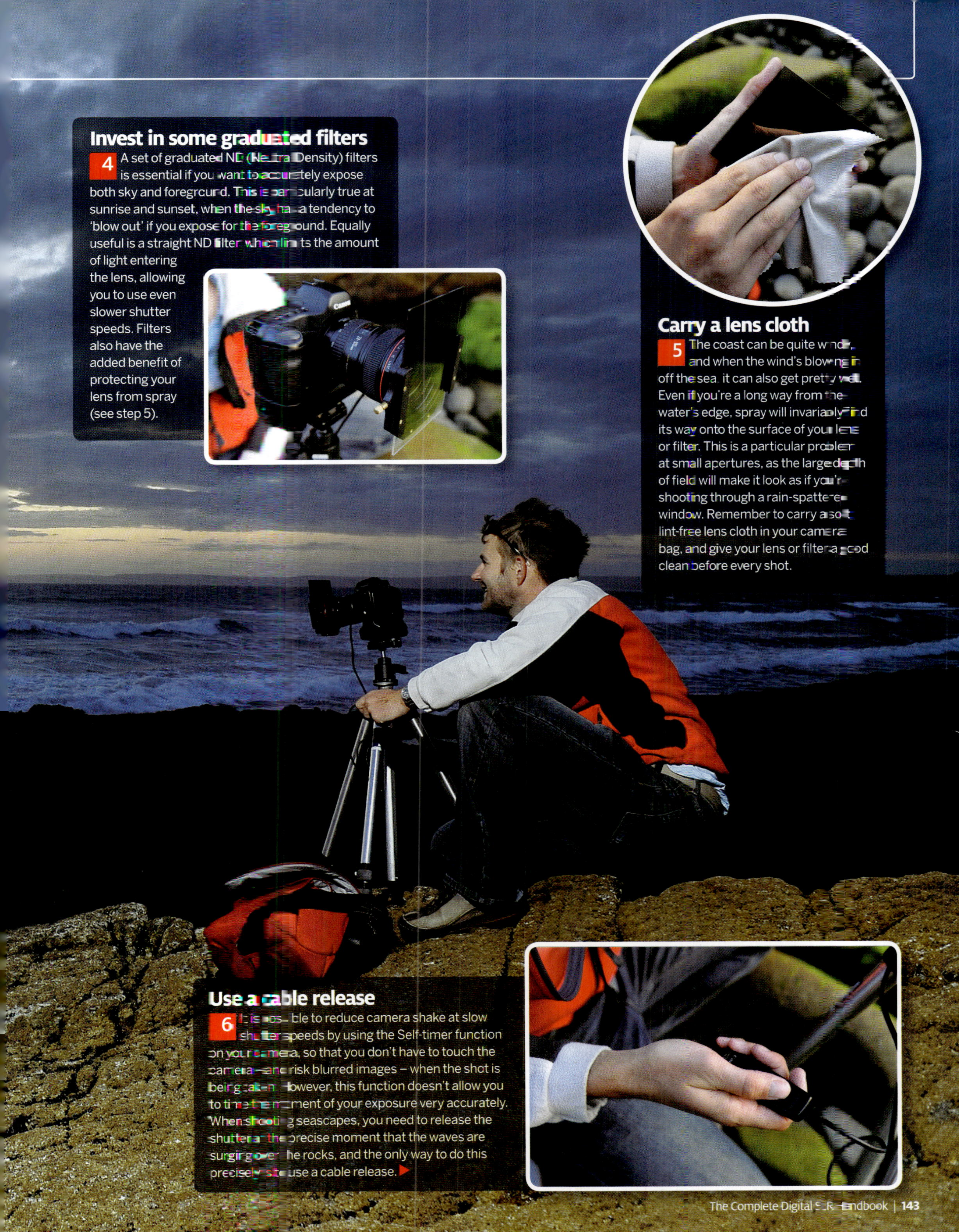

Invest in some graduated filters

4 A set of graduated ND (Neutral Density) filters is essential if you want to accurately expose both sky and foreground. This is particularly true at sunrise and sunset, when the sky has a tendency to 'blow out' if you expose for the foreground. Equally useful is a straight ND filter which limits the amount of light entering the lens, allowing you to use even slower shutter speeds. Filters also have the added benefit of protecting your lens from spray (see step 5).

Carry a lens cloth

5 The coast can be quite windy, and when the wind's blowing in off the sea, it can also get pretty wet. Even if you're a long way from the water's edge, spray will invariably find its way onto the surface of your lens or filter. This is a particular problem at small apertures, as the large depth of field will make it look as if you're shooting through a rain-spattered window. Remember to carry a soft lint-free lens cloth in your camera bag, and give your lens or filter a good clean before every shot.

Use a cable release

6 It is possible to reduce camera shake at slow shutter speeds by using the Self-timer function on your camera, so that you don't have to touch the camera – and risk blurred images – when the shot is being taken. However, this function doesn't allow you to time the moment of your exposure very accurately. When shooting seascapes, you need to release the shutter at the precise moment that the waves are surging over the rocks, and the only way to do this precisely is to use a cable release. ▶

Super Tip!

"The beauty of using layers is that you can go back and make adjustments to your image at any time, although you do have to remember to make the layers above invisible if you want to see the effect of your new adjustments. If you want to tweak the gradient mask, for example, you have to click the eye icon of the Corrected layer off. If you do make changes, you'll need to repeat steps 9 and 10, as the existing Corrected layer was created when you merged your *original* Gradient layer with the layer below."

STEP BY STEP 2 How to get exposure spot-on

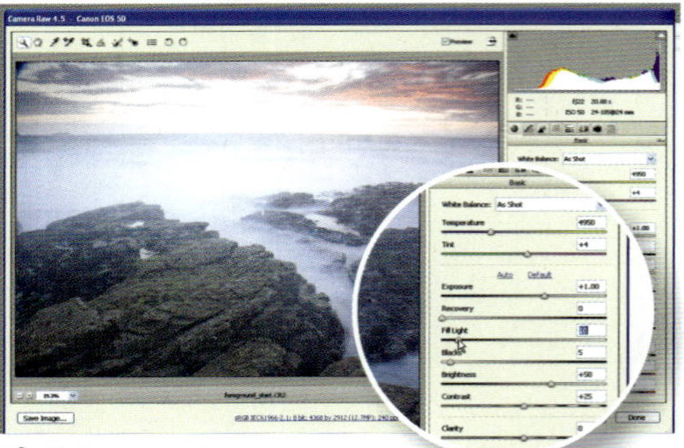

Lighten up!

1 Navigate to the folder called masterclass_start on your Video Disc and open the file called foreground_start.cr2 in Photoshop CS. The RAW file will automatically open in the Adobe Camera Raw interface. To lighten the foreground, drag the Exposure slider to +1.0 and the Fill Light slider to +10.

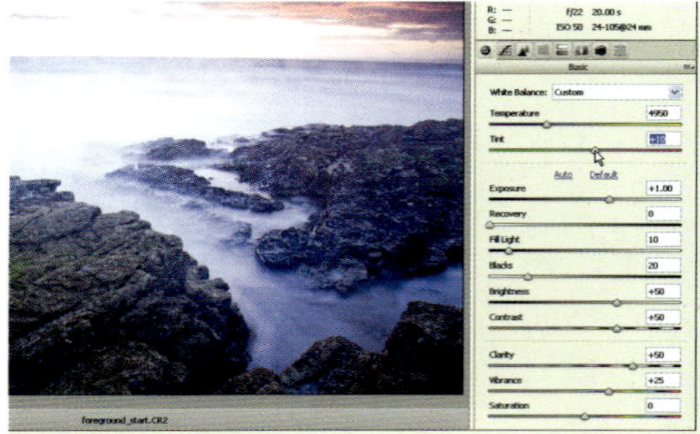

Cool it down

2 To boost contrast and colour, drag Blacks to +20, Contrast to +50, Clarity to 50 and Vibrance to +25. To cool down the foreground slightly without darkening it, move Tint to +10. To see the effect your edits have had on your original image, tick and untick Preview at the top of the window. Click on Open Image.

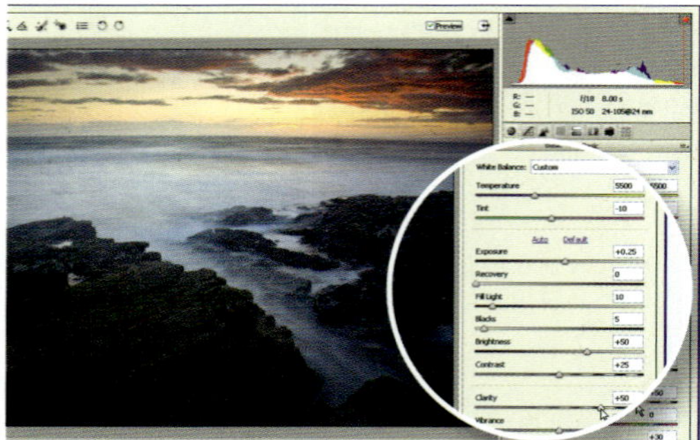

Red sky at night

3 Next, open the file called sky_start.cr2 from the Video Disc. To give the warm colours in the sky a gentle boost, drag the Temperature slider to around 5,500 and the Saturation slider to +30. To increase the overall brightness and contrast of the sky, drag Exposure to +0.25, Fill Light to +10 and Clarity to +50, then click on Open Image.

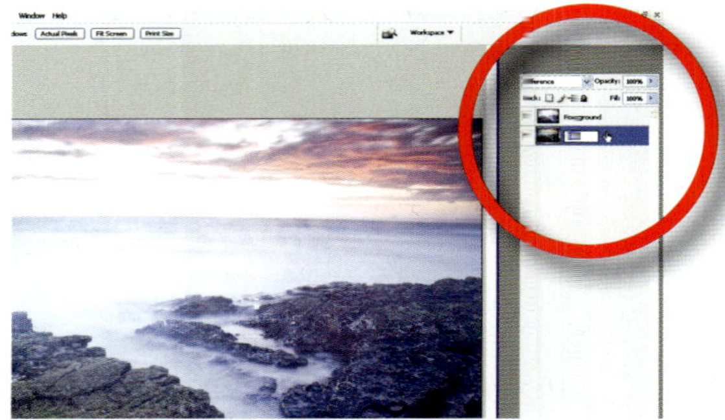

Merge the exposures

4 Press the F key to change views until both images are visible. Click on foreground_start.cr2, then click on its thumbnail in the Layers palette and drag it onto the main sky_start image. Close foreground_start.cr2, then double-click on the Background layer to rename it Sky, and Layer 1 to rename it Foreground. Press F until the image fills the screen.

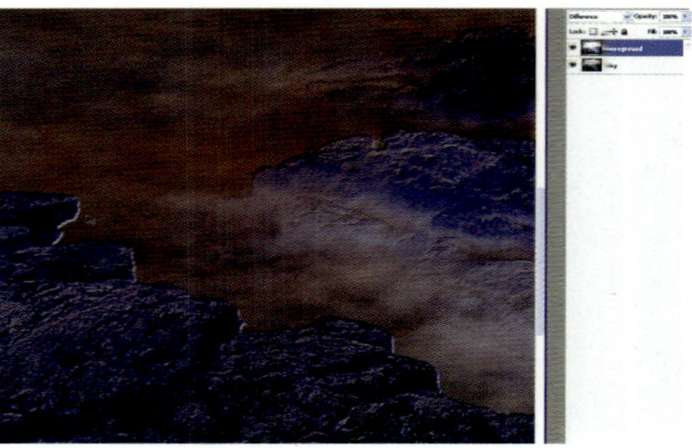

Line 'em up

5 To check that the two layers are aligned, click on the Foreground layer and select Difference from the Blending Mode menu. Zoom in on the edge of the rocks at the water's edge, select the Move tool and then use the arrow keys to nudge the Foreground layer around until it lines up with the Sky layer. Now return the Blending Mode to Normal and zoom back out.

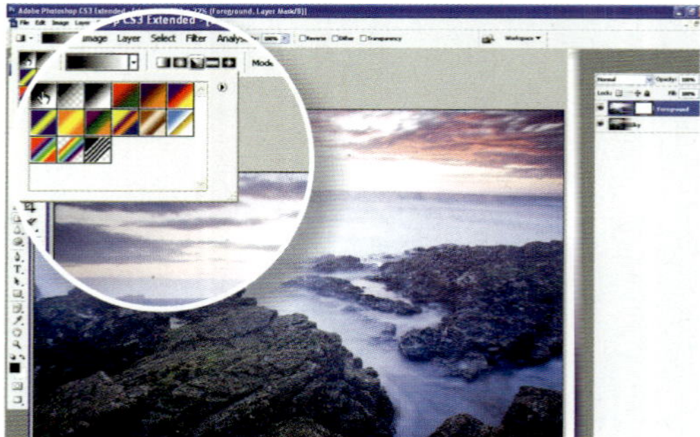

Add a Layer Mask

6 Next, select the Foreground layer and click on the Add Layer Mask icon in the Layers palette. Press the X key to set the foreground colour to black, then click on the Gradient tool and select Foreground to Background from the drop-down menu in the top bar.

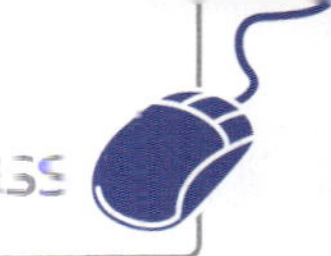

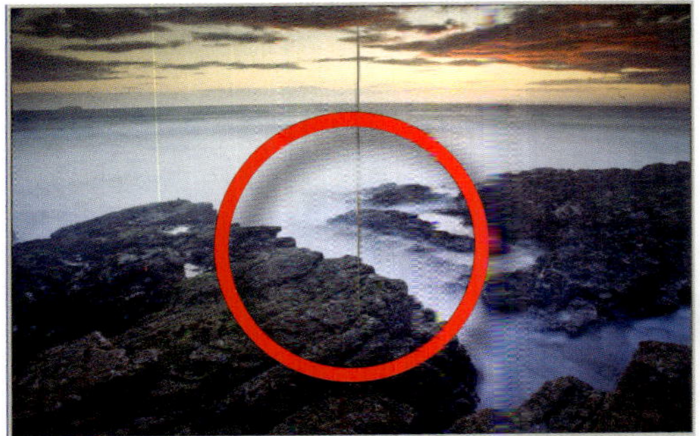

Draw a gradient

7 Click on the Linear Gradient icon in the top toolbar, then set the Blending Mode to Normal and the Opacity to 100%. Now draw a vertical line from the top-centre of the image to about three quarters of the way down. Don't worry if it looks a bit gradual at this stage, because we'll show you how to fine-tune the effect in the next step.

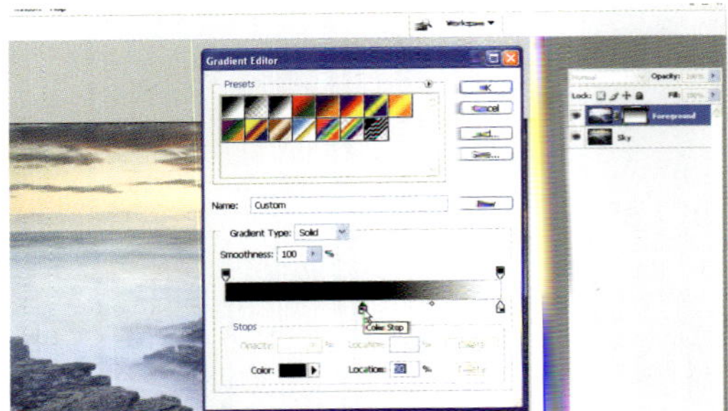

Reveal the sea

8 Click on the gradient bar in the top toolbar to open up the Gradient Editor. Drag the slider at the bottom left of the gradient bar to the right, until its location field reads 50%. This will make the edge of the mask less gradual. Click OK and draw a new line from the top of the image to about two thirds of the way down to reveal more detail in the sea from the layer below.

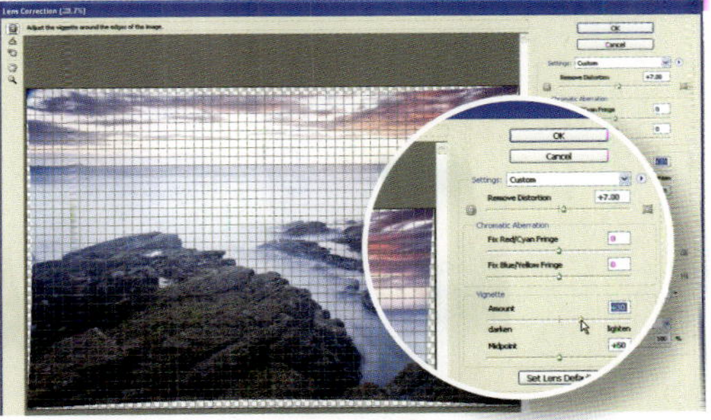

Straighten the horizon

9 Merge the visible layers into a new layer at the top of the layer stack by pressing Shift+Ctrl+Alt+E (or Shift+Apple+Alt+E on a Mac) and rename the layer Corrected. To straighten the curved horizon, and lighten the corners (see Phrase Book), go to Filter>Distort>LensCorrection. Drag Remove Distortion to +7 and Vignette to +30, then drag Scale to 107% to lose the transparent edges created by the correction. Hit OK.

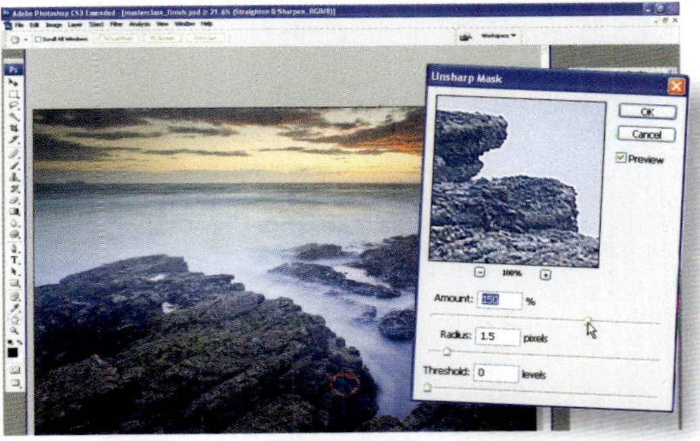

Look clean, look sharp

10 To clean up the image, grab the Clone Stamp tool from the Tools palette, set a brush Size of around 100 pixels, and zoom in on the sky and the milky sea to clone out any dust spots. Finally, to sharpen up the rocks slightly, go to Filter>Sharpen>UnsharpMask and set Amount to 150%, Radius to 1.5 and Threshold to 0.

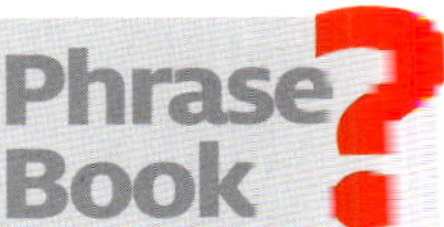

Phrase Book?

Barrelling
If you use a wide-angle lens to shoot landscapes the horizon may appear slightly curved, unless it is right in the middle of the viewfinder. The closer it is to the edge of the frame, the more obvious the curvature. This barrelling, as it's known, can be easily corrected using Photoshop's Lens Correction Filter (see step 9).

Scaling
In step 9 we scaled up the shot to lose the transparent edges created by the lens correction process. If you're starting with a low-res image and you don't want to make it bigger in case it starts to pixellate, you could crop the shot to lose the transparent edges.

Following the sun

When shooting sunsets, west is best!

One advantage of shooting seascapes after the sun has gone down is that the weather doesn't have to be perfect; not only do dark skies allow you to use slower shutter speeds for smoothing out moving water, they can also add drama to your final image.

However, if you are lucky enough to find yourself shooting a dramatic sunset, head for a beach that faces west and shoot towards the sun. Use a graduated Neutral Density filter on your lens to stop the sky from burning out and look out for reflections in rock pools. Boulders and seaweed can also add interest, and try to shoot in both landscape and portrait format. ■

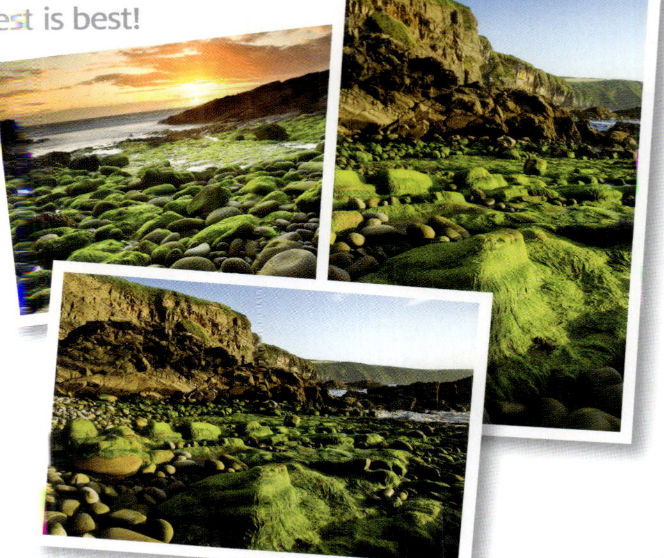

Super Tip!

"In step 8, it's worth playing around with the various sliders to see what effect they have on the linear gradient you've created – by adjusting how abruptly the gradient mask changes from black to white, you can fine-tune how much of the sea from the Sky layer is revealed. You can also reduce the opacity of the mask to reveal more of the darker rocks in the layer below."

Tackle lens-related problems

Correct the effects of vignetting and chromatic aberration in Adobe Camera Raw

Checklist
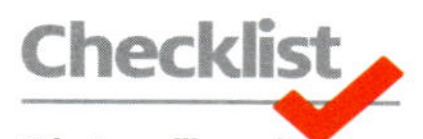

What you'll need
Photoshop CS or above

How long it'll take
10 minutes

The skills you'll learn
- ✔ How to get rid of chromatic aberration
- ✔ How to remove (or add) vignetting
- ✔ How to counteract lens distortion

Under some conditions, RAW files can suffer from lens-related flaws, or artefacts. High-contrast objects (the white sails on our windmill, for example) can be affected by chromatic aberration – where red or cyan fringes appear along bright edges. This occurs when a lens fails to focus different wave-lengths of light on the same part of a camera's sensor.

Other side effects of shooting with wide-angle lenses include curved horizons, caused by lens distortion (or 'barrelling'), and vignetting (dark areas in the corners of your shots), which occurs when the front edge of your lens (or filter) limits the amount of light entering the lens. Vignetting is most common at wide apertures in SLRs with full-frame sensors and it can be removed (or added) by lightening or darkening the corners in Photoshop.

Here we'll show you how to banish each of these common artefacts using Adobe Camera Raw and Photoshop's Lens Correction filter, plus how to *add* a touch of vignetting to creatively frame your shots.

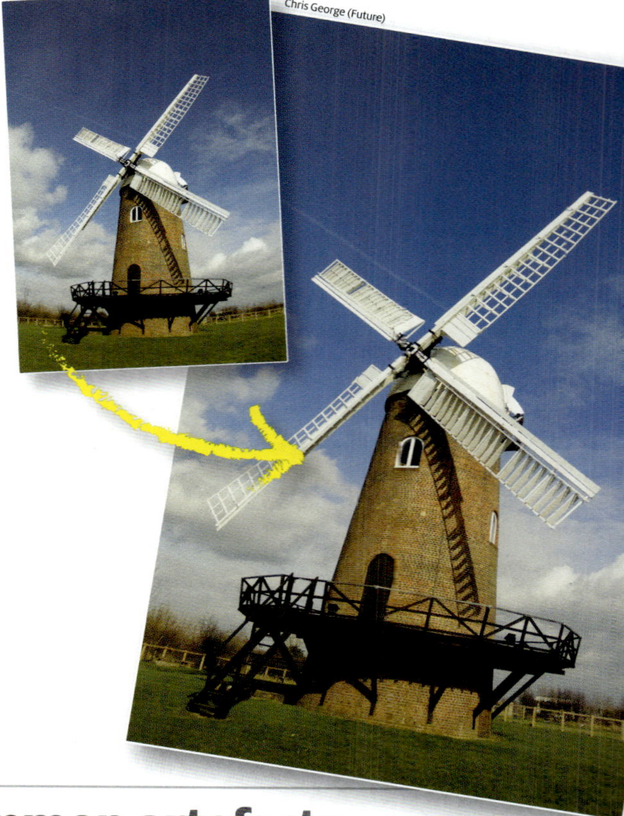
Chris George (Future)

Super Tip!

"When editing in Adobe Camera Raw, you need to zoom to at least 100% to spot problems such as chromatic aberration. To do this, use the Select Zoom Level control to quickly zoom in and out to specific sizes. To jump instantly to 100%, double-click on the Zoom Tool icon in the toolbar."

STEP BY STEP Banish common artefacts

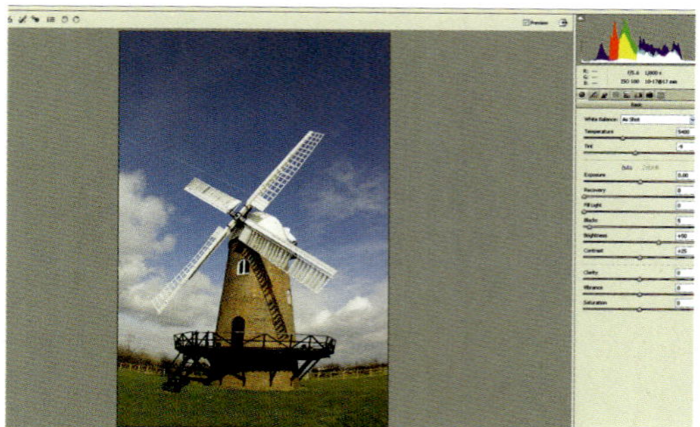

Getting started

1 First, open raw_start.CR2 from the Video Disc in Photoshop. The software will recognise that this is a RAW file and open it in the Adobe Camera Raw (ACR) editor. As well as lens-induced 'barrelling' and colour fringes along the edges of the windmill's sails, you'll notice that the shot tilts a little to the right, so there's plenty of work to be done.

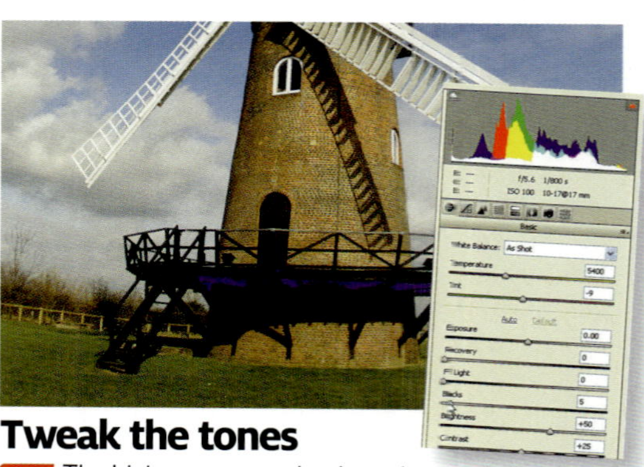

Tweak the tones

2 The histogram reveals a broad spread of shadows, midtones and highlights, so the shot's exposure is relatively healthy. Click the Shadow Clipping Warning icon (the white arrow) at the top-left of the histogram and the darkest parts of the shot will appear as blue patches. To reveal a little more detail in these areas, drag the Blacks slider to about 2. ▶

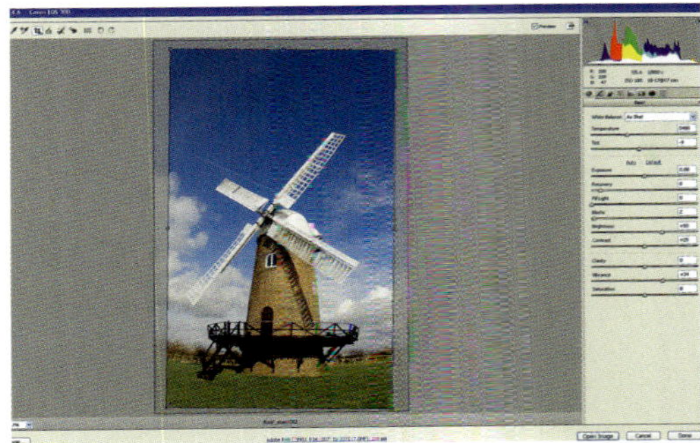

Straighten it up

3 The windmill is tilting slightly to the right. Grab the Straighten tool from the top toolbar and use it to draw a line along the windmill's horizontal wooden rail. This tells Photoshop which features should run parallel with the bottom edge of the frame. A rotated crop box will appear. Drag the crop handles in a little to lose some of the curved fence and sky.

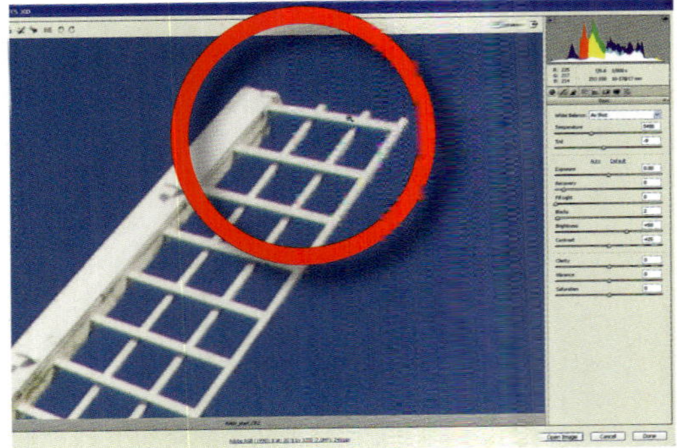

Chromatic aberration

4 Grab the Zoom tool from the top toolbar and click a few times on the top-right sail to zoom in to 300%. You'll see that there's a fringe of red clinging to the top edges of the white struts. This example of chromatic aberration is quite subtle, but it would still be enough for the file to be rejected if you submitted it to a stock photo library.

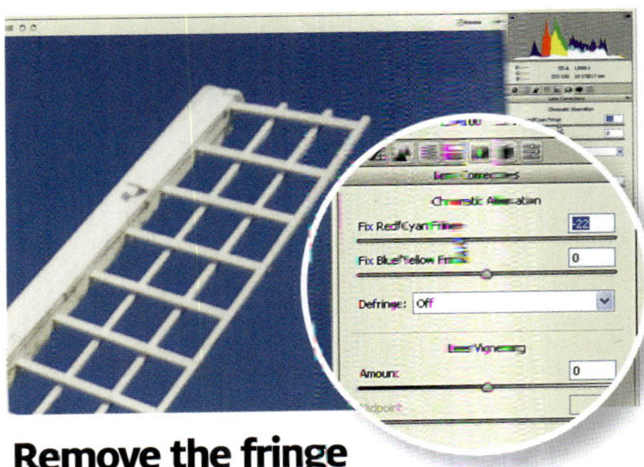

Remove the fringe

5 Click on the Lens Corrections tab, then drag the Fix Red/Cyan Fringe slider left to a value of around -22. This erases the red fringe, leaving a clean, white wooden sail. Zoom out to see the entire shot. You could use the Lens Vignetting slider to darken the corners, but as we're going to crop the edges when we remove the 'barrelling' we'll add a vignette later.

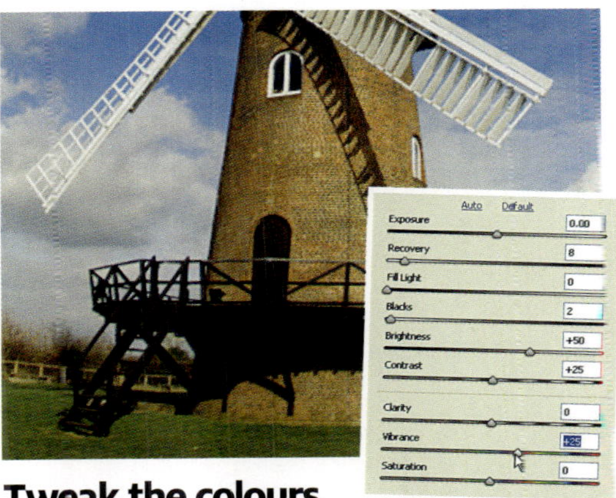

Tweak the colours

6 To create richer-looking blues and greens, click on the Basic tab and push the Vibrance slider up to +25. At this stage, you can't see the straightened horizon; to do that you need to open the edited image in Photoshop, which also has the tools you need to banish the 'barrelling' at the bottom of the image. Click Open Image to view it in Photoshop.

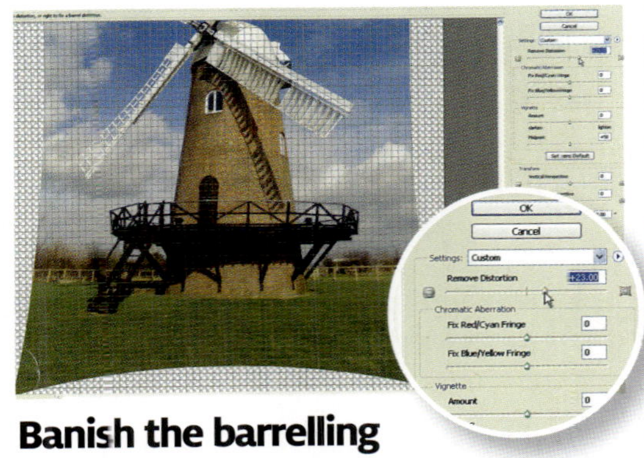

Banish the barrelling

7 Go to Filter>Distort>LensCorrection and a grey grid will appear. This will help you straighten out the curved horizon. Move the Remove Distortion slider to +23.00 to reduce the 'barrelling', then drag the Scale slider to 119% to lose the transparent edges produced by the lens correction procedure.

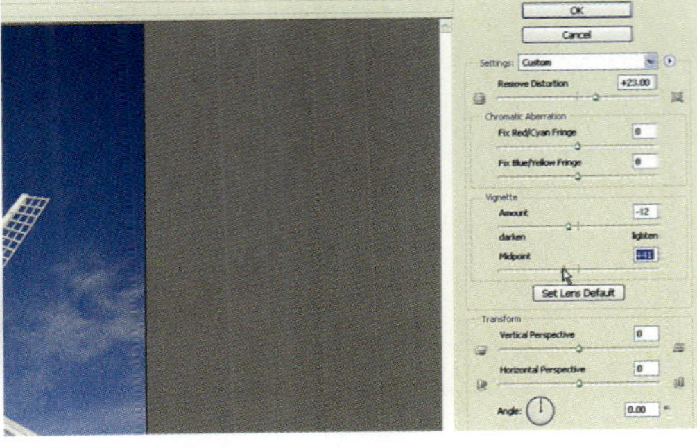

Add a vignette

8 Untick Show Grid to see the image clearly. The horizontal distortion has been eliminated. This image doesn't suffer from unwanted vignetting, but you can add a vignette to give texture to a bland blue sky and help draw attention to your subject. Drag Vignette Amount to -12 and push it to the corner edges by changing Midpoint to +41. Click OK. ■

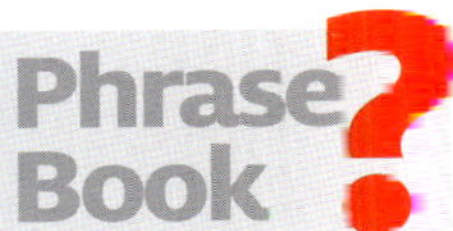

Barrelling
If you zoom out to a lens's widest setting, the horizontal lines in your pictures may become curved. This is called barrelling and can be counteracted using Photoshop's Lens Correction filter (see step 7).

Midpoint
The Vignette tool's Midpoint slider enables you to push the vignette out to the far corners or in towards the centre. This enables you to create more subtle or dominant vignettes.

.xmp
When you use the Camera Raw editor, all the changes you make are recorded in an .xmp file that's stored alongside your original file. Photoshop uses this information to 'remember' changes so you can fine-tune (or remove) them later.

Straighten
You can't change the content of a RAW file, which is why the shot doesn't immediately straighten up in step 3. Instead, you have to open the cropped version of the RAW file in Photoshop to see the straightened image. The original file remains unaffected.

Scale
In step 7 we scaled up the shot to lose the transparent edges created by the lens correction process. You could also crop the shot to lose the transparent edges.

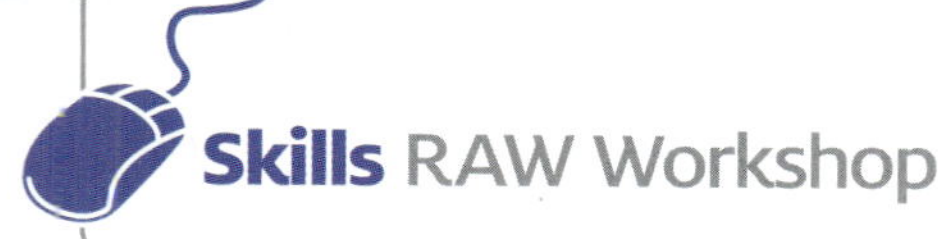

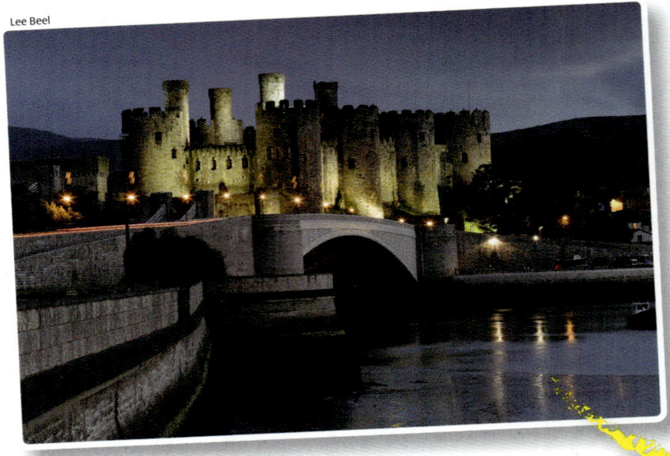
Lee Beel

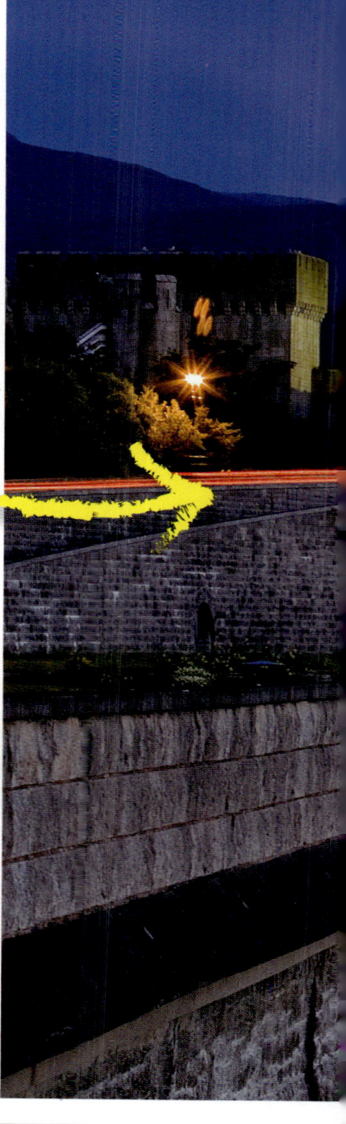

Maximise detail in low-light shots

Use Elements' Adobe Camera Raw editor to subtly adjust flat images – boosting detail in shadows *and* highlights

Shooting in challenging light conditions can be a nightmare, especially when it comes to getting the exposure right. Ideally, you'll want to keep the shadows and highlights balanced, but don't panic if you end up with flat images or over-exposed shots. Shoot in RAW and you can use Adobe Camera Raw to adjust flat tones, over-exposed highlights or detail-free dark spots. It's easy to make blacks richer and darker with the Blacks slider, which can also improve the overall contrast of your image. You can then use the Recovery and Fill Light sliders to recover detail in the highlights and shadows while maintaining balanced tones. Finally, try adding some subtle colour saturation with the editor's Vibrancy slider and you'll perfect your shots in minutes.

STEP BY STEP Add impact to your RAW shots

Checklist

What you'll need
Photoshop Elements 6 or 7

How long it'll take
10 minutes

The skills you'll learn
- How to improve a flat RAW shot
- How to recover detail in shadows and highlights
- How to increase an image's colour saturation

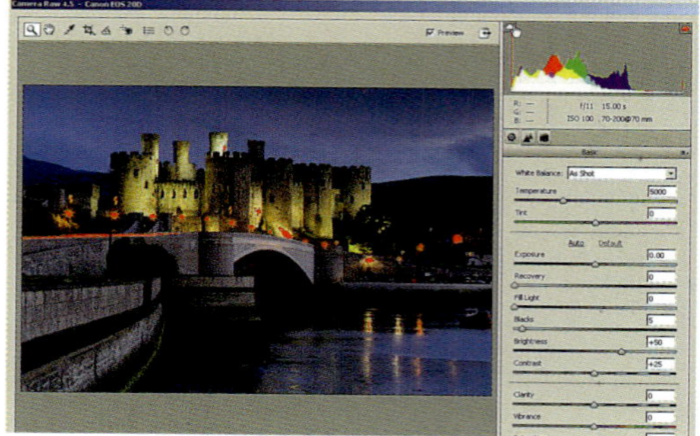

Use the clipping warning

1 First, open the image named raw_start.cr2 on the Video Disc in Photoshop Elements. The image will automatically appear in the Camera Raw interface. Next, turn on the clipping warning by clicking on the small triangular icons above the left and right of the histogram. Clipped highlights will flash red and clipped shadows will flash blue.

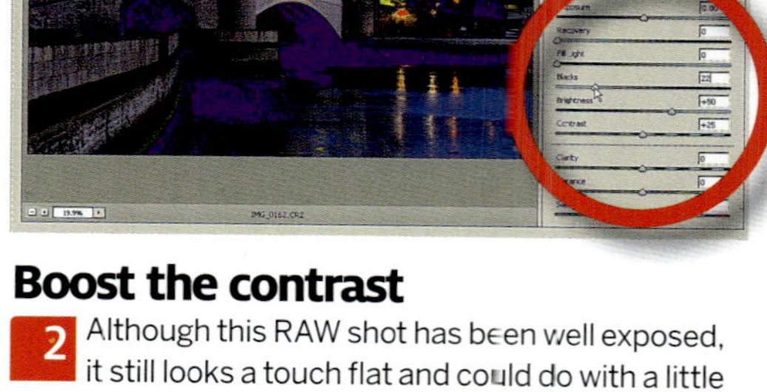

Boost the contrast

2 Although this RAW shot has been well exposed, it still looks a touch flat and could do with a little darkening to add contrast and deepen the black tones. Drag the Blacks slider to +22 and you'll see areas of black darken while the overall contrast improves. However, you'll also see more clipped shadows appear, meaning that detail has been lost in these areas.

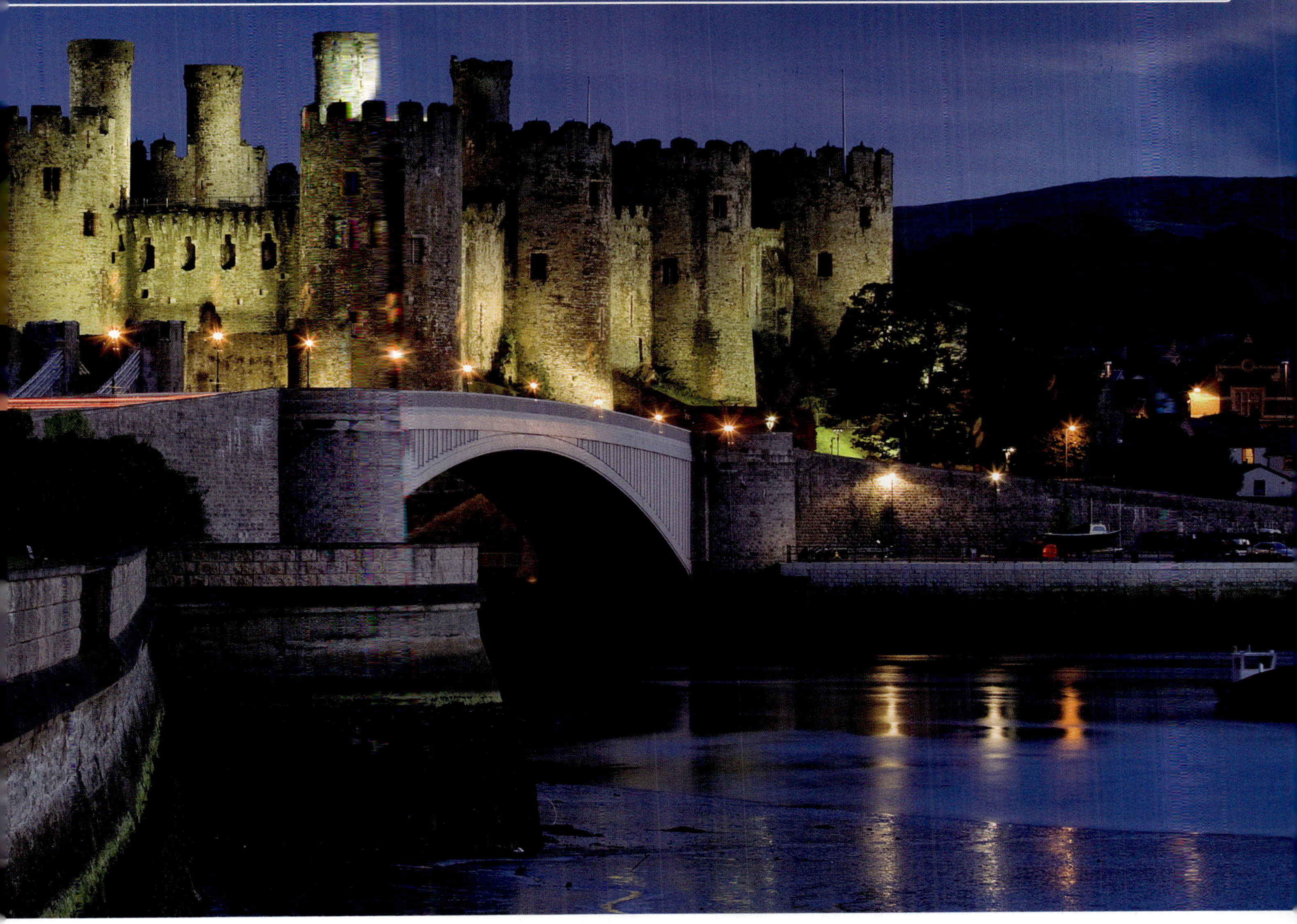

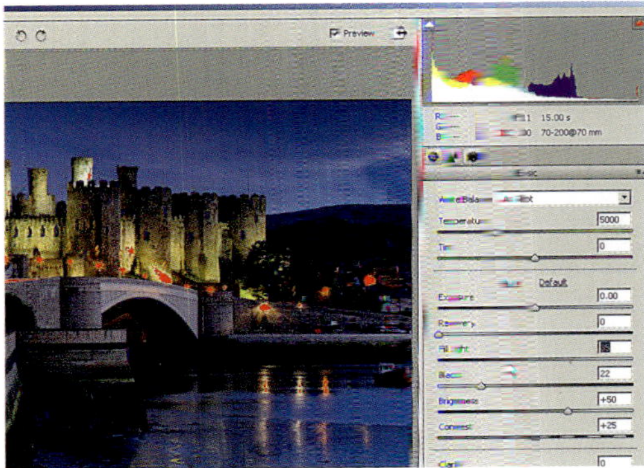

Recover shadow detail

3 This lack of detail can be recovered without compromising on the contrast. Using the Fill Light slider, you can 'shine a light' onto these areas to draw back the detail. Drag the slider to the right and watch as the blue clipping warning disappears. Areas that show red highlight clipping can be recovered in the same way, using the Recovery slider.

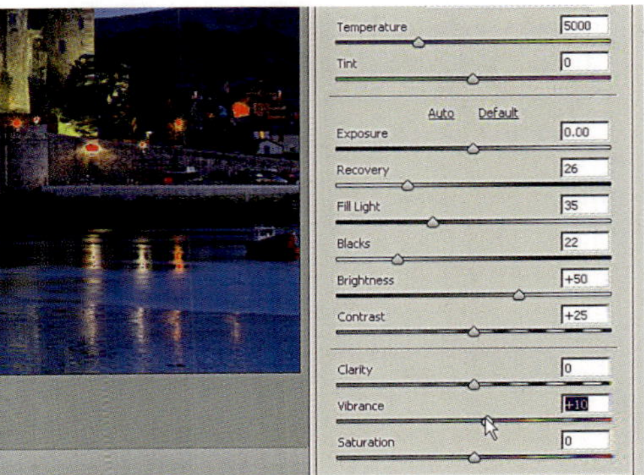

Increase saturation

4 The image would benefit from a slight saturation boost, and the easiest way to do this without adding garish blocks of colour is to use the Vibrance slider. As with all the previous adjustments, simply drag the slider to the right to increase the saturation. Let the slider come to rest at about +10 for a natural-looking result, and that's it! ■

Super Tip!

"The tools in Adobe Camera Raw can help you get the best out of your RAW shots, but they shouldn't be used as a substitute for getting exposure right first time. The Recovery and Fill Light sliders can be used to improve a good image that could be great, but they can't rescue a shot that's really over-exposed."

Chris George (Future)

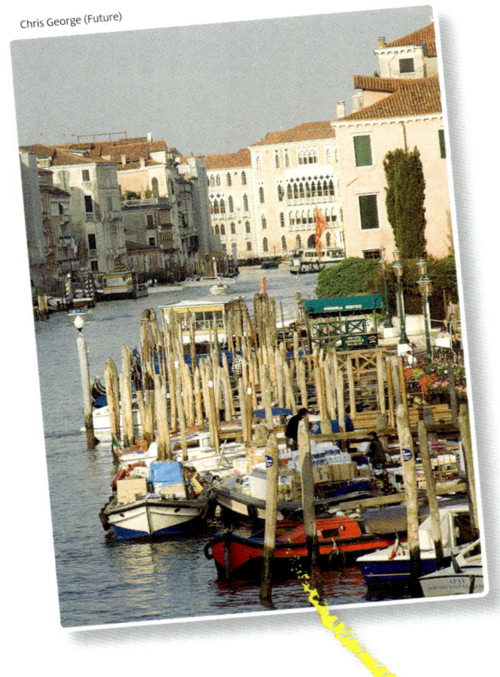

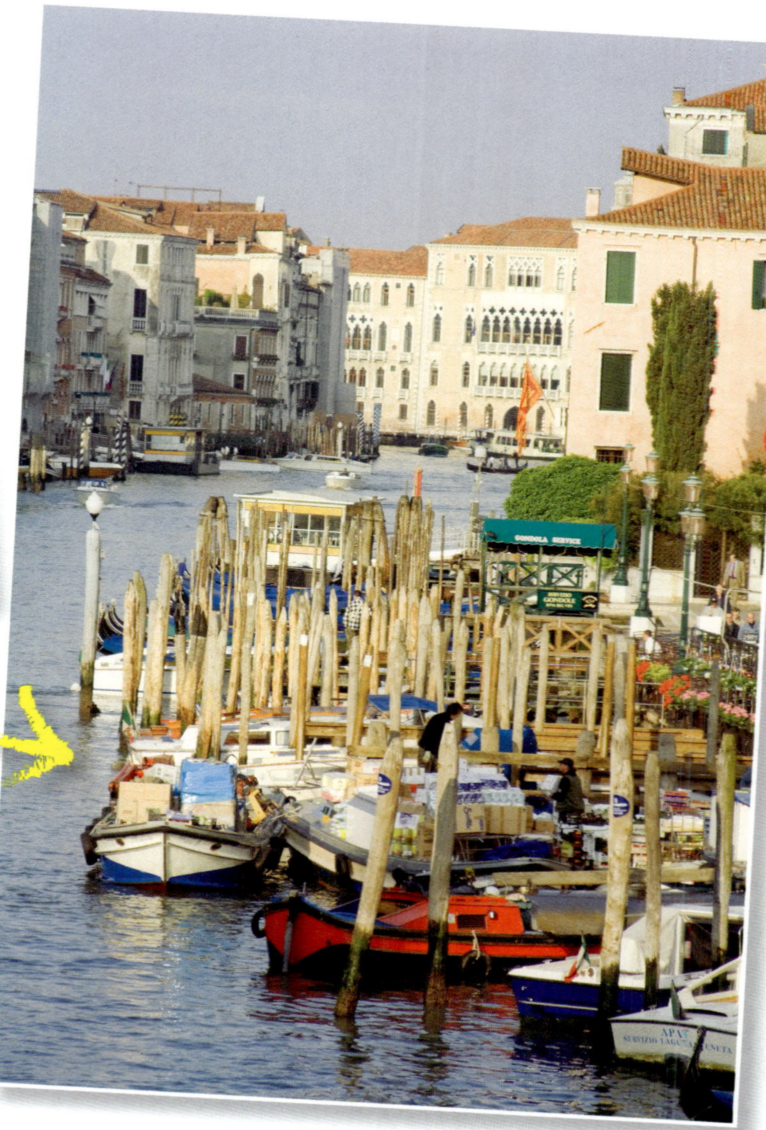

Harness RAW processing power

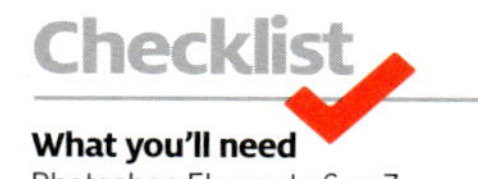

Checklist

What you'll need
Photoshop Elements 6 or 7

How long it'll take
10 minutes

The skills you'll learn
- How to improve the contrast and exposure of RAW files
- How to recover detail from shadows and highlights
- How to tweak a shot's colour and saturation

Learn how to manipulate colour, contrast and exposure like a pro using Photoshop's Adobe Camera Raw plug-in

To get great pictures from your digital SLR, you need to be shooting with the Quality option set to RAW. While other options save your pictures as JPEGs, RAW is a special format that provides significant advantages when it comes to editing your pictures.

RAW enables you to change key camera settings when you get home and gives you tremendous scope to adjust brightness and contrast on your computer. You can make similar changes with JPEGs, but RAW files can be manipulated more intensively without degrading the image quality. What's more, the shot is recorded with a greater range of tones and colours in the first place.

The RAW format used by each digital D-SLR is different, so the software you use must be compatible with your SLR. Rather than introduce a new version of Photoshop for every SLR that's launched, Adobe uses a special plug-in program called Adobe Camera Raw (ACR). Here are the key features of ACR in Elements 7.

Get to know... Adobe Camera Raw

Our at-a-glance guide to your RAW editor's key features and sliders

1 Histogram
This graph provides an instant guide to the contrast and exposure of your picture. It maps the distribution of tones, from the darkest on the left to the brightest on the right. You can use the sliders below to create a perfectly shaped graph.

2 Highlight Clipping Warning
Click on this yellow arrow to identify areas of the image that are too bright and where detail is being lost. A similar red arrow on the other side offers a Shadow Clipping Warning.

3 Camera settings
A handy reminder of the exposure settings and lens that were used to take the picture.

4 Settings
Drop-down menu that enables you to do things like saving your settings or re-using the ones from the last picture you edited.

5 Detail
Use this tab to access Sharpening and Noise Reduction options.

6 Colour temperature options
It doesn't matter what White Balance you set when you took your photo, as you can alter it in Camera Raw: the White Balance window gives you a range of presets; the Temperature slider enables you to tweak colour balance precisely; and Tint is an advanced option for fine tuning.

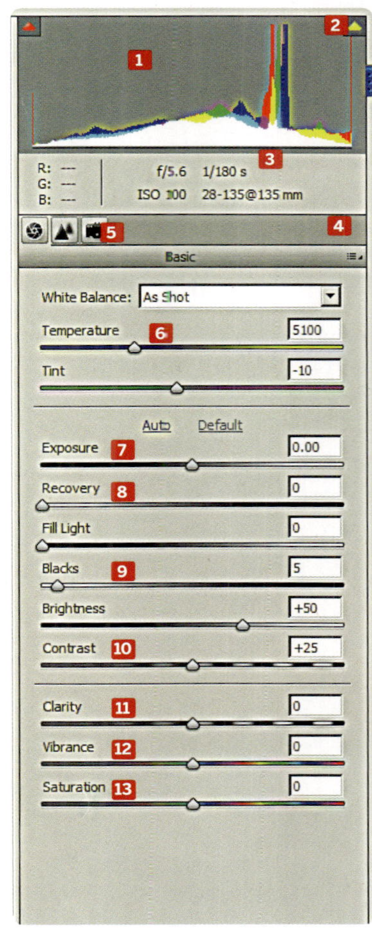

7 Exposure
Makes the whole image brighter or darker, shifting the histogram to the left or right.

8 Recovery & Fill Light
The Recovery slider can be used to rescue burnt-out highlights, while the Fill Light slider selectively lightens the shadow areas.

9 Blacks & Brightness
The Blacks slider makes the dark tones darker, and Brightness does the opposite by making the light tones lighter.

10 Contrast
This adjusts the contrast of the midtones in your image – it's best used when the five sliders above have already been set.

11 Clarity
Clarity makes your pictures look sharper by increasing contrast at subject edges. This feature is worth using, but don't overdo it.

12 Vibrance
The best way to make your image look more colourful. Unlike the Saturation slider, it works harder on colours that aren't already saturated

13 Saturation
This can be used to beef up colours (but it's best to start with the Vibrance slider) or to desaturate the image, giving a more monotone result.

STEP BY STEP Improve a RAW file in easy steps

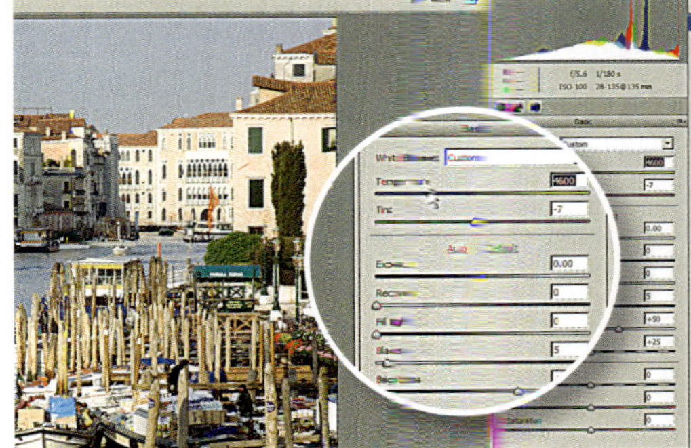

Adjust the colour balance
1 Open elements_start.cr2 from the Video Disc in Photoshop Elements. The image will automatically open in the Adobe Camera Raw interface. Tweak the overall colour balance using the Temperature slider, moving it to the left (from 5,100K to around 4,600K) to make the scene look more blue.

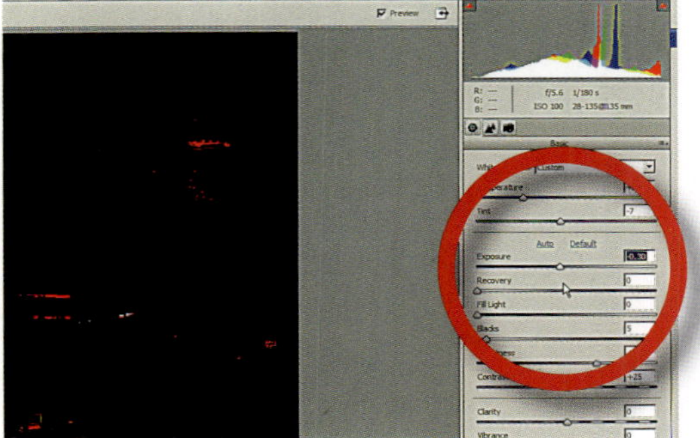

Use Threshold to set exposure
2 The Exposure slider makes an image darker or lighter – you can judge the effect visually or use the histogram. Switch to Threshold View by holding down Alt as you move the slider. This shows 'clipped' pixels. Move the slider to around -30 to improve the exposure and restore detail to the brightest areas.

Super Tip!
"Make sure you're using the most recent version of Adobe Camera RAW (ACR), because it may give you new features as well as support for more recent cameras. The latest version of ACR you can install will depend on which version of Adobe Photoshop Elements or Photoshop CS you're using."

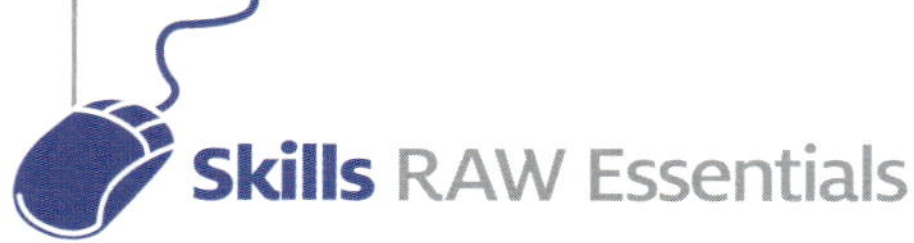

Super Tip!

"It doesn't matter what adjustments you make in Adobe Camera Raw, you aren't changing the RAW file itself. Your settings and slider positions are saved in a separate XMP file (see below). When you next open the RAW file, Camera Raw sees the XMP file and shows the sliders as you left them. Their position can be reset at any time."

Phrase Book?

XMP
Extensible Metadata Platform (XMP) is a labelling technology used by several Adobe programs, including Elements. It records information about a file and can be embedded in the file itself. XMP data for RAW files is stored in a separate file with the same name as the RAW original, but with an .xmp extension. It records adjustments made in Camera Raw without affecting the original.

Histogram
A graph that shows the tonal range of a photo. It plots the number of pixels in the image according to their brightness. In Photoshop Elements ACR, three graphs are provided – one for each of the primary colours recorded by the camera. The red, green and blue histograms are then shown superimposed onto each other.

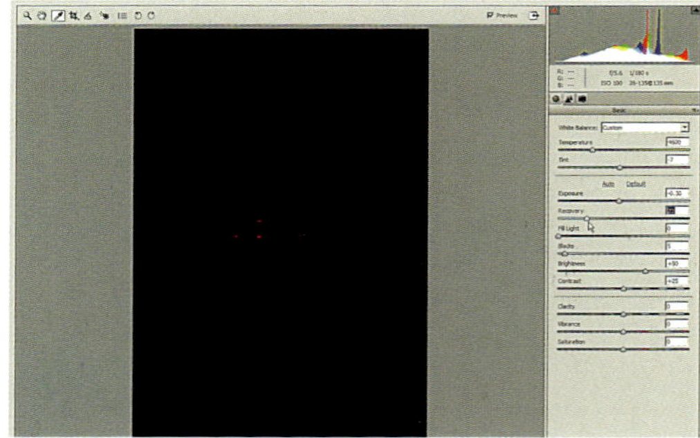

Tame the highlights

3 The Recovery slider is great for rescuing burnt-out areas. As with the Exposure slider, use the Threshold view to set this precisely. Hold down the Alt key as you move the slider to the right until most of the red areas disappear from the picture. Here, a setting of 22 does the trick. Don't worry if small areas of reflection on shiny objects still look clipped.

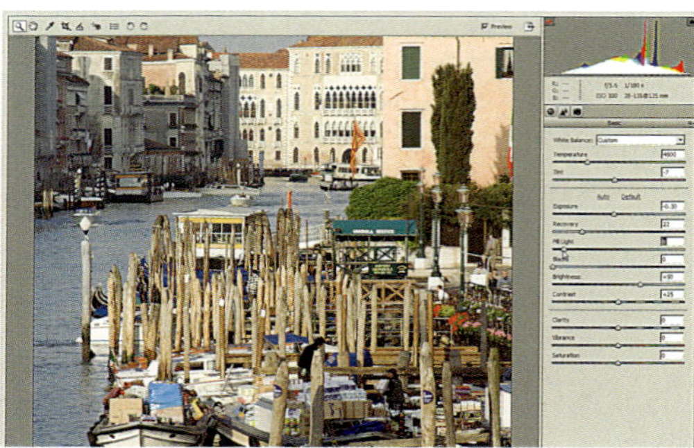

Lighten up the shadows

4 The Fill Light slider helps tone down the darkness of the shadows and is a good way to reduce the overall contrast of a sunlit scene. However, don't overdo it or the picture will start to look unnatural. You can't use the Threshold view with this slider, but notice how the left-hand side of the histogram moves inwards

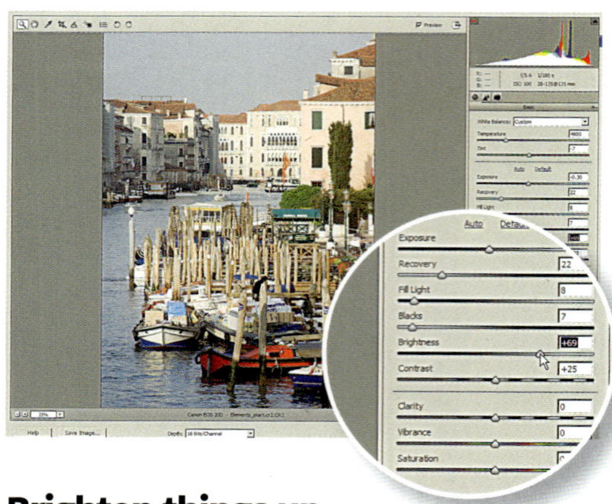

Brighten things up

5 The Brightness slider does a different job to the Exposure control. Rather than brightening up all the pixels in the picture, it has most effect on the midtones, so used with care it can make the image look lighter and brighter, without blowing out the highlights. We've used a setting of +69 for this shot.

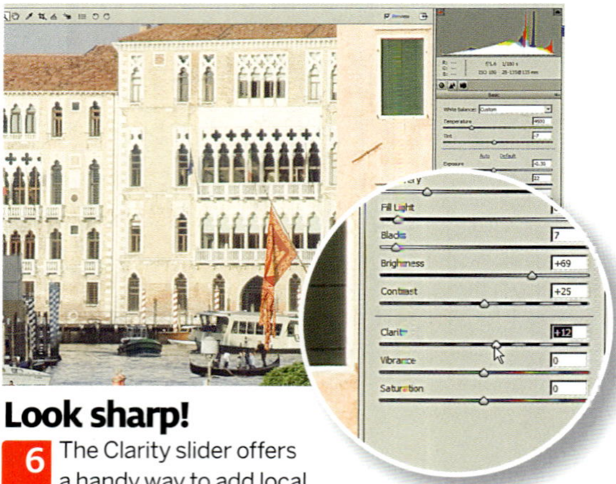

Look sharp!

6 The Clarity slider offers a handy way to add local contrast and, like a pinch of salt in your cooking, it's worth using a small amount to increase the apparent sharpness of all your pictures. A setting of +12 does the trick here and the effect is particularly noticeable in the windows of the Venetian palaces in the distance.

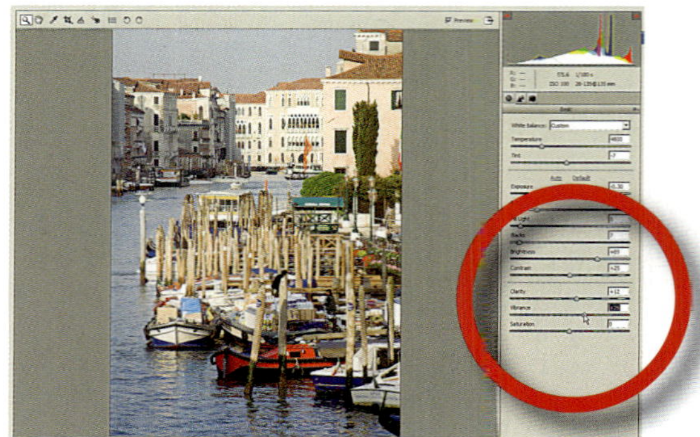

Crank up the colour

7 You can use the Vibrance and Saturation sliders to give images more punch. However, Vibrance is the intelligent choice because it adjusts saturation selectively, enabling you to beef up the hues without overcooking the colours that are already rich. Don't overdo it, though; +25 is more than enough here.

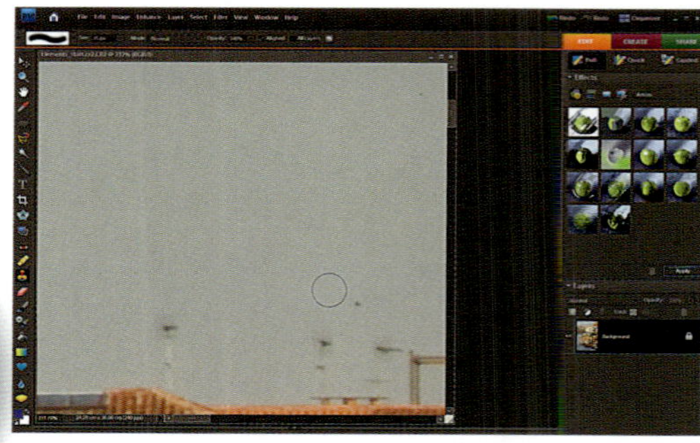

Get with the program

8 You can do most essential adjustments with Adobe Camera Raw, but you'll undoubtedly need to open the image in Photoshop Elements to finish the job. Click on Open Image and use the Rubber Stamp tool to remove some of the black blobs in the sky. You can also apply other effects here. Use Unsharp Mask to sharpen the edges of the image before saving it.

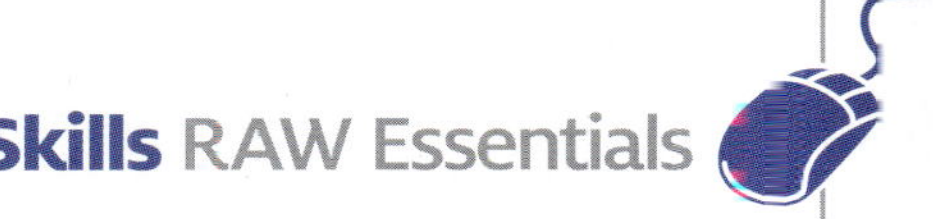

Advanced Technique

Get more from RAW

Use these handy shortcuts to speed up the image-editing process

Super Tip!

"When you click on Open Image to move from ACR to Photoshop Elements, you can choose to open the image in 16-bit mode rather than the usual 8-bit mode. This processes the picture to retain more of the colours that were recorded by the camera. The difference between the two modes is not visible, but the 16-bit mode is best if you're going to do lots of further manipulation using Photoshop Elements itself – it allows you more leeway before the picture quality is noticeably affected. The downside of 16-bit is that not all editing options will be available, and if you save the image in 16-bit the file will be twice the size. However, in Photoshop Elements it's easy to switch between the two by going to Image>Mode and selecting 8-bit or 16-bit."

The number of tools and options you have available in Adobe Camera Raw (ACR) depends on the version you're using. For example, you get more tools and features with the version of ACR that's designed for CS4 than you do with the one for CS3. Similarly, the ACR plug-in designed for CS3 will be more advanced than the version you get with Elements. Despite these differences, Elements users still get a huge array of buttons and options to work with – on top of the essential sliders that we've looked at – so there are plenty of tools at your fingertips.

Here's our choice of four top additional effects and tools that are worth using with your version of ACR. Try them out and improve your shots in an instant.

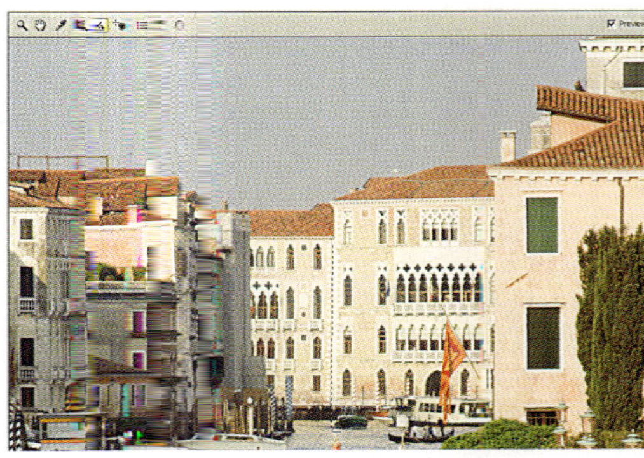

Straighten up

1 Open the file elements_start.cr2 in Photoshop Elements. This launches ACR. Use the Straighten tool to ensure that horizons and buildings are perfectly level. Click on the icon, then click and drag along a line in the picture that's meant to be either vertical or horizontal. For architectural shots such as this, draw down a line in a building in the centre of the frame (not at the side, as this may be affected by lens distortion).

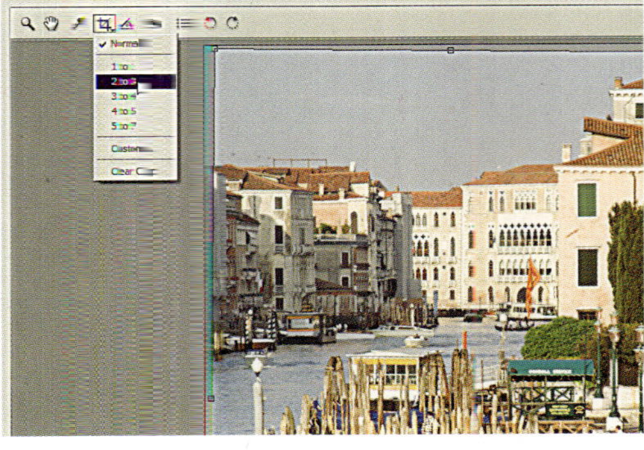

Crop in proportion

2 You can also use ACR to crop the image. The advantage of cropping in ACR is that the original RAW file isn't affected, so you can return to the uncropped image at any time. A neat refinement to the Crop tool is its drop-down menu, which provides preset aspect ratios. We chose a ratio of 2 to 3 because this ensures that however we cropped the shot it would have the same proportions as any original SLR image.

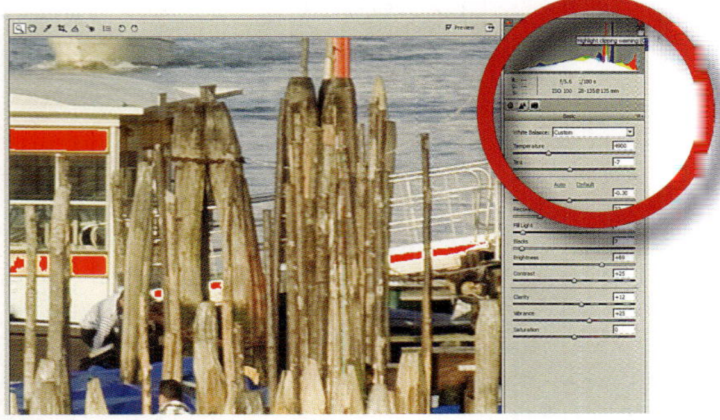

Highlight alert

3 Click the triangle at the top right of the histogram to toggle Highlight Clipping Warning on or off. With this on, you can see any areas of the image that are burnt out and then use the Exposure and Recovery sliders to correct the problem. This can sometimes be easier to use than the Threshold view. It's not so useful, however, if large areas of your image are already red.

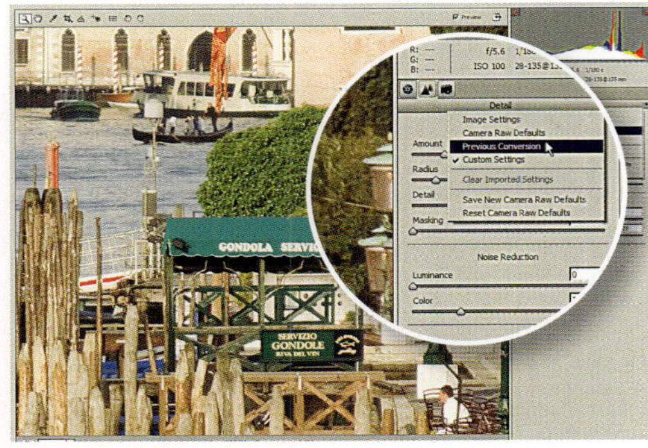

More of the same

4 You can process several files simultaneously in ACR, but there are other ways of re-using your settings so that you don't have to start from scratch with every RAW file you open. Try picking Previous Conversion from the drop-down menu (the icon to the right of the word Basic). This is ideal for processing the next shot you took of the same scene. If the lighting conditions and exposure were similar, you could process the shot in one easy step, tweaking the positions of individual sliders if necessary.

Discover the perfect method for...

Turning streets into model villages

Checklist

What you'll need
Photoshop CS or above

How long it'll take
Half a day

The skills you'll learn
- How to minimise depth of field with a specialist lens
- How to use Photoshop's Lens Blur filter
- How to use Layer Masks for depth of field effects
- How to boost colour

Get creative in Photoshop by minimising depth of field to turn urban landscapes into toy-towns. Here's how...

By minimising the depth of field in an image so that only a narrow band of the scene is in focus, it's possible to take a photograph of a busy street and make it look like a miniature model.

The illusion works because models are usually photographed using macro lenses, and these have a tendency to reduce depth of field and throw everything in the foreground and background out of focus. Our eyes are so used to this convention that when we see a scene with an extremely narrow depth of field, our brain is fooled into thinking that the objects in the scene must be tiny. This 'tilt-shift' effect is traditionally produced using a specialist lens, but you can also mimic the effect in Photoshop.

Over the next few pages, we'll show you how to create your own miniaturised version of a harbour scene in North Cornwall. We'll explain how to use a tilt-shift lens to produce the effect in-camera, and demonstrate how to fake it in Photoshop with the help of layers and Layer Masks. Let's get started...

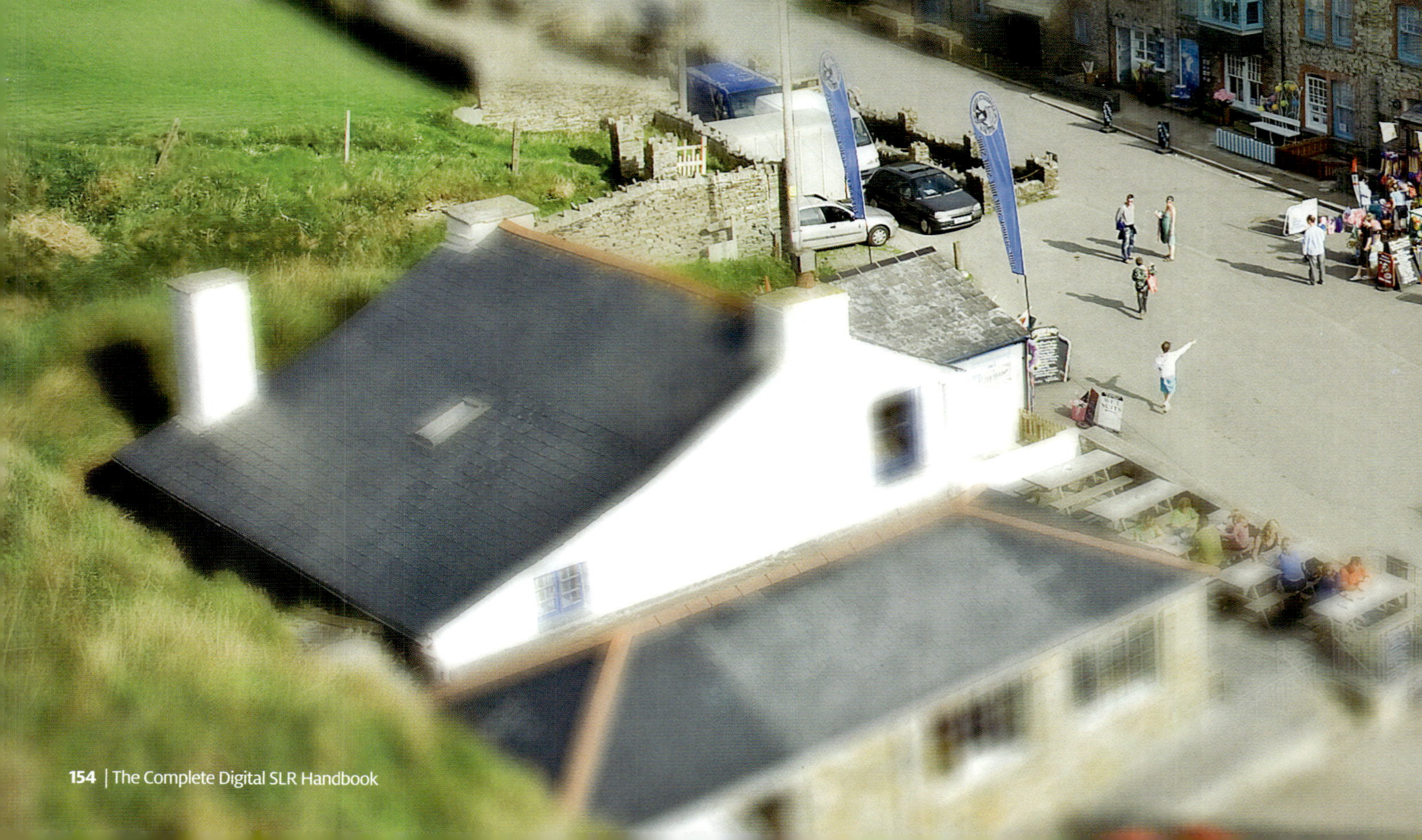

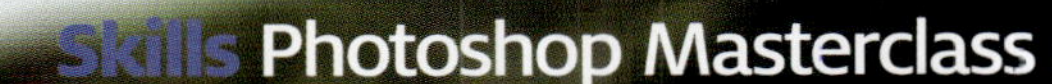
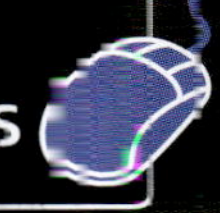

PRO SECRETS REVEALED

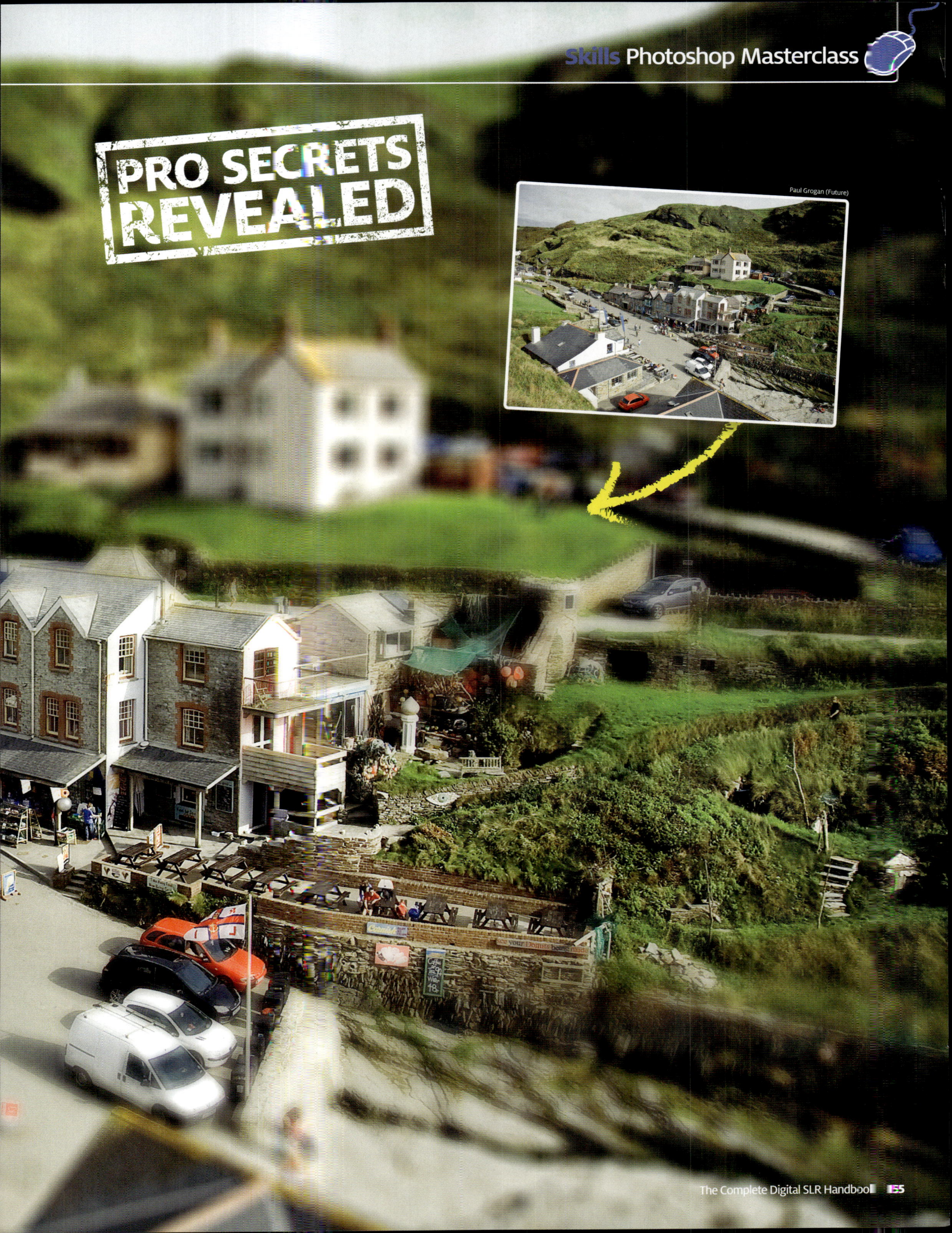

Paul Grogan (Future)

STEP BY STEP 1

It's a small world...

Six top tips for creating a world in miniature

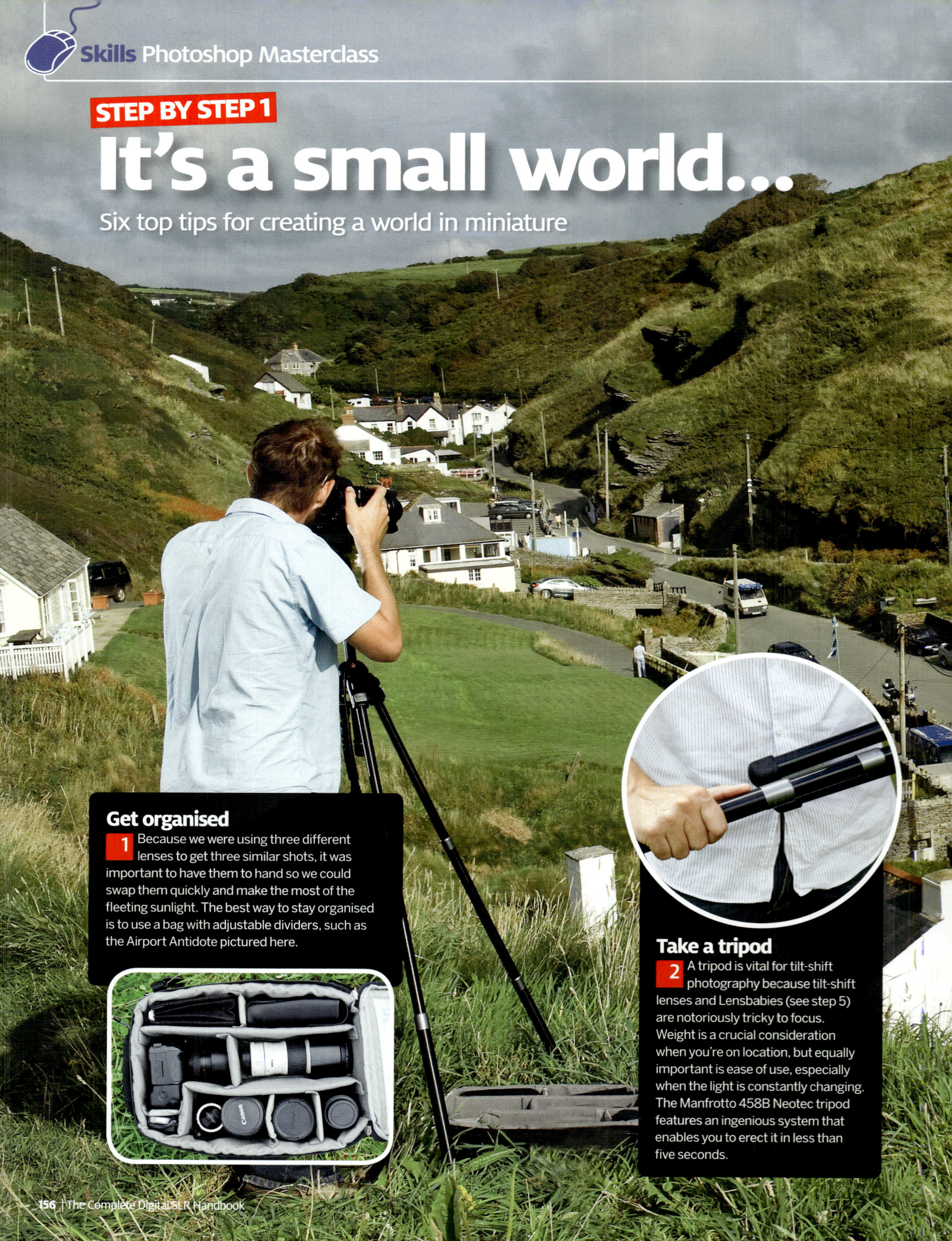

Get organised

1 Because we were using three different lenses to get three similar shots, it was important to have them to hand so we could swap them quickly and make the most of the fleeting sunlight. The best way to stay organised is to use a bag with adjustable dividers, such as the Airport Antidote pictured here.

Take a tripod

2 A tripod is vital for tilt-shift photography because tilt-shift lenses and Lensbabies (see step 5) are notoriously tricky to focus. Weight is a crucial consideration when you're on location, but equally important is ease of use, especially when the light is constantly changing. The Manfrotto 458B Neotec tripod features an ingenious system that enables you to erect it in less than five seconds.

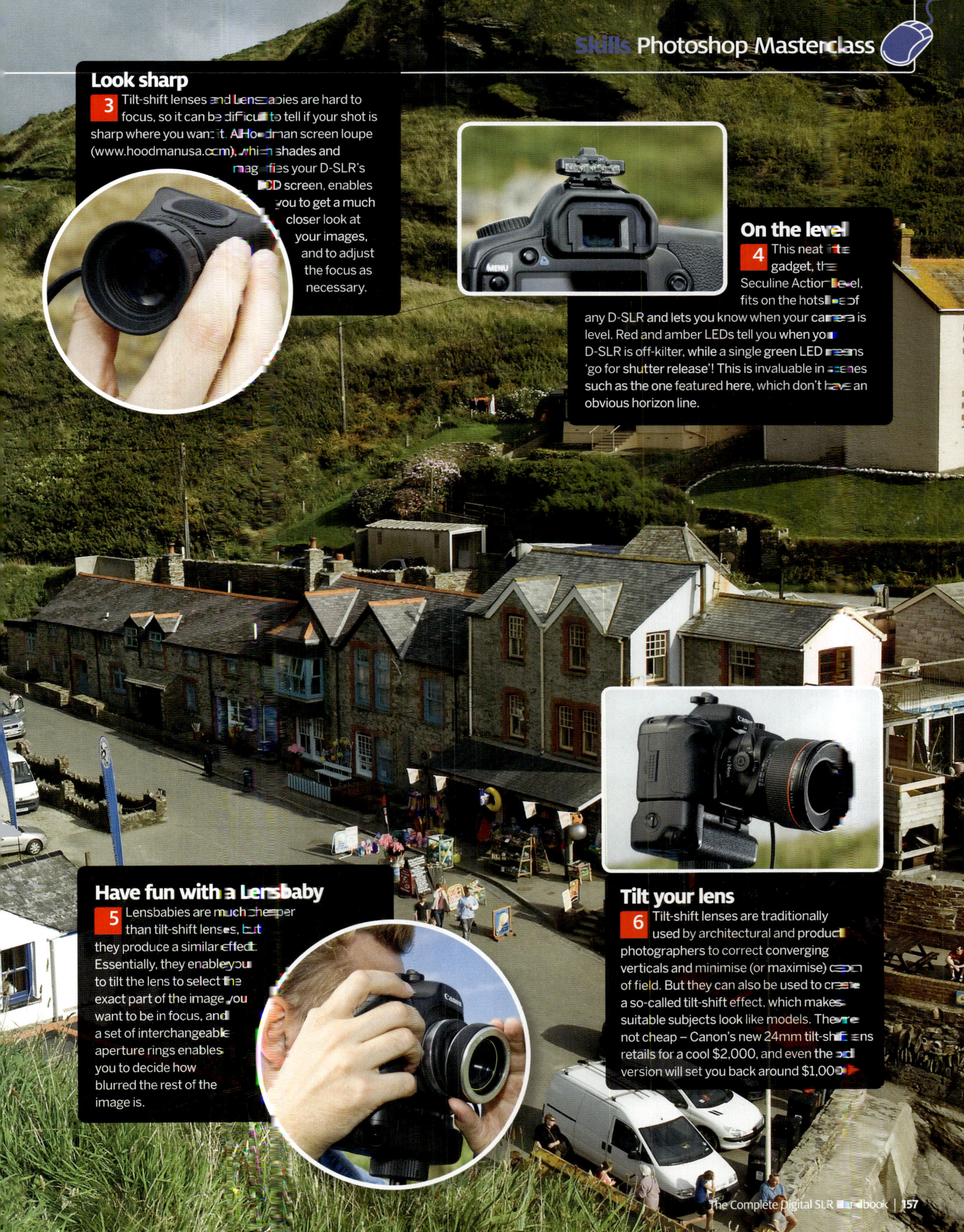

Look sharp

3 Tilt-shift lenses and Lensbabies are hard to focus, so it can be difficult to tell if your shot is sharp where you want it. A Hoodman screen loupe (www.hoodmanusa.com), which shades and magnifies your D-SLR's LCD screen, enables you to get a much closer look at your images, and to adjust the focus as necessary.

On the level

4 This neat little gadget, the Seculine Action Level, fits on the hotshoe of any D-SLR and lets you know when your camera is level. Red and amber LEDs tell you when your D-SLR is off-kilter, while a single green LED means 'go for shutter release'! This is invaluable in scenes such as the one featured here, which don't have an obvious horizon line.

Have fun with a Lensbaby

5 Lensbabies are much cheaper than tilt-shift lenses, but they produce a similar effect. Essentially, they enable you to tilt the lens to select the exact part of the image you want to be in focus, and a set of interchangeable aperture rings enables you to decide how blurred the rest of the image is.

Tilt your lens

6 Tilt-shift lenses are traditionally used by architectural and product photographers to correct converging verticals and minimise (or maximise) depth of field. But they can also be used to create a so-called tilt-shift effect, which makes suitable subjects look like models. They're not cheap – Canon's new 24mm tilt-shift lens retails for a cool $2,000, and even the old version will set you back around $1,000 ▶

Super Tip!

"The problem with applying the Lens Blur filter as a gradient, as in step 5, is that it tends to blur the tops of tall buildings or features; if you were shooting an actual toy-town using a very shallow depth of field, the building in the middle of your image would be sharp from top to bottom, as both are the same distance from the camera. For a more realistic toy-town effect, follow steps 6 and 7 to add to the mask over the top half of the building too. Press D on your keyboard to set the foreground colour to black, then paint over the buildings to reveal the sharp layer below."

STEP BY STEP 2 How to mimic a tilt-shift effect

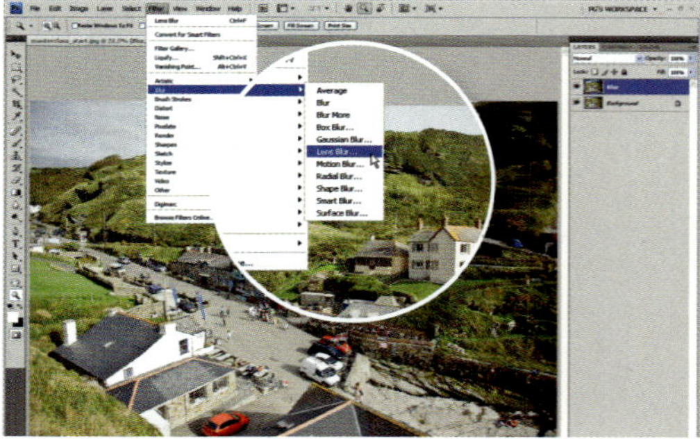

Get started

1 Open the image called masterclass_start.jpg, then go to Layer>DuplicateLayer. Call this layer Blur and click OK. Ensure the Blur layer is selected and then go to Filter>Blur>LensBlur. This will open up a new window that provides you with a number of sliders that can be used to mimic the effect of a tilt-shift lens.

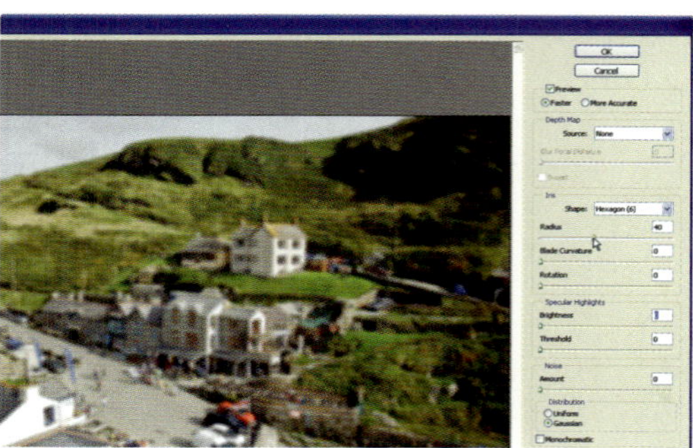

Apply Lens Blur

2 Make sure the Preview box is ticked and select Faster. Choose None from the Depth Map Box. Select Hexagon from the Iris shape drop-down menu, as this will ensure realistic-looking lens blur. Set Radius to 60 and leave Blade Curvature and Rotation at 0.

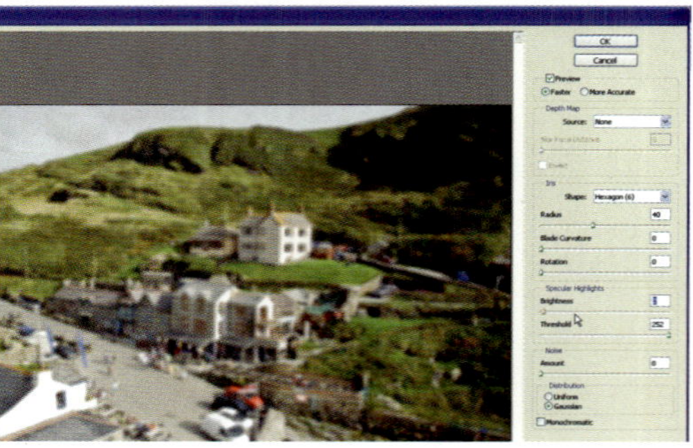

Light it up

3 Models are often illuminated by a lamp, so they tend to look like they've been lit from the side. The Specular Highlights option lets you lighten areas of bright, reflected light to mimic this. Set Threshold to 252 to brighten all pixels with a tonal value of higher than 252, and drag Brightness to 2. Click OK.

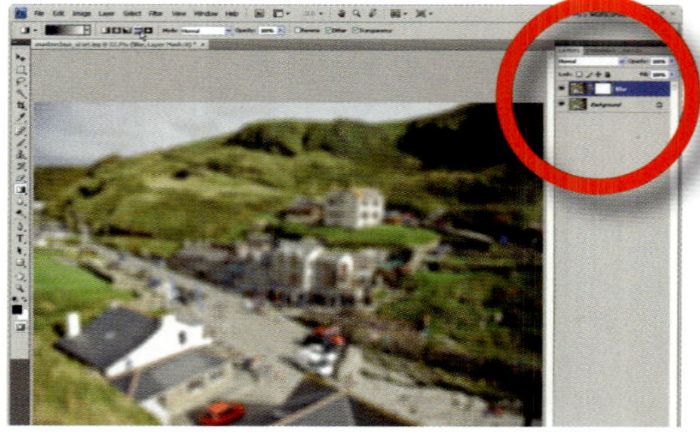

Go shallow

4 To get a shallow depth of field, you'll need to mask out the Blur layer in a horizontal band to reveal the sharp layer below. Click on Add Layer Mask in the Layers palette, grab the Gradient tool, select Reflected Gradient from the Options bar and set Mode to Normal.

How to get the shot in-camera

There's more than one way to make scenes look like models...

This harbour scene (right) was actually taken with a tilt-shift lens, and as you can see, our walkthrough does a pretty good job of mimicking the shallow depth of field that can be achieved with this lens.

To get this shot we used Canon's 24mm tilt-shift lens, set it to its widest aperture (f/4) to minimise depth of field, and then tilted the lens downwards as far as it would go to decrease depth of field further. This included too much foreground, so we used the lens's shift facility to re-frame the shot. We focused manually on the building in the middle of the frame. The result is that only the middle ground is in focus.

CANON TS-E 24MM

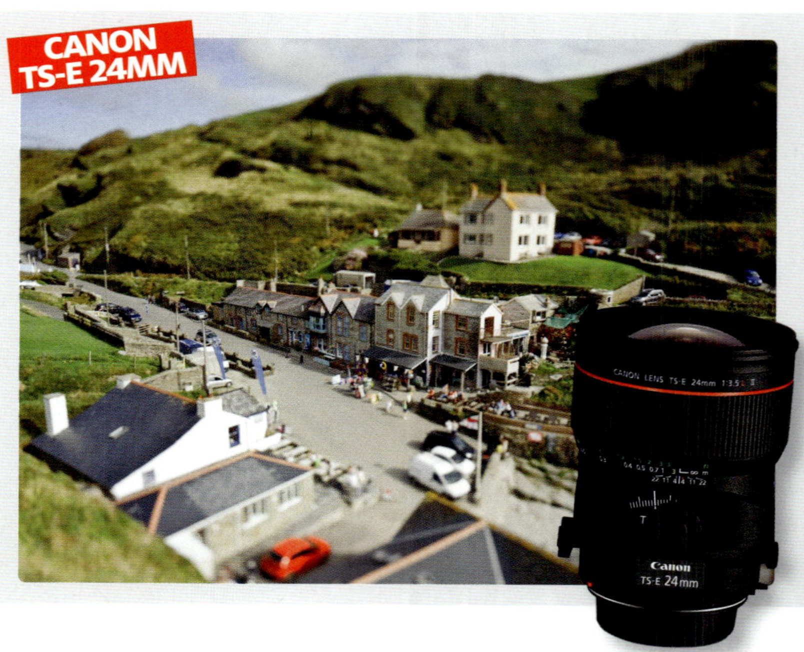

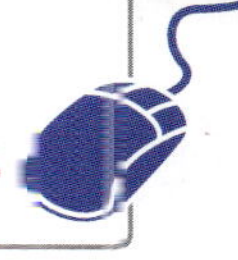

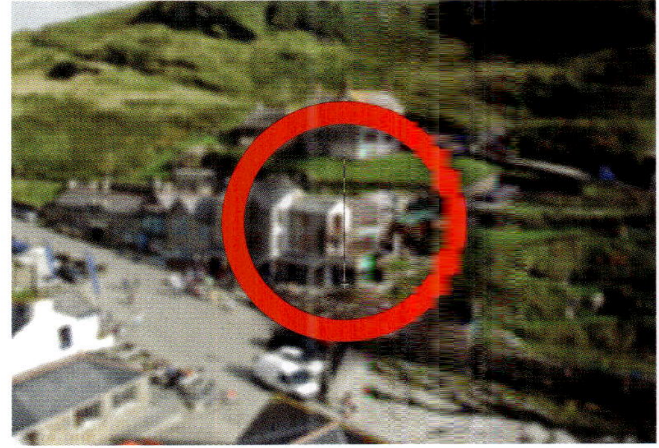

Create a gradient

5 Put your cursor on top of the flagpole near the middle of the image and then click and drag it up to the bottom of the white building on the hill, as shown in the image above. If you want more or less of the image in focus, you can re-draw the gradient so it's longer or shorter until you're happy with the effect.

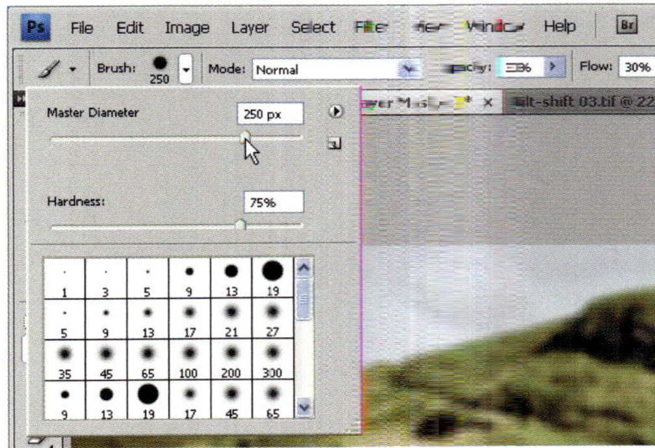

Grab a brush

6 For the shallow depth of field to be convincing, the building at the bottom-left of the frame should be out of focus, as it's closer to the camera than the buildings in the middle ground. To blur it, grab the Brush tool and set Size to 250, Hardness to 50%, and Opacity and Flow to 30% to give you some control.

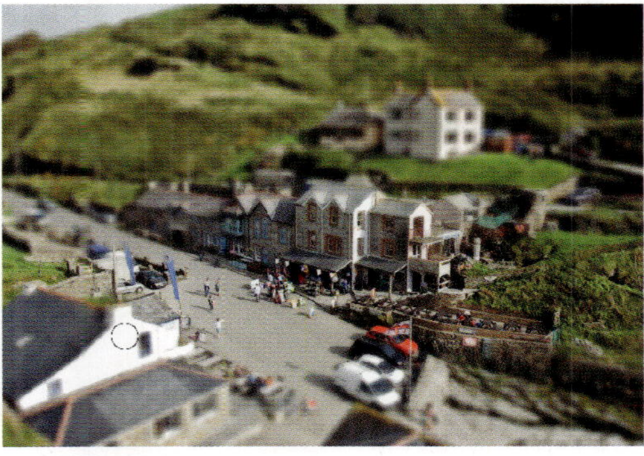

Blur by hand

7 Press the X key to set the foreground colour to white and then carefully paint over the building in the bottom left to blur it. You can also paint over the road at the far left, which is further from the camera than the buildings in the middle, and the sharp areas of harbour wall on the right, which are closer.

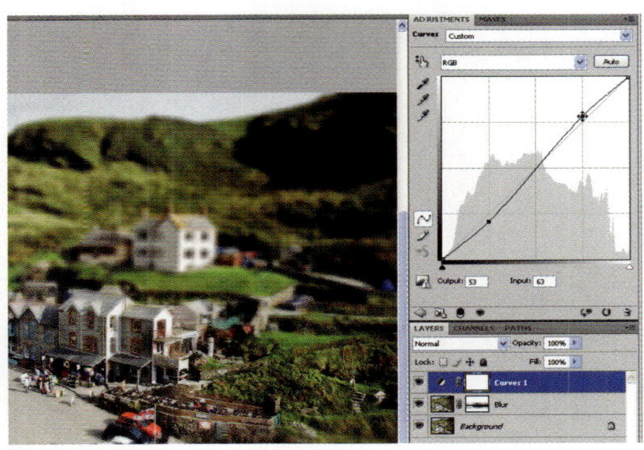

Toy-town

8 To make the colours more garish, so that the scene looks like it's made from toys and lichen, click on the Create New Adjustment Layer icon in the Layers palette and select Curves from the drop-down menu. In the new window that opens, drag the top and bottom of the line to create a subtle S-shaped curve.

Super Tip!

"One of the keys to making your final image look like a model is to get up high and shoot down. Model towns tend to be shot from above, so looking down on your scene adds to the illusion that what you're seeing is a world in miniature. You can also make the effect look more convincing by including some brightly coloured vehicles, such as cars or trains."

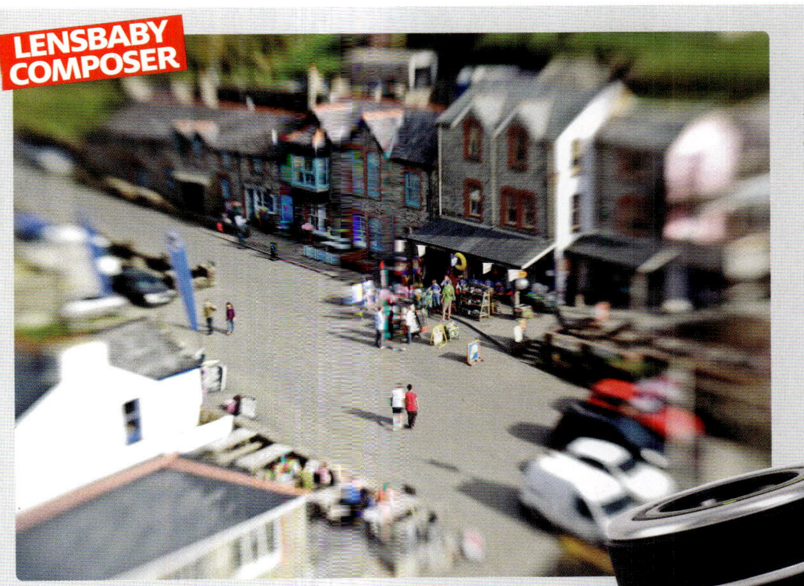

This second version (left) was shot using a Lensbaby. The Lensbaby has a focal length of around 50mm, so it has a narrower field of view than the 24mm tilt-shift lens (and the standard 24mm lens used for our start image).

In addition, the Lensbaby doesn't enable you to alter the aperture using the camera dials. Instead, it comes with six different aperture rings, ranging in size from f/2.8 to f/22, which have to be manually inserted into the front of the lens.

We used the f/4 ring (so that we could compare it with the tilt-shift version opposite, also shot at f/4) and set the shutter speed accordingly. We tilted the Lensbaby down slightly, composed our shot and then focused manually on the figures crossing the road. Because we didn't tilt it down very far, the 'sweet spot' of the lens was only just below the centre of the frame, resulting in a dramatic zoom blur effect. ■

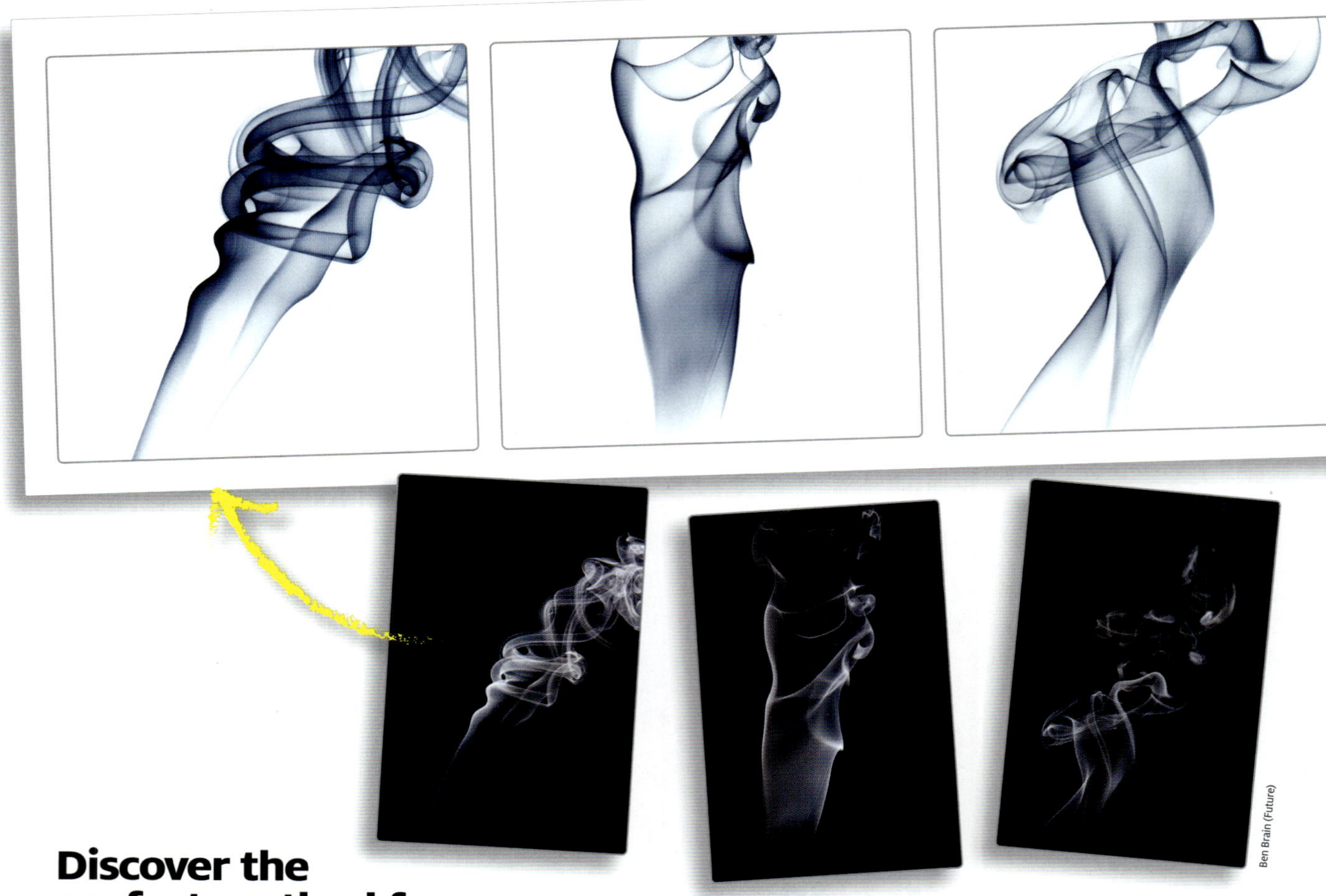

Discover the perfect method for...

Getting creative with smoke trails

Take shelter from the winter weather and learn the techniques you need to capture the graceful patterns of dancing smoke swirls from the comfort of your home

Checklist

What you'll need
Black cloth or velvet sheet
Incense sticks
Off-camera flash (such as a Canon Speedlite 430EX)
A dedicated flash cable
Photoshop Elements 5.0 or above, or Photoshop CS

How long it'll take
Half a day

The skills you'll learn
- How to set up a table-top studio
- How to photograph swirling patterns of smoke
- How to edit your smoke shots to create a stunning triptych

Just because it's cold, dark and probably raining outside doesn't mean you have to hang up your camera for the winter months. In fact, there are loads of great photographic projects you can enjoy at this time of year without leaving the house!

In this Masterclass, we'll take you step-by-step through a project that'll help you unleash your creativity. Using nothing more than a camera, a flashgun, some incense and a sheet of black velvet, we'll reveal how to capture swirls of smoke as they dance through the air.

After leading you through the process of setting up a mini makeshift home studio, we'll also show you how to take control of your camera and flashgun in Manual mode for ultimate control over your image making.

We'll then move on to Photoshop, sharing tips and techniques you can use to edit your pictures in the digital darkroom. We'll show you a simple way to convert your shots to black and white, invert them to create dark details against a white background, and then add a blue tint to the smoke swirls.

Finally, we'll explain how to convert your edited smoke shots into amazing art prints by creating a stunning triptych you'll be proud to print, frame and hang on your wall. So let's get started... ▶

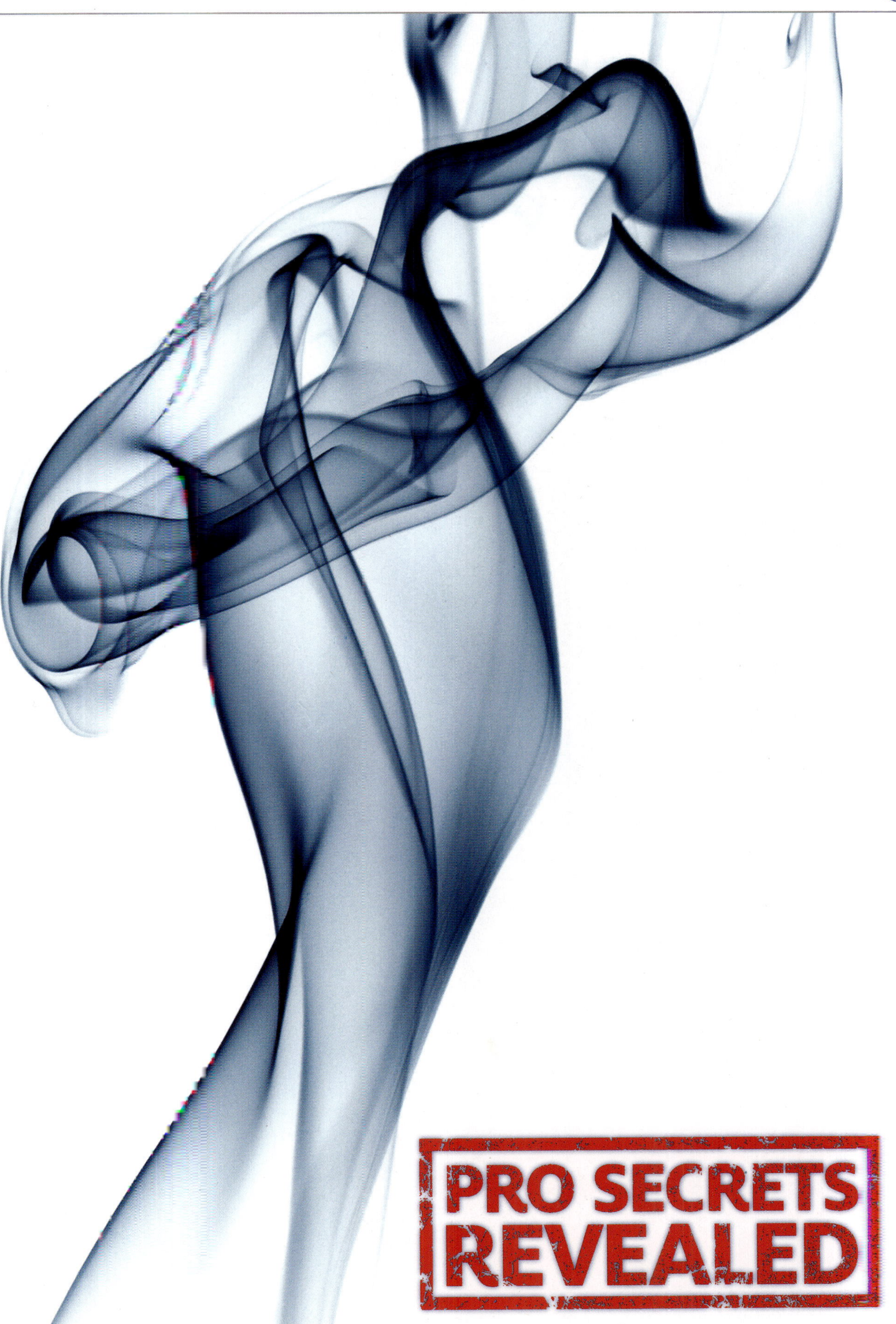

PRO SECRETS REVEALED

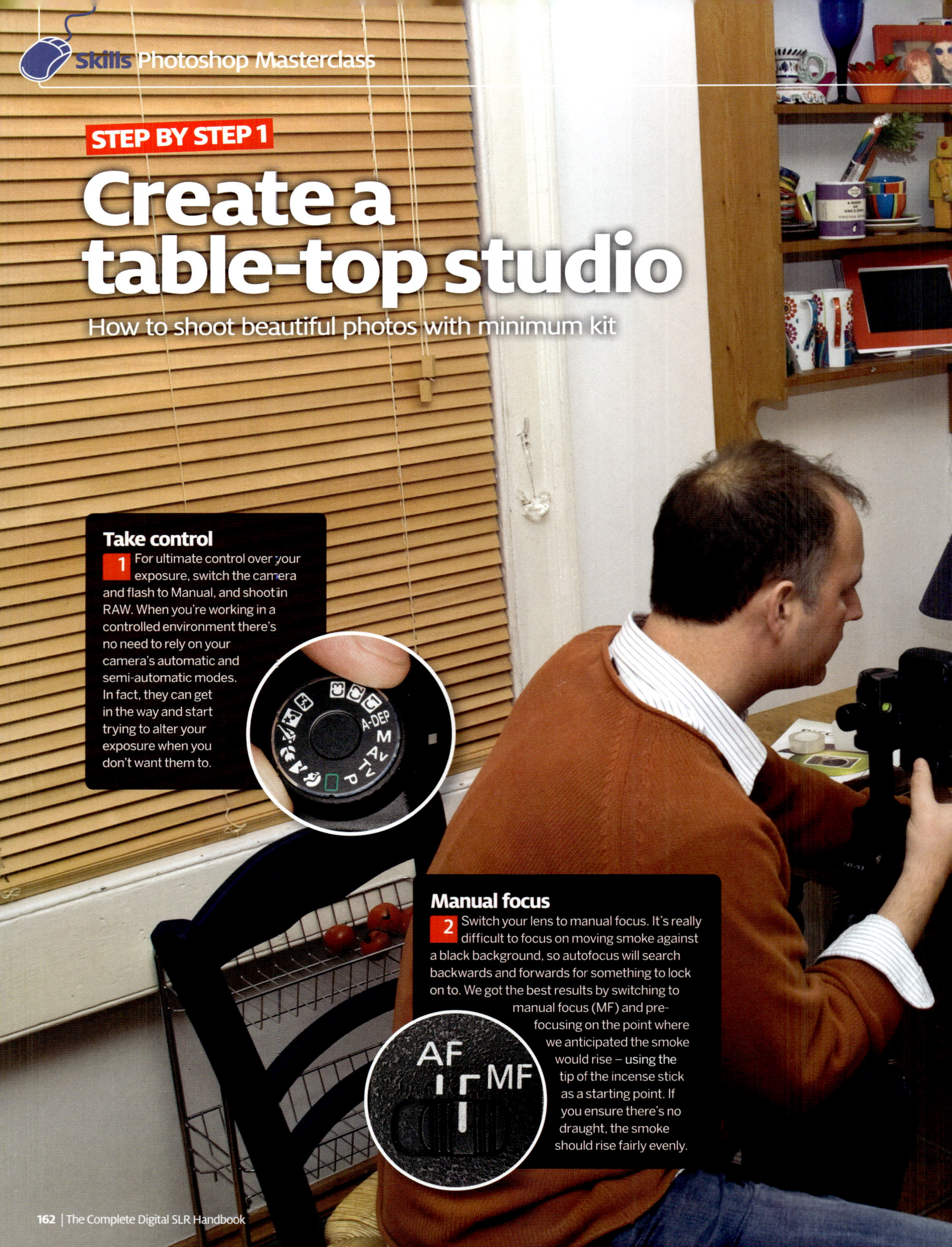

STEP BY STEP 1

Create a table-top studio

How to shoot beautiful photos with minimum kit

Take control

1 For ultimate control over your exposure, switch the camera and flash to Manual, and shoot in RAW. When you're working in a controlled environment there's no need to rely on your camera's automatic and semi-automatic modes. In fact, they can get in the way and start trying to alter your exposure when you don't want them to.

Manual focus

2 Switch your lens to manual focus. It's really difficult to focus on moving smoke against a black background, so autofocus will search backwards and forwards for something to lock on to. We got the best results by switching to manual focus (MF) and pre-focusing on the point where we anticipated the smoke would rise – using the tip of the incense stick as a starting point. If you ensure there's no draught, the smoke should rise fairly evenly.

Secure your flash

3 We used tape to secure our off-camera flash, which due to the short length of the remote cable, wouldn't stay in the correct position on the table-top. It's always a good idea to carry some kind of tape in your kit bag – it has some surprising uses!

Use a flashgun

4 We used a Canon Speedlite 580EX flashgun attached to our Canon via a dedicated flash cord, rather than our SLR's pop-up flash. This way, we could light the smoke from one side, rather than from straight on, and the cable kept the camera and flash synchronised.

Control the smoke

5 It's nearly impossible to control the pattern that smoke makes, so you'll need to experiment. First, set up your studio in a room free of draughts, because even the slightest air movement will interrupt the flow of smoke. We used a fly swatter to manipulate the smoke while looking through the viewfinder!

Take plenty of shots

6 Because capturing the perfect smoke pattern is going to be a little hit and miss, it's best to shoot as many images as possible, leaving you with plenty to choose from. Ensure you've got lots of space on your memory card and try different techniques to get the smoke to behave in different ways. ▶

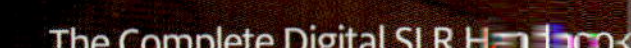

Phrase Book?

Triptych
A term borrowed from the art world. It's essentially any piece of art separated into three pieces. Triptychs are often seen in religious paintings or carvings with three hinged panels. This approach has also become popular with contemporary artists for presentations. Similarly, a piece of art with two pieces is known as a diptych.

Off-camera flash
By removing the flashgun from your digital SLR, you can illuminate your subject from different angles. If you use a dedicated remote cable, you'll be able to maintain TTL (through the lens) connectivity between the camera and flash. If you'd rather shoot cable-free, use an infrared trigger.

Super Tip!

"Try adding different effects to your smoke shots by applying a Gradient Map as an Adjustment Layer. In order to do this, go to Layer>New Adjustment Layer> GradientMap. In the window that appears (called the Gradient Editor), experiment with some of the presets and see what kind of results you get. You can also make maps using your own colour palettes if you prefer."

STEP BY STEP 2 Now get creative in Photoshop

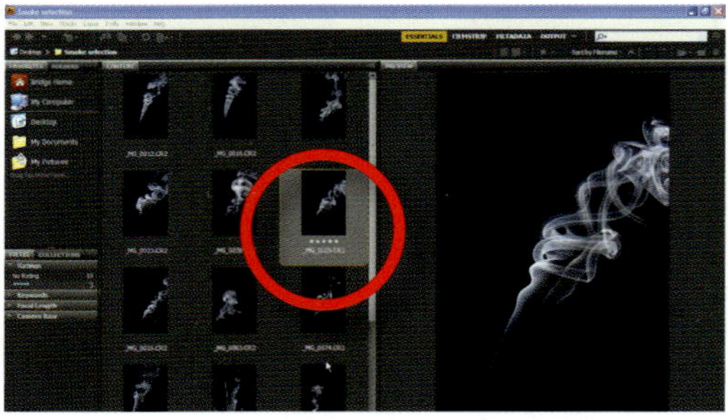

Edit in Adobe Bridge

1 One way to capture good smoke shots is to keep shooting until you've filled your memory card, although this means you'll have to spend time editing your images later. This could be time-consuming, but Adobe Bridge enables you to quickly browse your shots, checking them for focus and rating them with stars until you whittle down your selection.

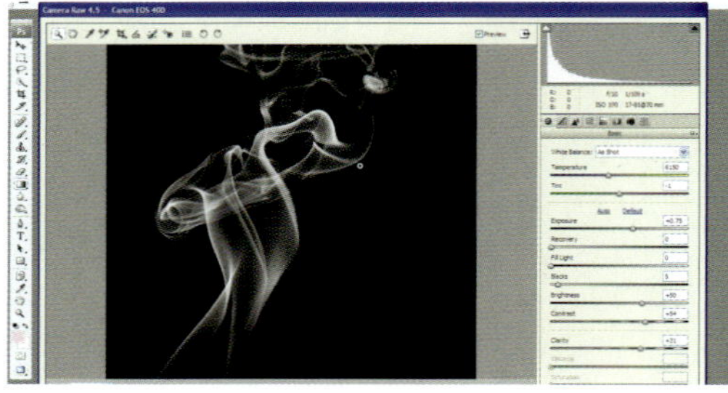

Perfect your RAW files

2 Once you've settled on three images that you'd like to use, open them in Adobe Camera Raw. Alternatively, you could choose to use the images provided on the Video Disc from this point onwards. Select the first image in the left-hand bar and set its Exposure to +0.75, Contrast to +50 and Clarity to +30. Now switch to the HSL/Greyscale tab and convert the image to black and white.

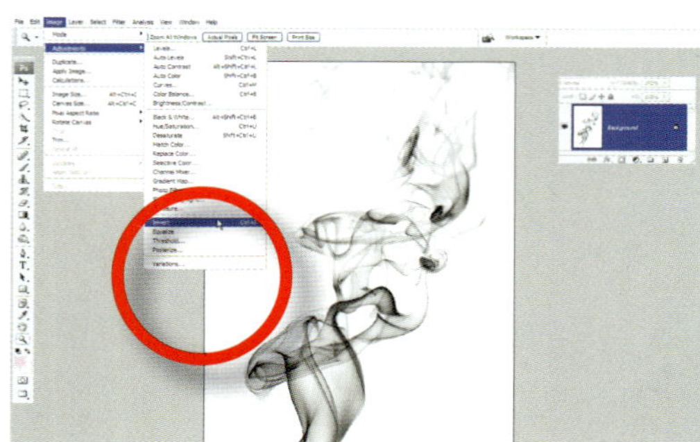

Invert the image

3 Click on Open Image and your shot should open in the main Photoshop CS interface. Now go to Image>Adjustments>Invert. This inverts the image's tones, creating a negative effect. We like the way this makes the smoke look like a delicate pencil drawing, but if you prefer the original black background you can simply miss this step out of the process.

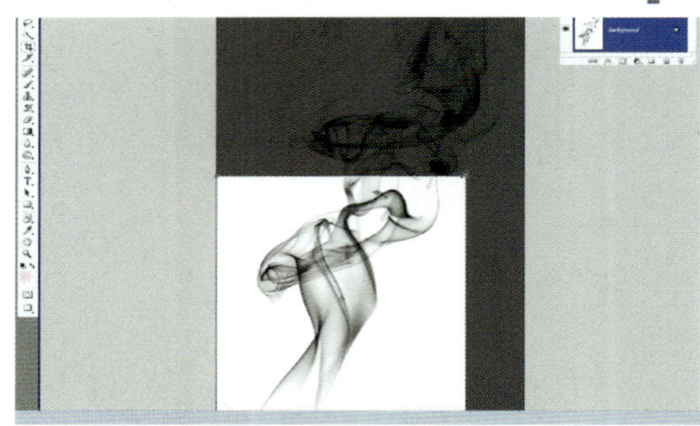

Crop to square

4 It's difficult to frame smoke patterns exactly as you shoot, but you can tweak this in Photoshop. To change the composition, select the Crop tool from the Tools palette. You'll need three square images for this project, so specify a Width and Height of 20cm in the Crop Parameters box and set the Resolution to 300 pixels per inch. Now mark out the area to crop.

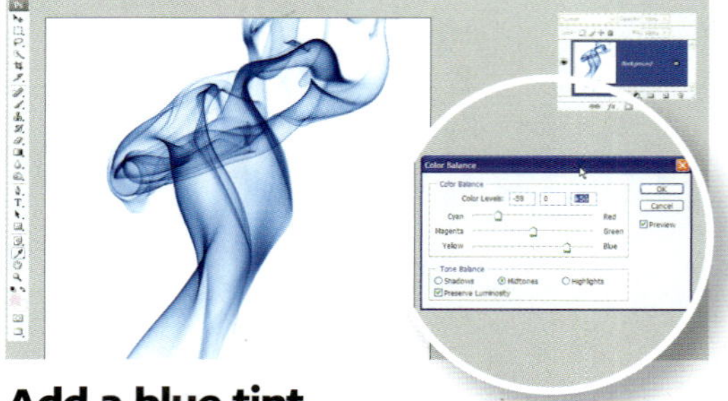

Add a blue tint

5 Go to Image>Mode>RGBColour. You can now add a blue tint by going to Image>Adjustments> ColourBalance and moving the Cyan/Red slider to -50 and the Yellow/Blue slider to +50. You don't have to stick with a blue tint – experiment with the sliders until you find a colour you're happy with.

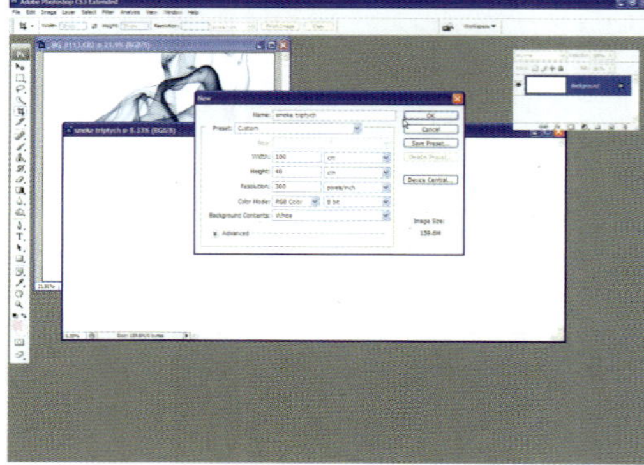

Create a new document

6 To put the triptych together you'll need to create a new document that's large enough to fit three 20cm squares side-by-side. To do this, go to File>New and name the document 'Smoke Triptych'. Specify a Width of 70cm and a Height of 30cm at a Resolution of 300 pixels per inch. Now set its Colour Mode to RGB Colour/8bit and Background Contents to White.

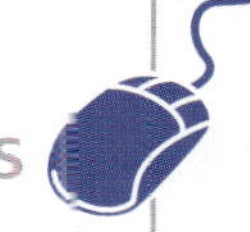

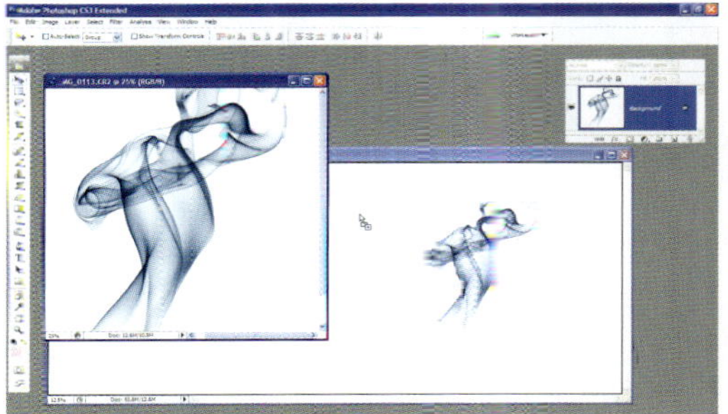

Grab and drop

7 Select the Grab tool from the Tools palette and drag and drop your first square smoke shot into the new 'Smoke Triptych' document. Now close the original smoke shot so you don't get confused as you open the remaining images in turn.

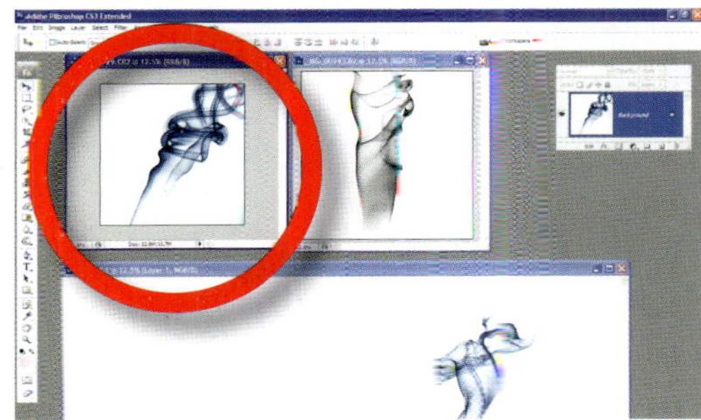

Repeat the process

8 Open the remaining shots and repeat steps 1 to 7 for each. Open the images in Adobe Camera Raw and select Previous Conversion from the drop-down menu at the top right of the sliders window. This will apply the changes you made to the first RAW file to your current image. Drag the edited images into the new document and move them into position, using a Guide (View>NewGuide) to ensure they are straight.

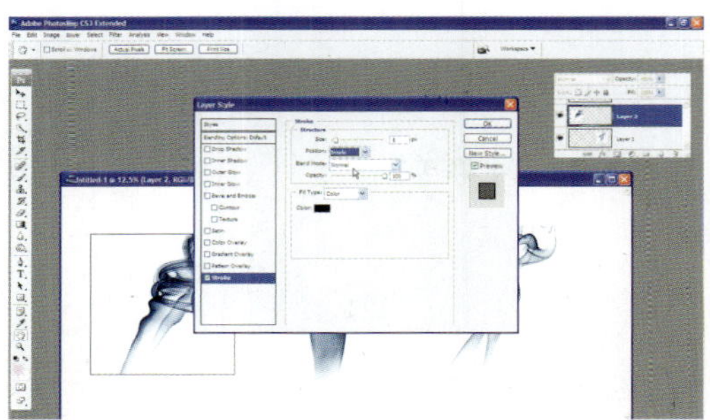

Add a stroke

9 Because the individual smoke layers all have a white background, they will bleed into the white document background. To prevent this, add a thin black border to each of the square smoke shots. To do this, click on each box and go to Layer>LayerStyle>Stroke. Once that's done, set the Colour to Black, Size to 8 pixels and Position to Inside.

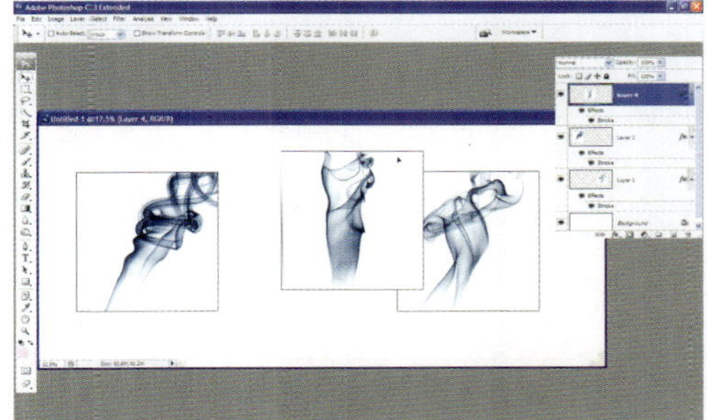

Final touches

10 Now there's a black border, you may find it easier to make final adjustments to the shots' positions with the Grab tool. Once the images are positioned correctly you can make any final tweaks to the colour or tone of the smoke, using Adjustment Layers at the top of the layer stack to affect all the layers beneath. Finally, save the image as a .PSD to retain the layers.

Super Tip!

"If you're looking for another table-top project, try capturing the magical swirls that coloured ink drops create as they hit water and disperse through it. You'll be able to use similar techniques to those we've revealed in this Masterclass, although the process is a lot slower because you'll need to refresh your water for every shot and be especially careful to keep your gear dry. If the process is successful, why not upload your images to a sharing website such as www.flickr.com? You'll find niche groups of photographers who specialise in shooting smoke swirls and ink drops. It's a great way to connect with other people that have similar interests and can also be a source of inspiration for new projects."

How we created our triptych

Create a beautiful still-life from the comfort of your home

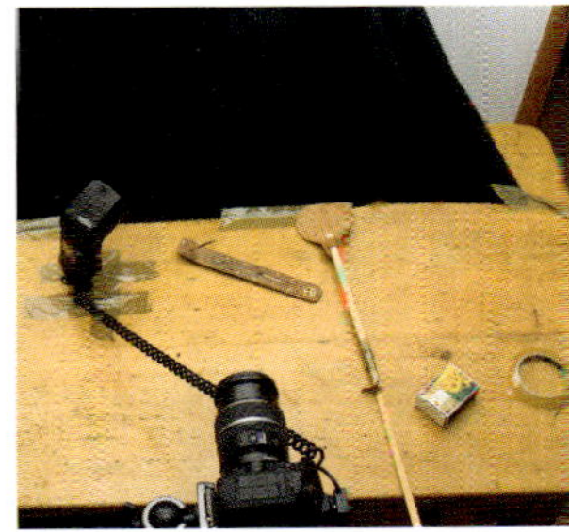

Create a home studio

1 Set up a table-top studio at home. Your kitchen table is ideal for this. Hang a piece of black velvet cloth to use as a background and burn incense to create a smoke pattern.

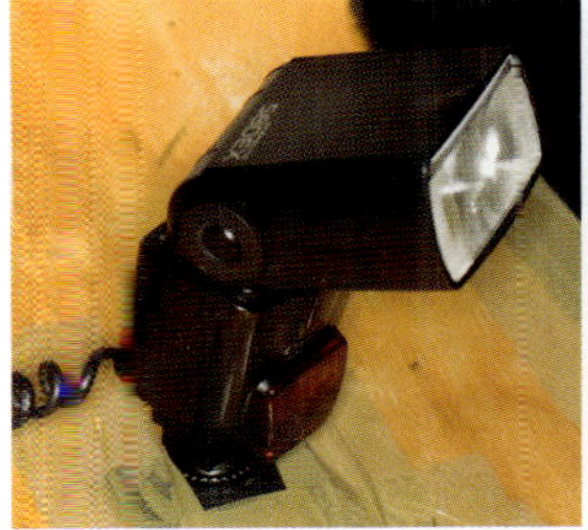

Light your scene

2 Use a Speedlite flashgun 'off camera' with a dedicated remote flash cable so that you can light the smoking incense from one side. Shoot in Manual mode for total control.

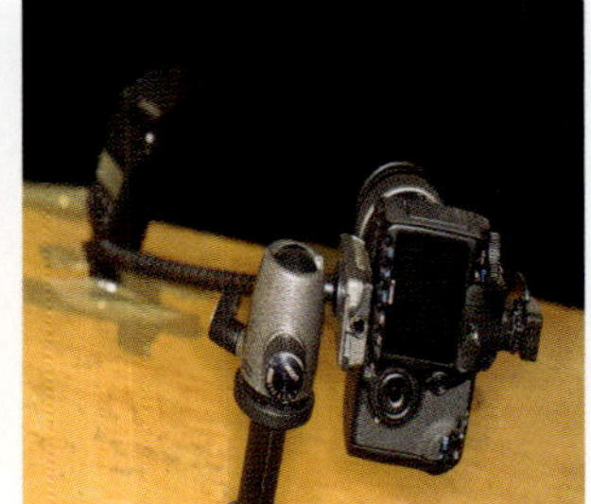

Start shooting

3 Once you've established a good exposure, shoot plenty of images. Stop when your memory card is full, and then use Adobe Bridge to narrow down your final selection.

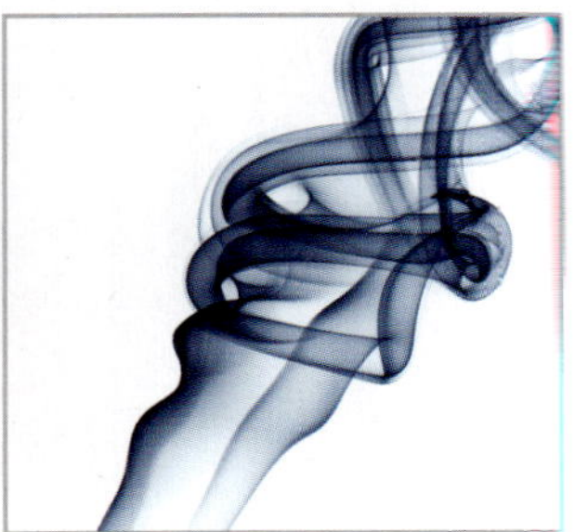

Edit your shots

4 Process the RAW files, convert them to mono, invert and crop them, then add a blue tint and import them into a new document. Add a thin black border to each image. ■

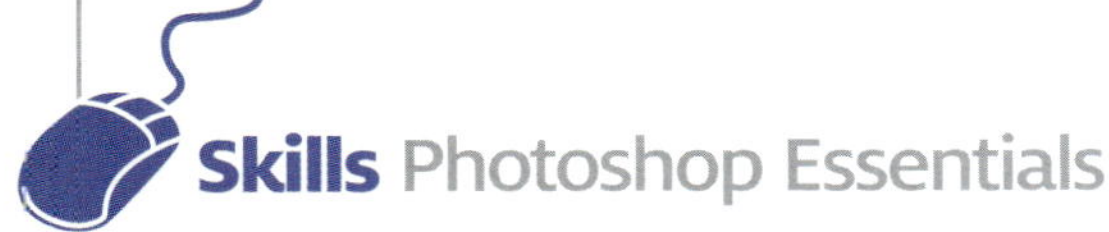

Peter Travers (Future)

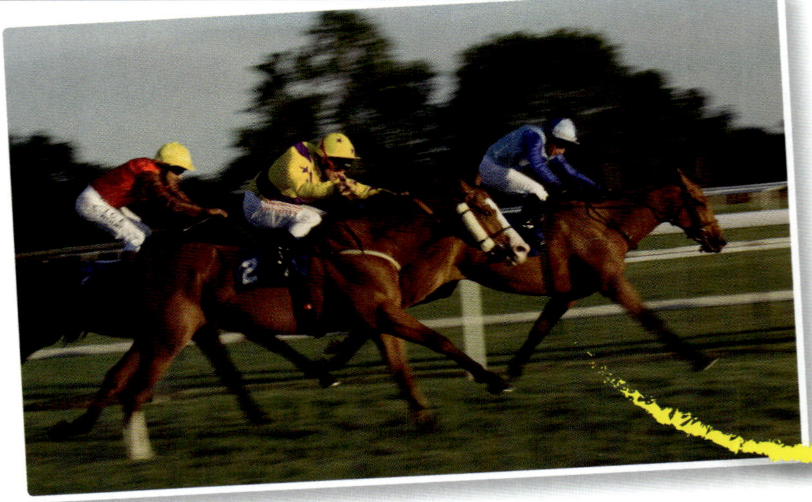

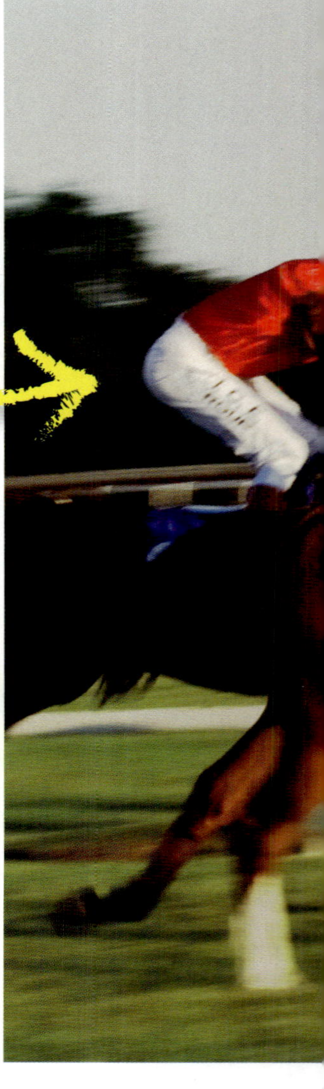

Boost contrast and colour in seconds

Use Photoshop Elements' Adjust Colour Curves command to transform uninspiring photos into vibrant stunners

Amateur photographers sometimes complain that their photos look flat straight out of the camera, but this isn't because there's anything wrong with the camera itself – digital sensors just produce images with less contrast and saturation than film. All these shots need is a helping hand to boost their contrast and colour.

Thankfully, there's a simple solution: the handy Adjust Colour Curves command in Photoshop Elements. This makes it easy to fine-tune your images' contrast and tones by adjusting highlights, midtones and shadows independently. You can also opt for one of the eight preset Styles provided, but we'd suggest building on those enhancements by tweaking the various sliders manually. Each time you move one of the four sliders, you'll see the curve on the graph in the bottom-right corner changing shape. Follow our guide to find out how it's done.

Checklist

What you'll need
Photoshop Elements 5.0 or above

How long it'll take
5 minutes

The skills you'll learn
- How to boost your images' tones and colours
- How to use the Adjust Colour Curves command
- What shape curve you need to boost tones and contrast

STEP BY STEP Adjust colour, tone and contrast

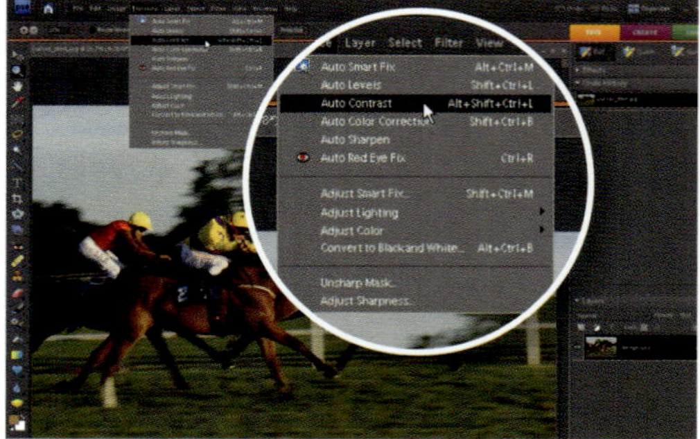

Out of the starting gate

1 Launch Photoshop Elements and open the curves_start.jpg image from your Video Disc. Elements has a fairly clever auto option to boost your shot's tones. Try it by going to Enhance> AutoContrast. However, to make more noticeable improvements with extra control, use Adjust Colour Curves. Go to Edit>Revert to undo the Auto Contrast.

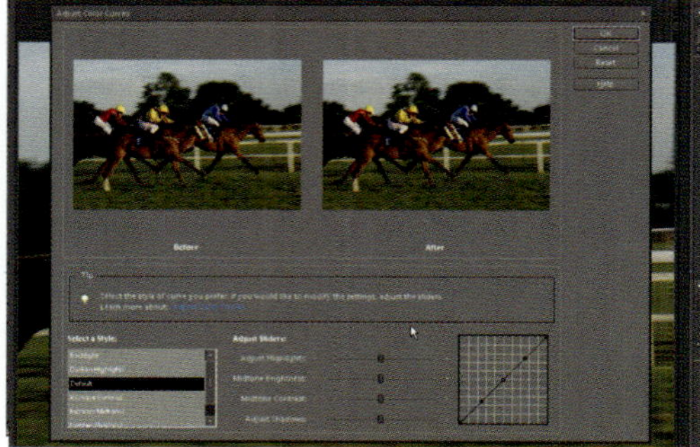

Pick a Style

2 Now go to Enhance>AdjustColour>AdjustColour Curves. You'll be greeted by the Adjust Colour Curves window and a display showing before and after images. You'll also find a number of different Styles to choose from: Backlight, Darken Highlights, Default, Increase Contrast, Increase Midtones, Lighten and Shadows. The last Style, Solarise, is an acquired taste.

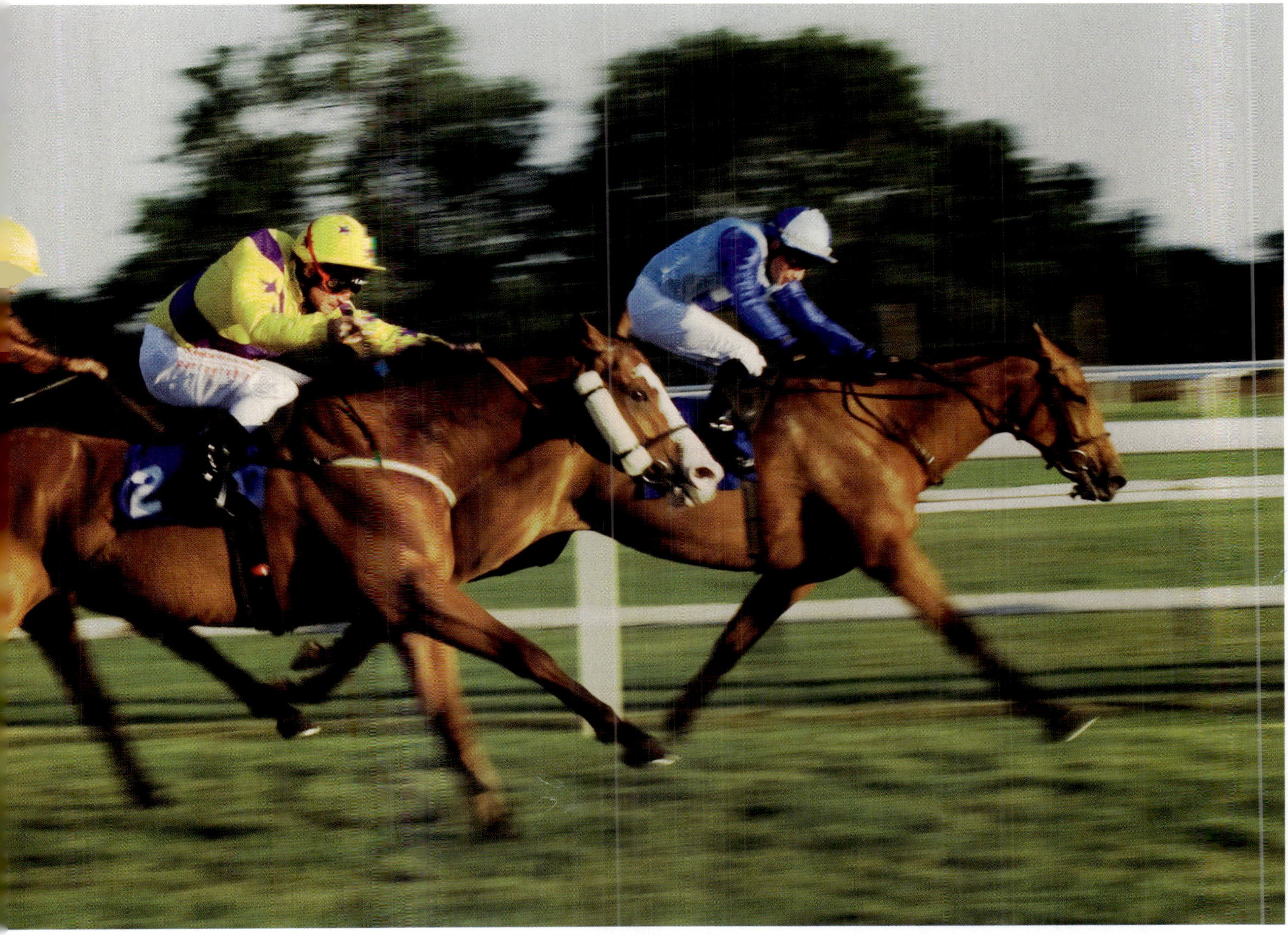

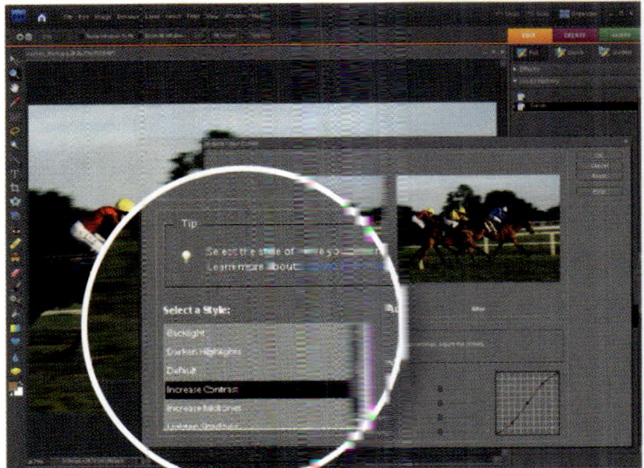

Select Increase Midtones

3 From these options you could just select the Increase Contrast Style to quickly enhance the overall contrast of this image. However, we're looking to boost the shot's overall tones, as well as brightening up the jockeys' colourful clothing and the green grass of the track. For this reason, we think the Increase Midtones Style works best. Choose this from the list.

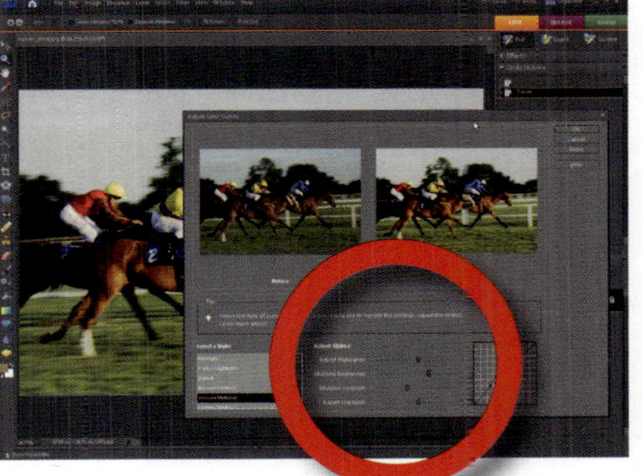

Take more control

4 Use the four sliders on the right to fine-tune your enhancements. Nudge the Adjust Highlights, Adjust Shadows and Midtone Brightness sliders to the right and the Midtones Contrast slider to the left. The curve on the graph changes shape as your image becomes brighter and the contrast increases. Finally, click on OK when you're happy with the result. ■

Super Tip!

"By using Adjust Colour Curves and its Highlight, Midtone Brightness, Midtone Contrast and Shadows sliders, you'll quickly get an idea of the shape of curve you need to create for different effects. This will come in handy should you upgrade to CS and use the more powerful Curves tool."

Peter Travers (Future)

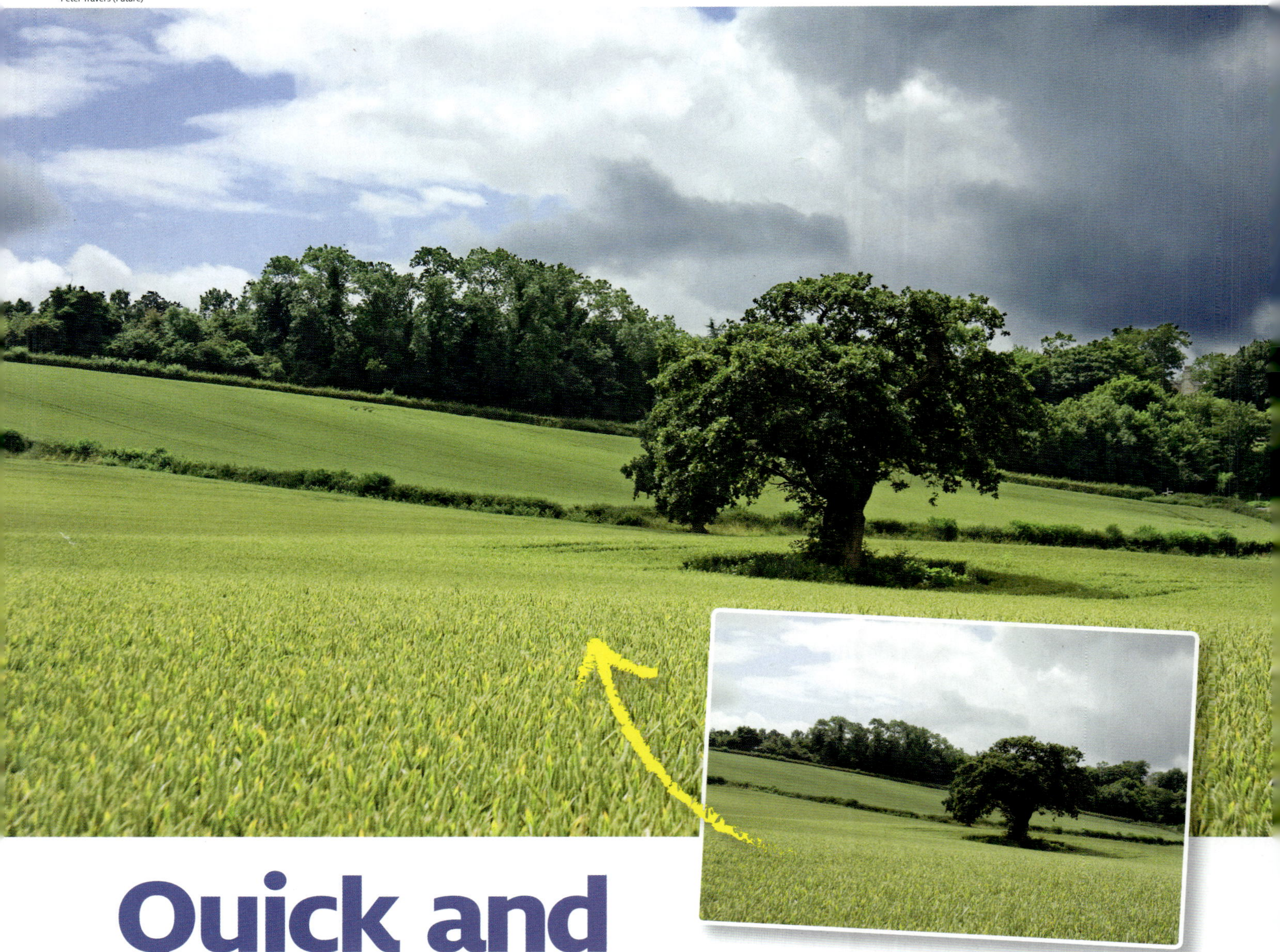

Quick and easy landscape fixes

Photoshop Elements' one-click Quick Fix solutions can help you to dramatically improve your photographs in a matter of seconds

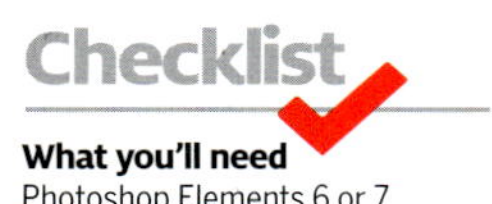

What you'll need
Photoshop Elements 6 or 7

How long it'll take
10 minutes

The skills you'll learn
- ✔ How to use Quick Fix to improve your images in an instant
- ✔ How to selectively boost the colour of skies and foregrounds

Some budding photographers are reluctant to start using image-editing software such as Photoshop or Photoshop Elements because they assume they will need to spend countless hours on their PCs, fruitlessly attempting to improve their photographs. However, technophobic photographers everywhere will be pleased to know that, by using Photoshop Elements' built-in Quick Fix tools, they can enhance their images quickly *and* accurately.

In the following tutorial, we'll guide you through each of these one-click Quick Fixes, showing you which Auto settings work well and which you should avoid. We'll explain which settings will help you successfully and realistically enhance your landscapes (such as the Levels and Contrast Auto buttons under the Lighting tab and the Saturation slider under the Colour tab) by improving the colour and tone of your foregrounds.

We'll also show you how to quickly select large sections of sky in your shots so you can instantly strengthen weak blues, enhance cloud detail to dramatic effect and transform lacklustre vistas into stunning scenes. So let's get started...

STEP BY STEP Improve your shot in a few clicks

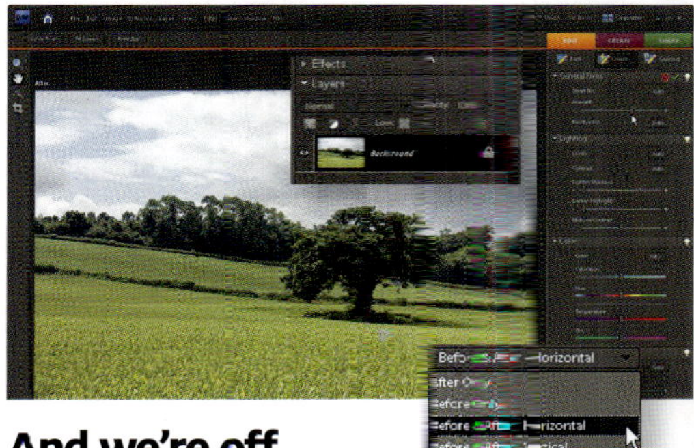

And we're off

1 Open quickfix_start.jpg from the Video Disc in Photoshop Elements and click on the Quick tab in the top right corner. Click the Fit Screen button in the top left of the new workspace. In the View box at the bottom left of the window you can choose to look at just the After image, or select Before and After so you can compare your original and edited images.

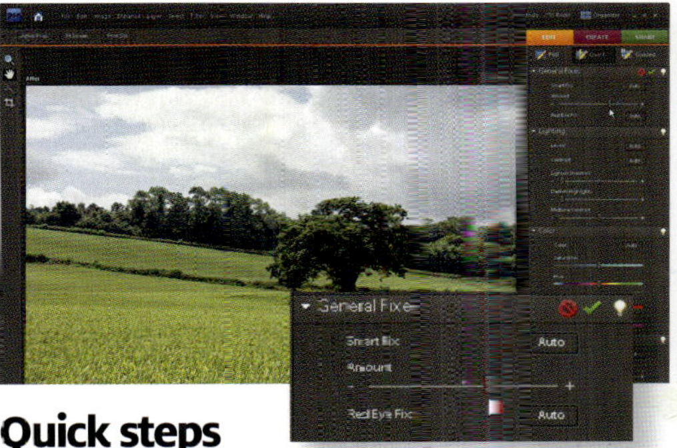

Quick steps

2 For quick enhancements, try the Smart Fix option under General Fixes. Click on Auto, or use the Amount slider to enhance your shot manually (watching out for image artefacts) before clicking the tick. If you're unfamiliar with Photoshop's Levels settings, click the Auto buttons for Levels and Contrast under the Lighting header. There's an Auto button under the Colour header, too (see Super Tip, right).

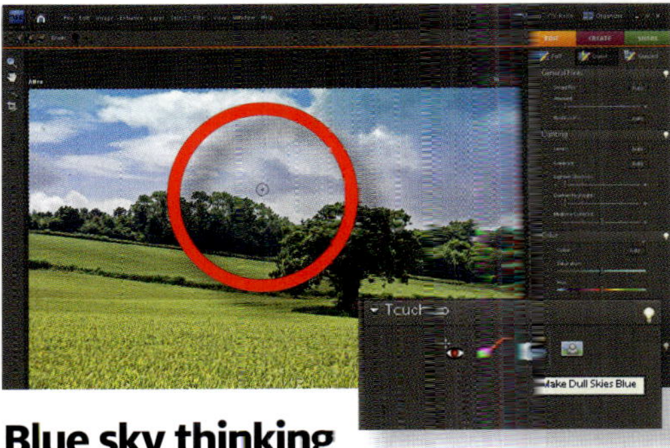

Blue sky thinking

3 One new addition to Quick Fix in Photoshop Elements 7 is a tool (under the Touch Up header) called Make Dull Skies Blue. Simply click on the icon, choose a brush size of around 200 pixels, then drag to select the sky and watch it turn bright blue. However, the effect is garish and you can't tweak the strength of the enhancement. You get a full-on blue sky or nothing!

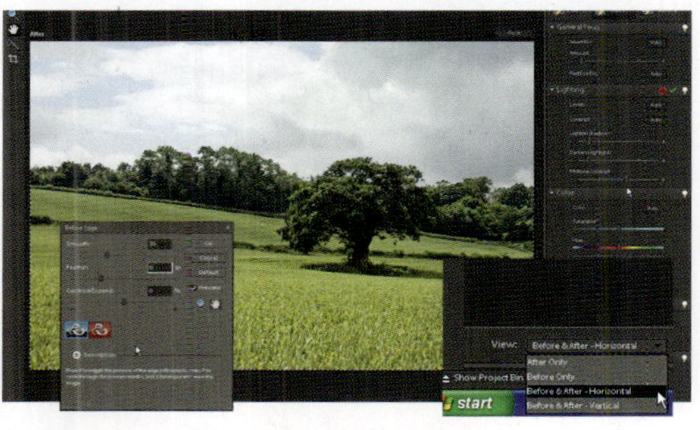

Targeted improvements

4 Click Reset, then pick the Quick Selection tool. Set Brush Size to 100 pixels, then click and drag to select the ground. Click Refine Edge, set Smooth to 35, Feather to 6, Contract/Expand to 0 and click OK. In Lighting, set Lighten Shadows to 15%, Darken Highlights to 15% and Midtone Contrast to 60%. In Colour, drag Saturation to around 60%. Click the tick.

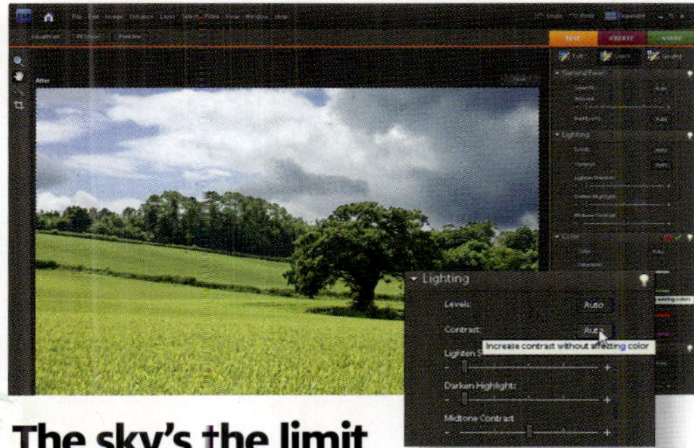

The sky's the limit

5 Go to Select>Inverse to quickly swap your selection from the ground to the sky. In the Lighting panel, move the Darken Highlights slider to 15% and the Midtone Contrast slider to about 40%. In the Colour panel, move the Saturation slider to 60%. Click the tick, then go to Select>Deselect to clear the sky selection.

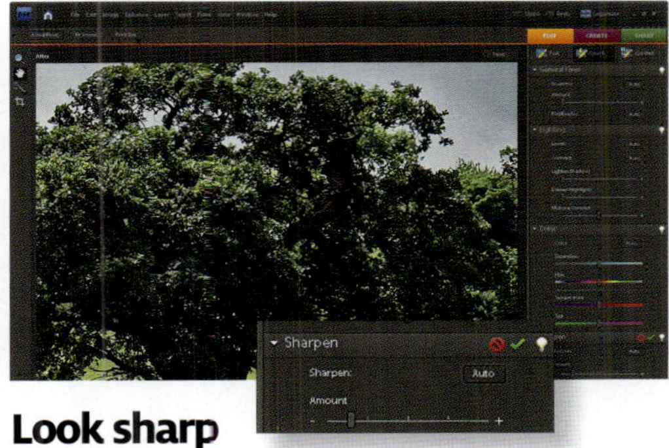

Look sharp

6 It's always good practice to make sharpening the last thing you do. If you sharpen your photo before going back to boost contrast, for example, the image quality will decrease. Only minor adjustments are necessary to make a difference when sharpening an image for printing. Zoom in to Actual Pixels (100% view), then push the Sharpen slider up to around 15%. Click the tick, then go to File>SaveAs to finish. ■

Super Tip!

"Be careful when using multiple auto enhancement settings in Quick Fix. If you use two or three adjustments combined – such as Auto Levels, Auto Contrast and Darken Highlights – the tweaks can quickly become noticeably destructive. This means that the image-editing process decreases the image quality and the pixels start to break up. This reduction in quality will be obvious when you zoom in to 100% view and will also show up when your image is printed. Follow the combinations we found successful in the tutorial to the left, or stick to using just one or two individual settings to retain your image's quality."

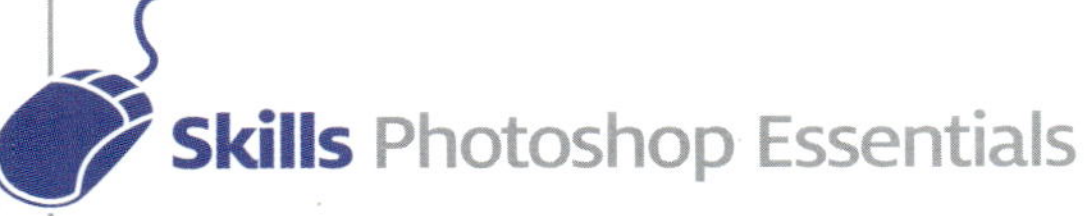

George Cairns

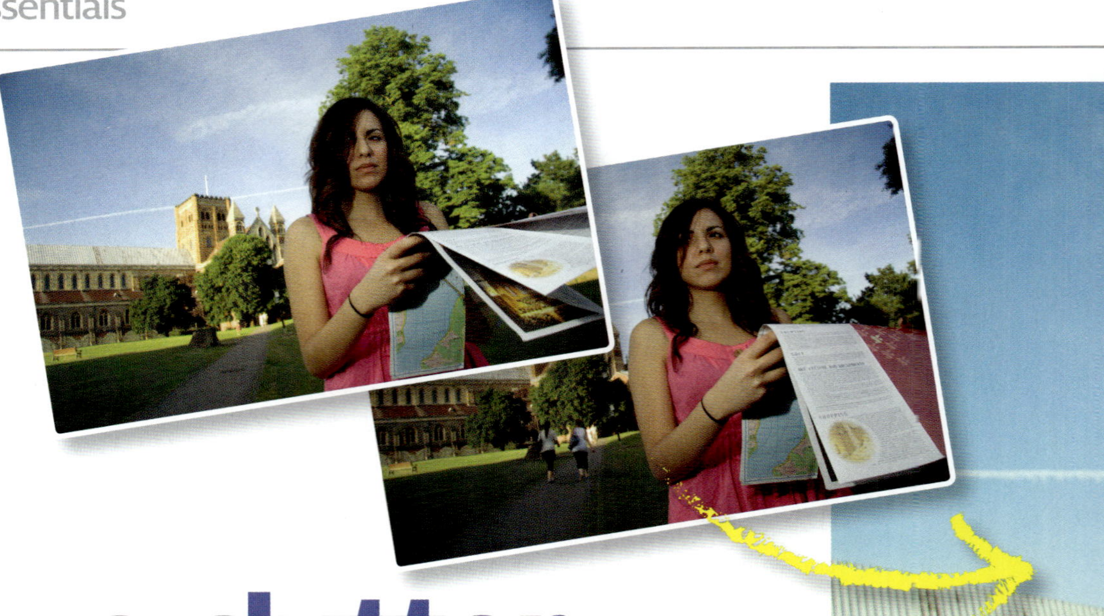

Remove clutter from your scenes

Use Elements' Photomerge Scene Cleaner to combine the best bits of two photos and eliminate unwanted distractions

When photographing friends or family against a popular landmark it can be a hard to capture them without ambling tourists walking into the frame. In the first shot (above), the background is empty but the subject has blinked. In the second image the subject looks good, but the background is too busy.

It is possible to combine the best bits of both shots in Photoshop by copying the first image and pasting it into a new layer above the second. You can then align the two layers as accurately as possible (they were shot without a tripod so this is quite tricky to do well) and use the Eraser tool to reveal the better background from the layer below.

However, there is another, more effective, way. Photoshop Elements 7.0's clever new Photomerge Scene Cleaner enables you to combine the two shots in a fraction of the time. Read on to find out how...

STEP BY STEP Merge the best parts of two shots

Checklist

What you'll need
Photoshop Elements 7.0

How long it'll take
10 minutes

The skills you'll learn

- ✔ How to use Photomerge Scene Cleaner to remove unwanted people or objects from a scene
- ✔ How to align two Photoshop layers accurately

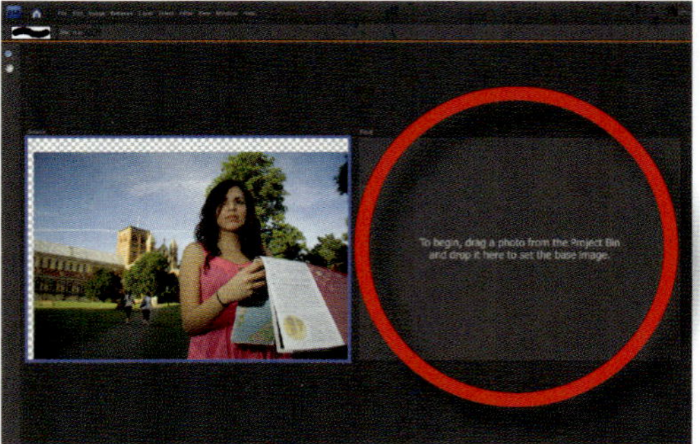

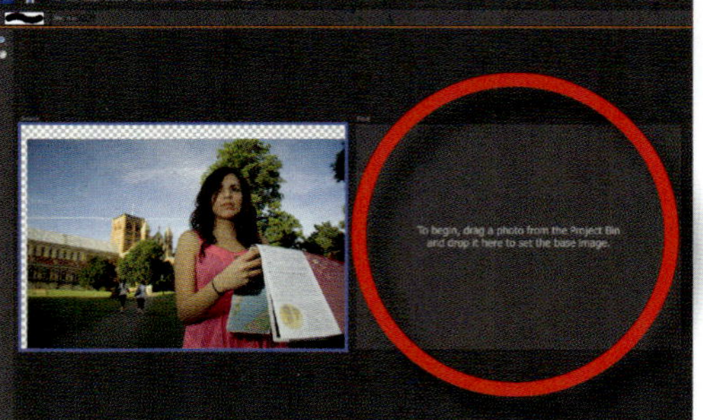

Import your images

1 In Photoshop Elements, go to File>Open and find cleaner_start01.jpg and cleaner_start02.jpg on your Video Disc. Hold down Shift and click to select both images, then click Open and the images will appear in the Project Bin. Next go to File>New> PhotomergeSceneCleaner. Click Open All and the images will open in the Scene Cleaner interface.

Choose a source image

2 Drag cleaner_start02.jpg into the Final window on the right, because this image features the girl's best pose, and then click on cleaner_start01.jpg to load it in the Source window. Select the Zoom tool and click on the image for a closer look at the unwanted background figures. Grab the Pencil tool from the panel on the right and set Size to 9 pixels.

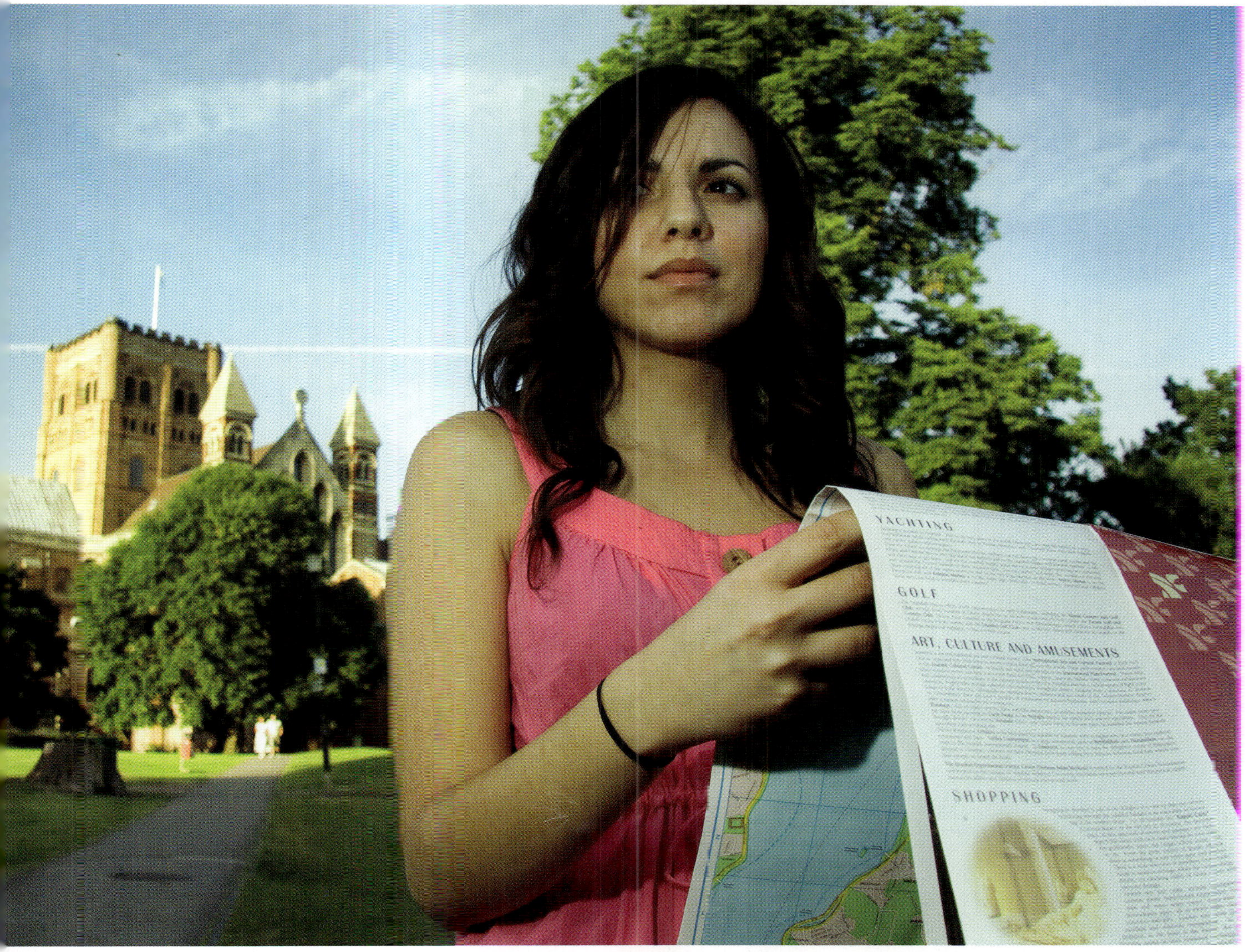

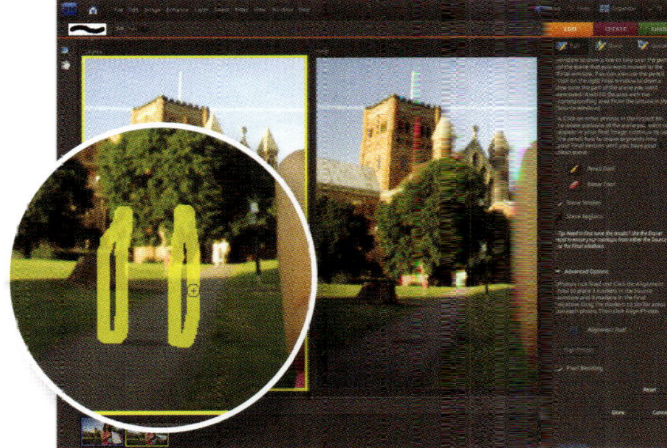

Start scribbling

3 Use the Pencil tool to circle the parts of the source file that you want to paste over the two figures in the background of the final file. Photomerge Scene Cleaner will then take this sampled area and transplant it over the unwanted figures. You may need to play around with it a bit – if you select too large an area you can use the Erase tool to fine-tune it.

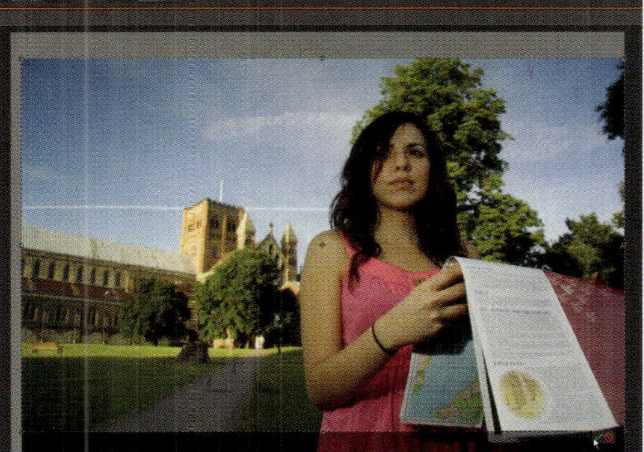

Blend it in

4 The transplanted area looks a bit rough around the edges. To fix this, scroll down and click on the Advanced Options tab, then tick Pixel Blending. This blends the two images together more effectively. Click Done. Next, use the Crop tool to remove any problem areas, such as the white edges caused by the automatic alignment. Click on the tick to finish. ■

Super Tip!

"To align your shots manually, click on Advanced Options and tick the Alignment tool. Place the numbered control points over the key areas in the Source window, then place the corresponding numbered control points in the same positions in the final window. Click Align Photos."

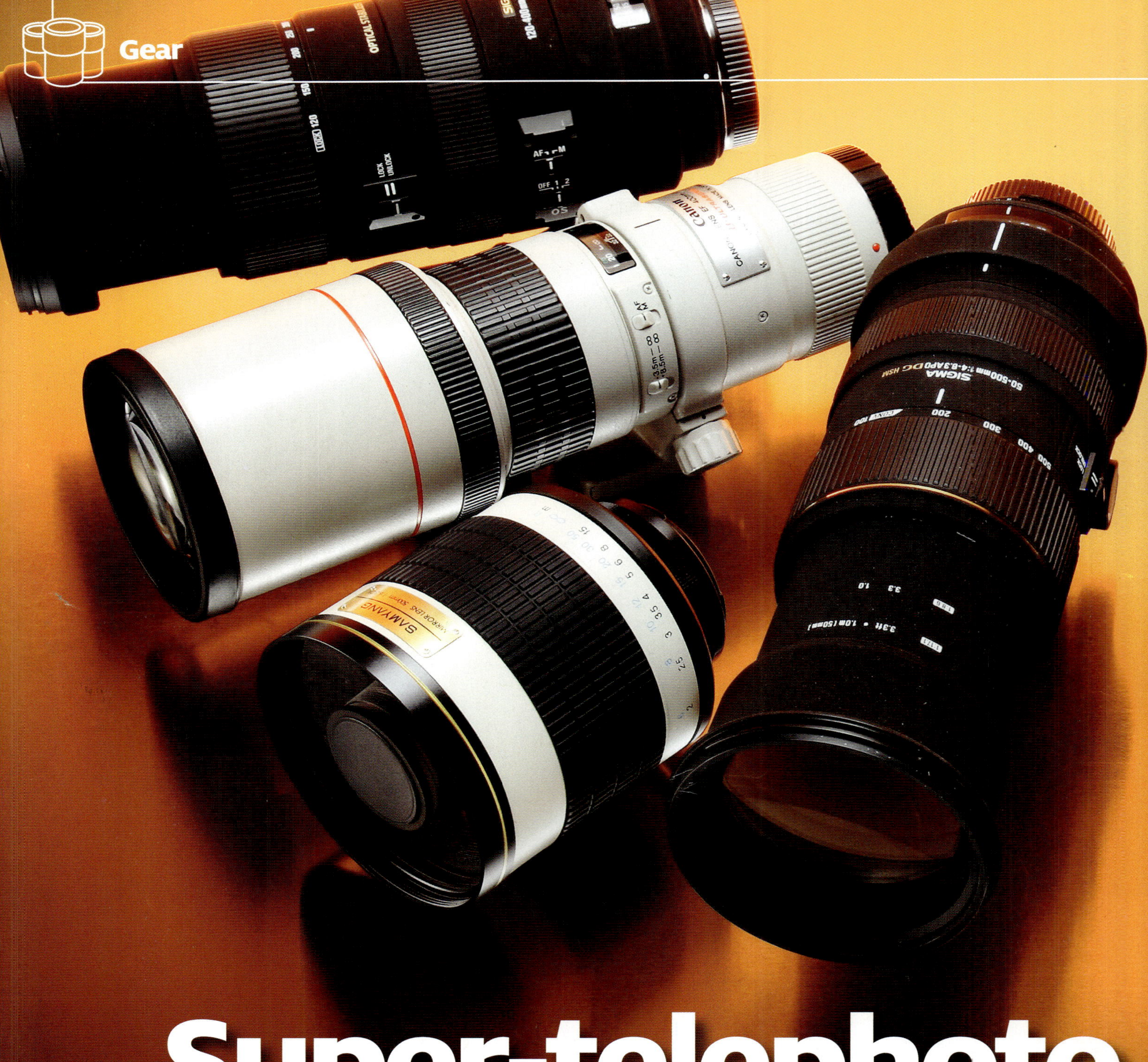

Super-telephoto

Get closer to the action, even from a distance with these monster telephoto lenses that are perfect for sports and wildlife

Turn to the sports pages at the back of just about any newspaper and you'll see remarkably close-up images of the action, even though the photographs themselves were taken at quite a distance. Follow the same sports on TV and you'll notice rows of press photographers on the sidelines using huge, wide-apertured telephoto lenses, most of which cost $5,000 and up. That kind of kit may be prohibitively expensive, but thankfully it's possible to get practically

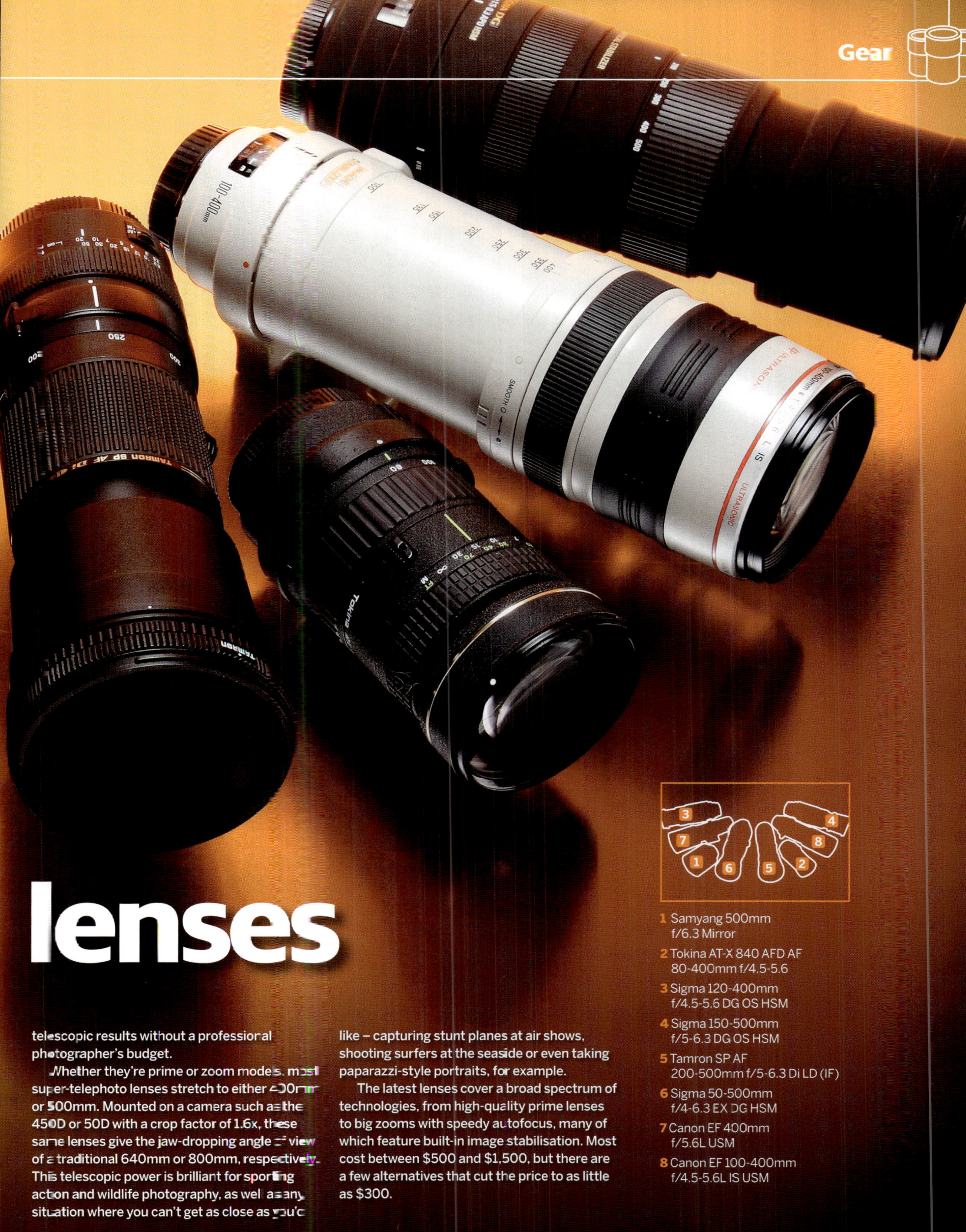

1 Samyang 500mm f/6.3 Mirror
2 Tokina AT-X 840 AFD AF 80-400mm f/4.5-5.6
3 Sigma 120-400mm f/4.5-5.6 DG OS HSM
4 Sigma 150-500mm f/5-6.3 DG OS HSM
5 Tamron SP AF 200-500mm f/5-6.3 Di LD (IF)
6 Sigma 50-500mm f/4-6.3 EX DG HSM
7 Canon EF 400mm f/5.6L USM
8 Canon EF 100-400mm f/4.5-5.6L IS USM

lenses

telescopic results without a professional photographer's budget.

Whether they're prime or zoom models, most super-telephoto lenses stretch to either 400mm or 500mm. Mounted on a camera such as the 450D or 50D with a crop factor of 1.6x, these same lenses give the jaw-dropping angle of view of a traditional 640mm or 800mm, respectively. This telescopic power is brilliant for sporting action and wildlife photography, as well as any situation where you can't get as close as you'd like – capturing stunt planes at air shows, shooting surfers at the seaside or even taking paparazzi-style portraits, for example.

The latest lenses cover a broad spectrum of technologies, from high-quality prime lenses to big zooms with speedy autofocus, many of which feature built-in image stabilisation. Most cost between $500 and $1,500, but there are a few alternatives that cut the price to as little as $300.

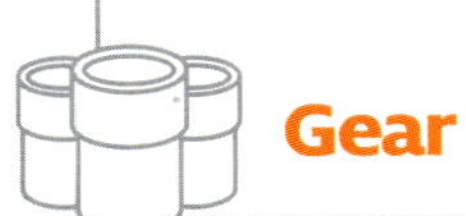

Super-telephotos up close

Put your eye to the telescope and get up close and personal with faraway subjects

Super Tip!

"Accurate focusing is especially important when using super-telephoto lenses, due to their minimal depth of field (the distance in front of and behind the point of focus that is rendered sharply). For example, using a 450D or 50D with a 500mm lens to shoot a subject that's 5m away with an aperture of f/5.6, the total depth of field is less than 2cm (nearly 1cm in front of and behind the focus point) – so focusing must be precise."

The battle between super-telephoto lenses is a heavyweight contest, with most models weighing in at up to 1.8kg. Fitted to a relatively lightweight body such as the 450D, it can seem as though the tail is wagging the dog, but the advantages are extreme when it comes to picking out details in the distance.

A tripod is useful, but a monopod works better to help take the weight when you're on the move. Almost all super-telephoto lenses come with a mounting collar that helps keep the camera and lens balanced when in use.

Super-telephoto lenses come into their own in sports and wildlife shooting, where your movements are often restricted, so there's a lot to be said for zoom lenses rather than primes, which give you more flexibility for framing your subjects. Unless you spend silly money, the maximum apertures of prime super-telephoto lenses tend to be similar to their zoom counterparts.

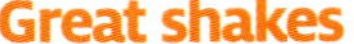

Great shakes

The single biggest problem when shooting with a super-telephoto lens is camera shake. The rule of thumb when handholding a camera is that you need a shutter speed at least as fast as the inverse of the focal length that you're using. So, continuing with our 450D by way of example, a 500mm lens is equivalent to an 800mm lens once you take the crop factor into account, which makes a shutter speed of 1/800 sec a safe minimum. Even in bright, sunny conditions, this is often impossible to achieve without increasing the ISO speed of your camera, so image stabilisation comes into its own.

Trusty IS (Image Stabilizer) technology is fitted to many own-brand zoom lensesand Sigma uses its similar OS (Optical Stabilizer) system on its new 120-400mm and 150-500mm lenses. However, there are plenty of long lenses that lack this useful feature.

A focal length of 300mm or longer is essential for most sports and wildlife

Get even closer

Extend your range with a teleconverter

A cost-effective alternative to getting more telescopic power is to fit a teleconverter, which typically magnifies the focal length by a factor of 1.4x or 2x. Canon Extender EF 1.4x II and EF 2x II models are suitable for use with Canon lenses. Remember, you can't use extenders with EF-S lenses such as the 55-250mm IS, because the rear element protrudes too far and may damage the teleconverter.

Sigma offers 1.4x and 2x EX DG APO teleconverters. Third-party teleconverters are available from the likes of Kenko, whose Pro 300 series costs $300 for 1.4x, 2x or 3x converters. Teleconverters cut down the light reaching the sensor. For instance, a 1.4x extender effectively makes the maximum aperture one stop slower and a 2x teleconverter makes it two stops slower. The autofocus is designed to work with maximum apertures of f/5.6 or wider, so you'll often need to use manual focus.

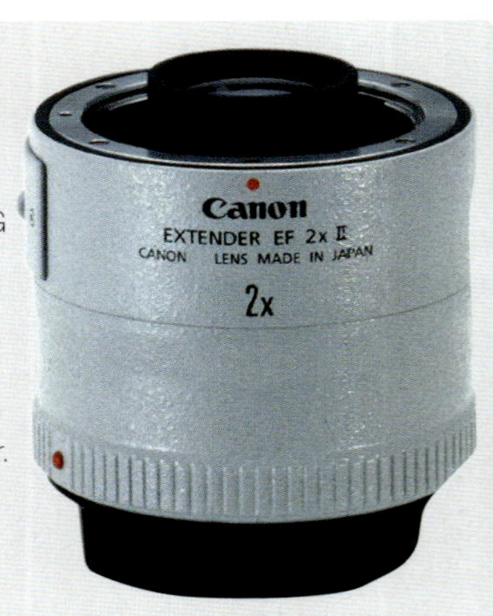

The Canon Extender EF 2x II effectively gives the EF 100-400mm lens a zoom range of 200-800mm, although you'll only have an f/11 maximum aperture

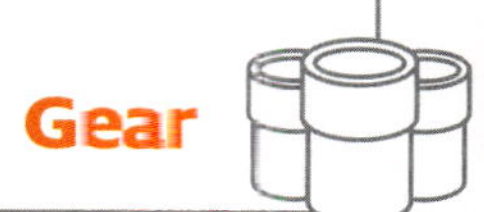

SUPER-LONG LENSES AT A GLANCE

Get the best out of your monster lens

How to use your telephoto lens to capture perfect detail from a distance

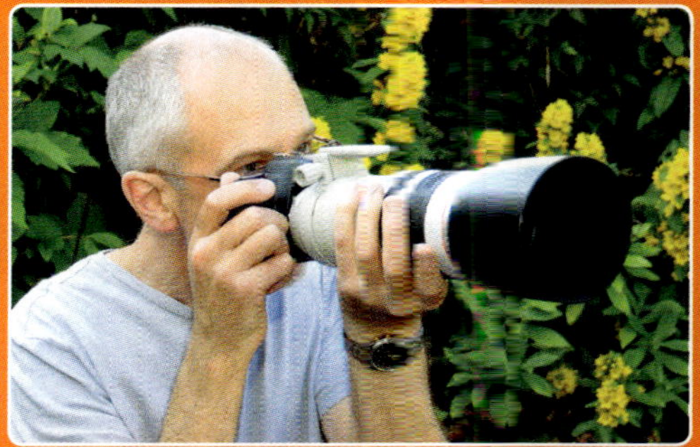

Handholding technique

1 To avoid camera shake when handholding, take a firm, relaxed grip of the body with your right hand and use your left hand to support the underside of the lens barrel, taking care not to foul the focus ring if it rotates during autofocus.

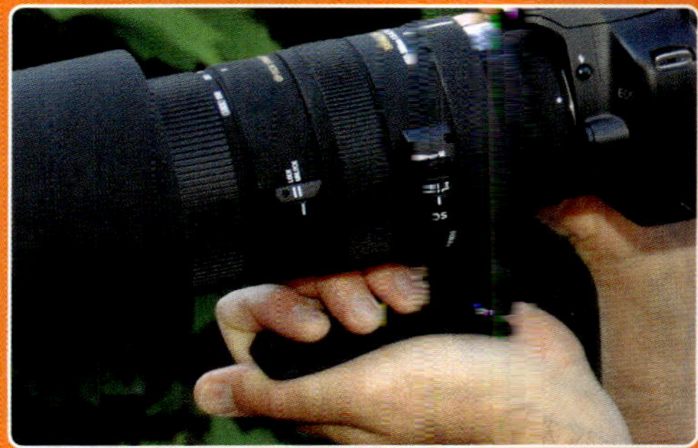

Get a grip

2 For lenses with short, stubby tripod mounting collars, it's best to rotate the collar upwards or remove it when handholding, so it's not in your way. However, some collar mounts double up as hand grips, with moulded grooves to act as finger slots.

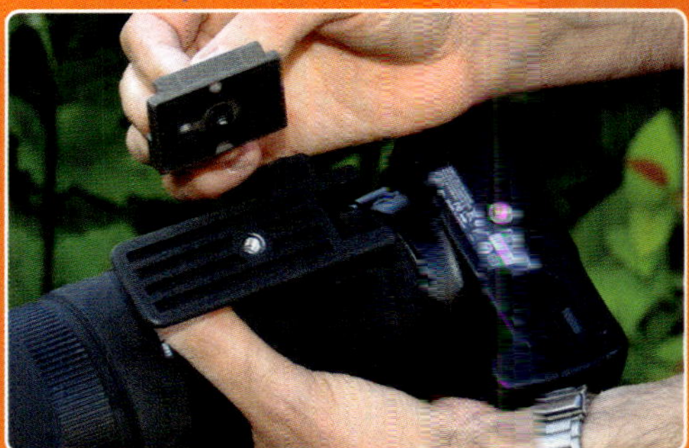

Quick release

3 Most tripods have quick-release plates for fitting to the camera or lens. Attach these firmly to the lens's tripod collar mount and consider investing in a second quick-release plate which you can leave attached to the lens permanently.

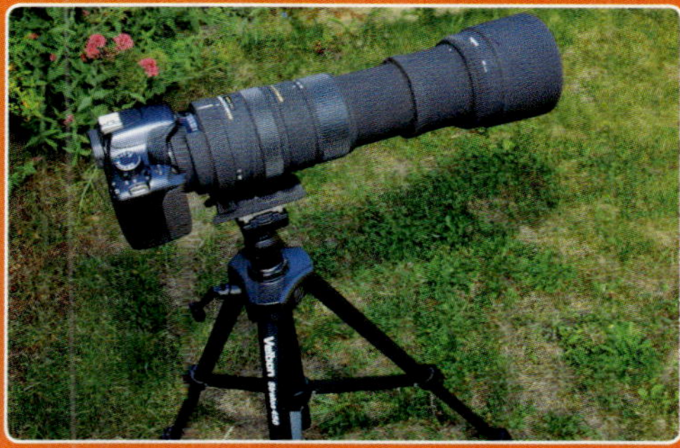

Tripod mounting

4 When fully extended, a super-telephoto lens can double in length. To stop your tripod toppling over, make sure the lens is directly over one of the legs. The tripod collar enables you to rotate the camera through 90° for upright shots.

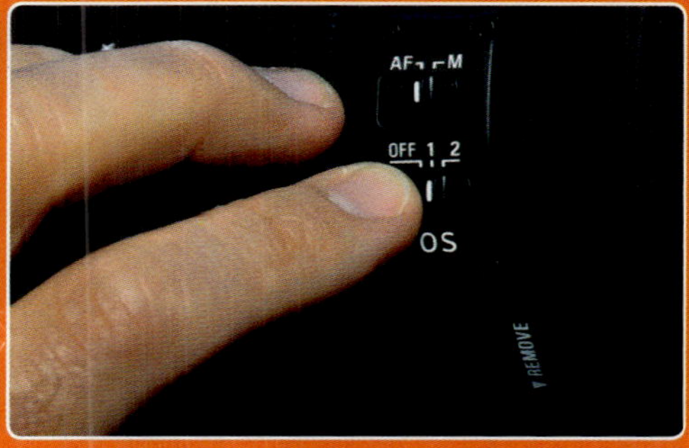

Stabilisation modes

5 The Canon and Sigma lenses have two image stabilisation modes. Mode 1 corrects for vibration in both the vertical and horizontal planes, while Mode 2 applies correction only in the vertical plane, which makes it ideal for panning shots.

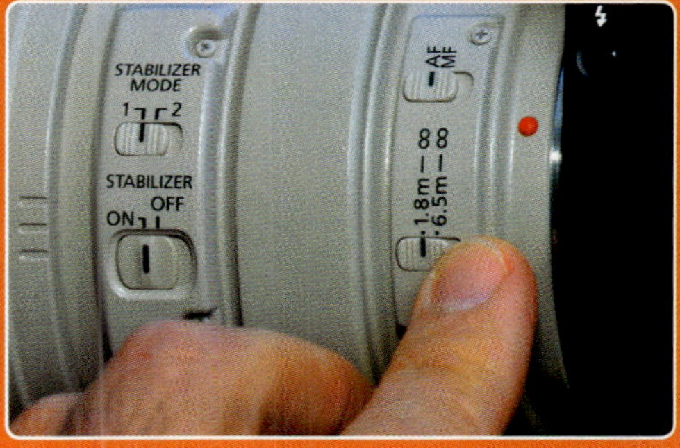

Extra AF speed

6 Despite the speed of some lenses' ultrasonic motors, autofocus can be slow if the lens misses its mark and has to cycle all the way from infinity and back. If your lens has a focus limit switch, use it to reduce the amount of autofocus travel.

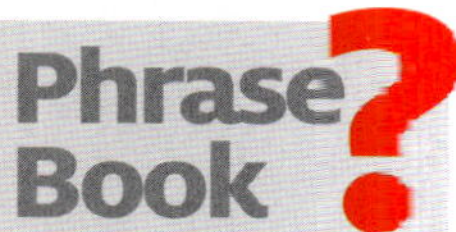

Phrase Book?

Crop factor
Cameras such as the EOS 5D Mark II have a 'full-frame' image sensor the same size as a frame of 35mm film, but most D-SLRs have smaller sensors that don't capture as much of the image produced by the camera's lens. Most D-SLRs have a crop factor of 1.6x, so a 100mm lens is equivalent to using a 160mm on a full-frame camera, for example.

Image stabilisation
An optically stabilised lens uses an extra group of lens elements to counteract the effects of camera shake. Any movement or vibration is sensed by the lens, and microprocessor-controlled servo motors move the IS group by a relative amount in the opposite direction in order to cancel it out.

Focal length
This is a measure of how strongly a lens converges rays of light reflected from the subject that's being photographed. Wide-angle lenses with short focal lengths (18mm, for example) actually have greater converging power than telephoto lenses, which don't need to 'bend in' the paths of light so strongly.

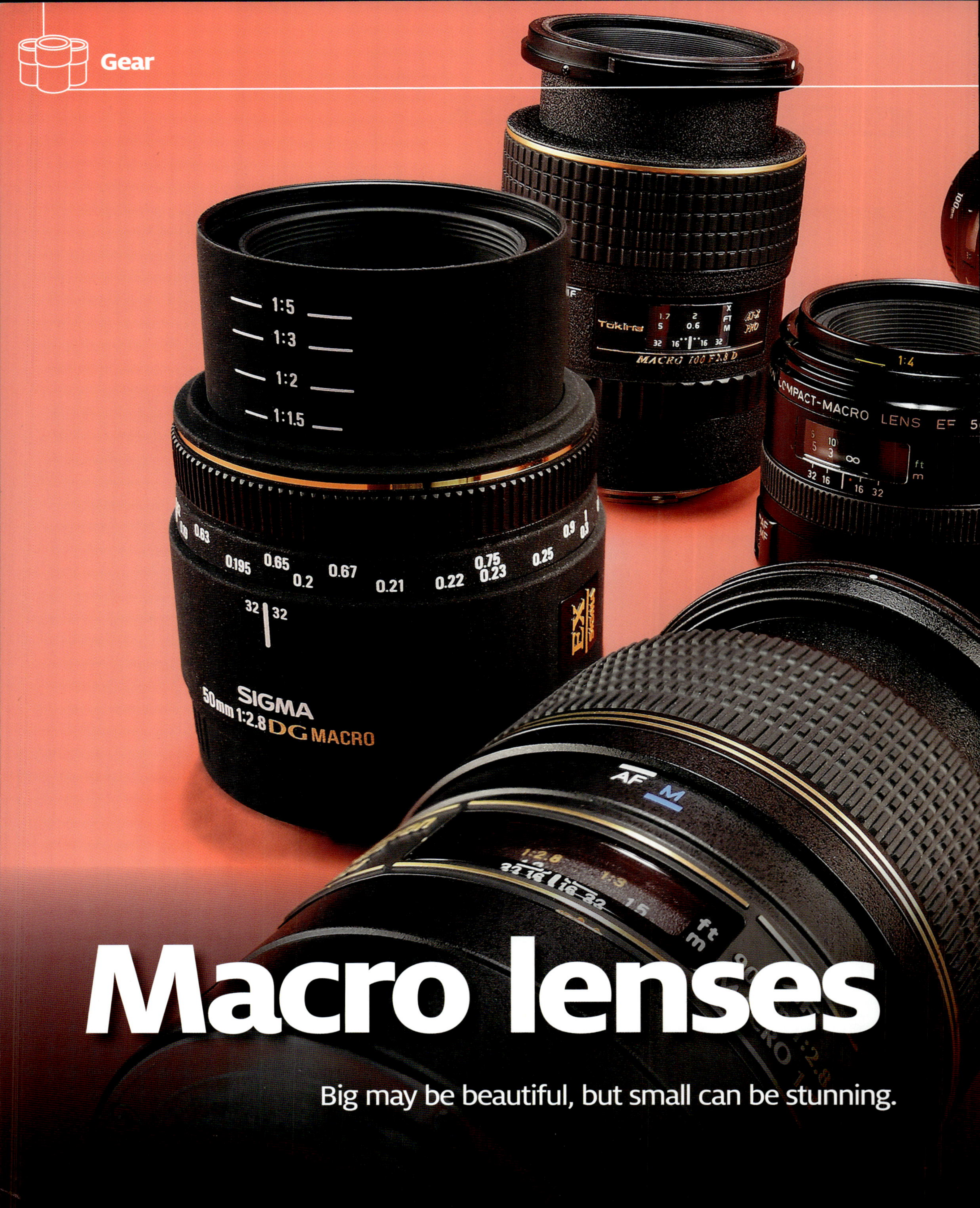

Macro lenses

Big may be beautiful, but small can be stunning.

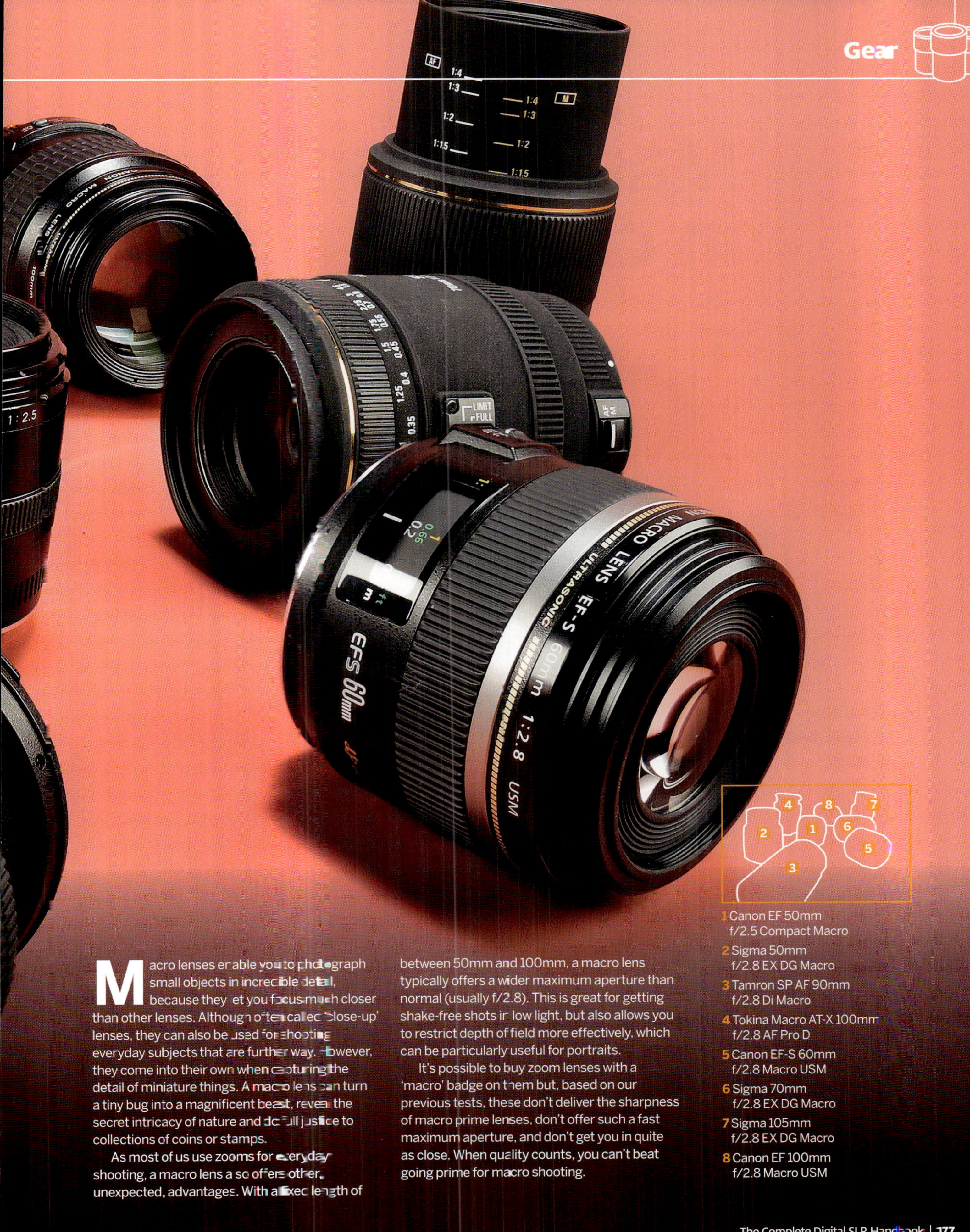

1 Canon EF 50mm f/2.5 Compact Macro
2 Sigma 50mm f/2.8 EX DG Macro
3 Tamron SP AF 90mm f/2.8 Di Macro
4 Tokina Macro AT-X 100mm f/2.8 AF Pro D
5 Canon EF-S 60mm f/2.8 Macro USM
6 Sigma 70mm f/2.8 EX DG Macro
7 Sigma 105mm f/2.8 EX DG Macro
8 Canon EF 100mm f/2.8 Macro USM

Macro lenses enable you to photograph small objects in incredible detail, because they let you focus much closer than other lenses. Although often called 'close-up' lenses, they can also be used for shooting everyday subjects that are further away. However, they come into their own when capturing the detail of miniature things. A macro lens can turn a tiny bug into a magnificent beast, reveal the secret intricacy of nature and do full justice to collections of coins or stamps.

As most of us use zooms for everyday shooting, a macro lens also offers other, unexpected, advantages. With a fixed length of between 50mm and 100mm, a macro lens typically offers a wider maximum aperture than normal (usually f/2.8). This is great for getting shake-free shots in low light, but also allows you to restrict depth of field more effectively, which can be particularly useful for portraits.

It's possible to buy zoom lenses with a 'macro' badge on them but, based on our previous tests, these don't deliver the sharpness of macro prime lenses, don't offer such a fast maximum aperture, and don't get you in quite as close. When quality counts, you can't beat going prime for macro shooting.

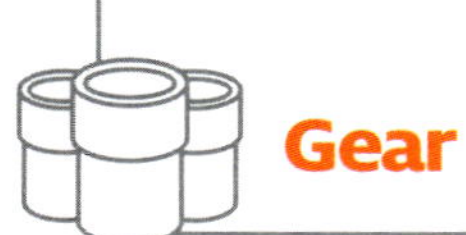

Macro lenses in close-up detail

Take a look at the finer points of these powerful lenses

Super Tip!

"Just like very long telephoto lenses, macro lenses are extremely prone to shake. A strong light source is essential for macro photography, but even so you'll need to keep the camera as still as possible. A sturdy tripod is a great place to start but it also makes sense to enable Mirror Lock-up, from your camera's Custom Function settings, via the main menu. Use this with the Self-timer, so that the camera isn't unsettled by the mirror flipping up before the shutter fires."

There's an all-important x-factor in macro lenses, which indicates the maximum magnification you can expect to get. This will always be at the closest focus distance enabled by the lens and a true macro lens has an x-factor of 1.0x, also referred to as 1:1. In plain English, this means that it can create a 'life-sized' image of a small object being photographed, which is the same size on the camera's sensor (or 35mm film frame in older cameras) as the object itself. So, for instance, a lens with a lesser magnification factor of 0.5x, or 1:2, would create an image on the sensor that's only half the size of the object being photographed.

The ability to create a life-sized image on the sensor might not sound particularly impressive in theory, but bear in mind that (just as with a frame of 35mm film) this is only the recording medium and the resulting print or on-screen image will be very much larger than the sensor itself. In real terms, when you take a macro photograph of a small object with a 1.0x lens, it will appear 50x larger on a computer screen when you view it at 100% zoom. Printed enlargements of the image, showing off all that detail, will look equally amazing.

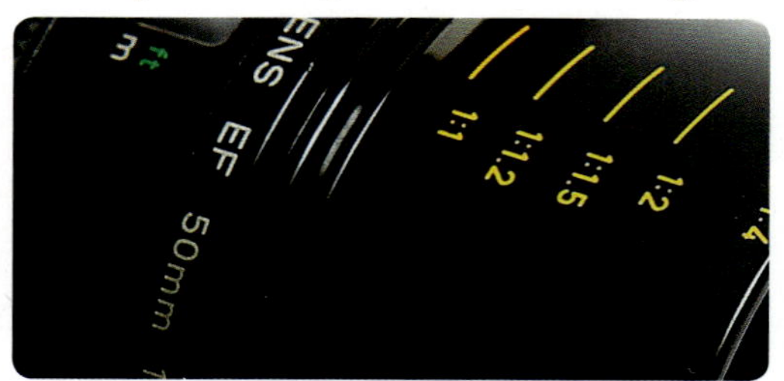

A macro lens with an x-factor of 1:1 is able to create a life-sized image of a small object on the sensor

Speed trap

One drawback with macro photography is that, because the level of detail you're recreating is so fine, focusing has to be incredibly accurate. This is also because depth of field (the distance between the closest and furthest parts of an object that appear sharp) is minimal in macro photography. For example, shooting at f/2.8 with an EF-S 60mm lens at the closest focus setting of 20cm, the depth of field is less than a single millimetre.

With such precise focusing required, the travel of the focus ring tends to be much longer than with standard lenses, so autofocus is generally slow. Some lenses feature a focus limit switch (see Phrase Book, right), but even so, don't expect blistering autofocus speed. Apart from that, macro lenses have a lot to offer, as you'll discover on these pages.

How we tested the lenses

Supersize your macro

Keep your distance with a lens that has a longer focal length

In most situations, a focal length of between 50mm and about 100mm is most practical for macro photography, but this isn't always the case. For example, if you want to shoot tiny insects without getting too close to them, a more telephoto focal length of about 180mm is a real advantage. There are various lenses available, including the Canon EF 180mm f/3.5L USM, Sigma 180mm f/3.5 EX DG HSM and the Tamron 180mm f/3.5 SP Di.

The downside of a longer focal length is that there's a significant increase in price, with the Sigma and Tamron 180mm lenses costing about $700 and the Canon weighing in at a whopping $1,500. A more cost-effective alternative is to stick to a macro lens of around 100mm and take advantage of the high resolution of 12 megapixels or more offered by most new D-SLRs, creatively cropping your photos in the digital darkroom for the best effect.

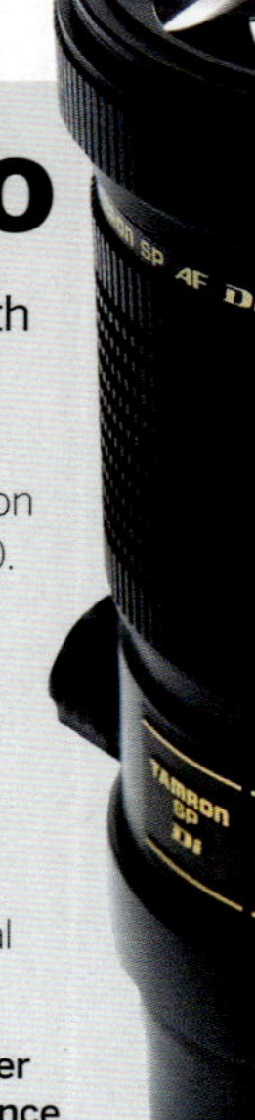

A 180mm macro lens offers better reach so you can keep your distance, but there's a major hike in the purchase price for these lenses

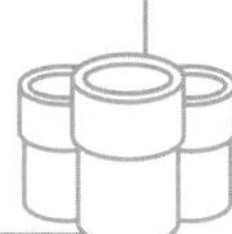

STEP BY STEP Focus effectively with macro lenses

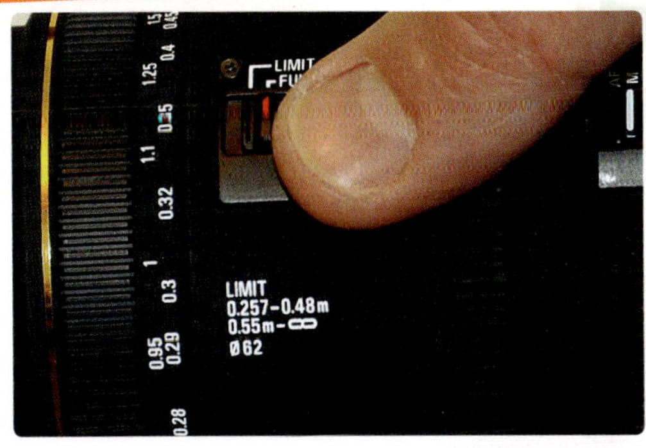

Focus limit switch

1 In autofocus mode, macro lenses can be slow to achieve focus, because of the extended travel of the focus ring. With most macro lenses, you can avoid autofocus having to hunt through the entire range by engaging the focus limit switch, which normally limits focus either side of a mid-distance setting.

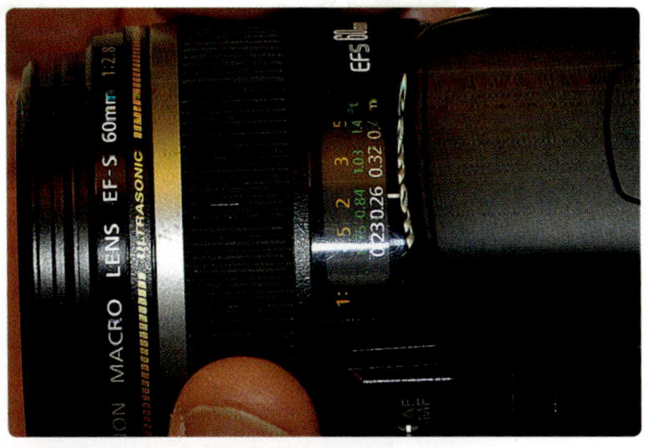

Full-time manual override

4 One particularly good feature of the Canon EF-S 60mm and EF 100mm lenses is that they have Ultrasonic autofocus with full-time manual override. This enables you to use autofocus in the normal way, then tweak the focus manually without having to flip any switches – great for quick and accurate focusing.

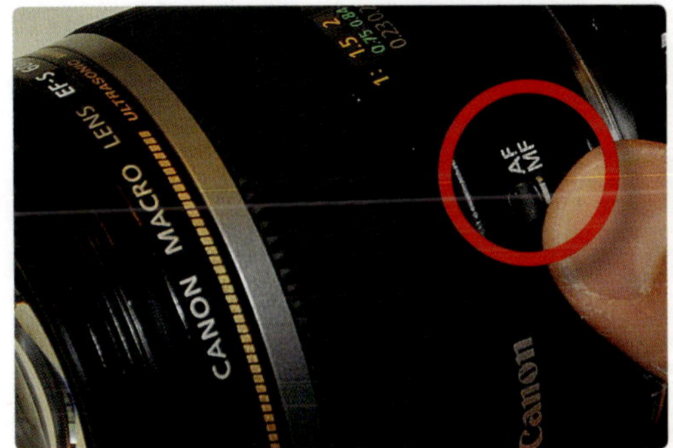

AF/Manual

2 It's often the case that none of the camera's autofocus points will coincide with the particular part of an object on which you wish to focus, and it's best not to move the camera after autofocus because focusing is critical. It's often a good idea to set the AF/MF switch on the lens to MF and focus manually.

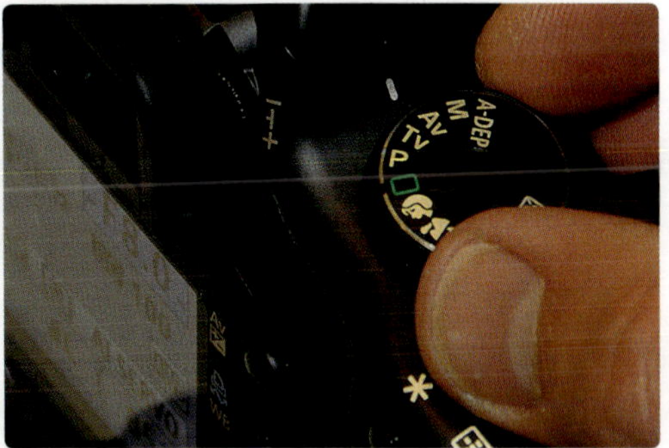

Depth of field

5 Wide apertures enable faster shutter speeds but, in macro photography, give a very small depth of field. Unless you want to creatively blur most of an object, switch to Av mode and use a smaller aperture of around f/11 to f/16. You may need to increase the sensitivity (ISO) to enable a sensibly fast shutter speed.

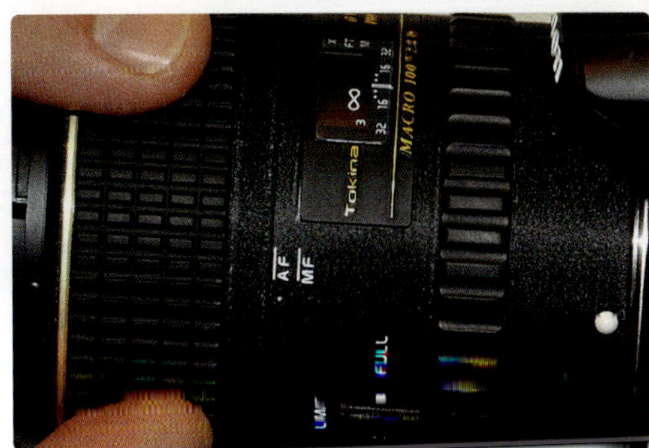

Push-pull manual

3 The Tamron and Tokina lenses on test here feature a neat push-pull focus ring for switching between autofocus and manual focus. Start in autofocus mode and then pull the focus ring towards you to engage manual focus mode, so that you can make any fine adjustments that are necessary.

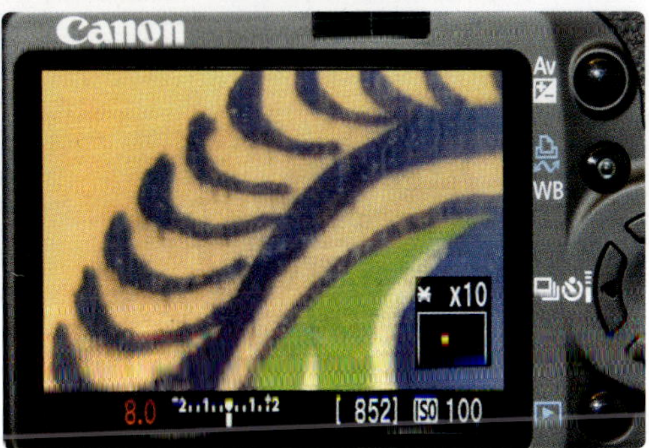

Live View

6 Using Live View mode, available on many of Canon's latest D-SLRs, you can zoom the LCD display before shooting, typically giving up to 10x magnification, which enables incredibly precise manual focus. It's often easier to alter the position of the camera or object rather than moving the focus ring.

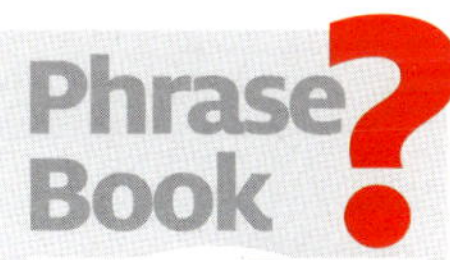

Phrase Book?

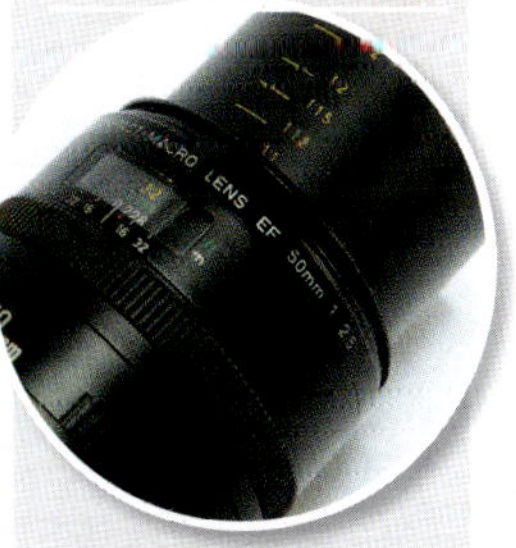

Fast lens

These have a wide maximum aperture, typically of between f/1.2 and f/2.8, and are so named because they can enable a fast shutter speed, even in dull lighting conditions. Compared with a standard zoom lens that has a maximum aperture of f/5.6, an aperture of f/2.8 enables a shutter speed that's about four times as fast – 1/250 sec instead of 1/60 sec, for example.

Focus distance scale

Many macro lenses include a focus distance scale, which gives a handy visual reference. However, it's important to remember that the distance shown is between the object being photographed and the sensor (also called the film plane), rather than the front end of the lens, as this distance would be a few inches shorter.

Focus limit switch

When engaged, most focus limit switches limit the focus travel either side of a specific distance, rather than enabling the full focus range. For example, with the Sigma 50mm macro lens, it limits travel between the shortest focus distance of 19cm and 2.5m, or between 2.5m and infinity.

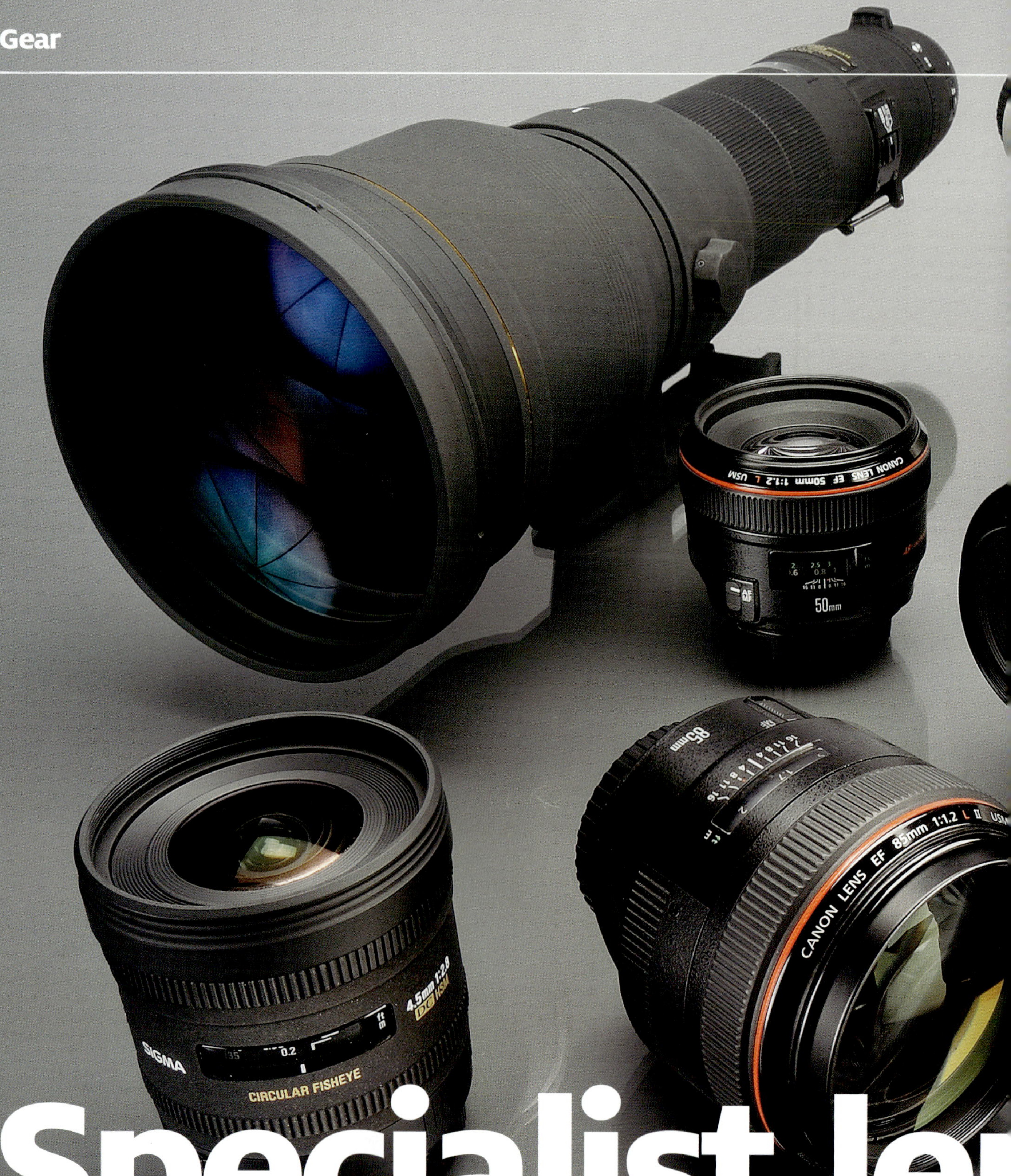

Specialist le

Want to break through the constraints imposed by normal lenses? These specialist lenses give your shots a whole new perspective

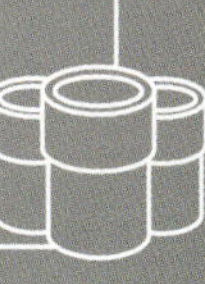

nses

A standard 'kit' zoom lens, such as the EF-S 18-55mm supplied with the Canon 450D, delivers everything from a modest wide-angle to a short telephoto focal length. Many photographers complement this with a second lens for extra telephoto reach and think that will cover pretty much any eventuality. Not so.

The most amazing thing about D-SLRs is that you can fit all manner of different types of lenses from an incredibly diverse range. From the magnifying effect of an ultra-macro and the all-seeing nature of a fisheye, to the telescopic range of a super-telephoto, these so-called 'specialist' lenses are big on wow-factor.

For decades, manufacturers have made lenses to suit practically every need, and with 100s of lenses currently available, there are plenty to choose from. Third-party lens makers tend to stick to making lenses for the mass-market.

OUR EIGHT CONTENDERS

1 Sigma 4.5mm f/2.8 EX DC HSM Circular Fisheye

2 Canon EF 15mm f/2.8 Fisheye

3 Canon MP-E 65mm f/2.8 1-5x Macro

4 Canon TS-E 24mm f/3.5

5 Canon EF 50mm f/1.2L USM

6 Canon EF 85mm f/1.2L II USM

7 Sigma 800mm f/5.6 APO EX DG HSM

8 Canon EF 500mm f/4L IS USM

Specialist lenses in detail

There's a special effects lens for practically every occasion and requirement. Here's what's on offer...

Digital photography is usually about reproducing what's seen with the naked eye. Specialist lenses go further. For example, an ultra-macro lens enables you to capture almost microscopic levels of detail, far beyond what a standard macro lens can do.

Another prime example of a lens that shows the world as the human eye cannot see it is the fisheye. These lenses were originally developed for tracking the weather as their 180° field of view could capture the whole sky in one shot. In modern fisheye lenses, that's not always the case, but they do all have the effect of bending straight horizontal or vertical lines into curves for artistic effect.

There are two types of fisheye on the market. A diagonal fisheye lens creates an image that covers the whole sensor, while a circular fisheye lens creates a small image circle in the middle, leaving the outer area blank.

Even more bizarre is the tilt-and-shift family of lenses. These come complete with controls to 'shift' the perspective, cancelling out the effect of converging parallels as they stretch into the distance. They're useful for shots of tall buildings, because you can prevent vertical lines from leaning towards each other. The 'tilt' adjustment lets you to get great depth of field, even with a large aperture, which is handy for landscape shots.

The big guns

Other types of specialist lens include very fast prime lenses, which are great for blurring the background with a very small depth of field and for working in low light without flash. The real monsters are the super-telephoto lenses, which weigh up to 5kg without the camera attached and can feel a bit like the tail wagging the dog.

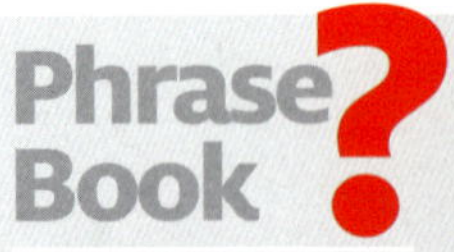

Crop factor

Instead of using conventional film, digital cameras use an image sensor to capture photographs. Full-frame D-SLRs like the EOS 5D Mark II have an image sensor that's the same size as a frame of 35mm film, whereas cameras like the 400D and 50D have an image sensor that's smaller. The net result is that instead of capturing the full image projected by a regular lens, the image is 'cropped' and only the central portion of the image is recorded. Most D-SLRs have a 1.6x crop factor, which means you need to multiply the focal length of the lens by 1.6 to get its 'effective' focal length. So using a 100mm lens on a 450D is like using a 160mm lens on a 5D Mark II. For full-frame SLRs, the actual and 'effective' focal lengths will be the same.

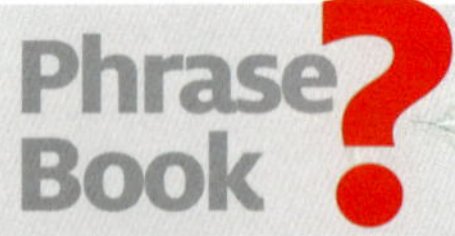

Super-telephoto

Telephoto lenses generally have focal lengths up to about 300mm. Anything more than this is a 'super-telephoto', is larger and heavier, and offers focal lengths of between 400mm and 800mm. Once you add the crop factor of cameras such as the 450D, an 800mm super-zoom lens takes on the almost astronomic focal length of 1,280mm.

Fast lens

This has nothing to do with the speed of autofocus or any other moving parts – instead it refers to the lens having a very large maximum aperture, typically between f/1.8 and f/2.8. A few of the lenses on test here are ultra-fast prime lenses, with huge maximum apertures of f/1.2.

Macro

Traditionally, a macro lens projects 'life-sized' images. So if you take a picture of a 5p piece measuring 18mm in diameter, its image would occupy a circle of 18mm across on the camera's sensor. In real terms, a 1x or 1:1 macro lens on a camera such as the 450D produces an image about 50x larger than life when viewed at 100% zoom on a computer screen, so just think what a 5x ultra-macro can do!

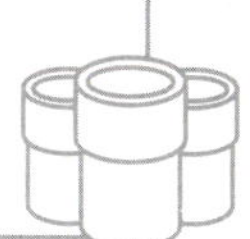

STEP BY STEP Ensure the best lens performance

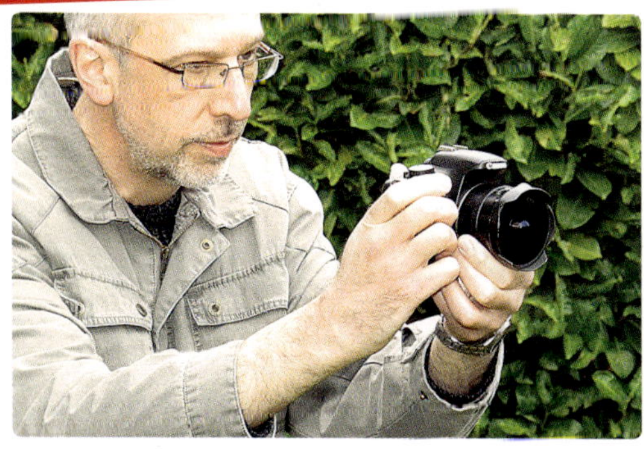

Fisheye

1 Most fisheye lenses have a phenomenal angle of view, up to a massive 180°. But this means that it's all too easy to end up with your feet or tripod legs in the picture. You can avoid this by using Live View (a feature included on most new digital SLRs) and holding the camera at arm's length, taking advantage of the very short focal length's inherent resistance to camera shake.

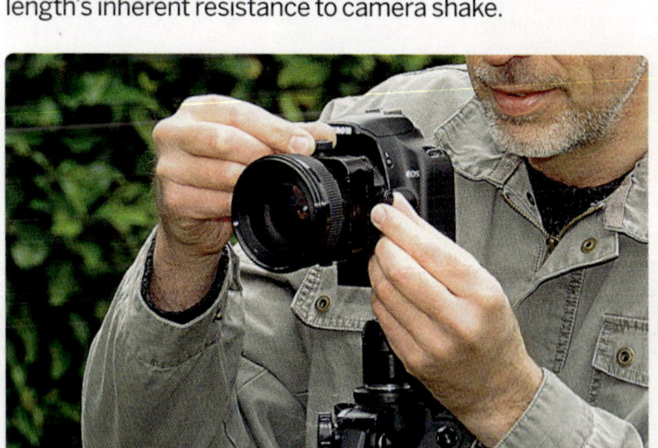

Tilt and shift

2 Tilt-and-shift lenses can be rather fiddly to use and they require precise set-up of the tilt-and-shift controls in order to get the best from them. For this reason, it's best to mount your camera on a tripod before you start making any adjustments to it, so that everything's fixed in place before you lock the tripod head.

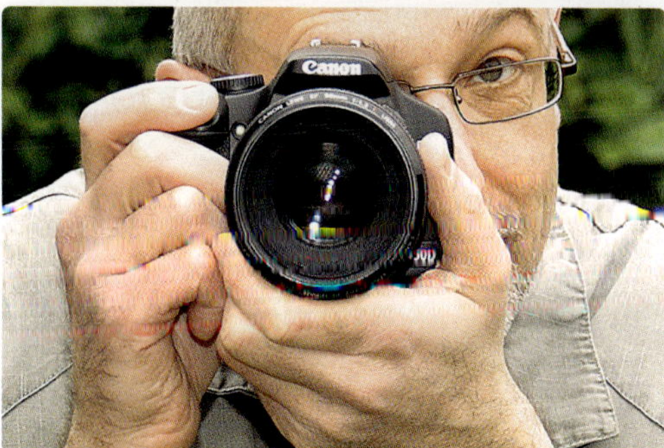

Ultra-fast

3 As well as offering a shallow depth of field with their very large maximum apertures, ultra-fast lenses are useful in low-light conditions because they allow faster shutter speeds. Unlike image stabilisation lenses, these faster shutter speeds help to freeze any movement on the part of the subject, as well as negating camera shake.

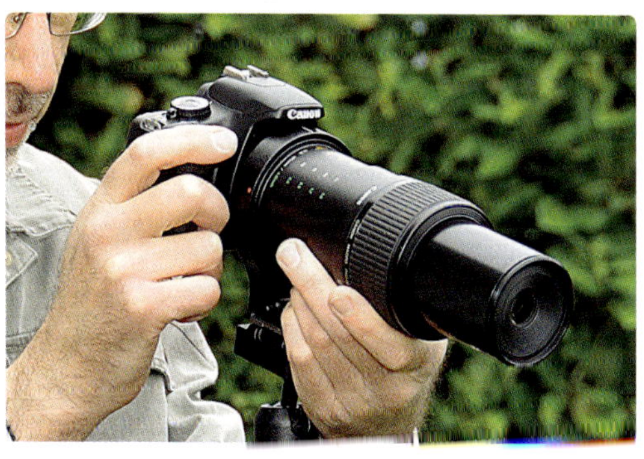

Super-macro

4 Even when using a small aperture, the depth of field of a super-macro lens is paper-thin, so it's essential to ensure that your focusing is accurate. To do this, mount the camera on a tripod and use Live View (if you have it) with maximum magnification to adjust the focus. It's also often easier to make tiny adjustments to the position of the camera or subject rather than altering lens focus.

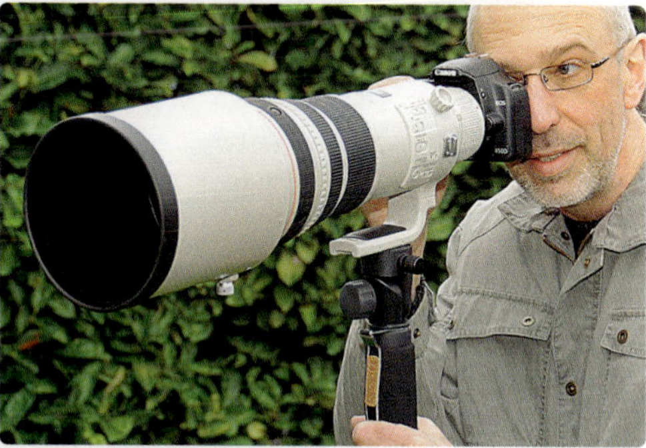

Super-telephoto (IS)

5 The image stabilisation (IS) feature built into some super-telephoto lenses offers protection against the ever-present problem of shake when handholding the camera. They're still heavy though so, even if your lens has IS, a sturdy monopod offers a good compromise between handholding and using a cumbersome tripod.

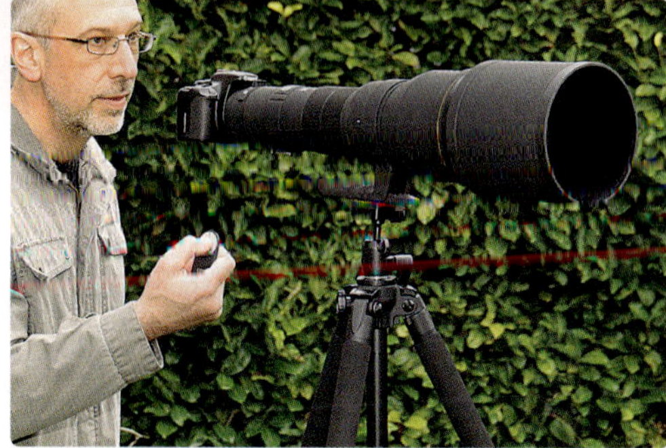

Super-telephoto (non IS)

6 It's notoriously difficult to get sharp, shake-free shots with super-telephoto lenses that don't have image stabilisation. It's best to mount these lenses on a sturdy tripod and, where possible, to use your camera's Mirror Lock-up function in conjunction with a remote shutter release to keep the camera and lens steady.

On your CD-ROM

Here's how to get the most from the packed disc that accompanies *The Complete Digital SLR Handbook*

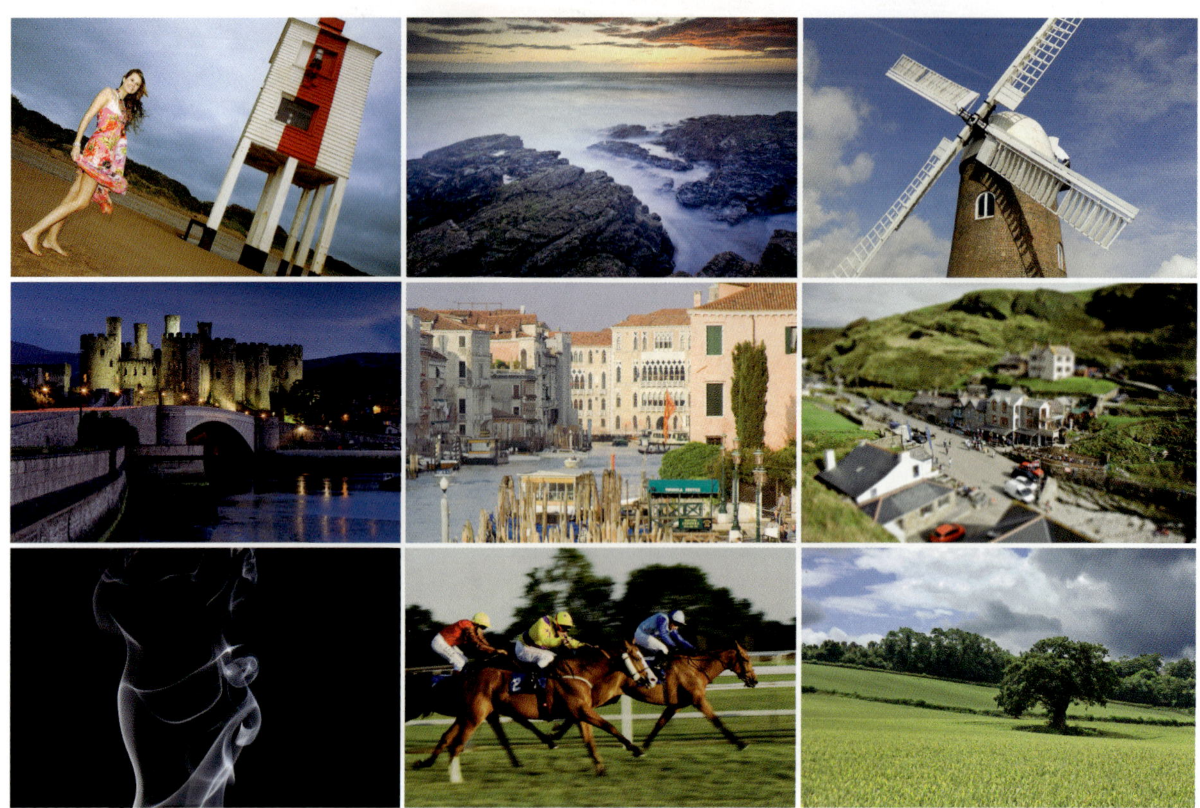

Important
About copyright

Please note that all the images on your CD are copyright. They are not 'royalty-free' or 'library' images. They are supplied solely for your own private use, so you can work along with our tutorials. They must not be sold on, redistributed in any form (whether as-supplied or edited), made available on any server or website, or used for any commercial purpose.

STEP BY STEP How to use the disc interface

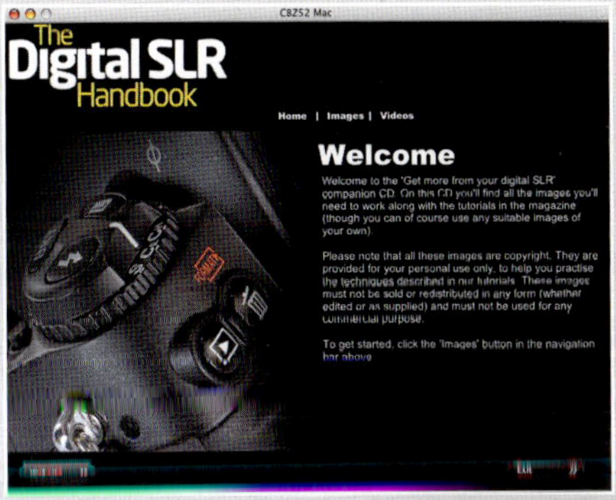

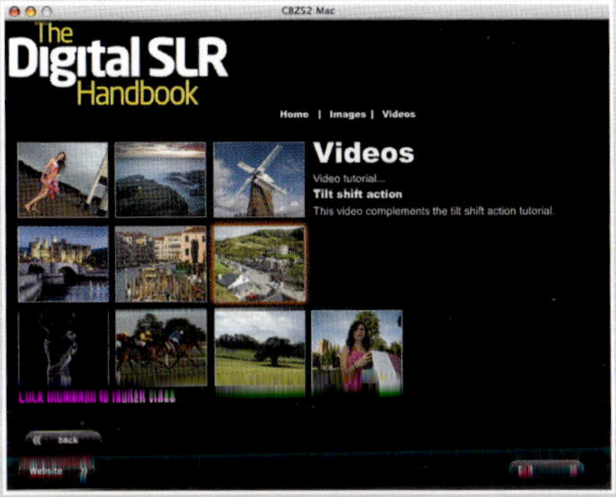

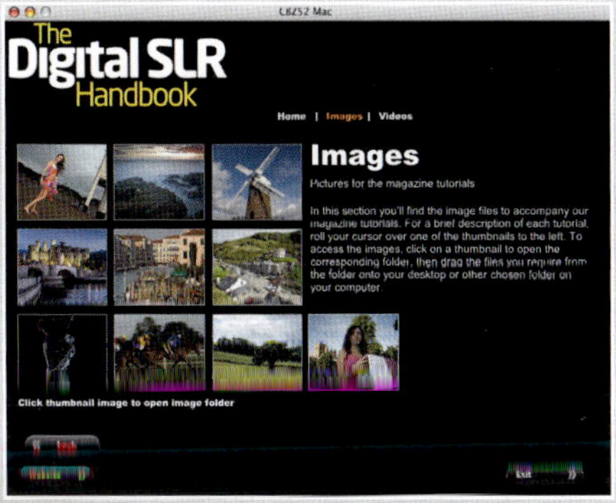

Welcome to the disc

1 After the disc interface launches and you've accepted the terms of use, you'll see this Welcome screen. To access the images on the disc, simply click the 'Images' link at the top of the screen. The button at the bottom left will take you to the new PhotoRadar web pages, including image galleries, news, reviews, videos and lively magazine forums. Naturally, this button will work only if you have an active internet connection.

Images and Videos

2 To view our exclusive video tutorials, click on the 'Videos' link, then click on one of the preview images to load that video. Click the 'Play' arrow button at the bottom-left of the screen to begin playing the video.

Click on the 'Images' link and you'll be able to preview some of the images included on the disc. You can jump to the next screen, or back again, using the 'Previous' and 'Next' links towards the bottom of the preview screen.

Accessing the images

3 Hover your cursor over one of the image previews and you'll see a text description telling you which tutorial it's associated with. If you want to try out the techniques in the tutorial, click the image preview and the folder containing the relevant image will open on your desktop (this might be behind your interface window). You can then simply drag the image to your own hard disk to open it in Photoshop Elements.

Your free CD-ROM includes exclusive video tutorials, plus all the 'start' images you'll need to complete the step-by-step projects in this book. You'll find our little 'On the disc' sticker on the page to remind you. Note that not all the tutorials in this book will be accompanied by source images: some don't require you to work along with a project.

To access the files on this disc, first insert the CD into your drive. Whether you're using a Mac or a Windows PC, the disc should work equally well. If the disc interface doesn't run automatically, look at the 'Starting the interface manually' box on this page for help.

Before you go on

The first item that should appear on your screen is the disclaimer window: here you'll need to click on 'I Accept'. Please remember that this disc has been scanned and tested at all stages of production, but – as with all new software – we still recommend that you run a virus checker before use. We also recommend that you have an up-to-date backup of your hard disk before using this disc. Future Publishing does not accept responsibility for any disruption, damage and/or loss to your data or computer system that may occur while using this disc, or the data and programs on it. Please consult your network administrator before attempting to install software on a networked PC.

Installation

Once the CD is running you'll see a range of options in the menu bar. Click on a link to access the section you require (see above for a brief guide to finding your way around the disc). If you prefer, you can access the source images directly from your desktop rather than via the disc interface: you'll find them all within the 'Images' folder on the CD.

Some files may need to be extracted from a Zip archive; try using WinZip (www.winzip.com) to do this if your version of Windows doesn't have a de-archiving utility.

Questions and queries

If you have a query about using your disc's interface or its content, please visit our reader support website at www.futurenet.co.uk/support, where you can find solutions to many common problems. In the unlikely event of your disc being defective, please e-mail our support team at support@futurenet.com for assistance. Please note that we can only provide basic advice on using the interface and disc content. We cannot give in-depth help on any applications or on your particular hardware or operating system.

Expert tip

Starting the disc interface manually

If the disc interface doesn't load automatically when you insert the disc, here's what to do.

PC users: Click on the Windows Start button and click Run. Now click Browse and go to the CD directory in My Computer. Look for a file called CBZ52.exe and double-click on it. Click OK in the Run dialog, and the interface should open.

Mac users: Double-click the disc icon to view its contents, then double-click 'CBZ52 Mac' to launch the interface.

Index

More Great Books from Fox Chapel Publishing

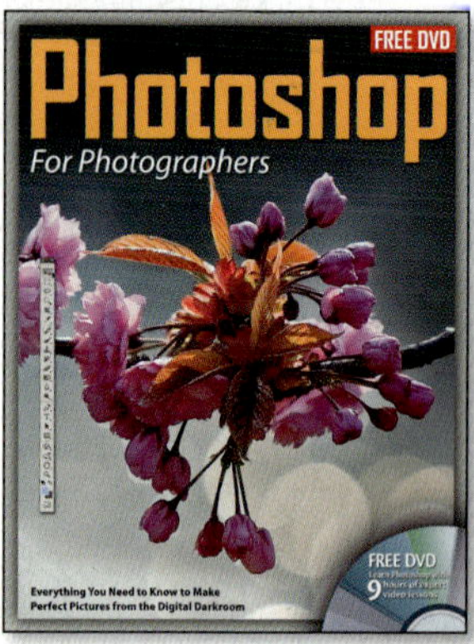

Photoshop For Photographers

Everything You Need to Know to Make Perfect Pictures from The Digital Darkroom

By Editors of PhotoPlus Magazine

This expert guide shows you how to get even better results from your digital SLR photography using Photoshop's photo-editing tools.

ISBN 978-1-56523-721-6
$27.95 • 216 Pages

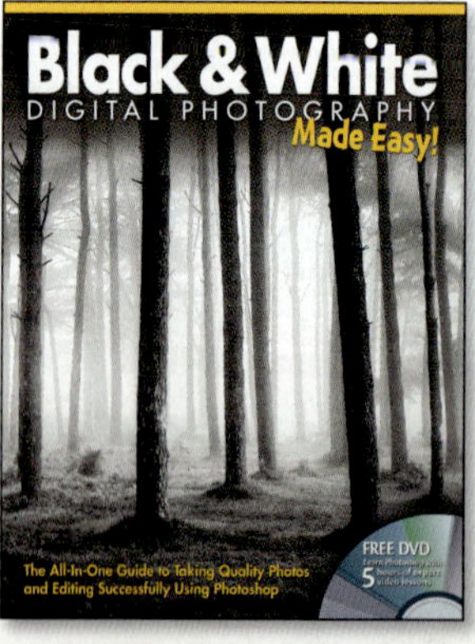

Black & White Digital Photography

The All-In-One Guide to Taking Quality Photos and Editing Successfully Using Photoshop

By Editors of PhotoPlus Magazine

This book explores the evocative world of black and white photography and looks at exhilarating new ways to approach the mono medium.

ISBN: 978-1-56523-718-6
$27.95 • 224 Pages

How to Draw and Paint Anatomy

Professional Artists Teach You Practical Drawing Techniques

By Editors of ImagineFX Magazine

Art students, professional illustrators, and creative amateurs alike will find inspiration and encouragement to develop their core skills and embrace innovative digital techniques.

ISBN: 978-1-56523-716-2
$27.95 • 112 Pages

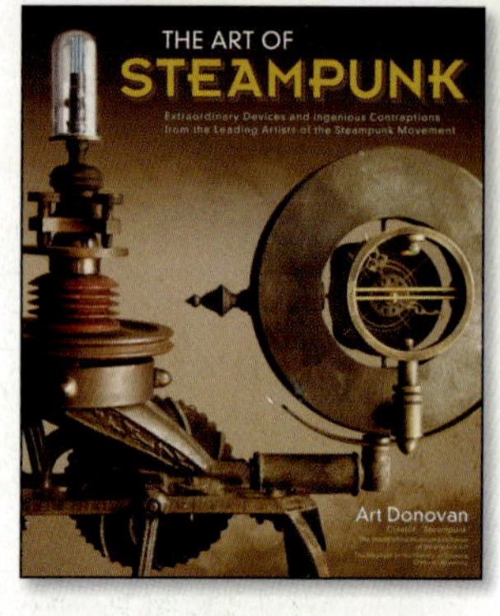

The Art of Steampunk

Extraordinary Devices and Ingenious Contraptions from the Leading Artists of the Steampunk Movement

By Art Donovan

Dive into the world of Steampunk where machines are functional pieces of art and the design is only as limited as the artist's imagination.

ISBN: 978-1-56523-573-1
$19.95 • 128 Pages

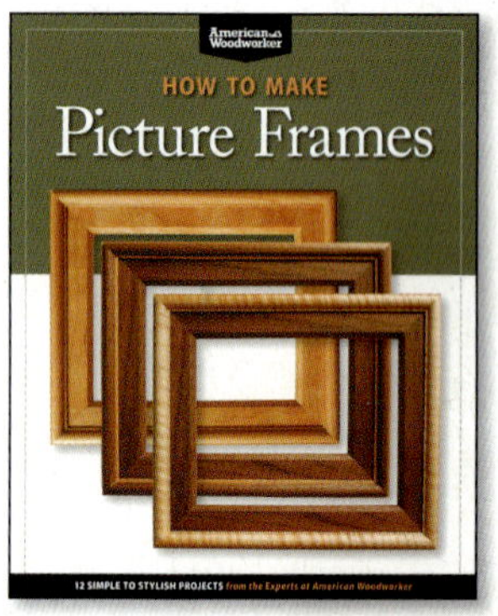

How to Make Picture Frames

12 Simple to Stylish Projects from the Experts at American Woodworker

Edited by Randy Johnson

Add a special touch to cherished photos or artwork with hand-made picture frames. The experts at American Woodworker give step-by-step instructions using a variety of woods and styles.

ISBN: 978-1-56523-459-8
$19.95 • 120 Pages

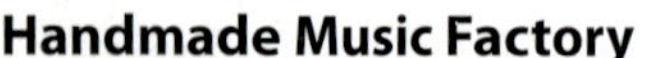

Labeling America: Popular Culture on Cigar Box Labels

The Story of George Schlegel Lithographers, 1849-1971

By John Grossman

Discover the beauty of cigar box labels and bands from the 19th and 20th centuries, printed by George Schlegel Lithographers and collected by John Grossman; currently being housed at the Winterthur Museum in Delaware.

ISBN: 978-1-56523-545-8
$39.95 • 320 Pages

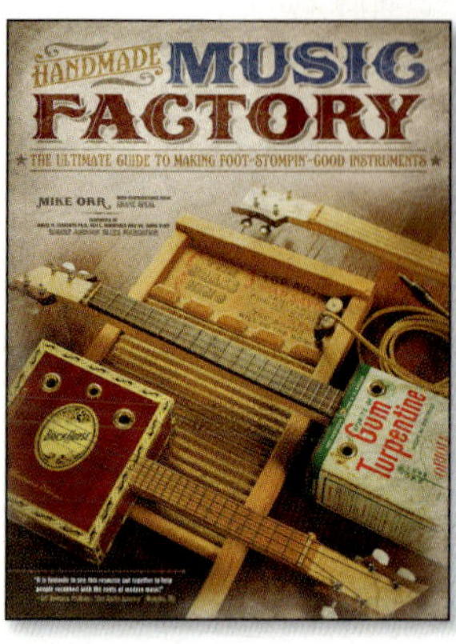

Handmade Music Factory

The Ultimate Guide to Making Foot-Stompin Good Instruments

By Mike Orr

Learn how to make eight of the most unique and imaginative instruments found anywhere—from a one-string guitar made from a soup can, to a hubcap banjo. Author Mike Orr takes you inside the growing trend of handmade music and shows you how with a little creativity and some salvaged parts, you can create your own arsenal of instruments that look good, sound great, and deliver some foot stompin' fun!

ISBN: 978-1-56523-559-5
$22.95 • 160 Pages

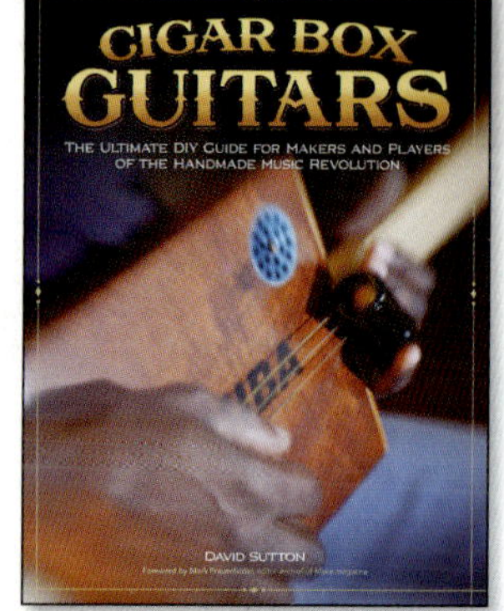
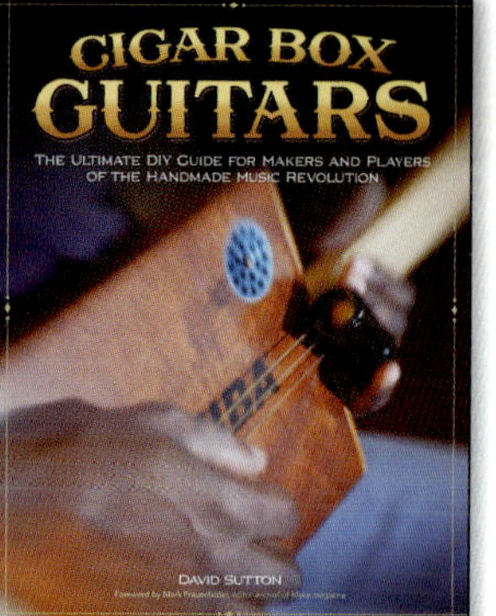

Cigar Box Guitars

The Ultimate DIY Guide for the Makers and Players of the Handmade Music Revolution

By David Sutton

Part DIY guide, part scrapbook—this book takes you behind the music to get a glimpse into the faces, places and workshops of the cigar box revolution.

ISBN: 978-1-56523-547-2
$29.95 • 224 Pages

Look for These Books at Your Local Bookstore or Specialty Retailer

To order direct, call **800-457-9112** or visit *www.FoxChapelPublishing.com*

By mail, please send check or money order + S&H to:

Fox Chapel Publishing, 1970 Broad Street, East Petersburg, PA 17520

# Item	US Shipping Rate
1 Item	$3.99
Each Additional	.99

Canadian & International Orders – please email info@foxchapelpublishing.com or visit our website for actual shipping costs.